ASPECTS OF WORLD CIVILIZATION

Problems and Sources in History

Volume I

Edited by

PERRY M. ROGERS

Prentice
Hall

Upper Saddle River, New Jersey 07458

Library of Congress Cataloging-in-Publication Data

Aspects of World civilization: problems and sources in history /
  edited by Perry M. Rogers. —1st ed.
      p. cm.
    ISBN 0–13–080828–8
    1. World History—Sources. 2. Religions—History—Sources.
  3. History—Philosophy   I. Rogers, Perry McAdow.
  D20 .A87 2003
  909—dc21   202007628

Editor-in-chief: Charlyce Jones-Owen
Executive editor: Todd Armstrong
Acquisitions editor: Emsal Hasan
Editorial assistant: Holly Jo Brown
Managing editor: Jan Stephan
Production liaison: Fran Russello
Editorial/production supervision: Russell Jones (Pine Tree Composition)
Prepress and manufacturing buyer: Sherry Lewis
Cover director: Jayne Conte
Cover Image Specialist: Karen Sanatar
Cover designer: Kiwi Design
Cover art: "Li T'ai-po Viewing the Waterfall," Painting, Japan, Asian Art Museum of San Francisco,
The Avery Brundage Collection, Chong-Moon Lee Center for Asian Art and Culture B62 D11.
Director, Image Resource Center: Melinda Lee Reo
Manager, rights & permissions: Zina Arabia
Interior Image specialist: Beth Boyd
Photo researcher: Teri Stratford
Marketing manager: Sheryl Adams

This book was set in 10/11½ Baskerville by Pine Tree Composition, Inc.,
and was printed and bound by R.R. Donnelley & Sons, Inc.
The cover was printed by Phoenix Color Corp.

© 2003 by Pearson Education, Inc.
Upper Saddle River, New Jersey 07458

Printed in the United States of America

10 9 8 7 6 5 4 3 2 1

ISBN 0-13-080828-8

Pearson Education Ltd., *London*
Pearson Education Australia Pty, Limited, *Sydney*
Pearson Education Singapore, Pte. Ltd.
Pearson Education North Asia Ltd. *Hong Kong*
Pearson Education Canada, Ltd., *Toronto*
Pearson Educatión de Mexico, S.A. de C.V.
Pearson Education—Japan, *Tokyo*
Pearson Education Malaysia, Pte. Ltd.
Pearson Education, *Upper Saddle River, New Jersey*

For Ann
Elisa, Kit, and Tyler

Brief Contents

HISTORICAL INTERSECTIONS

VOLUME II   The Early Modern Era Through the Contemporary World

HISTORICAL INTERSECTIONS

Contents

Caesar and Christ   146

The Historical Intersection   GERMANY: 1938   *157*

The Cycle of Empire (180–500 C.E.)   161

PART IV   TRANSITIONS TO THE MODERN WORLD (1450-1650)

10 The Age of the Renaissance and Reformation   311

SECTION 1: THE RENAISSANCE MOVEMENT   312

The Humanist Movement   314

The Political Life of Florence   316

Renaissance Arts and Manners   320

SECTION II: THE REFORMATION ERA   326

The Lutheran Reformation   328

Geographical Contents

Volume I

Africa and the Middle East

Asia

Europe

Ancient Greek Civilization

Ancient Roman Civilization

The Americas

The Maya Civilization

Preface

The Roman orator Cicero once remarked that "History is the witness of the times, the torch of truth, the life of memory, the teacher of life, the messenger of antiquity." In spite of these noble words, historians have often labored under the burden of justifying the value of studying events that are over and done. Humankind is practical, more concerned with its present and future than with its past. And yet the study of history provides us with unique opportunities for human self-knowledge. It teaches us what we have done and therefore helps define what we are. On a less abstract level, the study of history enables us to judge present circumstance by drawing on the laboratory of the past. Those who have lived and died, through their recorded attitudes, actions and ideas, have left a legacy of experience.

One of the best ways to travel through time and space and perceive the very "humanness" that lies at the root of history is through the study of primary sources. These are the documents, coins, letters, inscriptions and monuments of past ages. The task of historians is to evaluate this evidence with a critical eye and then construct a narrative that is consistent with the "facts" as they have established them. Such interpretations are inherently subjective and are therefore open to dispute. History is thus filled with controversy as historians argue their way toward the "truth." The only way to work toward an understanding of the past is through personal examination of the primary sources.

Yet, for the beginning student, this poses some difficulties. Such inquiry casts the student adrift from the security of accepting the "truth" as revealed in a textbook. In fact, history is too often presented in a deceptively objective manner; one learns "facts and dates" in an effort to obtain the "right answers" for multiple-choice tests. But the student who has wrestled with primary sources and has experienced voices from the past on a more intimate level accepts the responsibility of evaluation and judgment. He or she understands that history does not easily lend itself to "right answers," but demands reflection on the problems that have confronted past societies and are at play even in our contemporary world. Cicero was right in viewing history as the "life of memory." But human memory is fragile and the records of the past can be destroyed or distorted. Without the past, people have nothing with which to judge what they are told in the present.

Truth then becomes the preserve of the ruler or government, no longer relative, but absolute. The study of history, and primary sources in particular, goes far in making people aware of the continuity of humankind and the progress of civilization.

Aspects of World Civilization offers the student an opportunity to evaluate the primary sources of the past and to do so in a structured and organized format. The documents provided are diverse in nature and include state papers, secret dispatches, letters, diary accounts, poems, newspaper articles, papal encyclicals, and propaganda flyers. Occasionally, the assessments of modern historians are included to lend perspective. All give testimony to human endeavor in world societies. Yet, this two-volume book has been conceived as more than a simple compilation of primary sources. The subtitle of the work, *Problems and Sources in History*, gives true indication of the nature of its premise. It is meant to provide the student with thoughtful and engaging material, that is focused around individual units that encompass time periods, specific events, and historical questions. Students learn from the past most effectively when posed with problems that have meaning for their own lives. In evaluating the material from *Aspects of World Civilization*, the student will discover that issues are not nearly as simple as they may appear at first glance. Historical sources often contradict each other and truth then depends on logic and one's own experience and outlook on life. Throughout these volumes, the student is confronted with basic questions regarding historical development, human nature, moral action, and practical necessity. The text is therefore broad in its scope and incorporates a wide variety of political, social, economic, religious, intellectual, and scientific issues. It is internally organized around *eight major themes* that provide direction and cohesion to the text while allowing for originality of thought in both written and oral analysis:

1. *Imperialism.* How has imperialism been justified throughout world history and what are the moral implications of gaining and maintaining empire? Is defensive imperialism a practical foreign policy option? This theme is often juxtaposed with subtopics of nationalism, war, altruism, and human nature.

2. *Church/State Relationships.* Is there a natural competition between these two controlling units in society? Which is more influential, which legacy more enduring? How has religion been used as a means of securing political power or of instituting social change?

3. *Beliefs and Spirituality.* The diverse religious heritage of world civilization forms the basis of this theme. In particular, the text covers the primary tenets and historical development of Judaism, Christianity, Islam, Hinduism, and Buddhism. It also focuses on the impact of ideas and philosophical movements on society. How have religious values and moral attitudes affected the course of world history? To what extent have spiritual reform movements resulted in a change of political or social policy? Are ideas more powerful than any army? Why have so many people died fighting for religions that abhor violence? Does every society need a spiritual foundation?

4. *Systems of Government.* This theme seeks to introduce the student to the various systems of rule that have shaped world civilization: classical democracy, representative democracy (republican government), oligarchy, constitutional monarchy, divine-right monarchy, theocracy, and dictatorship (especially fascism and totalitarian rule). What are the advantages and drawbacks to each? This rubric also includes the concepts of balance of power and containment, principles of succession, geopolitics, and social and economic theories such as capitalism, communism, and socialism.

5. *Revolution.* This theme seeks to define and examine the varieties of revolution: political, intellectual, economic, and social. What were the underlying and precipitating causes of political revolution? How essential is the intellectual foundation? Are social demands and spontaneity more important elements in radical action?

6. *Propaganda.* What is the role of propaganda in history? Many sections examine the use and abuse of information, often in connection with absolute government, revolution, imperialism, or genocide. How are art and architecture, as well as written material, used in the "creation of belief"? This theme emphasizes the relativity of truth and stresses the responsibility of the individual in assessing the validity of evidence.

7. *Women in History.* The text intends to help remedy the widespread omission of women from history and to develop an appreciation of their contributions to the intellectual and political framework of world civilization. At issue is how women have been viewed—or rendered invisible—throughout history and how individually and collectively their presence is inextricably linked with the development and progress of civilization. This inclusive approach stresses the importance of achieving a perspective that lends value and practical application to history.

8. *Historical Change and Transition.* What are the main determinants of change in history? How important is the individual in effecting change, or is society regulated by unseen social and economic forces? What role does chance play? What are the components of civilization and how do we assess progress or decline? Are civilizations biological in nature? Is a crisis/response theory of change valid? This theme works toward providing the student with a philosophy of history and against the tendency to divide history into strict periods. It stresses the close connection between the past and the present.

The *overriding theme* that provides a foundation and overall unity to the text is that of *cultural interaction.* How have the diverse cultures of the world been linked by political systems, economic contact, social and religious movements, philosophy, art, literature, and such variables as disease and war? In what ways have world civilizations over the centuries struggled with similar challenges and contributed to the progress or destruction of humanity? How has the world community become increasingly dependent on cooperation and international understanding in achieving domestic stability, security, and prosperity?

STRUCTURE OF THE BOOK

Each chapter begins with a *timeline chronology* so that students may visualize the historical parameters of the chapter. This is generally followed by a *series of quotations* from various historians, diplomats, philosophers, literary figures, or religious spokespersons who offer insight on the subject matter of the chapter. These quotations may well be used in conjunction with the study questions at the end of the unit. After the quotations, *chapter themes* are listed and framed by several questions that direct the reader to broader issues and comparative perspectives with ideas and events in other chapters. This feature acknowledges the changing perspectives of different eras while linking historical problems that emphasize the continuity of history. A *general introduction* then provides a brief historical background and focuses the themes or questions to be discussed in the chapter.

Following this general introduction, the primary sources are presented with extensive direction for the student. A *headnote* explains in more detail the historical or biographical background for each primary source and focuses attention on themes or interrelationships with other sources. Each chapter concludes with a *chronology* designed to orient the student to the broader context of history, and a series of *study questions* that can form the basis of oral discussion or written analysis. The questions do not seek mere regurgitation of information, but demand a more thoughtful response based on reflective analysis of the primary sources.

This analysis is even more specifically focused by the inclusion of *TimeLink* chapters throughout the sectional divisions. These chapters function as assessments of particular eras or historical problems that are connected intimately to the subject matter in the section and provide a direct comparison between societies. *TimeLink* chapters frame the readings with initial questions to consider and followup questions that provide links to visual and written sources in previous chapters. Each volume also contains eight to ten comparative sources in a feature called *The Historical Intersection*. These readings provide the student with an immediate opportunity to compare two documents, which, although from different eras and societies, are linked through one of the historical themes mentioned above. This interactive feature will help students analyze the continuity of the past and appreciate the relevancy of historical inquiry.

USE OF THE BOOK

Aspects of World Civilization offers the instructor a wide variety of didactic applications. The chapters fit into a more or less standard lecture format and are ordered chronologically. An entire chapter may be assigned for oral discussion, or sections from each chapter may satisfy particular interests or requirements. Some of the chapters provide extensive treatment of a broad historical topic ("Medieval Civilization in the West: The Sword of Faith"; "A Wealth of Riches, A Sea of Sorrows: The Linking of Transatlantic Economies"). In order to make them manageable and effective, some have been grouped them into topical sections (with correspondingly labeled study questions) that can be utilized separately, if so desired.

The chapters may also be assigned for written analysis. One of the most important concerns of both instructor and student in an introductory class is the written assignment. *Aspects of World Civilization* has been designed to provide self-contained topics that are problem-oriented, promote reflection and analysis, and encourage responsible citation of particular primary sources. The study questions for each chapter should generally produce an eight- to ten-page paper.

ACKNOWLEDGMENTS

This book has evolved over the years through contact with many colleagues and friends, who offered their insight and analysis of history, poetry, literature, and art. I would like to recognize in particular the influence of Susan Altan, Marsha Ryan, Jack Guy, Frank O'Grady, Thomas Tappan, Dan Hall, Mary Ann Leonard, and Diane Abel, whose frequent conversations stimulated my interest and whose perception often opened new avenues of thought. Linda Swarlis paved the way by investing me with new research skills and by connecting me with obscure sources at crucial times. Thanks to my colleagues who took the time to review both volumes: Thomas Saylor and Paul Hillmer, Concordia University, St. Paul; Robert Bucholz, Loyola University, Chicago; and Elaine Spencer and Nancy M. Wingfield, Northern Illinois University. Thanks also to the students of Columbus School for Girls, who continue to "test" the chapters in this book with their typical diligence and hard work; the final product has benefitted greatly from their suggestions and ideas. Finally, I owe the largest debt to my wife, Ann, whose strength and gentle confirmation of what is most valuable in life offers the greatest perspective of all, and to my children, who always help me laugh.

Perry M. Rogers
Westerville, Ohio

Part I

THE FOUNDATIONS OF CIVILIZATION

1

The Earliest Civilizations: Mesopotamia, Egypt, and China

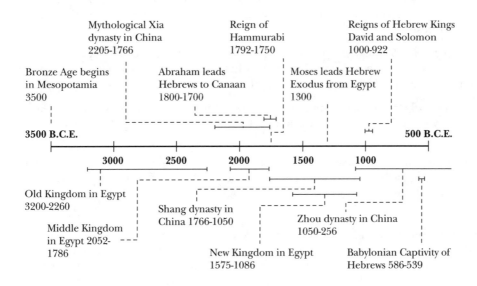

Mythological Xia dynasty in China 2205-1766

Reign of Hammurabi 1792-1750

Reigns of Hebrew Kings David and Solomon 1000-922

Bronze Age begins in Mesopotamia 3500

Abraham leads Hebrews to Canaan 1800-1700

Moses leads Hebrew Exodus from Egypt 1300

3500 B.C.E.   **500 B.C.E.**

3000   2500   2000   1500   1000

Old Kingdom in Egypt 3200-2260

Middle Kingdom in Egypt 2052-1786

Shang dynasty in China 1766-1050

Zhou dynasty in China 1050-256

New Kingdom in Egypt 1575-1086

Babylonian Captivity of Hebrews 586-539

If a man destroy the eye of another man, they shall destroy his eye.

—Code of Hammurabi

You are a lifespan in yourself; one lives by you.

—Hymn to Aten

Let the king be serious in what he does. He should not neglect to be serious with virtue.

—Book of History

A very handsome gentleman/Waited for me in the lane /I am sorry I did not go with him.

—*Book of Songs*

By the willows of the Eastern Gate/Whose leaves are so thick/At dusk we were to meet/And now the morning star is bright.

—*Book of Songs*

CHAPTER THEMES

- *Systems of Government:* How did the monarchies in Mesopotamia, Egypt, and China differ from one another? What is the best form of government for primitive societies?

- *Beliefs and Spirituality:* How did the belief systems of the ancient Near East and China contribute to the unity of society? In what ways were these societies primarily spiritual in nature? How radical a conception is monotheism?

- *Historical Change and Transition:* What were the main contributions of the early river valley societies to world civilization? In what specific ways did civilization progress during this time?

- *The Big Picture:* What are the most important political, social, and spiritual characteristics that each society must possess in order to lay the foundations for the transmission of culture?

The development of the many civilizations that we encounter in world history is an exciting and powerful story. It is a saga of human interaction, of creative brilliance and irresponsible destruction. This panorama of human history is set amid a confluence of languages, cultural traditions, and spiritual values. We can speak of separate human cultures, particular civilizations, empires, and political or spiritual movements, but human society is truly interconnected beyond geographical and linguistic boundaries. We are human, after all, and possess the same nature, the same capacity for greed, shame, love, hate, and desire. So when we study a particular culture at a particular time in history, we must be aware that this is a limited window—a moment in time, viewed from a focused perspective. In order to truly appreciate the moment and to learn from it, we must be expansive. Human beings are interactive in their relationships and we need to view history as such. It is the story of the ongoing relationships between peoples with different traditions and perspectives.

Historians and anthropologists who study human interaction and development are broadening their scope in an attempt to understand not just the relationships within a culture, but more importantly the relationships between cultures. This is especially important in prehistoric periods. Anthropologists designate early human cultures by their tools. In the Paleolithic ("old stone") Age, the human population was small and survived by hunting and gathering their limited food supply. The transition to the Neolithic ("new stone") Age was a major change that has been likened to a revolution of sorts. The earliest Neolithic societies appeared in the Near East about 8000 B.C.E., in India about 5500 B.C.E. and in China about 4000 B.C.E. The Mesoamerican cultures in modern Mexico and Central America and the Andean region of South America were still developing Neolithic societies by 2500 B.C.E. During this time, human beings made the transition from food gatherers to growers and agriculture was born. They no longer simply hunted, but domesticated and bred their animals for a more consistent food supply. The result was a tremendous growth in population. The Neolithic revolution in the Near East and India was based on wheat. In China, it was based on millet and rice, and in the Americas on corn, beans, and other crops.

Between about 4000 and 3000 B.C.E., there was another major transition in cultural development. This move was characterized by the appearance of urban centers with monumental architecture and complex hierarchical societies. This emergence of civilization was also characterized by the invention of writing and the discovery of a method for smelting copper and tin in order to produce bronze, a harder and useful metal. The four earliest Bronze Age civilizations developed around dominant river systems: the Tigris and Euphrates Rivers in Mesopotamia; the valley of the Nile River in Egypt; the Yellow River basin in China; and the Indus Valley in India. The civilizations of the Americas developed later and differently.

Beginning about 3500 B.C.E., there was an influx of people into the region of the Fertile Crescent, the land north of the Persian Gulf that now encompasses Iran and Iraq. This area was devoid of natural barriers, such as mountain ranges, and so provided easy access for nomadic peoples. It was here that world civilization first began, in the land watered by the flooding of the Tigris and Euphrates Rivers, whose silt allowed for abundant harvests and prosperity. The region became known as Mesopotamia ("the land between the rivers") and it fostered many distinct cultures. The Sumerians, who occupied the southern area at the confluence of the two rivers, assumed cultural leadership over the region by developing a syllabic writing script called cuneiform. Although conquerors would establish military control over the region, Sumerian literary and religious ideas and values proved a continuing influence.

Mesopotamia, at least initially, was organized on the basis of independent city-states. Each city had its own king and priests and conducted its own foreign policy, often in alliance with other city-states. The king's responsibilities included political and military leadership as well as supervision of the priests and their sacrifices to the gods. It is important to note that Mesopotamian kings were not considered to be divine themselves, but rather acted as representatives of the gods. The independence of the city-states often gave way to conquerors like Sargon the Great, who united the area briefly about 2300 B.C.E. Because of the open geographical access to the region, Mesopotamia was overrun by a succession of invaders, such as the Babylonians, Kassites, Assyrians, and finally Persians in the sixth century B.C.E. But the insecurity of the region did not limit the development of literature and law, which were its special contributions.

The second great civilization of the ancient Near East was Egypt. While Mesopotamia suffered from the uncertainties of invasion and swift transition, Egypt was generally secure and isolated because of the surrounding, prohibitive deserts. Egypt remains a land with an aura of mystery, reinforced by a fascination for the colossal statues of Ramses II at Abu Simbel, the Temple of Karnak at Luxor, the overwhelming presence of the pyramids, mummification, and the wealth of Tutankhamon's tomb. But it is perhaps the Egyptian religion with its emphasis on death and the netherworld that most reflects the endless order and regulation of life. Just as the Nile River promotes unity within the country and its annual flooding symbolizes the recurring cycle of life, so too did the pharaoh serve as a unifying presence. He was a god incarnate and was worshiped as such while he was living; in death he rose to the sky to be born anew each day with the cycle of the sun. Thus the Egyptians' close connection between state and religion, a theocracy of sorts, serves as a foundation for one of the more enduring themes in history.

The Indus culture was unknown to the modern world until archaeologists first discovered it at the site of Harappa in the 1920s. This Harappan civilization had large cities, bronze tools, writing, and a complex social organization, but we are somewhat limited in our knowledge because the civilization disappeared before 1500 B.C.E. and we have yet to decipher their writing. Our primary knowledge comes from archeological evidence.

The Bronze Age began in China about 2000 B.C.E., about a thousand years later than in Mesopotamia and five hundred years later than in India. China's traditional history tells of three ancient dynasties: Xia (2205–1766 B.C.E.), Shang (1766–1050 B.C.E.), and Zhou (1050–256 B.C.E.). Until the beginning of this century, historians believed that the first two dynasties were legendary. But archaeologists have uncovered the ruins of several Shang cities and thousands of "oracle bones" with writing in an early Chinese script. These bones of birds, animals, and turtle shells were used to predict the future. Some of these bone inscriptions confirmed the names and dates of Shang rulers that were noted in other written sources from the second century B.C.E. This and other archaeological evidence has removed the Shang dynasty from legend, but most of what we know about Shang society and religion must be attributed to these oracle bones. The Shang believed in a supreme "Deity Above" who had control over the human world. As in Mesopotamia, kings were not considered divine, but were the high priests of the state. Most interesting perhaps is the Shang institution of human sacrifice, which demonstrates a distinct hierarchy of class life in the Chinese city-state.

This chapter investigates three civilizations of the ancient Near East and China, with special concern for the relationships between kingship and religion, for it is through adherence to principles of government and religion that society is ordered and civilization proceeds.

MESOPOTAMIAN CIVILIZATION

Secular Authority and Order

The Reign of Sargon

The city-states that developed in the region of Mesopotamia after about 3500 B.C.E. were ruled by various kings who established local control. One of the first kings to successfully conquer and control the region was Sargon of Akkad, who ruled around 2300 B.C.E. The following excerpt from a tablet in the British Museum recounts his authority.

Sargon, King of Akkad, through the royal gift of Ishtar was exalted, and he possessed no foe nor rival. His glory over the world he poured out.

The Sea in the East he crossed, and in the eleventh year the Country of the West in its full extent his hand subdued. He united them

---

"The Reign of Sargon" is from George W. Botsford, ed., *A Source-Book of Ancient History* (New York: Macmillan, 1912), pp. 27–28.

under one control; he set up his images in the West; their booty he brought over at his word. Over the hosts of the world he reigned supreme. Against Kassala he marched, and he turned Kassala into mounds and heaps of ruins; he destroyed the land and left not enough for a bird to rest thereon. Afterward in his old age all the lands revolted against him, and they besieged him in Akkad; and Sargon went forth to battle and defeated them; he accomplished their overthrow, and their wide-spreading host he destroyed. Afterward he attacked the land of Subartu in his might, and they submitted to his arms, and Sargon settled that revolt, and defeated them; he accomplished their overthrow, and their wide-spreading host he destroyed, and he brought their possessions into Akkad. The soil from the trenches of Babylon he removed, and the boundaries of Akkad he made like those of Babylon. But because of the evil which he had committed, the great lord Marduk was angry, and he destroyed his people by famine. From the rising of the sun unto the setting of the sun they opposed him and gave him no rest.

The Code of Hammurabi

From 2000 to 1600 B.C.E., the city-states of Mesopotamia endured a period of nearly continuous warfare that saw shifting alliances and frequent chaos. The most dominant personality of the age, Hammurabi, established his control over the region from about 1800 to 1750 B.C.E. and ruled from the city of Babylon. His great contribution to Western civilization was a series of laws that sought to establish justice within his empire. This concept of equity, which remedied a large number of abuses, influenced law codes yet to come, most notably those of Greece and Rome. In the following passages, note the continual emphasis on fairness in the regulation of property, trade, debt, family relations, and personal injury.

When the lofty Anu, king of the Anunnaki gods, and Enlil, lord of heaven and earth, he who determines the destiny of the land . . . pronounced the lofty name of Babylon; when they made it famous among the quarters of the world and in its midst established an everlasting kingdom whose foundations were firm as heaven and earth; [they] . . . named me, Hammurabi, the exalted prince, the worshiper of the gods, to cause justice to prevail in the land, to destroy the wicked and the evil, to prevent the strong from oppressing the weak, to go forth like the sun over the black-headed people, to enlighten the land to further the welfare of the people. Hammurabi, the shepherd named by Enlil, am I, who brought about plenty and abundance; . . . the powerful king, the sun of Babylon, who caused light to go forth over the lands of Sumer and Akkad; the king who caused the four quarters of the world to render obedience; the favorite of Ishtar, am I.

When Marduk sent me to rule the people and to bring help to the country, I established law and justice in the language of the land and promoted the welfare of the people. At that time [I decreed]:

1. If a man bring accusation against another man, charging him with murder, but cannot prove it, the accuser shall be put to death.
3. If a man bear false witness in a case, or does not establish the testimony that he has given, if that case be a case involving life, that man shall be put to death.
4. If he bear [false] witness concerning grain or money, he shall himself bear the penalty imposed in that case.

"The Code of Hammurabi" is from Robert F. Harper, trans., *The Code of Hammurabi* (Chicago: University of Chicago Press, 1904).

5. If a judge pronounce a judgment, render a decision, deliver a verdict duly signed and sealed, and afterward alter his judgment, they shall call that judge to account for the alteration of the judgment which he has pronounced, and he shall pay twelve-fold the penalty in that judgment; and, in the assembly, they shall expel him from his seat of judgment, and with the judges in a case he shall not take his seat.

22. If a man practice robbery and is captured, that man shall be put to death.

23. If the robber is not captured, the man who has been robbed shall, in the presence of god, make an itemized statement of his loss, and the city and the governor in whose province and jurisdiction the robbery was committed shall compensate him for whatever was lost.

24. If it be a life [that is lost], the city and governor shall pay one mina [about one pound] of silver to his heirs.

53. If a man neglects to maintain his dike and does not strengthen it, and a break is made in his dike and the water carries away the farmland, the man in whose dike the break has been made shall replace the grain which has been damaged.

54. If he is not able to replace the grain, they shall sell him and his goods, and the farmers whose grain the water has carried away shall divide [the results of the sale].

55. If a man opens his canal for irrigation and neglects it and the water carries away an adjacent field, he shall pay out grain on the basis of the adjacent field.

109. If bad characters gather in the house of a wine seller and he does not arrest those bad characters and bring them to the palace, that wine seller shall be put to death.

110. If a priestess who is not living in a convent opens a wine shop or enters a wine shop for a drink, they shall burn that woman.

117. If a man be in debt and sell his wife, son, or daughter, or bind them over to service, for three years they shall work in the house of their purchaser or master; in the fourth year they shall be given their freedom.

128. If a man takes a wife and does not arrange a contract for her, that woman is not a wife.

129. If the wife of a man is caught lying with another man, they shall bind them and throw them into the water.

138. If a man wishes to put away his wife who has not borne him children, he shall give her money to the amount of her marriage price and he shall make good to her the dowry which she brought from her father's house and then he may put her away.

142. If a woman hates her husband and says, "You may not have me," the city council shall inquire into her case; and if she has been careful and without reproach and her husband has been going about and greatly belittling her, that woman has no blame. She may take her dowry and go to her father's house.

143. If she has not been careful but has gadded about, neglecting her house, and belittling her husband, they shall throw that woman into the water.

168. If a man set his face to disinherit his son and say to the judges, "I will disinherit my son," the judges shall inquire into his record, and if the son has not committed a crime sufficiently grave to cut him off from sonship, the father may not cut off his son from sonship.

195. If a son strike his father, they shall cut off his hand.

196. If a man destroy the eye of another man, they shall destroy his eye.

197. If he break another man's bone, they shall break his bone.

199. If he destroy the eye of a man's slave or break a bone of a man's slave, he shall pay one-half his price.

200. If a man knock out a tooth of a man of his own rank, they shall knock out his tooth.

229. If a builder build a house for a man and does not make its construction sound, and the house which he has built collapses and causes the death of the owner of the house, that builder shall be put to death.

233. If a builder build a house for a man and does not make its construction sound, and a wall cracks, that builder shall strengthen that wall at his own expense.

[These are] the just laws which Hammurabi, the wise king, established and by which he gave the land stable support and good government. Hammurabi, the perfect king, am I.

The great gods called me, and I am the guardian shepherd whose scepter is just and whose beneficent shadow is spread over my city. In my bosom I carried the people of the land of Sumer and Akkad; under my protection they prospered; I governed them in peace; in my wisdom I sheltered them.

In order that the strong might not oppress the weak, that justice be given to the orphans and the widow, in Babylon, . . . for the pronouncing of judgments in the land, for the rendering of decisions for the land, and to give justice to the oppressed, my weighty words I have written upon my monument, and in the presence of my image as king of justice have I established it.

Mesopotamian Thought and Religion

The Epic of Gilgamesh

The Sumerians who inhabited the southern region of Mesopotamia were the first people in Western civilization to produce epic tales about deities and human heroes. The Epic of Gilgamesh *dates from about 2000 B.C.E. and is a collection of stories about the Sumerian king of Uruk. In the following passages, Gilgamesh, confronted with the reality of his friend Enkidu's death, sets out to find Utnapishtim, the only man to whom the gods have given eternal life. Gilgamesh discovers that he must accept the inevitability of his own death.*

There follows the Mesopotamian tale of the Flood and the biblical account contained in the Old Testament. Flood epics were quite common in ancient literature and represented a cleansing of the community in accordance with a higher ethical law. But compare the two accounts closely, especially with regard to the attitudes and actions of the deities.

The Quest for Eternal Life

Bitterly Gilgamesh wept for his friend Enkidu; he wandered over the wilderness as a hunter, he roamed over the plains; in his bitterness he cried, "How can I rest, how can I be at peace? Despair is in my heart. What my brother is now, that shall I be when I am dead. Because I am afraid of death I will go as best I can to find Utnapishtim whom they call the Faraway, for he has entered the assembly of the gods." So Gilgamesh traveled over the wilderness, he wandered over the grasslands, a long journey, in search of Utnapishtim, whom the gods took after the deluge; and they set him to live in the land of Dilmin, in the garden of the sun; and to him alone of men they gave everlasting life. . . .

The Epic of Gilgamesh translated by N.K. Sandars (Penguin Classics, 1960, Third edition 1972) copyright © N. K. Sandars, 1960, 1964, 1972, pp. 94, 102–110. Reproduced with permission of Penguin Books Ltd.

Gilgamesh said to him [Utnapishtim], "Why should not my cheeks be starved and my face drawn? Despair is in my heart and my face is the face of one who has made a long journey. It was burned with heat and with cold. Why should I not wander over the pastures? My friend, my younger brother who seized and killed the Bull of Heaven and overthrew Humbaba in the cedar forest, my friend who was very dear to me and endured dangers beside me, Enkidu, my brother whom I loved, the end of mortality has overtaken him. I wept for him seven days and nights till the worm fastened on him. Because of my brother I am afraid of death; because of my brother I stray through the wilderness. His fate lies heavy upon me. How can I be silent, how can I rest? He is dust and I shall die also and be laid in the earth for ever. . . . Oh, father Utnapishtim, you who have entered the assembly of the gods, I wish to question you concerning the living and the dead, how shall I find the life for which I am searching?"

Utnapishtim said, "There is no permanence. Do we build a house to stand forever, do we seal a contract to hold for all time? Do brothers divide an inheritance to keep forever, does the flood-time of rivers endure? It is only the nymph of the dragonfly who sheds her larva and sees the sun in his glory. From the days of old there is no permanence. The sleeping and the dead, how alike they are, they are like a painted death. What is there between the master and the servant when both have fulfilled their doom? When the Annunaki, the judges, come together, and Mammetun the mother of destinies, together they decree the fates of men. Life and death they allot but the day of death they do not disclose." . . .

The destiny was fulfilled which the father of the gods, Enlil of the mountain, had decreed for Gilgamesh: "In nether-earth the darkness will show him a light; of mankind, all that are known, none will leave a monument for generations to come to compare with his. The heroes, the wise men, like the new moon have their waxing and waning. Men will say, "Who has ever ruled with might and with power like him?" As

in the dark month, the month of shadows, so without him there is no light. O Gilgamesh, this was the meaning of your dream. You were given the kingship, such was your destiny, everlasting life was not your destiny. Because of this do not be sad at heart, do not be grieved or oppressed; he has given you power to bind and to loose, to be the darkness and the light of mankind. He has given unexampled supremacy over the people, in victory in battle from which no fugitive returns, in forays and assaults from which there is no going back. But do not abuse this power, deal justly with your servants in the palace, deal justly with the face of the Sun."

The Story of the Flood

Then Gilgamesh said . . ."I look at you now, Utnapishtim, and your appearance is no different than mine; there is nothing strange in your features. . . . Tell me truly, how was it that you came to enter the company of the gods and to possess everlasting life?" Utnapishtim said to Gilgamesh, "I will reveal to you a mystery, I will tell you a secret of the gods."

"You know the city Shurrupak, it stands on the banks of Euphrates? That city grew old and the gods that were in it were old. There was Anu, lord of the firmament, their father, and warrior Enlil their counsellor, Ninurta the helper, and Ennugi watcher over canals; and with them also was Ea. In those days the world teemed, the people multiplied, the world bellowed like a wild bull, and the great god was aroused by the clamour. Enlil heard the clamour and he said to the gods in council, 'The uproar of mankind is intolerable and sleep is no longer possible by reason of the babel.' So the gods in their hearts were moved to let loose the deluge; but my lord Ea warned me in a dream. He whispered their words to my house of reeds, . . . 'O man of Shurrupak, . . . tear down your house and build a boat, abandon possessions and look for life, despise worldly goods and save your soul alive. . . . These are the measurements of the barque as you shall build her: let her beam equal her length, let her deck be roofed like the vault that covers the abyss; then take up into the boat the seed of all living creatures.'

"When I had understood I said to my lord, 'Behold, what you have commanded I will honor and perform, but how shall I answer the people, the city, the elders?' Then Ea opened his mouth and said to me, his servant, 'Tell them this: I have learnt that Enlil is wrathful against me, I dare no longer walk in his land nor live in his city; I will go down to the Gulf to dwell with Ea my lord. But on you he will rain down abundance, rare fish and shy wild-fowl, a rich harvest-tide. In the evening the rider of the storm will bring you wheat in torrents.'

"In the first light of dawn all my household gathered round me, the children brought pitch and the men whatever was necessary. . . . On the seventh day the boat was complete. . . . I loaded into her all that I had of gold and of living things, my family, my kin, the beasts of the field both wild and tame, and all the craftsmen. I sent them on board, for the time that Shamash had ordained was already fulfilled when he said, 'In the evening, when the rider of the storm sends down the destroying rain, enter the boat and batten her down.' This time was fulfilled, the evening came, the rider of the storm sent down the rain. I looked out at the weather and it was terrible, so I too boarded the boat and battened her down. . . .

"With the first light of dawn a black cloud came from the horizon. . . One whole day the tempest raged gathering fury as it went, it poured over the people like the tides of battle; a man could not see his brother nor the people be seen from heaven. Even the gods were terrified at the flood, they fled to the highest heaven, . . . they crouched against the walls, cowering like curs. . . . The great gods of heaven and of hell wept, they covered their mouths.

"For six days and six nights the winds blew, torrent and tempest and flood overwhelmed the world . . . like warring hosts. When the seventh day dawned the storm from the south subsided, the sea grew calm, the flood was stilled; I looked at the face of the world and there was silence, all mankind was turned to clay. The surface of the sea stretched as flat as a roof-top; I opened a hatch and the light fell on my face. Then I bowed low, I sat down and I wept, the tears streamed down my face, for on every side was the waste of water. . . . I threw everything open to the four winds, made a sacrifice and poured out a libation on the mountain top. . . . When the gods smelled the sweet savor, they gathered like flies over the sacrifice. . . .

"When Enlil had come, when he saw the boat, he was wrath and swelled with anger at the gods, the host of heaven, 'Has any of these mortals escaped? Not one was to have survived the destruction.' . . . Then Ea opened his mouth and spoke to warrior Enlil, 'Wisest of gods, hero Enlil, how could you so senselessly bring down the flood?

'Lay upon the sinner his sin,
Lay upon the transgressor his
    transgression,
Punish him a little when he breaks loose,
Do not drive him too hard or he perishes;
Would that a lion had ravaged mankind
Rather than the flood,
Would that a wolf had ravaged mankind
Rather than the flood,
Would that famine had wasted the world
Rather than the flood,
Would that pestilence had wasted
    mankind
Rather than the flood.

It was not I that revealed the secret of the gods; the wise man learned it in a dream. Now take your counsel what shall be done with him.'

"Then Enlil went up into the boat, he took me by the hand and my wife and made us enter the boat and kneel down on either side, he standing between us. He touched our foreheads to bless us saying, 'In time past Utnapishtim was a mortal man; henceforth he and his wife shall live in the distance at the mouth of the rivers.' Thus it was that the gods took me and placed me here to live in the distance at the mouth of the rivers."

The Biblical Flood

God said to Noah, "I have decided that the end has come for all living things, for the earth is full of lawlessness because of human beings. So I am now about to destroy them and the earth. Make yourself an ark out of resinous wood. Make it of reeds and caulk it with pitch inside and out. This is how to make it: the length of the ark is to be three hundred cubits, its breadth fifty cubits, and its height thirty cubits. . . .

"For my part, I am going to send the flood, the waters, on earth, to destroy living things having the breath of life under heaven: everything on earth is to perish. But with you I shall establish my covenant and you will go aboard the ark, yourself, your sons, your wife, and your sons' wives along with you. From all living creatures, from all living things, you must take two of each kind aboard the ark, to save their lives with yours; they must be a male and a female. Of every species of bird, of every kind of animal and of every kind of creature that creeps along

Excerpt from *The Jerusalem Bible,* copyright © 1966 by Darton, Longman & Todd, Ltd. and Doubleday, a division of Random House, Inc., pp. 24–26. Reprinted by permission.

the ground, two must go with you so that their lives may be saved. . . ." Noah did this, exactly as God commanded him. . . .

The flood lasted forty days on earth. The waters swelled, lifting the ark until it floated off the ground. . . . The waters rose higher and higher above the ground until all the highest mountains under the whole of heaven were submerged. . . . Every living thing on the face of the earth was wiped out, people, animals, creeping things and birds; they were wiped off the earth and only Noah was left, and those with him in the ark. . . .

Then God said to Noah, "Come out of the ark, you, your wife, your sons, and your sons' wives with you. Bring out all the animals with you, all living things. . . ." Then Noah built an altar to Yahweh and, choosing from all the clean animals and all the clean birds, he presented burnt offerings on the altar. Yahweh smelt the pleasing smell and said to himself, "Never again will I curse the earth because of human beings, because their heart contrives evil from their infancy. Never again will I strike down every living thing as I have done. . . ." God blessed Noah and his sons and said to them, "Breed, multiply and fill the earth."

The Mesopotamian View of Death

Historians can often tell much about a civilization by the way it regards the finality of death or the existence of an afterlife. The following poems are good examples of the Mesopotamian view.

The Mother Sings

Hark the piping!
My heart is piping in the wilderness
    where the young man once went free.
He is a prisoner now in death's kingdom,
    lies bound where once he lived.
The ewe gives up her lamb
and the nanny-goat her kid.

Poems of Heaven and Hell from Ancient Mesopotamia translated by N. K. Sandars (Penguin Classics, 1971) copyright © N. K. Sandars, 1971, pp. 163–164. Reproduced with permission of Penguin Books Ltd.

My heart is piping in the wilderness
    an instrument of grief.
Now she is coming to death's kingdom,
she is the mother desolate
in a desolate place; where once
he was alive, now he lies
like a young bull felled to the ground.
Into his face she stares, seeing
what she has lost—his mother
who has lost him to death's kingdom.
O the agony she bears,
shuddering in the wilderness,
she is the mother suffering so much.

"It is you,"
she cried to him,
  "but you are changed."
The agony, the agony she bears.
Woe to the house and the inner room.

The Son's Reply

There can be no answer
  to her desolate calling,
it is echoed in the wilderness,
  for I cannot answer.
Though the grass will shoot

from the land
I am not grass, I cannot come
  to her calling.
The waters rise for her,
I am not water to come
  for her wailing,
I am not shoots of grass
  in a dead land.

Poems of Heaven and Hell from Ancient Mesopotamia translated by N. K. Sandars (Penguin Classics, 1971) copyright © N. K. Sandars, 1971, pp. 163–164. Reproduced with permission of Penguin Books Ltd.

EGYPTIAN CIVILIZATION

The Authority of the Pharaohs

The king of Egypt, or Pharaoh (meaning "Great House"), possessed an authority rarely achieved in world civilization. He was regarded as a god incarnate who upon death rose to take his place in the sky as the deity, Horus. In the Old Kingdom (3200–2260 B.C.E.), pharaonic authority was great and the pyramids were built to house the body of the dead king. Egyptians considered preservation of the body essential for use in the afterlife, so they perfected the art of mummification. The following selections from the Greek historian Herodotus show the great authority of the Pharaoh in the Old Kingdom. Herodotus describes the commitment demanded by Cheops, for whom the Great Pyramid is named. An account of the process of mummification follows.

Building the Pyramids

HERODOTUS

After Cheops had ascended the throne, he brought the country into every manner of evil. First closing all the temples, he forbade sacrificing there, then ordered all the Egyptians to work for him. Some he told to draw stones from the quarries in the Arabian mountains about the Nile; others were ordered to receive them after they had been carried over the river in boats, and to draw them to the Libyan mountains. And they worked in groups of 100,000 men, each group for three months continually. Ten years of oppression for the people were required for making the

causeway by which they dragged the stones. This causeway which they built was not a much inferior work to the pyramid itself, as it seems to me; . . . it is made of polished stones and engraved with the figures of living beings. Ten years were required for this, and for the works on the mound, where the pyramids stand, and for the underground chambers in the island, which he intended as sepulchral vaults for his own use, and lastly for the canal which he dug from the Nile. The pyramid was built in 20 years; it is square; each side measures 800 feet and its height is the same; the stones are polished and fitted together with the utmost exactness. Not one of them is less than 30 feet in length.

The pyramid was built in steps, in the manner of an altar. After laying the base, they lifted the remaining stones to their places by means of machines, made of short pieces of wood. The first machine raised them from the ground to the top

"Building the Pyramids" is from Herodotus, *History*, 2.124, in *A Source-Book of Ancient History*, ed. George W. Botsford (New York: Macmillan, 1912), pp. 6–8.

of the first step; and when the stone had been lifted thus far, it was drawn to the top of the second step by another machine; for they had as many machines as steps. . . . At any rate, the highest parts were finished first, then the next, and so on till they came to the parts resting on the ground, namely the base. It is set down in Egyptian writing on the pyramid how much was spent on radishes and leeks and onions for the workmen; and I remember well the interpreter read the sum of 1600 talents of silver. Now if these figures are correct, how much more must have been spent on the iron with which they worked, and on the food and clothing of the workmen, considering the length of time which the work lasted, and an additional period, as I understand, during which they cut and brought the stones, and made the excavations.

Mummification

HERODOTUS

There are a set of men in Egypt who practice the art of embalming, and make it their proper business. These persons, when a body is brought to them, show the bearers various models of corpses made in wood, and painted so as to resemble nature. . . . The mode of embalming, according to the most perfect process, is the following:—They take first a crooked piece of iron, and with it draw out the brain through the nostrils, thus getting rid of a portion, while the skull is cleared of the rest by rinsing with drugs; next they make a cut along the flank with a sharp Ethiopian stone, and take out the whole contents of the abdomen, which they then cleanse, washing it thoroughly with palm wine, and again frequently with an infusion of pounded aromatics. After this they fill the cavity with the purest bruised myrrh, with cassia, and every other sort of spice, except frankincense, and sew up the opening. Then the body is

placed in natron [hydrated sodium carbonate] for seventy days, and covered entirely over. After the expiration of that space of time, which must not be exceeded, the body is washed, and wrapped round, from head to foot, with bandages of fine linen cloth, smeared over with gum, which is used generally by the Egyptians in the place of glue, and in this state it is given back to the relations, who enclose it in a wooden case which they have had made for the purpose, shaped into the figure of a man. Then fastening the case, they place it in a sepulchral chamber, upright against the wall. Such is the most costly way of embalming the dead.

If persons wish to avoid expense, and choose the second process, the following is the method pursued:—Syringes are filled with oil made from the cedar-tree, which is then, without any incision or disemboweling, injected into the abdomen. The passage by which it might be likely to return is stopped, and the body laid in natron the prescribed number of days. At the end of the time the cedar-oil is allowed to make its escape; and such is its power that it brings with it the whole stomach and intestines in a liquid state. The natron meanwhile has dissolved the flesh, and so nothing is left of the dead body but the skin and the bones. It is returned in this condition to the relatives, without any further trouble being bestowed upon it.

The third method of embalming, which is practised in the case of the poorer classes, is to rinse out the intestines and let the body lie in natron the seventy days, after which it is at once given to those who come to fetch it away. . . .

Whensoever any one, Egyptian or foreigner, has lost his life by falling prey to a crocodile, or by drowning in the river, the law compels the inhabitants of the city near which the body is cast up to have it embalmed, and to bury it in one of the sacred repositories with all possible magnificence. No one may touch the corpse, not even any of the friends or relatives, but only the priests of the Nile, who prepare it for burial with their own hands—regarding it as something more than the mere body of a man—and themselves lay it in the tomb.

"Mummification" is from Herodotus, *History*, 2.86, 87, 90, in *The History of Herodotus*, trans. George Rawlinson (New York: E. P. Dutton, 1910), pp. 154–156.

Ramses the Great

Ramses II (1301–1234 B.C.E.) was one of the greatest of all Egyptian pharaohs. His reign has been immortalized by his magnificent construction projects, such as the temple of Karnak at Luxor and the enormous statues of Abu Simbel. In addition, his fame is recorded in the Old Testament as the Pharaoh under whom the Exodus of the Hebrews took place. His mummy has been remarkably well preserved; we can tell that he died in his nineties and that he suffered from acne, tuberculosis, and poor circulation of the blood. His tomb had been plundered by ancient grave robbers, and one can only imagine its former gold and splendor. The following passage is from an inscription found on the temple at Abu Simbel. In it, the god Ptah speaks to his son, Ramses.

Thus speaks Ptah-Totunen with the high plumes, armed with horns, the father of the gods, to his son who loves him. . . .

Num and Ptah have nourished your childhood, they leap with joy when they see you made after my likeness, noble, great, exalted. The great princesses of the house of Ptah and the Hathors of the temple of Tem are in festival, their hearts are full of gladness, their hands take the drum with joy, when they see your person beautiful and lovely like my Majesty. . . . King Ramses, I grant you to cut the mountains into statues immense, gigantic, everlasting; I grant that foreign lands find for you precious stone to inscribe the monuments with thy name.

I give you to succeed in all the works which you have done. I give you all kinds of workmen, all that go on two or four feet, all that fly and all that have wings. I have put in the heart of all nations to offer you what they have done; themselves, princes great and small, with one heart seek to please you, King Ramses. You have built a great residence to fortify the boundary of the land, the city of Ramses; it is established on the earth like the four pillars of the sky; you have constructed within a royal palace, where festivals are celebrated to you as is done for me within. I have set the crown on your head with my own hands, when you appear in the great hall of the double throne; and men and gods have praised your name like mine when my festival is celebrated.

You have carved my statues and built my shrines as I have done in times of old. You reign in my place on my throne; I fill your limbs with life and happiness, I am behind you to protect you; I give you health and strength; I cause Egypt to be submitted to you; and I supply the two countries with pure life. King Ramses, I grant that the strength, the vigor, and the might of your sword be felt among all countries; you cast down the hearts of all nations; I have put them under your feet; you come forth every day in order that foreign prisoners be brought to you; the chiefs and the great of all nations offer you their children. I give them to your gallant sword that you may do with them what you like. King Ramses, I grant that the fear of you be in the minds of all and your command in their hearts. I grant that your valor reach all countries, and that the dread of you be spread over all lands; the princes tremble at your thought, and your majesty is [evident]; they come to you as supplicants to implore your mercy. You give life to whomever you please; the throne of all nations is in your possession. . . .

King Ramses, . . . the mountains, the water, and the stone walls which are on the earth are shaken when they hear your excellent name, since they have seen what I have accomplished for you; which is that the land of the Hittites

"Ramses the Great" is from George W. Botsford, ed., *A Source-Book of Ancient History* (New York: Macmillan, 1912), pp. 10–12. Translation modernized by the editor.

The temple of Ramses II at Abu Simbel is remarkable for its four colossal figures of the Pharaoh. They reflect the great authority of the famous Egyptian king. (*Eugene Gordon/Pearson Education/PH College*)

should be subjected to your rule. . . . Their chiefs are prisoners, all their property is the tribute in the dependency of the living king. Their royal daughter is at the head of them; she comes to soften the heart of King Ramses; her merits are marvelous, but she does not know the goodness which is in your heart.

Egyptian Values

Egyptian literature abounds with didactic writings intended to instruct an individual on right action or proper conduct in life. A sense of "limit" and thoughtful discretion pervade the following suggestions to a royal administrator named Kagemni by a sage whose identity is unknown. These maxims were found on a piece of papyrus dating from the Old Kingdom. The love songs in this section date from the New Kingdom and reveal a private side to the Egyptian.

Instructions of Kagemni

The respectful man prospers,
Praised is the modest one,

Lichtheim, Miriam, trans. & ed. *Ancient Egyptian Literature: A Book of Readings*, Vol. 1. Copyright © 1973–1980 Regents of the University of California, pp. 59–60. Reprinted with permission.

The tent is open to the silent,
The seat of the quiet is spacious.
Do not chatter!
Knives are sharp against the blunderer,
Without hurry except when he faults.

When you sit with company,
Shun the food you love,

Restraint is a brief moment,
Gluttony is base and is reproved.
A cup of water quenches thirst,
A mouthful of herbs strengthens the
    heart,
One good thing stands for goodness,
A little something stands for much.
Vile is he whose belly covets when
    [meal]-time has passed,
He forgets those in whose house his belly
    roams.

When you sit with a glutton,
Eat when his greed has passed,
When you drink with a drunkard,
Take when his heart is content.
Don't fall upon meat by the side of a
    glutton,
Take when he gives you, don't refuse it,
Then it will soothe.
He who is blameless in matters of food,
No word can prevail against him;
He who is gentle, even timid,

The harsh is kinder to him than to his
    mother,
All people are his servants.

Let your name go forth,
While your mouth is silent,
When you are summoned, don't boast of
    strength
Among those your age, lest you be
    opposed.
One knows not what may happen,
What god does when he punishes.

The vizier had his children summoned, after he had understood the ways of men, their character having become clear to him. Then he said to them: "All that is written in this book, heed it as I said it. Do not go beyond what has been set down." Then they placed themselves on their bellies. They recited it as it was written. It

seemed good to them beyond anything in the whole land.

Love Song: "Would You Then Leave Me?"

If good fortune comes your way, [you still
    cannot find] happiness.
But if you try to touch my thighs and
    breasts,
[then you'll be satisfied.]

Because you remember you are hungry
    would you then leave?
Are you a man
    thinking only of his stomach?
Would you [walk off from me
    concerned with] your stylish clothes
and leave me with the sheet?

Because of hunger
    would you then leave me?
    [or because you are thirsty?]
Take then my breast:
    for you its gift overflows.
Better indeed is one day in your arms . . .
    than a hundred thousand [anywhere]
    on earth.

My love for you is mixed throughout my
    body
like [salt] dipped in water,
like a medicine to which gum is added,
like milk shot through [water]. . . .

So hurry to see your lady,
like a stallion on the track,
or like a falcon [swooping down] to its
    papyrus marsh.
Heaven sends down the love of her
as a flame falls in the [hay]. . . .

Simpson, William Kelley, ed., *The Literature of Ancient Egypt.* Copyright © 1972 by Yale University Press, p. 298. Reprinted with permission.

Love Song: "I Am Your Best Girl"

I am your best girl:
I belong to you like an acre of land
which I have planted
with flowers and every sweet-smelling grass.

Pleasant is the channel through it
which your hand dug out

Simpson, William Kelley, ed., *The Literature of Ancient Egypt.* Copyright © 1972 by Yale University Press, pp. 308–309. Reprinted with permission.

for refreshing ourselves with the breeze,
a happy place for walking
with your hand in my hand.

My body is excited, my heart joyful,
at our traveling together.

Hearing your voice is pomegranate wine,
for I live to hear it,
and every glance which rests on me
means more to me than eating and
    drinking.

Egyptian Religion

The Pyramid Texts

The Pyramid Texts *date from the Old Kingdom and were carved on the walls of the sarcophagus chambers of the pyramids at Saqqara. They were discovered in 1881, and their purpose was to promote the resurrection of the pharaoh from the dead. Each utterance is separated from the others by dividing lines and thus represents a self-contained prayer. The following incantations are from the pyramids of Pepi I, a king in the Sixth Dynasty (ca. 2400 B.C.E.).*

The Pharaoh Prays for Admittance to the Sky

Awake in peace, O Pure One, in peace!
Awake in peace, Horus-of-the-East, in
    peace!
Awake in peace, Soul-of-the-East, in peace!
Awake in peace, Horus-of-Lightland, in
    peace!
You lie down in the Night-bark,
You awake in the Day-bark,
For you are he who gazes on the gods,
There is no god who gazes on you!

O father of Pepi, take Pepi with you
Living, to you mother Nut!
Gates of sky, open for Pepi,
Gates of heaven, open for Pepi,
Pepi comes to you, make him live!

Command that this Pepi sit beside you,
Beside him who rises in lightland!
O father of Pepi, command to the goddess
    beside you
To make wide Pepi's seat at the stairway of
    heaven!

Command the Living One, the son of
    Sothis,
To speak for this Pepi,
To establish for Pepi a seat in the sky!
Commend this Pepi to the Great Noble,
The beloved of Ptah, the son of Ptah,
To speak for this Pepi,
To make flourish his jar-stands on earth,
For Pepi is one with these four gods:
Imsety, Hapy, Duamutef, Kebhsenuf,
Who live by maat [truth],

Poems from the *Pyramid Texts* are from Miriam Lichtheim, trans. and ed., *Ancient Egyptian Literature: A Book of Readings*, vol. 1 (Berkeley: University of California Press, 1973), pp. 44, 49–50. © 1973 The Regents of the University of California. Reprinted by permission.

Hyksos

Who lean on their staffs,
Who watch over Upper Egypt.

He flies, he flies from you men as do
  ducks,
He wrests his arms from you as a falcon,
He tears himself from you as a kite,
Pepi frees himself from the fetter of
  earth,
Pepi is released from bondage!

The Pharaoh Prays to the Sky Goddess

O Great One who became Sky,
You are strong, you are mighty,
You fill every place with your beauty,
The whole earth is beneath you, you
  possess it!
As you enfold earth and all things in your
  arms,
So have you taken this Pepi to you,
An indestructible star within you!

The Book of the Dead: Negative Confession

The Book of the Dead is a collection of texts dating from the Middle and New Kingdoms that re-
flect a growing concern for the welfare of the dead and their search for eternal happiness. The Egyp-
tians believed that upon death, one was judged by Osiris, god of the underworld, who determined
*one's fate on the basis of truth (*maat*) and moral purity. The "negative confession" that follows was*
part of the summation of one's life in the presence of Osiris. The emphasis is not on one's positive ac-
complishments in life, but rather on the unrighteous acts that were not committed—hence the term
"negative confession." The following selection is from the tomb of Nu, an administrator of the Eigh-
teenth Dynasty (1570–1085 B.C.E.).

Homage to thee, O Great God [Osiris], . . . I
have come to thee, O my Lord, I have brought
myself hither that I may behold thy beauties. . . .
In truth I have come to thee, and I have
brought maat to thee, and I have expelled
wickedness for thee.

1. I have not done evil to mankind.
2. I have not oppressed the members of my
   family.
3. I have not wrought evil in the place of
   right and truth.
4. I have had no knowledge of worthless
   men.
7. I have not brought forward my name for
   exaltation to honors.
8. I have not ill-treated servants.
9. I have not belittled a god.
10. I have not defrauded the oppressed one
    of his property.

11. I have not done that which is an abomi-
    nation unto the gods.
14. I have made no man to suffer hunger.
15. I have made no one to weep.
16. I have done no murder.
17. I have not given the order for murder to
    be done for me.
18. I have not inflicted pain upon man-
    kind.
22. I have not committed fornication.
26. I have not encroached upon the fields of
    others.
29. I have not carried away the milk from
    the mouths of children.
30. I have not driven away the cattle which
    were upon their pastures.
38. I have not obstructed a god in his pro-
    cession. I am pure! I am pure!
    I am pure! I am pure!

"The Book of the Dead: Negative Confession" is from E. A. Wallace Budge, trans., *The Book of the Dead Ac-*
cording to the Theban Recension (New York: E. P. Dutton, 1922), Ch. 125. Reprinted by permission of George Routledge and Sons, Ltd.

Hymn to the Aten

AKHENATEN

Egyptian civilization was noted for its tradition, respect for authority, and unchanging cycles that gave unity and stability to the land for thousands of years. Yet one of the most radical changes in this pattern took place briefly during the reign of Amenhotep IV (1372–1355 B.C.E.). He changed the very course of Egyptian religion by eliminating the several gods and goddesses that were the basis for Egyptian polytheism. He replaced them with one god, a solar disk, whom he called Aten. In accordance with these new principles, Amenhotep IV ("Amon rests") changed his name to Akhenaten ("Aten is satisfied") and constructed a new capital at Amarna. Systematically, the names of the old gods were erased from temple walls and public inscriptions. All worship was to be directed toward Aten, a universal deity. Thus Akhenaten sacrificed his own divinity to promote himself as the son and interpreter of Aten.

Akhenaten's monotheism has been hotly debated. Some regard it as a unique and creative approach to religion that even influenced later Hebrew monotheism; others see it as the development of earlier Egyptian thought with new elements included. In any event, Akhenaten's new religion was considered a heresy and did not survive his reign. The following prayer to Aten is the quintessential expression of Akhenaten's devotion to his universal god.

You rise in perfection on the horizon of
   the sky,
living [Aten], who started life.
Whenever you are risen upon the eastern
   horizon
you fill every land with your perfection.
You are appealing, great, sparkling, high
   over every land;
your rays hold together the lands as far as
   everything you have made.
Since you are Re, you reach as far as they
   do,
and you curb them for your beloved son.
Although you are far away, your rays are
   upon the land;
you are in their faces, yet your departure is
   not observed.

Whenever you set on the western horizon,
the land is in darkness in the manner of
   death.
They sleep in a bedroom with heads
   under the covers,
and one eye does not see another.

If all their possessions which are under
   their heads were stolen,
they would not know it.
Every lion who comes out of his cave and
   all the serpents bite,

for darkness is a blanket.
The land is silent now, because he who
   made them
is at rest on his horizon.

But when day breaks you are risen upon
   the horizon,
and you shine as the [Aten] in the
   daytime.
When you dispel darkness and you give
   forth your rays
the two lands are in festival,
alert and standing on their feet,
now that you have raised them up.
Their bodies are clean, and their clothes
   have been put on;
their arms are [lifted] in praise at your
   rising.

Simpson, William Kelley, ed., *The Literature of Ancient Egypt.* Copyright © 1972 by Yale University Press, pp. 290–295. Reprinted with permission.

The entire land performs its works:
all the cattle are content with their fodder,
trees and plants grow,
birds fly up to their nests,
their wings [extended] in praise for your
    Ka.
All the kine prance on their feet;
everything which flies up and alights,
they live when you have risen for them.
The barges sail upstream and downstream
    too,
for every way is open at your rising.
The fishes in the river leap before your face
when your rays are in the sea.

You who have placed seed in woman
and have made sperm into man,
who feeds the son in the womb of his
    mother,
who quiets him with something to stop his
    crying;
you are the nurse in the womb,
giving breath to nourish all that has been
    begotten.
When he comes down from the womb to
    breathe
on the day he is born,
you open up his mouth [completely], and
    supply his needs.
When the fledgling in the egg speaks in
    the shell,
you give him air inside it to sustain him.
When you grant him his allotted time to
    break out from the egg,

he comes out from the egg to cry out at
    his fulfillment,
and he goes upon his legs when he has
    come forth from it.
How plentiful it is, what you have made,
although they are hidden from view,
sole god, without another beside you;
you created the earth as you wished,
when you were by yourself, [before]
mankind, all cattle and kine,
all beings on land, who fare upon their
    feet,

and all beings in the air, who fly with their
    wings.

The lands of Khor and Kush
and the land of Egypt:
you have set every man in his place,
you have allotted their needs,
every one of them according to his diet,
and his lifetime is counted out.
Tongues are separate in speech,
and their characters as well;
their skins are different,
for you have differentiated the foreigners.
In the underworld you have made a Nile
that you may bring it forth as you wish
to feed the populace,
since you made them for yourself, their
    utter master,
growing weary on their account, lord of
    every land.
For them the [Aten] of the daytime arises,
great in awesomeness.

All distant lands,
you have made them live,
for you have set a Nile in the sky
that it may descend for them
and make waves upon the mountains like
    the sea
to irrigate the fields in their towns.
How efficient are your designs,
Lord of eternity:
a Nile in the sky [meaning "rain"] for the
    foreigners
and all creatures that go upon their feet,
a Nile coming back from the underworld
    for Egypt.

Your rays give suck to every field:
when you rise they live,
and they grow for you.
You have made the seasons
to bring into being all you have made:
the Winter to cool them,
the Heat that you may be felt.
You have made a far-off heaven
in which to rise

in order to observe everything you have
  made.
Yet you are alone,
rising in your manifestations as the Living
  [Aten]:
appearing, glistening, being afar, coming
  close;
you make millions of transformations of
  yourself.
Towns, harbors, fields, roadways,
  waterways:
every eye beholds you upon them,
for you are the [Aten] of the daytime on
  the face of the earth.
When you go forth
every eye [is upon you].
You have created their sight
but not to see [only] the body . . .
which you have made.

You are my desire,
and there is no other who knows you
except for your son . . .
for you have apprised him of your designs
  and your power.
The earth came forth into existence by
  your hand,

and you made it.
When you rise, they live;
when you set, they die.
You are a lifespan in yourself;
one lives by you.
Eyes are upon your perfection until you
  set:
all work is put down when you rest in the
  west.

When [you] rise, [everything] grows
for the King and [for] everyone who
  hastens on foot,
because you have founded the land
and you have raised them for your son
who has come forth from your body,
the King of Upper and Lower Egypt, the
  one Living on Maat,
Lord of the Two Lands . . .
son of Re, the one Living on Maat, Master
  of Regalia,
[Akhenaten], the long lived,
and the Foremost Wife of the King, whom
  he loves,
the Mistress of the Two Lands, . . .
living and young, forever and ever.

EARLY CHINESE CIVILIZATION

Early Chinese history is clouded in mythology with vague, semi-divine heroes who are said to have led the Chinese people toward civilization. They were in turn succeeded by a series of three wise kings who founded and ruled the first Chinese dynasty called the Xia. This dynasty, which is based only in legend, was supposed to have existed from 2205 to 1766 B.C.E. It ended when the last Xia king, a degenerate and incompetent ruler, was overthrown by a new dynasty called the Shang (or Yin). As noted in the chapter introduction, we have archeological proof of its existence and oracle bones with inscriptions that tell us something of the life of the period. We find frequent references to a supreme "Deity Above," who apparently watched over human society and regulated the working of the universe. Beneath him were lesser deities of the sun, moon, stars, wind, and rain. In addition to these, the early Chinese believed that their ancestors should also be honored through sacrifices because they continued to affect the prosperity of their descendants on earth.

The Shang dynasty existed from 1766 to 1050 B.C.E. and then was overthrown by a new dynasty of kings who had been able to unite disaffected city-states and conquer the Shang. This new dynasty, called the Zhou (1050-256 B.C.E.), assimilated Shang culture but took many steps to establish the legitimacy of its political rule.

Having overthrown the Shang, the founders of the Zhou dynasty had to justify their right to rule. Consequently, they developed a doctrine called the "Mandate of Heaven." According to this doctrine, human destiny depended not on the whim of some spiritual force, but on the individual's own good words and deeds. The Zhou, therefore, asserted that the Shang rulers, because of their wickedness, had forfeited their right to rule. The mandate for good government had passed on to the new dynasty. Under the Zhou, the concept of "Heaven," (now more of an abstract metaphysical force than an anthropomorphic deity) replaced the "Deity Above" and subsequent Chinese dynasties all ruled by invoking the supreme power that governed all creation—as the Son of Heaven. Therefore, the security of dynastic rule was carefully linked to virtue in human affairs. Should a ruler falter in maintaining a kingdom based on virtue, he too could be legitimately replaced, in accordance with the will of Heaven.

The early Chinese in the Shang and Zhou dynasties generally believed in:
- *A supreme deity or moral force that ruled the world and took a personal interest in human affairs.*
- *The existence and influence of nature spirits and the spirits of ancestors who were served by sacrifices.*
- *The divine sanction of political order and the necessity of ruling with virtue.*

The Book of Songs

The following selections are from The Book of Songs, *one of a series of texts that became known as the "Confucian Classics." The great philosopher Confucius (551–479 B.C.E.) and his followers were important transmitters and conservators of tradition. To that end they idealized the early Shang and Zhou kings as paragons of virtue. These Classics preserve, edit, and comment on the speeches, poems, and rituals of early Chinese history.*

The Book of Songs, *an anthology of 305 poems, contains some of the oldest material of Chinese literature. It is composed of folk songs, ritual hymns, and ballads all drawn from various levels of Zhou society dating from about 1000 to 600 B.C.E. The poetry speaks with an inner simplicity and purity that educates the human heart and has provided the foundation for all classical and even modern Chinese poetry.*

Cypress Boat

Tossed is that cypress boat,
Wave-tossed it floats.
My heart is in turmoil, I cannot sleep.
But secret is my grief.
Wine I have, all things needful
For play, for sport.

My heart is not a mirror,
To reflect what others will.
Brothers too I have;
I cannot be snatched away.

But lo, when I told them of my plight
I found that they were angry with me.

My heart is not a stone;
It cannot be rolled.
My heart is not a mat;
It cannot be folded away.
I have borne myself correctly
In rites more than can be numbered.

My sad heart is consumed, I am harassed
By a host of small men.
I have borne vexations very many,
Received insults not few.
In the still of night I brood upon it;
In the waking hours I rend my breast.

O sun, ah, moon,
Why are you changed and dim?
Sorrow clings to me
Like an unwashed dress.
In the still of night I brood upon it,
Long to take wing and fly away.

Of Fair Girls

Of fair girls the loveliest
Was to meet me at the corner of the
    Wall.
But she hides and will not show
    herself;
I scratch my head, pace up and down.

Of fair girls the prettiest
Gave me a red flute.
The flush of that red flute
Is pleasure at the girl's beauty.

She has been in the pastures and brought
    for me rush-wool,
Very beautiful and rare.
It is not you that are beautiful;
But you were given by a lovely girl.

From *The Book of Songs* edited and translated by Arthur Waley. Copyright © 1937 by Arthur Waley, pp. 26–27. Used by permission of Grove/Atlantic, Inc.

Sun and Moon

O sun, ah, moon
That shine upon the earth below.
A man like this
Will not stand firm to the end.
How can such a one be true?
Better if he had never noticed me.

O sun, ah, moon
That cover the earth below,
A man like this
Will not deal kindly to the end.
How can such a one be true?
Better if he had not requited me.

O sun, ah, moon
That rise out of the east,
A man like this,
Of whom no good word is said,
How can he be true?
I wish I could forget him.

O sun, ah, moon
That from the east do rise,
Heigh, father! Ho, mother,
You have nurtured me to no good end.
How should he be true?
He requited me, but did not follow up
    [our love meeting].

From *The Book of Songs* edited and translated by Arthur Waley. Copyright © 1937 by Arthur Waley, p. 36. Used by permission of Grove/Atlantic, Inc.

The Mandate of Heaven

The following selections are from The Book of Songs. *They reflect the transition from the Shang to the Zhou dynasty when the "Mandate of Heaven" was given to King Wen, the founder of the Zhou dynasty and his successors. Note carefully that political stability was dependent on virtuous government.*

The Charge That Heaven Gave

The charge that Heaven gave
Was solemn, was for ever.

From *The Book of Songs* edited and translated by Arthur Waley. Copyright © 1937 by Arthur Waley, p. 291. Used by permission of Grove/Atlantic, Inc.

And ah, most glorious
King Wen in plenitude of power!
With blessings he has whelmed us;
We need but gather them in.
High favors has King Wen vouchsafed to
    us;
May his descendants hold them fast.

King Wen

King Wen is on high;
Oh, he shines in Heaven!
Zhou is an old people,
But its charge is new.
The land of Zhou became illustrious,
Blessed by God's charge.
King Wen ascends and descends
On God's left hand, on His right.

Very diligent was King Wen,
His high fame does not cease;
He spread his bounties in Zhou,
And now in his grandsons and sons,
In his grandsons and sons
The stem has branched
Into manifold generations,
And all the knights of Zhou
Are glorious in their generation.

Glorious in their generation,
And their counsels well-pondered.
Mighty were the many knights
That brought this kingdom to its birth.
This kingdom well they bore;
They were the prop of Zhou.
Splendid were those many knights
Who gave comfort to Wen the king.

August is Wen the king;
Oh, to be reverenced in his glittering
    light!

Mighty the charge that Heaven gave him.
The grandsons and sons of the Shang.
Shang's grandsons and sons,
Their hosts were innumerable.
But God on high gave His command,
And by Zhou they were subdued.

By Zhou they were subdued;
Heaven's charge is not for ever.
The knights of Yin [people overthrown by
    the Zhou], big and little,
Made libations and offerings at the capital;
What they did was to make libations
Dressed in skirted robe and close cap.
O chosen servants of the king,
May you never thus shame your ancestors!

May you never shame your ancestors,
But rather tend their inward power,
That for ever you may be linked to
    Heaven's charge
And bring to yourselves many blessings.
Before Yin lost its army
It was well linked to God above.
In Yin you should see as in a mirror
That Heaven's high charge is hard to
    keep.

The charge is not easy to keep.
Do not bring ruin on yourselves.
Send forth everywhere the light of your
    good fame;
Consider what Heaven did to the Yin.
High Heaven does its business
Without sound, without smell.
Make King Wen your example,
In whom all the peoples put their trust.

From *The Book of Songs* edited and translated by Arthur
Waley. Copyright © 1937 by Arthur Waley, pp. 227–228.
Used by permission of Grove/Atlantic, Inc.

The Spirit World

During the Zhou period, families, both noble and common, sacrificed to their ancestors. These sacrifices were of the utmost importance and any neglect would bring about misfortune and calamity, for ancestors had the power to aid or punish their descendants.

Human sacrifice was practiced extensively during the Shang dynasty and to a lesser extent down to the third century B.C.E. *The third selection decries the practice that "takes all our good men" in following the king in death. Duke Mu of Qin died in 621* B.C.E. *The last selection is a conversation between a Zhou king and his minister and demonstrates the Chinese belief in the close interaction between the spirit world and the political environment. The king could not afford to lose the favor and protection of Heaven.*

Abundant Is the Year

Abundant is the year, with much millet,
    much rice;
But we have tall granaries,
To hold myriads, many myriads and
    millions of grain.
We make wine, make sweet liquor,
We offer it to ancestor, to ancestress,
We use it to fulfill all the rites,
To bring down blessings upon each and
    all.

Glorious Ancestors

Ah, the glorious ancestors–
Endless, their blessings,
Boundless their gifts are extended;
To you, too, they needs must reach.
We have brought them clear wine;
They will give victory.
Here, too, is soup well seasoned,
Well prepared, well mixed.
Because we come in silence,
Setting all quarrels aside,
They make safe for us a ripe old age,
We shall reach the withered cheek, we
    shall go on and on.
With our leather-bound naves, our bronze-
    clad yokes,
With eight bells a-jangle
We come to make offering.
The charge put upon us is vast and
    mighty,

From Heaven dropped our prosperity,
Good harvests, great abundance.
They come [the ancestors], they accept,
They send down blessings numberless.
They regard the paddy-offerings, the
    offerings of first-fruits
That Tang's descendant brings.

Human Sacrifice

"Kio" sings the oriole
As it lights on the thorn-bush.
Who went with Duke Mu to the grave?
Yan-xi of the clan Zi-ju.
Now this Yan-xi
Was the pick of all our men;
But as he drew near the tomb-hole
His limbs shook with dread.
That blue one, Heaven,
Takes all our good men.
Could we but ransom him
There are a hundred would give their lives.

"Kio" sings the oriole
As it lights on the thorn-bush.
Who went with Duke Mu to the grave?
Zhong-hang of the clan Zi-ju.
Now this Zhong-hang
Was the sturdiest of all our men;
But as he drew near the tomb-hole
His limbs shook with dread.
That blue one, Heaven,
Takes all our good men.
Could we but ransom him
There are a hundred would give their
    lives.

From *The Book of Songs* edited and translated by Arthur Waley. Copyright © 1937 by Arthur Waley, p. 297. Used by permission of Grove/Atlantic, Inc.

From *The Book of Songs* edited and translated by Arthur Waley. Copyright © 1937 by Arthur Waley, p. 319. Used by permission of Grove/Atlantic, Inc.

From *The Book of Songs* edited and translated by Arthur Waley. Copyright © 1937 by Arthur Waley, p. 103. Used by permission of Grove/Atlantic, Inc.

"Kio" sings the oriole
As it lights on the thorn-bush.
Who went with Duke Mu to the grave?
Quan-hu of the clan Zi-ru.
Now this Quan-hu
Was the strongest of all our men;

But as he drew near the tomb-hole
His limbs shook with dread.
That blue one, Heaven,
Takes all our good men.
Could we but ransom him
There are a hundred would give their lives.

CHRONOLOGY: The Earliest Civilizations: Mesopotamia, Egypt, and China (All dates are approximate)

3500 B.C.E.   Bronze Age cultures develop in Mesopotamia, "the land between the rivers."

3200–2260 B.C.E.   Old Kingdom in Egypt: strong pharaonic authority as reflected by the building of the pyramids.

3000 B.C.E.   The Sumerians found the first "Western civilization" in the southern portion of the Tigris and Euphrates River Valley; development of writing and agriculture.

2340 B.C.E.   Sargon of Akkad, Semitic king, extends his empire over Sumer to the "cedar forests of Lebanon," on the west coast of the Mediterranean.

2250–1750 B.C.E.   Harappan civilization flourishes on the Indus River in India.

2205–1766 B.C.E.   Mythological Xia dynasty in China. Neolithic settlements. Transition to Bronze Age about 2000 B.C.E.

2052–1786 B.C.E.   Middle Kingdom in Egypt: Pharaonic authority reestablished after civil war among nomarchs (regional governors).

2000 B.C.E.   The Epic of Gilgamesh, a collection of stories about the Sumerian king of Uruk, is written. Hittites, who were among the first to use iron, appear in Anatolia.

1800–1700 B.C.E.   Hebrew patriarch, Abraham, leaves Ur in Sumer and establishes himself in Canaan. Joseph continues to Egypt.

1800–1500 B.C.E.   Aryan peoples invade northwestern India.

1792–1750 B.C.E.   Reign of Hammurabi, Amorite (Babylonian) king who ruled from Babylonia and established order in the region through the fullest and best-preserved law code extant from Mesopotamia.

1766–1050 B.C.E.   Shang dynasty in China traditionally founded by King Wen. Development of writing, fine bronze artifacts, social classes, and human sacrifice.

1575–1086 B.C.E.   New Kingdom in Egypt: period of expansion and authority throughout the eastern Mediterranean. Led by conquerors, Thutmose III (1490–1436) and Ramses II (1301–1234), and the enigmatic Akhenaton (1367–1350), whose insistence on monotheism disrupts this traditional culture. King Tutankhamon dies ca. 1350 B.C.E.

1050–256 B.C.E.   Zhou dynasty in China. "Mandate of Heaven" defined to link virtue with successful political rule. Rise of Iron Age territorial states (*ca.* 770 B.C.E.), commerce, and ruthless military tactics.

STUDY QUESTIONS

1. In the preface to the Code of Hammurabi, why does Hammurabi feel justified in setting forth this law code? What are some of the penalties? Do they seem too harsh to be fair? Why is a law code such as this a sign of progress in civilization?

2. What makes *The Epic of Gilgamesh* such an enduring story? Compare the two accounts of the Flood. Which account do you find more vivid or exciting? What are the reasons given for the Flood and what does it signify? Compare especially the roles of the deities. How does God of the Old Testament differ in manner and action from Enlil or Ea?

3. Kingship and authority are major themes in ancient Near Eastern civilization. What do the readings reveal as true indicators of the authority of the Egyptian Pharaoh?

4. Compare the selections from the *Pyramid Texts* and *The Book of the Dead.* When were they written and what were they expected to accomplish? Can you draw any conclusions from your analysis? What do your conclusions say about Egyptian religion? Explain the term "negative confession." What is the rationale behind this practice?

5. Compare Egyptian and Mesopotamian views of religion by analyzing the various selections on the nature of the gods, death, and the afterlife. What general conclusions can you draw? The geography of a region often influences the development of a civilization. In what ways did geography influence the religious outlooks of Mesopotamia and Egypt?

6. What was the Amarna "revolution" and why was it a radical change for Egyptians? What does the "Hymn to the Aten" reveal about Akhenaton's conception of the deity?

7. Among the various poems contained in *The Book of Songs*, which is your favorite? In what ways do they "educate the heart"?

8. What was the "Mandate of Heaven" and how is it reflected in the various selections presented. Specifically, how do you interpret the phrase, "Zhou is an old people/But its charge is new"?

9. What role did spirits play in the lives of the Chinese? Why was it important to placate them? Why are the elderly revered in Chinese society? How was human sacrifice regarded by the Chinese? Why was it practiced? Who went with Duke Mu to the grave and why? What does this tell you about the power of early Chinese kings?

10. How did the duties and responsibilities of a king differ among the Mesopotamians, Egyptians, and Chinese? Compare especially Sargon, Hammurabi, Akhenaton, Ramses II, and King Wen.

2

The Spiritual and Philosophical Bases of Early World Civilizations

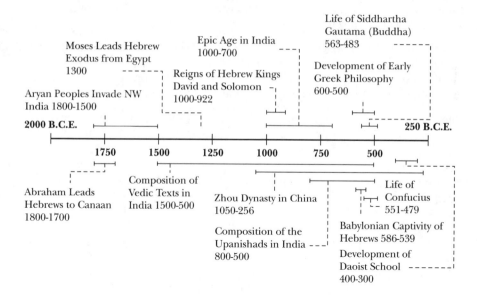

Philosophy is an attitude toward life based on a greater or lesser, but always limited comprehension of the universe as far as we happen to know it.

—Lin Youtang

The whole life of the philosopher is a preparation for death.

—Plato

Religion. A daughter of Hope and Fear, explaining to Ignorance the nature of the Unknowable.

—Ambrose Bierce

Religions die when they are proved to be true. Science is the record of dead religions.

—*Oscar Wilde*

Religion—that voice of the deepest human experience.

—*Matthew Arnold*

CHAPTER THEMES

- *Beliefs and Spirituality:* How did the belief systems of ancient India, China, Israel, and Greece provide a stabilizing foundation for the cultural development of each civilization? How radical a conception is monotheism? Is it more natural for a society to accept many deities, or does polytheism complicate spiritual organization and lead to a less unified religion?

- *Church/State Relationships:* In what ways were the political structures in China and ancient Israel supported or challenged by the spiritual and philosophical movements within these civilizations? Must a government adopt or support a particular belief in order to make the state efficient and secure from popular discontent?

- *The Big Picture:* Do people need religion and philosophy to provide meaning in life? Without an intellectual and spiritual focus, can a civilization thrive?

As we sit at the outset of the twenty-first century, we are in a unique position to assess our past and contemplate our future. This is not simply a new decade or even a new century. We have entered a new millennium, replete with harbingers of doom and destruction and with visions of progress and possibility. We have an opportunity to assess not only our technological progress in transistors, microchips, medicine, and nuclear weaponry, but also our more abstract progress in the cultivation of the human spirit. Are we better people than we were two hundred or two thousand years ago? Are we any further on the pathway toward understanding the nature of our creative potential or our capacity to destroy or to forgive? Has our human nature changed at all? Does each society at some point in time grapple with its own fears of the future and contemporary expectation of moral conduct? Ultimately, where are we headed as travelers in this life, and what lies for us after death?

These questions define some of the fundamental problems of human existence—all seem to deal with abstract intangibles that have troubled and challenged humankind over the centuries. The basic questions don't seem to change and the answers are still out there, just beyond our grasp, forcing us to be individuals in search of definition, hoping to find a "key" belief that will allow us some security and refuge from the vagaries of our human world. We want an answer, something to shoot for, some goal to attain. Life is hard or joyous often depending on how a person reconciles the competing demands of everyday life and finds the answers to many of the eternal questions of existence and moral conduct.

This is not just our contemporary problem. The search for meaning, security, and reconciliation forms the heart of human philosophical and religious study. And so, it is most appropriate for us in this chapter to enter a more abstract world of the mind and of the spirit to study some of the early religions and philosophies that were created to help human societies cope with the eternal questions that have been posed to each human generation.

Many people have sought answers to life's questions through philosophy and religion. We use these terms loosely and often interchangeably to the point that we often don't differentiate between disciplines. The word *philosophy* derives from a Greek root meaning "love of wisdom." Philosophy searches for the underlying causes and principles of reality. Inherent in philosophical speculation is a quest for truth through logical reasoning and factual observation rather than through faith. Philosophy is often organized around three principal areas: knowledge (epistemology), being (metaphysics), and moral conduct (ethics).

Religion can also offer solace and structure to people coping with the demands of a changing world. Rather than logical argument, religion is based primarily on faith and involves a personal commitment to God or gods through worship and conduct in accordance with divine commands found in accepted sacred writings or declared by authoritative teachers. Religions usually organize a body of true believers who are convinced of the existence of a supreme being or of supernatural powers that influence, if not completely control, the destiny of human beings or all nature.

Most people today, however, are not "true believers" and often partake of religion or philosophy only temporarily under duress in order to maintain balance. It has been said, for example, that in time of war, when soldiers are pinned down in foxholes, there are no atheists. But utilitarian or short-term religion is not the subject of this chapter. The philosophies and religious systems here presented are primary to the human experience and have influenced millions of people for thousands of years. They have had "staying power" and have provided the seed bed for intellectual and religious movements that continue to affect us today. It is true that ideas can rarely be contained in a void. Their permutations often threaten the status quo of governments, religious organizations, even universities. The ideas presented in this chapter were sometimes considered radical in origin, but have evolved to frame the intellectual foundation of world civilization.

The evolution of human thought is a fascinating and complex topic. In order to understand the belief systems of other cultures, you must be open to new ideas that might challenge your assumptions. And you must be willing to struggle with concepts that are foreign to your conditioned patterns of thought. In this chapter, we will look at the early foundations of human thought and faith in Europe and South, Southwest, and East Asia. It is an intellectual voyage of great adventure.

HEBREW CIVILIZATION

In the beginning, God created heaven and earth.

—Genesis 1:1

And what does the Lord require of you, but to do justly, and to love mercy, and to walk humbly with your God.

—Micah 6:8

They that wait upon the Lord shall renew their strength; they shall mount up with wings as eagles; they shall run and not be weary; and they shall walk and not faint.

—*Isaiah 40:31*

Origins, Oppression, and the Exodus of the Hebrews from Egypt

Nowhere did religion play a greater role than in the development of Hebrew civilization. The Hebrews were a nomadic people whose wanderings and eventual establishment in the promised land of Canaan (modern-day Israel) form the narrative story of the Old Testament of The Bible. *But more than this, the story concerns the relationship of Yahweh (or God) to his chosen people, the Hebrews. Many other Near Eastern conquerors held more land and ruled more people, but no one influenced the course of Western civilization more emphatically than did the Hebrews. Their concern with moral law, right action, and adherence to monotheistic principles has formed the basis for Christianity and Islam in the modern world.*

The first few pages from Genesis in the Old Testament of The Bible *contain some of the most powerful and influential ideas in world civilization. Genesis explains the origins of the universe by one omnipotent and omniscient God, who created human beings in his likeness, gave them dominion over nature, and endowed them with an inherent goodness. It is the story of the creation of woman, the origins of sin, and the fall from God's grace. This concept of monotheism and the ethical and social structure that derived from the development of these ideas were the primary contributions of the Hebrews to world civilization.*

The story of the Hebrews in the Old Testament begins with the wandering patriarch Abraham, who led his family from Ur in Sumer around 1800 B.C.E. to the promised land of Canaan by about 1700 B.C.E. A group of Hebrews led by Joseph continued south to Egypt, where they were hospitably received by the Hyksos, a Semitic people like the Hebrews, who had conquered Egypt about 1710 B.C.E. Joseph, according to the Old Testament, actually ruled Egypt for a time. But by 1570 B.C.E., a resurgent Egypt had ended the Hyksos' control, and the pharaohs enslaved the Hebrews and forced them to build new Egyptian cities. Shortly after 1300 B.C.E., Moses was directed by God to lead his people out of Egypt, across the Red Sea, and back to the promised land of Canaan.

The Creation of the World

In the beginning, God created heaven and earth. Now the earth was a formless void, there was darkness over the deep, with a divine wind sweeping over the waters.

God said, "Let there be light," and there was light. God saw that light was good, and God divided light from darkness. God called light "day," and darkness he called "night." Evening came and morning came: the first day.

God said, "Let there be a vault through the middle of the waters to divide the waters in two." And so it was. God made the vault, and it divided the waters under the vault from the waters above the vault. God called the vault "heaven." Evening came and morning came: the second day.

God said, "Let the waters under heaven come together into a single mass, and let dry land appear." And so it was. God called the dry land "earth" and the mass of waters "seas," and God saw that it was good.

God said, "Let the earth produce vegetation: seed-bearing plants, and fruit trees on earth, bearing fruit with their seed inside, each corresponding to its own seed-bearing fruit with their seed inside, each corresponding to its own species." And so it was. . . . God saw that it was good. Evening came and morning came: the third day.

God said, "Let there be lights in the vault of heaven to divide day from night, and let them indicate festivals, days and years. Let them be lights in the vault of heaven to shine on the earth." And so it was. God made the two great lights, the greater light to govern the day, the smaller light to govern the night, and the stars. . . . God saw that it was good. Evening came and morning came: the fourth day.

God said, "Let the waters be alive with a swarm of living creatures, and let birds wing their way above the earth across the vault of heaven." And so it was. God created great sea-monsters and all the creatures that glide and teem in the waters in their own species, and winged birds in their own species. God saw that it was good. God blessed them, saying, "Be fruitful, multiply, and fill the waters of the seas; and let the birds multiply on land." Evening came and morning came: the fifth day.

God said, "Let the earth produce every kind of living creature in its own species: cattle, creeping things and wild animals of all kinds." And so it was. . . . God saw that it was good. God said, "Let us make man in our own image, in the likeness of ourselves, and let them be masters of the fish of the sea, the birds of heaven, the cattle, all the wild animals, and all the creatures that creep along the ground."

God created man in the image of himself,
in the image of God he created him,
male and female he created them.

God blessed them, saying to them, "Be fruitful, multiply, fill the earth and subdue it. Be masters of the fish of the sea, the birds of heaven and all the living creatures that move on earth." God also said, "Look, to you I give all the seed-bearing plants everywhere on the surface of the earth, and all the trees with seed-bearing fruit; this will be your food. And to all the wild animals, all the birds of heaven and all the living creatures that creep along the ground, I give all the foliage of the plants as their food." And so it was. God saw all he had made, and indeed it was very good. Evening came and morning came: the sixth day.

Thus heaven and earth were completed with all their array. On the seventh day God had completed the work he had been doing. He rested on the seventh day after all the work he had undertaken. God blessed the seventh day and made it holy, because on that day he rested after all his work of creating.

The Historical Intersection

NIGERIA, AFRICA

The Mother Goddess

Creation myths often allow us to glimpse the social and religious values of a culture. They are expressions of the mystery of being and the relationship of the cosmos with the earth and the self. The earliest written accounts of orally transmitted African myths were provided by explorers and missionaries who came into contact with African societies and filtered these myths through their own biases. Christian missionaries, for example, emphasized a Supreme Creator who was male, and therefore often judged the relevance of African myths on this basis. But the word "God" stems from the Sanskrit root "Gheu," meaning "to invoke," or "to offer sacrifice," and does not necessarily carry a sexual designation. The Shona tribe in Africa, for instance, describe God as simultaneously "Father, Mother, and Son." The following account flows from the rich oral tradition of the Ijo tribe in southern Nigeria. It sanctifies the primary role of the Mother Goddess, Woyengi, in the creation of human beings.

Keep In Mind. . .

- Note the interaction between the deity and human beings in the process of creation.

Once there was a large field, and in this field stood an enormous iroko tree with large buttresses. One day, the sky darkened, and there descended on the field a large table, a large chair, and an immense "creation stone." And on the table was a large quantity of earth. Then there was lightning and thunder, and Woyengi, the Mother, descended. She seated herself on the chair and placed her feet on the "creation stone." Out of the earth on the table Woyengi molded human beings. But they had no life and were neither man nor woman, and

(contd)

Woyengi, embracing them one by one, breathed her breath into them, and they became living beings. But they were still neither men nor women, and so Woyengi asked them one by one to choose to be man or woman, and she made them so, each according to his or her choice.

Next Woyengi asked them, one by one, what manner of life each would like to lead on earth. Some asked for riches, some for children, some for short lives, and all manner of things. And these Woyengi bestowed on them one by one, each according to his or her wish. Then Woyengi asked them one by one by what manner of death they would return to her. And out of the diseases that afflict the earth they each chose a disease. To all of these wishes Woyengi said, "So be it."

Consider This:

- Compare the previous passage from Genesis on the Biblical creation of human beings with this Nigerian account. How are they different in terms of the relationship between humans and God? Do these differences have anything to do with the sex of the deity?
- Joseph Campbell in his book, *Transformations of Myth*, noted that the relationship of a woman with her baby was the "basic image of mythology." He argued that "when one can feel oneself in relation to the universe in the same complete and natural way as that of the child with the mother, one is in complete harmony and tune with the universe. Getting into harmony and tune with the universe and staying there is the principal function of mythology." Given this idea, does it seem more natural to view "God, the Creator" as female?

Beier, Ulli, ed., *The Origin of Life and Death: African Creation Myths,* Heinemann, 1966, pp. 23–24.

Paradise and the Fall from Grace

At the time when Yahweh God made earth and heaven, there was as yet no wild bush on the earth nor had any wild plant yet sprung up, for Yahweh God had not sent rain on the earth, nor was there any man to till the soil. Instead, water flowed out of the ground and watered all the surface of the soil. Yahweh God shaped man from the soil of the ground and blew the breath of life into his nostrils, and man became a living being.

Excerpt from *The Jerusalem Bible,* copyright © 1966 by Darton, Longman & Todd, Ltd. and Doubleday, a division of Random House, Inc., pp. 18–21. Reprinted by permission.

Yahweh God planted a garden in Eden, which is in the east, and there he put the man he had fashioned. From the soil, Yahweh God caused to grow every kind of tree, enticing to look at and good to eat, with the tree of life in the middle of the garden, and the tree of the knowledge of good and evil. . . .

Yahweh God took the man and settled him in the garden of Eden to cultivate and take care of it. Then Yahweh God gave the man this command, "You are free to eat of all the trees in the garden. But of the tree of the knowledge of good and evil you are not to eat; for, the day you eat of that, you are doomed to die."

Yahweh God said, "It is not right that the man should be alone. I shall make him a helper. . . ." Then Yahweh God made the man fall into a deep sleep. And, while he was asleep, he took one of his ribs and closed the flesh up again forthwith. Yahweh God fashioned the rib he had taken from the man into a woman, and brought her to the man. And the man said: "This one at last is bone of my bones and flesh of my flesh! She is to be called Woman, because she was taken from Man."

This is why a man leaves his father and mother and becomes attached to his wife, and they become one flesh. Now, both of them were naked, the man and his wife, but they felt no shame before each other.

Now the snake was the most subtle of all the wild animals that Yahweh God had made. It asked the woman, "Did God really say you were not to eat from any of the trees in the garden?" The woman answered the snake, "We may eat the fruit of the trees in the garden. But of the fruit of the tree in the middle of the garden God said, 'You must not eat it, nor touch it, under pain of death.'" Then the snake said to the woman, "No! You will not die! God knows in fact that the day you eat it your eyes will be opened and you will be like gods, knowing good from evil." The woman saw that the tree was good to eat and pleasing to the eye and that it was enticing for the wisdom that it could give. So she took some of the fruit and ate it. She also gave some to her husband who was with her, and he ate it. Then the eyes of both of them were opened and they realized that they were naked. So they sewed fig leaves to make themselves loincloths.

The man and his wife heard the sound of Yahweh God walking in the garden in the cool of the day, and they hid from Yahweh God among the trees of the garden. "Where are you?" he asked. . . . ."Have you been eating from the tree I forbade you to eat?" The man replied, "It was the woman you put with me; she gave me some fruit from the tree, and I ate it." Then Yahweh God said to the woman, "Why did you do that?" The woman replied, "The snake tempted me and I ate." Then Yahweh God said to the snake,

"Because you have done this,
Accursed be you
of all animals wild and tame!
On your belly you will go
and on dust you will feed
as long as you live.
I shall put enmity
between you and the woman,
and between your offspring and hers;
it will bruise your head
and you will strike its heel."

To the woman he said:
"I shall give you intense pain in
    childbearing,
you will give birth to your children in
    pain.
Your yearning will be for your husband,
and he will dominate you."

To the man he said:
"Because you listened to the voice of your
    wife and ate from the tree of which I
    had forbidden you to eat,
Accursed be the soil because of you!
Painfully will you get your food from it
as long as you live. . . .
By the sweat of your face
will you earn your food,
until you return to the ground,
as you were taken from it.
For dust you are
and to dust you shall return."

The man named his wife "Eve" because she was the mother of all those who live. Yahweh made tunics of skins for the man and his wife and clothed them. Then Yahweh God said, "Now that the man has become like one of us in knowing good from evil, he must not be allowed to reach out his hand and pick from the tree of life too, and eat and live forever!" So Yahweh God expelled him from the garden of Eden, to till the soil from which he had been taken. He banished the man, and in front of the garden of Eden he posted the great winged creatures and the fiery flashing sword to guard the way to the tree of life.

The Hebrew Bondage

Then there came to power in Egypt a new king who knew nothing of Joseph. "Look," he said to his subjects, "these people, the sons of Israel, have become so numerous and strong that they are a threat to us. We must be prudent and take steps against their increasing any further, or if war should break out, they might add to the number of our enemies. They might take arms against us and so escape out of the country." Accordingly they put slave-drivers over the Israelites to wear them down under heavy loads. In this way they built the store-cities of Pithom and Ramses for Pharaoh. But the more they were crushed, the more they increased and spread, and men came to dread the sons of Israel. The Egyptians forced the sons of Israel into slavery, and made their lives unbearable with hard labor, work with clay and brick, all kinds of work in the fields; they forced on them every kind of labor. . . .

The Burning Bush

During this long period the king of Egypt died. The sons of Israel, groaning in their slavery, cried out for help and from the depths of their slavery their cry came up to God. God heard their groaning and he called to mind his covenant with Abraham, Isaac, and Jacob. God looked down upon the sons of Israel, and he knew. . . .

Moses was looking after the flock of Jethro, his father-in-law, priest of Midian. He led his flock to the far side of the wilderness and came to Horeb, the mountain of God. There the angel of Yahweh appeared to him in the shape of a flame of fire, coming from the middle of a bush. Moses looked; there was the bush blazing, but it was not being burnt up. "I must go and look at this strange sight," Moses said, "and see why the bush is not burnt." Now Yahweh saw him go forward to look, and God called to him from the middle of the bush. "Moses, Moses!" He said. "Here I am," he answered. "Come no nearer," He said. "Take off your shoes, for the place on which you stand is holy ground. I am the God of your father," he said, "the God of Abraham, the god of Isaac and the God of Jacob." At this Moses covered his face, afraid to look at God. . . .

The Mission of Moses

God spoke to Moses and said to him, "I am Yahweh. To Abraham and Isaac and Jacob I appeared as El Shaddai; I did not make myself known to them by my name Yahweh. Also, I made my covenant with them to give them the land of Canaan, the land they lived in as strangers. And I have heard the groaning of the sons of Israel, enslaved by the Egyptians, and have remembered my covenant. Say this, then, to the sons of Israel, 'I am Yahweh. I will free you of the burdens which the Egyptians lay on you. I will release you from slavery to them, and with my arm outstretched and my strokes of power I will deliver you. I will adopt you as my own people, and I will be your God. Then you shall know that it is I, Yahweh your God, who have freed you from the Egyptians' burdens. Then I will bring you to the land I swore that I would give to Abraham, and Isaac, and Jacob, and will give it to you for your own; I, Yahweh, will do this!'" Moses told this to the sons of Israel, but they would not listen to him, so crushed was their spirit and so cruel their slavery.

Yahweh then said to Moses, "Go to Pharaoh, king of Egypt, and tell him to let the sons of Israel leave his land." But Moses answered to Yahweh's face: "Look," said he, "since the sons of Israel have not listened to me, why should Pharaoh listen to me, a man slow of speech?" Yahweh spoke to Moses and Aaron and ordered them to both go to Pharaoh, king of Egypt, and to bring the sons of Israel out of the land of Egypt.

The Departure of the Israelites

When Pharaoh had let the people go, God did not let them take the road to the land of the Philistines, although that was the nearest way. God thought that the prospect of fighting would make the people lose heart and turn back to Egypt. Instead, God led the people by the roundabout way of the wilderness to the Sea of Reeds [Red Sea]. . . .

Yahweh went before them, by day in the form of a pillar of cloud to show them the way, and by night in the form of a pillar of fire to give them light: thus they could continue their march by day and by night. The pillar of cloud never failed to go before the people during the day, nor the pillar of fire during the night. . . .

When Pharaoh, king of Egypt, was told that the people had made their escape, he and his courtiers changed their minds about the people. "What have we done," they said, "allowing Israel to leave our service?" So Pharaoh had his chariot harnessed and gathered his troops about him, taking six hundred of the best chariots and all the other chariots in Egypt, each manned by a picked team. Yahweh made Pharaoh, king of Egypt, stubborn, and he gave chase to the sons of Israel as they made their triumphant escape. So the Egyptians gave chase and came up with them where they lay encamped beside the sea—all the horses, the chariots of Pharaoh, his horsemen, his army—near Pi-hahiroth, facing Baalzephon. And as Pharaoh approached, the sons of Israel looked round— and there were the Egyptians in pursuit of them! The sons of Israel were terrified and cried out to Yahweh. To Moses they said, "Were there no graves in Egypt that you must lead us out to die in the wilderness? What good have you done us, bringing us out of Egypt? We spoke of this in Egypt, did we not? Leave us alone, we said, we would rather work for the Egyptians! Better to work for the Egyptians than die in the wilderness!" Moses answered the people, "Have no

fear! Stand firm, and you will see what Yahweh will do to save you today: the Egyptians you see today, you will never see again. Yahweh will do the fighting for you: you have only to keep still."

Yahweh said to Moses, "Why do you cry to me so? Tell the sons of Israel to march on. For yourself, raise your staff and stretch out your hand over the sea and part it for the sons of Israel to walk through the sea on dry ground. I for my part will make the heart of the Egyptians so stubborn that they will follow them. So shall I win myself glory at the expense of Pharaoh, of all his army, his chariots, his horsemen. And when I have won glory for myself, at the expense of Pharaoh and his chariots and his army, the Egyptians will learn that I am Yahweh."

Then the angle of Yahweh, who marched at the front of the army of Israel, changed station and moved to their rear. The pillar of cloud changed station from the front to the rear of them, and remained there. It came between the camp of the Egyptians and the camp of Israel. The cloud was dark, and the night passed without the armies drawing any closer the whole night long. Moses stretched out his hand over the sea. Yahweh drove back the sea with a strong easterly wind all night, and he made dry land of the sea. The waters parted and the sons of Israel went on dry ground right into the sea, walls of water to right and to left of them. The Egyptians gave chase: after them they went, right into the sea, all Pharaoh's horses, his chariots, and his horsemen. . . . Yahweh said to Moses "that the waters may flow back on the Egyptians and their chariots and their horsemen." Moses stretched out his hand over the sea and, as day broke, the sea returned to its bed. The fleeing Egyptians marched right into it, and Yahweh overthrew the Egyptians in the very middle of the sea. The returning waters overwhelmed the chariots and the horsemen of Pharaoh's whole army, which had followed the Israelites into the sea; not a single one of them was left. But the sons of Israel had marched through the sea on dry ground, walls of water to right and to left of them. That day, Yahweh rescued Israel from the Egyptians, and Israel saw the Egyptians lying dead on the shore. Israel witnessed the great act that Yahweh had performed against the Egyptians, and the people venerated Yahweh; they put their faith in Yahweh and in Moses, his servant.

Covenant and Commandments

After the exodus of the Hebrews from Egypt, Yahweh established the nation of Israel and through Moses made a covenant with His chosen people that He would protect them in return for their obedience to His laws. The law code that God handed down to Moses on Mt. Sinai is called the Decalogue or Ten Commandments and is absolute in nature. Other laws that are less absolute and generally reflect the needs and values of Hebrew society are called the Covenant Code; they are included after the Ten Commandments and were probably written centuries later. Note the similarity between this Covenant Code and the laws of Hammurabi.

The Ten Commandments

Three months after they came out of the land of Egypt . . . on that day the sons of Israel came to the wilderness of Sinai. . . .

Moses then went up to God, and Yahweh called to him from the mountains, saying, "Say this to the House of Jacob, declare this to the sons of Israel, 'You yourselves have seen what I did with the Egyptians, how I carried you on eagle's wings and brought you to myself. From this you know that now, if you obey my voice and hold fast to my covenant, you of all the nations shall be my very own for all the earth is mine. I will count you a kingdom of priests, a consecrated nation.' Those are the words you are to speak to the sons of Israel." . . .

Yahweh said to Moses, "Go to the people and tell them to prepare themselves today and tomorrow. Let them wash their clothing and hold themselves in readiness for the third day, because on the third day Yahweh will descend on the mountain of Sinai in the sight of all the people. You will mark out the limits of the mountain and say, 'Take care not to go up the mountain or to touch the foot of it. Whoever touches the mountain will be put to death. No one must lay a hand on him: he must be stoned or shot down

Excerpt from *The Jerusalem Bible*, copyright © 1966 by Darton, Longman & Todd, Ltd. and Doubleday, a division of Random House, Inc., pp. 100–102. Reprinted by permission.

by arrow, whether man or beast; he must not remain alive.' When the ram's horn sounds a long blast, they are to go up the mountain." . . .

Now at daybreak on the third day there were peals of thunder on the mountain and lightning flashes, a dense cloud, and a loud trumpet blast, and inside the camp all the people trembled. Then Moses led the people out of the camp to meet God; and they stood at the bottom of the mountain. The mountain of Sinai was entirely wrapped in smoke, because Yahweh had descended on it in the form of fire. Like smoke from a furnace the smoke went up, and the whole mountain shook violently. Louder and louder grew the sound of the trumpet, Moses spoke, and God answered him with peals of thunder. Yahweh came down on the mountain of Sinai, on the mountain top, and Yahweh called Moses to the top of the mountain; and Moses went up. . . .

Then God spoke all these words. He said, "I am Yahweh your God who brought you out of the land of Egypt, out of the house of slavery.

"You shall have no gods except me.

"You shall not make yourself a carved image or any likeness of anything in heaven or on earth beneath or in the waters under the earth; you shall not bow down to them or serve them. For I, Yahweh your God, am a jealous God and I punish the father's fault in the sons, the grandsons, and the great-grandsons of those who hate me; but I show kindness to thousands of those who love me and keep my commandments.

"You shall not utter the name of Yahweh your God to misuse it, for Yahweh will not leave unpunished the man who utters his name to misuse it.

"Remember the sabbath day and keep it holy. For six days you shall labor and do all your work, but the seventh day is a sabbath for Yahweh your God. You shall do no work that day, neither you nor your son nor your daughter nor your servants, men or women, nor your animals nor the stranger who lives with you. For in six days Yahweh made the heavens and the earth and the sea and all that these hold, but on the seventh day he rested; that is why Yahweh has blessed the sabbath day and made it sacred.

"Honor your father and your mother so that you may have a long life in the land that Yahweh your God has given to you.

"You shall not kill.

"You shall not commit adultery.

"You shall not steal.

"You shall not bear false witness against your neighbor.

"You shall not covet your neighbor's house. You shall not covet your neighbor's wife, or his servant, man or woman, or his ox, or his donkey, or anything that is his."

The Covenant Code

"This is the ruling you [Moses] are to lay before them: . . .

'Anyone who strikes a man and so causes his death, must die. If he has not lain in wait for him but God has delivered him into his hands, then I will appoint you a place where he may seek refuge. But should a man dare to kill his fellow by treacherous intent, you must take him even from my altar to be put to death.

'Anyone who strikes his father or mother must die. Anyone who abducts a man—whether he has sold him or is found in possession of him—must die. Anyone who curses father or mother must die.

'If men quarrel and one strikes the other a blow with stone or fist so that the man, though he does not die, must keep his bed, the one who struck the blow shall not be liable provided the other gets up and can go about, even with a stick. He must compensate him, however, for his enforced inactivity, and care for him until he is completely cured.

'If a man beats his slave, male or female, and the slave dies at his hands, he must pay the penalty. But should the slave survive for one or two days, he shall pay no penalty because the slave is his by right of purchase.

'If, when men come to blows, they hurt a woman who is pregnant and she suffers a miscarriage, though she does not die of it, the man responsible must pay the compensation demanded of him by the woman's master; he shall hand it over, after arbitration. But should she die, you shall give life for life, eye for eye, tooth for tooth, hand for hand, foot for foot, burn for burn, wound for wound, stroke for stroke. . . .

'You must not molest the stranger or oppress him, for you lived as strangers in the land of Egypt. You must not be harsh with the widow, or with the orphan; if you are harsh with them, they will surely cry out to me, and be sure I shall hear their cry; my anger will flare and I shall kill you with the sword, your own wives will be widows, your own children orphans.

'If you lend money to any of my people, to any poor man among you, you must not play the usurer with him: you must not demand interest from him.

'If you take another's cloak as a pledge, you must give it back to him before sunset. It is all the covering he has; it is the cloak he wraps his body in; what else would he sleep in? If he cries to me, I will listen, for I am full of pity. . . .'"

Moses went and told the people all the commands of Yahweh and all the ordinances. In answer, all the people said with one voice, "We will observe all the commands that Yahweh has decreed." Moses put all the commands of Yahweh into writing.

The Hebrew Monarchy and a New Covenant

When the Hebrews settled in the land of Canaan (modern Israel) after the exodus from Egypt in the early thirteenth century B.C.E., it soon became apparent that the loose confederacy of Hebrew tribes was ineffective when faced with enemies. Of special concern were the Philistines, who settled in the region about 1200 B.C.E., destroyed the Hebrew sanctuary at Shiloh about 1050 B.C.E., and carried off the Ark of the Covenant. In response to this, the Hebrew people demanded strong leadership and elected a king named Saul. He was not a particularly effective leader and died in battle with the Philistines. His successor was the famous David (1020–1000 B.C.E.) whose personal defeat of the Philistine Goliath led to security and domestic reform. David established the Hebrew capital at Jerusalem and equipped it with a central administration. At last, a united Israel was born.

David's progressive spirit was continued by his son Solomon (961–922 B.C.E.), who strengthened centralized control of the state by the king. His construction of the Temple and palace complex required frequent taxes and even oppressive forced labor. Still, Solomon developed a reputation for wisdom and fairness. It was only later in his reign that he incurred the wrath of God.

Solomon's oppressive policies split the Hebrew nation into two parts after his death: Israel became the northern kingdom and Judah formed in the south. Such division made the two kingdoms vulnerable to rising new empires. Israel fell to the Assyrians in 722 B.C.E. and Judah to the Chaldeans in 586 B.C.E., whereupon the Jews were removed from the land of Canaan in what was called the Babylonian Captivity. They were finally released when the Persian Cyrus the Great conquered the Chaldean empire and liberated Babylon in 539 B.C.E.

During the years 750–550 B.C.E., when the Hebrews were trying to survive in the face of foreign invasion, they were also struggling internally. A succession of prophets arose who claimed to speak for Yahweh and condemned social injustice and the people's general disregard for the covenant they had made with God under Moses. The most influential of these prophets was Jeremiah (626–586 B.C.E.). He not only decried the faithlessness of the people of Israel and warned of the wrath of God, but also offered a solution to the problem: a new covenant. God destroys, but he also builds anew. Of utmost importance was a new covenant within each individual (rather than with the nation as a whole) that would renew moral and spiritual commitment.

"Deep Within Them I Will Plant My Law"

The word that was addressed to Jeremiah by Yahweh, "Go and stand at the gate of the Temple of Yahweh and there proclaim this message. Say, 'Listen to the word of Yahweh, all you men of Judah who come in by these gates to worship Yahweh. Yahweh Sabaoth, the God of Israel, says this: Amend your behavior and your actions and I will stay with you here in this place. Put no trust in delusive words like these: This is the sanctuary of Yahweh, the sanctuary of Yahweh, the sanctuary

of Yahweh! But if you do amend your behavior and your actions, if you treat each other fairly, if you do not exploit the stranger, the orphan, and the widow (if you do not shed innocent blood in this place), and if you do not follow alien gods, to your own ruin, then here in this place I will stay with you, in the land that long ago I gave to your fathers forever. Yet here you are, trusting delusive words, to no purpose! Steal, would you, murder, commit adultery, perjure yourselves, burn incense to Baal, follow alien gods that you do not know?—and then come presenting yourselves in this Temple that bears my name, saying: Now we are safe—safe to go on committing all these abominations! Do you take this Temple that bears my name for a robbers' den? I, at any rate, am not blind—it is Yahweh who speaks. . . .

"'And now, since you have committed all these sins—it is Yahweh who speaks—and have refused to listen when I spoke so urgently, so persistently, or to answer when I called you, I will treat this Temple that bears my name, and in which you put your trust, and the place I have given to you and your ancestors, just as I treated Shiloh. I will drive you out of my sight, as I drove all your kinsmen, the entire race of Ephraim.'". . . See, the days are coming—it is Yahweh who speaks—when I am going to sow the seed of men and cattle on the House of Israel and on the House of Judah. And as I once watched them to tear up, to knock down, to overthrow, destroy and bring disaster, so now I shall watch over them to build and to plant. It is Yahweh who speaks. In those days people will no longer say: 'The fathers have eaten unripe grapes; the children's teeth are set on edge.' But each is to die for his own sin. Every man who eats unripe grapes is to have his own teeth set on edge.

"See, the days are coming—it is Yahweh who speaks—when I will make a new covenant with the House of Israel (and the House of Judah), but not a covenant like the one I made with their ancestors on the day I took them by the hand to bring them out of the land of Egypt. They broke that covenant of mine, so I had to show them who was master. It is Yahweh who speaks. No, this is the covenant I will make with the House of Israel when those days arrive—it is Yahweh who speaks. Deep within them I will plant my Law, writing it on their hearts. Then I will be their God and they shall be my people. There will be no further need for neighbour to try to teach neighbour, or brother to say to brother, 'Learn to know Yahweh!' No, they will all know me, the least no less than the greatest—it is Yahweh who speaks—since I will forgive their inequity and never call their sin to mind."

RELIGION IN INDIA

Samsara, the transmigration of life, takes place in one's mind. Let one therefore keep the mind pure, for what a man thinks that he becomes.

—*Maitri Upanishad*

And then he saw that *Brahman* was joy. For from joy all beings have come, by joy they all live, and unto joy they all return.

—*Taittiriva Upanishad*

He who sees that the Lord of all is ever the same in all that is, immortal in the field of mortality— he sees the Truth. And when a man sees that God in himself is the same God in all that is, he hurts not himself by hurting others: then he goes indeed to the highest Path.

—*Bhagavad Gita*

But even dearer to me are those who have faith and love, and who have me as their End Supreme: those who hear my words of Truth, and who come to the waters of Everlasting Life.

—*Bhagavad Gita*

Glossary of Hindu and Buddhist Terms

Atman (the "Self" or "Individual Soul"): In Hinduism, the essence of impermanence in this transitory life; encompasses the limited nature of this world; the pathway to Brahman (the "Infinite") is through knowledge of the Self. This concept is denied in Buddhism.

Bodhisattva: A person who wishes to win full enlightenment, or to become a Buddha.

Brahman (the "Absolute," the "Infinite," "Universal Soul," "Spirit Supreme"): The ultimate source of all reality in the universe, not subject to the limitations of existence; the permanent spiritual force of the world.

Buddha: In Sanskrit, a "fully enlightened" individual. Buddhism was formed around the teachings of Siddhartha Gautama, who became a Buddha about 500 B.C.E. and remained on earth until 479 B.C.E. to guide people through compassion toward the joy of Nirvana. Siddhartha Gautama is referred to as "the Buddha."

Dharma ("Spiritual Merit," "Right Action," "Moral Conduct"): This Hindu solution ("Ordinary Norm") to the endless "redeath" (*Samsara*) focuses on living a moral life and accepting the responsibilities of one's social position. *Dharma* accepts the impermanence of life and seeks to accumulate spiritual merit for rebirth in a more evolved state. In Buddhism, the natural laws by which all things are ordered; the teaching of the Buddha; Truth.

The Eightfold Path: In Buddhism, the acquisition of eight perfections that lead to the cessation of suffering: right views, right intent, right speech, right conduct, right means of livelihood, right endeavor, right mindfulness, right meditation.

The Four Noble Truths: In Buddhism, the Truth of suffering, the Truth of the origin of suffering, the Truth of the cessation of suffering, and the Truth of the Eightfold Path that leads to the cessation of suffering.

Karma ("Action"): Physical or mental "action" in life. *Karma* perpetuates the process of *Samsara*, the endless cycle of existence. To attain Nirvana, one must obtain *Moksha* ("Release") from all karmic contagion.

Moksha ("Release," "Liberation"): The solution ("Extraordinary Norm") to the problem of Samsara emphasizes a life of study, spiritual meditation, ascetic denial, a renunciation, and withdrawal from personal attachments to the world. By withdrawing from "normal existence" one eliminates *Karma* ("Action") that may allow the most evolved spirits to break free of *Samsara* and attain *Nirvana*.

Nirvana ("Extinction"): In Hinduism, the state of spiritual freedom and complete joy obtained by realizing the "oneness" of the Self (*Atman*) with the Infinite (*Brahman*). Upon death of the physical body, the soul is released from *Samsara* and resides in *Nirvana*, the perpetual state of bliss. Note that *Nirvana* is not a place like Heaven where gods may reside, but a limitless state of existence.

(contd)

In Buddhism, the ultimate goal of all endeavor, the extinction of craving and separate selfhood, a life that has gone beyond death.

Samsara ("Journeying," "Transmigration"): The endless cycle of existence. The process of endless "redeath" for all beings. The constancy of *Samsara* can only be broken by the elimination of *Karma* ("Action").

Sangha ("Crowd," "Host"): the Buddhist monastic community.

The Triple Refuge: In Buddhism, "take refuge in the Buddha, the Law, and the Sangha."

The Rig Veda *and Cosmic Order*

The religion today known as Hinduism traces its origins to the migration of an Indo-European people called the "Aryans" around 2000 B.C.E. into the Indian subcontinent. They entered in waves and came to dominate the existing Harappan civilization on the Indus River. The Aryans brought with them their own religious beliefs and a pantheon of naturalistic gods. This migration was part of a larger pattern of southern and western movement of Indo-European peoples into Europe and Iran. In fact, the gods of Persia, Greece, and Rome were closely linked, indicating a common religious origin in prehistoric times.

The Aryan religion mingled with other beliefs of the indigenous Indian population and by 500 B.C.E. came to be collected in a body of hymns, philosophical treatises, and ritual texts called the Veda. The authority of this scripture has been accepted to some extent by all Hindus as embodying the essential truths of Hinduism. The most comprehensive of the four Vedic texts is the Rig Veda, a collection of 1,028 hymns composed between 1500 and 1000 B.C.E. that serves as the earliest expression of the Aryan religion.

The hymns of the Rig Veda express a wonder for the brilliance and the power of nature. All life revolves around establishing a positive relationship with cosmic deities who regulate the physical world. In turn the gods provide security and prosperity. In the following passages from the Rig Veda, note the emphasis on nature and the personalities and functions of some of the most important gods.

Indra: The Warrior King

Indra is the most prominent god in the Rig Veda. Originally a god of thunder, his actions in defeating the snake god Vritra and thus ordering the world focused his identity as a heroic warrior. He is invoked to vanquish human and supernatural forces that threaten or jeopardize the prosperity of the Aryan community. This selection recounts the fierce battle between Indra and Vritra. With Indra's victory, the waters of the world were released and the cosmic order established.

Now I shall proclaim the mighty deeds of Indra, those foremost deeds that he, the wielder of the mace, has performed. He smashed the serpent.

He released the waters. He split the sides of the mountains.

From *Sources of Indian Tradition* 2/e, by Ainslie Embree, ed., © 1988 Columbia University Press, Vol. 1, pp. 12–13. Reprinted with permission of the publisher.

[Indra] smashed the serpent, which was resting on the mountain—for him [the god Tvashtari] had fashioned a mace that shone like the sun. Like lowing cattle, the waters, streaming out, rushed straight to the sea. . . .

When you, Indra, smashed the first-born of serpents, you overcame even the tricks of the tricky. Then you brought forth the sun, the heaven, and the dawn, and since then you have never had a rival.

With his mace, that great murderous weapon, Indra smashed Vritra, the very great obstacle, whose shoulders were spread. Like branches hewn away by an axe, the serpent lies, embracing the earth.

A feeble warrior, in his drunkenness he challenged the great hero, the overwhelming. . . . He did not withstand the attack of Indra's weapons. Broken completely, Indra's rival was crushed.

Handless and footless, he gave battle to Indra. Indra smashed his mace against his neck. A bullock who wished to be the measure of a bull, Vritra lay there, broken to pieces.

As he lay in that way, like a broken reed, the waters, consigning themselves to man, rushed over him. Whom Vritra in his greatness [had once] surrounded, at their feet [now] lay the serpent. . . .

After Indra and the serpent fought, [Indra], the Provider, became the conqueror for all time. . . .

Indra, holding the mace, is the king of both that which stands and moves, of the horned and the not-horned. So, as king, he rules over the peoples. As a rim of the spokes of a wheel, he encompasses them.

Varuna: Regulator of Cosmic Law

Varuna is the chief administrative deity of Hinduism. He regulates all activities in this world and administers cosmic law. He set the earth and sun in motion, causes the rain, and maintains the proper balance of life in the world. He is also seen as the lord of human morality and assures that no transgression of cosmic or human law goes unnoticed. He embodies the image of a king as ruler and judge, a counterpart to Indra who presents the image of king as warrior. In this selection, the poet of this hymn is seeking repentance and forgiveness.

Wise are the races [of gods and men] through the greatness of him who propped apart the two wide worlds. He pressed forth the high, lofty vault of heaven and, likewise, the stars. And he spread out the earth [beneath].

In my own person, I speak this together [with him]: "When shall I be in [obedience to] Varuna? Might he take pleasure in my oblation, becoming free of anger? When shall I contentedly look upon his mercy?"

I ask about that trouble, Varuna, desiring to understand; I approach those who know to ask [about it]. The knowing say the same thing to me: "Varuna is now angry with you."

Was the offense so great, Varuna, that you want to crush your friend and praiser? O you who are impossible to deceive, wholly self-sustaining, you will explain this to me. I would swiftly humble myself before you with reverence to be free of guilt.

Release from us the deceits of our ancestors and those that we have done ourselves. Release Vasishtha, O King, like a cattle-stealing thief [from his bondage] or a calf from its rope.

This mistake was not my intention: it was liquor, pride, dice, ignorance. The elder is [caught] in the offense of the younger. Even sleep does not ward off untruth.

From *Sources of Indian Tradition* by Ainslie Embree, ed., © 1988 Columbia University Press, Vol. 1, P. 11. Reprinted with permission of the publisher.

Like a slave, I shall serve my master; I, without offending, [shall serve] the angry one. The civilizing god has enlightened those without understanding. The more knowing man hastens to the clever one for riches.

This praise is for you, Varuna, the self-sustaining: may it repose in your heart. May prosperity in peace be ours, prosperity also in war. Protect us always with well-being.

Agni: Lord of Fire

The Aryans developed the worship of Agni or Fire to a remarkable degree. The god Agni is the personification of sacrificial fire. He embodies the forms of terrestrial fire, of atmospheric lightning, and of celestial sun. Agni also serves as a liaison between the gods and man and is seen as the priest of gods and the god of priests. In the Rig Veda, *he is second only to Indra in importance.*

I extol Agni, the household priest, the divine minister of the sacrifice, the chief priest, the bestower of blessings.

May that Agni, who is to be extolled by ancient and modern seers, conduct the gods here.

Through Agni may one gain day by day wealth and welfare which is glorious and replete with heroic sons.

O Agni, the sacrifice and ritual which you encompass on every side, that indeed goes to the gods.

May Agni, the chief priest, who possesses the insight of a sage, who is truthful, widely renowned, and divine, come here with the gods.

O Agni, O Angiras ["messenger"], whatever prosperity you bring to the pious is indeed in accordance with your true function.

O Agni, illuminator of darkness, day by day we approach you with holy thought bringing homage to you,

Presiding at ritual functions, the brightly shining custodian of the cosmic order, thriving in your own realm.

O Agni, be easy of access to us as a father to his son. Join us for our well being.

Dawn: The Path of Truth

The poets of the Rig Veda *often focused their elegant images of beauty and peace on Dawn. In this hymn, Dawn is a lovely woman who ushers in the new day by driving her chariot across the sky. In her regularity, Dawn also embodies the renewal of the divine order.*

High aloft on her shining course, she who follows the truth according to her truth, [breathing out her] ruddy breath [the morning mists], radiant—responding to her, the goddess Dawn, who brings the sun, the inspired [priests] awaken with their poems.

This beautiful [goddess], awakening the peoples, making their paths easy, drives [her chariot] at the beginning. High in her lofty chariot, arousing every creature, Dawn spreads out her light at the beginning of days.

Yoking [her chariot] with ruddy cows, without fail she continually creates wealth [for us]. Making her path toward prosperity, the much-praised goddess, bringing all desirable things, becomes radiant.

From *Sources of Indian Tradition,* 2/e, by Ainslie Embree, ed., © 1988 Columbia University Press, Vol. 1, p. 9. Reprinted with permission of the publisher.

From *Sources of Indian Tradition,* 2/e, by Ainslie Embree, ed., © 1988 Columbia University Press, pp. 14–15. Reprinted with permission of the publisher.

Dappled, she becomes doubly strong as she reveals herself from the east. She follows unswervingly the path of truth. Like one who understands, she confuses not the directions.

Like a girl who has become aware of the radiance of her body, she seems to rise from her bath for us to see. Pressing away hostilities and darkness, Dawn the daughter of heaven, has come with her light.

The daughter of heaven, facing men, slips down her garments, like a beautiful young woman [before her husband]. Opening up all desirable things for him who serves her, the youthful maiden once again, as before, has created her light.

The Origin of the World

The mystery of creation is the subject of this abstract and searching hymn. No human being nor god can penetrate with certainty the mysteries of the origin of the world.

There was no nonexistent; and there was no existent at that time. There was neither the midspace nor the heaven beyond. What stirred? And in whose control? Was there water? The abyss was deep.

Neither death nor deathlessness was there then. There was no sign of night or day. That One breathed without wind through its independent power. There was nothing other than it.

Darkness there was, hidden by darkness, in the beginning. A signless ocean was everything here. The potential that was hidden by emptiness—that One was born by the power of heat.

Desire evolved then in the beginning, which was the first seed of thought. Searching in their hearts through inspired thought, sages found the connection of the existent in the nonexistent.

Their cord was stretched crosswise. Was there [something] above? [Something] below? Were there powers of insemination and powers of expansion? Was independence below, offering above?

Who really knows? Who shall here proclaim it?—whence things came to be, whence this creation. The gods are on this side, along with the creation of this [world]. So then who does know whence it came to be?

This creation, whence it came to be, whether it was made or not—he who is its overseer in the highest heaven, he surely knows. Or if he does not know . . . ?

The Upanishads *and the Nature of Ultimate Reality*

Hindu Rituals

The Vedic hymns of the Aryans established a complex system of deities and defined their relationships with humans in this world. In order to maintain the balance of civilization, this religion advocated a strict moral stance in its cults and rituals. Explanations of sacrificial rituals and detailed instructions for their performance abound in the Vedic hymns. The institution of sacrifice in fact is very intricate and complex and the role of the priest who knew the proper words was most im-

From *Sources of Indian Tradition*, 2/e, by Ainslie Embree, ed., © 1988 Columbia University Press, Vol. 1, p. 21. Reprinted with permission of the publisher.

portant. The magical power, inherent in sacrificial prayers, developed into spells. He who recited them was a "pray-er" (brahman). From this concept developed the brahman or priestly class.

The Hindu worshiper submitted himself to considerable preparation: food restrictions and fasting, body postures and finger gesticulation, breath control, and even habitation of the physical body by a deity. Purity is the essential watchword of Hinduism and ritual purification rites are a daily obligation. Hindu prayer consists of silent recitation (japa) of sacred formulas (mantra) that are repeated indefinitely. This type of syllabic prayer often invokes the names of deities and aids the mental concentration necessary to promote right action and achieve virtue. Prayer three times a day (morning, noon, and evening) is accompanied by offerings to the gods, to recognized sages, and to ancestors. Study of the Vedic texts and meditation, above all, strengthened by yoga exercises, can release tension and accomplish the ultimate end of all Indian religious thought: a state of perfect union with the Absolute, the Ultimate Reality, the Infinite.

The *Upanishads* and the Nature of Ultimate Reality

This great abstraction of the Absolute is a major feature of Indian religious thought and finds its expression and development in Hinduism, Jainism, and Buddhism. The concept of the Absolute, and more importantly its relationship with the concept of the Self, is first enunciated in the Upanishads, *a group of philosophical speculations that were attached to the Vedic literature almost as a kind of commentary between 800 and 500 B.C.E. The* Upanishads *do not present a consistent, unified philosophical system, but certain doctrines are held in common for which antecedents can be found in earlier Vedic texts. The* Upanishads, *therefore, probe earlier Vedic thought in order to obtain a more coherent view of the universe and of humanity's place within it.*

The ideas contained in the Upanishads *represent a major turning point in human thought on a level with the monotheism of the Hebrews and the philosophical speculations of the Chinese and Greeks. In reaction to the Vedic Aryan traditions that emphasized ritual and right action in the pursuit of an afterlife in heaven among the gods, the* Upanishads *emphasize knowledge as the ultimate source of freedom and power. This pursuit of ultimate wisdom will allow one to transcend the limitations of an afterlife in heaven and escape from existence in any earthly, heavenly, or other form.*

The goal is to achieve a perfect union with the Absolute—the source of all reality in the universe. It is impossible to define this Absolute. No words can express the freedom or help conceptualize the power of the Infinite. Suffice it to say that the Absolute is a force that exists apart from all physical embodiment. It exists in the mind and in the unlimited dimensions of the souls of all things, plants and animals, human and even divine, since the gods themselves are merely a part of creation and are subject to the limitations of existence.

The goal, therefore, is to become one with the Absolute or "universal soul" (Brahman) through an awareness and clear understanding of the Self or "individual soul" (Atman). The pathway to the Absolute is through the Self. Everything in the realm of life is impermanent and changing: the physical world, the body, success, happiness—everything is transient. Only the Absolute is permanent. How then does one link with the Absolute? The real difficulty is in recognizing the Self and the Absolute while one is enmeshed in normal existence. How can one understand the Infinite when confined by the impermanence of this world? The answer in different variations forms the basis of Hinduism, Jainism, and Buddhism.

The first two selections come from the Kena Upanishad *and seek to define the universal and infinite nature of Brahman, the Absolute, the Spirit. The second in particular presents an allegorical conversation demonstrating that* Brahman *is superior to all the gods, who attempt to control it and simply do not understand the greatness of the Absolute. The knowledge of* Brahman *is intuitive and comes to the soul as a flash of wonder. The last selection is from the* Chandogya Upanishad *and identifies and links the Absolute with the Self.*

The Nature of *Brahman*

Who sends the mind to wander afar? Who first drives life to start on its journey? Who impels us to utter these words? Who is the Spirit behind the eye and the ear?

It is the ear of the ear, the eye of the eye, and the Word of words, the mind of mind, and the life of life. Those who follow wisdom pass beyond and, on leaving this world, become immortal.

There the eye goes not, nor words, nor mind. We know not, we cannot understand, how he can be explained: He is above the known and he is above the unknown. Thus have we heard from the ancient sages who explained this truth to us.

What cannot be spoken with words, but that whereby words are spoken: Know that alone to be *Brahman*, the Spirit; and not what people here adore.

What cannot be thought with the mind, but that whereby the mind can think: Know that alone to be *Brahman*, the Spirit; and not what people here adore.

What cannot be seen with the eye, but that whereby the eye can see: Know that alone to be *Brahman*, the Spirit; and not what people here adore.

What cannot be heard with the ear, but that whereby the ear can hear: Know that alone to be *Brahman*, the Spirit; and not what people here adore.

What cannot be indrawn with breath, but that whereby breath is indrawn: Know that alone to be *Brahman*, the Spirit; and not what people here adore.

The Supremacy of *Brahman*

Once upon a time, *Brahman*, the Spirit Supreme, won a victory for the gods. And the gods thought in their pride: "We alone attained this victory, ours alone is the glory."

Brahman saw it and appeared to them, but they knew him not. "Who is that being that fills us with wonder?" they cried.

And they spoke to Agni, the god of fire: "O god all-knowing, go and see who is that being that fills us with wonder."

Agni ran towards him and *Brahman* asked: "Who are you?" "I am the god of fire," he said, "the god who knows all things."

"What power is in you?" asked *Brahman*. "I can burn all things on earth."

And *Brahman* placed a straw before him, saying: "Burn this." The god of fire strove with all his power, but was unable to burn it. He then returned to the other gods and said: "I could not find out who was that being that fills us with wonder."

Then they spoke to Vayu, the god of the air. "O Vayu, go and see who is that being that fills us with wonder."

Vayu ran towards him and *Brahman* asked: "Who are you?" "I am Vayu, the god of the air," he said, "Matarisvan, the air that moves in space."

"What power is in you?" asked *Brahman*. "In a whirlwind I can carry away all there is on earth."

And *Brahman* placed a straw before him saying: "Blow this away." The god of the air strove with all his power, but was unable to move it. He returned to the other gods and said: "I could not find out who was that being that fills us with wonder."

Then the gods spoke to Indra, the god of thunder: "O giver of earthly goods, go and see who is that being that fills with wonder." And Indra ran towards *Brahman*, the Spirit Supreme, but he disappeared.

Then in the same region of the sky the god saw a lady of radiant beauty. She was Uma, divine wisdom, the daughter of the mountains of snow. "Who is that being that fills us with wonder?" he asked.

"He is *Brahman*, the Spirit Supreme," she answered. "Rejoice in him, since through him you attained the glory of victory."

And the gods, Agni, Vayu, and Indra excelled the other gods, for they were the first that came near *Brahman* and they first knew he was the Spirit Supreme.

And thus Indra, the god of thunder, excelled all other gods, for he came nearest to *Brahman* and he first knew that he was the Spirit Supreme.

Concerning whom it is said: He is seen in Nature in the wonder of a flash of lightning. He comes to the soul in the wonder of a flash of vision . . . .

"All This Universe Is *Brahman*"

All this universe is in truth *Brahman*. He is the beginning and end and life of all. As such, in silence, give unto him adoration.

Man in truth is made of faith. As his faith is in this life, so he becomes in the beyond: with faith and vision let him work.

There is a Spirit that is mind and life, light and truth and vast spaces. He contains all works and desires and all perfumes and all tastes. He enfolds the whole universe, and in silence is loving to all.

This is the Spirit that is in my heart, smaller than a grain of rice, or a grain of barley, or a grain of mustard-seed, or a grain of canary-seed, or the kernel of a grain of canary-seed. This is the Spirit that is in my heart, greater than the earth, greater than the sky, greater than heaven itself, greater than all these worlds.

He contains all works and desires and all perfumes and all tastes. He enfolds the whole universe and in silence is living to all. This is the Spirit that is in my heart, this is *Brahman*. To him I shall come when I go beyond this life. And to him will come he who has faith and doubts not. Thus said Sandilya, thus said Sandilya.

The Upanishads translated by Juan Mascaro (Penguin Classics, 1965) copyright © Juan Mascaro, 1965, p. 114. Reproduced with permission of Penguin Books Ltd.

Dharma: The "Ordinary Norm"

The Upanishads *present difficult existential propositions that cut to the heart of life's most intangible questions. What is the ultimate reality and purpose of life? What is the relationship of the individual to the Infinite? How does one proceed through life and to what end? The answers that emerged out of the* Upanishads *were developed in subsequent Hindu thought and provide a structure for individual existence in this world and in the next.*

Existence, according to Hindu thought, is an eternal alternation between life and death. This endless cycle of existence is called Samsara. Samsara is not a secure, liberating experience, but a burden, a process of endless "redeath" (or "rebirth") for all beings, plant, animal, human, or divine. You are born into life in some form, you die and are reborn endlessly. The key to resolving the constancy of Samsara and to attaining spiritual freedom lies in the concept of Karma or "action." As long as there is physical or mental action in life, there is a continued effect and existence is perpetu-ated. Good deeds in life result in rebirth on a more elevated scale, perhaps in this world as a more evolved entity, a person of greater wealth or status, or perhaps rebirth in heaven as a god. Con-versely, bad deeds might result in a diminution of status or existence in a hell. Since good, as well as evil, are temporary conditions, existence knows only eternal change. Only Brahman or the Absolute is permanent. The only way to halt the cycle of Samsara is for the individual Self to eliminate Karma, the action that maintains the cycle of life and death.

Therefore, true liberation of the soul can only be achieved by the evolution of the Self from an en-tity existing within an impermanent world of stress and strain to a Self that is fully evolved, fully connected to the Absolute, to the "oneness" of the Infinite and the Self.

To achieve this "oneness," to break the cycle of Samsara and attain spiritual freedom, one must end all Karma—to absolve the Self from all mental and physical action. This is a complex process, requiring years, rather "lifetimes" of Vedic study, meditation, ascetic self-denial, and self-illumina-tion. Only the most evolved souls can attain "Nirvana" with its complete freedom from Samsara and oneness with the Absolute. So what is a human being to do? There are two primary solutions to the problem of Samsara. One is called the "Ordinary Norm" or Dharma *and the other is the "Extra-ordinary Norm" or* Moksha.

Dharma has been variously defined as "the right order of things," "moral law," "right conduct," or even "duty." How does one deal with the endless cycle of Samsara? The "Ordinary Norm" focuses on living a life of moral action, of right conduct in political, social, economic, and religious affairs. A life according to Dharma will lead to a more evolved birth in the next round of existence. This "Ordinary Norm" of right action is the majority solution for most Hindus. But it has important im-plications in life:

- *Accepts Samsara: The "Ordinary Norm" accepts the endless cycle of birth and rebirth as legiti-mate and appropriate.*
- *Acceptance of Responsibilities: Dharma or "right action" accepts all responsibilities that are appropriate to one's sex, class or caste group, stage in life, and so on. One accepts the world and one's position in society as it is without trying to change it.*
- *Self-Interest: The "Ordinary Norm" solution necessarily implies that it is one's duty to do good and to acquire merit in this world for one's Atman (Self). One must avoid actions that will re-sult in harm to any life form, for each is an evolving entity, trapped in Samsara, coping with the limitations of existence.*
- *Rebirth in Heaven: This is the highest goal attainable by living a life in accordance with Dharma.*
- *Impermanence: Still, all attainments and achievements in the world of Dharma, even the at-tainment of Heaven, is impermanent and subject to change. One never overcomes Samsara— one simply seeks to make the best of the impermanence that defines existence.*

The Transmigration of the Soul

The following selections illuminate these points by discussing the transmigration or evolution of the soul in the world of Samsara and the accumulation of merit through Dharma or right action. Note the fatalistic resignation about the constancy of Samsara.

"The Transmigration of the Soul" is from *Manu-Smrti,* 12.3-9, 11,14, in G. Buhler, *The Laws of Manu* (Oxford: Clarendon Press, 1886).

Action [*Karma*], which springs from the mind, from speech, and from the body, produces either good or evil results; by action are caused the various conditions of men, the highest, the middling, and the lowest.

Know that the mind is the instigator here below, even to that action which is connected with the body, and which is of three kinds, has three locations, and falls under ten heads.

Coveting the property of others, thinking in one's heart of what is undesirable, and adherence to false doctrines are the three kinds of sinful mental action.

Abusing others, speaking untruth, detracting from the merits of all men, and talking idly shall be the four kinds of evil verbal action.

Taking what has not been given, injuring creatures without the sanction of the law, and holding criminal intercourse with another man's wife are declared to be the three kinds of wicked bodily action.

A man obtains the result of a good or evil mental act in his mind, that of a verbal act in his speech, that of a bodily act in his body.

In consequence of many sinful acts committed with his body, a man becomes in the next birth something inanimate, in consequence of sins committed by speech, a bird, or a beast, and in consequence of mental sins he is reborn in a low caste.

Spiritual Merit

Giving no pain to any creature, let him slowly accumulate spiritual merit [*Dharma*], for the sake of acquiring a companion to the next world, just as the white ant gradually raises its hill.

For in the next world neither father, nor mother, nor wife, nor sons, nor relations stay to be his companions; spiritual merit alone remains with him.

Single is each being born; single it dies; single it enjoys the reward of its virtue; single it suffers the punishment of its sin.

Leaving the dead body on the ground like a log of wood, or a clod of earth, the relatives depart with averted faces; but spiritual merit follows the soul.

Let him therefore always slowly accumulate spiritual merit, in order that it may be his companion after death; for without merit as his companion he will traverse a gloom difficult to traverse.

That companion speedily conducts the man who is devoted to duty and effaces his sins by austerities, to the next world, radiant and clothed with an ethereal body.

"Death Will Not Wait"

Virtue alone will follow an individual, wherever he may go; therefore do you duty unflinchingly in this wretched world.

Tomorrow's business should be done today, and the afternoon's business in the forenoon; for death will not wait, whether a person has done it or not. While his mind is fixed upon his field, or traffic, or his house, or while his thoughts are engrossed by some other beloved object, death suddenly carries him away as his prey, as a she-wolf catches a lamb.

Time is no one's friend and no one's enemy; when the effect of his acts in a former existence, by which his present existence is caused, has expired, he snatches a man away forcibly.

He will not die before his time has come, even though he has been pierced by a thousand shafts; he will not live after his time is out, even though he has only been touched by the point of a blade of Kusa grass.

Neither drugs, nor magical formulas, nor burnt offerings, nor prayers will save a man who is in the bonds of death or old age. An impending

---

"Spiritual Merit" is from *Manu-Smrti*, 4.238-243, in G. Buhler, *The Laws of Manu* (Oxford: Clarendon Press, 1886).

"'Death Will Not Wait'" is from *Vishnu-Smrti*, 20.39–53, in J. Jolly, *The Institutes of Vishnu* (Oxford: Clarendon Press, 1900).

evil cannot be averted even by a hundred precautions; what reason then for you to complain?

Even as a calf finds his mother among a thousand cows, an act formerly done is sure to find the perpetrator. Of existing beings the beginning is unknown, the middle of their career is known, and the end again unknown; what reason then for you to complain?

As the body of mortals undergoes the vicissitudes of infancy, youth, and old age, even so will it be transformed into another body hereafter; a sensible man is not mistaken about that.

As a man puts on new clothes in this world, throwing aside those which he formerly wore, even so the self of man puts on new bodies, which are in accordance with his acts in a former life.

No weapons will hurt the self of man, no fire burn it, no waters moisten it, and no wind dry it up. It is not to be hurt, not to be burnt, not to be moistened, and not to be dried up; it is imperishable, perpetual, unchanging, immovable, without beginning.

It is further said to be immaterial, passing all thought, and immutable. Knowing the self of man to be such, you must not grieve for the destruction of his body.

Moksha: The "Extraordinary Norm"

As we have noted, the dilemma of Samsara, or the endless process of death and rebirth is fueled by mental or physical action (Karma) in the world. The "Ordinary Norm" solution for the majority of Hindus is to accept this process and strive through moral action (Dharma) to improve one's lot in subsequent lives. But some Hindus choose another solution, the "Extraordinary Norm," and seek "liberation" (Moksha) from Samsara. The highest goal for these Hindus is not rebirth in Heaven, but release from Samsara, from all rebirth and redeath.

In order to accomplish this spiritual freedom one must not contribute to Karma. "Non-action" is achieved only by withdrawal from "normal existence." One must renounce the responsibilities of family and abandon all personal attachments to this world, for they create Karma and therefore are impediments to spiritual purity. By living a solitary existence as a monk or hermit, and through Vedic study, spiritual meditation, and ascetic denial, the purified Self, cleansed of all Karmic contagion, can break free from Samsara. Moksha is lasting and permanent with no suffering in the realm of Samsara. The Self transcends the limitations of the world and becomes at one with the infinite nature of the universe, at one with the Absolute—the soul has achieved Nirvana.

Those few who embark upon this path are greatly respected in Hindu tradition. They must be cared for by the Hindu laity, who offer shelter and food as necessary. Some who attain Nirvana become sages and teachers and in the time remaining in their "last life" on earth serve as spiritual advisors.

The following selections are from perhaps the greatest poem in all of Sanskrit literature, the Bhagavad Gita. *Written about 500 B.C.E., it was included as a small section in the Mahabharata, the longest poem in world literature. The Mahabharata centers around a great struggle between the forces of good and evil. There is little doubt that the war described in the Mahabharata is not simply symbolic and may in fact be based on fact. But the* Bhagavad Gita *is very symbolic and the battle described here is a battle for the kingdom of the soul.*

The Bhagavad Gita *is a dialogue primarily between Arunja, symbolizing the soul of man and Krishna, the god who is charioteer of the soul. The wheels of the chariot are "right effort" and the driver is Dhamma or Truth. The chariot leads to Nirvana, the realm of the Absolute. It is described as "the land which is free from fear." Therefore, the* Bhagavad Gita *crystallizes the essence of Moksha. Spiritual release, freedom from pain and anxiety, and the process of spiritual unity with the In-*

finite are elemental to the understanding of the poem. In this regard, the concept of love is especially important. If life is finite and knowledge is the Infinite, then love is the bond of union between the finite and Infinite. Love is the power that moves the Universe. All creation comes from love and love returns all things to Eternity after their time has passed. All energy is love and love leads to Light, the joy of the Infinite.

The Manifestations and Will
of the Divine

Polytheism, or the worship of many gods, is an important component of Hinduism. There are hundreds of deities and there is great emphasis on individual devotion to a personal god. And yet, Hindu gods are born in many forms many times for the benefit of humankind. Krishna, for example, is one of the many incarnations of Vishnu. What could be inherently confusing is simplified by the notion that the universe is filled with the manifestations of God, or the forms in which the Absolute chooses to show Itself. To worship any god, therefore, is to worship the Absolute, "the beginning, the middle, and the end of all that lives." In the following excerpts from the Bhagavad Gita, *Arunja, the soul of man, questions and learns of the will of Krishna, the manifestation of the Infinite.*

Krishna:

4.5: I have been born many times, Arunja, and many times hast thou been born. But I remember my past lives, and thou hast forgotten thine.

4.6: Although I am unborn, everlasting, and I am the Lord of all, I come to my realm of nature and through my wondrous power I am born.

4.7: When righteousness [*Dharma*] is weak and fails and unrighteousness exults in pride, then my Spirit arises on earth.

4.8: For the salvation of those who are good, for the destruction of evil in men, for the fulfilment of the kingdom of righteousness, I come to this world in the ages that pass.

4.9: He who knows my birth as God and who knows my sacrifice, when he leaves his mortal body, goes no more from death to death, for he in truth comes to me.

4.10: How many have come to me, trusting in me, filled with my Spirit, in peace from passions and fears and anger, made pure by the fire of wisdom!

4.11: In any way that men love me in that same way they find my love; for many are the paths of men, but they all in the end come to me.

4.19: He whose undertakings are free from anxious desire and fanciful thought, whose work is made pure in the fire of wisdom: he is called wise by those who see.

4.23: He has attained liberation: he is free from all bonds, his mind has found peace in wisdom, and his work is a holy sacrifice. The work of such a man is pure.

4.24: Who in all his work sees God, he in truth goes unto God: God is his worship, God is his offering, offered by God in the fire of God.

4.34: Those who themselves have seen the Truth can be thy teachers of wisdom. Ask from them, bow unto them, be thou unto them a servant.

4.35: When wisdom is thine, Arunja, never more shalt thou be in confusion; for thou shalt see all things in thy heart, and thou shalt see thy heart in me.

4.39: He who has faith has wisdom, who lives in self-harmony, whose faith is his life; and he who finds wisdom, soon finds the peace supreme.

9.23: Even those who in faith worship other gods, because of their love they worship me, although not in the right way.

9.27: Whatever you do, or eat, or give, or offer in adoration, let it be an offering to me; and whatever you suffer, suffer it for me.

9.28: Thus thou shalt be free from the bonds of *Karma* which yield fruits that are evil and good; and with thy soul one in renunciation thou shalt be free and come to me.

9.29: I am the same to all beings, and my love is ever the same; but those who worship me with devotion, they are in me and I am in them.

9.34: Give me thy mind and give me thy heart, give me thy offerings and thy adoration; and thus with thy soul in harmony, and making me thy goal supreme, thou shalt in truth come to me.

Arunja:

10.18: Speak to me again in full of thy power and of thy glory, for I am never tired, never, of hearing thy words of life.

Krishna:

10:19: Listen and I shall reveal to thee some manifestations of my divine glory. Only the greatest, Arunja, for there is no end to my infinite greatness.

10.20: I am the soul, prince victorious, which dwells in the heart of all things. I am the beginning, the middle, and the end of all that lives.

10.21: Among the sons of light I am Vishnu, and of luminaries the radiant sun. I am the lord of the winds and storms, and of the lights in the night I am the moon.

10.22: Of the Vedas I am the Veda of songs, and I am Indra, the chief of the gods. Above man's senses I am the mind, and in all living beings I am the light of consciousness.

10.40: There is no end of my divine greatness, Arunja. What I have spoken here to thee shows only a small part of my Infinity.

10.41: Know thou that whatever is beautiful and good, whatever has glory and power is only a portion of my own radiance.

10.42: But of what help is it to thee to know this diversity? Know that with one single fraction of my Being I pervade and support the Universe, and know that I AM.

Arunja:

11.15: I see in thee all the gods, O my God; and the infinity of the beings of thy creation. I see god Brahma on his throne of lotus, and all the seers and serpents of light.

11.16: All around I behold thy Infinity: the power of thy innumerable arms, the visions from thy innumerable mouths, and the fire of life of thy innumerable bodies. Nowhere I see a beginning or middle or end of thee, O God of all, Form Infinite!

11.17: I see the spendour of an infinite beauty which illumines the whole universe. It is thee! with thy crown and sceptre and circle. How difficult thou art to see! But I see thee: as fire, as the sun, blinding, incomprehensible.

11.18: Thou art the Imperishable, the highest End of knowledge, the support of this vast universe. Thou, the everlasting ruler of the law of righteousness, the Spirit who is and who was at the beginning.

The Perfect Being

The perfection of the spirit is a common goal of many of the world's religions. This characterization of the perfect being embodies many of the principal teachings of the Bhagavad Gita. *Only a Yogin, or spiritual devotee, who is dedicated to purity and truth, may attain the release from suffering and enjoy the peace of Nirvana.*

Arunja:

2.54: How is the man of tranquil wisdom, who abides in divine contemplation? What are his words? What is his silence? What is his work?

Krishna:

2.55: When a man surrenders all desires that come to the heart and by the grace of God finds the joy of God, then his soul has indeed found peace.

2.56: He whose mind is untroubled by sorrows, and for pleasures he has no longings, beyond passion, and fear and anger, he is the sage of unwavering mind.

2.57: Who everywhere is free from all ties, who neither rejoices nor sorrows if fortune is good or is ill, his is a serene wisdom.

2.58: When in recollection he withdraws all his senses from the attractions of the pleasures of sense, even as a tortoise withdraws all its limbs, then his is a serene wisdom.

2.59: Pleasures of sense, but not desires, disappear from the austere soul. Even desires disappear when the soul has seen the Supreme.

6.12: On that seat let him rest and practise Yoga for the purification of the soul: with the life of his body and mind in peace; his soul in silence before the One.

6.14: With soul in peace, and all fear gone, and strong in the vow of holiness, let him rest with mind in harmony, his soul on me, his God supreme.

6.15: The Yogi who, lord of his mind, ever prays in this harmony of soul, attains the peace of Nirvana, the peace supreme that is in me.

6.21: Then the seeker knows that joy of Eternity: a vision seen by reason far beyond what senses can see. He abides therein and moves not from Truth.

6.22: He has found joy and Truth, a vision for him supreme. He is therein steady: the greatest pain moves him not.

6.23: In this union of Yoga there is liberty: a deliverance from the oppression of pain. This Yoga must be followed with faith, with a strong and courageous heart.

6.24: When all desires are in peace and the mind, withdrawing within, gathers the multitudinous straying senses into the harmony of recollection,

6.25: Then, with reason armed with resolution, let the seeker quietly lead the mind into the Spirit, and let all his thoughts be silence.

6.26: And whenever the mind unsteady and restless strays away from the Spirit, let him ever and forever lead it again to the Spirit.

6.27: Thus joy supreme comes to the Yogi whose heart is still, whose passions are peace, who is pure from sin, who is one with *Brahman*, with God.

6.31: He who in this oneness of love, loves me in whatever he sees, wherever this man may live, in truth this man lives in me.

THE WISDOM OF THE BUDDHA

Suffering is the lot of everyone, everywhere and all the time; therefore, my friend, do not hanker after the glittering objects of this world! And, once this hankering is extinct in you, then you will clearly see that this entire world of the living can be said to be on fire.

—*Buddhaghosa, Buddhist Path of Purification*

The Life of the Buddha

Buddhism, as a historical movement, is a vast subject. The effect of Buddhist teachings on the social and cultural traditions of several countries in the world community is a long and complex study. As a religion, however, Buddhism is relatively simple in its basic and persistent ideals.

Buddhism was born in India, within the Hindu culture, and assumed many of the fundamental principles of Indian religious thought. The concepts of Dharma (right action), Samsara (eternal rebirth), and Moksha (release) are common to both religions. But unlike Hinduism, Buddhism had a historical founder, a set of fundamental scriptures, and an order of monks. Buddhism renounced the Indian caste system with its static social hierarchy and rejected the authority of the Brahmin priests who regulated the religious life cycle in India. Because of these inherent differences, Buddhism vanished from the Indian subcontinent by the twelfth century C.E. and spread beyond the Himalayas to Tibet, China, Korea, and Japan. In southeast Asia, Buddhism gained acceptance as the principal religion of Myanmar, Thailand, Cambodia, Laos, and Vietnam. Today over 6 percent of the world's population identifies itself as Buddhist. This section of the chapter will present some of the most important concepts that define Buddhist thought.

In trying to understand the religious tenets of Buddhism, it is important to remember that "Buddha" is not the name of a specific person, but is Sanskrit for someone who is "fully enlightened" about the nature and meaning of life. In the stream of cosmic time, there are numerous Buddhas who appear at successive intervals to teach and inject spiritual reality into this world.

About 500 B.C.E., there appeared a "historical Buddha" named Siddhartha Gautama (also called Shakyamuni), who decided to enter this world in order to promote the pathway of spiritual enlightenment. He did so as a Bodhisattva, a title for one who intends to become a Buddha. This process of becoming fully enlightened usually involves birth and rebirth in many historical lives. So, prior to Gautama's achieving Nirvana and becoming a Buddha in his last life on earth about 500 B.C.E., he had lived many previous incarnations. In the following story, the "historical Buddha," Siddhartha Gautama, narrates a story of one of his preparatory lives to his student Ananda.

Previous Lives: The Tale of the Hungry Tigress

The Buddha told the following story to Ananda: "Once upon a time, in the remote past, there lived a king, Maharatha by name. He was rich in gold, grain, and chariots, and his power, strength, and courage were irresistible. He had three sons who were like young gods to look at. They were named Mahapranada, Mahadeva, and Mahasattva.

One day the king went for relaxation into a park. The princes, delighted with the beauties of the park and the flowers which could be seen everywhere, walked about here and there until they came to a large thicket of bamboos. There they dismissed their servants, in order to rest for a while. But Mahapranada said to his two brothers: "I feel rather afraid here. There might easily be some wild beasts about, and they might do us harm." Mahadeva replied: "I also feel ill at ease. Though it is not my body I fear for. It is the thought of separation from those I love which terrifies me." Finally, Mahasattva said:

"No fear feel I, nor any sorrow either,
In this wide, lonesome wood, so dear to
   Sages.
My heart is filled with bursting joy,
For soon I'll win the highest boon."

As the princes strolled about in the solitary thicket they saw a tigress, surrounded by five cubs, seven days old. Hunger and thirst had exhausted the tigress, and her body was quite weak. On seeing her, Mahapranada called out: "The poor animal suffers from having given birth to the seven cubs only a week ago! If she finds nothing to eat, she will either eat her own young, or die from hunger!" Mahasattva replied: "How can this poor exhausted creature find food?" Mahapranada said: "Tigers live on fresh

meat and warm blood." Mahadeva said: "She is quite exhausted, overcome by hunger and thirst, scarcely alive and very weak. In this state she cannot possibly catch any prey. And who would sacrifice himself to preserve her life?" Mahapranada said: "Yes, self-sacrifice is so difficult!" Mahasattva replied: "It is difficult for people like us, who are so fond of our lives and bodies, and who have so little intelligence. It is not at all difficult, however, for others, who are true men, intent on benefitting their fellow-creatures, and who long to sacrifice themselves. Holy men are born of pity and compassion. Whatever the bodies they may get, in heaven or on earth, a hundred times will they undo them, joyful in their hearts, so that the lives of others may be saved."

Greatly agitated, the three brothers carefully watched the tigress for some time, and then went towards her. But Mahasattva thought to himself: "Now the time has come for me to sacrifice myself! For a long time I have served this putrid body and given it beds and clothes, food and drink, and conveyances of all kinds. Yet it is doomed to perish and fall down, and in the end it will break up and be destroyed. How much better to leave this ungrateful body of one's own accord in good time! It cannot subsist forever, because it is like urine which must come out. Today I will use it for a sublime deed. Then it will act for me as a boat which helps me to cross the ocean of birth and death. When I have renounced this futile body, a mere ulcer, tied to countless becomings, burdened with urine and excrement, unsubstantial like foam, full of hundreds of parasites—then I shall win the perfectly pure *Dharma*-body, endowed with hundreds of virtues, full of such qualities as trance and wisdom, immaculate, free from all Substrata, changeless and without sorrow." So, his heart filled with boundless compassion, Mahasattva asked his brothers to leave him alone for a while, went to the lair of the tigress, hung his cloak on a bamboo, and made the following vow:

"For the [benefit] of the world I wish to win enlightenment, incomparably wonderful. From deep compassion I now give away my body, so hard to quit, unshaken in my mind. That enlightenment I shall now gain, in which nothing hurts and nothing harms. . . .Thus shall I cross to the Beyond of the fearful ocean of becoming which fills the triple world!"

The friendly prince then threw himself down in front of the tigress. But she did nothing to him. The *Bodhisattva* noticed that she was too weak to move. As a merciful man he had taken no sword with him. He therefore cut his throat with a sharp piece of bamboo, and fell down near the tigress. She noticed the *Bodhisattva's* body all covered with blood, and in no time ate up all the flesh and blood, leaving only the bones.

"It was I, Ananda, who at that time and on that occasion was that prince Mahasattva."

The Birth of the *Bodhisattva*

After many preparatory lives, the Bodhisattva *was ready for his last life on earth when he would achieve full enlightenment and become a Buddha. The Buddha, as an historical figure, was born as Siddhartha Gautama about 563 B.C.E. in Northwest India at the foot of the Himalaya mountains. All we know about the life and teachings of the Buddha come from much later accounts that were embellished by his followers. Therefore, the following account of the birth of the* Bodhisattva *reflects the anticipation of a great event.*

There lived once upon a time a king of the Shakyas, a scion of the solar race, whose name was Shuddhodana. He was pure in conduct, and beloved of the Shakyas like the autumn moon. He had a wife, splendid, beautiful, and steadfast, who was called the Great Maya, from her resemblance to Maya the Goddess. These two tasted of love's delights, and one day she conceived the fruit of her womb, but without any defilement, in the same way in which knowledge joined to trance bears fruit. Just before her conception she had a dream. A white king elephant seemed to enter her body, but without causing her any pain. So Maya, queen of that god-like king, bore in her womb the glory of his dynasty. But she remained free from the fatigues, depressions, and fancies which usually accompany pregnancies. Pure herself, she longed to withdraw into the pure forest, in the loneliness of which she could practice trance. She set her heart on going to Lumbini, a delightful grove, with trees of every kind, like the grove of Citraratha in Indra's Paradise. She asked the king to accompany her, and so they left the city, and went to that glorious grove.

When the queen noticed that the time of her delivery was approaching, she went to a couch overspread with an awning, thousands of waiting-women looking on with joy in their hearts. The propitious constellation of Pushya shone brightly when a son was born to the queen, for the benefit of the world. He came out of his mother's side, without causing her pain or injury. . . .So he issued from the womb as befits a Buddha. He did not enter the world in the usual manner, and he appeared like one descended from the sky. And since he had for many aeons been engaged in the practice of meditation, he now was born in full awareness, and not thoughtless and bewildered as other people are. When born, he was so lustrous and steadfast that it appeared as if the young sun had come down to the earth. And yet, when people gazed at his dazzling brilliance, he held their eyes like the moon. His limbs shone with the radiant hue of precious gold, and lit up the space all around. Instantly he walked seven steps, firmly and with long strides. In that he was like the constellation of the Seven Seers. With the bearing of a lion he surveyed the four quarters, and spoke these

words full of meaning for the future: "For enlightenment I was born, for the good of all that
lives. This is the last time that I have been born
into this world of becoming."

The Awakening

*Siddhartha Gautama's father was a chief of the Shakya tribe and a member of the warrior caste. He
was informed that his son would become either a great emperor or a great religious teacher. The chief
recognized this potential and tried to shelter his son from the realities of the world by providing him
with a life of luxury and privilege. At the age of 29, Siddhartha's wife bore him a son and all elements were in place for a life of continued prestige and prosperity.*

*Yet inwardly Siddhartha was not at peace. He became aware of the inevitable suffering of life in
the universal experience of sickness, old age, and death. He agonized over the impermanence of
things, and reflected on the pain of separation from what is loved, and loving what cannot be attained. Since he shared the common Indian belief in reincarnation, he feared that life with all its
suffering would be repeated in countless rebirths. How could one attain release and achieve ultimate
deliverance from the pain and suffering of the world?*

*Siddhartha at age 29 resolved to seek the answer to this question and renounced his worldly life,
that of his wealth and family, in exchange for the way of a homeless mendicant. For six years he
wandered as an ascetic, seeking the wisdom of teachers and enduring the pain of starvation and
physical deprivation. He found no answers and abandoned his religious quest as profitless. In his
frustration, he began to meditate under a tree. For forty-nine days he concentrated and rejected the
temptations of Mara, the spirit of this world, who offered him rewards and threatened him with
punishments if he would not renounce his meditation. Finally, Siddhartha overcame the illusions of
Mara's threats and experienced the inner illumination that he had sought for so long. Upon attaining Nirvana, he had made the transition from Bodhisattva to a fully enlightened state. He had become the Enlightened One, the Buddha. The following selections recount the story of his spiritual
transformation.*

In the course of time the women told him how
much they loved the groves near the city, and
how delightful they were. So, feeling like an elephant locked up inside a house, he set his heart
on making a journey outside the palace. The
king heard of the plans of his dearly beloved
son, and arranged a pleasure excursion which
would be worthy of his own affection and royal
dignity, as well as of his son's youth. But he gave
orders that all the common folk with any kind of
affliction should be kept away from the royal
road, because he feared that they might agitate
the prince's sensitive mind. Very gently all crip-
ples were driven away, and all those who were
crazy, aged, ailing, and the like, and also all

wretched beggars. So the royal highway became
supremely magnificent.

The citizens jubilantly acclaimed the prince.
But the Gods of the Pure Abode, when they saw
that everyone was happy as if in Paradise, con-
jured up the illusion of an *old man*, so as to induce the king's son to leave his home. The
prince's charioteer explained to him the meaning of old age. The prince reacted to this news
like a bull when a lightning-flash crashes down
near him. For his understanding was purified by
the noble intentions he had formed in his past
lives and by the good deeds he had accumulated
over countless aeons. In consequence his lofty
soul was shocked to hear of old age. He sighed

deeply, shook his head, fixed his gaze on the old man, surveyed the festive multitude, and, deeply perturbed, said to the charioteer: "So that is how old age destroys indiscriminately the memory, beauty, and strength of all! And yet with such a sight before it the world goes on quite unperturbed. This being so, my son, turn round the horses, and travel back quickly to our palace! How can I delight to walk about in parks when my heart is full of fear of aging?" So at the bidding of his master's son, the charioteer reversed the chariot. And the prince went back into his palace, which now seemed empty to him, as a result of his anxious reflections.

On a second pleasure excursion the same gods created a *man with a diseased body.* When this fact was explained to him, the son of Shuddhodana was dismayed, trembled like the reflection of the moon on rippling water, and in his compassion he uttered these words in a low voice: "This then is the calamity of disease, which afflicts people! The world sees it, and yet does not lose its confident ways. Greatly lacking in insight it remains gay under the constant threat of disease. We will not continue this excursion, but go straight back to the palace! Since I have learned of the danger of illness, my heart is repelled by pleasures and seems to shrink into itself."

On a third excursion the same gods displayed a *corpse,* which only the prince and his charioteer could see being borne along the road. The charioteer again explained the meaning of this sight to the prince. Courageous though he was, the king's son, on hearing of death, was suddenly filled with dismay. Leaning his shoulder against the top of the chariot rail, he spoke these works in a forceful voice: "This is the end which has been fixed for all, and yet the world forgets its fears and takes no heed! The hearts of men are surely hardened to fears, for they feel quite at ease even while traveling along the road to the next life. Turn back the chariot! This is no time or place for pleasure excursions. How could an intelligent person pay no heed at a time of disaster, when he knows of his impending destruction?"

The Flight

The beauties of the landscape and [the prince's] longing for the forest carried him deep into the countryside. There he saw the soil being ploughed, and its surface, broken with the tracks of the furrows, looked like rippling water. The ploughs had torn up the sprouting grass, scattering tufts of grass here and there, and the land was littered with tiny creatures who had been killed and injured, worms, insects, and the like. The sight of all this grieved the prince as deeply as if he had witnessed the slaughter of his own kinsmen. He observed the ploughmen, saw how they suffered from wind, sun, and dust, and how the oxen were worn down by the labor of drawing. And in the supreme nobility of his mind he performed an act of supreme pity. He then alighted from his horse and walked gently and slowly over the ground, overcome with grief. He reflected on the generation and the passing of all living things, and in his distress he said to himself: "How pitiful all this!"

His mind longed for solitude, he withdrew from the good friends who walked behind him, and went to a solitary spot at the foot of a rose-apple tree. The tree's lovely leaves were in constant motion, and the ground underneath it salubrious and green like beryl. There he sat down, reflected on the origination and passing away of all that lives, and then he worked on his mind in such a way that, with this theme as a basis, it became stable and concentrated. When he had won through to mental stability, he was suddenly freed from all desire for sense-objects and from cares of any kind. He had reached the first stage of trance, which is calm amidst applied and discursive thinking. In his case it had already at this stage a supra mundane purity. He had obtained that concentration of mind which is born of detachment, and is accompanied by the highest rapture and joy, and in this state of

Buddhist Scriptures translated by Edward Conze (Penguin Classics, 1959), copyright © Edward Conze, 1959, pp. 41–43. Reproduced with permission of Penguin Books Ltd.

trance his mind considered the destiny of the world correctly, as it is: "Pitiful, indeed, that these people who themselves are helpless and doomed to undergo illness, old age, and destruction, should, in the ignorant blindness of their self-intoxication, show so little respect for others who are likewise victims of old age, disease, and death! But now that I have discerned this supreme *Dharma*, it would be unworthy and unbecoming if I, who am so constituted, should show no respect for others whose constitution is essentially the same as mine." When he thus gained insight into the fact that the blemish of disease, old age, and death vitiate the very core of this world, he lost at the same moment all self-intoxication, which normally arises from pride in one's own strength, youth, and vitality. He now was neither glad nor grieved; all doubt, lassitude, and sleepiness disappeared; sensuous excitements could no longer influence him; and hatred and contempt for others were far from his mind.

The Enlightenment

Now that he had defeated Mara's violence [Evil, Death] by his firmness and calm, the *Bodhisattva*, possessed of great skill in Transic meditation, put himself into trance, intent on discerning both the ultimate reality of things and the final goal of existence. After he had gained complete mastery over all the degrees and kinds of trance:

1. In the *first watch* of the night he recollected the successive series of his former births. "There was I so and so; that was my name; deceased from there I came here"—in this way he remembered thousands of births, as though living them over again. When he had recalled his own births and deaths in all these various lives

Buddhist Scriptures translated by Edward Conze (Penguin Classics, 1959), copyright © Edward Conze, 1959, pp. 49–52. Reproduced with permission of Penguin Books Ltd.

of his, the Sage, full of pity, turned his compassionate mind towards other living beings, and he thought to himself: "Again and again they must leave the people they regard as their own, and must go on elsewhere, and that without ever stopping. Surely this world is unprotected and helpless, and like a wheel it turns round and round." As he continued steadily to recollect the past thus, he came to the definite conviction that this world of *Samsara* is as unsubstantial as the pith of a plantain tree.

2. Second to none in valor, he then, in the *second watch* of the night, acquired the supreme heavenly eye, for he himself was the best of all those who have sight. Thereupon with the perfectly pure heavenly eye he looked upon the entire world, which appeared to him as though reflected in a spotless mirror. He saw that the decease and rebirth of beings depend on whether they have done superior or inferior deeds. And his compassion grew still further. It became clear to him that no security can be found in this flood of Samsaric existence, and that the threat of death is ever-present. Beset on all sides, creatures can find no resting place. In this way he surveyed that five places of rebirth with his heavenly eye. And he found nothing substantial in the world of becoming, just as no core of heartwood is found in a plantain tree when its layers are peeled off one by one.

3. Then, as the *third watch* of that night drew on, the supreme master of trance turned his meditation to the real and essential nature of this world: "Alas, living beings wear themselves out in vain! Over and over again they are born, they age, die, pass on to a new life, and are reborn! What is more, greed and dark delusion obscure their sight, and they are blind from birth. Greatly apprehensive, they yet do not know how to get out of this great mass of ill.". . .

When the great seer had [stopped all *Karma*-formations]. . . and had achieved a correct knowledge of all there is to be known, he stood out in the world as a Buddha. He passed through the eight stages of Transic insight, and quickly reached their highest point. From the summit of the world downwards he could detect no self anywhere. Like the fire, when its fuel is burnt up, he became tranquil. He had reached perfection, and he thought to himself: "This is the authentic Way on which in the past so many great seers, who also knew all higher and all lower things, have traveled on to ultimate and real truth. And now I have obtained it!"

4. At that moment, in the *fourth watch* of the night, when dawn broke and all the ghosts that move and those that move not went to rest, the great seer took up the position which knows no more alteration, and the leader of all reached the state of all-knowledge. Then through his Buddhahood, he had cognized this fact, the earth swayed like a woman drunken with wine, the sky shone bright,. . . and the mighty drums of thunder resounded through the air. Pleasant breezes blew softly, rain fell from a cloudless sky, flowers and fruits dropped from the trees out of season—in an effort, as it were, to show reverence for him. . . . All living things rejoiced and sensed that things went well. . . .

For seven days He dwelt there—his body gave him no trouble, his eyes never closed, and he looked into his own mind. He thought: "Here I have found freedom," and he knew that the longings of his heart had at last come to fulfillment. Now that he had grasped the principle of causation, and finally convinced himself of the lack of self in all that is, he roused himself again from his deep trance, and in his great compassion he surveyed the world with his Buddha-eye, intent on giving it peace. . . .

As soon as Indra and Brahma, the two chiefs of those who dwell in the heavens, had grasped the Buddha's intention to proclaim the path to Peace, they shone brightly and came up to him, the benefit of the world their concern. . . . "Please do not condemn all those that live as unworthy of such treasure! Oh, please engender pity in your heart for beings in this world! So varied is their endowment, and while some have much passion, others have only very little. Now that you, O Sage, have yourself crossed the ocean of the world of becoming, please rescue also the other living beings who have sunk so deep into suffering!". . . Having made this request to the great seer, the two gods returned to their celestial abode by the way they had come. And the sage pondered over their words. In consequence he was confirmed in his decision to set the world free.

The "Middle Path" of Buddhism

When Siddhartha Gautama had finally attained the spiritual illumination of Nirvana and had become the Buddha, he arose with strength, joy, and a new purpose. He had seen the cause and cure of world suffering. With the greatest compassion for all creatures suffering in ignorance, he went forth to spend the remaining forty-five years of his life as a wandering teacher, to share with others his pathway to spiritual freedom and release from the suffering of life.

What had Buddha discovered? He offered the new conviction that desire and passion were the primary causes of suffering in the world. This craving for sense-gratification, for transitory illusions and objects that can never satisfy, is the cause of continuing rebirth into lives filled with suffering. If suffering is truly to cease, cravings and misplaced desire must end. This could be achieved by disciplining the mind and by focusing it on right action, and ethical conduct through compassion for all living creatures. Through discipline, right action, and compassion, craving gradually ceases and the joy of complete spiritual attachment leads to Nirvana. One cannot describe such a transcendent state of emancipation because it is beyond anything we can understand in the realm of existence. Whoever attains Nirvana will never again be reborn into this world. It is the final deliverance.

*In the following excerpts from the Buddha's First Sermon after his own enlightenment, he reveals the Four Noble Truths that describe the nature of existence and the Noble Eightfold Path that leads to the cessation of suffering. These basic doctrines or teaching of Buddha (*Dharma*) provide a* *"middle path" to enlightenment, one between complete asceticism and personal abandonment to the pleasures of life.*

The First Sermon of the Buddha

And the Blessed One [Buddha] thus addressed the five monks: There are two extremes, monks, which he who has given up the world ought to avoid.

What are these two extremes? A life given to pleasures, devoted to pleasures and lusts—this is degrading, sensual, vulgar, ignoble, and profitless. And a life given to mortifications—this is painful, ignoble, and profitless.

By avoiding these two extremes, monks, the [Buddha] has gained the knowledge of the Middle Path which leads to insight, which leads to wisdom, which conduces to calm, to knowledge, to Supreme Enlightenment, to Nirvana. . . .

The Four Noble Truths

This, monks, is the Noble Truth of Suffering: birth is suffering; decay is suffering; illness is suffering; death is suffering; presence of objects we hate is suffering; separation from objects we love is suffering; not to obtain what we desire is suffering. In brief, the five aggregates which spring from grasping, they are painful.

This, monks, is the Noble Truth concerning the Origin of Suffering: verily, it originates in that craving which causes the renewal of becomings, is accompanied by sensual delight, and seeks satisfaction now here, now there; that is to say, craving for pleasures, craving for becoming, craving for not becoming.

This, monks, is the Noble Truth concerning the Path which leads to the Cessation of Suffering: verily it is passionlessness, cessation without remainder of this very craving; the laying aside of, the giving up, the being free from, the harboring no longer of, this craving.

This, monks, is the Noble Truth concerning the Path which leads to the Cessation of Suffering: verily, it is this Noble Eightfold Path, that is to say, right views, right intent, right speech, right conduct, right means of livelihood, right endeavor, right mindfulness, and right meditation. . . .

Thus the Blessed One spoke. The five monks were delighted, and they rejoiced at the words of the Blessed One. . . . [And] having overcome uncertainty, having dispelled all doubts, having won confidence, dependent on nobody else for knowledge of the religion of the Teacher, they thus spoke to the Blessed One: "Lord, let us become a recluse under the Blessed One and receive ordination."

"Come, monks," said the Blessed One, "well taught is the *Dhamma* [doctrine]; lead a holy life for the sake of the complete ending of Suffering." Thus these venerable persons received ordination.

"The First Sermon of the Buddha" is from *Buddhism: A Religion of Infinite Compassion*, edited and trans. by Clarence H. Hamilton (New York: The Liberal Arts Press, 1951), pp. 28–29, 32. Copyright © The Liberal Arts Press, 1951. Reprinted by permission.

The Nature of the Self

The Buddha's teachings about the cycle of life, about rebirth and release, were all consistent with the Hindu concepts of Samsara *and* Moksha. *Yet there were differences. Since Buddha taught that all things were impermanent, he believed that neither an immortal soul (Atman) or immortal gods existed.*

"The Nature of the Self" is from *Buddhism: A Religion of Infinite Compassion*, edited and trans. by Clarence H. Hamilton (New York: The Liberal Arts Press, 1951), pp. 33–34. Copyright © The Liberal Arts Press, 1951. Reprinted by permission.

Buddha's rejection of the concept of eternal gods clearly placed him outside Indian religious traditions. His rejection of caste as an organizing principle for Indian society and his rejection of the religious authority of the priestly (Brahmin) class brought him into direct confrontation with the ruling hierarchy of Indian society. This granted him many followers from the lower rungs of society, but also created powerful enemies that eventually led to the rejection of Buddhism on the Indian subcontinent and its success outside the region. The following excerpt helps to define the Buddha's concept of the Self.

[And the Blessed One spoke thus to the five holy men: The body, monks, is not the Self. If the body, monks, were the Self, the body would not be subject to disease. . . . But since the body, monks, is not the Self, therefore the body is subject to disease] . . .

Now what do you think, monks, is the body permanent or perishable?

It is perishable, Lord.

And that which is perishable, does that cause pain or joy?

It causes pain, Lord.

And that which is perishable, painful, subject to change, is it possible to regard that in this way? This is mine, this am I, this is myself?

That is impossible, Lord.

[The same dialogue follows with regard to feelings, perceptions, impulses, and consciousness]]

Therefore, monks, whatever body has been, will be, and is now, belonging or not belonging to sentient beings, gross or subtle, low or exalted, distant or near, all that body is not mine, is not me, is not my Self; thus it should be considered by right knowledge according to the truth.

Considering this, monks, the wise and noble disciple turns away from the body, turns away from sensation, turns away from perception, turns away from the impulses, turns away from body and mind.

Turning away he loses passion, losing passion he is liberated, in being liberated the knowledge comes to him: "I am liberated," and he knows rebirth is exhausted, the holy life is completed, duty is fulfilled; there is no more living in these conditions.

Thus the Blessed One spoke. The five monks were delighted and rejoiced at the words of the Blessed One. And when this exposition had been propounded, the minds of the five monks became free from attachment to the world, and were released from the suffering.

The Death of the Buddha

This account of the death of the Buddha testifies to the impact of his influence. There was no point in trying to find a successor because the Buddha had never styled himself as a leader, but was content only to give advice. In the years following his death, monks developed different orders that emphasized particular aspects of the Master's teachings. A personality of such dimension as the Buddha required interpretation. Early Buddhism was focused around two important elements: first, the actual teaching of Buddha concerning the pathway to Nirvana (Four Noble Truths and Noble Eightfold Path); second, the example of Buddha's life and spirit exemplified in the profound compassion of Buddha, who sought to help others find release from suffering. The last element gave rise to a social ideal, that of limitless unselfish devotion to the highest welfare of others.

By the first century C.E., *through a series of general councils that had codified key doctrines, there had formed two principal branches of Buddhism. The* Theravada *("Doctrine of the Elders") branch supported the* Hinayana *or "Lesser Vehicle" approach that focused on the teaching of the Buddha.*

The second branch called Mahayana *("Greater Vehicle") accepted the primacy of Buddha's compassion for human beings and sought enlightenment for the sake of others.*

In Sri Lanka and southeast Asia (except for Vietnam), Theravadan Buddhism prevails. In China, Korea, Japan, and Tibet, the Mahayanist vision of the compassionate Buddha has been exalted, hoping to promote the ideal of living first as a merciful, self-denying Bodhisattva, and ultimately as a Buddha, the completely enlightened savior of others.

Thereupon the Buddha turned to his Disciples, and said to them: "Everything comes to an end, though it may last for an aeon. The hour of parting is bound to come in the end. Now I have done what I could do, both for myself and for others. To stay here would from now on be without any purpose. I have disciplined, in heaven and on earth, all those whom I could discipline, and I have set them in the stream. Hereafter this my *Dharma*, O monks, shall abide for generations and generations among living beings. Therefore, recognize the true nature of the living world, and do not be anxious; for separation cannot possibly be avoided. Recognize that all that lives is subject to this law; and strive from today onwards that it shall be thus no more! When the light of [knowledge] has dispelled the darkness of ignorance, when all existence has been seen as without substance, peace ensues when life draws to an end, which seems to cure a long sickness at last. Everything, whether stationary or movable, is bound to perish in the end. Be ye therefore mindful and vigilant! The time for my entry into Nirvana has now arrived! These are my last words!"

Thereupon, supreme in his mastery of the trances, he at that moment entered into the first trance, emerged from it and went on to the second, and so in due order he entered all of them without omitting one. And then, when he had ascended through all the nine stages of meditational attainment, the great Seer reversed the process, and returned again to the first trance. Again he emerged from that, and once more he ascended step by step to the fourth trance. When he emerged from the practice of that, he came face to face with everlasting Peace.

And when the Sage entered Nirvana, the earth quivered like a ship struck by a squall, and firebrands fell from the sky. The heavens were lit up by a preternatural fire, which burned without fuel, without smoke, without being fanned by the wind. Fearsome thunderbolts crashed down on the earth, and violent winds raged in the sky. The moon's light waned, and, in spite of a cloudless sky, an uncanny darkness spread everywhere. The rivers, as if overcome with grief, were filled with boiling water. Beautiful flowers grew out of season on the Sal trees above the Buddha's couch, and the trees bent down over him and showered his golden body with their flowers. . . .

In due course the five hundred [Holy Persons] assembled in Rajagriha, on the slope of one of its five mountains, and there and then they collected the sayings of the great Sage, so that his *Dharma* [doctrines] might abide. . . .They have in the past led to Nirvana those who have made the effort fully to master the Scriptures. They still today help them to Nirvana, and they will continue to do so in the future.

CHINESE PHILOSOPHICAL TRADITIONS

Humanity is the distinguishing characteristic of man. When embodied in man's conduct, it is the Way.

—Mencius

To know what you know and what you don't know is characteristic of one who knows.

—Confucius

A good traveler has no fixed plans and is not intent upon arriving.

—Laozi

Knowing others is intelligence; knowing yourself is true wisdom.
Mastering others is strength; mastering yourself is true power.
If you realize that you have enough, you are very rich.

—Laozi

The Confucian Tradition

Over the last two thousand years, no single individual has so deeply influenced the intellectual development of Chinese civilization as the great philosopher, Confucius. As a teacher and transmitter of ancient literature, he molded the Chinese mind and established foundations of thought that have affected the subsequent political organization and social mores of Chinese civilization to this day. The values and ideas of Confucius as they were developed over the centuries were less a creed to be professed or rejected, but more a way of life, an inseparable part of society that permeated the administration, the arts, and education of Chinese civilization for thousands of years. Although the Chinese have often professed themselves to be Buddhists, Daoists, or even Christians, they have rarely stopped being Confucianists.

For such an influential individual, we know little about the details of the life of Confucius. He was born in 551 B.C.E. to a family of the lesser aristocracy that had declined to poverty and insignificance. His father died when Confucius was quite young, leaving him to make his own way in the world. Confucius struggled to secure an education and finally landed a position of some authority in the administration of his home province.

Confucius hoped to bring order to the chaotic political world of the Zhou dynasty where assassination and betrayal were often the watchwords of existence. But he failed in his political career and turned instead to teaching where he hoped to mold the leaders of society from the ground up. In this occupation, he was an unequivocal success. By all accounts, Confucius was a teacher of rare enthusiasm and great authority who challenged his students to think beyond the confines of their immediate society and establish in themselves a discipline of thought and action. By the time of Confucius' death in 479 B.C.E. he had taught over 3,000 students, who developed and applied his ideas in a world of chaos and misdirection.

What was the solution that Confucius offered for the ills and evils of the world? It was a simple notion, one that has been articulated by philosophers throughout the ages: a return to virtue. Confucius, however, developed his simple idea with a compelling logic and rationale that was attractive to many who sought to touch the ideal world and believe that it could be made practical and effective in society. Although he lived in a society dominated by a primitive fear of the supernatural and marred by superstitions, he rejected the spiritual world and focused his concern on a good society based on good government and harmonious human relations. Confucius believed in a natural order that was also a moral order. The family maintained balance through filial respect, the society through proper conduct, and the government through virtue rather than by threat or punishment. Confucius conceived of a "mean" in society, a relationship between people, and between the government and the governed that reflected control and balance, not simply moderation.

Most important of all, Confucius evoked a new concept of jen or "humanity." Confucius made humanity the main theme of his teachings. No other topic so engaged the attention of the Master and his disciples than jen. In particular, Confucius spoke of jen as the balanced and harmonized aspects of the self and society. The man of jen *is the perfect man. He establishes his own character in harmony with himself, and by so doing establishes the character of others. As he seeks prominence, he helps others to be prominent. The one thread running through all of Confucius' teachings is this humanity, born of diligence and altruism. The "golden mean" of life is in fact the Golden Rule. It is because of Confucius' optimistic view that human beings are essentially good and perfectible that led later Chinese philosophers to promote the unity of Man and Nature, and of Man and Heaven.*

The following selections are from the Analects, *which is the record of the Master's thoughts compiled probably by his disciples' disciples. This work is generally the most reliable source of Confucius' doctrines and consists of 497 verses, some of which are only the briefest aphorisms. Nevertheless, they have exercised a profound influence on the thought and language of the peoples of East Asia.*

The Analects

CONFUCIUS

Learning and Teaching

1. Confucius said: "At fifteen, I set my heart on learning. At thirty, I was firmly established. At forty, I had no more doubts. At fifty, I knew the will of Heaven. At sixty, I was ready to listen to it. At seventy, I could follow my heart's desire without transgressing what was right." (2:4)

2. Confucius said: "When walking in a party of three, I always have teachers. I can select the good qualities of the one for imitation, and the bad ones of the other and correct them in myself." (7:21)

3. There were four things that Confucius was determined to eradicate: a biased mind, arbitrary judgments, obstinacy, and egotism. (9:4)

4. Confucius said: "Having heard the Way [*Dao*] in the morning, one may die content in the evening." (4:8)

5. Confucius said: "By nature men are pretty much alike; it is learning and practice that set them apart." (17:2)

6. Confucius said: "In education there are no class distinctions." (15.38)

7. Confucius said: "The young are to be respected. How do we know that the next generation will not measure up to the present one? But if a man has reached forty or fifty and nothing has been heard of him, then I grant that he is not worthy of respect." (9:22)

8. Confucius said: "I won't teach a man who is not anxious to learn, and will not explain to one who is not trying to make things clear to himself. If I hold up one corner of a square and a man cannot come back to me with the other three, I won't bother to go over the point again." (7:8)

9. Confucius said: "Learning without thinking is labor lost; thinking without learning is perilous." (2:15)

10. Confucius said: "A young man's duty is to be filial to his parents at home and respectful to his elders abroad, to be circumspect and truthful, and, while overflowing with love for all men, to associate himself with humanity [*jen*]. If, when all that is done, he has any energy to spare, then let him study the polite arts." (1:6)

11. Confucius said: "Personal cultivation begins with poetry, is made firm by rules of decorum, and is perfected by music." (8:8)

12. Confucius took four subjects for his teaching—literature, conduct, loyalty, and truthfulness. (7:24)

13. Shu-sun Wu-she said to the officials at court: "Zi Gong is a better man than Confucius." Zifu Qingbo told this to Zi Gong: "It is like the matter of house walls. My

From *Sources of Chinese Tradition* by William Theodore de Bary, ed. © 1960 Columbia University Press, pp. 24–29, 33–35. Reprinted with permission of the publisher.

house wall comes up only to the shoulder, and the people outside are therefore able to see my handsome dwelling, whereas the wall of Confucius rises fathoms high, and unless one is let in by the gate, one does not see the palatial beauty of the ancestral temple and the grandeur of the hundred [compartments] inside. But few are they who have found the gate. What Shu-sun says is therefore perfectly easy to understand." (19:23)

The Unitary Principle of Humanity

14. Zi Gong asked: "Is there any one word that can serve as a principle for the conduct of life?" Confucius said: "Perhaps the word 'reciprocity': do not do to others what you would not want others to do to you." (15:23)
15. Confucius said: "It is man that can make the Way [Truth] great, not the Way that can make man great." (15:28)
16. Confucius said: "The humane man, desiring to be established himself, seeks to establish others; desiring himself to succeed, he helps others to succeed. To judge others by what one knows of oneself is the method of achieving humanity." (6:28)
17. Fan Chi asked about humanity. Confucius said: "Love men." (22:22)
18. Zi Zhang asked Confucius about humanity. Confucius said: "To be able to practice five virtues everywhere in the world constitutes humanity." Zi Zhang begged to know what these were. Confucius said: "Courtesy, magnanimity, good faith, diligence, and kindness. He who is courteous is not humiliated, he who is magnanimous wins the multitude, he who is of good faith is trusted by the people, he who is diligent attains his objective, and he who is kind can get service from the people." (17:6)
19. Someone inquired: "What do you think of 'requiting injury with kindness'?"

Confucius said: "How will you then requite kindness? Requite injury with justice, and kindness with kindness." (14:36)
20. Confucius said: "Riches and honor are what every man desires, but if they can be obtained only by transgressing the right way, they must not be held. Poverty and lowliness are what every man detests, but if they can be avoided only by transgressing the right way, they must not be evaded. If a gentleman departs from humanity, how can he bear the name? Not even for the lapse of a single meal does a gentleman ignore humanity. In moments of haste he cleaves to it: in seasons of peril he cleaves to it."
21. Zi Lu asked about the worship of ghosts and spirits. Confucius said: "We don't know yet how to serve men, how can we know about serving the spirits?" "What about death?" was the next question. Confucius said: "We don't know yet about life, how can we know about death?" (11:11)

The Qualities of a Gentleman

22. Zi Gong asked about the gentleman. Confucius said: "The gentleman first practices what he preaches and then preaches what he practices." (2:13)
23. Confucius said: "The gentleman is always calm and at ease; the inferior man is always worried and full of distress." (7:36)
24. Confucius said: The gentleman understands what is right; the inferior man understands what is profitable." (4:16)
25. Confucius said: "The gentleman makes demands on himself; the inferior man makes demands on others." (15:20)

Government by Personal Virtue

26. Confucius said: "If a ruler himself is upright, all will go well without orders. But if he himself is not upright, even though

he gives orders they will not be obeyed." (13:6)

27. Confucius said: "Lead the people by laws and regulate them by penalties, and the people will try to keep out of jail, but will have no sense of shame. Lead the people by virtue and restrain them by the rules of decorum, and the people will have a sense of shame, and moreover will become good." (2:3)

28. Zi Gong asked about government. Confucius said: "The essentials are sufficient food, sufficient troops, and the confidence of the people." Zi Gong said: "Suppose you were forced to give up one of these three, which would you let go first?" Confucius said: "The troops." Zi Gong asked again: "If you are forced to give up one of the two remaining, which would you let go?" Confucius said: "Food. For from of old, death has been the lot of all men, but a people without faith cannot survive."

The Basis of Humane Government
MENCIUS

The most influential advocate of the ideas of Confucius was Mencius (372-289 B.C.E.?). In many ways, his career was similar to that of Confucius in that he became a professional teacher during a period of political disintegration in which his ideas of virtue and humanism went unheeded by the rulers of the day. Although Mencius' teaching derived from Confucius, he articulated a new stance on the topic of human nature. While Confucius implied that human nature is good, Mencius declared that humans were originally good and that they have an innate knowledge of good and an innate ability to develop the mind and fulfill their destiny by doing good in the world.

Mencius believed that political leaders should be guided by humanity and righteousness without a thought to utility, political advantage, or economic profit. In fact, he was the first to use the term "humane government." Since moral power was inherent in everyone's nature, each individual is complete in himself and equal to everyone else. Mencius argued that the ruler who neglects or oppresses his people is no true ruler and his subjects are absolved of their loyalty to him. This "right to revolution" was a novel and dangerous concept that caused Mencius' writings to be condemned by some rulers. But he remains the greatest advocate of political democracy in Chinese history.

Gao Zi said: "The nature of man may be likened to a swift current of water: you lead it eastward and it will flow to the east; you lead it westward and it will flow to the west. Human nature is neither disposed to good nor to evil, just as water is neither disposed to east nor west." Mencius replied: "It is true that water is neither disposed to east nor west, but is it neither disposed to flowing upward nor downward? The tendency of human nature to do good is like that of water to flow downward. There is no man who does not tend to do good; there is no water that does not flow downward. Now you may strike water and make it splash over your forehead, or you may even force it up the hills. But is this in the nature of water? It is of course due to the force of circumstances. Similarly, man may be brought to do evil, and that is because the same is done to his nature.". . .

The disciple Gongtu Zi said: "Gao Zi says that human nature is neither good nor bad. Some say that human nature can be turned to be good

From *Sources of Chinese Tradition* by William Theodore de Bary, ed. © 1960 Columbia University Press, pp. 103–104, 107–108. Reprinted with permission of the publisher.

or bad. . . . Now, you say that human nature is good. Are the others then all wrong? Mencius replied: "When left to follow its natural feelings human nature will do good. This is why I say it is good. If it becomes evil, it is not the fault of man's original capability. The sense of mercy is found in all men; the sense of shame is found in all men; the sense of respect is found in all men; the sense of right and wrong is found in all men. The sense of mercy constitutes humanity; the sense of shame constitutes righteousness; the sense of respect constitutes decorum; the sense of right and wrong constitutes wisdom. Humanity, righteousness, decorum, and wisdom are not something instilled into us from without; they are inherent in our nature. Only we give them no thought. Therefore it is said: 'Seek and you will find them, neglect and you will lose them.' Some have these virtues to a much greater degree than others—twice, five times, and incalculably more—and that is because those others have not developed to the fullest extent their original capability.". . .

Mencius said: "When men are subdued by force, it is not that they submit from their hearts but only that their strength is unavailing. When men are won by virtue, then their hearts are gladdened and their submission is sincere. . . . States have been won by men without humanity, but the world, never."

Mencius said: "It was because Qin and Zhou lost the people that they lost the empire, and it was because they lost the hearts of the people that they lost the people. Here is the way to win the empire: win the people and you win the empire. Here is the way to win the people: win their hearts and you win the people. Here is the way to win their hearts: give them and share with them what they like, and do not do to them what they do not like. The people turn to a humane ruler as water flows downward or beasts take to wilderness.". . .

[Mencius said to King Xuan]: "If your Majesty wishes to practice humane government, would it not be well to go back to the root of the matter?. . . Let attention be paid to teaching in schools and let the people be taught the principles of filial piety and brotherly respect, and white-headed old men will not be seen carrying loads on the road. When the aged wear silk and eat meat and the common people are free from hunger and cold, never has the lord of such a people failed to become king."

Mo Zi and the Doctrine of Universal Love

Among the "hundred philosophers" of ancient China, Mo Zi (fl. 470-400 B.C.E.?) holds a special place. Up to the beginning of the Han dynasty in 206 B.C.E., the two greatest philosophical schools were Confucianism and Moism. They were bitter rivals on the intellectual battlefield because they were diametrically opposed in their doctrines.

The Confucian ethical system based itself on the concept of humanity (jen), whereas Moism was based on righteousness as dictated by the will of Heaven. To a Confucianist, Heaven is the Supreme Being who reigns but does not directly influence the human world, leaving His moral law to operate by itself. This is somewhat fatalistic. Life will evolve as it will without a particularly active human involvement in the affairs of Heaven. To Mo Zi, however, the will of Heaven determined all and humans should actively seek a guiding relationship in life. The people should obey their leaders, who themselves obey the will of Heaven. Since all was dependent on cultivating an active will of Heaven, the Confucianist emphasis on fatalism was particularly abrasive for Moists.

The divergence between Confucianism and Moism centered on the issue of human relations. What truly distinguishes the Moist movement is its emphasis on universal love: Other people's possessions, family members and even countries should be treated as if they were your own. This is incompatible with the Confucian belief that there is always a gradation of love: While love should em-

brace all, it should start with love for one's parents (filial piety) and then branch out accordingly. If the Moist vision of universal love were embraced, then the Confucian system (and the established social order) would be threatened and destroyed. This is why the Confucian philosopher Mencius attacked Moism so mercilessly.

Mo Zi set the most exacting standards for himself and his followers. At times, when he heard of one state's war plans against a neighbor, he would walk miles to dissuade the ruler from his aggressive stance. If consultation failed, he and his followers would rush to the aid of the threatened state, often organizing defensive measures. The following selections emphasize his primary ideas on universal love and the will of Heaven.

"Universal Love Is Right"

MO ZI

Mo Zi said: "Humane men are concerned about providing benefits for the world and eliminating its calamities. Now among all the current calamities, which are the worst? I say that the attacking of small states by large states, the making of inroads on small houses by large houses, the plundering of the weak by the strong, the oppression of the few by the many, the deception of the simple by the cunning, the disdain of the noble towards the humble—these are some of the calamities in the world. Again, the want of kindness on the part of the ruler, the want of loyalty on the part of the ruled, the want of affection on the part of the father, the want of filial piety on the part of the son—these are some further calamities in the world. Added to these, the mutual injury and harm which the vulgar people do to one another with weapons, poison, water, and fire is still another kind of calamity in the world.

"When we come to inquire about the cause of all these calamities, whence have they arisen? Is it out of people's loving others and benefitting others? We must reply that it is not so. We should say that it is out of people's hating others and injuring others. If we should classify one by one all those who hate others and injure others, should we find them too universal or partial in their love? Of course, we should say they are

From *Sources of Chinese Tradition* by William Theodore de Bary, ed. © 1960 Columbia University Press, pp. 42–43, 46. Reprinted with permission of the publisher.

partial. Now, since partiality among one another is the cause of the major calamities in the world, then partiality is wrong."

Mo Zi continued: "He who criticizes others must have something to offer in replacement. Criticism without an alternative proposal is like trying to stop flood with flood and put out fire with fire. It will surely be worthless."

Therefore Mo Zi said: "Partiality is to be replaced by universality. But how is partiality to be replaced by universality? Now, when everyone regards the states of others as he regards his own, who would attack the other's state? One would regard others as one's self. When everyone regards the cities of others as he regards his own, who would seize the others' cities? One would regard others as one's self. When everyone regards the houses of others as he regards his own, who would disturb the other's houses? One would regard others as one's self. Now when the states and cities do not attack and seize each other, and when the clans and individuals do not disturb and harm one another—is this a calamity or a benefit to the world? Of course it is a benefit.

"When we come to inquire about the cause of all these benefits, whence have they arisen? Is it out of men's hating and injuring others? We must reply that it is not so. We should say that it is out of men's loving and benefitting others. If we should classify one by one all those who love others and benefit others, should we find them to be partial or universal in their love? Of course we would say they are universal. Now, since universal love is the cause of the major benefits in the world, therefore Mo Zi proclaims that universal love is right. . . .

"Now, as to universal love and mutual aid, they are incalculably more beneficial and less difficult. It seems to me that the only trouble is that there is no ruler who will encourage them. If there were a ruler who would encourage them, bringing to bear the lure of reward and the threat of punishment, I believe the people would tend toward universal love and mutual aid like fire tending upward and water downwards—nothing in the world could stop them."

"Obey the Will of Heaven"

MO ZI

The gentlemen of the world who desire to do righteousness have no other recourse than to obey the will of Heaven. One who obeys the will of Heaven will practice universal love; one who

From *Sources of Chinese Tradition* by William Theodore de Bary, ed. © 1960 Columbia University Press, p. 49. Reprinted with permission of the publisher.

opposes the will of Heaven will practice partial love. According to the doctrine of universality the standard of conduct is righteousness; according to the doctrine of partiality the standard is force. What is it like when righteousness is the standard of conduct? The great will not attack the small, the strong will not plunder the weak, the many will not oppress the few, the cunning will not deceive the simple, the noble will not disdain the humble, the rich will not mock the poor, and the young will not encroach upon the old, poison, and weapons. Such a regime will be auspicious to Heaven above, to the spirits in the middle sphere, and to the people below. Being auspicious to these three, it is beneficial to all. This is called the disposition of Heaven. He who follows it is sagacious and wise, humane and righteous, kind as a ruler and loyal as a minister, affectionate as a father and filial as a son, and all such good names in the world are gathered and attributed to him. Why? Because such conduct is in accordance with the will of Heaven.

Daoism: The Way of Life

Next to the Confucian school, no philosophy has had such an impact on the Chinese mind over the centuries than Daoism. The teachings of this mystical, natural philosophy were attributed first to Laozi, perhaps in the third century B.C.E., whose thoughts were later compiled in the Dao De Jing. *This small book contains only about 5,250 words, yet is one of the most provocative and inspired works in all Chinese literature.*

The teaching of Laozi is based on a great abstract principle called the Dao, *which is perhaps best translated as the "Way." It refers to the underlying principle of life, undefined, eternal, spontaneous, and indescribable. The* Dao *is the source of all being and the regulator of all life. It is the foundation of all that exists, both human and natural, and is the unifying principle around which all contradictions are ultimately resolved.*

The Dao *is thus possessed by all things and provides that character for the ideal life of the individual, the ideal order of society, and the ideal system of government. The* Dao *denotes simplicity and tranquility, and promotes the concept of "nonaction" in the resolution of all conflict. The passivity of this doctrine should not imply "inactivity" or "weakness," but rather "taking no course that is contrary to Nature." If you do not oppose that natural order of life, the "Way" of all things, and instead become "One" with what is, then you are empowered with the confidence of resolution. A mind that is resolved and in tune with the underlying principle of life can lead an engaged and active life. The philosophy of the* Dao *is not for hermits and is not a philosophy of withdrawal. By resolving your strife and not opposing the natural order of things, human nature is fulfilled.*

The following selections from the Dao De Jing *are mystical and paradoxical, yet wonderfully open to personal insight and enlightenment. Think of them as prompts that allow you to open new windows to your soul. These verses were not meant to convince the mind by cogent argument, but rather to startle and capture the mind and the heart through symbolic association and poetic vision.*

Living in Harmony With the Dao

LAOZI

What Is the Dao?

1

The Dao that can be told
is not the eternal Dao.
The name that can be named
is not the eternal name.

The unnamable is the eternally real.
Naming is the origin
of all particular things.

Free from desire, you realize the mystery.
Caught in desire, you see only the
    manifestations.

Yet mystery and manifestations
arise from the same source.
This source is called darkness.

Darkness within darkness.
The gateway to all understanding.

4

The Dao is like a well:
used but never used up.
It is like the eternal void:
filled with infinite possibilities.

It is hidden but always present.
I don't know who gave birth to it.
It is older than God.

6

The Dao is called the great Mother:
empty yet inexhaustible,

Tao Te Ching by Lao Tzu, A New English Version, With Forward and Notes by Stephen Mitchell. Translation copyright © 1988 by Stephen Mitchell, numbers 1, 4, 6–7, 9, 16–17, 22–23, 25, 34, 37, 47, 57, 66–67. Reprinted by permission of Harper Collins Publishers, Inc. and Pan Macmillan.

it gives birth to infinite worlds.
It is always present within you.
You can use it any way you want.

7

The Dao is infinite, eternal.
Why is it eternal?
It was never born;
thus it can never die.
Why is it infinite?
It has no desires for itself;
thus it is present for all beings.

The Master stays behind;
that is why she is ahead.
She is detached from all things;
that is why she is one with them.
Because she has let go of herself,
she is perfectly fulfilled.

25

There was something formless and
    perfect
before the universe was born.
It is serene. Empty.
Solitary. Unchanging.
Infinite. Eternally present.
It is the mother of the universe.
For lack of a better name,
I call it the Dao.

It flows through all things,
inside and outside, and returns
to the origin of all things.

The Dao is great.
The universe is great.
Earth is great.
Man is great.
These are the four great powers.

Man follows the earth.
Earth follows the universe.

The universe follows the Dao.
The Dao follows only itself.

34

The great Dao flows everywhere.
All things are born from it,
yet it doesn't create them.
It pours itself into its work,
yet it makes no claim.
It nourishes infinite worlds,
yet it doesn't hold on to them.
Since it is merged with all things
and hidden in their hearts,
it can be called humble.
Since all things vanish into it
and it alone endures,
it can be called great.
It isn't aware of its greatness;
thus it is truly great.

The Quiet Mind

16

Empty your mind of all thoughts.
Let your heart be at peace.
Watch the turmoil of beings,
but contemplate their return.

Each separate being in the universe
returns to the common source.
Returning to the source is serenity.

If you don't realize the source,
you stumble in confusion and sorrow.
When you realize where you come from,
you naturally become tolerant,
disinterested, amused,
kindhearted as a grandmother,
dignified as a king.
Immersed in the wonder of the Dao,
you can deal with whatever life brings you,
and when death comes, you are
    ready.

23

Express yourself completely,
then keep quiet.

Be like the forces of nature:
when it blows, there is only wind;
when it rains, there is only rain;
when the clouds pass, the sun shines
    through
If you open yourself to the Dao,
you are at one with the Dao
and you can embody it completely.
If you open yourself to insight,
you are at one with insight
and you can use it completely.
If you open yourself to loss,
you are at one with loss
and you can accept it completely.
Open yourself to the Dao,
then trust your natural responses;
and everything will fall into place.

Harmony and Political Leadership

9

Fill your bowl to the brim
and it will spill.
Deep sharpening your knife
and it will blunt.
Chase after money and security
and your heart will never unclench.
Care about people's approval
and you will be their prisoner.

Do your work, then step back.
The only path to serenity.

22

If you want to become whole,
let yourself be partial.
If you want to become straight,
let yourself be crooked.
If you want to become full,
let yourself be empty.
If you want to be reborn,
let yourself die.
If you want to be given everything,
give everything up.

The Master, by residing in the Dao,
sets an example for all beings.

Because he doesn't display himself,
people can see his light.
Because he has nothing to prove,
people can trust his words.
Because he doesn't know who he is,
people recognize themselves in him.
Because he has no goal in mind,
everything he does succeeds.
When the ancient Masters said,
"If you want to be given everything,
give everything up,"
they weren't using empty phrases.
Only in being lived by the Dao
can you be truly yourself.

47

Without opening your door,
you can open your heart to the world.

Without looking out your window,
you can see the essence of the Dao.

The more you know,
the less you understand.

The Master arrives without leaving,
sees the light without looking,
achieves without doing a thing.

17

When the Master governs, the people
are hardly aware that he exists.
Next best is a leader who is loved.
Next, one who is feared.
The worst is one who is despised.

If you don't trust the people,
you make them untrustworthy.

The Master doesn't talk, he acts.
When his work is done,
the people say, "Amazing:
we did it, all by ourselves!"

37

The Dao never does anything,
yet through it all things are done.

If powerful men and women
could center themselves in it,
the whole world would be transformed
by itself, in its natural rhythms.
People would be content
with their simple, everyday lives,
in harmony, and free of desire.

When there is no desire,
all things are at peace.

57

If you want to be a great leader,
you must learn to follow the Dao.
Stop trying to control.
Let go of fixed plans and concepts,
and the world will govern itself.

The more prohibitions you have,
the less virtuous people will be.
The more weapons you have,
the less self-reliant people will be.

Therefore the Master says:
I let go of the law,
and people become honest.
I let go of economics,
and people become prosperous.
I let go of religion,
and people become serene.
I let go of all desire for the common good,
and the good becomes common as grass.

66

All streams flow to the sea
because it is lower than they are.
Humility gives it its power.

If you want to govern the people,
you must place yourself below them.
If you want to lead the people,
you must learn how to follow them.

The Master is above the people,
and no one feels oppressed.
She goes ahead of the people,
and no one feels manipulated.

The whole world is grateful to her.
Because she competes with no one,
no one can compete with her.

67

Some say that my teaching is nonsense.
Others call it lofty but impractical.
But to those who have looked inside
   themselves,
this nonsense makes perfect sense.
And to those who put it into practice,
this loftiness has roots that go deep.

I have just three things to teach:
simplicity, patience, compassion.
These three are your greatest
   treasures.
Simple in actions and in thoughts,
you return to the source of being.
Patient with both friends and enemies,
you accord with the way things are.
Compassionate toward yourself,
you reconcile all beings in the world.

GREEK RATIONALISM

You could not step twice in the same river, for other and yet other waters are ever flowing on.

—*Heraclitus*

Wonder is the feeling of a philosopher, and philosophy begins in wonder.

—*Socrates*

The Greeks were the originators of philosophy in the Western historical tradition. Philosophy means "love of wisdom," and in this the Greeks had no rivals in Western civilization for originality of thought and beauty of expression. The Greek language is endowed with a formidable vocabulary that allows for an expressive discussion of abstract thoughts. This amazing civilization, which would produce the likes of Plato and Aristotle, began its intellectual journey with Thales of Miletus (ca. 600 B.C.E.), who asked the simple question, "What are things made of?" The inspiration of the question alone reveals much about the inquiring nature of the Greeks, but its answer would lead Thales and other "monists" like Anaximenes to reduce the world to one primary element around which all others existed. For Thales, it was water; for Anaximenes, air. For others, like Pythagoras (ca. 550 B.C.E.), the world could best be explored through numerical ratios and resulting harmonies. Indeed, life itself, through the transmigration of the soul, was a cycle of rebirth.

Thales of Miletus: "Water Is the Primary Element"

ARISTOTLE

Some say that the earth rests on water. This in fact is the oldest view that has been transmitted

Early Greek Philosophy translated by Jonathan Barnes (Penguin Classics, 1987), copyright © Johnathan Barnes, 1987, p. 63. Reproduced with permission of Penguin Books Ltd.

to us, and they say that it was advanced by Thales of Miletus who thought that the earth rests because it can float like a log or something else of that sort (for none of these things can rest on air, but they can rest on water)—as though the same must not hold of the water supporting the earth as holds of the earth itself.

Most of the first philosophers thought that principles in the form of matter were the only principles of all things. For they say that the element and first principle of the things that exist is that from which they all are and from which they first come into being and into which they are finally destroyed, its substance remaining and its properties changing. . . . There must be some nature—either one or more than one—from which the other things come into being, it being preserved. But as to the number and form of this sort of principle, they do not all agree. Thales, the founder of this kind of philosophy, says that it is water (that is why he declares that the earth rests on water). He perhaps came to acquire this belief from seeing that the nourishment of everything is moist and that heat itself comes from this and lives by this (for that from which anything comes into being is its first principle)—he came to his belief both for this reason and because the seeds of everything have a moist nature, and water is the natural principle of moist things.

Anaximenes: "The First Principle Is Infinite Air"
HIPPOLYTUS

Anaximenes, son of Eurystratus, was also a Milesian. He said that the first principle is infinite air, from which what is coming into being and what has come into being and what will exist and gods and divinities come into being, while everything else comes into being from its offspring. The form of the air is this: when it is most uniform it is invisible, but it is made apparent by the hot and the cold and the moist and the moving. It is always in motion; for the things that change would not change if it were not in motion. For as it is condensed and rarefied it appears different: when it dissolves into a more rarefied condition it becomes fire; and winds, again, are condensed air, and cloud is produced from air by compression. Again, when it is more condensed it is water, when still further condensed it is earth, and when

it is as dense as possible it is stones. Thus the most important factors in coming into being are opposites—hot and cold.

The earth is flat and rides on air; in the same way the sun and the moon and the other heavenly bodies, which are all fiery, ride the air because of their flatness. The heavenly bodies have come into being from earth, because mist rose from the earth and was rarefied and produced fire, and the heavenly bodies are composed of this fire when it is aloft. There are also some earthly substances in the region of the heavenly bodies which orbit with them. He says that the heavenly bodies move not under the earth, as others have supposed, but round the earth—just as a felt cap turns on the head. And the sun is hidden not because it goes under the earth but because of its greater distance from us. The heavenly bodies do not heat us because of their great distance.

Winds are generated when the air is condensed and driven along. As it collects together and is further thickened, clouds are generated and in this way it changes into water. Hail comes about when the water falling from the clouds solidifies, and snow when these same things solidify in a more watery form. Lightning occurs when the clouds are parted by the force of winds; for when they part a bright and fiery flash occurs. Rainbows are generated when the sun's rays fall on compacted air; earthquakes when the earth is considerably altered by heating and cooling. These are the views of Anaximenes. He flourished in the first year of the fifty-eighth Olympiad [548/547 B.C.E.].

Pythagoras on the Transmigration of the Soul
DIODORUS

Pythagoras believed in metempsychosis [transmigration of the soul] and thought that eating meat was an abominable thing, saying that the souls of all animals enter different animals after death. He himself used to say that he remembered being, in Trojan times, Euphorbus, Panthus' son, who was killed by Menelaus. They say that once when he was staying at Argos he saw a shield from the spoils of Troy nailed up, and burst into tears. When the Argives asked him the reason for his emotion, he said that he himself had borne that shield at Troy when he was Euphorbus. They did not believe him and judged him to be mad, but he said he would provide a true sign that it was indeed the case; on the inside of the shield there had been inscribed in archaic lettering EUPHORBUS. Because of the extraordinary nature of his claim they all urged that the shield be taken down—and it turned out that on the inside the inscription was found.

CHRONOLOGY: The Spiritual and Philosophical Bases of Early World Civilizations

Religion in India/Buddhism

1800–1500 B.C.E.   Aryan peoples invade northwestern India. Establish themselves in the Ganges river valley ca. 1000 B.C.E., cultivating it with iron tools.

1000–700 B.C.E.   Brahminic Age in India, dominated by the priestly religion of the Brahman class. Also called the "epic age" because it provides the setting for two classical epic poems: the *Mahabharata* and *Ramayana* (both composed 400–200 B.C.E.).

800–500 B.C.E.   Composition of the *Upanishads*, commentaries on the Vedic texts. These great works of philosophical speculation focus on the quest for "ultimate truth."

563–483 B.C.E.   Life of Siddhartha Gautama, the historical Buddha.

540–468 B.C.E.   Life of Mahavira, founder of Jainism.

321 B.C.E.   Mauryan dynasty of northern India founded by Chandragupta.

273–232 B.C.E.   Reign of Chandragupta's grandson, Asoka, a zealous supporter of Buddhism; Buddhist missionaries sent by Asoka to regions bordering the Mauryan empire.

100 C.E.   Buddhist activity in Central Asia and China.

500–600 C.E.   Traces of Theravada Buddhism appear in Burma and Thailand. Introduction of Buddhism into Japan by Korean monks.

Chinese Philosophical Traditions

1050–256 B.C.E.   Zhou dynasty in China. "Mandate of Heaven" defined to link virtue with successful political rule. Rise of Iron Age territorial states (ca. 770 B.C.E.), commerce, and ruthless military tactics.

551–479 B.C.E.   Life of the great philosopher Confucius. Inaugurates an age of expansive philosophical thought.

481–256 B.C.E.	Warring States Period. The quasi-feudal, multistate Zhou system gives way to the centralized bureaucratic government of the Qin dynasty. Great Wall of China begun in order to keep out Xiongnu invaders (completed in 214 B.C.E.).
470–391 B.C.E.	Life of the philosopher, Mo Zi, who criticized Confucius by emphasizing the ethic of universal love to overcome a selfish human nature.
400–300 B.C.E.	School of Daoist thought attributed to Laozi.
370–290 B.C.E.	The philosopher Mencius represents the most idealistic expression of Confucian thought: The role of education is to cultivate innate human goodness.
256–221 B.C.E.	Political upheaval and breakdown of Chinese society as Zhou dynasty is overthrown and replaced by the Qin dynasty.
221–207 B.C.E.	Qin dynasty established by First Emperor, Qin Shi Huangdi. Revolts lead to breakdown by 207 B.C.E.
206 B.C.E.**–220** C.E.	Han dynasty. Often divided into Former Han (206 B.C.E.–8 C.E.) and Later Han (25–220 C.E.).

Hebrew Civilization and Greek Rationalism

1200 B.C.E.	Destruction throughout Mediterranean. "Sea Peoples" attack Egypt, destroy Hittites, and disrupt Mycenaean Greek culture. Power vacuum filled by developing cultures of Phoenicians and Hebrews.
1000–922 B.C.E.	Reigns of King David and King Solomon. Establishment of law and military presence.
722 B.C.E.	Assyrian conquest of Israel (Northern Kingdom).
600–500 B.C.E.	Development of early Greek philosophy. Thales of Miletus (ca. 600 B.C.E.) and Pythagoras (ca. 550 B.C.E.) search for the primary elements around which life revolves and the numerical relationships and harmonies within the universe.
586 B.C.E.	Destruction of Jerusalem; fall of Judah (Southern Kingdom); the Babylonian Captivity begins.
539 B.C.E.	Persians defeat Babylonians and end the Babylonian Captivity of Jews.
508 B.C.E.	Development of democracy in Athens under the leadership of Clisthenes.

STUDY QUESTIONS

Hebrew Civilization

1. After reading the selections from Genesis on the origin of the world, paradise, and the fall from grace, analyze why these have been so influential in world civilization. What do the Garden of Eden and the Tree of Life represent? What are the two stories about the creation of woman? What is the relative position of women to men at the biblical origin of life? How have these passages from Genesis been used to structure social attitudes and expectations throughout the centuries? Do they still have impact today?

2. What was Moses' mission as recorded in the Old Testament? Why is the exodus from Egypt central to the Jewish experience? What does it say about Yahweh's relationship with the Hebrews? How does the "new covenant" of Jeremiah differ from the original (as embodied in the Ten Commandments) established by Yahweh with Moses? Why the need for a new covenant? Be specific in your use of the primary sources.

3. Note the Hebrew concern for moral instructions and law. Compare the Covenant Code with the Code of Hammurabi in Chapter 1 (pages 7–9). In what ways are they similar? Were the Mesopotamians, Egyptians, and Hebrews all concerned with living a good, moral life? What values were most appreciated?

Religion in India

4. The hymns of the *Rig Veda* focus on cosmic order. What qualities characterize the gods Indra, Varuna, and Agni? Why are these qualities important in the establishment of cosmic order? Note the importance of the sun and its equation with Dawn and Truth. Compare these selections with the Egyptian "Hymn to the Aten" by the Pharaoh Akhenaten in Chapter 1 (pages 20–22). In the New Testament of the Bible, Jesus proclaims, "I am the light of the world" (John 8:12). Why is the sun or the image of light such an important religious symbol?

5. Compare the Vedic hymn on the "Origin of the World" with the selection from Genesis in the Old Testament on the "Creation of the World." How do these accounts differ? What does this say about Hinduism and Judaism? How do you interpret the last line of the Vedic hymn: "Or if he does not know. . ."?

6. How would you define the Indian religious concepts of *Brahman* and *Atman*? What is their relationship? What is the relationship of the Hindu gods to *Brahman*? How does their power compare? How do you interpret this phrase from "The Nature of *Brahman*": "He is seen in Nature in the wonder of a flash of lightning. He comes to the soul in the wonder of a flash of vision"? Why is the idea of "wonder" so essential to the concept of *Brahman*?

7. How would you define the process of *Samsara* and how is it related to *Karma*? What are the specific physical and mental sins that produce greater *Karma*? How does one obtain spiritual merit, or *Dharma*?

8. In the selection "Death Will Not Wait," why must people not "grieve for the destruction of the body"? What is meant by the phrase "time is no one's friend and no one's enemy"?

9. How would you define the concept of *Moksha*? In the dialogue between Krishna and Arunja contained in the *Bhagavad Gita*, what is the nature of God? How would you best define the concept of a supreme deity in Hinduism? What does it mean when Krishna says (10.22): "I am the mind, and in all living things, I am the light of consciousness"?

10. In the selection entitled "The Perfect Being," how would you describe the vision of Varuna? What specifically must one do to know "that joy of Eternity"?

11. Section 10.20 of the *Bhagavad Gita* states: "I am the beginning, the middle, and the end of all that lives." Compare this with the following Biblical passage from Revelation (1:8) where God says, "I am the Alpha and the Omega, who is, who was, and who is to come, the Almighty." What are the meanings of these passages? Is there a difference in the conception of a Supreme Being in a polytheistic religion like Hinduism and in a monotheistic religion like Judaism, Christianity, or Islam?

The Wisdom of the Buddha

12. In what ways does Buddhism differ from Hindu beliefs? Why was Buddhism unsuccessful in India even though it grew out of basic Hindu beliefs?

13. According to the accounts of the life of the Buddha, why was he troubled and why did he decide to forsake society in order to win enlightenment? How did he achieve this enlightenment? Was it a difficult process? Why did the Buddha decide to remain on earth after he had achieved Nirvana?

14. In the First Sermon of the Buddha, what are the Four Noble Truths and what is the Noble Eightfold Path toward enlightenment? What is the "Middle Path" to enlightenment that helps differentiate Buddhism from Hinduism?

15. Buddhism has been termed a religion of "infinite compassion." Why? What was the purpose of the Buddha? Is the Buddhist emphasis on compassion similar to that of Christianity? Are Judaism or Islam "compassionate" religions?

Chinese Philosophical Traditions

16. Confucius contributed a new concept to Chinese society, that of *jen* or humanity. How would you further define this concept and how is it reflected in the *Analects*? Which are your favorite selections from the *Analects* and why are they important to you?

17. What was Mencius's contribution to Confucianism? Do you agree with his view of human nature? Can you make a counterargument?

18. How would you explain Mo Tzu's doctrine of universal love? What is the difference between partiality and universality? Note his statement: "When everyone regards the houses of others as he regards his own, who would disturb that other's house?" Compare this with Confucius' idea (14): "Do not do to others what you would not want others to do to you." Isn't this a similar philosophy? Why were Moists opposed to Confucianists? Is the Golden Rule basic to many religions and philosophies?

19. How would you define the concept of the *Dao* ("Way")? Which among the several statements of Laozi have the greatest meaning for you? Why? Who is the Master? Compare the nature of the *Dao* with that of the Hindu concept of *Brahman* (the "Infinite," the "Absolute"). Is the concept of the *Dao* as powerful as any army? Why?

20. What are the most important ideas of the *Dao* on leadership? Can you apply them to our contemporary political or business world? How should leaders govern? How would you compare them to Confucius' ideas on leadership?

21. What constitutes "power" in Daoist philosophy? What constitutes "power" in human relationships or between humans and God? Must one have power over another in order to be influential?

22. Note that Laozi says (67): "I have just three things to teach: simplicity, patience, compassion." Is this a unifying idea in this chapter? Would you argue that this is the thrust behind Hinduism and Buddhism? Could you apply this idea to Judaism?

Early Greek Philosophy

23. What were the main ideas of Thales of Miletus? Why is his fundamental question about the composition of things in the world so expressive of the Greek spirit of inquiry? What were the contributions of Anaximenes and Pythagoras? Why has it been proposed that the Greeks invented Western philosophy?

24. How is Pythagoras' idea on the "transmigration of the soul" similar to that contained in Hinduism? What is so attractive or frightening about the idea of reincarnation? What is the difference between reincarnation and the Christian and Islamic vision of a soul living forever in Heaven?

Part II

THE ANCIENT WORLD
(500 B.C.E. – 500 C.E.)

3

The Glory of Greece

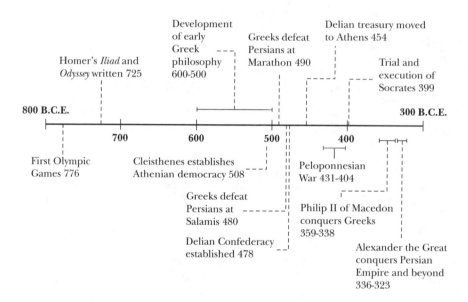

Development of early Greek philosophy 600-500

Greeks defeat Persians at Marathon 490

Delian treasury moved to Athens 454

Homer's *Iliad* and *Odyssey* written 725

Trial and execution of Socrates 399

800 B.C.E.

300 B.C.E.

700   600   500   400

First Olympic Games 776

Cleisthenes establishes Athenian democracy 508

Peloponnesian War 431-404

Greeks defeat Persians at Salamis 480

Philip II of Macedon conquers Greeks 359-338

Delian Confederacy established 478

Alexander the Great conquers Persian Empire and beyond 336-323

CHAPTER THEMES

- *Systems of Government:* How would you define democracy in the classical sense of the term? Was Athens a democracy? Is democracy the best and most natural form of government for people?

- *Imperialism:* How did Athens gain and maintain its empire? Can a democracy possess an empire, or is this a moral contradiction? Alexander the Great expanded his empire beyond the known limits of the Greek world. By bringing Greek culture to the East, was Alexander a force for progress? Can imperialism be progressive?

- *Propaganda:* Who was Alexander the Great? To what extent were his exploits the stuff of legend, with little foundation in reality? How do we separate the myth from the man? Is the "hero" in history simply a myth?

- *Beliefs and Spirituality:* What role did the gods play in the imagination of the early Greeks? How sophisticated was the pantheon of Greek gods when compared with the monotheism of the Hebrews? What was the Greek view of the afterlife? How do the stories and legends regarding the Greek gods and their interaction with humans reflect the creativity of Greek culture?

- *Women in History:* How were women portrayed in early Greek society as viewed in the *Odyssey* of Homer? Is this picture consistent with the view of women during the Golden Age of Greece in the fifth century B.C.E.? Did the Athenian democracy consider women to be political equals?

- *Historical Change and Transition:* The history of fifth-century Greece has generally been viewed as a great success story. Is success in war or government a necessary foundation for success in the arts? How essential is arrogance to the progress of civilization? Was Athens created and then destroyed by its hubris?

- *The Big Picture:* Do the great artistic and literary creations of civilization justify the means of obtaining them? Is there a political price to pay for cultural progress?

In trying to establish just what happened in the past and why, historians focus on a wide variety of sources, most of which were not originally composed or constructed to serve as a window to the past: secret dispatches, letters, diary accounts, poems, newspaper articles, propaganda fliers, coins, pottery, and even wall graffiti can open a new world to the historian. One of the more uncertain and controversial historical sources is the evidence of legend and myth.

The mythology of a culture—the stories of heroism, deities, moral instruction—often seems reflective of a fantasy world where reality is suspended and the pure joy of creativity is unleashed. But the legends of a culture not only tell us about the values of a people, they can also lead historians toward reconstruction of the past. This question of the appropriateness of legend in the reconstruction of the past is nowhere more evident than in the debate regarding the Trojan War.

Can we accept as valid historical sources the *Iliad* and the *Odyssey*, monumental narrative poems that deal with the legendary Troy and its fight to the death with the forces from mainland Greece about 1230 B.C.E.? Or must they be relegated to the world of fantasy? The skepticism is even more fundamental: Did their author, Homer, even exist? Was he one person or several, or simply the compiler of oral legends that had been handed down and amplified by several singers over the centuries? What can they tell us of the developing values and ideals of Greek society?

A second focus of this chapter will be on the greatness and moral contradictions apparent in classical Greek society during its Golden Age. The city-state of Athens has been widely admired for its contributions to world civilization during the fifth century B.C.E. This was a time of great intellectual energy, producing enduring works of art, architecture, philosophy, drama, and history. The confidence necessary to achieve such heights was granted early in the century when the Greek city-states united to repel two invasions by the mighty Persian empire. The Spartan military machine had proved its worth at the battle of Thermopylae, and the Athenian reputation for cleverness was established by Themistocles at the battle of Salamis in 480 B.C.E. On this note of triumph, the Golden Age of Athens began.

During the period from 480 to 430 B.C.E., leaders such as Pericles extolled the superiority of Athenian democratic government and the freedom essential to Athenian greatness. Yet, critics of the time pointed out the shortcomings of the democracy and of its leadership. At root, it might be argued that the greatness of Athenian civilization was dependent upon her "allies," or fellow members of the Delian Confederacy. This Confederacy was established in 478 B.C.E., after the Persian wars, to ensure that the Greeks would not be attacked by Persia again. Further, Greek cities on the coast of Asia Minor were to be freed and booty obtained from Persia to offset the costs of Confederate expeditions and past losses. Theoretically, Athens had no greater vote than any of her Confederates, but almost from the outset she held the keys to power, contributing both the administrators of the treasury on the island of Delos and the commanders of the military expeditions. By 466 B.C.E., after several Confederate victories, it became evident that Persia no longer posed a threat to the city-states of Greece or the islands in the Aegean Sea. Some members wished to secede (Naxos in 469, Thasos in 465 B.C.E.), but they were opposed and militarily crushed by Athens. Secession from the Confederacy would not be tolerated. In 454 B.C.E., the treasury was moved from the island of Delos to Athens. The patron goddess, Athena, supervised the protection of all tribute that came into Athens and took a piece of the action (called the "first fruits") for her trouble. The great Athenian orator Pericles maintained the Athenian Empire (as the Delian Confederacy came to be called) partly to counter Spartan land power, and managed it efficiently so as to produce revenues essential to the glorification of Athens. By 447 B.C.E., work on the Parthenon had begun, and several other building projects, artists, and sculptors would be financed by funds contributed by Athenian "allies."

Athens controlled its empire rigidly, maintaining order by imposing its own laws and customs on subject cities. Every four years its subjects would come to Athens to participate in the Panatheneia, a celebration honoring the patron goddess Athena. There they would gather to learn what their tax assessment would be for the next four years. The Athenians inscribed these assessments on a great monolith, located on the Acropolis, called the Tribute Lists. Such a blatant reminder of their subservience must have been difficult for the Athenian allies to bear.

From 431 to 404 B.C.E., the Spartans and Athenians entered into a great conflict that came to be called the Peloponnesian War. This war was born of Spartan distrust for the growing Athenian power and trade influence in areas heretofore controlled by Sparta and its allies. The two city-states, so different in outlook and political orientation, fought, as the historian Thucydides noted, the greatest war "in Greek history, affecting a large part of the non-Greek world, and I might also say, the whole of mankind."

In the end, Athens lost not only the physical struggle and its empire, but also the edge of confidence that had propelled its democracy and inspired its poets and statesmen. Perhaps the greatest indication of this loss was the execution of the philosopher Socrates. His penetrating questions demanded reflection on Athenian values and ideals. He considered himself a gadfly whose job it was to prod Athens to self-awareness by challenging the very foundation of its beliefs. Socrates was condemned to death in 399 B.C.E. on rather nebulous charges. His death was symbolic of the rigid defensiveness of a decaying democracy.

The historical problem at issue here involves the compatibility of democracy and empire. From a moral standpoint, should a state that espouses freedom for all of its citizens control an empire that is maintained by fear and force? Is it even possible for a democratic government to rule an empire effectively? Finally, do the beauty and cultural worth of the monuments of a civilization justify the means of obtaining them? In other words, what price civilization?

GREEK VALUES: THE ODYSSEY OF HOMER

The Iliad *and the* Odyssey *were perhaps the most influential works in Greek history. Greek and Roman education was fundamentally concerned with the values expressed in these two works. Alexander the Great was even said to have slept with a copy of the* Iliad *under his pillow. And yet the* Odyssey *is very different in temperament and theme from the* Iliad. *The* Odyssey *speaks of homecoming, of love, longing, and revenge. It is the story of Odysseus, a great fighter for the Greeks at Troy whose inspired ploy of the Trojan horse resulted in the Greek victory over the Trojans. But in spite of his brilliance, or perhaps because of it, his homecoming was delayed for ten years as the gods conspired with monsters and witches to interrupt his life. His adventure with the one-eyed Cyclops and his dramatic visit to the underworld, where he meets the souls of the great warriors Achilles and Agamemnon, are two of the most dramatic stories in literature. But Odysseus' return to his island of Ithaca, his introduction to his adult son, Telemachus, his vengeance on the suitors of his wife, Penelope, and their tearful recognition capture the brilliance of the poet history has called Homer.*

Tell me, Muse, of the man of many devices, who wandered far and wide after he had sacked Troy's sacred city, and saw the towns of many men and knew their mind.

—Homer

I will drink life to the lees: all times I have enjoyed greatly, have suffered greatly, both with those that love me, and alone. . . . I am become a name; for always roaming with a hungry heart much have I seen and known; cities of men and manners, climates, councils, governments. . . . and drunk delight of battle, with my peers, far on the ringing plains of windy Troy. I am a part of all that I have met.

—Alfred Lord Tennyson ("Ulysses")

The Adventure of the Cyclops

HOMER

"When [the Cyclops] had done with his business and finished all his jobs, he lit up the fire, spied us, and began asking questions."

"'Strangers!" he said. 'And who may you be? Where do you hail from over the highways of the sea? Is yours a trading venture; or are you cruising the main on chance, like roving pirates, who risk their lives to ruin other people?'"

"Our hearts sank within us. The booming voice and the very sight of the monster filled us with panic. Still, I managed to find words to answer him."

"We are Achaeans," I said, on our way back from Troy, driven astray by contrary winds across a vast expanse of sea. Far from planning to come here, we meant to sail straight home; but we lost our bearings, as Zeus, I suppose, intended that we should. We are proud to be-

The Odyssey by Homer, translated by E.V. Rieu (Penguin Classics, 1947), copyright © 1950 the Estate of E.V. Rieu, pp. 146–150, 152–153. Reproduced with permission of Penguin Books Ltd.

long to the forces of Agamemnon, Atreus' son, who by sacking the great city of Ilium [Troy] and destroying all its armies has made himself the most famous man in the world today. We, less fortunate, are visiting you here as suppliants, in the hope that you may give us friendly entertainment or even go further in your generosity. You know the laws of hospitality: I beseech you, good sir, to remember your duty to the gods. For we throw ourselves on your mercy; and Zeus is there to avenge the suppliant and the guest. He is the travellers' god; he guards their steps and he invites them with their rights."

"So," said I, and promptly he answered me out of his pitiless heart: 'Stranger, you must be a fool, or must have come from very far afield, to preach to me of fear or reverence for the gods. We Cyclopes care not a jot for Zeus with his aegis [shield], nor for the rest of the blessed gods, since we are much stronger than they. It would never occur to me to spare you or your men against my will for fear of trouble from Zeus. But tell me where you moored your good ship when you came. Was it somewhere up the coast, or near by? I should like to see her.'

"He was trying to get the better of me, but I knew enough of the world to see through him and I met him with deceit. 'As for my ship,' I answered, 'it was wrecked by the Earth-shaker Poseidon on the confines of your land. The wind had carried us onto a lee shore. He drove the ship up to a headland and hurtled it on the rocks. But I and my friends managed to escape with our lives.'"

"To this the cruel brute made no reply. Instead, he jumped up, and reaching out towards my men, seized a couple and dashed their heads against the floor as though they had been puppies. Their brains ran out on the ground and soaked the earth. Limb by limb he tore them to pieces to make his meal, which he devoured like a mountain lion, never pausing till entrails and flesh, marrow and bones, were all consumed, while we could do nothing but weep and lift up our hands to Zeus in horror at the ghastly sight, paralysed by our sense of utter helplessness. When the Cyclops had filled his great belly with this meal of human flesh, which he washed down with unwatered milk, he stretched himself out for sleep among his flocks inside the cave. . . .'"

"'Here Cyclops, have some wine to wash down that meal of human flesh, and find out for yourself what kind of vintage was stored away in our ship's hold. I brought it for you by way of an offering in the hope that you would be charitable and help me on my homeward way. But your savagery is more than we can bear. Cruel monster, how can you expect ever to have a visitor again from the world of men, after such deeds as you have done?'"

"The Cyclops took the wine and drank it up. And the delicious draught gave him such exquisite pleasure that he asked me for another bowlful. . . . Three times I filled it up for him; and three times the fool drained the bowl to the dregs. At last, when the wine had fuddled his wits, I addressed him with disarming suavity."

"'Cyclops, I said, 'you wish to know the name I bear. I'll tell it to you; and in return I should like to have the gift you promised me. My name is Nobody. That is what I am called by my mother and father and by all my friends.'"

"The Cyclops answered me with a cruel jest. 'Of all his company I will eat Nobody last, and the rest before him. That shall be your gift.'"

"He had hardly spoken before he toppled over and fell face upwards on the floor, where he lay with his great neck twisted to one side, conquered, as all men are, by sleep. His drunkenness made him vomit, and a stream of wine mixed with morsels of men's flesh poured from his throat. I went at once and thrust our pole deep under the ashes of the fire to make it hot, and meanwhile gave a word of encouragement to all my men, to make sure that no one should play the coward and leave me in the lurch. When the fierce glow from the olive stake warned me that it was about to catch alight in the flames, green as it was, I withdrew it from the fire and brought it over to the spot where my men were standing ready. Heaven now inspired them with a reckless courage. Seizing the olive pole, they drove its sharpened end into the Cyclops' eye, while I used my weight from above to twist it home, like a man boring a ship's timber with a drill which his mates below him twirl with a strap they hold at either end, so that it spins continuously. [In much the same way we handled our pole with its red-hot point and twisted it in his eye till the blood boiled up round the burning wood. The fiery smoke from the blazing eyeball singed his lids and brow all round, and the very roots of his eye crackled in the heat. I was reminded of the loud hiss that comes from a great axe . . . when a smith plunges it into cold water—to temper it and give strength to the iron.] That is how the Cyclops' eye hissed round the olive stake. He gave a dreadful shriek, which echoed round the rocky walls, and we backed away from him in terror, while he pulled the stake from his eye, streaming with blood. Then he hurled it away from him with frenzied hands and raised a great shout for the other Cyclopes who lived in neighboring caves along the windy heights. These, hearing his screams, came from every quarter, and gathering outside the cave asked him what ailed him:

"'What on earth is wrong with you, Polyphemus? Why must you disturb the peaceful night and spoil our sleep with all this shouting? Is a robber driving off your sheep, or is somebody trying by treachery or violence to kill you?'

"Out of the cave came Polyphemus' great voice in reply: 'O my friends, it's Nobody's treachery, no violence, that is doing me to death.'

"'Well then,' they answered, in a way that settled the matter, 'if nobody is assaulting you in your solitude, you must be sick. Sickness comes from almighty Zeus and cannot be helped. All

you can do is to pray to your father, the Lord Poseidon.'

[The next morning, Odysseus and his men escaped from the Cyclops' cave by holding on to the underside of Polyphemus' sheep. The blinded Cyclops felt the top of each sheep as they left the cave, but did not detect any of Odysseus' men.]

"When we had put a little distance between ourselves and the courtyard of the cave, I first freed myself from under my ram and next untied my men from theirs. Then, quickly, though with many a backward look, we drove our long-legged sheep right down to the ship. . . . With a nod, [I made clear my will to each man], bidding them make haste to tumble all the fleecy sheep on board and put to sea. So in they jumped, ran to the benches, sorted themselves out, and plied the grey water with their oars.

"But before we were out of earshot, I let Polyphemus have a piece of my mind. 'Cyclops!' I called. 'So he was not such a weakling after all, the man whose friends you meant to overpower and eat in that snug cave of yours! And your crimes came home to roost, you brute, who have not even the decency to refrain from devouring your own guests. Now Zeus and all his fellow-gods have paid you out.'

"My taunts so exasperated the angry Cyclops that he tore the top off a great pinnacle of rock and hurled it at us. The rock fell just ahead of our blue-painted bows. As it plunged in, the water rose and the backwash, like a swell from the open sea, swept us landward and nearly drove us on the beach. . . . After I roused my crew with urgent nods, . . . they buckled to and rowed with a will . . . and brought us across the water to twice our previous distance. . . . My spirit was up, and in my rage I called to him once more:

"'Cyclops, if anyone ever asks you how you came by your unsightly blindness, tell him your eye was put out by Odysseus, Sacker of Cities, the son of Laertes, who lives in Ithaca.'"

Odysseus in the Underworld

HOMER

[I saw the soul of Agamemnon, which] burst into tears, stretching his arms out in my direction in his eagerness to reach me. But this he could not do, for all the strength and vigor had gone forever from those once supple limbs. Moved to compassion at the sight, I too gave way to tears and spoke to him from my heart:

"'Illustrious son of Atreus, Agamemnon, King of men, tell me what mortal stroke of fate it was that laid you low. Did Poseidon rouse the winds to fury and overwhelm your ships? Or did you fall to some hostile tribe on land as you were rounding up their cattle and their flocks or fighting with them for their town and women?'

"'Royal son of Laertes, Odysseus of the nimble wits,' he answered me at once, 'Poseidon did not wreck my ships; nor did I fall to any hostile tribe on land. It was Aegisthus who plotted my destruction and with my accursed wife put me to death. He invited me to the palace, he feasted me, and he killed me as a man fells an ox at its manger. That was my most miserable end. And all around me my companions were cut down in ruthless succession, like white-tusked swine slaughtered in the mansion of some great and wealthy lord, for a wedding, a club banquet, or a sumptuous public feast. You, Odysseus, have witnessed the deaths of many men in single combat or the thick of battle, but none with such horror as you would have felt had you seen us lying there by the wine-bowl and the laden tables in the hall, while the whole floor swam with our blood. Yet the most pitiable thing of all was the cry I heard from Cassandra, daughter of Priam, whom that foul traitress Clytemnestra [Agamemnon's wife] murdered at my side. As I lay on the ground, I raised my hands in a dying effort to grip Clytemnestra's sword. But the harlot turned her face aside, and had not even the grace, though I was on my way to Hades, to shut my eyes with her hands or to close my mouth. And so I say that for brutality and infamy there is no one to equal a woman who can contemplate such deeds. Who else could conceive so hideous a crime as her deliberate butchery of her husband and her lord? Indeed, I had looked forward to a rare welcome from my children and my servants when I reached home. But now, in the depth of her villainy, she has branded not herself alone but the whole of her sex and every honest woman for all time to come.'

"'Alas!' I exclaimed. 'All-seeing Zeus has indeed proved himself a relentless foe to the House of Atreus, and from the beginning he has worked his will through women's crooked ways. It was for Helen's sake that so many of us met our deaths, and it was Clytemnestra who hatched the plot against her absent lord.'

"'Let this be a lesson to you also,' replied Agamemnon. 'Never be too gentle even with your wife, nor show her all that is in your mind. Reveal a little of your counsel to her, but keep the rest of it to yourself. Not that *your* wife, Odysseus, will ever murder you. Icarius' daughter is far too sound in heart and brain for that. The wise Penelope! She was a young bride when we said goodbye to her on our way to the war. She had a baby son at her breast. And now, I suppose, he has begun to take his seat among the men. The lucky lad! His loving father will come home and see him, and he will kiss his father. That is how things should be. Whereas that wife of mine refused me even the satisfaction of setting eyes on my son. She could not wait so long before she killed his father. And now let me give you a piece of advice which I hope you will take to heart. Do not sail openly into port when you reach your home-country. Make a secret approach. Women, I tell you, are no longer to be trusted. . . .'

"Such was the solemn conversation that we two had as we stood there with our sorrows and the tears rolled down our cheeks. And now there came the souls of Peleus' son Achilles, of Patroclus, of the noble Antilochus, and of Aias. . . . It was the soul of Achilles, the great runner, who recognized me. In mournful, measured tones he greeted me by my titles, and went on: 'What next, Odysseus, dauntless heart? What greater exploit can you plan to cap your voyage here? How did you dare to come below to Hades' realm, where the dead live on without their wits as disembodied ghosts?'

"'Achilles,' I answered him, 'son of Peleus and flower of Achaean chivalry, I came to consult with Teiresias in the hope of finding out from him how I could reach my rocky Ithaca. For I have not managed to come near Achaea yet, nor set foot on my own island, but have been dogged by misfortune. How different from you, Achilles, the most fortunate man that ever was or will be! For in the old days when you were on earth, we Argives honored you as though you were a god; and now, down here, you are a mighty prince among the dead. For you, Achilles, Death should have lost his sting.'

"'My lord Odysseus,' he replied, 'spare me your praise of Death. Put me on earth again, and I would rather be a serf in the house of some landless man, with little enough for himself to live on, than king of all these dead men that have done with life.'"

The Return of Odysseus

HOMER

Amid all the Suitors' banter, the cool-headed Odysseus had poised the great bow and given it a final inspection. And now . . . he strung the great bow without effort or haste and with his right hand proved the string, which gave a lovely sound in answer like a swallow's note. The Suitors were confounded. The color faded from

their cheeks; while to mark the signal moment there came a thunderclap from Zeus, and Odysseus' long-suffering heart leapt up for joy at this sign of favor from the son of Chronos. . . .

One arrow lay exposed on the table beside him, the rest, which the Achaean lords were soon to feel, being still inside their hollow quiver. He picked up this shaft, set it against the bridge of the bow, drew back the grooved end and the string together, all without rising from his stool, and aiming straight ahead he shot. Not a single axe did he miss. From the first axe, right through them all and out at the last, the arrow sped with its burden of bronze. Odysseus turned to his son.

"'Telemachus,' he said, 'the stranger sitting in your hall has not disgraced you. I scored no miss, nor made hard work of stringing the bow. My powers are unimpaired, and these gentlemen were mistaken when they scornfully rated them so low. . . .'

"As he finished, Odysseus gave a nod. Whereupon his son and heir, Prince Telemachus, slung on his sharp-edged sword and gripping his spear took his stand by the chair at his father's side, armed with resplendent bronze.

"Shedding his rags, the indomitable Odysseus leapt onto the great threshold with his bow and his full quiver, and poured out the winged arrows at his feet.

"'That match is played and won!' he shouted to the Suitors. 'Now for another target! No man has hit it yet; but with Apollo's help I'll try.' And with that he levelled a deadly shaft straight at Antinous.

"Antinous had just reached for his golden cup to take a draught of wine, and the rich, two-handled beaker was balanced in his hands. No thought of bloodshed had entered his head. For who could guess, there in that festive company, that one man, however powerful he might be, would bring calamity and death to him against such odds? Yet Odysseus shot his bolt and struck him in the throat. The point passed clean through the soft flesh of his neck. Dropping the cup as he was hit, he lurched over to one side. His life-blood gushed from his nostrils in a turbid jet. His foot lashed out and kicked the table from him; the food was scattered on the ground, and his bread and meat were smeared with gore. . . .

"The unconquerable Odysseus looked down on the Suitors with a scowl. 'You curs!' he cried. 'You never thought to see me back from Troy. So you ate me out of house and home; you raped my maids; you wooed my wife on the sly though I was alive—with no more fear of the gods in heaven than of the human vengeance that might come. I tell you, one and all, your doom is sealed.'

[Odysseus and his son Telemachus then killed all of the suitors who were trapped in the Great Hall. After the battle, Odysseus met his wife, Penelope, for the first time in nineteen years. Penelope, who had resisted all overtures from the suitors, decided to confirm Odysseus' identity by subjecting him to a test.]

"'What a strange creature!' Odysseus exclaimed. 'Heaven made you as you are, but for sheer obstinacy you put all the rest of your sex in the shade. No other wife could have steeled herself to keep as long out of the arms of a husband she had just got back after nineteen years of misadventure. Well, nurse, make a bed for me to sleep alone in. For my wife's heart is just about as hard as iron.'

"'You too are strange,' said the cautious Penelope. 'I am not being haughty or indifferent. I am not even unduly surprised. But I have too clear a picture of you in my mind as you were when you sailed from Ithaca in your long-oared ship. Come, Eurycleia, make him a comfortable bed outside the bedroom that he built so well himself. Place the big bed out there, and make it up with rugs and blankets, and with laundered sheets.'

"This was her way of putting her husband to the test. But Odysseus flared up at once and rounded on his loyal wife. 'Penelope,' he cried, 'you exasperate me! Who, if you please, has moved my bed elsewhere? Short of a miracle, it would be hard even for a skilled workman to shift it somewhere else, and the strongest young fellow alive would have a job to budge it. For a great secret went into the making of that complicated bed; and it was my work and mine alone. Inside

the court there was a long-leaved olive tree, which had grown to full height with a stem as thick as a pillar. Round this I built my room of close-set stone-work, and when that was finished, I roofed it over thoroughly, and put in a solid, neatly fitted, double door. Next I lopped all the twigs off the olive, trimmed the stem from the root up, rounded it smoothly and carefully with my adze and trued it to the line, to make my bedpost. This I drilled through where necessary, and used as a basis for the bed itself, which I worked away at till that too was done, when I finished it off with an inlay of gold, silver, and ivory, and fixed a set of purple straps across the frame.

'There is our secret, and I have shown you that I know it. What I don't know, madam, is whether my bedstead stands where it did, or whether someone has cut the tree-trunk through and shifted it elsewhere.'

"Her knees began to tremble as she realized the complete fidelity of his description. All at once her heart melted. Bursting into tears she ran up to Odysseus, threw her arms round his neck and kissed his head. 'Odysseus,' she cried, 'do not be cross with me, you who were always the most reasonable of men.   our unhappiness is due to the gods, who couldn t bear to see us share the joys of youth and reach the threshold of old age together. But don't be angry with me now, or hurt because the moment when I saw you first I did not kiss you as I kiss you now. For I had always had the cold fear in my heart that somebody might come here and bewitch me with his talk. There are plenty of rogues who would seize such a chance. . . . But now all's well. You have faithfully described our token, the secret of our bed, which no one ever saw but you and I. . . . You have convinced your unbelieving wife.'

"Penelope's surrender melted Odysseus' heart, and he wept as he held his dear wife in his arms, so loyal and so true. Sweet moment too for her, sweet as the sight of land to sailors struggling in the sea. . . . If that is bliss, what bliss it was for her to see her husband once again! She kept her white arms round his neck and never quite let go. Dawn with her roses caught them at their tears."

THE GREEK POLIS: TWO WAYS OF LIFE

Democracy is based on the conviction that man has the moral and intellectual capacity, as well as the inalienable right, to govern himself with reason and justice.

—Harry S. Truman

In the strict sense of the term, a true democracy has never existed and never will exist.

—Jean-Jacques Rousseau

The City-State of Sparta

The city-state, or polis, evolved during the period 1200–500 B.C.E. and offered a unique organization for the Greeks. Each polis was independent in its particular form of government, provided for its own defensive arrangements, and conducted its own foreign policy. Thus one city-state might be a monarchy, another a democracy, and a third an oligarchy. One of the most fascinating city-states was Sparta. In the eighth century B.C.E., it had prospered in a rather open political and economic environment. But in the late seventh century, Sparta, under the leadership of Lycurgus, adopted a rigid military system that produced one of the most efficient and feared armies in antiquity. The Spartans enslaved some of the surrounding population (calling them helots) and used them to work the land while Spartan warriors honed their military skills. The following account describes the Spartan way of life. Though they never produced great literature or ideas, the Spartans were admired because they prevented chaos in their society.

Spartan Discipline

PLUTARCH

Nor was it in the power of the father to dispose of the child as he thought fit; he was obliged to carry it before certain officials at a place called Lesche; these were some of the elders of a tribe to which the child belonged; their business it was carefully to view the infant, and, if they found it strong and well formed, they gave order for its rearing, and allowed to it one of the nine thousand shares of land above mentioned for its maintenance, but if they found it puny and ill-shaped, ordered it to be taken to . . . a sort of chasm [and exposed to the elements]; as thinking it neither for the good of

the child itself, nor for the public interest, that it should be brought up, if it did not, from the very outset, appear . . . healthy and vigorous. There was much care and art, too, used by the nurses; they had no swaddling bands; the children grew up free and unconstrained in limb and form, and not dainty and fanciful about their food; not afraid in the dark, or of being left alone; without any irritability or ill humor or crying. Upon this account, Spartan nurses were often . . . hired by people of other countries. . . .

Lycurgus would not have tutors brought out of the market for his young Spartans; nor was it lawful, indeed, for the father himself to raise the children after his own fancy; but as soon as they were 7 years old they were to be enrolled in certain companies and classes, where they lived under the same order and discipline, doing their exercises and playing together. Of these, he who showed the most conduct and courage

"Spartan Discipline" is from Plutarch, Lycurgus, 16–19, in *Readings in Ancient History*, vol. 1, ed. William S. Davis (New York: Allyn and Bacon, 1912), pp. 107–111. Translation modernized by the editor.

was made captain; they had their eyes always upon him, obeyed his order, and underwent patiently whatsoever punishment he inflicted; so that the whole course of their education was one continued exercise of a ready and perfect obedience. The old men, too, were spectators of their performances, and often raised quarrels and disputes among them, to have a good opportunity of finding out their different characters, and of seeing which would be valiant, which a coward, when they should come to more dangerous encounters. Reading and writing they gave them, just enough to serve their turn; their chief care was to make them good subjects, and to teach them to endure pain and conquer in battle. To this end, as they grew in years, their discipline was proportionably increased; their heads were close clipped, and they were accustomed to go barefoot, and for the most part to play naked.

The Second Stage of the Spartan Education

After they were 12 years old, they were no longer allowed to wear any undergarment; they had one coat to serve them a year; their bodies were hard and dry, with but little acquaintance of baths and unguents; these human indulgences they were allowed only on some few particular days in the year. They lodged together in little bands upon beds made of the reeds which grew by the banks of the river, which they were to break off with their hands without a knife; if it were winter, they mingled some thistledown with their reeds, which it was thought had the property of giving warmth. . . . [Spartan youths were required to steal wood and herbs], which they did by creeping into the gardens, or conveying themselves cunningly and closely into the eating houses: if they were taken in the act, they were whipped without mercy, for thieving so poorly and awkwardly. They stole, too, all other meat they could lay their hands on, looking out and watching all opportunities, when people were asleep or more careless than usual. If they were caught, they were not only punished with whipping, but hunger, too, being reduced to their ordinary allowance, which was very slender, and so contrived on purpose, that they might set about to help themselves, and be forced to exercise their energy and ingenuity.

So seriously did the Spartan children go about their stealing, that a youth, having stolen a young fox and hid it under his coat, allowed it to tear out his very guts with its teeth and claws, and died upon the place, rather than let it be seen. What is practiced to this very day in Sparta is enough to gain credit to this story, for I myself have seen several of the youths endure whipping to death. . . .

They taught them, also, to speak in a natural and graceful manner, and to express much in few words. . . . Children in Sparta, by a habit of long silence, came to give just and wise answers; for, indeed, as loose and incontinent livers are seldom fathers of many children, so loose and incontinent talkers seldom originate many sensible words. When some Athenian laughed at their short swords, . . . King Agis answered him, "We find them long enough to reach our enemies"; and as their swords were short and sharp, so, it seems to me, were their sayings. They reach the point and arrest the attention of the hearers better than any other kind.

The City-State of Athens

The Athenian polis was, in most respects, the opposite of Sparta. In 510 B.C.E., under the leadership of Cleisthenes, Athens adopted a democratic system in which all citizens were expected to vote, serve in public office, and offer themselves as jurors. Active participation in political affairs was demanded, and one who shunned such responsibility was called "idiotes," or "private person"; the word has come down to us as "idiot," with all its pejorative connotations.

The leader of the Athenian democracy in the middle of the fifth century B.C.E. was the great orator Pericles. After the first year of the Peloponnesian War (430 B.C.E.), Pericles spoke to the wives and parents of those who had died in the fighting in an attempt to justify their loss. The famous Funeral Oration that follows was recorded by the Athenian historian Thucydides; it is the quintessential expression of the structure and values of the Athenian democracy.

"Freedom Depends on Being Courageous": The Funeral Oration of Pericles (430 B.C.E.)

THUCYDIDES

"I have no wish to make a long speech on subjects familiar to you all: so I shall say nothing about the warlike deeds by which we acquired our power or the battles in which we or our fathers gallantly resisted our enemies, Greek or foreign. What I want to do is, in the first place, to discuss the spirit in which we faced our trials and also our constitution and the way of life which has made us great. After that I shall speak to praise of the dead, believing that this kind of speech is not inappropriate to the present occasion, and that this whole assembly, of citizens and foreigners, may listen to it with advantage.

"Let me say that our system of government does not copy the institutions of our neighbours. It is more the case of our being a model to others, than of our imitating anyone else. Our constitution is called a democracy because power is in the hands not of a minority but of the whole people. When it is a question of settling private disputes, everyone is equal before the law; when it is a question of putting one person before another in positions of public responsibility, what counts is not membership of a particular class, but the actual ability which the man possesses. No one, so long as he has it in him to be of service to the state, is kept in political obscurity because of poverty. And, just as our political life is free and open, so is our day-to-day life in our relations with each

other. . . . We are free and tolerant in our private lives; but in public affairs we keep to the law. This is because it commands our deep respect.

"We give our obedience to those whom we put in positions of authority, and we obey the laws themselves, especially those which are for the protection of the oppressed, and those unwritten laws which it is an acknowledged shame to break.

"And here is another point. When our work is over, we are in a position to enjoy all kinds of recreation for our spirits. There are various kinds of contests and sacrifices regularly throughout the year; in our own homes we find a beauty and a good taste which delight us every day and which drive away our cares. Then the greatness of our city brings it about that all the good things from all over the world flow in to us, so that to us it seems just as natural to enjoy foreign goods as our own local products.

"Then there is a great difference between us and our opponents, in our attitude towards military security. Here are some examples: our city is open to the world, and we have no periodical deportations in order to prevent people observing or finding out secrets which might be of military advantage to the enemy. This is because we rely, not on secret weapons, but on our own real courage and loyalty. There is a difference, too, in our educational systems. The Spartans, from their earliest boyhood, are submitted to the most laborious training in courage; we pass our lives without all these restrictions, and yet are just as ready to face the same dangers as they are. . . . There are certain advantages, I think, in our way of meeting danger voluntarily, with an easy mind, instead of with a laborious training, with natural rather than with state-induced courage. We do not have to spend our time practising to meet sufferings which are still in the future; and when they are actually upon us we show ourselves just as brave as these others who are always in strict training. This is one point in which, I think, our city deserves to be admired. There are also others:

"Our love of what is beautiful does not lead to extravagance; our love of the things of the mind does not make us soft. We regard wealth as something to be properly used, rather than as something to boast about. As for poverty, no one need be ashamed to admit it: the real shame is in not taking practical measures to escape from it. Here each individual is interested not only in his own affairs but in the affairs of the state as well: even those who are mostly occupied with their own business are extremely well-informed on general politics—this is a peculiarity of ours: we do not say that a man who takes no interest in politics is a man who minds his own business; we say that he has no business here at all. We Athenians, in our persons, take our decisions on policy or submit them to proper discussions: for we do not think that there is an incompatibility between words and deeds; the worst thing is to rush into action before the consequences have been properly debated. And this is another point where we differ from other people. We are capable at the same time of taking risks and of estimating them beforehand. Others are brave out of ignorance; and, when they stop to think, they begin to fear. But the man who can most truly be accounted brave is he who best knows the meaning of what is sweet in life and of what is terrible, and then goes out undeterred to meet what is to come.

"Again, in question of general good feeling there is a great contrast between us and most other people. We make friends by doing good to the more reliable, since we want to keep alive the gratitude of those who are in our debt by showing continued good will to them. . . . We are unique in this. When we do kindnesses to others, we do not do them out of any calculations of profit or loss: we do them without afterthought, relying on our free liberality. Taking everything together then, I declare that our city is an education to Greece, and I declare that in my opinion each single one of our citizens, in all the manifold aspects of life, is able to show himself the rightful lord

and owner of his own person, and do this, moreover, with exceptional grace and exceptional versatility. And to show that this is no empty boasting for the present occasion, but real tangible fact, you have only to consider the power which our city possesses and which has been won by those very qualities which I have mentioned. Athens, alone of the states we know, comes to her testing time in a greatness that surpasses what was imagined of her. In her case, and in her case alone, no invading enemy is ashamed at being defeated, and no subject can complain of being governed by people unfit for their responsibilities. Mighty indeed are the marks and monuments of our empire which we have left. Future ages will wonder at us, as the present age wonders at us now. . . . For our adventurous spirit has forced an entry into every sea and into every land; and everywhere we have left behind us everlasting memorials of good done to our friends or suffering inflicted on our enemies.

"This, then, is the kind of city for which these men, who could not bear the thought of losing her, nobly fought and nobly died. It is only natural that every one of us who survive them should be willing to undergo hardships in her service. And it was for this reason that I have spoken at such length about our city, because I wanted to make it clear that for us there is more at stake than there is for others who lack our advantages; also I wanted my words of praise for the dead to be set in the bright light of evidence. And now the most important of these words has been spoken. I have sung the praises of our city; but it was the courage and gallantry of these men, and of people like them, which made her splendid. Now would you find it true in the case of many of the Greeks, as it is true of them, that no words can do more than justice to their deeds.

"To me it seems that the consummation which has overtaken these men shows us the meaning of manliness in its first revelation and in its final proof. Some of them, no doubt, had their faults; but what we ought to remember first is their gallant conduct against the enemy in defence of their native land. They have blotted out evil with good, and done more service to

The rocky plateau of the ancient Acropolis overlooks the city of Athens. The Parthenon (center), temple of the patron goddess Athena, was built with funds garnered from the Athenian Empire. What price civilization? (*Photo Researchers, Inc.*)

the commonwealth than they ever did harm in their private lives. . . .

"So and such they were, these men—worthy of their city. We who remain behind may hope to be spared their fate, but must resolve to keep the same daring spirit against the foe. It is not simply a question of estimating the advantages in theory. I could tell you a long story (and you know it as well as I do) about what is to be gained by beating the enemy back. What I would prefer is that you should fix your eyes every day on the greatness of Athens as she really is, and should fall in love with her. When you realize her greatness, then reflect that what made her great was men with a spirit of adventure, men who knew their duty, men who were ashamed to fall below a certain standard. If they ever failed in an enterprise, they made up their minds that at any rate the city should not find their courage lacking to her, and they gave to her the best contribution they could. They gave her their lives, to her and to all of us, and for their own selves they won praises that never grow old, the most splendid of sepulchres—not the sepulchre in which their bodies are laid, but where their glory remains eternal in men's minds, always there on the right occasion to stir others to speech or to action. For famous men have the whole earth as their memorial: it is not only the inscriptions on their graves in their own country that mark them out; no, in foreign lands also, not in any visible form but in people's hearts, their memory abides and grows. It is for you to try to be like them. Make up your minds that happiness depends on being free, and freedom depends on being courageous. Let there be no relaxation in face of the perils of the war. The people who have most excuse for despising death are not the wretched and unfortunate, who have no hope of doing well for themselves, but those who run the risk of a complete reversal in their lives, and who would feel the difference most intensely, if things went wrong for them. Any intelligent man would find a humiliation caused by his own slackness more painful to bear than death, when death comes to him unperceived, in battle, and in the confidence of his patriotism."

Theme: Systems of Government

The Historical Intersection

NORMANDY: 1994

Fiftieth Anniversary of D-Day: "When They Were Young, These Men Saved the World"

PRESIDENT BILL CLINTON

During World War II, with Allied victories in Northern Africa, Italy, and Russia begin-ning to turn the tide of battle by 1944, the Allied High Command, led by General Dwight Eisenhower, developed plans for the invasion of Europe. The Germans were aware that an invasion was imminent and had constructed formidable defenses along the French coast at Normandy under the direction of Field Marshal Erwin Rommel.

An amphibious assault is a delicate operation, and even the most meticulous plans are vulnerable to changes of wind and weather. The D-Day operation was a high-risk gamble that cost thousands of lives but resulted in the establishment of a "second front" against the Germans. The next drive was to Berlin itself. The fiftieth anniversary commemorative speech by President Clinton on June 6, 1994, offers perspective on the cost and importance of this day.

Compare and Contrast:

- Paying tribute to soldiers who have sacrificed their lives during war is an important obligation for the political head of a state. Compare the speech of Pericles during the Peloponnesian War in 430 B.C.E. with Presi-dent Bill Clinton's commemoration of the fiftieth anniversary of the D-Day invasion of Europe. What did the soldiers die for?

In these last days of ceremonies, we have heard wonderful words of tribute. Now we come to this hallowed place that speaks, more than anything else, in silence.

(contd)

Here on this quiet plateau, on this small piece of American soil, we honor those who gave their lives for us fifty crowded years ago.

Today, the beaches of Normandy are calm. If you walk these shores on a summer's day, all you might hear is the laughter of children playing on the sand, or the cry of seagulls overhead, or perhaps the ringing of a distant church bell—the simple sounds of freedom barely breaking the silence.

But June 6th, 1944 was the least ordinary day of the twentieth century. On that chilled dawn, these beaches echoed with the sounds of staccato gunfire, the roar of aircraft, the thunder of bombardment. And through the wind and the waves came the soldiers, out of their landing craft and into the water, away from their youth and toward a savage place many of them would sadly never leave.

They had come to free a continent—the Americans, the British, the Canadians, the Poles, the French Resistance, the Norwegians and the others—they had all come to stop one of the greatest forces of evil the world has ever known. . . .

During those first hours on bloody Omaha nothing seemed to go right. Landing craft were ripped apart by mines and shells. Tanks sent to protect them had sunk, drowning their crews. Enemy fire raked the invaders as they stepped into chest-high water and waded past the floating bodies of their comrades. And as the stunned survivors of the first wave huddled behind a seawall, it seemed the invasion might fail.

Hitler and his followers had bet on it. They were sure the Allied soldiers were soft, weakened by liberty and leisure, by the mingling of races and religion. They were sure their totalitarian youth had more discipline and zeal. But then, something happened. Although many of the American troops found themselves without officers on unfamiliar ground, next to soldiers they didn't know, one by one, they got up. They inched forward and together in groups of threes and fives and tens, the sons of democracy improvised and mounted their own attacks. At that exact moment on these beaches, the forces of freedom turned the tide of the twentieth century. . . .

Today, many of them are here among us. Oh, they may walk with a little less spring in their step and their ranks are growing thinner, but let us never forget—when they were young, these men saved the world. . . .

Millions of our GIs did return home from that war to build up our nations and enjoy life's sweet pleasures. But on this field, there are 9,386 who did not. . . . They were the fathers we never knew, the uncles we never met, the friends who never returned, the heroes we can never repay. They gave us our world. And those simple sounds of freedom we hear today are their voices speaking to us across the years. . . .

Fifty years ago, the first Allied soldiers to land here in Normandy came not from the sea, but from the sky. They were called Pathfinders, the first paratroopers to make the jump. Deep in the darkness they descended upon these fields to light beacons for the airborne assaults that would soon follow. Now, near the dawn of a new century, the job of lighting those beacons falls to our hands.

(contd)

To you who brought us here, I promise, we will be the new pathfinders, for we are the children of your sacrifice.

Consider This:

- What are the most impressive phrases from Pericles' Funeral Oration and President Clinton's tribute? What emotions do they evoke from their respective audiences? Is this kind of speech the privilege of the victors? Why did Spartan or German soldiers die? For the same reasons? For the same causes? Why did American soldiers die in Vietnam? Why did they never receive such a verbal testimonial?

"Fiftieth Anniversary of D-Day" is from President Bill Clinton, speech delivered at the United States National Cemetery above Omaha Beach, Colleville-sur-Mer, France, on June 6, 1994. Contained in *Vital Speeches of the Day,* July 1, 1994, pp. 546–547.

THE PERSIAN WARS AND THE ATHENIAN EMPIRE

The Spartans at Thermopylae (480 B.C.E.)

HERODOTUS

In 499 B.C.E., the Ionian city-state of Miletus rebelled against Persian rule and asked the Athenians for support. Athens not only aided the rebels, but marched inland and burned one of the Persian capitals at Sardis. Such impulsive aggression could not go unpunished, and the Persian king Darius launched an invasion against Athens in 490 B.C.E., which the Greeks heroically repulsed on the plains of Marathon. The Persian defeat at Marathon served only to anger and frustrate an empire now bent on revenge. The new king, Xerxes, decided to take no chances and formed a massive army of about 250,000 men; this force made its way by land and sea north across the Dardanelles and down into Greece itself. In the face of such power, many Greek city-states surrendered to the Persian horde. While the Athenians evacuated their city, a Spartan force of 300 warriors and one of their kings (Leonidas) left to prevent a Persian invasion of Greece by making a stand in a pass called Thermopylae. A disgruntled Greek shepherd named Ephialtes told Xerxes of a way around the pass. The following selection by the Greek historian Herodotus recounts the Spartan heroism.

The barbarians under Xerxes began to draw near; and the Greeks under Leonidas, as they now went forth determined to die, advanced much farther than on previous days, until they reached the more open portion of the pass. Hitherto they had held their station within the wall, and from this had gone forth to fight at the point where the pass was the narrowest. Now they joined battle . . . and carried a slaughter among the barbarians, who fell in heaps. Behind [the Persians] the captains of the squadrons, armed with whips, urged their men

"The Spartans at Thermopylae" is from Herodotus, *The Histories,* 7.223–228, trans. George Rawlinson, in *The History of Herodotus* (New York: E. P. Dutton, 1910), pp. 207–209. Translation modernized by the editor.

forward with continual blows. Many were thrust into the sea, and there perished; a still greater number were trampled to death by their own soldiers; no one heeded the dying. For the Greeks, reckless of their own safety and desperate, since they knew that, as the mountain had been crossed, their destruction was nigh at hand, exerted themselves with the most furious valor against the barbarians.

By this time the spears of the greatest number were all shivered, and with their swords they hewed down the ranks of the Persians; and here, as they strove, Leonidas [the Spartan king] fell fighting bravely, together with many other famous Spartans, whose names I have taken care to learn on account of their great worthiness, as indeed I have those of all the three hundred. There fell too at the same time very many famous Persians: among them, two brothers of Xerxes. . . .

And now there arose a fierce struggle between the Persians and the Spartans over the body of Leonidas, in which the Greeks four times drove back the enemy, and at last by their great bravery succeeded in bearing off the body. This combat was scarcely ended when the Persians with Ephialtes approached; and the Greeks, informed that they drew near, made a change in the manner of their fighting. Drawing back into the narrowest part of the pass, and retreating even behind the cross wall, they posted themselves upon a hillock, where they stood all drawn up to-

gether in one close body. The hillock whereof I speak is at the entrance of the pass, where the stone lion stands which was set up in honor of Leonidas. Here they defended themselves to the last, such as still had swords using them, and the others resisting with their hands and teeth; till the barbarians, who in part had pulled down the wall and attacked them in front, in part had gone round and now encircled them upon every side, overwhelmed and buried the remnant left beneath showers of missile weapons.

Thus nobly did the whole body of Spartans behave, but nevertheless one man is said to have distinguished himself above all the rest, . . . Dieneces the Spartan. A speech which he made before the Greeks engaged the Persians remains on record. One of the Trachinians told him, "Such was the number of the barbarians [Persians], that when they shot forth their arrows the sun would be darkened by their multitude." Dieneces, not at all frightened at these words, but making light of the Persian numbers, answered, "Our Trachinian friend brings us excellent tidings. If the Persians darken the sun, we shall have our battle in the shade." . . .

The slain were buried where they fell; and in their honor, not less in honor of those who died before Leonidas sent the allies away, an inscription was set up, which said. . . .
Go, stranger, and to Sparta tell
That here, obedient to her laws, we fell.

The Battle of Salamis (480 B.C.E.)

AESCHYLUS

With the destruction of the Spartan force at Thermopylae, the Persians poured into Greece. After evacuating Athens, the Greeks made a desperate stand. Through a clever trick, Themistocles lured the Persians into the narrow straits between the Greek shore and the island of Salamis. There, they were crushed in a surprise attack by the Athenian fleet. Xerxes, the Persian king, watched impotently from a nearby hill. This dramatic account of the battle is excerpted from the play The Persians *by Aeschylus.*

Persian Messenger: The Persians knew
their error; fear gripped every man.

They were not fugitives who sang that
terrifying

Paean, but Hellenes [Greeks] charging
with courageous hearts
To battle. The loud trumpet flamed along
their ranks.
At once their frothy oars moved with a
single pulse,
Beating the salt waves to the bo'sons'
chant; and soon
Their whole fleet hove clear into view;
their right wing first
In precise order, next their whole array
came on,
And at that instant a great shout beat on
our ears:
Forward, you sons of Hellas! Set your
country free!
Set free your sons, your wives, tombs of
your ancestors,
And temples of your gods. All is at stake:
Now fight!
Then from our side in answer rose the
manifold
Clamour of Persian voices; and the hour
had come.
At once ship into ship battered its brazen
beak.
A Hellene ship charged first, and chopped
off the whole stern

Of a Phoenician galley. Then charge
followed charge
On every side. At first by its huge impetus
Our [Persian] fleet withstood them. But
soon, in that narrow space,
Our ships were jammed in hundreds;
none could help another.
They rammed each other with their prows
of bronze; and some
Were stripped of every oar. Meanwhile the
enemy [Greeks]
Came round us in a ring and charged.
Our vessels heeled
Over; the sea was hidden, carpeted with
wrecks
And dead men; all the shores and reefs
were full of dead. . . .

This depth of horror Xerxes saw, close to
the sea
On a high hill he sat, where he could
clearly watch
His whole force both by sea and land. He
wailed aloud,
And tore his clothes, weeping; and
instantly dismissed
His army, hastening them to a disordered
flight.

From Confederacy to Empire

THUCYDIDES

By 479 B.C.E., the combined Greek armies had defeated the Persian forces, which returned home never to invade Greece again. Still, many of the Greek city-states thought it wise to establish an organization intended to protect against any future Persian invasion, to gain booty, and to liberate Greek city-states on the coast of Ionia still under Persian control. Toward this end, many Greek islands pledged their eternal unity to the cause, formed the Delian Confederacy, and contributed money or ships for use against the Persians. Although all members had the same voting weight, the Athenians initially led the organization by supplying the generals and controlling the treasury. Gradually, however, the Athenian allies became Athenian subjects. The historian Thucydides discusses this transition in the following selection.

At first the allies were independent and deliberated in a common assembly under the leadership of Athens. But in the interval between the

Persian and Peloponnesian wars, by their military success and by policy in dealing with the barbarian, with their own rebellious allies and

"From Confederacy to Empire" is from Thucydides, *History of the Peloponnesian War,* 1.97, 1.99, in *A Source-Book of Ancient History,* ed. George W. Botsford (New York: Macmillan, 1912), pp. 177–178.

with the Peloponnesians [Spartans] who came across their path from time to time, the Athenians made immense strides in power. . . .

The causes which led to the defection of the allies were of different kinds, the principal one being their neglect to pay the tribute or to furnish ships, and, in some cases, failure of military service. For the Athenians were exacting and oppressive, using coercive measures toward men who were neither willing nor accustomed to work hard. And for various reasons they soon began to prove less agreeable leaders than at first. They no longer fought upon an equality with the rest of the confederates, and they had no difficulty in reducing them when they revolted. Now the allies brought all this upon themselves; for the majority of them disliked military service and absence from home, and so they agreed to contribute a regular sum of money instead of ships. Whereby the Athenian navy was proportionately increased, while they themselves were always untrained and unprepared for war when they revolted.

THE GOLDEN AGE OF ATHENS

Zeus spoke, and nodded with his darkish brows, and immortal locks fell forward from the lord's deathless head, and he made great Olympus tremble.

—Homer

Of all the wondrous things on earth, the greatest of these is man.

—Sophocles

Oedipus the King (430 B.C.E.)
SOPHOCLES

The greatness of Athenian civilization in the fifth century B.C.E. was evident in many ways. Not only was the city decorated with temples such as the Parthenon and other monuments on the Acropolis, but Athens was also glorified by the splendor of her intellectual accomplishment. During the century, three dramatists emerged who are comparable in quality to Shakespeare: Aeschylus, Sophocles, and Euripides. Aeschylus, a true patriot, wanted to be remembered only as having fought at the battle of Marathon. Sophocles, a commander in the Athenian navy, won first place in dramatic competition for his play about Oedipus, an unfortunate king of Thebes who unwittingly killed his father (Laius) and married his mother. Such sin, even if unintended and unperceived, cannot go unpunished by the gods: When the truth is revealed, Jocasta (his mother/wife) commits suicide and Oedipus blinds himself. The Athenians loved the "no-win" situation, both for the problems it presented and for the moral choices it demanded. In the following selection, note the importance of self-discovery and truth, no matter the outcome.

Attendant: O you most honourable lords of the city of Thebes,
Weep for the things you shall hear, the things you must see,
If you are true sons and loyal to the house of Labdacus.
Not all the water of Ister, the waters of Phasis,

The Theban Plays by Sophocles, translated by E.F. Watling (Penguin Classics, 1947), copyright © E. F. Watling, 1947, pp. 59–61. Reproduced with permission of Penguin Books Ltd.

Can wash this dwelling clean of the foulness within,
Clean of the deliberate acts that soon shall be known,
Of all horrible acts most horrible, wilfully chosen.

Chorus: Already we have wept enough for the things we have known,
The things we have seen. What more will your story add?

Attendant: First, and in brief—Her Majesty is dead.

Chorus: Alas, poor soul: what brought her to this end?

Attendant: Her own hand did it. You that have not seen,
And shall not see, this worst, shall suffer the less.
But I that saw, will remember, and will tell what I remember
Of her last agony.
You saw her cross the threshold
In desperate passion. Straight to her bridal-bed
She hurried, fastening her fingers in her hair.
There in her chamber, the doors flung sharply to,
She cried aloud to Laius long since dead,
Remembering the son she bore long since, the son
By whom the sire was slain, the son to whom
The mother bore yet other children, fruit
Of luckless misbegetting, there she bewailed
The twice confounded issue of her wifehood—
Husband begotten of husband, child of child.
So much we heard. Her death was hidden from us.
Before we could set out her tragedy,
The King broke in with piercing cries, and all

Had eyes only for him. This way and that
He strode among us. 'A sword, a sword!' he cried;
'Where is that wife, no wife of mine—that soil
Where I was sown, and whence I reaped my harvest!'
While thus he raved, some demon guided him—
For none of us dare to speak—to where she was.
As if in answer to some leader's call
With wild hallooing cries he hurled himself
Upon the locked doors, bending by main force
The bolts out of their sockets—and stumbled in.
We saw a knotted pendulum, a noose,
A strangled woman swinging before our eyes.
The King saw too, and with heart rending groans
Untied the rope, and laid her on the ground.
But worse was yet to see. Her dress was pinned
With golden brooches, which the King snatched out
And thrust, from full arm's length, into his eyes—
Eyes that should see no longer his shame, his guilt,
No longer see those they should never have seen,
Nor see, unseeing, those he had longed to see,
Henceforth seeing nothing but night. . . . To this wild tune
He pierced his eyeballs time and time again,
Till bloody tears ran down his beard—not drops
But in full spate a whole cascade descending
In drenching cataracts of scarlet rain.
Thus two have sinned; and on two heads, not one—
On man and wife—falls mingled punishment.
Their old long happiness of former times
Was happiness earned with justice; but to-day
Calamity, death, ruin, tears, and shame,
All ills that there are name for—all are here.

Antigone (441 B.C.E.)

SOPHOCLES

Sophocles continued the story of Oedipus in Antigone, *a play about Oedipus' tainted children. The play won first prize in the dramatic competition and again demonstrates the tragedy of those who are not guilty but are condemned by the misdeeds of others. In the following excerpt, Antigone and her sister Ismene must decide whether to bury the body of their brother, thus satisfying the laws of the gods, or to leave it unburied as the king (Creon) has decreed.*

Scene: Before the Palace at Thebes

Enter Ismene from the central door of the Palace. Antigone follows, anxious and urgent; she closes the door carefully, and comes to join her sister.

Antigone: O sister! Ismene dear, dear sister Ismene!
You know how heavy the hand of God is upon us;
How we who are left must suffer for our father, Oedipus.
There is no pain, no sorrow, no suffering, no dishonour
We have not shared together, you and I.
And now there is something more. Have you heard this order,
This latest order that the King has proclaimed to the city?
Have you heard how our dearest are being treated like enemies?

Ismene: I have heard nothing about any of those we love,
Neither good nor evil—not, I mean, since the death
Of our two brothers, both fallen in a day.
The Argive army, I hear, was withdrawn last night.
I know no more to make me sad or glad.

Antigone: I thought you did not. That's why I brought you out here,
Where we shan't be heard, to tell you something alone.

Ismene: What is it, Antigone? Black news, I can see already.

Antigone: O Ismene, what do you think? Our two dear brothers. . . .
Creon has given funeral honours to one,
And not to the other; nothing but shame and ignominy.
Eteocles has been buried, they tell me, in state,
With all honourable observances due to the dead.

But Polynices, just as unhappily fallen—the order
Says he is not to be buried, not to be mourned;
To be left unburied, unwept, a feast of flesh
For keen-eyed carrion birds. The noble Creon!
It is against you and me he has made this order.
Yes, against me. And soon he will be here himself
To make it plain to those that have not heard it,
And to enforce it. This is not idle threat;
The punishment for disobedience is death by stoning.
So now you know. And now is the time to show
Whether or not you are worthy of your high blood.

Ismene: My poor Antigone, if this is really true,
What more can I do, or undo, to help you?

Antigone: Will you help me? Will you do something with me? Will you?

Ismene: Help you do what, Antigone? What do you mean?

Antigone: Would you help me lift the body. . . you and me?

Ismene: You cannot mean . . . to bury him? Against the order?

Antigone: Is he not my brother, and yours, whether you like it
Or not? I shall never desert him, never.

Ismene: How could you dare, when Creon has expressly forbidden it?

Antigone: He has no right to keep me from my own.

Ismene: O sister, sister, do you forget how our father
Perished in shame and misery, his awful sin
Self-proved, blinded by his own self-mutilation?
And then his mother, his wife—for she was both—
Destroyed herself in a noose of her own making.
And now our brothers, both in a single day
Fallen in an awful exaction of death for death.

Blood for blood, each slain by the other's hand.
Now we two left; and what will be the end of us,
If we transgress the law and defy our king?
O think, Antigone; we are women; it is not for us
To fight against men; our rulers are stronger than we,
And we must obey in this, or in worse than this.
May the dead forgive me, I can do no other
But as I am commanded; to do more is madness.

Antigone: No; then I will not ask for your help.
Nor would I thank you for it, if you gave it.
Go your own way; I will bury my brother;
And if I die for it, what happiness!
Convicted of reverence—I shall be content
To lie beside a brother whom I love.
We have only a little time to please the living,
But all eternity to love the dead.
There I shall lie for ever. Live, if you will;
Live, and defy the holiest laws of heaven.

Ismene: I do not defy them; but I cannot act
Against the State. I am not strong enough.

Antigone: Let that be your excuse, then. I will go
And heap a mound of earth over my brother.

Ismene: I fear for you, Antigone; I fear—

Antigone: You need not fear for me. Fear for yourself.

Ismene: At least be secret. Do not breathe a word.
I'll not betray your secret.

Antigone: Publish it
To all world! Else I shall hate you more.

Ismene: Your heart burns! Mine is frozen at the thought.

Antigone: I know my duty, where true duty lies.

Ismene: If you can do it; but you're bound to fail.

Antigone: When I have tried and failed, I shall have failed.

Ismene: No sense in starting on a hopeless task.

Antigone: Oh, I shall hate you if you talk like that!
And he will hate you, rightly. Leave me alone
With my own madness. There is no punishmen
Can rob me of my honourable death.

Ismene: Go then, if you are determined, to your folly.
But remember that those who love you. . . . love you still.

[Condemned to death for defying the king and burying her brother, Antigone explains her actions]

Antigone: So to my grave,
My bridal-bower, my everlasting prison,
I go, to join those many of my kinsmen
Who dwell in the mansions of Persephone,
Last and unhappiest, before my time.
Yet I believe my father will be there
To welcome me, my mother greet me gladly,
And you, my brother, gladly see me come.
Each one of you my hands have laid to rest,
Pouring the due libations on your graves.

It was by this service to your dear body, Polynices,
I earned the punishment which now I suffer,
Though all good people know it was for your honour.
O but I would not have done the forbidden thing
For any husband or for any son.
For why? I could have had another husband
And by him other sons, if one were lost;
But, father and mother lost, where would I get
Another brother? For thus preferring you,
My brother, Creon condemns me and hales me away,
Never a bride, never a mother, unfriended,
Condemned alive to solitary death.
What law of heaven have I transgressed? What god
Can save me now? What help or hope have I,
In whom devotion is deemed sacrilege?
If this is God's will, I shall learn my lesson
In death; but if my enemies are wrong,
I wish them no worse punishment than mine. . . .

[Antigone, thus condemned by Creon, commits suicide as does her intended husband, Haemon, son of Creon. In this passage, Creon realizes that he was blind to wisdom and that his laws have defied the gods and cost him the lives of his son and also his wife.]

Enter Creon with the body of Haemon.

Creon: The sin, the sin of the erring soul

Drives hard unto death.
Behold the slayer, the slain,
The father, the son.
O the curse of my stubborn will!
Son, newly cut off in the newness of youth,
Dead for my fault, not yours.

Chorus: Alas, too late you have seen the truth.

Creon: I learn in sorrow. Upon my head
God has delivered this heavy punishment,
Has struck me down in the ways of wickedness,
And trod my gladness under foot.
Such is the bitter affliction of mortal man.

Enter the Messenger from the palace.

Messenger: Sir, you have this and more than this to bear.
Within there's more to know, more to your pain.

Creon: What more? What pain can overtop this pain?

Messenger: She is dead—your wife, the mother of him that is dead—
The death-wound fresh in her heart. Alas, poor lady!

Creon: Insatiable Death, wilt thou destroy me yet?
What say you, teller of evil?
I am already dead,
And there is more?
Blood upon blood?
More death? My wife?

The central doors open, revealing the body of Eurydice.

Chorus: Look then, and see; nothing is hidden now.

Creon: O second horror!
What fate awaits me now?
My child here in my arms . . . and there, the other. . . .
The son . . . the mother. . . .

Messenger: There at the altar with the whetted knife
She stood, and as the darkness dimmed her eyes
Called on the dead, her elder son and this,
And with her dying breath cursed you, their slayer.

Creon: O horrible. . . .

Is there no sword for me
To end this misery?

Messenger: Indeed you bear the burden of two deaths.
It was her dying word.

Creon: And her last act?

Messenger: Hearing her son was dead, with her own hand she drove the sharp sword home into her heart.

Creon: There is no man can bear this guilt but I.
It is true, I killed him.
Lead me away, away. I live no longer.

Chorus: 'Twere best, if anything is best in evil times.
What's soonest done, is best, when all is ill.

Creon: Come, my last hour and fairest,
My only happiness . . . come soon.
Let me not see another day.
Away . . . away. . . .

Chorus: The future is not to be known; our present care
Is with the present; the rest is in other hands.

Creon: I ask no more than I have asked.

Chorus: Ask nothing.
What is to be, no mortal can escape.

Creon: I am nothing. I have no life.
Lead me away. . . .
That have killed unwittingly
My son, my wife.
I know not where I should turn,
Where look for help.
My hands have done amiss, my head is bowed
With fate too heavy for me.

Chorus: Of happiness the crown
And chiefest part
Is wisdom, and to hold
The gods in awe
This is the law
That, seeing the stricken heart
Of pride brought down,
We learn when we are old.

[The last excerpt from Antigone is the famous choral passage that expresses the Greek view of man.]

Chorus: Wonders are many on earth, and the greatest of these
Is man, who rides the ocean and takes his way
Through the deeps, through wind-swept valleys of perilous seas
That surge and sway.
He is master of ageless Earth, to his own will bending
The immortal mother of gods by the sweat of his brow,
As year succeeds year, with toil unending
Of mule and plough.
He is lord of all things living; birds of the air,
Beasts of the field, all creatures of sea and land
He taketh, cunning to capture and ensnare
With sleight of hand;
Hunting the savage beast from the upland rocks,
Taming the mountain monarch in his lair,
Teaching the wild horse and the roaming ox

His yoke to bear.
The use of language, the wind-swift motion of brain
He learnt; found out the laws of living together
In cities, building him shelter against the rain
And wintry weather.
There is nothing beyond his power. His subtlety
Meeteth all chance, all danger conquereth.
For every ill he hath found its remedy,
Save only death.
O wondrous subtlety of man, that draws
To good or evil ways! Great honour is given
And power to him who upholdeth his country's laws
And the justice of heaven.
But he that, too rashly daring, walks in sin
In solitary pride to his life's end.
At door of mine shall never enter in
To call me friend.

THE PELOPONNESIAN WAR AND THE DECLINE OF ATHENS (431–404 B.C.E.)

Excessive freedom leads to anarchy, which in turn results in despotism, the most burdensome and most brutal slavery.

—*Plato*

When the Athenians finally wanted not to give to society, but for society to give to them, when the freedom they wished for was freedom from responsibility, then Athens ceased to be free.

—*Edward Gibbon*

The Melian Dialogue (416 B.C.E.)
THUCYDIDES

The Peloponnesian War (431–404 B.C.E.) was fought primarily over the threat that Athens posed to the security and economic well-being of Sparta and her allies. After the first two years of the war, Pericles died from a plague raging in Athens. With the loss of this far-sighted statesman, the democracy fell prey to more demagogic leaders who could influence people with effective oratory but whose policies were often extreme. The island of Melos, located off the southern tip of the Peloponnesus, was a Spartan colony. Even so, the Melians maintained a strict neutrality during the Peloponnesian War. Thucydides, the Athenian historian, wrote this contrived dialogue to demonstrate the

"The Melian Dialogue" from Thucydides—Reprinted from *The History of The Peloponnesian War,* edited and translated by Richard Livingstone (1943), by permission of Oxford University Press, pp. 266–274.

brutal force used by Athens in maintaining her empire. The ideals expounded by Pericles in the Fu-neral Oration are thus balanced by power politics in which logic is no defense and might makes right. Melos was conquered by Athens in 416 B.C.E.

The next summer the Athenians made an expedition against the isle of Melos. The Melians are a colony of Sparta that would not submit to the Athenians like the other islanders, and at first remained neutral and took no part in the struggle, but afterwards, upon the Athenians using violence and plundering their territory, assumed an attitude of open hostility. The Athenian generals encamped in their territory with their army, and before doing any harm to their land sent envoys to negotiate. . . . The Athenian envoys then said:

Athenians: "If you have met us in order to make surmises about the future, or for any other purpose than to look existing facts in the face and to discuss the safety of your city on this basis, we will break off the conversations; otherwise, we are ready to speak."

Melians: "In our position it is natural and excusable to explore many ideas and arguments. But the problem that has brought us here is our security, so, if you think fit, let the discussion follow the line you propose."

Athenians: "Then we will not make a long and unconvincing speech, full of fine phrases, to prove that our victory over Persia justifies our empire, or that we are now attacking you because you have wronged us, and we ask you not to expect to convince us by saying that you have not injured us, or that, though a colony of Sparta, you did not join her. . . ."

Melians: "As you ignore justice and have made self-interest the basis of discussion, we must take the same ground, and we say that in our opinion it is in your interest to maintain a principle which is for the good of all—that anyone in danger should have just and equitable treatment and any advantage, even if not strictly his due, which he can secure by persuasion. This is your interest as much as ours, for your fall would involve you in a crushing punishment that would be a lesson to the world."

Athenians: "We have no apprehensions about the fate of our empire, if it did fall; those who rule other peoples, like the Spartans, are not formidable to a defeated enemy. Nor is it the Spartans with whom we are now contending: the danger is from subjects who of themselves may attack and conquer their rulers. But leave that danger to us to face. At the moment we shall say we are seeking the safety of your state; for we wish you to become our subjects with least trouble to ourselves, and we would like you to survive in our interests as well as your own."

Melians: "It may be your interest to be our masters: how can it be ours to be your slaves?"

Athenians: "By submitting you would avoid a terrible fate, and we should gain by not destroying you."

Melians: "Would you not agree to an arrangement under which we should keep out of the war, and be your friends instead of your enemies, but neutral?"

Athenians: "No: your hostility injures us less than your friendship. That, to our subjects, is an illusion of our weakness, while your hatred exhibits our power."

Melians: "Is this the construction which your subjects put on it? Do they not distinguish between states in which you have no concern, and peoples who are most of them your colonies, and some conquered rebels?"

Athenians: "They think that one nation has as good rights as another, but that some survive because they are strong and we are afraid to attack them. So, apart from the addition of our empire, your subjection would give us security: the fact that you are islanders (and weaker than others) makes it more important that you should not get the better of the mistress of the sea."

Melians: "But do you see no safety in our neutrality? Will you not make enemies of all neutral powers when they see your conduct and reflect that some day you will attack them? Will not your action strengthen your existing opponents, and induce those who would otherwise never be your enemies to become so against their will?"

Athenians: "No. The mainland states, secure in their freedom, will be slow to take defensive measures against us, and we do not consider them so formidable as independent island powers like yourselves, or subjects already smarting under our yoke. These are most likely to take a thoughtless step and bring themselves and us into obvious danger."

Melians: "Surely, then, if you are ready to risk so much to maintain your empire, and the enslaved peoples so much to escape from it, it would be criminal cowardice in us, who are still free, not to take any and every measure before submitting to slavery?"

Athenians: "No, if you reflect calmly: for this is not a competition in heroism between equals, where your honor is at stake, but a question of self-preservation to save you from a struggle with a far stronger Power."

Melians: "Still, we know that in war fortune is more impartial than the disproportion in numbers might lead one to expect. If we submit at once, our position is desperate; if we fight, there is still a hope that we shall stand secure."

Athenians: "Hope encourages men to take risks; men in a strong position may follow her without ruin, if not without loss. But when they stake all that they have to the last coin (for she is a spendthrift), she reveals her real self in the hour of failure, and when her nature is known she leaves them without means of self-protection. You are weak, your future hangs on a turn of the scales; avoid the mistake most men make, who might save themselves by human means, and then, when visible hopes desert them, in their extremity turn to the invisible—prophecies and oracles and all those things which delude men with hopes, to their destruction."

Melians: "We too, you can be sure, realize the difficulty of struggling against your power and against Fortune if she is not impartial. Still we trust that Heaven will not allow us to be worsted by Fortune, for in this quarrel we are right and you are wrong. Besides, we expect the support of Sparta to supply the deficiencies in our strength, for she is bound to help us as her kinsmen, if for no other reason, and from a sense of honor. So our confidence is not entirely unreasonable."

Athenians: "As for divine favor, we think that we can count on it as much as you, for neither our claims nor our actions are inconsistent with what men believe about Heaven or desire for themselves. We believe that Heaven, and we know that men, by a natural law, always rule where they are stronger. We did not make the law nor were we the first to act on it; we found it existing, and it will exist forever, after we are gone; and we know that you and anyone else as strong as we are would do as we do. As to your expectations from Sparta and your belief that she will help you from a sense of honor, we congratulate you on your innocence but we do not admire your folly. So far as they themselves and their natural traditions are concerned, the Spartans are a highly virtuous people; as for their behavior to others, much might be said, but we can put it shortly by saying that, most obviously of all people we know, they identify their interests with justice and the pleasantest course with honor. Such principles do not favor your present irrational hopes of deliverance."

Melians: "That is the chief reason why we have confidence in them now; in their own interest they will not wish to betray their own colonists and so help their enemies and destroy the confidence that their friends in Greece feel in them."

Athenians: "Apparently you do not realize that safety and self-interest go together, while the path of justice and honor is dangerous; and danger is a risk which the Spartans are little inclined to run. . . . Here experience may teach you like others, and you will learn that Athens has never abandoned a siege from fear of another foe. You said that you proposed to discuss the safety of your city, but we observe that in all your speeches you have never said a word on which any reasonable expectation of it could be founded. Your strength lies in deferred hopes; in comparison with the forces now arrayed against you, your resources are too small for any hope of success. You will show a great want of judgment if you do not come to a more reasonable decision after we have withdrawn. Surely you will not fall back on the idea of honor, which has been the ruin of so many when danger and disgrace were staring them in the face. How often, when men have seen the fate to which they were tending, have they been enslaved by a phrase and drawn by the power of this seductive word to fall of their own free will into irreparable disaster, bringing on themselves by their folly a greater dishonor than fortune could inflict! If you are wise, you will avoid that fate. The greatest of cities makes you a fair offer, to keep your own land and become her tributary ally: there is not dishonor in that. The choice between war and safety is given you; do not obstinately take the worse alternative. The most successful people are those who stand up to their equals, behave properly to their superiors, and treat their inferiors fairly. Think it over when we withdraw, and reflect once again that you will have only one country, and that its prosperity or ruin depends on one decision."

The Athenians then withdrew from the conference; and the Melians, left to themselves, came to a decision corresponding with what they had maintained in the discussion, and answered, "Our resolution, Athenians, is unaltered. We will not in a moment deprive of freedom a city by which the gods have preserved it until now, and in the help of men, that is, of the Spartans; and so we will try and save ourselves. Meanwhile we invite you to allow us to be friends to you and foes to neither party, and to retire from our country after making such a treaty as shall seem fit to us both."

Such was the answer of the Melians. The Athenians broke up the conference saying, "To judge from your decision, you are unique in regarding the future as more certain than the present and in allowing your wishes to convert the unseen into reality; and as you have staked most on, and trusted most in, the Spartans, your fortune, and your hopes, so will you be most completely deceived."

The Athenian envoys now returned to the army, and as the Melians showed no signs of yielding the generals at once began hostilities, and drew a line of circumvallation round the Melians . . . besieged the place. . . .

Summer was now over . . . and the siege was now pressed vigorously; there was some treachery in the town, and the Melians surrendered at discretion to the Athenians, who put to death all the grown men whom they took, and sold the women and children for slaves. . . .

The Trojan Women (415 B.C.E.)

EURIPIDES

One year after the destruction of Melos, the great Athenian dramatist Euripides reacted to the incident by composing The Trojan Women. *The subject of his play is the fate of the women of Troy after their husbands had been killed and their city destroyed by the Greek force in 1230 B.C.E. In the following passage, Andromache, wife of the valiant Trojan leader Hector, is informed of the fate proscribed for her young son. Note how her argument parallels that of "The Melian Dialogue." The* Trojan Women *failed to win a prize in the dramatic competition that year.*

From "The Women of Troy" from *The Bacchae and Other Plays* by Euripides, translated by Phillip Vellacott (Penguin, 1954), pp. 105–107. Copyright © Philip Vellacott, 1954, 1972. Reproduced by permission of Penguin Books Ltd.

Talthybius: Andromache, widow of the bravest of the Trojans: do not hate me. It is with great reluctance that I have to convey to you the decision unanimously reached by the Greeks and their two generals, the sons of Pelops.

Andromache: What is this? Your words hint at the worst.

Talthybius: It was decided that your son—how can I say it?

Andromache: He is to have a different master from mine?

Talthybius: No Greek will ever be his master.

Andromache: What? Is he to be the one Trojan left behind in Troy?

Talthybius: My news is bad. It is hard to find words.

Andromache: Thank you for your sympathy. What have you to say?

Talthybius: You must know the worst: they mean to kill your son.

Andromache: Oh, gods! His sentence is worse than mine.

Talthybius: In a speech delivered before the whole assembly Odysseus carried his point—

Andromache [sobbing passionately]: Oh, Oh! This is more than I can bear.

Talthybius:—that the son of so distinguished a father must not be allowed to attain manhood—

Andromache: May he hear the same sentence passed on his own son!

Talthybius:—but should be thrown down from the battlements of Troy. Now show yourself a sensible woman, and accept this decision. Don't cling to him, or imagine you have any chance of resisting: you have none. Bear what must be like a queen. There is no one who can help. You can see for yourself: your city and your husband are gone; you are in our hands. Shall we match our strength against one woman? We can. So I hope that you won't feel inclined to struggle, or to call down curses on the Greeks, or do anything that might lead to violent measures or resent-ment. If you say anything to anger the army, this child will die without rites of pity, without burial. If you are quiet, and accept the inevitable in a proper spirit, you will be allowed to lay your child in his grave, and you will find the Greeks more considerate to yourself.

Andromache: Darling child, precious beyond all price! You will die, killed by our enemies, leaving your mother to mourn. Your noble father's courage, which saved others, has condemned you; his spirit was a fatal inheritance. I thought, on that day when I entered Hector's house as a bride, on that ill-fated night, that my son would rule the teeming multitudes of the East—not die by a Greek ritual of murder.

Are you crying, little one? Do you understand? Why do you tug my hand, cling to my dress, nestling like a bird under its mother's wing? No Hector will rise from the grave and step forth to save you, gripping his glorious spear; none of your father's brothers, no army of Phrygians. You must leap from that horrible height, and fall, and break your neck, and give up your life, and be pitied by no one.

My baby, so young in my arms, and so dear! O the sweet smell of your skin! When you were newly born, how I wrapped you up and gave you my breast, and tended you day and night, and was worn out with weariness—all for nothing, for nothing! Now say good-bye to me for the last time; come close to your mother, wind your arms round my neck, and put your lips to mine.

O men of Hellas, inventors of cruelty unworthy of you! Why will you kill him? What has he done?—Helen, child of Hyndareus, you are no daughter of divine Majesty! You had many fathers, and I can name them: the Avenging Curse was one, Hate was the next, then Murder and Death and every evil that lives on earth! I will swear that Zeus never fathered you to ruin men's lives by tens of thousands through Asia and Hellas! My curse on you! With the shining glance of your beauty you have brought this rich and noble country to a shameful end.

Take him! Carry him away, throw him down, if your edict says 'Throw!' Feast on his flesh! God is destroying us! I have no power to save my child from death. Hide my miserable body, throw me on board! I go to my princely marriage, and leave behind me my dear child.

Women and War: Lysistrata (411 B.C.E.)

ARISTOPHANES

Athens not only produced great tragedians such as Sophocles and Euripides, but also great comic dramatists as well. The brilliant playwright Aristophanes poked fun at the major personalities of the day (Socrates included) and influenced public opinion about the most divisive political issues. Aristophanes was born about 447 B.C.E. at a time when Athens was at the height of her power and influence. He was often critical of the democracy and especially the prosecution of the Peloponnesian War. After the tragic destruction of Athenian forces at Syracuse in 413 B.C.E. and the impotent leadership in the years that followed, Aristophanes contrived his own solution for the end of the war, which he presented in 411 B.C.E. in the play Lysistrata. *The women of both Sparta and Athens would take the initiative in stopping the war by withholding sex while their husbands were on leave until the men came to their senses!*

Of special note here is the presentation of women in Athenian society. Although it is debated whether women were allowed to attend the theater (Plato gives evidence that they did), in other ways their lives were extremely restricted. They were not allowed to leave their homes unescorted, could not vote, hold public office, own property, or even attend social gatherings in their own homes. They were essentially bound to the will and decisions of their husbands or fathers. Perhaps the biggest joke in Athens after the presentation of Lysistrata *was that women could have conceived and organized such a bold and effective plan for ending the Peloponnesian War. In this scene, the leader of the Athenian women, Lysistrata, and her compatriot, Stratyllis, confront the male Athenian leadership.*

Magistrate: Anyway, what business are war and peace of yours?

Lysistrata: I'll tell you.

Magistrate [restraining himself with difficulty]: You'd better or else.

Lysistrata: I will if you'll listen and keep those hands of yours under control.

Magistrate: I can't—I'm too livid. . . . Say what you have to say.

Lysistrata: In the last war we were too modest to object to anything you men did—and in any case you wouldn't let us say a word. But don't think we approved! We knew everything that was going on. Many times we'd hear at home about some major blunder of yours, and then when you came home we'd be burning inside but we'd have to put on a smile and ask what it was you'd decided to inscribe in the pillar underneath the Peace Treaty. And what did my husband always say?—'Shut up and mind your own business!' And I did.

Stratyllis: I wouldn't have done!

Magistrate: He'd have given you one if you hadn't.

Lysistrata: Exactly—so I kept quiet. But sure enough, next thing we knew you'd make an even sillier decision. And if I so much as said, 'Darling, why are you carrying on with this silly policy?' he would glare at me and say, 'Back to your weaving, woman, or you'll have a headache for a month. Go and attend to your work; let war be the care of the menfolk.'

Magistrate: Quite right too, by Zeus.

Lysistrata: Right? That we should not be allowed to make the least little suggestion to you, no matter how much you mismanage the City's affairs? And now, look, every time two people meet in the street, what do they say? 'Isn't there a man in the country?' and the answer comes, 'Not one.' That's why we women got together and decided we were going to save Greece. What was the point of waiting any longer, we asked ourselves. Well now, we'll make a deal. You listen to us—and we'll talk sense, not like you used to—listen to us and keep quiet, as we've had to do up to now, and we'll clear up the mess you've made.

Magistrate: Insufferable effrontery! I will not stand for it!

Lysistrata [magisterially]: Silence!

Magistrate: You, confound you, a woman with your face veiled, dare to order me to be silent! Gods, let me die! . . .

Leader: Disgraceful!—women venturing to prate
In public so about affairs of State!
They even (men could not be so naive)
The blandishments of Sparta's wolves believe!
The truth the veriest child could surely see:
This is a Monarchist Conspiracy.
I'll fight autocracy until the end:

My freedom I'll unswervingly defend. . . .
And from this place
I'll give this female one upon the face!
[He slaps Stratyllis hard on the cheek.]
Stratyllis [giving him a blow in return that sends him reeling]:
Don't trifle with us, rascals, or we'll show you
Such fisticuffs, your mothers will not know you!

Chorus of Women: My debt of love today
To the City I will pay,
And I'll pay it in the form of good advice;
For the City gave me honour
(Pallas' blessing be upon her!),
And the things I've had from her deserve their price. . . .

Stratyllis: See why I think I have a debt to pay?
'But women can't talk politics,' you say.
Why not? What is it you insinuate?
That we contribute nothing to the State?
Why, we give more than you! See if I lie:
We cause men to be born, you make them die.
What's more, you've squandered all the gains of old;
And now, the taxes you yourselves assess
You do not pay. Who's got us in this mess?
Do you complain? Another grunt from you,
And you will feel the impact of this shoe! . . .

Leader: If once we let these women get the semblance of a start,
Before we know, they'll be adept at every manly art!

The Trial of Socrates (399 B.C.E.)

PLATO

The Peloponnesian War came to an end in 404 B.C.E. The Athenians suffered a humiliating defeat and were divested of their empire, military forces, and dignity. A Spartan occupation force assumed control of the city and replaced Athenian democracy with the reactionary rule of the Thirty Tyrants, vindictive Athenian citizens who used the months from 404 to 403 B.C.E. to settle scores with their former political enemies. Although a democracy was reinstituted, it no longer espoused the tolerance

"The Trial of Socrates" is from Plato, *Apology*, in *The Dialogues of Plato*, 3rd ed., trans. Benjamin Jowett (Oxford: The Clarendon Press, 1875). Translation modernized by the editor.

of ideas and freedom of speech that had been such a part of former Athenian glory. A true indicator of this decline was the trial of Socrates.

Socrates, a stonecutter by trade, had dutifully served the Athenian state in a political capacity and also as a soldier in war. He disliked the advances of popular teachers called "sophists" who claimed to be able to teach anything for a fee. Socrates instead claimed that he knew nothing and set about informally teaching people to question in the hope of finding wisdom. He considered himself the gadfly whose responsibility it was to prod the democracy continually in hopes that self-reflection might produce wise policy. His "services" were free of charge, and he became quite influential among the youth of Athens. In 399 B.C.E. he was accused by various Athenian leaders of not believing in the gods of the state and of corrupting the youth. His most famous pupil, Plato, watched the proceedings in the court and wrote an account of Socrates' defense, called the Apology; *an excerpt is presented below. In the end, Socrates was condemned to death and actually insisted on drinking the poisonous hemlock. In his martyrdom lay the destruction of Athenian ideals.*

This inquisition has led to my having many enemies of the worst and most dangerous kind, and has given occasion also to many injuries. . . .

There is another thing: young men of the richer classes, who have not much to do, come about me of their own accord; they like to hear the pretenders examined, and they often imitate me, and proceed to examine others; there are plenty of persons, as they quickly discover, who think they know something, but really know little or nothing; and then those who are examined by them instead of being angry with themselves are angry with me: This confounded Socrates, they say; this villainous misleader of youth!—and then if somebody asks them, Why, what evil does he practice or teach? they do not know, and cannot tell; but in order that they may not appear to be at a loss, they repeat the ready-made charges which are used against all philosophers about teaching things up in the clouds and under the earth, and having no gods, and making the worse appear the better cause; for they do not like to confess that their pretense of knowledge has been detected—which is the truth: and as they are numerous and ambitious and energetic, and are drawn up in battle array and have persuasive tongues, they have filled your ears with their loud and inveterate slanders. And this is the reason why my three accusers, Meletus and Anytus and Lycon, have set upon me. . . .

Some one will say: And are you not ashamed, Socrates, of a course of life which is likely to bring you to an untimely end? To him I may fairly answer: There you are mistaken: a man who is good for anything ought not to calculate the chance of living or dying; he ought only to consider whether in doing anything he is doing right or wrong—acting the part of a good man or of a bad. . . . And therefore if you let me go now, . . . if you say to me, Socrates, this time we will not mind Anytus, and you shall be let off, but upon one condition, that you are not to enquire and speculate in this way any more, and that if you are caught doing so again you shall die; if this was the condition on which you let me go, I should reply: Men of Athens, I honor and love you; but I shall obey God rather than you, and while I have life and strength I shall never cease from the practice and teaching of philosophy, exhorting anyone whom I meet and saying to him after my manner: You, my friend—a citizen of the great and mighty and wise city of Athens—are you not ashamed of heaping up the greatest amount of money and honor and reputation, and caring so little about wisdom and truth and the greatest improvements of the soul, which you never regard or heed at all? And if the person with whom I am arguing, says: Yes, but I do care; then I do not leave him or let him go at once; but I proceed to interrogate and examine and cross-examine him, and if I think that he has no virtue in him, but only says that he has, I reproach him with undervaluing the greater, and overvaluing the less. . . . This is my teaching, and if this is the doctrine which corrupts youth, I am a mischievous person. . . .

And now, Athenians, I am not going to argue for my own sake, as you may think, but for yours, that you may not sin against God by condemning me, who am his gift to you. For if you kill me you will not easily find a successor to me, who, if I may use such a ludicrous figure of speech, am a sort of gadfly, given to the state by God; and the state is a great and noble steed who is tardy in his motions owing to his very size, and requires to be stirred into life. I am that gadfly which God has attached to the state, and all day long and in all places am always fastening upon you, arousing and persuading and reproaching you. You will not easily find another like me, and therefore I would advise you to spare me. I dare say that you may feel out of temper (like a person who is suddenly awakened from sleep), and you think that you might easily strike me dead as Anytus advises, and then you would sleep on for the remainder of your lives, unless God in his care of you sent you another gadfly. . . .

And now, O men who have condemned me, I would give prophecy to you; for I am about to die, and in the hour of death men are gifted with prophetic power. And I prophecy to you who are my murderers, that immediately after my departure punishment far heavier than you have inflicted on me will surely await you. Me you have killed because you wanted to escape the accuser, and not to give an account of your lives. But that will not be as you suppose: far otherwise. For I say that there will be more accusers of you than there are now; accusers whom hitherto I have restrained: and as they are younger they will be more inconsiderate with you, and you will be more offended at them. If you think that by killing me you can prevent someone from censuring your evil lives, you are mistaken; that is not a way of escape which is either possible or honorable; the easiest and noblest way is not to be disabling others, but to be improving yourselves. This is the prophecy which I utter before my departure to the judges who have condemned me. . . .

Still I have a favor to ask of them. When my sons are grown up, I would ask you, O my friends, to punish them; and I would have you trouble them, as I have troubled you if they seem to care about riches, or anything, more than about virtue; or if they pretend to be something when they are really nothing—then reprove them, as I have reproved you, for not caring about that for which they ought to care, and thinking that they are something when they are really nothing. And if you do this, both I and my sons will have received justice at your hands.

The hour of departure has arrived, and we go on our ways—I to die, and you to live. Which is better God only knows.

THE AGE OF ALEXANDER THE GREAT

During the first half of the fourth century B.C.E., Greece in general and Athens in particular were in a state of domestic chaos. Nearly continuous warfare and political strife interfered with trade and thus contributed to economic dislocation and depression. A widening gulf developed between rich and poor, and this was reflected in political dissension and indecision. There was a genuine desire to return to the days of glory and honor when Athens commanded the respect of the world; yet there was much debate on how to regain such a position. Many eyes turned toward the Persians, whose defeat in 480 B.C.E. by Greek tenacity and ingenuity had ushered in the Golden Age. The Athenian orator Isocrates strongly advocated foreign conquest as the panacea for depression but also knew that the Greeks had to be unified in order to defeat Persian power. His solution was to support the leadership of the King of Macedon, Philip II. In this Isocrates was opposed by perhaps the greatest orator of all, Demosthenes. Demosthenes firmly believed that to accept the leadership of Philip in such a cause was in fact to accept the end of Greek freedom. His speeches against Philip (called the

"Philippics") are models of persuasive argument. Demosthenes influenced the democracy to resist the advances of Philip, but in 338 B.C.E. Athens was militarily defeated and made to join the League of Corinth in support of Macedon.

With Greece securely under his control, Philip could now afford to move ahead with his plans to invade Persia. But in 336 B.C.E. he was assassinated during a wedding feast. His 20-year-old son Alexander, who had inherited his ambition for the conquest of Persia, assumed his position as King of Macedon. Alexander certainly capitalized on his father's plans and preparations, and his conquest of the Persian empire became the stuff of legends. It is difficult to decide which of his adventures are fact and which are fiction. His influence on the world around him and on the course of history has also been hotly debated. It is easy to degenerate into "historical what-ifs": What if Alexander had not decided to conquer Persia, but had turned west instead toward the infant Roman civilization? What would have happened to Greece if Alexander had died early in the Persian campaign? Had he lived longer, would he still be called the Great? These questions are unanswerable, but his conquest of the world was a feat of amazing endurance and determination. It is important to ask the right questions of it in order to obtain meaningful answers.

The period after Alexander's death in 323 B.C.E. is called Hellenistic, or "Greek-like." The age of Greek political domination was past, and soon the Romans would conquer and control the region. Still, the Greeks of the fourth and third centuries continued to influence Western civilization with the philosophies of Plato, Aristotle, and various schools of Stoics, Epicureans, and Cynics. The Greeks continued to dominate artistic style, education, and scholarship, providing tutors and oratorical instruction for the Mediterranean world. Scientific inquiry was one of the great advancements of the age, and urban planning can largely be traced to the Greeks of this period. In all, we see transition from the dying ideals of the Greeks to the more realistic and practical foundations of Roman civilization.

The Figure of Alexander

"Carve out a Kingdom Worthy of Yourself!"
PLUTARCH

One of the most fascinating and controversial figures of history was Alexander III of Macedon. After Philip's assassination in 336 B.C.E., Alexander was elected to the kingship and continued with his father's plans to invade and conquer Persia. His exploits became legendary and it is difficult to separate fact from fiction. The following selection recounts an early indication of Alexander's special abilities when he tamed a horse too wild for others to control.

Philonicus the Thessalian brought the horse Bucephalus to Philip, offering to sell him for thirteen talents; but when they went into the field to try him, they found him so very vicious and unmanageable, that he reared up when they endeavored to mount him, and would not so much as endure the voice of any of Philip's attendants. Upon which, as they were leading him away as wholly useless and intractable, Alexander, who stood by, said, "What an excellent horse do they

"Carve Out A Kingdom Worthy of Yourself!" is from Plutarch, *Life of Alexander,* 5, in *Readings in Ancient History,* vol. 1, ed. William S. Davis (Boston: Allyn and Bacon, 1912), pp. 301–302.

lose, for want of skill and boldness to manage him!" Philip at first took no notice of what he said; but when he heard him repeat the same thing several times, and saw he was very frustrated to see the horse sent away, "Do you criticize," said Philip, "those who are older than yourself, as if you knew more, and were better able to manage him then they?" "I could manage this horse," replied Alexander, "better than others do." "And if you do not," said Philip, "what will you forfeit for your rashness?" "I will pay," answered Alexander, "the whole price of the horse." At this the whole company fell laughing; and as soon as the wager was settled among them, he immediately ran to the horse, and, taking hold of the bridle, turned him directly towards the sun, having, it seems, observed that he was disturbed at and afraid of the motion of his own shadow; then letting him go forward a little, still keeping the reins in his hand, and stroking him gently when he began to grow eager and fiery, . . . with one nimble leap, Alexander securely mounted him, and when he was seated, by little and little drew in the bridle, and curbed him without either striking or spurring him. Presently, when he found him free from all rebelliousness, and only impatient for the course, he let him go at full speed, inciting him now with a commanding voice, and urging him also with his heel. Philip and his friends looked on at first in silence and anxiety for the result, [but when he came] back rejoicing and triumphing for what he had performed, they all burst out into acclamations of applause; and his father, shedding tears, it is said, for joy, kissed him as he came down from his horse, and in his transport said, "O my son, carve out a kingdom equal to and worthy of yourself, for Macedonia is too small for you."

A mosaic of Alexander the Great leading his Macedonian troops into battle. Alexander conquered but never consolidated his vast empire. (*Art Resource*)

The Leadership of Alexander

ARRIAN

Alexander's military abilities are beyond question, but it takes more than tactical knowledge to inspire and encourage a force to move thousands of miles away from their homeland in pursuit of the unknown. Finally, deep in India, Alexander's troops forced him to forget the "ends of the earth" and to return to Macedon. The journey home was difficult, and Alexander lost many men to the hardship of the desert. His leadership, as the following account reveals, was never in doubt.

At this point in my story I must not leave unrecorded one of the finest things Alexander ever did. . . . The army was crossing a desert of sand; the sun was already blazing down upon them, but they were struggling on under the necessity of reaching water, which was still far away. Alexander, like everyone else, was tormented by thirst, but he was none the less marching on foot at the head of his men. It was all he could do to keep going, but he did so, and the result (as always) was that the men were the better able to endure their misery when they saw that it was equally shared. As they toiled on, a party of light infantry which had gone off looking for water found some—just a wretched little trickle collected in a shallow gully. They scooped up with difficulty what they could and hurried back, with their priceless treasure, to Alexander; then, just before they reached him, they tipped the water into a helmet and gave it to him. Alexander, with a word of thanks for the gift, took the helmet, and, in full view of his troops, poured the water on the ground. So extraordinary was the effect of this action that the water wasted by Alexander was as good as a drink for every man in the army. I cannot praise this act too highly; it was a proof, if anything was, not only of his power of endurance, but also of his genius for leadership.

The Campaigns of Alexander by Arrian, translated by Aubrey de Sélincourt, revised by J. R. Hamilton (Penguin Classics 1958, Revised edition 1971), copyright © Aubrey de Sélincourt, 1958, pp. 338–339. Reproduced with permission of Penguin Books Ltd.

The Thought of the Age

Allegory of the Cave

PLATO

Plato was one of the greatest philosophers in world civilization. His influence has been so decisive that one scholar remarked that all subsequent thought is but a series of footnotes to Plato. He was a student of Socrates and shared his view that universal truths exist and can be discovered. Plato went further by developing a system called the "Theory of Ideas," which defies simple explanation but rather requires a kind of immersion in thought to understand its tenets. Plato's doctrine is founded on the belief that there are two worlds, one we can readily see and experience with our senses and the other unseen and eternal. All objects in the sensory world are imperfect and transitory; the only true and perfect things, the eternal Ideas, exist in the abstract realm. Man's task in life is to struggle toward the ideal realm, the world of thought and spirit, by pursuing reason and logic. In this way, Plato hoped to address the concerns of his day. For Plato, democracy had failed, misdirect-

"Allegory of the Cave" is from Plato, *The Republic*, 7.514–7.521, in *The Dialogues of Plato*, vol. II, trans. Benjamin Jowett (Boston: The Aldine Publishing Company, 1911), pp. 265–274. Translation modernized by the editor.

ing society into constant turmoil, war, doubt, and depression. He saw a need to look to a higher ideal, a realm that was secure and offered answers and organization in a chaotic world. As Plato noted in his work The Republic, *"Until philosophers are kings or the kings and rulers of this world have the spirit of philosophy, until political power and wisdom are united . . . states will never have rest from their evils, nor . . . will the human race."*

The following passage from The Republic *explains Plato's Theory of Ideas. In the "Allegory of the Cave," he stresses the need to move away from the "shadows," which exist in the everyday realm of the senses, into the world of eternal truth and spiritual reality. Notice that Plato also believes that those who see the light, move toward it, and are thus freed from the captivity of the shadows, need to return in order to enlighten others; this is how civilization will progress.*

Behold! human beings living in an underground den, which has a mouth open toward the light and reaching all along the den; here they have been from their childhood, and have their legs and necks chained so that they cannot move, and can only see before them, being prevented by the chains from turning round their heads. Above and behind them a fire is blazing at a distance, and between the fire and the prisoners there is a raised way; and you will see, if you look, a low wall built along the way, like the screen which marionette players have in front of them, over which they show the puppets. And do you see men passing along the wall carrying all sorts of vessels, and statues and figures of animals made of wood and stone and various materials, which appear over the wall? Some of them are talking, others silent.

You have shown me a strange image, and they are strange prisoners.

Like ourselves, I replied; and they see only their own shadows, or the shadows of one another, which the fire throws on the opposite wall of the cave?

True, he said; how could they see anything but the shadows if they were never allowed to move their heads?

And of the objects which are being carried in like manner they would only see the shadows. And if they were able to converse with one another, would they not suppose that they were naming what was actually before them?

Very true.

And suppose further that the prison had an echo which came from the other side, would they not be sure to notice when one of the passersby spoke that the voice which they heard came from the passing shadows? To them the truth would be literally nothing but the shadows of the images.

And now look again, and see what will naturally follow if the prisoners are released and exonerated of their error. At first, when any of them is liberated and compelled suddenly to stand up and turn his neck around and walk and look toward the light, he will suffer sharp pains; the glare will distress him, and he will be unable to see the realities of which in his former state he had seen the shadows; and then conceive someone saying to him, that what he saw before was an illusion, but that now, when he is approaching nearer to being and his eye is turned toward more real existence, he has a clearer vision—what will be his reply? And you may further imagine that his instructor is pointing to the objects as they pass and requiring him to name them—will he not be perplexed? Will he not think that the shadows which he formerly saw are truer than the objects which are now shown him?

And if he is compelled to look straight at the light, will he not have a pain in his eyes which will make him turn away to take refuge in the objects of vision which he can see, and which he will conceive to be in reality clearer than the things which are now being shown to him?

And suppose once more, that he is reluctantly dragged up a steep and rugged ascent, and held fast until he is forced into the presence of the sun himself, is he not likely to be pained and irritated? When he approaches the light his eyes will be dazzled, and he will not be able to see anything at all of what are now called realities. He will require to grow accustomed to the sight of the upper world. And first he will see the shadows best, next the reflection of men and other objects in the water, and then the objects themselves; then he will gaze upon the light of the moon and the stars and the spangled heaven; and he will see the sky and the stars by night better than the sun or the light of the sun by day. Last of all he will be able to see the sun, and not mere reflections of him in the water, but he will see him in his own proper place, and not in another; and he will contemplate him as he is. He will then proceed to argue that this is he who gives the seasons and the years, and is the guardian of all that is in the visible world, and in a certain way the cause of all things which he and his fellows have accustomed to behold.

And when he remembered his old habitation, and the wisdom of the den and his fellow prisoners, do you not suppose that he would be happy about the change, and pity them? And if they were in the habit of conferring honors among themselves on those who were quickest to observe the passing shadows and to remark which of them went before, and which followed after, and which were together; and who were therefore best able to draw conclusions as to the future, do you think that he would care for such honors and glories or envy the possessors of them? Would he not say with Homer, "Better to be the poor servant of a poor master," and to endure anything, rather than think as they do and live after their manner?

Imagine once more such a one coming suddenly out of the sun to be replaced in his old situation; would he not be certain to have his eyes full of darkness? And if there were a contest, and he had to compete in measuring the shadows with the prisoners who had never moved out of the den, while his sight was still weak, and before his eyes had become steady (and the time which he needed to acquire this new habit of sight might be very considerable), would he not be ridiculous? Men would say of him that up he went and down he came without his eyes;

and that it was better not even to think of ascending; and if anyone tried to loose another and lead him up to the light, let them only catch the offender, and they would put him to death.

This entire allegory, you may now append, dear Glaucon, to the previous argument; the prison-house is the world of sight, the light of the fire is the sun, and you will not misunderstand me if you interpret the journey upwards to be the ascent of the soul into the intellectual world according to my poor belief, which, at your desire, I have expressed—whether rightly or wrongly God knows. But, whether true or false, my opinion is that in the world of knowledge the idea of good appears last of all, and is seen only with an effort: and, when seen, is also inferred to the universal author of all things beautiful and right, parent of light, and of the lord of light in this visible world, and the immediate source of reason and truth in the intellectual; and that this is the power upon which he who would act rationally either in public or private life must have his eye fixed.

I agree, he said, as far as I am able to understand you.

Moreover, you must not wonder that those who attain to this beatific vision are unwilling to descend to human affairs; for their souls are ever hastening into the upper world where they desire to dwell; which desire of theirs is very natural, if our allegory may be trusted.

Yes, very natural. . . .

Then the business of us who are the founder of the State will be to compel the best minds to attain that knowledge which has been already declared by us to be the greatest of all—they must continue to ascend until they arrive at the good; but when they have ascended and seen enough we must not allow them to do as they do now.

What do you mean?

I mean that they remain in the upper world: but this must not be allowed; they must be made to descend again among the prisoners in the den, and partake of their labors and honors, whether they are worth having or not.

But is not this unjust? he said; ought we to give them an inferior life, when they might have a superior one?

You have forgotten, my friend, the intention of the legislator, who did not aim at making any one class in the State happy above the rest; the happiness was to be in the whole State, and he held the citizens together by persuasion and necessity, making them benefactors of the State, and therefore benefactors of one another; to this end he created them, not that they should please themselves, but they were to be his instruments in binding up the State.

True, he said, I had forgotten.

Observe, Glaucon, that there will be no injustice in compelling our philosophers to have a care and providence of others; we shall explain to them that in other States, men of their class are not obliged to share in the toils of politics: and this is reasonable, for they grow up at their own sweet will, and the government would rather not have them. Now the wild plant which owes culture to nobody, has nothing to pay for culture. But we have brought you into the world to be rulers of the hive, kings of yourselves and of the other citizens, and have educated you far better and more perfectly than they have been educated, and you are better able to share in the double duty. Wherefore each of you, when his turn comes, must go down to the general underground abode, and get the habit of seeing in the dark; for all is habit; and by accustoming yourselves you will see ten thousand times better than the dwellers in the den, and you will know what the images are, and of what they are images, because you have seen the beautiful and just and good in their truth. And thus the order of our State, and of yours, will be a reality, and not a dream only, as the order of States too often is, for in most of them men are fighting with one another about shadows and are distracted in the struggle for power, which in their eyes is a great good. Whereas the truth is that the State in which the rulers are most reluctant to govern is best and most quietly governed, and the State in which they are most willing, the worst.

Quite true, he replied.

And will our pupils, when they hear this, refuse to share in turn the toils of State, when they are allowed to spend the greater part of their time with one another in the heaven of ideas? Impossible, he answered; for they are just men, and the commands which we impose upon them are just; there can be no doubt that every one of them will take office as a stern necessity, and not like our present ministers of State.

Yes, my friend, and there lies the point. You must contrive for your future rulers another and a better life than that of a ruler, and then you may have a well-ordered State; for only in the State which offers this, will they rule who are truly rich, not in silver and gold, but in virtue and wisdom, which are the true blessings of life. Whereas if they go to the administration of public affairs, poor and hungering after their own private advantage, thinking that hence they are to snatch the good of life, order there can never be; for they will be fighting about office, and the civil and domestic broils which thus arise will be the ruin of the rulers themselves and of the whole State.

Most true, he replied.

Against Communism

ARISTOTLE

Aristotle (384–322 B.C.E.) was another of the great philosophers of this era who would greatly influence thinkers in the Middle Ages. A student of Plato and tutor to Alexander the Great, Aristotle believed that ideal forms and truths existed but were not found in some abstract world apart from everyday life. In fact, one could discover Truth by observing sensory objects and then logically (through the process of induction) discerning their universal characteristics. Thus Aristotle was very

"Against Communism" is from Aristotle, *Politics,* 2.5, in *The Politics of Aristotle,* trans. Benjamin Jowett (Oxford: Oxford University Press, 1905), pp. 62–64.

practical and believed that all theories must be abandoned if they could not be observed to be true. Aristotle wrote widely on politics and ethics and is very contemporary in application. Note how many of the following ideas can be applied to our own world.

Next let us consider what should be our arrangements about property; should the citizens of the perfect state have possessions in common or not? . . .

There is always a difficulty in men living together and having things in common, but especially in their having common property. . . . Property should be in a certain sense common, but, as a general rule, private. For when everyone has his separate interest, men will not complain of one another, and they will make more progress, because everyone will be attending to his own business. Yet among good men, and as regards use, "friends," as the proverb says, "will have all things common." . . . For although every human has his own property, some things he will place at the disposal of his friends, while of others he shares the use of them. . . .

Again, how immeasurably greater is the pleasure, when a man feels a thing to be his own! For love of self is a feeling implanted by nature and not given in vain, although selfishness is rightly condemned. This, however, is not mere love of self, but love of self in excess, like the miser's love of money; for all, or almost all, men love money, and other such objects in a measure. Furthermore, there is the greatest pleasure in doing a kindness or service to friends or guests or companions, which can only be done when a man has private property. These advantages are lost by the excessive unification of the state. . . . No one, when men have all things in common, will any longer set an example of liberality or do any liberal action; for liberality consists in the use a man makes of his own property.

Such [communistic] legislation may have a specious appearance of benevolence. Men readily listen to it, and are easily induced to believe that in some wonderful manner everybody will become everybody's friend, especially when someone is heard denouncing the evils now existing in states, suits about contracts, convictions for perjury, flatteries of rich men and the like, which are said to arise out of the possession of private property. These evils, however, are due to a very different cause—the wickedness of human nature. Indeed, we see that there is much more quarreling among those who have all things in common, though there are not many of them when compared with the vast numbers who have private property.

Again, we ought to reckon, not only the evils from which the citizens will be saved, but also the advantages which they will lose. . . . Unity there should be, both of the family and of the state, but in some respects only. For there is a point at which a state may attain such a degree of unity as to be no longer a state, or at which, without actually ceasing to exist, it will become an inferior state, like harmony passing into unison, or rhythm which has been reduced to a single foot. The state, as I was saying, is a plurality, which should be united and made into a community by education. . . .

Virtue and Moderation: The Doctrine of the Mean
ARISTOTLE

Aristotle's principle concern in his Ethics is moral virtue, which might best be described as "good character." One obtains a good character by continually doing right acts until they become second

Nichomachean Ethics, Ostwald. Reprinted by permission of Pearson Education, Inc., Upper Saddle River, NJ., pp. 41–44.

nature. In defining "right action," Aristotle offers his Doctrine of the Mean, which serves as a guide toward achieving moral virtue and happiness. Right acts are those that lie between two extremes: courage, therefore, is the mean between the extremes of cowardice and rashness. Aristotle explains this in the following passage.

It is not sufficient, however, merely to define virtue in general terms as a characteristic: we must also specify what kind of characteristic it is. It must, then, be remarked that every virtue or excellence (1) renders good the thing itself of which it is the excellence, and (2) causes it to perform its function well. For example, the excellence of the eye makes both the eye and its function good, for good sight is due to the excellence of the eye. Likewise, the excellence of a horse makes it both good as a horse and good at running, at carrying its rider, and at facing the enemy. Now, if this is true of all things, the virtue or excellence of man, too, will be characteristic which makes him a good man, and which causes him to perform his own function well. . . .

Of every continuous entity that is divisible into parts it is possible to take the larger, smaller, or equal either in relation to the entity itself, or in relation to us. The "equal" part is something median between excess and deficiency. By the median of an entity I understand a point equidistant from both extremes, and this point is one and the same for everybody. By the median relative to us I understand an amount neither too large nor too small, and this is neither one nor the same for everybody. To take an example. . . if ten pounds of food is much for a man to eat and two pounds little, it does not follow that the trainer will prescribe six pounds, for this may in turn be much or little for him to eat; it may be little for Mile [the wrestler] and much for someone who has just begun to take up athletics. The same applies to running and wrestling. Thus we see that an expert in any field avoids excess and deficiency, but seeks the median and chooses it—not the median of the object but the median relative to us.

If this, then, is the way in which every science perfects its work, by looking to the median and by bringing its work up to that point—and this is the reason why it is usually said of a successful piece of work that it is impossible to detract from it or to add to it, the implication being that excess and deficiency destroy success while the mean safeguards it (good craftsmen, we say, look toward this standard in the performance of their work)—and if virtue, like nature, is more precise and better than any art, we must conclude that virtue aims at the median. I am referring to moral virtue: for it is moral virtue that is concerned with emotions and actions, and it is in emotions and actions that excess, deficiency, and the median are found. Thus we can experience fear, confidence, desire, anger, pity, and generally any kind of pleasure and pain either too much or too little, and in either case not properly. But to experience all this at the right time, toward the right objects, toward the right people, for the right reason, and in the right manner—that is the median and the best course, the course that is a mark of virtue.

Similarly, excess, deficiency, and the median can also be found in actions. Now virtue is concerned with emotions and actions; and in emotions and actions excess and deficiency miss the mark, whereas the median is praised and constitutes success. . . .

We may thus conclude that virtue or excellence is a characteristic involving choice, and that it consists in observing the mean relative to us, a mean which is defined by a rational principle, such as a man of practical wisdom would use to determine it. It is the mean by reference to two vices: the one of excess and the other of deficiency. It is, moreover, a mean because some vices exceed and the others fall short of what is required in emotion and in action, whereas virtue finds and chooses the median.

Epicureanism: Golden Maxims

EPICURUS

Hellenistic philosophy (after 323 B.C.E.) was concerned with surviving in an insecure world where political and social chaos was fast becoming a normal standard of life. Many people found consolation in the Stoic philosophy, which was fatalistic and advocated adherence to duty and responsibility (see Chapter 4: "The Roman Peace and the Dimensions of Empire"). One of the most popular schools of Hellenistic thought was founded by Epicurus (342–270 B.C.E.). The Epicureans denied that there was any interference of gods in human affairs or any life after death. All things were composed of atoms, which eventually returned to the "void." For an Epicurean, pleasure was the key to life. The following selections are maxims of Epicurus himself.

Pleasure is an original and natural good, but we do not choose every pleasure. Sometimes we avoid pleasures when a greater pain follows them; and many pains we consider preferable to pleasure when they lead eventually to a greater pleasure. Self-sufficiency is to be sought. Luxuries are hard to get, but natural things are easy and give us much pleasure.

When we say pleasure is the purpose of life, we do not mean the pleasures of the sensually self-indulgent, as some assert, but rather freedom from bodily pain and mental disturbance. The life of pleasure does not come from drinking or revels, or other sensual pleasures. It comes from sober thinking, the sensible investigation of what to choose and to avoid, and getting rid of ideas which agitate the soul. Common sense is our best guide. It tells us that we cannot live happily unless we live wisely, nobly, and justly without being happy. The virtues are inseparably linked with pleasure. For whom do you rate higher than the man who has correct beliefs about God, who has no fear of death, who has understood the purpose of Nature, who realizes that pain does not last long, and that Necessity, which some people consider the directing force of the world, is partly a matter of luck, and partly in our power?

• • •

Gods exist, but they are not as they are popularly thought to be. To destroy the gods as they are commonly thought to be is not impious; actually it is impious to have such distorted notions. The divine powers, blessed and incorruptible, neither are troubled themselves nor do they feel anger or gratitude toward men.

• • •

Accustom yourself to think that death means nothing to us. For what is good and bad is a matter of sensation, and death is an end of sensation. Grasping this principle makes human life pleasant, not by giving us any promise of immortality, but by freeing us from any desire for immortality. For there is nothing in life to be afraid of for a man who understands that he need not be afraid of its extinction. So death, usually regarded as the greatest of calamities, is actually nothing to us; for while we are, death is not, and when death is here, we are not. So death means nothing to either the living or the dead, for it has nothing to do with the living and the dead do not exist.

CHRONOLOGY: The Glory of Greece

776 B.C.E.   First Olympic Games. Athletic competition develops between small developing Greek city-states. Greek chronology reckoned in four-year periods from this date called "olympiads."

750–700 B.C.E.   Greeks emerge from Dark Ages and begin process of trading and colonizing throughout the Mediterranean. Greek alphabet based on letters, not syllables, adapted by Greeks, probably from the Phoenician example, and writing develops. The *Iliad* and the *Odyssey,* epic poems passed down through the Dark Ages by oral tradition, compiled and composed, perhaps by a poet named Homer (ca. 725 B.C.E.).

650 B.C.E.   Sparta quells a rebellion of helots (Messenian slaves) and defeats Argos in a long war. Reforms of Lycurgus make Spartan state into a military academy and camp.

600–550 B.C.E.   Age of Tyrants. Because of difficult economic conditions, factional divisions within the ruling Greek aristocracies often resulted in the establishment of tyrants, strongmen who restructured society and oversaw public works and security within the polis.

600–500 B.C.E.   Development of Early Greek Philosophy. Thales of Miletus (ca. 600 B.C.E.) and Pythagoras (ca. 550 B.C.E.) search for the primary elements around which life revolves and the numerical relationships and harmonies within the universe.

594 B.C.E.   Reforms of Solon in Athens to relieve debt slavery.

546–510 B.C.E.   Athens under the control of the tyrant Pisistratus and his sons.

508–501 B.C.E.   Cleisthenes institutes democratic reforms in Athens.

499–494 B.C.E.   Greek cities on the coast of Persian territory (Ionia) rebel.

490 B.C.E.   Battle of Marathon. Athenians led by Miltiades defeat Persian forces sent by Darius.

480 B.C.E.   Persian forces under Xerxes invade Greece, overcome Spartan resistance at Thermopylae, and burn Athens before being defeated under the command of Themistocles at the Battle of Salamis.

478 B.C.E.   Delian Confederacy established among Aegean islands and cities in order to protect against future Persian attacks. Athens supplies the commanders and administers the treasury on the island of Delos.

454 B.C.E.   Treasury of the Delian Confederacy moved from Delos to Athens. Confederacy is transformed into the Athenian Empire.

447 B.C.E.   Parthenon begun with funds garnered from the Delian Confederacy's treasury in Athens.

441 B.C.E.   *Antigone* by Sophocles performed at Athens. Wins first prize in the competition. Climax of Athenian tragic drama.

431–404 B.C.E.   The Peloponnesian War pits Athens against Sparta for leadership of the Greek world. Pericles expounds on Athenian greatness in his funeral oration (430 B.C.E.). "The Melian Dialogue" (416 B.C.E.) by Thucydides and *The Trojan Women* (415 B.C.E.) by Euripides emphasize the hypocrisy between the ideals of Athenian democracy and the brutalities of imperial rule.

399 B.C.E.   Trial and execution of Socrates, whose role as "gadfly" forced self-reflection upon the Athenian democracy.

404–403 B.C.E.   End of the Peloponnesian War and rule of the Thirty Tyrants in Athens.

400–371 B.C.E.   Spartan hegemony over Greece. Second Athenian Confederation established (378 B.C.E.).

371–362 B.C.E.   Rise of Thebes under the leadership of Epaminondas. Theban hegemony over Greece.

347 B.C.E.   Death of Plato, whose philosophy reflects disillusionment with democracy and advocates the rule of enlightened philosopher-kings.

359–338 B.C.E.   Philip II becomes King of Macedon (359 B.C.E.) and seeks involvement in Greek affairs. Debate in Athens between supporters who want Philip's leadership (Isocrates) and those who believe him dangerous to Greek freedom (Demosthenes). League of Corinth established (338 B.C.E.) after Greek defeat at Chaeronea.

336–323 B.C.E.   Reign of Alexander III, the Great. Accedes to power after assassination of his father, Philip II. Alexander invades Persia (334 B.C.E.), defeats King Darius III, and reaches Indus Valley (327 B.C.E.). Dies of fever and his generals carve up the parts of his empire that did not fall away immediately. Transition to Hellenistic ("Greek-like") era.

322 B.C.E.   Death of the philosopher Aristotle, student of Plato, teacher of Alexander.

STUDY QUESTIONS

1. What human themes dominate the *Odyssey?* Note specific passages in the selections from the *Odyssey* that support your ideas. How are Odysseus' cleverness and wit demonstrated in the story of the Cyclops? What qualities in a warrior are most appreciated? Compare Odysseus and Achilles in this respect. What do we learn about the Greek view of death from Odysseus' visit to the underworld? How do you interpret Achilles' reply to Odysseus' statement, "For you, Achilles, Death should have lost its sting"?

2. In the excerpt in which Odysseus returns to Ithaca, why does he decide to kill all the suitors of Penelope? What informal law in Greek society have the suitors violated? How did the Cyclops, Polyphemus, violate this same law? How did Penelope "test" Odysseus before she would accept him as her true husband? Why is Homer's *Odyssey* considered a classic of world literature?

3. How were the city-states of Athens and Sparta diametrically opposed? According to Pericles in his Funeral Oration, what qualities made Athens great? What was the basis of Spartan achievement?

4. Were the Persians justified in their invasions of Greece? In the accounts of the Persian Wars, what, for you, is the most memorable scene? In what ways did the Persian Wars benefit the Greeks?

5. In his Funeral Oration, how does Pericles justify Athenian imperialism? What benefits does Athens give her allies and what does she get in return? Is this equitable? Are there any weaknesses or defects in Pericles' arguments?

6. Note the dramatic selections by Sophocles. What are some of his main ideas about justice, responsibility, and law? How do these ideas reflect a prosperous civilization?

7. In "The Melian Dialogue," what is the basic argument of the Athenians? of the Melians? Choose the most effective phrases from this source and explain why they are important and what they reveal about the nature of power and democracy. Is Thucydides a moralist? What is his view of human nature?

8. In what ways does the excerpt from *The Trojan Women* by Euripides parallel the arguments of "The Melian Dialogue"? Be specific in your answer. What is Euripides trying to say about power and innocence? What does the production of this play say about the nature of freedom in Athens?

9. Thucydides, the historian, maintained that one of the reasons Athens lost the Peloponnesian War was that it was guilty of "hubris," or going beyond the limits imposed by the gods. Does this belief appear in Sophocles' plays? Be specific in your answer.

10. What can you discern from Aristophanes' *Lysistrata* about the treatment of women in Greek society? Note how critical the women are about how the war has been conducted. What was Aristophanes trying to do—criticize the state or make light of the impotent status of women? Do you regard satire as a legitimate vehicle for reform?

11. How is Socrates critical of the Athenian leaders in his Apology? What does he say in particular about freedom and virtue? Why is the condemnation of Socrates symbolic of the failure of Athenian civilization?

12. After reading the sources on Alexander the Great, describe what kind of man he was. Be specific in your answer. Do you think his actions warrant the epithet "the Great"? Does "greatness" imply more than conquest? Is it more difficult to conquer than it is to consolidate and rule territory? To what extent can an individual change the course of history?

13. In Plato's "Allegory of the Cave," how do you interpret the fire, shadows, and prisoners? How does Plato express his Theory of Ideas in this allegory?

14. How does Aristotle's philosophy differ from that of Plato? Do you agree with his assessment of communism? Define the "Doctrine of the Mean." Why is Aristotle called a "practical philosopher"?

15. Explain the nature of pleasure for an Epicurean philosopher. How would he define pleasure and what does it consist of? Do you consider Epicureanism to be a practical philosophy? Why or why not?

16. Can we call the fourth century B.C.E. and Hellenistic period an age of decline? How does it show decline, and how does it show progress? Be specific in your answer.

4

The Roman Peace
and the Dimensions of Empire

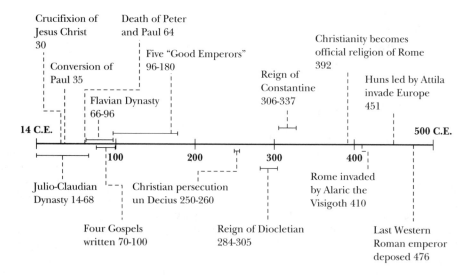

Crucifixion of
Jesus Christ
30

Death of Peter
and Paul 64

Five "Good Emperors"
96-180

Christianity becomes
official religion of Rome
392

Conversion of
Paul 35

Reign of
Constantine
306-337

Huns led by Attila
invade Europe
451

Flavian Dynasty
66-96

14 C.E.

500 C.E.

100   200   300   400

Julio-Claudian
Dynasty 14-68

Christian persecution
un Decius 250-260

Rome invaded
by Alaric the
Visigoth 410

Four Gospels
written 70-100

Reign of Diocletian
284-305

Last Western
Roman emperor
deposed 476

But you, Roman, must remember that you have to guide nations by your authority, for this is to be your skill, to graft tradition onto peace, to show mercy to the conquered, and to wage war until the haughty are brought low.

—*Virgil, Aeneid*

As yourselves, your empires fall. And every kingdom hath a grave.

—*William Hobbington*

We can destroy ourselves by cynicism and disillusionment just as effectively as by bombs.

—*Kenneth Clark*

Civilization is a stream with banks. The stream is sometimes filled with blood from people killing, stealing, shouting and doing things historians usually record, while on the banks, unnoticed, people build homes, make love, raise children, sing songs, [and] write poetry. . . . The history of civilization is the story of what happened on the banks.

—*Will and Ariel Durant*

CHAPTER THEMES

- *Systems of Government:* The system of government instituted by Augustus, called the "principate," functioned as a complex blend of power and authority. How well did his successors as emperors of Rome maintain his system of rule? Is freedom most im-

This contemporary view of the Roman Forum from the Palatine hill, which contained the palaces of the emperors, can now only hint at the majesty of the great capital of the Roman Empire and the busy "emporium of the world." (*Perry M. Rogers*)

portantly a thing of the mind? If the institutions of government are controlled, yet *appear* to be free, and if you *feel* that you are free, are you free?

- *Imperialism:* How did the Romans control their empire? Were they efficient rulers who were respected by their subjects? Is imperialism that results in political and social stability necessarily a bad thing?

- *Church/State Relationships:* What are the basic tenets of the Christian religion? Why did the Romans, who easily tolerated so many other religious cults, find the Christian religious movement so dangerous? Why were Christians persecuted? Can one serve both Caesar and Christ at the same time with equal devotion?

- *Historical Change and Transition:* What were the components of Roman decline? Did the Romans make specific mistakes, or is decline a natural and inevitable fate of each society? How much can a society change and adapt before it loses the elements that gave it purpose and success?

- *The Big Picture:* Is each civilization biological in nature and does it have a "life span" like human beings? What are the most important remnants of one civilization that form the seeds of the succeeding civilization?

The Roman Republic had once been hailed as a progressive society of balance and restraint, where freedom was guaranteed by law and defended with the blood of those committed to such ideals. Yet during the first century B.C.E., the Republic was destroyed, a victim of extremist political factions, domestic dissension, and violence. Roman armies, which had once silenced foreign foes, became the preserve of generals who were committed more to their personal advancement than to the security of the state. The Republic died amid the clash of civil war, and in its place flourished a "restored republic," the principate of Augustus.

The Augustan principate was designed to establish and maintain peace and harmony in the state. The institutions of the Republic were retained; people voted in the assemblies, senators vied for office and discussed issues in much the same way as they had done for years. Augustus, in his role as *princeps* (first citizen), merely advised the senate on issues that he thought were important for the welfare of the empire. But since the army was loyal to him and represented the true power in the state, Augustus' opinions and suggestions assumed the greatest importance. Yet Augustus maintained a political equilibrium by stressing his authority, not his blatant military power. He respected the dignity of the senators and their need to feel as if they actually controlled the government; in return, they generally supported his political solutions to the chaos of the Roman Republic. And although some senators grumbled and decried this facade of freedom, nevertheless the system worked for over two hundred years. Those succeeding emperors who played the game well, respected the dignity of the senate, and maintained control of the army usually survived and prospered. Those who did not, like the emperors Caligula and Domitian, were assassinated. Since the Augustan system of government brought political security to the state, the Roman Empire flourished in peace, a universal peace known as the Pax Romana. It was during this time that the city of Rome served as the emporium of the world. All roads indeed ended sooner or later in the center of the magnificent city, whose population swelled to a million inhabitants. To hail from the provinces of the empire and to see Rome for the first time must have been a numbing experience. The theaters, baths, sewers, aqueducts, and monuments provided services and entertainment on a magnificent scale. And the spectacle was even more impressive in the Coliseum, where gladiators fought, or in the Circus Maximus, where over 250,000 people could thrill to the chariot races.

Outside the city, a road system was built that connected the provinces of the empire and unified Europe as never before. The provincials were allowed to retain their own customs, languages, and religions; all Rome demanded in return were taxes and peace. It is testament to the loyalty and satisfaction of provincial subjects that Rome maintained the security of her enormous empire with only about 350,000 soldiers.

One aspect of civilization that stabilized Roman society was religion. The Romans had traditionally considered religion an important part of the prosperity of the state. They had established an intricate system of worship that employed nature gods, pagan deities syncretized from the Greeks, and a priesthood that saw to it the state enjoyed a close relationship with the gods by divining the future through the reading of animal entrails and the interpretation of omens. The state religion during the first century C.E. also came to include the worship of the emperor. Sacrifices to his health, however, were primarily patriotic in nature and did not demand or even encourage the emotional involvement of the people. For such satisfaction, many turned to the consoling logic of philosophy, the emotional excitement of oriental mystery cults, or to a new religion established in the early first century—Christianity.

The growth of Christianity from an obscure Jewish sect to the official religion of the Roman Empire during the first through fourth centuries is one of the most fascinating dramas in history. But success for Christianity did not come easily. In addition to facing competition from religious cults and philosophies, Christianity labored under misunderstandings fostered by anti-Christian propaganda. The Roman state was concerned not only with what was described as a morally dissolute religion, but perhaps most of all with the threat Christianity posed to the political stability of the state. Christians refused to worship the emperor (merely a token of political allegiance), and their talk of a "messiah" and a "kingdom" connoted political unrest and agitation. Rome tried to punish and even eradicate the religion in sporadic persecutions (Nero in 64, Decius in 250, Diocletian and Galerius from 303 to 311), but Roman policy was often confused and ambivalent. By 311, Christianity was tolerated and later endorsed by the Emperor Constantine. By the end of the fourth century, Christianity had become the official religion of the Roman Empire.

Perhaps the greatest failure in Western civilization was Rome's inability to sustain her hegemony. Confronted with political, social, and economic dislocation in the third century C.E., Rome struggled to survive. External pressures by Germanic tribes also took their toll on an increasingly overburdened army that no longer reflected the efficiency and tenacity of the famous Roman legions. The Roman Empire declined gradually, losing its unity and organization by the fifth century C.E. The eternal question is: Why?

This chapter will evaluate the Roman Empire during its era of strength and its period of decline. This is a particularly relevant chapter because many have compared Roman society to American society. Some have thus viewed Roman civilization as a laboratory in which we might see the seeds of our own destruction. But what are the components of greatness and decline? And can we ascertain our position along the way? Rome has many lessons to offer that continue to make its history important and meaningful.

THE ESTABLISHMENT OF THE AUGUSTAN PRINCIPATE

After the assassination of Julius Caesar in 44 B.C.E., a civil war ensued between the forces of Mark Antony, Caesar's chief lieutenant, and Octavian, Caesar's grand nephew and designated heir. By 27 B.C.E., Antony was dead and Octavian, by virtue of his military support, controlled the entire Roman Empire. At this point, he went to the senate and proclaimed that he had restored the Republic. Upon request of the senators, he decided to assume the advisory position of princeps or "first citizen" and the honorary title of "Augustus." The Republic was to function as it had in the past, with voting in the assemblies, election of magistrates, and traditional freedom. But as long as Augustus controlled the army, his "advice" could not be safely ignored. His system of government, called the principate, lasted in the same basic form until 180 C.E. The following accounts describe the powers of the princeps (or emperor, as he was also called). Note especially the cynicism of the historian Tacitus, who saw through the facade of republicanism and decried the loss of liberty.

The Powers and Authority of the Emperor

DIO CASSIUS

In this way the power of both people and senate passed entirely into the hands of Augustus, and from this time there was, strictly speaking, a monarchy; for monarchy would be the truest name for it. . . . Now, the Romans so detested the title "monarch" that they called their emperors neither dictators nor kings nor anything of this sort. Yet, since the final authority for government devolves upon them. . . . In order to preserve the appearance of having this authority not through their power but by virtue of the laws, the emperors have taken themselves all the offices (including the titles) which under the Republic possessed great power with the consent of the people. . . . Thus, they very often become consuls . . . instead of the . . . "king" or "dictator." These latter titles they have never assumed since they fell out of use in the constitution but the actuality of those offices is secured to them. . . . By virtue of the titles named, they secure the right to make levies, collect funds, declare war, make peace, and rule foreigners and citizens alike everywhere and always. . . .

From *Roman Civilization, Sourcebook II: The Empire* by N. Lewis and M. Reinhold, eds., © 1955 Columbia University Press, pp. 89–90. Reprinted with permission of the publisher.

Thus by virtue of these Republican titles they have clothed themselves with all the powers of the government, so that they actually possess all the prerogatives of kings without the usual title. For the appellation "Caesar" or "Augustus" confers upon them no actual power but merely shows in the one case that they are the successors of their family line, and in the other the splendour of their rank. The name "Father" perhaps gives them a certain authority over us all— the authority which fathers once had over their children; yet it did not signify this at first, but betokened honor and served as an admonition both to them to love their subjects as they would their children, and to their subjects to revere them as they would their fathers. . . .

Augustus did not enact all laws on his sole responsibility, but some of them he brought before the popular assembly in advance, in order that, if any features caused displeasure, he might learn it in time and correct them; for he encouraged everybody whatsoever to give him advice, in case anyone could think of any improvement in them, and he accorded them great freedom of speech; and he actually changed some provisions. Most important of all, he took as advisors. . . the consuls, . . . one of each of the other kinds of officials, and fifteen men chosen by lot from the remainder of the senatorial body, so that it was his custom to communicate proposed legislation after a fashion through these to all the other senators. For although he brought some matters before the whole senate, he generally followed this course, considering it better to take under preliminary advisement in a leisurely fashion most matters, and especially the most important ones, in consultation with a few; and sometimes he even sat with these men in trials. The senate as a body, it is true, continued to sit in judgment as before, and in certain cases transacted business with embassies and envoys from both peoples and kings; and the people and the plebs, moreover, continued to come together for the election; but nothing was actually done that did not please Caesar. At any rate, in the case of those who were to hold office, he himself selected and nominated some; and though he left the election of others in the hands of the people and the plebs, in accordance with the ancient practice, yet he took care that no persons should hold office who were unfit or elected as the result of factious combinations or bribery.

The Transition from Republic to Principate

TACITUS

Augustus won over the soldiers with gifts, the populace with cheap [grain], and all men with

"The Transition from Republic to Principate" is from Tacitus, *Annals*, 1.2–4, trans. Alfred Church and William Brodribb (New York: Macmillan and Co., 1891).

the sweets of repose, and so grew greater by degrees, while he concentrated in himself the functions of the Senate, the magistrates, and the laws. He was wholly unopposed, for the boldest spirits had fallen in battle, or in the proscription, while the remaining nobles, the readier they were to be slaves, were raised the higher by wealth and promotion, so that, aggrandised by revolution, they preferred the safety of the present to the dangerous past. Nor did the provinces dislike that condition of affairs, for they distrusted the government of the Senate and the people, because of the rivalries between the leading men and the rapacity of the officials. . . . At home all was tranquil, and there were magistrates with the same titles; there was a younger generation, sprung up since the victory of Actium, and even many of the older men had been born during the civil wars. How few were left who had seen the Republic.

Thus the State had been revolutionized, and there was not a vestige left of the old sound morality. Stripped of equality, all looked up to the commands of a sovereign without the least apprehension for the present, while Augustus in the vigour of life, could maintain his own position, that of his house, and the general tranquility.

STRENGTH AND SUCCESS
(14–180 C.E.)

Political and Military Control

The Augustan system of government generally functioned well during the first century C.E., outlasting bad emperors and a brief civil war, and prospering especially during the reigns of Tiberius, Claudius, and Vespasian. Rome's greatest achievement during this period was the establishment of peace throughout the empire, which was maintained by an efficient and dedicated army.

"The Whole World Speaks in Unison"

AELIUS ARISTEIDES

Extensive and sizable as the Empire is, perfect policing does much more than territorial boundaries to make it great. . . . Like a well-swept and fenced-in front yard . . . the whole world speaks in unison, more distinctly than a chorus; and so well does it harmonize under this director-in-chief that it joins in praying this Empire may last for all time. All everywhere are ruled equally. The mountain people are lowlier in their submissiveness than the inhabitants of the most exposed plains. The owners and occupants of rich plains are your peasants. Continent and island are no longer separate. Like one continuous country and one people, all the world quietly obeys. Everything is carried out by command or nod, and it is simpler than touching a string. If a need arises, the thing has only to be decided on, and it is done. The governors assigned to cities and provinces govern their various subjects; but among themselves and in relation to one another, all of them alike are governed . . . [by] the supreme governor, the chief executive [the emperor]. They are convinced that he knows what they are doing better than they know it themselves. They fear and respect him more than any slave could fear his master standing over him personally and giving orders. None of them are so proud that they can sit still if they so much as hear his name. They leap up, praise him, bow, and utter a double prayer—to the gods on behalf of him, and to him on their own behalf. If they felt the slightest doubt about their subjects' lawsuits, public or private, or whether petitions should be granted, they immediately send to him and ask what to do, and they wait for a signal from him, as a chorus from its director. No need for him to wear himself out making the rounds of the whole Empire, or to be in one place after another adjusting the af-

fairs of each people whenever he sets foot in their country. Instead, he can very easily sit and manage the whole world by letters, which are practically no sooner written than delivered, as if flown by birds. . . . The constitution is a universal democracy under the one man that can rule and govern best.

The Imperial Army

FLAVIUS JOSEPHUS

If one goes on to study the organization of [the Roman] army as a whole, it will be seen that this vast empire of theirs has come to them as the prize of valor, and not as a gift of fortune. For they do not wait for the outbreak of war, nor do they sit with folded hands in peacetime only to put them in motion in the hour of need. On the contrary, as though they had been born with weapons in hand, they never have a truce from training, never wait for the emergencies to arise. Moreover, their peacetime maneuvers are no less strenuous than veritable warfare; each soldier daily throws all his energy into his drill, as though he were in action. Hence that perfect ease with which they sustain the shock of battle. . . .

The Romans never lay themselves open to a surprise attack; for, whatever hostile territory they may invade, they engage in no battle until they have fortified their camp. . . . Thus an improvised city, as it were, springs up, with its market place, its artisan quarter, its judgment seats, where officers adjudicate any differences which may arise. The outer wall and all the installations within are completed more quickly than thought, so numerous and skilled are the workmen. . . . Once entrenched, the soldiers take up their quarters in their tents by companies, quietly and in good order. All their fatigue duties are performed with the same discipline, the same regard for security: the procuring of wood, of food supplies, and water, as required—each company having its allotted task. The hour for supper and breakfast is not left to individual discretion; all take their meals together. The hours for sleep, sentinel duty, and rising are announced by the sound of trumpets; nothing is done without a word of command. At daybreak the rank and file report to their respective centurions, the centurions go to salute the tribunes, the tribunes with all the officers then wait on the commander-in-chief, and he gives them according to custom the watchword and other orders to be communicated to the lower ranks. The same precision is maintained on the battlefield; the troops wheel smartly round in the requisite direction, and, whether advancing to the attack or retreating, all move as a unit.

When the camp is to be broken up, the trumpet sounds a first call; at that none remain idle; instantly, at this signal, they strike the tents and make all ready for departure. The trumpets sound a second call to prepare the march; at once they pile their baggage on the mules and other beasts of burden, and stand ready to start. . . . They then set fire to the encampment, both because they can easily construct another. . . and to prevent the enemy from ever making use of it. A third time the trumpets give a similar signal for departure, to hasten the movements of stragglers, whatever the reason for their delay, and to ensure that none is out of his place in the ranks. Then the herald, standing on the right of the commander, inquires in their native tongue whether they are ready for war. Three times they loudly and lustily shout in reply, "We are ready," some even anticipating the question; and worked up to a kind of martial frenzy, they raise their right arms in the air along with the shout. . . .

The infantry are armed with cuirasses and helmets and carry a sword on either side; that on the left is far the longer of the two, the dagger on the right being no longer than a span. The picked infantry, forming the general's

The Pont du Gard, perhaps the most majestic of all Roman ruins, was an aqueduct that carried water through southern France. The provinces were thus served by Roman engineering genius. (*Perry M. Rogers*)

guard, carry a spear and round shield, the regiments of the line a javelin and oblong shield; the equipment of the latter includes, further, a saw, a basket, a pick, and an axe, not to mention a strap, a bill-hook, a chain, and three days' rations, so that an infantry man is almost as heavily laden as a pack mule. . . .

By their military exercises the Romans instill into their soldiers fortitude not only of body but also of soul; fear, too, plays its part in their training. For they have laws which punish with death not merely desertion but even a slight neglect of duty; and their generals are held in even greater awe than the laws. For the high honors with which they reward the brave prevent the offenders whom they punish from regarding themselves as treated cruelly.

This perfect discipline with regard to their generals makes the army an ornament of peacetime, and in battle welds the whole into a single body; so compact are their ranks, so alert their movements in wheeling, so quick their ears for orders, their eyes for signals, their hands for tasks. Prompt as they consequently ever are in action, none are slower than they in succumbing to suffering, and never have they been known in any predicament to be beaten by numbers, by ruses, by difficulties of terrain, or even by fortune; for victory is more certain for them than fortune.

Submission and Safety

TACITUS

Although Rome was generally a benign master, there were rebellions, especially on the part of the Jews, whose revolt from 66 to 70 C.E. ended with the methodical elimination of the rebels at Masada and the consequent destruction of the Temple at Jerusalem. The following excerpt relates the aftermath of a rebellion of the Gauls in 70 C.E. The Roman commander bluntly and realistically sums up the imperial policy of submission and safety and the advantages to be obtained through cooperation.

"Gaul always had its petty kingdoms and intestine wars, till you submitted to our authority. We, though so often provoked, have used the right of conquest to burden you only with the cost of maintaining peace. For the tranquility of nations cannot be preserved without armies; armies cannot exist without pay; pay cannot be furnished without tribute; all else is common between us. You often command our legions. You rule these and other provinces. There is no privilege, no exclusion. From worthy Emperors you derive equal advantage, though you dwell so far away, while cruel rulers are most formidable to their neighbors. Endure the passions and rapacity of your masters, just as you bear barren seasons and excessive rains and other natural evils. There will be vices as long as there are men. But they are not perpetual, and they are compensated by the occurrence of better things. . . . Should the Romans be driven out (which God forbid) what can result but wars between all these nations? By the prosperity and order of eight hundred years has this fabric of empire been consolidated, nor can it be overthrown without destroying those who overthrow it. Yours will be the worst peril, for you have gold and wealth, and these are the chief incentives to war. Give therefore your love and respect to the cause of peace, and to that capital in which we, conquerors and conquered, claim an equal

"Submission and Safety" is from Tacitus, *Histories*, 4.73–74, trans. Alfred Church and William Brodribb (New York: Macmillan, 1894).

right. Let the lessons of fortune in both its forms teach you not to prefer rebellion and ruin to submission and safety." With words to this ef-fect he quieted and encouraged his audience, who feared harsher treatment.

"They Make a Desolation and Call It Peace"

TACITUS

These famous words were written by Tacitus, a senator and later critic of Rome. The following selec-tion is a speech that Tacitus attributes to the Caledonian chieftain Galgacus, just before his defeat at the hands of Roman armies. His sentiments balance the view of Rome as the protector of freedom. Not everyone believed it.

Whenever I consider the origin of this war and the necessities of our position, I have a sure con-fidence that this day, and this union of yours, will be the beginning of freedom to the whole of Britain. . . . Now, however, the furthest limits of Britain are thrown open, and the unknown al-ways passes for the marvelous. But there are no tribes beyond us, nothing indeed but waves and rocks, and the yet more terrible Romans, from whose oppression escape is vainly sought by obe-dience and submission. Robbers of the world, having by their universal plunder exhausted the land, they rifle the deep. If the enemy be rich, they are rapacious; if he be poor, they lust for dominion; neither the east nor the west has been able to satisfy them. Alone among men they covet with equal eagerness poverty and riches. To robbery, slaughter, plunder, they give the lying name of empire; they make a desola-tion and call it "peace."

"'They Make a Desolation and Call It Peace'" is from Tacitus, *Agricola*, 29–30, trans. Alfred Church and William Brodribb (New York: Macmillan, 1877).

"All Roads Lead to Rome!"

The city of Rome was the vibrant center of this extensive empire. It provided services and entertain-ment to a teeming population of about one million inhabitants from all over the world. The follow-ing excerpts reveal the advantages and disadvantages of city life.

The Glory of the City

STRABO

[The Romans] paved the roads, cut through hills, and filled up valleys, so that the merchan-dise may be conveyed by carriage from the ports. The sewers, arched over with hewn stones, are large enough in parts for actual hay wagons to pass through, while so plentiful is the supply of water from the aqueducts, that rivers may be said to flow through the city and the sew-ers, and almost every house is furnished with water pipes and copious fountains.

We may remark that the ancients [of Re-publican times] bestowed little attention upon the beautifying of Rome. But their successors,

"The Glory of the City" is from Strabo, *Geography*, 5.3.8, in *Readings in Ancient History*, vol. 2, ed. William S. Davis (Boston: Allyn and Bacon, 1913), pp. 179–181.

A view of the Arch of Titus and the magnificent Roman Coliseum beyond. Each successive building "caused you speedily to forget that which you have seen before. Such then is Rome!"— Strabo. (*Perry M. Rogers*)

and especially those of our own day, have at the same time embellished the city with numerous and splendid objects. Pompey, the Divine Caesar [i.e., Julius Caesar], and Augustus, with his children, friends, wife, and sister have surpassed all others in their zeal and munificence in these decorations. The greater number of these may be seen in the Campus Martius which to the beauties of nature adds those of art. The size of the plain is remarkable, allowing chariot races and the equestrian sports without hindrance, and multitudes [here] exercise themselves with ball games, in the Circus, and on the wrestling grounds. . . . The summit of the hills beyond the Tiber, extending from its banks with panoramic effect, present a spectacle which the eye abandons with regret.

Near to this plain is another surrounded with columns, sacred groves, three theaters, an amphitheater, and superb temples, each close to the other, and so splendid that it would seem idle to describe the rest of the city after it. For this cause the Romans esteeming it the most sacred place, have erected funeral monuments there to the illustrious persons of either sex. The most remarkable of these is that called the "Mausoleum" [the tomb of Augustus] which consists of a mound of earth raised upon a high foundation of white marble, situated near the river, and covered on the top with evergreen shrubs. Upon the summit is a bronze statue of Augustus Caesar, and beneath the mound are the funeral urns of himself, his relatives, and his friends. Behind is a large grove containing charming promenades. . . . If then you proceed to visit the ancient Forum, which is equally filled with basilicas, porticoes, and temples, you will there behold the Capitol, the Palatine, and the noble works that adorn them, and the piazza of Livia [Augustus' Empress],—each successive work causing you speedily to forget that which you have seen before. Such then is Rome!

Rome: The Emporium of the World

AELIUS ARISTEIDES

Around [the Mediterranean] lie the continents far and wide, pouring an endless flow of goods to you. There is brought from every land and sea whatever is brought forth by the seasons and is produced by all countries, rivers, lakes, and the skills of Greeks and foreigners. So that anyone who wants to behold all these products must either journey through the whole world to see them or else come to this city. For whatever is raised or manufactured by each people is assuredly always here to overflowing. So many merchantmen arrive here with cargoes from all over, at every season, and with each return of the harvest, that the city seems like a common warehouse of the world. . . . The arrival and departure of ships never ceases, so that it is astounding that the sea—not to mention the harbor—suffices for the merchantmen. . . . And all things converge here, trade, seafaring, agriculture, metallurgy, all the skills which exist and have existed, anything that is begotten and grows. Whatever cannot be seen here belongs completely to the category of nonexistent things.

The Dark Side of Rome

JUVENAL

I cannot bear, Romans, a Greek Rome; and yet, how small a portion of our dregs is from Greece! Long since, Syrian Orontes [a river] has flowed into the Tiber, and has brought with it its language and manners. . . . The coming of the Greek has brought us a Jack-of-all-trades—grammarian, rhetorician, geometrician, painter,

From *Roman Civilizatin, Sourcebook II: The Empire* by N. Lewis and M. Reinhold, eds., © 1955 Columbia University Press, pp. 208–209. Reprinted with permission of the publisher.

"The Dark Side of Rome" is from Juvenal, *Satires*, 3, trans. J. D. Lewis (London: Trubner, 1873).

wrestling manager, prophet, rope-walker, physician, magician; he knows everything. Bid the hungry Greekling go to heaven, he will go. . . . The poor among the Romans ought to have emigrated in a body long ago. Not easily do those emerge from obscurity whose noble qualities are cramped by domestic poverty. But at Rome the attempt is still harder for them; a great price must be paid for a wretched lodging, a great price for slaves' keep, a great price for a modest little dinner. A man is ashamed to dine off earthenware. . . . Here splendour of dress is carried beyond people's means; here something more than is enough is occasionally borrowed from another man's strongbox. This vice is common to all of us; here all of us live in a state of pretentious poverty. In a word, in Rome everything costs money. . . .

Many a sick man dies here from want of sleep, the sickness itself having been produced by undigested food clinging to the fevered stomach. For what rented lodgings allow of sleep? It takes great wealth to sleep in the city. Hence the origin of the disease. The passage of carriages in the narrow winding streets, and the abuse of the drivers of the blocked teams would rob even [the heaviest sleepers] of sleep.

If a social duty calls him, the rich man will be carried through the yielding crowd and will speed over their heads on his huge Liburnian litter bearers; he will read on his way, or write, or even sleep inside, for a litter with closed windows induces sleep. Yet he will arrive before us. We in our hurry are impeded by the wave in front, while the multitude which follows us presses on our back in dense array; one strikes me with his elbow, another with a hard pole, one knocks a beam against my head, another a wine jar. My legs are sticky with mud; before long I am trodden on all sides by large feet, and the hobnails of a soldier stick into my toe. . . .

Observe now the different and varied dangers of the night. What a height it is to the lofty roofs, from which a tile brains you, and how often cracked and broken utensils fall from windows—with what a weight they mark and damage the pavement when they strike it! You may well be accounted remiss and improvident about sudden accidents if you go out to supper without making a will. There are just so many fatal chances as there are wakeful windows open at night when you are passing by. Hope, then, and carry this pitiable prayer about with you, that they may be content merely to empty broad wash basins over you.

"Bread and Circuses"

FRONTO

The emperors were very careful not to neglect the basic needs of the inhabitants of Rome. Since an idle population was prone to boredom and rioting, the emperors promoted building programs that not only increased the glory of the city but also employed the masses. A sizable number of citizens were on the grain dole, a welfare program, that offered free grain for those who could not afford to buy it. It was therefore essential that grain ships arrived from Egypt on a regular basis, for a hungry populace was also prone to disturbance. Finally, the people demanded entertainment, and Rome responded with gladiatorial games in the Coliseum and chariot races in the Circus Maximus. The Circus was especially popular and could hold 250,000 people at one time—a quarter of the population of Rome! "Bread and Circuses" were the essential ingredients of harmony in the great city.

It was the height of political wisdom for the emperor not to neglect even actors and the other performers of the stage, the circus, and the arena, since he knew that the Roman people is held fast by two things above all, the grain supply and the shows, that the success of the government depends on amusements as much as on serious things. Neglect of serious matters entails the greater detriment, of amusements

the greater unpopularity. The money largesses are less eagerly desired than the shows; the largesses appease only the grain-doled plebs singly and individually, while the shows keep the whole population happy.

Gladiatorial Combat

SENECA

By chance I attended a mid-day exhibition, expecting some fun, wit, and relaxation—an exhibition at which men's eyes have respite from the slaughter of their fellow-men. But it was quite the reverse. The previous combats were the essence of compassion; but now all the trifling is put aside and it is pure murder. The men have no defensive armour. They are exposed to blows at all points, and no one ever strikes in vain. . . . In the morning they throw men to the lions and the bears; at noon, they throw them to the spectators. The spectators demand that the slayer shall face the man who is to slay him in his turn; and they always reserve the latest conqueror for another butchering. The outcome of every fight is death, and the means are fire and sword. This sort of thing goes on while the arena is empty. You may retort: "But he was a highway robber; he killed a man!" And what of it? Granted that, as a murderer, he deserved this punishment, what crime have you committed, poor fellow, that you should deserve to sit and see this show? In the morning they cried "Kill him! Lash him! Burn him! Why does he meet the sword in so cowardly a way? Why does he strike so feebly? Why doesn't he die game? Whip him to meet his wounds! Let them receive blow for blow, with chests bare and exposed to the stroke!" And when the games stop for the intermission, they announce: "A little throat-cutting in the meantime, so that there may still be something going on!"

From *Roman Civilization, Sourcebook II: The Empire* by N. Lewis and M. Reinhold, eds., © 1955 Columbia University Press, pp. 229–230. Reprinted with permission of the publisher.

"Gladiatorial Combat" is reprinted by permission of the publishers and the Loeb Classical Library from Seneca, *Moral Epistles*, 7.3–5, trans. Richard Gummere, vol. 1 (Cambridge, MA: Harvard University Press, 1917), pp. 31, 33.

The Stoic Philosophy

The Romans were never known for their contributions to abstract thought and did not produce a unique philosophy. Still, they borrowed well and adapted ideas that complemented their values. For the Roman, duty and organization were particularly important; consequently, the Stoic philosophy, which had originated in Greece in the third century B.C.E., was especially popular among the aristocracy. According to Stoic tenets, a divine plan ordered the universe, so whatever lot or occupation fell to one in life should be accepted and coped with appropriately. Restraint and moderation characterized the ideal Stoic, and he advocated tolerance as an essential component of the "brotherhood of man." To a Stoic who felt that his honor was somehow compromised, suicide was an acceptable and dutiful way of preserving his dignity. The following selections come from the writings of three Stoics of diverse backgrounds. Epictetus was the slave of a rich freedman; Seneca was tutor to the emperor Nero and finally committed suicide at his command in 66 C.E.; Marcus Aurelius became emperor in 161 C.E., an occupation he did not seek, but dutifully executed.

"How Will I Die?"
EPICTETUS

I must die: if instantly, I will die instantly; if in a short time, I will dine first; and when the hour comes, then I will die. How? As becomes one who restores what is not his own.

Do not you know that both sickness and death must overtake us? At what employment? The husbandman at his plough; the sailor on his voyage. At what employment would you be taken? For my own part, I would be found engaged in nothing but in the regulation of my own Will; how to render it undisturbed, unrestrained, uncompelled, free. I would be found studying this, that I may be able to say to God, "Have I transgressed Thy commands? Have I perverted the powers, the senses, the instincts, which Thou hast given me? Have I ever accused Thee, or censured Thy dispensations? I have been sick, because it was Thy pleasure, like others; but I willingly. I have been poor, it being Thy will; but with joy. I have not been in power, because it was not Thy will; and power I have never desired. Hast Thou ever seen me saddened because of this? Have I not always approached Thee with a cheerful countenance; prepared to execute Thy commands and the indications of Thy will? Is it Thy pleasure that I should depart from this assembly? I depart. I give

Thee all thanks that Thou hast thought me worthy to have a share in it with Thee; to behold Thy works, and to join with Thee in comprehending Thy administration." Let death overtake me while I am thinking, while I am writing, while I am reading such things as these.

"What Is the Principal Thing in Life?"
SENECA

What is the principal thing in human life? . . . To raise the soul above the threats and promises of fortune; to consider nothing as worth hoping for. For what does fortune possess worth setting your heart upon? . . . What is the principal thing? To be able to endure adversity with a joyful heart; to bear whatever occurs just as if it were the very thing you desired to have happen to you. For you would have felt it your duty to desire it, had you known that all things happen by divine decree. Tears, complaints, lamentations are rebellion [against divine order]. . . .

What is the principal thing? To have life on the very lips, ready to issue when summoned. This makes a man free, not by right of Roman citizenship but by right of nature. He is, moreover, the true freeman who has escaped from

"'How Will I Die?'" is from T. W. Higginson, ed., *The Works of Epictetus* (Boston: Little Brown, 1886).

"'What Is the Principal Thing in Life?'" is from Seneca, *Natural Questions*, 3. Preface, 10–17, trans. J. Clarke (London, 1910).

bondage to self; that slavery is constant and unavoidable—it presses us day and night alike, without pause, without respite. To be a slave to self is the most grievous kind of slavery; yet its fetters may easily be struck off, if you will cease to make large demands upon yourself, if you will cease to seek a personal reward for your services, and if you will set before your eyes your nature and your age, even though it be the bloom of youth; if you will say to yourself, "Why do I rave, and pant, and sweat? Why do I ply the earth? Why do I haunt the Forum? Man needs but little, and that not for long."

Meditations

MARCUS AURELIUS

1. He who acts unjustly acts impiously. For since the universal nature has made rational animals for the sake of one another to help one another according to their deserts, but in no way to injure one another, he who transgresses her will, is

"Meditations" is from Marcus Aurelius, *Meditations*, trans. George Long (London: The Chesterfield Library, 1862), pp. 241–242, 253.

clearly guilty of impiety towards the highest divinity. And he too who lies is guilty of impiety to the same divinity; for there is a universal nature of things that are; and things that are have a relation to all things that come into existence.

2. It would be a man's happiest lot to depart from mankind without having had any taste of lying and hypocrisy and luxury and pride. However, to breathe out one's life when a man has had enough of these things is the next best voyage, as the saying goes. . . .

3. Do not despise death, but be well content with it, since this too is one of those things which nature wills. For such as it is to be young and to grow old, and to increase and to reach maturity, and to have teeth and beard and grey hairs, and to beget, and to be pregnant and to bring forth, and all the other natural operations which the seasons of thy life bring, such also is dissolution. This, then, is consistent with the character of a reflecting man, to be neither careless nor impatient nor contemptuous with respect to death, but to wait for it as one of the operations of nature. . . .

4. Wipe out imagination: check desire: extinguish appetite: keep the ruling faculty in its own power.

CAESAR AND CHRIST

The Message of Jesus

The New Testament of the Bible records the life of Jesus in four Gospels (Matthew, Mark, Luke, and John), the Acts of the Apostles, twenty-one Epistles (didactic letters), and the book of Revelation. The New Testament is the primary source for the teaching of Jesus, who was crucified by the Romans about 30 C.E. The following excerpts relate some of the more pacifistic Christian beliefs regarding love, sympathy, forgiveness, and the nature of the Kingdom of God.

The Baptism of Jesus

Jesus left Galilee and went to the Jordan River to be baptized by John. But John kept objecting

The Baptism of Jesus from Matthew 3:13–17, 4:17 from the *Good News Translation*-Second Edition; Today's English Version © 1992 American Bible Society, New York, NY 10023, www.americanbible.org. Used by permission.

and said, "I ought to be baptized by you. Why have you come to me?" Jesus answered, "For now this is how it should be, because we must do all that God wants us to do." Then John agreed.

So Jesus was baptized. And as soon as he came out of the water, the sky opened, and he saw the Spirit of God coming down on him like a dove. Then a voice from heaven said, "This is my own dear Son, and I am pleased with him.". . .

Then Jesus started preaching, "Turn back to God! The kingdom of heaven will soon be here."

The Sermon on the Mount

Jesus Teaches, Preaches, and Heals

Jesus went all over Galilee, teaching in the Jewish meeting places and preaching the good news about God's kingdom. He also healed every kind of disease and sickness. News about him spread all over Syria, and people with every kind of sickness or disease were brought to him. Some of them had a lot of demons in them, others were thought to be crazy, and still others could not walk. But Jesus healed them all. Large crowds followed Jesus from Galilee and the region around the ten cities known as Decapolis. They also came from Jerusalem, Judea, and from across the Jordan River.

The Beatitudes

When Jesus saw the crowds, he went up on the side of a mountain and sat down. Jesus' disciples gathered around him, and he taught them: God blesses those people who depend only on him. They belong to the kingdom of heaven! God blesses those people who grieve. They will find comfort! God blesses those people who are humble. The earth will belong to them! God blesses those people who want to obey him more than to eat or drink. They will be given what they want! God blesses those people who are merciful. They will be treated with mercy! God blesses those people whose hearts are pure. They will see him! God blesses those people who make peace. They will be called his children! God blesses those people who are treated badly for doing right. They belong to the kingdom of heaven. God will bless you when people insult you, mistreat you, and tell all kinds of evil lies about you because of me.

Be happy and excited! You will have a great reward in heaven. People did these same things to the prophets who lived long ago.

Salt and Light

You are like salt for everyone on earth. But if salt no longer tastes like salt, how can it make food salty? All it is good for is to be thrown out and walked on. You are like light for the whole world. A city built on top of a hill cannot be hidden, and no one would light a lamp and put it under a clay pot. A lamp is placed on a lampstand, where it can give light to everyone in the house. Make your light shine, so that others will see the good that you do and will praise your Father in heaven.

The Law of Moses

Don't suppose that I came to do away with the Law and the Prophets. I did not come to do away with them, but to give them their full meaning. Heaven and earth may disappear. But I promise you that not even a period or comma will ever disappear from the Law. Everything written in it must happen. If you reject even the least important command in the Law and teach others to do the same, you will be the least important person in the kingdom of heaven. But if you obey and teach others its commands, you will have an important place in the kingdom. You must obey God's commands better than the Pharisees and the teachers of the Law obey them. If you don't, I promise you that you will never get into the kingdom of heaven.

Anger

You know that our ancestors were told, "Do not murder" and "A murderer must be brought to trial." But I promise you that if you are angry with someone, you will have to stand trial. If you call someone a fool, you will be taken to court. And if you say that someone is worthless, you will be in danger of the fires of hell. So if you

The Sermon on the Mount from Matthew 4:23–25; 5:1–25; 5:38–48; 6:5–15 from the *Good News Translation*-Second Edition; Today's English Version © 1992 American Bible Society, New York, NY 10023, www.americanbible.org. Used by permission.

are about to place your gift on the altar and remember that someone is angry with you, leave your gift there in front of the altar. Make peace with that person, then come back and offer your gift to God.

Revenge

You know that you have been taught, "An eye for an eye and a tooth for a tooth." But I tell you not to try to get even with a person who has done something to you. When someone slaps your right cheek, turn and let that person slap your other cheek. If someone sues you for your shirt, give up your coat as well. If a soldier forces you to carry his pack one mile, carry it two miles. When people ask you for something, give it to them. When they want to borrow money, lend it to them.

Love

You have heard people say, "Love your neighbors and hate your enemies." But I tell you to love your enemies and pray for anyone who mistreats you. Then you will be acting like your Father in heaven. He makes the sun rise on both good and bad people. And he sends rain for the ones who do right and for the ones who do wrong. If you love only those people who love you, will God reward you for that? Even tax collectors love their friends. If you greet only your friends, what's so great about that? Don't even unbelievers do that? But you must always act like your Father in heaven.

Prayer

When you pray, don't be like those show-offs who love to stand up and pray in the meeting places and on the street corners. They do this just to look good. I can assure you that they already have their reward. When you pray, go into a room alone and close the door. Pray to your Father in private. He knows what is done in private, and he will reward you. When you pray, don't talk on and on as people do who don't know God. They think God likes to hear long prayers. Don't be like them. Your Father knows what you need before you ask. You should pray like this:

> Our Father in heaven,
> help us to honor your name.
> Come and set up your kingdom,
>   so that everyone on earth will obey you,
>   as you are obeyed in heaven.
> Give us our food for today.
> Forgive us for doing wrong, as we forgive
>   others.
> Keep us from being tempted and protect
>   us from evil.

If you forgive others for the wrongs they do to you, your Father in heaven will forgive you. But if you don't forgive others, your Father will not forgive your sins.

The Good Samaritan

An expert in the Law of Moses stood up and asked Jesus a question to see what he would say. "Teacher," he asked, "what must I do to have eternal life?" Jesus answered, "What is written in the Scriptures? How do you understand them?" The man replied, "The Scriptures say, 'Love the Lord your God with all your heart, soul, strength, and mind.' They also say, 'Love your neighbors as much as you love yourself.'" Jesus said, "You have given the right answer. If you do this, you will have eternal life."

But the man wanted to show that he knew what he was talking about. So he asked Jesus, "Who are my neighbors?" Jesus replied: "As a man was going down from Jerusalem to Jericho, robbers attacked him and grabbed everything he had. They beat him up and ran off, leaving him half dead. A priest happened to be going down the same road. But when he saw the man, he walked by on the other side. Later a temple helper came to the same place. But when he saw the man who had been beaten up, he also went

The Good Samaritan from Luke 10:25–37 from the *Good News Translation*-Second Edition; Today's English Version © 1992 American Bible Society, New York, NY 10023, www. americanbible.org. Used by permission.

by on the other side. A man from Samaria then came traveling along that road. When he saw the man, he felt sorry for him and went over to him. He treated his wounds with olive oil and wine and bandaged them. Then he put him on his own donkey and took him to an inn, where he took care of him. The next morning he gave the innkeeper two silver coins and said, 'Please take care of the man. If you spend more than this on him, I will pay you when I return.'" Then Jesus asked, "Which one of these three people was a real neighbor to the man who was beaten up by robbers?" The teacher answered, "The one who showed pity." Jesus said, "Go and do the same!"

The Mission of Jesus

One of the more difficult regions of the empire for the Roman government to manage was the province of Judea. Encompassing the Jewish homeland, it was a continual hotbed of disagreement and dissatisfaction. The career of a Roman administrator might easily be placed in jeopardy if he failed to maintain peace. Although much of this dissent was in response to Roman occupation of the area, various Jewish sects also competed among themselves for influence in the region. Thus, the appearance of a young, popular leader who was proclaimed by some as "King of the Jews" and who himself claimed to be the long-awaited Messiah, gave pause to both the Jewish hierarchy and Roman authorities. The following selections from Matthew reveal Jesus's own conception of his mission.

Instructions to the Twelve Disciples

Jesus Chooses His Twelve Apostles

Jesus called together his twelve disciples. He gave them the power to force out evil spirits and to heal every kind of disease and sickness. The first of the twelve apostles was Simon, better known as Peter. His brother Andrew was an apostle, and so were James and John, the two sons of Zebedee. Philip, Bartholomew, Thomas, Matthew the tax collector, James the son of Alphaeus, and Thaddaeus were also apostles. The others were Simon, known as the Eager One, and Judas Iscariot, who later betrayed Jesus.

Instructions for the Twelve Apostles

Jesus sent out the twelve apostles with these instructions: "Stay away from the Gentiles and don't go to any Samaritan town. Go only to the people of Israel, because they are like a flock of lost sheep. As you go, announce that the kingdom of heaven will soon be here. Heal the sick, raise the dead to life, heal people who have leprosy, and force out demons. You received without paying, now give without being paid. Don't take along any gold, silver, or copper coins. And don't carry a traveling bag or an extra shirt or sandals or a walking stick. Workers deserve their food.

So when you go to a town or a village, find someone worthy enough to have you as their guest and stay with them until you leave. When you go to a home, give it your blessing of peace. If the home is deserving, let your blessing remain with them. But if the home isn't deserving, take back your blessing of peace. If someone won't welcome you or listen to your message, leave their home or town. And shake the dust from your feet at them. I promise you that the day of judgment will be easier for the towns of Sodom and Gomorrah than for that town.

Warning about Trouble

I am sending you like lambs into a pack of wolves. So be as wise as snakes and as innocent as doves. Watch out for people who will take you to court and have you beaten in their meeting places. Because of me, you will be dragged before rulers and kings to tell them and the Gentiles about your faith. But when someone arrests you, don't worry about what you will say or how you will say it. At that time you will be given the words to say. But you will not really be the one speaking. The Spirit from your Father will tell you what to say.

Brothers and sisters will betray one another and have each other put to death. Parents will betray their own children, and children will turn against their parents and have them killed. Everyone will hate you because of me. But if you remain faithful until the end, you will be saved. When people mistreat you in one town, hurry to another one. I promise you that before you have gone to all the towns of Israel, the Son of Man will come. . . .

Not Peace, but Trouble

"Don't think that I came to bring peace to the earth! I came to bring trouble, not peace. I came to turn sons against their fathers, daughters against their mothers, and daughters-in-law against their mothers-in-law. Your worst enemies will be in your own family. If you love your father or mother or even your sons and daughters more than me, you are not fit to be my disciples. And unless you are willing to take up your cross and come with me, you are not fit to be my disciples. If you try to save your life, you will lose it. But if you give it up for me, you will surely find it.

Rewards

"Anyone who welcomes you welcomes me. And anyone who welcomes me also welcomes the one who sent me. Anyone who welcomes a prophet, just because that person is a prophet, will be given the same reward as a prophet. Anyone who welcomes a good person, just because that person is good, will be given the same reward as a good person. And anyone who gives one of my most humble followers a cup of cool water, just because that person is my follower, will surely be rewarded.

Peter: The Rock

Who Is Jesus?

When Jesus and his disciples were near the town of Caesarea Philippi, he asked them, "What do people say about the Son of Man?" The disciples answered, "Some people say you are John the Baptist or maybe Elijah or Jeremiah or some other prophet." Then Jesus asked them, "But who do you say I am?" Simon Peter spoke up, "You are the Messiah, the Son of the living God." Jesus told him: "Simon, son of Jonah, you are blessed! You didn't discover this on your own. It was shown to you by my Father in heaven. So I will call you Peter, which means 'a rock.' On this rock I will build my church, and death itself will not have any power over it. I will give you the keys to the kingdom of heaven, and God in heaven will allow whatever you allow on earth. But he will not allow anything that you don't allow." Jesus told his disciples not to tell anyone that he was the Messiah.

Suffering, Persecution, and the Son of Man

From then on, Jesus began telling his disciples what would happen to him. He said, "I must go to Jerusalem. There the nation's leaders, the chief priests, and the teachers of the Law of Moses will make me suffer terribly. I will be killed, but three days later I will rise to life." Peter took Jesus aside and told him to stop talking like that. He said, "God would never let this happen to you, Lord!" Jesus turned to Peter and said, "Satan, get away from me! You're in my way because you think like everyone else and not like God."

Peter: The Rock from Matthew 16:13–18 from the *Good News Translation*-Second Edition; Today's English Version © 1992 American Bible Society, New York, NY 10023, www.americanbible.org. Used by permission.

Suffering, Persecution, and the Son of Man from Matthew 16:21–28, 24:3–14, 29 from the *Good News Translation*-Second Edition; Today's English Version © 1992 American Bible Society, New York, NY 10023, www.americanbible.org. Used by permission.

Then Jesus said to his disciples: "If any of you want to be my followers, you must forget about yourself. You must take up your cross and follow me. If you want to save your life, you will destroy it. But if you give up your life for me, you will find it. What will you gain, if you own the whole world but destroy yourself? What would you give to get back your soul? The Son of Man will soon come in the glory of his Father and with his angels to reward all people for what they have done. I promise you that some of those standing here will not die before they see the Son of Man coming with his kingdom.". . .

Warning about Trouble

Later, as Jesus was sitting on the Mount of Olives, his disciples came to him in private and asked, "When will this happen? What will be the sign of your coming and of the end of the world?"

Jesus answered: "Don't let anyone fool you. Many will come and claim to be me. They will say that they are the Messiah, and they will fool many people. You will soon hear about wars and threats of wars, but don't be afraid. These things will have to happen first, but that isn't the end. Nations and kingdoms will go to war against each other. People will starve to death, and in some places there will be earthquakes. But this is just the beginning of troubles.

"You will be arrested, punished, and even killed. Because of me, you will be hated by people of all nations. Many will give up and will betray and hate each other. Many false prophets will come and fool a lot of people. Evil will spread and cause many people to stop loving others. But if you keep on being faithful right to the end, you will be saved. When the good news about the kingdom has been preached all over the world and told to all nations, the end will come. . . ."

When the Son of Man Appears

Right after those days of suffering, "The sun will become dark, and the moon will no longer shine. The stars will fall, and the powers in the sky will be shaken." Then a sign will appear in the sky. And there will be the Son of Man. All nations on earth will weep when they see the Son of Man coming on the clouds of heaven with power and great glory. At the sound of a loud trumpet, he will send his angels to bring his chosen ones together from all over the earth.". . .

The Final Judgment

When the Son of Man comes in his glory with all of his angels, he will sit on his royal throne. The people of all nations will be brought before him, and he will separate them, as shepherds separate their sheep from their goats. He will place the sheep on his right and the goats on his left. Then the king will say to those on his right, "My father has blessed you! Come and receive the kingdom that was prepared for you before the world was created. When I was hungry, you gave me something to eat, and when I was thirsty, you gave me something to drink. When I was a stranger, you welcomed me, and when I was naked, you gave me clothes to wear. When I was sick, you took care of me, and when I was in jail, you visited me." Then the ones who pleased the Lord will ask, "When did we give you something to eat or drink? When did we welcome you as a stranger or give you clothes to wear or visit you while you were sick or in jail?" The king will answer, "Whenever you did it for any of my people, no matter how unimportant they seemed, you did it for me."

Then the king will say to those on his left, "Get away from me! You are under God's curse. Go into the everlasting fire prepared for the devil and his angels! I was hungry, but you did not give me anything to eat, and I was thirsty, but you did not give me anything to drink. I was a stranger, but you did not welcome me, and I was naked, but you did not give me any clothes to wear. I was sick and in jail, but you did not take care of me." Then the people will ask, "Lord, when did we fail to help you when you were hungry or thirsty or a stranger or naked or sick or in jail?" The king will say to them, "Whenever you failed to help any of my people, no matter how unimportant they seemed, you failed to do it for me." Then Jesus said, "Those people will be punished forever. But the ones who pleased God will have eternal life."

The Work of Paul

Paul of Tarsus (ca.10–65 C.E.) was a Hellenized Jew who had once persecuted Christians before his conversion. He was instrumental in establishing fundamental doctrines and in spreading the teachings of Jesus throughout the Roman Empire, seeking converts among Jews and Gentiles alike on faith, love, and the Resurrection of Christ.

Paul's Answer to the Intellectuals

Christ did not send me to baptize. He sent me to tell the good news without using big words that would make the cross of Christ lose its power.

Christ Is God's Power and Wisdom

The message about the cross doesn't make any sense to lost people. But for those of us who are being saved, it is God's power at work. As God says in the Scriptures, "I will destroy the wisdom of all who claim to be wise. I will confuse those who think they know so much." What happened to those wise people? What happened to those experts in the Scriptures? What happened to the ones who think they have all the answers? Didn't God show that the wisdom of this world is foolish?

God was wise and decided not to let the people of this world use their wisdom to learn about him. Instead, God chose to save only those who believe the foolish message we preach. Jews ask for miracles, and Greeks want something that sounds wise. But we preach that Christ was nailed to a cross. Most Jews have problems with this, and most Gentiles think it is foolish. Our message is God's power and wisdom for the Jews and the Greeks that he has chosen. Even when God is foolish, he is wiser than everyone else, and even when God is weak, he is stronger than everyone else.

My dear friends, remember what you were when God chose you. The people of this world didn't think that many of you were wise. Only a few of you were in places of power, and not many of you came from important families. But God chose the foolish things of this world to put the wise to shame. He chose the weak things of this world to put the powerful to shame. What the world thinks is worthless, useless, and nothing at all is what God has used to destroy what the world considers important. God did all this to keep anyone from bragging to him. . . .

Telling about Christ and the Cross

Friends, when I came and told you the mystery that God had shared with us, I didn't use big words or try to sound wise. In fact, while I was with you, I made up my mind to speak only about Jesus Christ, who had been nailed to a cross. At first, I was weak and trembling with fear. When I talked with you or preached, I didn't try to prove anything by sounding wise. I simply let God's Spirit show his power. That way you would have faith because of God's power and not because of human wisdom.

We do use wisdom when speaking to people who are mature in their faith. But it isn't the wisdom of this world or of its rulers, who will soon disappear. We speak of God's hidden and mysterious wisdom that God decided to use for our glory long before the world began. The rulers of this world didn't know anything about this wisdom. If they had known about it, they would not have nailed the glorious Lord to a cross.

"All of You Are God's Children"

The Law [of the Jews] controlled us and kept us under its power until the time came when we would have faith. In fact, the Law was our teacher. It was supposed to teach us until we

Paul's Answer to the Intellectuals from 1 Corinthians 1:7–2:8 from the *Good News Translation*-Second Edition; Today's English Version © 1992 American Bible Society, New York, NY 10023, www.americanbible.org. Used by permission.

had faith and were acceptable to God. But once a person has learned to have faith, there is no more need to have the Law as a teacher.

All of you are God's children because of your faith in Christ Jesus. And when you were baptized, it was as though you had put on Christ in the same way you put on new clothes. Faith in Christ Jesus is what makes each of you equal with each other, whether you are a Jew or a Greek, a slave or a free person, a man or a woman. So if you belong to Christ, you are now part of Abraham's family, and you will be given what God has promised.

The Resurrection of Christ

Christ Was Raised to Life

My friends, I want you to remember the message that I preached and that you believed and trusted. You will be saved by this message, if you hold firmly to it. But if you don't, your faith was all for nothing.

I told you the most important part of the message exactly as it was told to me. That part is: Christ died for our sins, as the Scriptures say. He was buried, and three days later he was raised to life, as the Scriptures say. Christ appeared to Peter, then to the twelve. After this, he appeared to more than five hundred other followers. Most of them are still alive, but some have died. He also appeared to James, and then to all of the apostles. Finally, he appeared to me, even though I am like someone who was born at the wrong time.

I am the least important of all the apostles. In fact, I caused so much trouble for God's church that I don't even deserve to be called an apostle. But God was kind! He made me what I am, and his wonderful kindness wasn't wasted. I worked much harder than any of the other apostles, although it was really God's kindness at work and not me. But it doesn't matter if I preached or if they preached. All of you believed the message just the same.

The Resurrection of Christ from 1 Corinthians 15:1–22, 31–32, 35–39, 42–55 from the *Good News Translation*-Second Edition; Today's English Version © 1992 American Bible Society, New York, NY 10023, www.americanbible.org. Used by permission.

God's People Will Be Raised to Life

If we preach that Christ was raised from death, how can some of you say that the dead will not be raised to life? If they won't be raised to life, Christ himself wasn't raised to life. And if Christ wasn't raised to life, our message is worthless, and so is your faith. If the dead won't be raised to life, we have told lies about God by saying that he raised Christ to life, when he really did not.

So if the dead won't be raised to life, Christ wasn't raised to life. Unless Christ was raised to life, your faith is useless, and you are still living in your sins. And those people who died after putting their faith in him are completely lost. If our hope in Christ is good only for this life, we are worse off than anyone else.

But Christ has been raised to life! And he makes us certain that others will also be raised to life. Just as we will die because of Adam, we will be raised to life because of Christ. Adam brought death to all of us, and Christ will bring life to all of us. And why do we always risk our lives and face death every day? The pride that I have in you because of Christ Jesus our Lord is what makes me say this. What do you think I gained by fighting wild animals in Ephesus? If the dead are not raised to life, "Let's eat and drink. Tomorrow we die."

What Our Bodies Will Be Like

Some of you have asked, "How will the dead be raised to life? What kind of bodies will they have?" Don't be foolish. A seed must die before it can sprout from the ground. Wheat seeds and all other seeds look different from the sprouts that come up. This is because God gives everything the kind of body he wants it to have. People, animals, birds, and fish are each made of flesh, but none of them are alike. Everything in the heavens has a body, and so does everything on earth. But each one is very different from all the others.

That's how it will be when our bodies are raised to life. These bodies will die, but the bodies that are raised will live forever. These ugly and weak bodies will become beautiful and strong. As surely as there are physical bodies, there are spiritual bodies. And our physical bodies will be changed into spiritual bodies. The first man was named Adam, and the Scriptures tell us that he was a living person. But Jesus, who may be called the last Adam, is a life-giving spirit. We see that the one with a spiritual body did not come first. He came after the one who had a physical body. The first man was made from the dust of the earth, but the second man came from heaven. Everyone on earth has a body like the body of the one who was made from the dust of the earth. And everyone in heaven has a body like the body of the one who came from heaven. Just as we are like the one who was made out of earth, we will be like the one who came from heaven.

My friends, I want you to know that our bodies of flesh and blood will decay. This means that they cannot share in God's kingdom, which lasts forever. I will explain a mystery to you. Not every one of us will die, but we will all be changed. It will happen suddenly, quicker than the blink of an eye. At the sound of the last trumpet the dead will be raised. We will all be changed, so that we will never die again. Our dead and decaying bodies will be changed into bodies that won't die or decay. The bodies we now have are weak and can die. But they will be changed into bodies that are eternal. Then the Scriptures will come true:

"Death has lost the battle!
Where is its victory?
Where is its sting?"

On Love

What if I could speak all languages of humans and of angels? If I did not love others, I would be nothing more than a noisy gong or a clanging cymbal. What if I could prophesy and understand all secrets and all knowledge? And what if I had faith that moved mountains? I would be nothing, unless I loved others. What if I gave away all that I owned and let myself be burned alive? I would gain nothing, unless I loved others. Love is kind and patient, never jealous, boastful, proud, or rude. Love isn't selfish or quick tempered. It doesn't keep a record of wrongs that others do. Love rejoices in the truth, but not in evil. Love is always supportive, loyal, hopeful, and trusting. Love never fails! Everyone who prophesies will stop, and unknown languages will no longer be spoken. All that we know will be forgotten. We don't know everything, and our prophecies are not complete. But what is perfect will someday appear, and what isn't perfect will then disappear. When we were children, we thought and reasoned as children do. But when we grew up, we quit our childish ways. Now all we can see of God is like a cloudy picture in a mirror. Later we will see him face to face. We don't know everything, but then we will, just as God completely understands us. For now there are faith, hope, and love. But of these three, the greatest is love.

On Love from 1 Corinthians 13:1–13 from the *Good News Translation*-Second Edition; Today's English Version © 1992 American Bible Society, New York, NY 10023, www.american-bible.org. Used by permission.

Roman Imperial Policy

The Persecution under Nero (64 C.E.)
TACITUS

At the beginning of their movement, Christians had difficulty in achieving an identity distinct from the Jews. But by the middle of the first century C.E., they had begun to spread Jesus' beliefs into the provinces. Christianity was not immediately popular, and many despised the missionaries for their zealous conversion methods. Paul himself had difficulty appealing to the Athenians in 51 C.E. The first recorded persecution of Christians took place in 64 C.E. when the emperor Nero blamed a de-

"The Persecution under Nero" is from Tacitus, *Annals*, 15.44, trans. Alfred Church and William Brodribb (New York: Macmillan, 1891).

structive fire in Rome on them in order to deflect suspicion from himself. It was in this persecution, confined to the city of Rome, that Saint Peter and Saint Paul were killed.

All human efforts, all the lavish gifts of the emperor, and the propitiations of the gods, did not banish the sinister belief that the fire was the result of an order. Consequently, to get rid of the report, Nero fastened the guilt and inflicted the most exquisite tortures on a class hated for their abominations, called Christians by the populace. Christus, from whom the name had its origin, suffered the death penalty during the reign of Tiberius at the hands of one of our procurators, Pontius Pilate, and a most mischievous superstition, thus checked for the moment, again broke out not only in Judea, the first source of the evil, but even in Rome, where all things hideous and shameful from every part of the world find their centre and become popular. Accordingly, an arrest was first made of all who pleaded guilty; then, upon their information, an immense multitude was convicted, not so much of the crime of firing the city, as of hatred against mankind. Mockery of every sort was added to their deaths. Covered with the skins of beasts, they were torn by dogs and perished, or were nailed to crosses, or were doomed to the flames and burnt, to serve as a nightly illumination, when daylight had expired. . . . Even for criminals who deserved extreme and exemplary punishment, there arose a feeling of compassion; for it was not, as it seemed, for the public good, but to glut one man's cruelty that they were being destroyed.

"A Religion of Lust": Anti-Christian Propaganda

MINUCIUS FELIX

In the confusion surrounding the Christian movement, many pagans were willing to believe whatever they heard about the religion. The following selection is by a Roman lawyer named Minucius Felix around 250 C.E. Note the emphasis on threatening political terms such as "faction" and "conspiracy."

Is it not deplorable that a faction . . . of abandoned, hopeless outlaws makes attacks against the gods? They gather together ignorant persons from the lowest dregs, and credulous women, easily deceived as their sex is, and organize a rabble of unholy conspirators, leagued together in nocturnal associations and by ritual fasts and barbarous foods not for the purpose of some sacred rite but for the sake of sacrilege—a secret tribe that shuns the light, silent in public but talkative in secret places. They despise the temples as if they were tombs, they spit upon the gods, they ridicule our sacred rites. Pitiable themselves, they pity . . . our priests; half-naked themselves, they despise offices and official robes. What amazing folly! What incredible arrogance! They despise present tortures yet dread uncertain future ones; while they fear to die after death, they have no fear of it in the meantime; deceptive hope soothes away their terror with the solace of a life to come.

Already . . . decay of morals spreads from day to day throughout the entire world, and the loathsome shrines of this impious conspiracy multiply. This plot must be completely rooted out and execrated. They recognize one another by secret signs and tokens; they love one another before they are acquainted. Everywhere a kind of religion of lust is also associated with them, and they call themselves promiscuously brothers and sisters, so that ordinary fornication, through the medium of a sacred name, becomes incest. And thus their vain and mad superstition glories in crimes. And for themselves, if there were not a basis of truth, knowing rumor would not tell of gross and unspeakable abominations. I hear that in some absurd conviction or other they consecrate and worship the head of an ass, the most repulsive of beasts—a religion worthy of the morals that begot it. Others say that they reverence the private parts of their director and high priest, and adore them as if belonging to a parent. Whether this is false I know not, but suspicion naturally attaches to secret and nocturnal rites. To say that a man put to death for a crime and the lethal wooden cross are objects of their veneration is to assign altars suitable for abandoned and impious men, the kind of worship they deserve. What is told of the initiation of neophytes is as detestable as it is notorious. An infant covered with a blanket to deceive the unsuspecting is set before the one to be initiated in the rites. The neophyte is induced to strike what seem to be harmless blows on the surface of the blanket, and this infant is killed by his random and unsuspecting blows. Its blood—oh, shocking!—they greedily lap up; the limbs they eagerly distribute; and by this victim they league themselves, and by this complicity in crime they pledge themselves to mutual silence. . . .

Their form of banqueting is notorious; everywhere all talk of it. . . . On an appointed day they assemble at a feast with all their children, sisters, and mothers, people of both sexes and every age. There, after much feasting, when the banquet has become heated and intoxication has inflamed the drunken passions of incestuous lust, a dog which has been tied to a lamp is incited to rush and leap forward after a morsel thrown beyond the range of the cord by which it was tied. The telltale light is upset and extinguished, and in the shameless dark they exchange embraces indiscriminately, and all, if not actually, yet by complicity are equally involved in incest. . . .

The Persecution under Diocletian (305 C.E.)

LACTANTIUS

Diocletian was an important emperor who in 285 C.E. instituted reforms that were crucial to the survival of the empire. Still, he persecuted Christians with a zeal not seen since that of the emperor Decius in 250 C.E. This was the last empire-wide persecution, but also the severest and most sustained, lasting from 303 to 311.

On the following day an edict was published providing that men of that religion should be deprived of all honors and rank; that they should be subjected to torture, from whatever rank and station they might come; that every legal action should be pressed against them, but they themselves were not to have the right to sue for any wrong or for adultery or theft; and finally, that they should be accorded no freedom and no voice. A certain person, although it was wrong, yet with great courage ripped down this edict and tore it up. . . .

Brought to judgment at once, he was not only tortured but was burned in the legal manner, and displaying admirable endurance was finally consumed by the flames.

But Galerius [Diocletian's colleague] was not satisfied with the terms of the edict and sought another way to influence Diocletian. For to drive him to a determination to employ an excess of cruelty in persecution, he employed private agents to set the palace on fire; and when some part of it had gone up in flames, the Christians were accused as public enemies, and

From *Roman Civilization, Sourcebook II: The Empire* by N. Lewis and M. Reinhold, eds., © 1955 Columbia University Press, pp. 598–599. Reprinted with permission of the publisher.

Theme: Propaganda

The Historical Intersection

GERMANY: 1938

"I Got You At Last, You Little German Girl!":
Anti-Jewish Propaganda

ERNST HIEMER

In 1936, Germany hosted the Olympic Games, and Hitler ordered the temporary removal of anti-Jewish placards in order to appease foreign opinion. Still, the propaganda continued to flow. The following excerpt is from a book for older children called Der Giftpilz (The Poisonous Mushroom), *which presented the Jew as an evil deviate who preyed on the innocence of children.*

Compare and Contrast:

- Compare the Roman propaganda directed against the Christians with Nazi propaganda directed against the Jews. Based on your analysis of these sources, what makes for effective or ineffective propaganda?

"It is almost noon," the teacher said, "now we want to summarize what we have learned in this lesson. What did we discuss?"

All the children raise their hands. The teacher calls on Karl Scholz, a little boy on the first bench. "We talked about how to recognize a Jew."

"Good! Now tell us about it!"

"I Got You at Last" is from the Office of the U.S. Chief of Counsel for the Prosecution of Axis Criminality, *Nazi Conspiracy and Aggression* (Washington, D.C.: Government Printing Office, 1947), vol. 4, pp. 358–359 (PS-1778).

(contd)

Little Karl takes the pointer, goes to the blackboard and points to the sketches.

"One usually recognizes a Jew by his nose. The Jewish nose is crooked at the end. It looks like the figure 6. Therefore it is called the "Jewish Six." Many non-Jews have crooked noses, too. But their noses are bent, not at the end but further up. Such a nose is called a hook nose or eagle's beak. It has nothing to do with a Jewish nose."

"Right!" says the teacher. "But the Jew is recognized not only by his nose. . . ." The boy continues. The Jew is also recognized by his lips.

His lips are usually thick. Often the lower lip hangs down. This is called "sloppy." And the Jew is also recognized by his eyes. His eyelids are usually thicker and more fleshy than ours. The look of the Jew is lurking and sharp.

Inge sits in the reception room of the Jew doctor. She has to wait a long time. She looks through the journals which are on the table. But she is almost too nervous to read even a few sentences. Again and again she remembers the talk with her mother. And again and again her mind reflects on the warnings of her leader of the BDM [League of German Girls]: "A German must not consult a Jew doctor! And particularly not a German girl! Many a girl that went to a Jew doctor to be cured, found disease and disgrace!"

When Inge had entered the waiting room, she experienced an extraordinary incident. From the doctor's consulting room she could hear the sound of crying. She heard the voice of a young girl: "Doctor, doctor leave me alone!"

Then she heard the scornful laughing of a man. And then all of a sudden it became absolutely silent. Inge had listened breathlessly.

"What may be the meaning of all this?" she asked herself and her heart was pounding. And again she thought of the warning of her leader in the BDM.

Inge was already waiting for an hour. Again she takes the journals in an endeavor to read. Then the door opens. Inge looks up. The Jew appears. She screams. In terror she drops the paper. Frightened she jumps up. Her eyes stare into the face of the Jewish doctor. And this face is the face of the devil. In the middle of this devil's face is a huge crooked nose. Behind the spectacles two criminal eyes. And the thick lips are grinning. A grinning that expresses: "Now I got you at last, you little German girl!"

And then the Jew approaches her. His fleshy fingers stretch out after her. But now Inge has her wits. Before the Jew can grab hold of her, she hits the fat face of the Jew doctor with her hand. Then one jump to the door. Breathlessly she escapes the Jew house.

Consider This:

- In these two propaganda selections, how does one recognize a Christian in 250 and how does one recognize a Jew in 1938? What role does rumor

(contd)

and exaggeration play in propaganda? Will people usually believe whatever they *want* to believe?

And How About . . .

- The portrayal of Communist sympathizers during the McCarthy hearings from 1953–1955 in the United States?
- The dehumanization of prisoners of war or "Enemies of the Revolution"?
- The treatment of Japanese Americans during World War II?

tremendous prejudice flared up against the very name of Christian as the palace burned. It was said that the Christians had plotted in concert with the eunuchs to destroy the princes, and that the two emperors had almost been burned alive in their own palace. But Diocletian, who always wanted to appear shrewd and intelligent, suspected nothing of the deception; inflamed with anger, he began immediately to torture all his domestics.

The Triumph of Christianity

On decree of the emperor Galerius in 311 C.E., Christianity proceeded from a persecuted to a tolerated sect. The emperor Constantine next raised Christianity to a favored position but still continued to erect pagan temples and was not formally baptized until on his deathbed in 337. After an unsuc-

The Coliseum in Rome, where hundreds of Christians were sporadically sacrificed to the lions as condemned reprobates during the imperial era in the first through fourth centuries C.E. "If the weather will not change, if there is an earthquake, a famine, a plague—straightway the cry is heard: 'Toss the Christians to the lions!'"—Tertullian (*Perry M. Rogers*)

cessful attempt to revive paganism under the emperor Julian the Apostate in 360, Christianity finally became the official religion of the Roman Empire under Theodosius the Great in 392. The following selections trace this successful rise.

The Edict of Toleration (311 C.E.)
EUSEBIUS

In view of our most gentle clemency and considering our consistent practice whereby we are wont to grant pardon to all men, we have thought fit in this case, too, to extend immediate indulgence, to wit: that they may be Christians once more and that they may reconstitute their places of assembly, on condition that they do nothing contrary to public order. In another letter, moreover, we shall indicate to governors of provinces what rules they are to observe. Wherefore, in accordance with this indulgence of ours, they are bound to implore their own god for our safety, for that of the state, and for their own, so that on every side the state may be rendered secure and they may be able to live tranquilly in their own homes.

The Edict of Milan (313 C.E.)
EUSEBIUS

When I, Constantine Augustus, and I, Licinius Augustus, met under happy auspices in Milan and had under discussion all matters that concerned the public advantage and security, among other measures that we saw would benefit most men we considered that first of all regulations should be drawn up to secure respect for divinity, to wit: to grant both to the Christians and to all men unrestricted right to follow the form of worship each desired, to the end that

whatever divinity thereby on the heavenly seat may be favorably disposed and propitious to us and all those placed under our authority. Accordingly, with salutary and most upright reasoning, we resolved on adopting this policy, namely that we should consider that no one whatsoever should be denied freedom to devote himself either to the cult of the Christians or to such religion as he deems best suited for himself, so that the highest divinity, to whose worship we pay allegiance with free minds, may grant us in all things his wonted favor and benevolence.

The Theodosian Code: Prohibition of Pagan Worship (392 C.E.)

Emperors Theodosius and Valentinian, Augustuses: To Isidorus, Praetorian Prefect:

We prohibit all persons of criminal pagan mind from the accursed immolation of victims, from damnable sacrifices, and from all other such practices that are prohibited by the authority of the more ancient sanctions. We command that all their . . . temples and shrines, if even now any remain entire, shall be destroyed by the command of the magistrates, and shall be purified by the erection of the sign of the venerable Christian religion. All men shall know that if it should appear, by suitable proof before a competent judge, that any person has mocked this law, he shall be punished with death.

THE CYCLE OF EMPIRE (180–500 C.E.)

Roman Dislocation and Decline

"Empire for Sale" (193 C.E.)

DIO CASSIUS

The Roman Empire generally prospered during the first and second centuries C.E. During the third century, however, the empire gradually fell prey to problems that had existed to some extent in preceding years, but had never reached crisis proportions. One of the main problems was a lack of leadership. Rome had survived bad emperors before, but during the fifty years from 235 TO 285 C.E., there were twenty-two emperors and only one died a natural death in his bed. The rest fell victim to assassination or violent death on the battlefield. The following excerpt describes the political chaos upon the death of the emperor Pertinax in 193 C.E. The empire was sold to the highest bidder by the emperor's personal troops, the Praetorian Guard. The "winner," Didius Julianus, ruled for three months before he himself was killed by these same Praetorian Guardsmen.

Didius Julianus, at once an insatiate money getter and a wanton spendthrift, who was always eager for revolution, and hence had been exiled by Commodus to his native city of Milan, now, when he heard of the death of Pertinax, hastily made his way to the [Praetorian] camp and, standing at the gates of the enclosure, made bids to the soldiers for the rule over the Romans. Then ensued a most disgraceful business and one unworthy of Rome. For, just as if it had been in some market or auction room, both the city and its entire Empire were auctioned off. The sellers were the ones who had slain their emperor, and the would-be buyers were Sulpicianus and Julianus, who vied to outbid each other, one from the inside, the other from outside. They gradually raised their bids up to 20,000 sesterces per soldier. Some of the soldiers would carry word to Julianus, "Sulpicianus offers so much; how much more do you bid?" And to Sulpicianus in turn, "Julianus promises so much; how much do you raise him?" Sulpicianus would have won the day, being inside and being prefect of the city and also the first to name the figure of 20,000, had not Julianus raised his bid no longer by a small amount but by 5,000 at one time, shouting it in a loud voice and also indicating the amount with his fingers. So the soldiers, captivated by this extravagant bid . . . received Julianus inside and declared him emperor.

Price Controls

The empire was saved for a time through the efforts of the emperor Diocletian (284–305). Diocletian developed a system of providing for peaceful succession and more efficient rule of the empire. He divided it into four prefectures, each with a leader responsible for the administration and security of his region. The system worked while Diocletian was in power but fell victim to ambitious generals once Diocletian retired.

Reprinted by permission the publishers and the Trustees of the Loeb Classical Library from *Dio Cassius: Roman History*, Loeb Classical Library Vol. IX, translated by Earnest Cary, Cambridge, Mass: Harvard University Press, 1927, pp. 143–145. The Loeb Classical Library ® is a registered trademark of the President and Fellows of Harvard College.

Frank, Tenney. *An Economic Survey of Ancient Rome: Rome and Italy of the Empire*, pp. 314–317, © 1940, Johns Hopkins University Press. Reprinted by permission of Johns Hopkins University Press.

One problem that Diocletian never solved was economic dislocation. As the first excerpt indicates, there was a general distrust of coinage issued by emperors whose short reigns did not inspire confidence in the value of money. Diocletian tried to control inflation by setting a maximum price that could be paid for goods. Note the penalty for transgressing the system.

Aroused justly and rightfully by all the facts set forth above, and in response to the needs of mankind itself, which appears to be praying for release, we have decided that maximum prices of articles for sale must be established. We have not set down fixed prices, for we do not deem it just to do this, since many provinces occasionally enjoy the good fortune of welcome low prices and the privilege, as it were, of prosperity. Thus, when the pressure of high prices appears anywhere—may the gods avert such a calamity!—avarice . . . will be checked by the limits fixed in our statute and by the restraining curbs of the law.

It is our pleasure, therefore, that the prices listed in the subjoined schedule be held in observance in the whole of our Empire. And every person shall take note that the liberty to exceed them at will has been ended, but that the blessing of low prices has in no way been impaired in those places where supplies actually abound. . . . Moreover, this universal edict will serve as a necessary check upon buyers and sellers whose practice it is to visit ports and other provinces. For when they too know that in the pinch of scarcity there is no possibility of exceeding the prices fixed for commodities, they will take into account in their calculations at the time of sale the localities, the transportation costs, and all other factors. In this way they will make apparent the justice of our decision that those who transport merchandise may not sell at higher prices anywhere.

It is agreed that even in the time of our ancestors it was the practice in passing laws to restrain offenses by prescribing a penalty. For rarely is a

A contemporary view of the ruins of the Roman Forum from the Temple of Saturn: "As yourselves, your empires fall. And every kingdom hath a grave."—William Hobbington (*Perry M. Rogers*)

situation beneficial to humanity accepted spontaneously; experience teaches that fear is the most effective regulator and guide for the performance of duty. Therefore it is our pleasure that anyone who resists the measures of this statute shall be subject to a capital [death] penalty for daring to do so. And let no one consider the statute harsh, since there is at hand a ready protection from danger in the observance of moderation. . . . We therefore exhort the loyalty of all, so that a regulation instituted for the public good may be observed with willing obedience and due scruple, especially as it is seen that by a statute of this kind provision has been made, not for single municipalities and peoples and provinces but for the whole world. . . .

Barbarian Invasions

JEROME

The most distressing and ultimately ruinous cause for the fall of the empire was the constant influx of Germanic invaders. Rome had been able to cope with Germanic incursions during the first and second centuries by either defeating them militarily or by allowing them to fight with Roman troops as confederates. In the latter circumstance, the barbarians were often "Romanized," learning the Latin language and respecting Roman traditions. Perhaps because of perceptions of Roman weakness, or in response to pressures from other nomadic eastern peoples (such as the Huns), in the mid-second and third centuries the Germanic tribes moved more aggressively into the empire, often overwhelming Roman armies that were hampered by a lack of political and military direction. The first selection is by Tacitus, who describes the values and lifestyle of the Germanic "barbarians" in the second century. By the fifth century, the empire had been overrun. Jerome, a Christian writer in the East, described the scene in the western provinces.

Innumerable and most ferocious people have overrun the whole of Gaul. The entire area bounded by the Alps, the Pyrenees, the ocean and the Rhine is occupied by the Quadi, Vandals, Carmatians, Alanni, Gepides, Saxons, Burgundians, Alammani—oh weep for the empire—and the hostile Pannonians. . . . Mainz, once a noble city, is captured and razed, and thousands have been massacred in the church. Worms has succumbed to a long siege. Rheims, the impregnable, Amiens, Artois . . . Tours, Nimes and Strasbourg are in the hands of the Germans. The provinces of Aquitaine, . . . of Lyons and Narbonne are completely occupied and devastated either by the sword from without or famine within. I cannot mention Toulouse without tears, for until now it has been spared, due to the merits of its saintly bishop Exuperus. The Spaniards tremble, expecting daily the invasion and recalling the horrors Spaniards suffer in continual anticipation.

Who would believe that Rome, victor over all the world, would fall, that she would be to her people both the womb and the tomb? Once all the East, Egypt and Africa acknowledged her sway and were counted among her men servants and her maid servants. Who would believe that holy Bethlehem would receive as beggars, nobles, both men and women, once abounding in riches? Where we cannot help we mourn and mingle with theirs our tears. . . . There is not an hour, not even a moment, when we are not occupied with crowds of refugees, when the peace of the monastery is not invaded by a horde of guests so that we shall either have to shut the gates or neglect the Scriptures for which the gates were opened. Consequently I have to snatch furtively the hours of the night, which now with winter approaching are growing longer, and try to dictate by candle light and thus . . . relieve a mind distraught. I am not boasting of our hospitality, as some may suspect, but simply explaining to you the delay.

The Rising Power in Africa: Axumite Ethiopia

As the Roman Empire began its slow disintegration after about 200 c.e., another power based in Africa was on the rise. The people of Axum in the highlands of Ethiopia had developed an organized, commercially powerful trading state just to the south of the kingdom of Kush. Kush had dominated the northern trade routes along the Nile River to Egypt and had plied the caravan trade to West Africa for centuries. But Kush's decline in the first century c.e. permitted Axum to seize the initiative. By the third century c.e., Axum was one of the most impressive civilizations in the African or western Asian world with imposing stone buildings and monuments in its primary cities. The Axumite empire was ruled by a King of Kings, who controlled fertile land and tribute-paying vassals in southern Arabia and the eastern Sudan. The chief port of Adulis on the Red Sea and the city of Axum itself became conduits for trade between the African interior and the Mediterranean and Southeast Asian markets along the lucrative Indian Ocean trade routes. Elephants, ivory, obsidian, slaves, and gold dust flowed to the ends of the known world.

The following description of the Axumite gold trade about 625 c.e. comes from the Greek-speaking monk and former Alexandrian merchant, Cosmas Indicopleustes.

The Axumite Gold Trade
COSMAS INDICOPLEUSTES

That country known as that of Sasu is itself near the ocean, just as the ocean is near the frankincense country [Somalia], in which there are many gold mines. The King of the Axumites accordingly, every other year, through the governor of Agau, sends thither special agents to bargain for the gold, and these are accompanied by many other traders—upwards, say of five hundred—bound on the same errand as themselves. They take along with them to the mining district oxen, lumps of salt, and iron, and when they reach its neighborhood they make a halt at a certain spot and form an encampment, which they fence round with a great hedge of thorns. Within this they live, and having slaughtered the oxen, cut them in pieces, and lay the pieces on the top of thorns, along with the lumps of salt and the iron. Then come the natives bringing gold in nuggets like peas, and lay one or two or more of these upon what pleases them–the pieces of flesh or the salt or the iron, and then they retire to some distance off. Then the owner of the meat approaches, and if he is satisfied he takes the gold away, and upon seeing this its owner comes and takes the flesh or the salt or the iron. If, however, he is not satisfied, he leaves the gold, when the native seeing that he has not taken it, comes and either puts down more gold, or takes up what he had laid down, and goes away. Such is the mode in which business is transacted with the people of that country, because their language is different and interpreters are hardly to be found.

"The Axumite Gold Trade" is from J. W. McCrindle, trans., *The Christian Topography of Cosmas, An Egyptian Monk* (London, 1898), pp. 52–54.

The Destruction at Meroe

EZANA, KING OF KINGS

During the third and fourth centuries C.E., as Rome was facing political disintegration and external invasion, Axum was on the move, extending its empire at the expense of the Kushite kingdom to its north. By about 330 C.E. the great Axumite king, Ezana, who later converted to Christianity, brought the kingdom of Kush under his control. In this inscription, dated about 360 C.E., Ezana recalls the defeat of a Kushite people he refers to as the Noba. Ezana went on to devastate other Kushite towns including the stronghold at Meroe. Although Axumite power was eclipsed in the seventh century by the rising Islamic tide under Arab leadership, Ethiopia continued to foster a vibrant Christian community, surrounded as it was by Muslim peoples and states.

By the power of the Lord of Heaven, Who in heaven and upon earth is mightier than everything which exists, Ezana, the son of Ella Amida, King of Axum and of Himyar, and of Raydan, and of Saba, and of Slhen, and of Bega and of Kasu, King of Kings, who is invincible to the enemy.

By the might of the Lord of Heaven, Who has made me Lord, Who to all eternity, the Perfect One, reigns, Who is invincible to the enemy, no enemy shall stand before, and after me no enemy shall follow.

By the might of the Lord of all, I made war upon Noba, for the peoples had rebelled and had made a boast of it. "And [the Axumites] will not cross the river Takkaze," said the peoples of Noba. And they were in the habit of attacking the peoples of Mangurto, and Khasa, and Barya [Axum's allies] . . . . And twice and thrice they had broken their solemn oaths, and had killed their neighbors mercilessly, and they had stripped bare and stolen the properties of our deputies and messengers, which I had sent to them to inquire into their thefts, and had stolen

from them their weapons of defense. And as I had sent warnings to them and they would not listen to me, and they refused to cease from their evil deeds, and then they ran away, I made war upon them. . . .

And I rose in the might of the Lord of the Land, and I followed after the fugitives for twenty-three days, killing some and making prisoners others, and capturing spoil wherever I stopped. . . . Meanwhile, I burned their towns, carried off their food, destroyed the statues in their houses, . . . and cast them into the River Seda [the Nile]. Many people died in the water; I do not know their number. Their ships were sunk together with numerous men and women who were in them.

And my peoples arrived at the frontier of the Red Noba and they returned safe and sound having captured prisoners and slain the Noba and taken spoil from them by the might of the Lord of Heaven. And I planted a throne in that country at the place where the Rivers Seda and Takkaze join.

Kirwan, L. P., "A Survey of Nubian Origins," *Sudan Notes and Records,* 20, 1937, Royal Geographical Society, pp. 50–51. Reprinted with permission.

CHRONOLOGY: The Roman Peace and the Dimensions of Empire

27 B.C.E.–14 C.E.   The principate of Augustus. Augustus "restores" the Roman Republic, yet controls it as emperor through his authority and military power.

4 B.C.E.–30 C.E.   Life span of Jesus of Nazareth. According to the New Testament, Jesus preached a message of love, charity, and humility. He was crucified in Judaea by Roman procurator, Pontius Pilate, after incurring the enmity of Jewish religious leaders.

35   Conversion of Paul of Tarsus to Christianity. Born Saul, he was a Roman citizen and Hellenized Jew who persecuted Christians until his own conversion.

14–68   Julio-Claudian Dynasty (Tiberius, Caligula, Claudius, Nero).

64–65   Roman emperor, Nero, blames the destructive fire in Rome on the Christians in order to deflect suspicion from himself. Both Paul and the apostle Peter were killed in the succeeding persecution.

66–70   Jewish rebellion crushed by Titus after siege at Masada. Temple destroyed. A final rebellion led by Simon Bar-Kochba brutally suppressed in 135.

69   Year of the Four Emperors. Civil war results in suicide of Nero and power struggle eventually won by Vespasian.

69–96   Flavian Dynasty (Vespasian, Titus, Domitian). Eruption of Vesuvius and destruction of Pompeii and Herculaneum (79).

70–100   Four Gospel accounts of Jesus' early life written (Matthew, Mark, Luke, John).

96–180   The five "Good Emperors" (Nerva, Trajan, Hadrian, Antoninus Pius, Marcus Aurelius) expand the Roman Empire and preside over the Pax Romana. Succession is based on an adoptive principle of choosing a leader who will maintain the efficiency and stability of the state. Breaks down with succession of Commodus (180–193).

180–284   Decline of Roman leadership ("Barrack emperors"), economic crisis, and Germanic invasions cause the "Crisis of the Third Century."

250–260   Major persecution of Christians under the emperors Decius (249–251) and Valerius (253–260).

284–305   Reign of Diocletian. Establishment of Dominate. Tetrarchy designed to provide a secure succession by dividing the Roman Empire among four emperors.

303   Empirewide persecution of Christians under the emperor Diocletian begins.

306–337   Rule of Constantine. Economic reforms postpone Roman collapse. Dedication of Constantinople as new capital of the empire (330).

311   Emperor Galerius issues the "Edict of Toleration."

325   Headed by Constantine, the Council of Nicaea resolves division of Christianity. Declares Arianism a heresy. Orthodox position: Jesus is both fully human and fully divine.

330	The Axumite King of Kings, Ezana, defeats the rival Kushite kingdom in Ethiopia and soon thereafter converts to Christianity. Axum becomes the conduit for the Indian Ocean trade with the interior of Africa until Axum's decline in the eighth century.
379–395	Rule of Theodosius, the last emperor to control both the eastern and western halves of the Roman Empire. Christianity becomes the official state religion.
410	Rome invaded by Visigoths under Alaric.
413–426	St. Augustine writes *The City of God.*
450	Anglo-Saxon invasion of Britain.
451–453	Huns invade Europe led by Attila, "Scourge of God."
455	Vandals overrun Rome.
476	Barbarian Odoacer deposes last Western Roman emperor, Romulus Augustulus.
489–493	Theodoric establishes Ostrogothic Kingdom in Italy.

STUDY QUESTIONS

1. Note carefully the opening document ("The Powers and Authority of the Emperor"). What were the specific rights of an emperor? Do they sound reasonable and necessary for efficient rule? Or were they arbitrary and prone to abuse? Was the emperor truly a "first citizen," or was he an autocratic monarch?

2. Discuss some of the benefits and drawbacks of life in imperial Rome. Do you consider the Romans barbaric because they often enjoyed such sports as chariot racing or gladiatorial combat? Can you think of any modern parallels to such activity in our own society?

3. Pick out specific passages from the selections on Stoicism that reflect the tenets of that philosophy as described in the section introduction. Why can this be considered a philosophy compatible with Roman values?

4. What was Jesus' basic message and mission? Discuss this with specific examples. Do you see anything in his message that might be considered politically threatening to the Roman state? Consider, in particular, the vocabulary.

5. What were Paul's contributions to the message of Jesus? How did the Pax Romana contribute to the success of missionaries like Paul who were spreading the word of Christ?

6. What was Roman policy on Christianity? Why was Rome concerned about the Christians? How did Christians threaten the Roman state, and why were they persecuted? If you had been an emperor during this period and were trying to maintain stability in the empire, what would your policy toward the Christians have been? Why were Christians finally tolerated by Constantine and Theodosius?

7. Analyze the Roman propaganda directed against the Christians. In your opinion, what makes it effective or ineffective propaganda?

8. What were some of the main reasons for the decline of the Roman Empire? Be specific in your analysis of the primary sources presented in the section "Roman Dislocation and Decline." In your opinion, which is the most important factor for the decline of a civilization and why?

9. The process of decline has fascinated humanity for centuries. Are civilizations biological in nature? Are they born and do they grow, mature, age, and die, as do other living entities? Does each civilization progress and transfer its benefits to the developing successor civilization? Are there any warning signs for decline, and can a civilization reverse the process once it has been started? Does technology have anything to do with decline? As we get more advanced technologically, does this speed up the process of decline? Compare Roman and American societies in this regard.

10. What do you learn about Ezana, the Axumite King of Kings, from the inscription commemorating his victory at Meroe? Why did Ezana make war on the Noba? How would you compare Ezana's attitude in this inscription with the Roman imperial vision as noted by the historian, Tacitus: "They make a desolation and call it peace"?

5

China's First Empire: The Qin and Han Dynasties (221 B.C.E. – 225 C.E.)

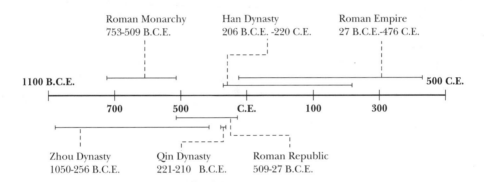

As we view Roman civilization in world perspective, it is important to realize that the rise and fall of this formidable empire did not occur in a historical void. Rome established trade and cultural contacts far beyond the Mediterranean region with civilizations that were developing along similar lines. China's first empire, which was established under the Qin and Han dynasties, existed concurrently with Rome from about 221 B.C.E. to 225 C.E. Rome and China were both Iron Age cultures that joined their developing technologies with superb organizational techniques that resulted in powerful, disciplined armies able to conquer vast territories and an administration that consolidated and preserved an efficient structure for hundreds of years. Both empires also proceeded from a firm intellectual foundation that confirmed the benefits of universal political control. Rome borrowed heavily from Greek precedents. The sophisticated bureaucratic system of the Han dynasty relied on the discipline of Confucian and Legalist thought developed during the Zhou Dynasty.

But there were also significant differences between the Roman and Chinese empires. In China the pervasive culture was Chinese and the empire developed from a homogenous base: language, social customs, religious traditions—all contributed to a cultural unity. In contrast, Rome's empire encompassed many older civilizations with peoples speaking diverse languages, worshiping an assortment of gods. This fundamental difference can be attributed primarily to the influence of geography. China was geopolitically more landlocked and Rome enjoyed the commercial benefits and access accorded by the Mediterranean Sea.

Comparisons between these two civilizations are important, and many others can be established, but this chapter focuses on the Qin and Han dynasties of China. Along the way, there will be ample opportunity to compare political and cultural development.

THE QIN ESTABLISHMENT OF POWER (232–210 B.C.E.)

The Zhou era in Chinese history from 1050–256 B.C.E. saw the development of several territorial states that ruled regionally without strong centralized political control. This was a feudal era and the regional kings often competed in establishing secure boundaries. Of all the territorial states of the late Zhou era, none was more efficiently organized or effective than that of Qin. In spite of its harsh laws and restrictive political environment, peasant farmers moved to Qin because it offered a stable society.

In 232 B.C.E., the king of Qin began a series of campaigns that eliminated the six remaining territorial states and established the new single state of China. This unification was accomplished in only a decade. The first Qin emperor named Qin Shi Huangdi extended the structure of the Qin state into each newly conquered territory. He substituted unfocused feudal government for an efficient centralized state, organized by impersonal bureaucrats chosen for their efficiency. China was divided into prefectures and subdivided into counties. An impressive road system allowed for the efficient and even ruthless collection of taxes. The First Emperor established a uniform system of weights and measures and established a standardized writing system. All thought also had to be unified and this resulted in the confiscation and burning of Confucian texts and the execution of scholars who opposed the strict Legalist philosophy. Such actions certainly united the state, but never established a loyalty borne of anything but fear. When the First Emperor died in 210 B.C.E., the system broke apart into chaos that lasted until 206 B.C.E.

The Unification of China

JIA YI

The following account of the unification of China by the First Emperor, Qin Shi Huangdi, during the years 232 to 221 B.C.E. is by the Han poet and statesman Jia Yi (201–169 B.C.E.). His essay had great influence on Chinese political thought.

Keep in Mind . . .

- How did the Qin dynasty establish control over China?

- According to the Han statesman, Jia Yi, what were the accomplishments of Qin?

With its superior strength Qin pressed the crumbling forces of its rivals, pursued those who had fled in defeat, and overwhelmed the army of a million until their shields floated upon a river of blood. Following up the advantages of its victory, Qin gained mastery over the empire and divided up the land as it saw fit. The powerful states begged to submit to its sovereignty and the weak ones paid homage at its court. . . .

The First Emperor [Qin Shi Huangdi] arose to carry on the glorious achievements of six generations. Cracking his long whip, he drove the universe before him, swallowing up the eastern and western Zhou and overthrowing the feudal lords. He ascended to the highest position and ruled the six directions, scourging the world with his rod, and his might shook the four seas. . . . Then he caused Meng Tian to build the Great Wall and defend the borders, driving back the Xiongnu . . . so that the barbarians no longer dared to come south to pasture their horses and their men dared not take up their bows to avenge their hatred.

Thereupon he discarded the ways and burned the writings of the hundred schools [Confucian scholarship] in order to make the people ignorant. He destroyed the major fortifications of the states, assassinated their powerful leaders, collected all the arms of the empire, and had them brought to his capital. . . . He garrisoned strategic points [along the Yellow River] with skilled generals and expert bowmen and stationed trusted ministers and well-trained soldiers to guard the land with arms and question all who passed back and forth. When he had thus pacified the empire, the First Emperor believed in his heart that with the strength of his capital within the Pass and his walls of metal extending a thousand miles, he had established a rule that would be enjoyed by his descendants for ten thousand generations.

Guardians of the Empire

In 1974, an army of 8,000 life-size terra-cotta soldiers were found by a farmer near Xian, China. These soldiers guarded the tomb of the First Emperor, Qin Shi Huangdi.

"Guardians of the Empire" [Terra-Cotta Soldiers] (*Bridgeman Art Library*)

Keep in Mind. . .

- What do these soldiers say about the rule of the First Emperor? What did the emperor think was important?

- How do the soldiers represent the emperor's efficient rule?

The Achievements of the First Emperor

SIMA QIAN

The unification of China in just over a decade could only have been achieved with great ruthlessness and violence of a type described in the preceding excerpt. The First Emperor, Qin Shi Huangdi, made note of his accomplishments in several stone inscriptions that he ordered to be established throughout the empire. From them, we can learn something of how he viewed his achievements and the values he wanted to promote.

Keep in Mind. . .

- According to these inscriptions, what were the values and achievements that Qin Shi Huangdi found important and worthy of remembering?

Then he [Qin Shi Huangdi] mobilized armies, and punished the unprincipled, and those who perpetrated rebellion were wiped out.

Armed force exterminates the violent and rebellious, but civil power relieves that guiltless of their labours, and the masses all submit in their hearts.

Achievements and toil are generously assessed, and the rewards even extend to cattle and horses, and his bounty enriches the land.

The August Emperor gave a vigorous display of his authority, and his virtue brought together all the states, and for the first time brought unity and supreme peace.

City walls were demolished, waterways were opened up, and obstacles were flattened.

When the physical features of the land had been determined, there was no conscript labour for the masses, and all under Heaven was pacified.

Men take pleasure in their farm-land, and women cultivate their tasks, and all matters have their proper arrangement.

His kindness protects all production, and for long they have been coming together in the fields, and everyone is content with his place. . . .

The August Emperor, glorious in the blessings he brought, pacified and unified everywhere within the universe, and his virtue and kindness will long survive.

In his thirty-seventh year, he in person toured all under Heaven, and everywhere inspected the distant regions. . . .

"The Achievements of the First Emperor" from Sima Qian—© Raymond Dawson 1994. Reprinted from *Sima Qian: Historical Records* translated with an introduction and notes by Raymond Dawson (World Classics, 1994) by permission of Oxford University Press.

The Historical Intersection

ROME: 14 C.E.

Res Gestae: The Accomplishments of Augustus

AUGUSTUS

The following document was written by the first Roman Emperor Augustus in 14 C.E., the year of his death. Although it is largely factual and therefore important as a historical source, it is nevertheless a subjective political document that summarizes his career as he wanted it remembered.

Compare and Contrast:

- Compare the following inscriptions that comprise the "Res Gestae" or "accomplishments" of Augustus in 14 C.E. with the achievements of Qin Shi Huangdi in the previous source. In what ways do the themes of pacification, order, and justice permeate these two legacy statements? Do successful governments generally promote these values and try to establish similar political and social conditions?

Below is a copy of the accomplishments of the deified Augustus by which he brought the whole world under the empire of the Roman people, and of the moneys expended by him on the state and the Roman people, as inscribed on two bronze pillars set up in Rome.

1. At the age of nineteen, on my own initiative and at my own expense, I raised an army by means of which I liberated the Republic, which was oppressed by the tyranny of a faction. For which reason the senate, with honorific decrees, made me a member of its order..., giving me at the same time consular rank in voting, and granted me the *imperium* [right of command]. It ordered me..., to

(contd)

see to it that the state suffered no harm. Moreover, in the same year, when both consuls had fallen in the war, the people elected me consul and a triumvir for the settlement of the commonwealth.

2. Those who assassinated my father [Julius Caesar] I drove into exile, avenging their crime by due process of law; and afterwards when they waged war against the state, I conquered them twice on the battlefield. . . .

3. I waged many wars throughout the whole by land and by sea, both civil and foreign, and when victorious I spared all citizens who sought pardon. Foreign peoples who could safely be pardoned I preferred to spare rather than to extirpate. . . .

4. Twice I celebrated ovations, three times curule triumphs, and I was acclaimed imperator twenty-one times. When the senate decreed additional triumphs to me, I declined them on four occasions. I deposited in the Capitol laurel wreaths . . . after fulfilling the vows which I had made in each war.

5. The dictatorship offered to me . . . by the people and by the senate, both in my absence and in my presence, I refused to accept. In the midst of a critical scarcity of grain I did not decline the supervision of the grain supply, which I so administered that within a few days I freed the whole people from the imminent panic and danger by my expenditures and efforts. The consulship, too, which was offered to me at that time as an annual office for life, I refused to accept. . . . I refused to accept any office offered me which was contrary to the traditions of our ancestors.

13.   The temple of Janus Quirinus, which our ancestors desired to be closed whenever peace with victory was secured by sea and by land throughout the entire empire of the Roman people, and which before I was born is recorded to have been closed only twice since the founding of the city, was during my principate three times ordered by the senate to be closed.

26.   I extended the frontiers of all the provinces of the Roman people on whose boundaries were peoples not subject to our empire. . . . I added Egypt to the empire of the Roman people.

34.   In my sixth and seventh consulships, after I had put an end to the civil wars, having attained supreme power by universal consent, I transferred the state from my own power to the control of the Roman senate and people. For this service of mine I received the title of Augustus by decree of the senate, and the doorposts of my house were publicly decked with laurels, the civic crown was affixed over my doorway, and a golden shield was set up in the Julian senate house, which, as the inscription of this shield testifies, the Roman senate and people gave me in recognition of my valor, clemency, justice, and devotion. After that time I excelled all in authority, but I possessed no more power than the others who were my colleagues in each magistracy.

35.   When I held my thirteenth consulship, the senate, the equestrian order, and the entire Roman people gave me the title of "father of the country" and decreed that this title should be inscribed in the vestibule of my house, in the

(contd)

Julian senate house, and in the Augustan Forum on the pedestal of the chariot which was set up in my honor by decree of the senate. At the time I wrote this document I was in my seventy-sixth year.

Consider This:

- Both Augustus and Qin Shi Huangdi had fashioned empires through their efficiency and military control. Note in particular the emphasis placed on the title. Both emperors are mentioned as "August." Why? What political and religious images were they trying to promote?

From *Roman Civilization, Sourcebook II: The Empire* by N. Lewis and M. Reinhold, eds., © 1955 Columbia University Press, pp. 9–11, 13–14, 16–19. Reprinted with permission of the publisher.

When the sage of Qin took charge of his state, he first determined punishments and names, and clearly set forth the ancient regulations.

He was the first to standardize the system of laws, examine and demarcate duties and responsibilities, so as to establish unchanging practices. . . .

[Rebels] were punished justly and with authority, their cruel rebelliousness was obliterated, and the criminals who spread disorder were wiped out. . . .

If a man commits adultery, to kill him is no crime, so men hang on to the standards of righteousness.

If a wife elopes to remarry, then the son will not have a mother, and so everyone is converted into chastity and purity.

His great rule cleanses morality, and all under Heaven come under his influence, and are the beneficiaries of his bountiful regime.

Everyone honuors the rules, and earnestly strives in harmony and tranquility, and nobody does not obey orders.

Compare and Contrast:

- Compare these inscriptions with the "Code of Hammurabi" on pp. 7–9. Which issues are of concern to both the Babylonian king Hammurabi in 1750 B.C.E. and Qin Shi Huangdi about 220 B.C.E.? What constitutes justice in each society?

- How important is it for a leader to promote "efficient" policies in the establishment of power? Does "efficient" mean "repressive?" Note that the absolute monarchies of seventeenth century Europe, as well as fascist and totalitarian regimes of the twentieth century, promoted efficiency and stability as virtues of a stable society. Can a government become "too efficient" and provoke popular resentment of its policies?

Legalism and the Justification of Power:
The Five Vermin of the State

HAN FEI ZI

The ideas of Confucius that were expounded in the 6th century B.C.E. during the Zhou Dynasty emphasized the cultivation of personal virtue in the establishment of a moral order that could regulate society around humanistic principles. Confucius and his principles were not well-respected or practiced by government officials during his day, and for centuries the Confucian school remained one among many competing philosophies. Perhaps the school of thought with the greatest influence on the political life of its time was Legalism. Its advocates were usually practicing politicians who sought to maintain the political order by advocating and justifying the harsh policies of the Qin dynasty.

The first selection is by Han Fei Zi, a student of Xun Zi, who taught that human nature was evil. His definition of the "Five Vermin of the State" is a powerful condemnation of those whose comments posed a threat to the ruling order. The second selection is by Li Si, a classmate of Han Fei who became chief minister to the First Emperor of the Qin dynasty. His advocacy of book burning was an extreme solution to the contagion of defiant ideas, but very consistent with the tenets of Legalism.

Keep in Mind. . .

• According to Han Fei Zi, who specifically are the "Five Vermin of the State" and why should they be eliminated?

The enlightened sovereign therefore employs a man's energies but does not heed his words, rewards men with meritorious services but without fail bans the useless. Accordingly, the people exert themselves to the utmost in obeying their superiors. Farming is hard toil indeed. . . . Naturally a hundred men will be attending to learning where one will apply his physical energies. When many attend to learning, the law will come to naught; when few apply their physical energies, the state will fall into poverty. That is the reason why the world is in chaos.

In the state ruled by an enlightened sovereign, one would find no recorded literature and the law would supply the only instruction; . . . As a result, the people in the state would all conform to the law in their discourse, would aim at meritori-

ous achievement in their actions, and would offer their services to the army out of bravery. Therefore, in time of peace the state would be rich; in time of war the army would be strong. These might be called the "kingly resources." When the "kingly resources" were stored up, the sovereign could avail himself of any situation that might arise in the state of the enemy. . . .

This then is the customary experience of a disorderly state: the learned men will exalt the ways of the early kings and make a show of humanity and righteousness. They will adorn their manners and clothes and embroider their arguments and speeches so as to scatter doubts on the law of the age and beguile the mind of the sovereign. The itinerant speakers will advocate deceptive theories and utilize foreign influence to accomplish their selfish purposes, being unmindful of the benefit of the state. The freelance fighters will gather pupils and followers and set up standards of fidelity and discipline, hoping thereby to spread their reputation. . . . The courtiers will congregate in the powerful

From *Sources of Chinese Tradition* by William Theodore de Bary, ed. © 1960 Columbia University Press, pp. 149–150. Reprinted with permission of the publisher.

houses, use all kinds of bribes, and exploit their contacts with influential men in order to escape the burden of military service. The tradesmen and craftsmen will produce inferior wares and collect cheap articles, and wait for good opportunities to exploit the farmers. These five types of men are the vermin of the state. Should the ruler fail to eliminate such people as the five vermin and should he not uphold men of firm integrity and strong character, then he can hardly be surprised if within the seas there should be states that decline and fall, and dynasties that wane and perish.

"Burn the Books!"

LI SI

Keep in Mind. . .

- Why does Li Si advocate the burning of books? What are the penalties he proposes for those who refer to the "past to criticize the present"? Why is the past so dangerous?

In earlier times the empire disintegrated and fell into disorder, and no one was capable of unifying it. Thereupon the various feudal lords rose to power. In their discourses they all praised the past in order to disparage the present and embellished empty words to confuse the truth. Everyone cherished his own favorite school of learning and criticized what had been instituted by the authorities. But at present Your Majesty possesses a unified empire, has regulated the distinctions of black and white and has firmly established for yourself a position of sole supremacy. And yet these independent schools, joining with each other, criticize the codes of laws and instructions. Hearing of the promulgation of a decree, they disapprove of it in their

From *Sources of Chinese Tradition* by William Theodore de Bary, ed. © 1960 Columbia University Press, pp. 154–155. Reprinted with permission of the publisher.

hearts; going out they criticize it in the thoroughfare. They seek a reputation by discrediting their sovereign; they appear superior by expressing contrary views, and they lead the lowly multitude in the spreading of slander. If such license is not prohibited, the sovereign power will decline above and partisan factions will form below. It would be well to prohibit this.

Your servant suggests that all books in the imperial archives, save the memoirs of Qin, be burned. All persons in the empire, except members of the Academy of Learned Scholars, in possession of the *Book of Odes*, the *Book of History*, and discourses of the hundred philosophers [Confucian scholars] should take them to the local governors and have them indiscriminately burned. Those who dare to talk to each other about the *Book of Odes* and the *Book of History* should be executed and their bodies exposed in the market place. Anyone referring to the past to criticize the present should, together with all members of his family, be put to death. Officials who fail to report cases that have come under their attention are equally guilty. After thirty days from the time of issuing the decree, those who have not destroyed their books are to be branded and sent to build the Great Wall. Books not to be destroyed will be those on medicine and pharmacy, divination by the tortoise and milfoil, and agriculture and arboriculture. People wishing to pursue learning should take the officials as their teachers.

Consider This:

- After reading the two previous excerpts, how would you define the main principles of Legalism?

- Compare these Legalistic ideas with the values of discipline and obedience that were a part of the education of Spartan warriors in 5th century Greece (see pp. 96–97). Does a strict control of society by the state produce a stable community or a rigid dictatorship that is vulnerable to revolution? Where does book burning lead?

"The Great Wall of China" (*Paolo Koch/ Photo*).

The Great Wall of China

After the First Emperor had defeated all rival armies by 221 B.C.E., he set about the consolidation of his gains. The Great Wall of China was started in 214 B.C.E. in order to prevent the incursions of barbarian tribes north of China. It was often extended and finally rebuilt during the Ming dynasty (1318–1644 C.E.).

Keep in Mind. . .

- Why is this wall such an impressive structure?

- What does the Great Wall of China say about the effectiveness of Chinese government during the Qin and Han dynasties? Is such a structure a clear indication of a dominant political control of society?

Compare and Contrast:

- Compare the Great Wall of China to the photo of the Pont du Gard on page 121. How does this Roman aqueduct demonstrate the stability and security of Roman society?

THE HAN MANDATE OF GOVERNMENT (206 B.C.E.–225 C.E.)

The Han Empire in China from 206 B.C.E. to 220 C.E. coincided chronologically with the period of expansion and decline of the Roman Empire in the West. It is a particularly fruitful comparison that can teach us much about the establishment and maintenance of empire, the evolving image of leadership, and the values that contribute to stable society.

After the death of Qin Shi Huangdi in 210 B.C.E., there was a four-year period of chaos before the rebels, Chen She and Liu Bang, overthrew the Qin and established the Han dynasty. Liu Bang ultimately succeeded to the throne of China and was supported by the popular discontent engendered by repressive Qin policies. Slowly he established his control and authority by reducing taxes and maintaining the efficient bureaucracy of the Qin, while avoiding its despotism. Liu Bang moved away from the strict Legalist philosophy and "Confucianized" the state with its emphasis on virtuous rule. The position of emperor became more strictly defined and more closely joined with both political and religious authority as the omnipotent "Son of Heaven." For his efforts, Liu Bang received the posthumous title, Gaozu ("Exalted Ancestor").

The following selections note the drawbacks of Qin rule and the establishment of the principles of Han authority. They give you an idea of the Han imperial system, the functions of the ruler, and the dynastic principles expounded by philosophers during the Han.

The Faults of Qin

JIA YI

Keep in Mind. . .

- According to the Han statesman, Jia Yi, what were the faults of Qin?

For a while after the death of the First Emperor, the memory of his might continued to awe the common people. Yet Chen She, born in a humble hut with tiny windows and wattle door, a day laborer in the fields and a garrison conscript, whose abilities could not match even the average, who had neither the worth of Confucius and Mo Zi nor the wealth of Dao Zhu or Yi Dun, stepped from the ranks of the common soldiers, rose up from the paths of the fields and led a band of some hundred poor, weary troops in revolt against the Qin. They cut down trees to make their weapons, raised their flags on garden poles, and the whole world in answer gathered about them like a great cloud, brought them provisions, and followed after them as shadows follow a form. In the end the leaders of the entire east rose up together and destroyed the House of Qin.

Now the empire of Qin at this time was by no means small or feeble . . . . The position of Chen She could not compare in dignity with the lords

of [the great Chinese feudal territories]. The weapons which he improvised of hoes and tree branches could not match the sharpness of spears and battle pikes; his little band of garrison conscripts was nothing beside the armies of the nine states; his plots and stratagems, his methods of warfare were far inferior to those of the men of earlier times. And yet Chen She succeeded in his undertaking where they had failed. Why was this, when in ability, size, power and strength his forces came nowhere near those of the state of the east that had formerly opposed Qin? Qin, beginning with an insignificant amount of territory, reached the power of a great state and for a hundred years made all the other great lords pay homage to it. Yet after it had become master of the whole empire, . . . a single commoner opposed it and its ancestral temples toppled, its ruler died by the hands of men, and it became the laughing stock of the world. Why? Because it failed to rule with humanity and righteousness and to realize that the power to attack and the power to retain what one has thereby won are not the same.

Consider This:

- Why was the Qin dynasty overthrown? Do you agree that "the power to attack and the power to retain what one has thereby won are not the same"? Which is a sign of true political greatness: the accumulation of territory or its consolidation and the maintenance of empire?

From *Sources of Chinese Tradition,* by William Theodore de Bary, ed. © 1960 Columbia University Press, p. 168. Reprinted with permission of the publisher.

The Dynastic Cycle

SIMA QIAN

After the establishment of the Han dynasty, the philosophy of Confucius with its emphasis on virtue, kindness, and learning became increasingly influential as the Han emperors sought ways of distancing themselves from the harsh rule of Qin. By the second century B.C.E., Confucianism had become the official creed of the nation and its ideas dominant among scholars and statesmen.

In the following selection, Sima Qian (ca. 145-90 B.C.E.), the Grand Historian of China, whose writings served to praise the Han dynasty as the embodiment of traditional political virtues, discusses the "dynastic cycle." This Confucian theory suggested that the success or failure of a dynasty was directly related to the moral strength of its leadership. The "mandate of Heaven" was a heavy responsibility for the first Han emperor to bear.

Keep in Mind. . .

- According to Sima Qian, what was the "dynastic cycle" and why "when it ends, must it begin over again"?

- In the opinion of Sima Qian, what must the leaders of the Han dynasty do to retain power?

The Grand Historian of China remarks: The government of the Xia dynasty was marked by good faith, which in time deteriorated until mean men had turned it into rusticity. Therefore the men of Shang who succeeded to the Xia reformed this defect through the virtue of piety. But piety degenerated until mean men had made it a superstitious concern for the spirits. Therefore the men of Zhou who followed corrected this fault through refinement and order. But refinement again deteriorated until it became in the hands of the mean a mere hollow show. Therefore what was needed to reform this hollow show was a return to good faith, for the way of the Three Dynasties of old is like a cycle which, when it ends, must begin over again.

It is obvious that in late Zhou and Qin times the earlier refinement and order had deteriorated. But the government of Qin failed to correct this fault, instead adding its own harsh punishments and laws. Was this not a grave error?

Thus when the Han rose to power it took over the faults of its predecessors and worked to change and reform them, causing men to be unflagging in their efforts and following the order properly ordained by Heaven. . . .

After the Qin ruler had assumed the title of emperor, he was fearful lest warfare should continue because of the presence of feudal lords. Therefore he refused to grant so much as a foot of land in fief, but instead destroyed the fortifications of the principal cities, melted down the lance and arrow points, and ruthlessly wiped out the brave men of the world, hoping thus to ensure the safety of his dynasty for countless generations to come. Yet from the lanes of the common people there arose a man with the deeds of a king whose alliances and campaigns of attack surpassed those of the three dynasties of Xia, Shang, and Zhou. Qin's earlier prohibitions against feudalism and the possession of arms, as it turned out, served only to aid worthy men and remove from their path obstacles they would otherwise have encountered. Therefore Gaozu [Liu Bang] had but to roar forth his indignation to become a leader of the world. Why should people say that one cannot become a king un-

From *Sima Qian: Records of the Grand Historian of China*, Vol. I by Burton Watson, trans., © 1961 Columbia University Press, pp. 118–125. Reprinted with permission of the publisher.

less he possesses land? Was this man not what the old books term a "great sage"? Surely this was the work of Heaven! Who but a great sage would be worthy to receive the mandate of Heaven and become emperor?

THOUGHT AND SOCIAL VALUES

"Men Do Not Become Ghosts"

WANG CHONG

From ancient times, the Chinese believed that the souls of the dead assumed human forms and appeared among men, often affecting their lives. In the next selection, the Han philosopher, Wang Chong, denies that phantoms are actively the souls of the dead. His denial of a conscious life after death had great significance in Chinese thought with the introduction of Buddhism.

Keep in Mind. . .

* How does Wang define "vital force" and why can't ghosts appear in form like living men? Does he deny the existence of ghosts?

* Does a man have consciousness before birth or after death? What is Wang's argument?

People say that when men die they become ghosts with consciousness and the power to harm others. If we try to test this theory by comparing men with other creatures, however, we find that men do not become ghosts, nor do they have consciousness or power to harm. . . . Man lives because of his vital force and when he dies this vital force is extinguished. The vital force is able to function because of the blood system, but when a man dies the blood system ceases to operate. With this the vital force is extinguished and the body decays and turns to clay. What is there to become a ghost then? If a man is without ears or eyes, he lacks faculties of consciousness. Hence men who are dumb and blind are like grass or trees. But when the vital force has left a man, it is a far more serious matter than simply being without ears or eyes. . . . The vital force produces man just as water becomes ice. As water freezes into ice, so the vital force coagulates to form man. When ice melts it becomes water and when a man dies he becomes spirit again. He is called spirit just as ice which has melted changes its name to water. People see that the name has changed, but they then assert that spirit has consciousness and can assume a form and harm others, but there is no basis for this assertion. . . .

It is the nature of Heaven and earth that, though new fires can be kindled, one cannot rekindle a fire that has burned out, and though new human beings can be born, one cannot bring back the dead. . . . Now people say that ghosts are the spirits of the dead. If this were true, then when men see them they ought to appear completely naked and not clothed in robes and sashes. Why? Because clothes have no spirits. When a man dies they all rot away along with his bodily form, so how could he put them on again? . . .

If dead men cannot become ghosts, then they also cannot have consciousness. How do we prove this? By the fact that before a man is born he has no consciousness. Before a man is born he exists in the midst of primal force, and after he dies he returns again to this primal force.

From *Sources of Chinese Tradition* by William Theodore de Bary, ed. © 1960 Columbia University Press, pp. 253–255. Reprinted with permission of the publisher.

The primal force is vast and indistinct and the human force exists within it. Before a man is born he has no consciousness, so when he dies and returns to this original unconscious state how could he still have consciousness? The reason a man is intelligent and understanding is that he possesses the forces of the five virtues [humanity, righteousness, decorum, wisdom, and faith]. The reason he possesses these is that he has within him the five organs [heart, liver, stomach, lungs, and kidneys]. If these five organs are unimpaired, a man has understanding, but if they are diseased, then he becomes vague and confused and behaves like a fool or an idiot. When a man dies, the five organs rot away and the five virtues no longer have any place to reside. Both the seat and the faculty of understanding are destroyed. The body must await the vital force before it is complete, and the vital force must await the body before it can have consciousness. Nowhere is there a fire that burns all by itself. How then could there be a spirit with consciousness existing without a body?

Compare and Contrast:

- Compare this source to the Apostle Paul's account of Christ's resurrection on pages 153–154. How does the Christian conception of "a physical body and a spiritual body" differ from Wang Chong's ideas?

Lessons for Women

BAN ZHAO

Ban Zhao (ca. 45–120 C.E.) has been described as China's "foremost woman scholar." She served as an instructor in history, astronomy, and mathematics to the Empress Deng and her court during the reign of the Emperor He (29–105 C.E.). Her Lessons for Women *is the first educational treatise written expressly for women so that they might comport themselves with dignity and not humiliate their ancestors. This image of the ideal woman proved most influential in Chinese society.*

Keep in Mind. . .

- According to Ban Zhao, what are the specific responsibilities of women at the Han court?

- What are the ideal qualities that women should strive to emulate? What was at stake if a woman didn't maintain an "upright character"?

I, the unworthy writer, am unsophisticated, unenlightened, and by nature unintelligent, but I am fortunate both to have received not a little favor from my scholarly father, and to have had a [cultured] mother and instructresses upon whom to rely for a literary education as well as for training in good manners. More than forty years have passed since at the age of fourteen I took up the dustpan and the broom in the Zhao family. During this time with trembling heart I feared constantly that I might disgrace my parents, and that I might multiply difficulties for both the women and the men [of my husband's family]. . . . Now and hereafter, however, I know how to escape [from such fears].

Being careless, and by nature stupid, I taught and trained [my children] without system. Consequently I fear that my son Gu may bring disgrace upon the Imperial Dynasty. . . . Nevertheless, now that he is a man and able to plan his own life, I need not again have concern for him. But I do grieve that you, my daughters, just now at the age for marriage, have not learned the proper customs for married women. I fear that by failure in good manners in other families you will humiliate both your ancestors and your clan. I am now seriously ill, life is uncertain. As I have thought of you all in so untrained a state, I have been uneasy many a time for you. At hours of leisure I have composed . . . these instructions under the title, "Lessons for Women." In order that you may have something wherewith to benefit your persons, I wish every one of you, my daughters, each to write out a copy for yourself. From this time on every one of you strive to practise these [lessons].

These . . . ancient customs epitomize a woman's ordinary way of life and the teachings of the traditional ceremonial rites and regulations. Let a woman modestly yield to others; let her respect others; let her put others first, herself last. Should she do something good, let her not mention it; should she do something bad, let her not deny it. Let her bear disgrace; let her even endure when others speak or do evil to her. Always let her seem to tremble and to fear. Then she may be said to humble herself before others. . . .

Let a woman be correct in manner and upright in character in order to serve her husband. Let her live in purity and quietness [of spirit], and attend to her own affairs. Let her love not gossip and silly laughter. Let her cleanse and purify and arrange in order the wine and the food for the offerings to the ancestors. Then she may be said to continue ancestral worship. . . .

The Way of husband and wife is intimately connected with *Yin* and *Yang*, and relates the individual to gods and ancestors. Truly it is the great principle of Heaven and Earth, and the great basis of human relationships.

If a husband does not control his wife, then the rules of conduct manifesting his authority are abandoned and broken. If a wife does not serve her husband, then the proper relationship [between men and women] and the natural order of things are neglected and destroyed. . . .

Now examine the gentlemen of the present age. They only know that wives must be controlled, and that the husband's rules of conduct manifesting his authority must be established.

They therefore teach their boys to read books and histories. But they do not in the least understand that husbands and masters must [also] be served, and that the proper relationship and the rites should be maintained.

Yet only to teach men and not to teach women—is that not ignoring the essential relation between them? According to the "Rites," it is the rule to begin to teach children to read at the age of eight years, and by the age of fifteen years they ought then to be ready for cultural training. Only why should it not be that [both girls' and boys' education adhere] to this principle? . . .

As *Yin* and *Yang* are not of the same nature, so man and woman have different characteristics. The distinctive quality of the *Yang* is rigidity; the function of the *Yin* is yielding. Man is honored for strength; a woman is beautiful on account of her gentleness. . . .

A woman [ought to] have four qualifications: 1) womanly virtue; 2) womanly words; 3) womanly bearing; and 4) womanly work. . . .

To guard carefully her chastity; to control circumspectly her behavior; in every motion to exhibit modesty; and to model each act on the best usage, this is womanly virtue.

To choose her words with care; to avoid vulgar language; to speak at appropriate times; and not to weary others [with too much conversation], may be called the characteristics of womanly words.

To wash and scrub filth away; to keep clothes and ornaments fresh and clean; to wash the head and bathe the body regularly, and to keep the person free from disgraceful filth, may be called the characteristics of womanly bearing.

With whole-hearted devotion to sew and to weave; to love not gossip and silly laughter; in cleanliness and order [to prepare] the wine and food for serving guests, may be called the characteristics of womanly work.

These four qualifications characterize the greatest virtue of a woman. No woman can afford to be without them. In fact they are very easy to possess if a woman only treasure them in her heart. . . .

Consider This:

- Why is it important to Ban Zhao to teach women as well as men? Does she believe that the sexes compete on an equal basis? Why or why not?

The Grand Historian of China

SIMA QIAN

During the Han dynasty, the Chinese acquired a sense of cultural and national identity. This sense was fostered by the first comprehensive history of an entire nation, called the Records of the Historian. *It was begun under the Emperor Wu by the Grand Historian, Sima Tan, until his death in 110 B.C.E., then continued by his son and successor, Sima Qian. In this reflective excerpt, Sima Qian discusses the importance of his work. In 98 B.C.E., Sima Qian was castrated on the orders of the Emperor Wu because he dared to defend a military leader whom the emperor believed had disgraced himself. In this letter to a friend, the historian explains why he chose castration over suicide.*

Keep in Mind. . .

- Why did Sima Qian decide not to commit suicide? What does he mean when he says, "The brave man does not always die for honor, while even the coward may fulfill his duty"?

My father had no great deeds that entitled him to receive territories or privileges from the emperor. He dealt with affairs of astronomy and the calendar, which are close to divination and the worship of the spirits. He was kept for the sport and amusement of the emperor, treated the same as the musicians and jesters, and made light of by the vulgar men of his day. If I fell before the law and were executed, it would make no more difference to most people than one hair off nine oxen, for I was nothing but a mere ant to them. The world would not rank me among those men who were able to die for their ideals, but would believe simply that my wisdom was exhausted and my crime great, that I had been unable to escape penalty and in the end had gone to my death. Why? Because all my past actions had brought this on me, they would say.

A man has only one death. That death may be as weighty as Mount Tai, or it may be as light as a goose feather. It all depends upon the way he uses it. . . . It is the nature of every man to love life and hate death, to think of his relatives and look after his wife and children. Only when a man is moved by higher principles is this not so. Then there are things which he must do. . . . The brave man does not always die for honor, while even the coward may fulfill his duty. Each takes a different way to exert himself. Though I might be weak and cowardly and seek shamefully to prolong my life, yet I know full well the difference between what ought to be followed and what rejected. How could I bring myself to sink into the same of ropes and bonds? If even the lowest slave and scullery maid can bear to commit suicide, why should not one like myself be able to do what has to be done? But the reason I have not refused to bear these ills and have continued to live, dwelling among this filth, is that I grieve that I have things in my heart that I have not been able to express fully, and I am shamed to think that after I am gone my writings will not be known to posterity. . . .

From *Sources of Chinese Tradition* by William Theodore de Bary, ed. © 1960 Columbia University Press, pp. 271–273. Reprinted with permission of the publisher.

I too have ventured not to be modest but have entrusted myself to my useless writings. I have gathered up and brought together the old traditions and events of the past and investigated the principles behind their success and failure, their rise and decay. . . . I wished to examine into all that concerns heaven and man, to penetrate the changes of the past and present, completing all as the work of one family. But before I had finished my rough manuscript, I met with this calamity. It is because I regretted that it had not been complete that I submitted to the extreme penalty without rancor. When I have truly completed this work, I shall deposit it in some safe place. If it may be handed down to men who will appreciate it and penetrate to the villages and great cities, then though I should suffer a thousand mutilations, what regret would I have?

Compare and Contrast:

- The greatest of Greek historians was Thucydides who, in the introduction to his history of the Peloponnesian War between the Athenians and the Spartans from 431–404 B.C.E., stated: "It will be enough for me, however, if these words of mine are judged useful by those who want to understand clearly the events which happened in the past and which (human nature being what it is) will, at some time or other and in much the same ways, be repeated in the future. My work is not a piece of writing designed to meet the taste of an immediate public, but was done to last for ever." How would you compare the depth of Thucydides' commitment to the importance of history as a discipline to that of Sima Qian?

Part III

THE CONSOLIDATION OF CIVILIZATION (500–1450)

6

Medieval Civilization in the West: The Sword of Faith

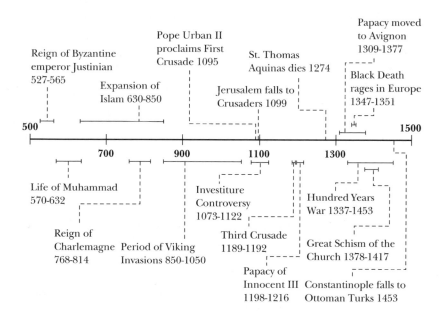

Understanding is the reward of faith. Therefore, do not seek to understand that you may believe, but believe that you may understand.

—*St. Augustine*

If the work of God could be comprehended by reason, it would no longer be wonderful.

—*Pope Gregory I*

There are two ways to slide through life: to believe everything or to doubt everything; both ways save us from thinking.

—*Alfred Korzybski*

To believe in God is impossible—not to believe in Him is absurd.

—Voltaire

Man is great only when he is kneeling.

—Pope Pius XII

CHAPTER THEMES

- *Beliefs and Spirituality:*   How did the establishment of the Christian church and the development of the papacy structure Christian beliefs, thus providing a spiritual foundation for the Middle Ages? How was devotion, whether Christian or Islamic, an encompassing theme for the period? Why did the church decline in the Late Middle Ages?

- *Church/State Relationships:*   Was medieval society primarily spiritual or secular in nature? In the confrontation between church and state, which authority was dominant, and which legacy more enduring? How did the papacy decline and lose influence in the face of royal control?

- *Imperialism:*   Some historians have considered the Crusades to be examples of a great "religious enterprise." To what extent were the Crusades about religion and to what extent about the assertion of blatant military imperialism and lust for conquest?

- *Women in History:*   What were the social and political positions of women during the European Middle Ages? Was the Middle Ages a period of relative freedom for women, and to what extent was this based on the popular worship of the Virgin Mary? Were women really placed on pedestals, and did the medieval concept of chivalry enhance their positions? Did the Islamic view of women differ?

- *Historical Change and Transition:*   How and why did Islamic religion and culture spread into Europe, Africa, and southwest Asia during the Middle Ages? How did trade promote the dissemination of Islamic culture? How did the political and religious struggle of the Crusades help blend European and Islamic civilizations by establishing economic and cultural links?

- *The Big Picture:*   To what extent can religion serve as a progressive and stabilizing force in society? Do people need religion? How can it be manipulated by the state in order to control a population? Are popes in essence the same as kings?

Some historians have argued that one of the greatest disasters in history was the failure of Rome to maintain her civilization. The internal economic and social decay of the third and fourth centuries, and the weakened military and political structure of the empire, paved the way for the barbarization of the realm by an uncontrolled influx of Germanic invaders. Western Europe was subjected to an era of chaos and disaster, marked by brutish force and devoid of the moderation that maintains civilized existence; by the fifth century, darkness had descended upon Europe. As the noted art historian Sir Kenneth Clark said, "In so far as we are the heirs of Greece and Rome, we got through by the skin of our teeth."

The period between the collapse of Roman civilization in the fifth century and the revival of classical learning in the European Renaissance of the fifteenth century is called the Middle Ages or the medieval world. Renaissance artists and intellectuals viewed their own era as one of light and progress, of renewed hope, where the emphasis centered no longer on God but on humanity. It was a secular era that condemned the chanting of prayers as mindless and viewed the collection of holy relics as absurd; it saw these practices as contradictory to the freedom of a new society focused on creativity. The Middle Ages were viewed with regret and scorn. Petrarch, a poet of the fourteenth century, lamented that "the Muse of History has been dead for a thousand years." When Rome fell, the Dark Ages settled over western Europe and civilization retreated—and then remained static.

This view of the Middle Ages was accepted and remained popular until perhaps the nineteenth century, when a more detached and less advocative scholarship began to assess critically the contributions and limitations of the medieval world. Perhaps the Middle Ages seemed so foreign because it was generally an age of faith, in contrast to the secular and rational emphasis of the modern world. The Christian church had been born during the height of Roman civilization and developed by drawing from Roman organization, making accommodation and enduring occasional persecution. Christianity survived and triumphed eventually as the official religion of the Roman Empire because of the broad appeal of its doctrine, its committed membership, and its superior organization. While the facade of Roman civilization gradually crumbled, the spiritual substructure of Christianity kept the Latin language, architectural styles, and other Roman cultural benefits alive. This was not easy given the dislocation that Europe experienced from about 500 to 1000 C.E. This period (called the Early Middle Ages) was indeed a difficult time. It was an era of transition, when leaders such as Charlemagne in Europe and Justinian in the eastern Byzantine empire were reestablishing political control. Waves of Viking invasions, starting around 850, led to major changes in social and political organization as peasants sought protection and nobles raised armies. Feudalism, which had its origin in late Roman times, became a complex, yet workable system of establishing authority and ordering society.

This period of disruption ended by 1100 as the Viking invasions dwindled in intensity and frequency. No longer was European civilization struggling to survive; anxiety gave way to confidence and confirmation that God held sway over the world. The years from about 1000 to 1300 (called the High Middle Ages) represent the acme of medieval civilization. During this era, universities were established and the great cathedrals were built as testaments of faith and devotion to God. This Christian devotion bordered on fanaticism as thousands marched off to the glory of the Crusades, hoping to achieve divine victory against the Muslims. The issue of authority was also brought more fully into question as popes and kings contended for ultimate supremacy in the earthly realm.

The conflict between religious and secular authority is one of the fundamental themes of Western civilization. Because of the diversity of human needs ranging from physical security to emotional support, establishing and maintaining order and harmony in a city or state is a complex and difficult task. It might be argued that two basic spheres of leadership exist in human affairs: the secular sphere, including matters of government, law, and domestic harmony, as well as defense and foreign affairs; and the spiritual sphere, generally, but not exclusively, attending to less tangible and more abstract human concerns. Questions of deity, creation, ethics, life, death, and afterlife are the concerns of religious leadership. In order for one person or a small group of people to rule effectively, they not only must control the apparatus of physical coercion in the state (military, police, etc.), but must also be recognized as head, or at least protector, of the people's religion. Thus the pharaohs of Egypt were revered as divine beings; in ancient Rome, the emperors bore the title Pontifex Maximus and served as head of the state religion, often to be deified after death. In modern totalitarian autocracies, control of party and state must be balanced by control of the state church or suppression of religion. Such is the essence of despotic authority.

We should therefore not be surprised to find that in the Middle Ages many kings and popes aspired to both secular and religious power. Both claimed supremacy over the other and based their positions on the evidence of scripture and logical argument. A king might well argue that the very survival of the church depended on his military strength; as defender of the faith, his will should prevail. On the other hand, the pope's position as successor to Saint Peter and representative of God on earth commanded the respect of all. For he was entrusted with the "Keys of Heaven," and there could be no exception to the ultimate authority of God.

The Late Middle Ages spanned the years from about 1300 to 1450 and was a time of stress as the church became more divided and declined in stature. The fourteenth century in particular saw the bloody Hundred Years' War between France and England, which was itself interrupted by perhaps the most destructive force yet encountered in world civilization—Black Death. The bubonic plague killed nearly half the population of Europe and contributed to massive economic and social change. It was this era of crisis that gave way to the ideals and attitudes of the Renaissance. The transition was made possible by a new human-centered energy, much as the transition from the ancient world was effected by energy sustained through devotion to God. But it should be remembered that the transition between the Middle Ages and the Renaissance was not abrupt, but gradual. We must resist the simplistic assumption that the medieval world was an "age of faith," rooted in mundane abstractions, and that the Renaissance was an "age of light," where man had thrown off the shackles of religion. In truth, such a gross distortion has little foundation in the historical evidence of the period.

It is difficult to assess the Middle Ages as a whole because there are so many different aspects to consider. However, one dominant theme is devotion. Devotion to God was a foundation of the medieval world; the ascetic principles and dutiful prayers of the monks had great purpose in maintaining a proper relationship with the Creator. Popular devotion was also evident in the construction of magnificent cathedrals like Notre Dame, Chartres, and Canterbury. Generations of construction workers labored to make their local cathedral impressive in the eyes of God. They were followed by generations of pilgrims who journeyed long distances simply to pray and offer gifts to an enshrined saint. The devotion of vassals to their lords also proved to be the foundation of political organization, and the abstract devotion of knights to chivalric ideals provided purpose and direction in life. The relationship of chaos and unity is another major theme. Much of the history of this period involves attempts to achieve unity by restraining the forces that contributed to chaos. In this respect, the conflicts between the representatives of church and state, as well as the Viking invasions and the Black Death, were primary threats to the unity of medieval civilization. They were countered by movements that organized and directed energy such as the Crusades or the cult of the Virgin

Mary (to whom so many cathedrals were dedicated), or by the security of the feudal relationship. In so many other ways, the European Middle Ages was an era of economic and technological progress—progress that flowed from a spiritual base.

This chapter is divided into three distinct sections, which can be studied individually or compared for analytic purposes; they are bound together by the theme of progress. The historical sources contained in this chapter reflect the problems and chaos of the medieval world and offer insight into the conditions and ideas that are truly representative of this important era.

SECTION I: THE EARLY MIDDLE AGES (500–1000)

BYZANTINE SPIRITUAL FOUNDATIONS

As the Western Roman Empire succumbed to Germanic invaders in the fourth and fifth centuries c.e., power shifted from Rome, which was at constant risk, to the city of Byzantium. The emperor Constantine the Great began the rebuilding of Byzantium in 324 and renamed the city Constantinople in 330. Its well-defended and critical location on the lucrative eastern trade routes at the entrance to the Black Sea augured a dynamic future. Greek culture dominated the region, and this eastern successor to the glory of Rome became known as the Byzantine Empire. Between 324 and its demise in 1453, the Byzantine Empire provided an important link between the Eastern and Western cultures of the former Roman Empire.

The religious history of the Byzantine Empire is particularly interesting, owing to the relatively unrestricted and speculative intellectual heritage of the Greek East. A free flow of ideas had always been a feature of Greek philosophy, and the Christian churches in the eastern Mediterranean had been absorbed in this tradition. The patriarchs of Constantinople, Alexandria, Antioch, and Jerusalem were especially influential and competitive. Many doctrinal differences arose between the pope in Rome and these eastern patriarchs over such issues as the nature of the Trinity and the worship of religious icons (representation of saints and other religious artifacts), not to mention whether papal authority held primacy for Byzantine Christians. Eventually these matters led to a split in the Christian church in 1054, with the establishment of Eastern Orthodox Christianity and Roman Catholic Christianity. The churches still remain split, though Pope John Paul II has renewed the call for unity.

Byzantine emperors had a long tradition of involvement with religious affairs. In fact, the term "Caesaro-papism" describes this melding of political power and religious authority in the person of the emperor. The first selection discusses the concern over the appearance of a dangerous heresy in the late third century, which threatened the unity of the early Christian church. Arius was an Egyptian priest who argued that Jesus was the Son of God and since sons always existed after fathers, then Jesus could not be both the Son of God and God at the same time. Jesus was a created being and therefore not eternal, nor made of the same substance (homoiousian) as the Father. Arius believed that Jesus was made of similar substance (homoiousian), but was primarily human. Constantine himself called the Council of Nicaea in 325 to settle the dispute and therein was formed the Nicene Creed, which settled the matter and provided a precedent for secular influence within the Eastern churches.

Heresy: The Threat of Arianism

EUSEBIUS

In this manner the emperor [Constantine], like a powerful herald of God, [wrote] to all the provinces, at the same time warning his subjects against superstitious error, and encouraging them in the pursuit of true godliness. But in the midst of his joyful anticipations of the success of this measure, he received tidings of a most serious disturbance which had invaded the peace of the Church. This intelligence he heard with deep concern, and at once endeavored to devise a remedy for the evil. The origin of this disturbance may be thus described.

The people of God were in a truly flourishing state, and abounding in the practice of good works. No terror from without assailed them, but a bright and most profound peace, through the favor of God, encompassed his Church on every side. Meantime, however, the spirit of envy was watching to destroy our blessings, which at first crept in unperceived, but soon revelled in the midst of the assemblies of the saints. At length it reached the bishops themselves, and arrayed them in angry hostility against each other, on pretense of a jealous regard for the doctrines of Divine truth. Hence it was that a mighty fire was kindled as it were from a little spark, and which, originating in the first instance in the Alexandrian church, overspread the whole of Egypt and Libya, . . . and eventually extended its ravages to the other provinces and cities of the empire; so that not only the prelates of the churches might be seen encountering each other in the strife of words, but the people themselves were completely divided, some adhering to one faction and others to another. So notorious did the scandal of these proceedings become, that the sacred matters of inspired teaching were exposed to the most shameful ridicule in the very theaters of the unbelievers. . . .

"Heresy: The Threat of Arianism" is from Eusebius, *The Life of the Blessed Emperor Constantine*, in *A Select Library of Nicene and Post-Nicene Fathers of the Christian Church*, vol. I, trans. Ernest C. Richardson (New York: The Christian Literature Company, 1890), pp. 515–516.

The Nicene Creed (325)

EUSEBIUS

[In accordance with the Emperor Constantine's instructions,] the bishops drew up this formula of faith:

"We believe in one God, the Father Almighty, Maker of all things visible and invisible: and in one Lord Jesus Christ, the Son of God, the only-begotten of the Father, that is of the substance of the Father; God of God, Light of light, true God of true God; begotten not made, consubstantial with the Father; by whom all things were made both which are in heaven and on earth; who for the sake of us men, and on account of our salvation, descended, became incarnate, was made man, suffered and rose again on the third day; he ascended into the heavens and will come to judge the living and the dead. We believe also in the Holy Spirit. But those who say 'There was a time when he was not,' or 'He did not exist before he was begotten,' or 'He was made of nothing,' or assert that 'He is of other substance or essence than the Father,' or that the Son of God is created, or mutable, or susceptible of change, the Catholic and apostolic Church of God rejects. . . ."

Consequently [Christ] is no creature like those which were made by him, but is of a substance far excelling any creature; which substance the Divine Oracles teach was begotten of the Father by such a mode of generation as cannot be explained nor even conceived by any creature. Thus also the declaration that "the Son is consubstantial [homoousios] with the Father" having been discussed, it was agreed that this must not be understood in a corporeal sense, or in any way analogous to mortal creatures; inasmuch as it is neither by division of substance, nor by any change of the Father's substance and power, since the underived na-

"The Nicene Creed" is from Eusebius, *The Life of the Blessed Emperor Constantine*, in *A Select Library of Nicene and Post-Nicene Fathers of the Christian Church*, vol. I, trans. Ernest C. Richardson (New York: The Christian Literature Company, 1890), pp. 515–518.

ture of the Father is inconsistent with all these things. That he is consubstantial with the Father then simply implies, that the Son of God has no resemblance to created things, but is in every respect like the Father only who begat him; and that he is of no other substance or essence but

of the Father. . . . Accordingly, since no divinely inspired Scripture contains the expression, "of things which do not exist" and "there was a time when he was not," and such other phrases as are therein subjoined, it seemed unwarrantable to utter and teach them.

Iconoclasm and Orthodoxy: The Second Council of Nicaea (787)

Another primary religious dispute within Eastern Christianity was the tradition of worshiping images of Christ, the Virgin, and the saints. Although this was acceptable practice in Western churches, in 726 the Byzantine emperor Leo IV abolished the cult of images by imperial edict. This was called "iconoclasm," and it is a primary example of Caesaro-papism. In 787, however, the empress Irene, who served as regent to her young son, reestablished the veneration of images at the Second Council of Nicaea, as the following source indicates. This policy remained under dispute for centuries.

We, therefore, following the royal pathway and the divinely inspired authority of our holy Fathers and the traditions of the Catholic Church for, as we all know, the Holy Spirit dwells in her, define with all certitude and accuracy, that just as the figure of the precious and life-giving cross, so also the venerable and holy images, as well in painting and mosaic, as of other fit materials, should be set forth in the holy churches of God. . . . For by so much the more frequently as they are seen in artistic representation, by so much the more readily are men lifted up to the memory of their prototypes, and to a longing after them; and to these should be given due salutation and honorable reverence, not indeed that true worship which pertains alone to the divine nature; but to these, as to the figure of the precious and life–giving cross, and to the book of the Gospels and

to other holy objects, incense and lights may be offered according to ancient pious custom. For the honor which is paid to the image passes on to that which the image represents, and he who shows reverence to the image shows reverence to the subject represented in it.

Those, therefore, who dare to think or teach otherwise, or as wicked heretics dare to spurn the traditions of the Church and to invent some novelty, or else to reject some of those things which the Church hath received, to wit, the book of the Gospels, or the image of the cross, or the pictorial icons, or the holy relics of a martyr, or to devise anything subversive of the lawful traditions of the Catholic Church, or to turn to common uses the sacred vessels and the venerable monasteries, if they be bishops or clerics we command that they be deposed [and] be cut off from communion.

"Iconoclasm and Orthodoxy" is from Joseph G. Ayer, Jr., ed. *A Source Book for Ancient Church History* (New York: Charles Scribner's Sons, 1913), pp. 696–697.

A Western Attitude toward the Byzantine Greeks (1147)

ODO OF DEUIL

One of the primary obstacles to the eventual success of the Crusades was the lack of trust and cooperation between the Roman Catholic Church in the West and the Greek Orthodox Church in the East.

"A Western Attitude toward the Byzantine Greeks" is from Odo of Deuil, *De Profectione Ludovici VII*, ed. and trans. Virginia G. Berry, p. 57. Copyright © 1948 by Columbia University Press. Reprinted by permission of the publisher.

These two Christian churches had separated in 1054 over doctrinal differences, and this rift fueled a political and economic competition between Western forces and those of the Byzantine emperor. The following selection notes Western disgust for the Byzantine Greeks at the beginning of the Second Crusade.

We know other heresies of theirs, both concerning their treatment of the Eucharist and concerning the procession of the Holy Ghost, but none of these matters would mar our page if not pertinent to our subject. Actually, it was for these reasons that the Greeks had incurred the hatred of our men, for their error had become known even among the lay people. Because of this they were judged not to be Christians, and the Franks considered killing them a matter of no importance and hence could with more difficulty be restrained from pillage and plundering.

And then the Greeks degenerated entirely . . . putting aside all manly vigor, both of words and of spirit, they lightly swore whatever they thought would please us, but they neither kept faith with us nor maintained respect for themselves. In general they really have the opinion that anything which is done for the holy empire [that is, Byzantium] cannot be considered perjury.

Islamic Civilization

The Religious Tenets of the Qur'an

The rise of Islamic civilization is a story of faith and confrontation amidst societies in political and cultural transition. The basic ideas of the Islamic worldview derived from a single prophetic revelation of the prophet Muhammad in the Qur'an: "There is but one God and his prophet is Muhammad." It is a simple revelation that has formed the basis of one of the world's most influential religions.

Muhammad (ca. 570–632) was an orphan who had worked on a caravan before marrying a wealthy widow. He was a man of great spiritual depth who had become troubled about the idolatry, worldliness, and lack of social conscience that plagued his society. Muhammad's discontent with this moral status quo and his searching nature positioned him to found a new religion that would address the needs of his particular Arabic community. On repeated occasions, he felt himself called by God (Allah) to "rise and warn" his fellow Arabs about their moral vacuousness. God's word had been delivered through other prophets prior to Muhammad, including Abraham, Moses, and Jesus. But the final revelation of God's work, the recitation (qur'an), was given to Muhammad by the messenger angel Gabriel. The message was clear: The Prophet Muhammad was to warn Arabs of God's displeasure with idolatrous worship and injustices to the weak and sick, the poor, widows, orphans, and women. God spoke of a judgment day where believers would enjoy the pleasures of paradise and nonbelievers would be cast into eternal hellfire, to be damned forever. God forgives the penitent and rewards those who respect his law and offer proper gratitude. Through submission (islam) to God's will, one becomes submissive (muslim) in worship and morality. A fervent monotheism is essential to the acceptance of the religion of Islam. Only humans have been given the choice either to obey or to reject the one true God.

At first Muhammad's revelations and strict demands invited opposition and even persecution in the city of Mecca, but his reputation as a moral leader increased and he was accepted in the city of Medina. This emigration (hegira) from Mecca to Medina in 622 became the starting point for year one of the Islamic calendar, signifying the creation of the Islamic community (umma).

Devotion to Islam is based on five basic principles or "pillars": (1) the acceptance of one God, Allah, and Muhammad as his prophet; (2) recitation of prayers five times a day toward Mecca after ritual purification before worship; (3) daytime fasting and abstinence from sexual relations from sunrise to sunset for one month a year; (4) payment of a tithe to support poor and unfortunate Muslims; and (5) a pilgrimage to Mecca at least once in a lifetime (hajj), *if one is able. The moral codes of Islam help define the religion: allegiance to the Islamic community, abstention from alcohol and pork, and modesty in personal affairs.*

After Muhammad's death in 632, the Islamic community struggled to maintain its unity since Muhammad had not named a successor. The success of Islam in organizing itself and in promoting the religion not only throughout Arab lands but beyond to Europe and the East is one of the great dramas of history. The influence of Islam on our contemporary world is formidable indeed, and it is important to understand the spiritual foundations of this impressive religion.

The following excerpts are primarily from the Qur'an and provide insight into some of the most important aspects of Islam.

The Heritage of Islam

In the Name of Allah, the Compassionate, the Merciful

This Book is not to be doubted. It is a guide for the righteous, who have faith in the unseen and are steadfast in prayer; who bestow in charity a part of what We have given them; who trust what has been revealed to you and to others before you, and firmly believe in the life to come. These are rightly guided by their Lord; these shall surely triumph.

As for the unbelievers, it is the same whether or not you forewarn them; they will not have faith. God has set a seal upon their hearts and ears; their sight is dimmed and grievous punishment awaits them. . . .

To Moses We gave the Scriptures and after him We sent other apostles. We gave Jesus the son of Mary veritable signs and strengthened him with the Holy Spirit. Will you then scorn each apostle whose message does not suit your fancies, charging some with imposture and slaying others? They say: "Our hearts are sealed." But God has cursed them for their unbelief. They have but little faith.

And now that a Book confirming their own has come to them from God, they deny it, although they know it to be the truth and have

The Koran translated by N.J. Dawood (Penguin Classics 1956, Fifth revised edition 1990) copyright © N.J. Sawood 1956, 1966, 1968, 1974, 1990, pp. 11, 18, 20–21, 23, 26–27, 29, 420. Reproduced with permission of Penguin Books Ltd.

long prayed for help against the unbelievers. God's curse be upon the infidels! Evil is that for which they have bartered away their soul. To deny God's own revelation, grudging the He should reveal His bounty to whom He chooses from among His servants! They have incurred God's most inexorable wrath. An ignominious punishment awaits the unbelievers. . . .

Many among the People of the Book [Jews and Christians] wish, through envy, to lead you back to unbelief, now that you have embraced the Faith and the truth has been made plain to them. Forgive them and bear with them until God makes known His will. God has power over all things.

Attend to your prayers and render the alms levy. Whatever good you do shall be rewarded by God. God is watching all your actions.

They declare: "None shall enter Paradise but Jews and Christians." Such are their wishful fancies. Say: "Let us have your proof, if what you say be true." Indeed, those that surrender themselves to God and do good works shall be rewarded by their Lord: they shall have nothing to fear or to regret.

The Jews say the Christians are misguided, and the Christians say it is the Jews who are misguided. Yet they both read the Scriptures. And the ignorant say the same of both. God will judge their disputes on the Day of Resurrection. . . .

They say: "Accept the Jewish or the Christian faith and you shall be rightly guided."

Say: "By no means! We believe in the faith of Abraham, the upright one. He was no idolater."

Say: "We believe in God and that which is revealed to us; in what was revealed to Abraham, Ishmael, Isaac, Jacob, and the tribes; to Moses and Jesus and the other prophets by their Lord. We make no distinction among any of them, and to God we have surrendered ourselves."

If they accept your faith, they shall be rightly guided; if they reject it, they shall surely be in schism. Against them God is your all-sufficient defender. He bears all and knows all. . . .

Believers, eat of the wholesome things with which We have provided you and give thanks to God, if it is Him you worship.

He has forbidden you carrion, blood, and the flesh of swine; also any flesh that is consecrated other than in the name of God. But whoever is compelled through necessity, intending neither to sin nor to transgress, shall incur no guilt. God is forgiving and merciful. . . .

Righteousness does not consist in whether you face towards the East or the West. The righteous man is he who believes in God and the Last Day, in the angels and the Book and the prophets; who, though he loves it dearly, gives away his wealth to kinsfolk, to orphans, to the destitute, to the traveller in need and to beggars, and for the redemption of captives; who attends to his prayers and renders the alms levy; who is true to his promises and steadfast in trial and adversity and in times of war. Such are the true believers; such are the God-fearing. . . .

Fight for the sake of God those that fight against you, but do not attack them first. God does not love the aggressors.

Slay them wherever you find them. Drive them out of the places from which they drove you. Idolatry is more grievous than bloodshed. But do not fight them within the precincts of the holy Mosque unless they attack you there; if they attack you put them to the sword. Thus shall the unbelievers be rewarded: but if they mend their ways, know that God is forgiving and merciful.

Fight against them until idolatry is no more and God's religion reigns supreme. But if they desist, fight none except the evil-doers. . . .

Give generously for the cause of God and do not with your own hands cast yourselves into destruction. Be charitable; God loves the charitable.

Make pilgrimage and visit the Sacred House [in Mecca] for His sake. If you cannot, send such offerings as you can afford and do not shave your heads until the offerings have reached their destination. But if any of you is ill or suffers from an ailment of the head, he must pay a ransom either by fasting or by almsgiving or by offering a sacrifice. . . .

When the sky is rent asunder; when the stars scatter and the oceans roll together; when the graves are hurled about; each soul shall know what it has done and what it has failed to do.

O man! What evil has enticed you from your gracious Lord who created you, gave you an upright form, and proportioned you? In whatever shape He willed He could have molded you. Yet you deny the Last Judgement. Surely there are guardians watching over you, noble recorders who know of all your actions.

The righteous will surely dwell in bliss. But the wicked shall burn in Hell upon the Judgement-day: nor shall they ever escape from it.

Would that you knew what the Day of Judgement is! Oh, would that you knew what the Day of Judgement is! It is the day when every soul will stand alone and God will reign supreme.

The Qur'an on Women

In the Name of Allah, the Compassionate, the Merciful

Men, have fear of your Lord, who created you from a single soul. From that soul He created its mate, and through them He bestrewed the earth with countless men and women.

Fear God, in whose name you plead with one another, and honor the mothers who bore you. God is ever watching you.

The Koran translated by N.J. Dawood (Penguin Classics 1956, Fifth revised edition 1990) copyright © N.J. Dawood 1956, 1966, 1968, 1974, 1990, pp. 60–62, 64, 74. Reproduced with permission of Penguin Books Ltd.

Give orphans the property which belongs to them. Do not exchange their valuables for worthless things or cheat them of their possessions; for this would surely be a great sin. If you fear that you cannot treat orphan [girls] with fairness, then you may marry other women who seem good to you: two, three, or four of them. But if you fear that you cannot maintain equality among them, marry one only or any slave-girls you may own. This will make it easier for you to avoid injustice.

Give women their dowry as a free gift; but if they choose to make over to you a part of it, you may regard it as lawfully yours. . . .

God has thus enjoined you concerning your children: A male shall inherit twice as much as a female. If there be more than two girls, they shall have two-thirds of the inheritance; but if there be one only, she shall inherit the half. Parents shall inherit a sixth each, if the deceased have a child; but if he leaves no child and his parents be his heirs, his mother shall have a third. If he has brothers, his mother shall have a sixth after payment of any legacy he may have bequeathed or any debt he may have owed.

You may wonder whether your parents or your children are more beneficial to you. But this is the law of God; God is all-knowing and wise. . . .

If any of your women commit fornication, call in four witnesses from among yourselves against them; if they testify to their guilt confine them to their houses till death overtakes them or till God finds another way for them. . . .

Men have authority over women because God has made the one superior to the other, and because they spend their wealth to maintain them. Good women are obedient. They guard their unseen parts because God has guarded them. As for those from whom you fear disobedience, admonish them and send them to beds apart and beat them. Then if they obey you, take no further action against them. God is high, supreme. . . .

If a woman fears ill-treatment or desertion on the part of her husband, it shall be no offence for them to seek a mutual agreement, for agreement is best. . . . Try as you may, you cannot treat all your wives impartially. Do not set yourself altogether against any of them, leaving her, as it were in suspense. If you do what is right and guard yourselves against evil, you will find God forgiving and merciful. If they separate, God will compensate both out of His own abundance: God is munificent and wise.

The Love of Allah

AL-GHAZZALI

The love of God is the highest of all topics, and is the final aim to which we have been tending hitherto. We have spoken of spiritual dangers as they hinder the love of God in a man's heart, and we have spoken of various good qualities as being the necessary preliminaries to it. Human perfection resides in this, that the love of God should conquer a man's heart and possess it wholly, and even if it does not possess it wholly it should predominate in the heart over the love of all other things. Nevertheless, rightly to understand the love of God is so difficult a matter that one sect of theologians have altogether denied that man can love a Being who is not of his own species, and they have defined the love of God as consisting merely in obedience. Those who hold such views do not know what real religion is.

All Muslims are agreed that the love of God is a duty. God says concerning the believers, "He loves them and they love Him," and the Prophet [Muhammad] said, "Till a man loves God and His Prophet more than anything else he has not the right faith. . . ."

When we apply this principle to the love of God we shall find that He alone is really worthy of our love, and that, if any one loves Him not, it is because he does not know Him. Whatever we love in any one we love because it is a reflection of Him. It is for this reason that we love Muhammad, because he is the Prophet and the Beloved of God, and the love of learned and pious men is really the love of God. We shall see this more

"The Love of Allah" is from Al-Ghazzali, *The Alchemy of Happiness*, trans. Claud Field, *The Wisdom of the East Series* (London: John Murray Publishers Ltd., 1910), pp. 51–54.

clearly if we consider what are the causes which excite love.

The first cause is this, that man loves himself and the perfection of his own nature. This leads him directly to the love of God, for man's very existence and man's attributes are nothing else but the gift of God, but for whose grace and kindness man would never have emerged from behind the curtain of nonexistence into the visible world. Man's preservation and eventual attainment to perfection are also entirely dependent upon the grace of God. It would indeed be a wonder, if one should take refuge from the heat of the sun under the shadow of a tree and not be grateful to the tree, without which there would be no shadow at all. Precisely in the same way, were it not for God, man would have no existence nor attributes at all; wherefore, then, should he not love God, unless he be ignorant of Him? Doubtless fools cannot love Him, for the love of Him springs directly from the knowledge of Him, and whence should a fool have knowledge?

Islamic Trade and Expansion

Within two centuries after the death of Muhammad in 632 C.E., the Muslim faith had spread to Spain and the Atlantic coast in the west, and to the borders of India and China in the east. This astonishing record of conversion was made possible by a centralized commitment to the faith of Islam even in the face of internal political turmoil, the strength and organization of a powerful Islamic military force, and very importantly, an Islamic interest in trade and exploration. After about 900, as the centralized caliphate administration gave way to the more flexible control of regional rulers, Islam spread to Afghanistan, India, and southeast Asia. Muslim maritime traders paved the way for this expansion of political control in the fifteenth and sixteenth centuries. Commercial interest was also responsible for Islamic expansion into sub-Saharan Africa from 850 to 1500. Caravans from Egypt, Libya, and Morocco in north Africa introduced the Islamic faith to the kingdoms of Ghana (ca. 700–1100) and Mali (1100–1400). The legendary trading center of Timbuktu on the Niger River near the Sahara became a major cultural center for Arabic and Muslim studies. By 1500, Islamic trade centers dotted the east coast of Africa.

The following selection is from one of the most celebrated story collections in the world. Under threat of death, Shahrazad, wife of the king of India and China, forestalled her execution by mesmerizing her husband with a new tale of love, deception, adventure, and conquest each night until in admiration, he lifted her sentence of death. Finally compiled in the fourteenth century, A Thousand and One Arabian Nights *reflects the rich folk traditions throughout the Islamic world. One of the most influential story cycles told of the adventures of Sinbad the Sailor. His seven voyages into the Indian Ocean reveal much about the Islamic spirit of adventure and attitude toward trade and risk.*

"We Begin Our Voyage": The Adventures of Sinbad

I dissipated the greatest part of my paternal inheritance in the excesses of my youth; but at length, seeing my folly, I became convinced that riches were not of much use when applied to such purposes as I had employed them in. . . . In short, I determined to employ to some profit the small sum I had remaining, and no sooner was this resolution formed than I put it into execution. I went to Basra [at the northern tip of the Persian Gulf], where I embarked with several merchants in a vessel which had been equipped at our united expense.

We set sail and steered toward the East Indies by the Persian Gulf. . . . One day, when in full sail, we were unexpectedly becalmed before a

"We Began Our Voyage" is from *The Arabian Nights' Entertainments*, trans. by Edward William Lane (London: George Routledge, 1890), pp. 113–114, 116.

small island appearing just above the water, and which, from its green color, resembled a beautiful meadow. The captain ordered the sails to be lowered, and gave permission to those who wished it to go ashore, of which number I formed one. But during the time that we were regaling ourselves with eating and drinking, by way of relaxation from the fatigues we had endured at sea, the island suddenly trembled, and we felt a severe shock.

They who were in the ship perceived the earthquake in the island, and immediately called to us to re-embark as soon as possible, or we should all perish, for what we supposed to be an island was no more than the back of a whale! The most active of the party jumped into the boat, while others threw themselves into the water to swim to the ship: as for me, I was still on the island, or, more properly speaking, on the whale, when it plunged into the sea, and I had only time to seize hold of a piece of wood which had been brought to make a fire with. Meantime the captain, willing to avail himself of a fair breeze which had sprung up, set sail with those who had reached his vessel, and left me to the mercy of the waves. I remained in this situation the whole of that day and the following night; and on the return of morning I had neither strength nor hope left, when a breaker happily dashed me on an island. The shore was high and steep, and I should have found great difficulty in landing, had not some roots of trees, which fortune seemed to have furnished for my preservation, assisted me. I threw myself on the ground, where I continued, more than half dead, till the sun rose.

Although I was extremely enfeebled by the fatigues I had undergone, I tried to creep about in search of some herb or fruit that might satisfy my hunger. I found some, and had also the good luck to meet with a stream of excellent water, which contributed not a little to my recovery. Having in a great measure regained my strength, I began to explore the island, and entered a beautiful plain. . . . I heard a voice of a man, who shortly after appeared, and coming to me, asked me who I was. I related by adventure

to him; after which he took me by the hand and led me into a cave, where there were some other persons, who were not less astonished to see me than I was to find them there.

I ate some food which they offered me; and having asked them what they did in a place which appeared so barren, they replied that they were grooms to King Mihrage, who was the sovereign of that isle, and that they came every year about that time with some mares belonging to the king, for the purpose of having a breed between them and a sea-horse which came on shore at that spot. . . .

The following day they returned to the capital of the island with the mares, where I accompanied them. On our arrival, King Mihrage, to whom I was presented, asked me who I was, and by what chance I had reached his dominions; and when I had satisfied his curiosity, he expressed pity at my misfortune. At the same time, he gave orders that I should be taken care of and have everything I might want. These orders were executed in a manner that proved the king's generosity, as well as the exactness of his officers.

As I was a merchant, I associated with persons of my own profession. I sought, in particular, foreigners, as much to hear some intelligence of Baghdad, as with the hope of meeting with some one whom I could return with; for the capital of King Mihrage is situated on the sea-coast, and has a beautiful port, where vessels from all parts of the world daily arrive. I also sought the society of the Indian sages, and found great pleasure in their conversation; this, however, did not prevent me from attending at court very regularly, nor from conversing with the governors of provinces, and some less powerful kings, tributaries of Mihrage, who were about his person. They asked me a thousand questions about my country; and I, on my part, was not less inquisitive about the laws and customs of their different states, or whatever appeared to merit my curiosity. . . .

As I was standing one day near the port, I saw a ship come toward the land; when they had cast anchor, they began to unload its goods, and the merchants, to whom they belonged, took them away to their warehouses. Happening to cast my eyes of some of the packages, I saw my name written, and, having attentively examined them, I concluded them to be those which I had embarked in the ship in which I left Basra. I also recollected the captain; but as I was persuaded that he thought me dead, I went up to him. . . . "Captain, I am that Sinbad, whom you supposed dead, but who is still alive, and these parcels are my property and merchandise." . . .

He was rather staggered at my discourse, but was soon convinced that I was not an impostor; for some people arriving from his ship knew and began to congratulate me on my fortunate escape. . . . I selected the most precious and valuable thing in by bales, as presents for King Mihrage. . . . After that, I took my leave of him, and re-embarked in the same vessel, having first exchanged what merchandise remained with that of the country, which consisted of aloes and sandal-wood, camphor, nutmegs, cloves, pep-

per, and ginger. We touched at several islands, and at last landed at Basra, from whence I came here, having realized [as profit] about a hundred thousand [gold coins]. I returned to my family, and was received by them with the joy which a true and sincere friendship inspires. I purchased slaves of each sex, and bought a magnificent house and grounds. I thus established myself, determined to forget the disagreeable things I had endured, and to enjoy the pleasures of life. . . .

I had resolved after my first voyage, to pass the rest of my days in tranquility at Baghdad. . . . But I soon grew weary of an idle life; the desire of seeing foreign countries, and carrying on some negotiations by sea returned: I bought some merchandise, which I thought likely to [sell], and set off a second time with some merchants, upon whose probity I could rely. We embarked in a good vessel, and having recommended ourselves to the care of the Almighty, we began our voyage. . . .

"O King, If You Believed in Allah": Islamic Conversion

AL-BAKRI

The Muslim geographer, Abu Ubaydallah al-Bakri (d. 1094), was a resident of Córdoba, Spain, and is most famous for his description of that region. In his Book of Routes and Realms *(1068), al-Bakri drew heavily on the oral information that Islamic merchants provided him about the peoples of West Africa. In this excerpt, he speaks of the conversion of a West African king to the tenets of Islam.*

On the opposite bank of the Nil [Niger River] is another great kingdom, stretching a distance of more than eight days' marching, the king of which has the title of Daw. The inhabitants of this region use arrows when fighting. Beyond this country lies another called Malal [Mali], the king of which is known as *al-musulmani* ["The Muslim"]. He is thus called because his country became afflicted with drought one year follow-

ing another; the inhabitants prayed for rain, sacrificing cattle till they had exterminated almost all of them, but the drought and the misery only increased. The king had as his guest a Muslim who used to read the Qur'an and was acquainted with the Sunna [traditions of Sunni Muslims]. To this man the king complained of the calamities that assailed him and his people. The man said: "O King, if you believed in Allah (who is exalted) and testified that He is One, and testified as to the prophetic mission of Muhammad (God bless him and give him peace) and if you accepted all the religious laws of Islam, I would pray for your deliverance from your plight and that God's mercy would envelop all the people of your country and that your enemies and adversaries might envy you on that account." Thus he continued to press the king until the latter accepted Islam and became a sincere Muslim. The man made the king recite from the Qur'an some easy passages and taught him religious obligations and practices which no one may be excused from knowing. Then the Muslim made him wait till the eve of the following Friday, when he ordered him to purify

himself by a complete ablution, and clothed him in a cotton garment which he had. The two of them came out towards a mound of earth, and there the Muslim stood praying while the king, standing at his right side, imitated him. Thus they prayed for a part of the night, the Muslim reciting invocations and the king saying "Amen." The dawn had just started to break when God caused abundant rain to descend upon them. So the king ordered the idols to be broken and expelled the sorcerers from his country. He and his descendants after him as well as his nobles were sincerely attached to Islam, while the common people of his kingdom remained polytheists. Since then their rulers have been given the title of *al-musulmani.*

Islamic Science and Mathematics

The Islamic community during the Middle Ages and beyond was not simply concerned with matters of faith and obedience to doctrine. As Muslim armies covered North Africa and the Middle East, even venturing into Europe, they carried with them some of the great advancements of Islamic civilization. Muslim learning was embraced in such academic centers as Córdoba, Spain, where Jewish scholars were central in establishing a conduit of knowledge to the West by translating Arabic science and medical texts into Spanish and Latin. Many of these ideas in astronomy, medicine, advanced mathematics, law, literature, poetry, philosophy, and history fell on deaf ears in the West because of the fear of doctrinal contamination. Indeed, for Western Christians, the followers of Allah were the "Infidel," to be feared and opposed through Crusades to recapture the Holy Land for the glory of a Christian God.

The following selections attest to the framework of learning and inquiry that was a most impressive benefit of Islamic civilization.

On the Separation of Mathematics and Religion

AL-GHAZZALI

Mathematics comprises the knowledge of calculation, geometry, and cosmography: it has no connection with the religious sciences, and proves nothing for or against religion; it rests on a foundation of proofs which, once known and

understood, cannot be refuted. Mathematics tend, however, to produce two bad results.

The first is this: Whoever studies this science admires the subtlety and clearness of its proofs. His confidence in philosophy increases, and he thinks that all its departments are capable of the same clearness and solidity of proof as mathematics. But when he hears people speak on the unbelief and impiety of mathematicians, of their professed disregard for the Divine Law, which is notorious, it is true that, out of regard for authority, he echoes these accusations, but he says to himself at the same time that, if there was truth in religion, it would not have escaped

"On the Separation of Mathematics and Religion" is from Al-Ghazzali, *The Confession of Al-Ghazzali,* trans. Claud Field, The Wisdom of the East Series (London: John Murray Publishers Ltd., 1908), pp. 33–34.

those who have displayed so much keenness of intellect in the study of mathematics.

Next, when he becomes aware of the unbelief and rejection of religion on the part of these learned men, he concludes that to reject religion is reasonable. How many of such men gone astray I have met whose sole argument was that just mentioned. . . .

It is therefore a great injury to religion to suppose that the defence of Islam involves the condemnation of the exact sciences. The religious law contains nothing which approves them or condemns them, and in their turn they make no attack on religion. The words of the Prophet, "The sun and the moon are two signs of the power of God; they are not eclipsed for the birth or the death of any one; when you see these signs take refuge in prayer and invoke the name of God"—these words, I say, do not in any way condemn the astronomical calculations which define the orbits of these two bodies, their conjunction and opposition according to particular laws.

On the Causes of Small-Pox

AL-RAZI

Although [scholars] have certainly made some mention of the treatment of the Small-Pox (but without much accuracy and distinctness), yet there is not one of them who has mentioned the cause of the existence of the disease, and how it comes to pass that hardly any one escapes it, or who has disposed the modes of treatment in

"On the Causes of Small-Pox" is from Abu Bekr Muhammad Ibn Zacariya Al-Razi, *A Treatise on Small-Pox and Measles,* trans. William A. Greenhill (London, 1848), pp. 28–31.

their right places. And for this reason I . . . have mentioned whatever is necessary for the treatment of this disease, and have arranged and carefully disposed everything in its right place, by GOD's permission. . . .

I say then that every man, from the time of his birth until he arrives at old age, is continually tending to dryness; and for this reason the blood of children and infants is much moister than the blood of young men, and still more so than that of old men. . . . Now the Small-Pox arises when the blood putrefies and ferments, so that the superfluous vapors are thrown out of it, and it is changed from the blood of infants, which is like must, into the blood of young men, which is like wine perfectly ripened: and the Small-Pox itself may be compared to the fermentation and the hissing noise which takes place in must at that time. And this is the reason why children, especially males, rarely escape being seized with this disease, because it is impossible to prevent the blood's changing from this state into its second state. . . .

As to young men, whereas their blood is already passed into the second state, its maturation is established, and the superfluous particles of moisture which necessarily cause putrefaction are now exhaled; hence it follows that this disease only happens to a few individuals among them, that is, to those whose vascular system abounds with too much moisture, or is corrupt in quality with a violent inflammation. . . .

And as for old men, the Small-Pox seldom happens to them, except in pestilential, putrid, and malignant constitutions of the air, in which this disease is chiefly prevalent. For a putrid air, which has an undue proportion of heat and moisture, and also an inflamed air, promotes the eruption of this disease.

The Dawn of the European Middle Ages

Charlemagne and the Empire of the Franks

Biographical writing constitutes a considerable part of medieval literature, but much of it cannot be relied upon for accuracy. Medieval biographers who wrote about the lives of saints or kings often exaggerated their accomplishments for the sake of providing solid examples of moral living. A major exception to this practice was Einhard, a secretary and public works administrator at Charlemagne's court. Although his biography has some inaccuracies, nevertheless it is regarded as a trustworthy account of the life and deeds of Charlemagne, ruler of the Frankish empire from 768 to 814.

The Moderate and Progressive King

EINHARD

Charles was large and strong, and of lofty stature, though not excessively tall. The upper part of his head was round, his eyes very large and animated, nose a little long, hair auburn, and face laughing and merry. His appearance was always stately and dignified, whether he was standing or sitting, although his neck was thick and somewhat short and his abdomen rather prominent. The symmetry of the rest of his body concealed these defects. His gait was firm, his whole carriage manly, and his voice clear, but not so strong as his size led one to expect. His health was excellent, except during the four years preceding his death, when he was subject to frequent fevers; toward the end of his life he limped a little with one foot. Even in his later years he lived rather according to his own inclinations than the advice of physicians; the latter indeed he very much disliked, because they wanted him to give up roasts, to which he was accustomed, and to eat boiled meat instead. In accordance with national custom, he took frequent exercise on horseback and in the chase, in which sports scarcely any people in the world can equal the Franks. He enjoyed the vapors from natural warm springs, and often indulged in swimming, in which he was so skillful that none could surpass him; and hence it was that he built his palace at Aix-la-Chapelle, and lived there constantly during his later years. . . .

Charles was temperate in eating, and especially so in drinking, for he abhorred drunkenness in anybody, much more in himself and those of his household; but he could not easily abstain from food, and often complained that

fasts injured his health. He gave entertainments but rarely, only on great feast-days, and then to large numbers of people. His meals consisted ordinarily of four courses not counting the roast, which his huntsmen were accustomed to bring in on the spit; he was more fond of this than of any other dish. While at table, he listened to reading or music. The subjects of the readings were the stories and deeds of olden time. He was fond, too, of St. Augustine's books, and especially of the one entitled The City of God. He was so moderate in the use of wine and all sorts of drink that he rarely allowed himself more than three cups in the course of a meal. . . .

Charles had the gift of ready and fluent speech, and could express whatever he had to say with the utmost clearness. He was not satisfied with ability to use his native language merely, but gave attention to the study of foreign ones, and in particular was such a master of Latin that he could speak it as well as his native tongue; but he could understand Greek better than he could speak it. He was so eloquent, indeed, that he might have been taken for a teacher of oratory. He most zealously cherished the liberal arts, held those who taught them in great esteem, and conferred great honors upon them. He took lessons in grammar of the deacon Peter of Pisa, at that time an aged man. Another deacon, Albin of Britain, surnamed Alcuin, a man of Saxon birth, who was the greatest scholar of the day, was his teacher in other branches of learning. The king spent much time and labor with him studying rhetoric, dialectic, and especially astronomy. He learned to make calculations, and used to investigate with much curiosity and intelligence the motions of the heavenly bodies. He also tried to write, and used to keep tablets and blanks in bed under his pillow, that at leisure hours he might accustom his hand to form the letters; however, as he began

"The Moderate and Progressive King" is from Frederick Ogg, ed., *A Source Book of Medieval History* (New York: American Book Company, 1907), pp. 109–114.

his efforts late in life, and not at the proper time, they met with little success.

He cherished with the greatest fervor and devotion the principles of the Christian religion, which had been instilled into him from infancy. Hence it was that he built the beautiful basilica at Aix-la-Chapelle, which he adorned with gold and silver and lamps, and with rails and doors of solid brass. He had the columns and marbles for this structure brought from Rome and Ravenna, for he could not find such as were suitable elsewhere. He was a constant worshipper at this church as long as his health permitted, going morning and evening, even after nightfall, besides attending mass. He took care that all the services there conducted should be held in the best possible manner, very often warning the sextons not to let any improper or unclean thing be brought into the building, or remain in it. He provided it with a number of sacred vessels of gold and silver, and with such a quantity of clerical robes that not even the door-keepers, who filled the humblest office in the church, were obliged to wear their everyday clothes when in the performance of their duties. He took great pains to improve the church reading and singing, for he was well skilled in both, although he neither read in public nor sang, except in a low tone and with others.

He was very active in aiding the poor, and in that open generosity which the Greeks call alms; so much so, indeed, that he not only made a point of giving in his own country and his own kingdom, but when he discovered that there were Christians living in poverty in Syria, Egypt, and Africa, at Jerusalem, Alexandria, and Carthage, he had compassion on their wants, and used to send money over the seas to them. The reason that he earnestly strove to make friends with the kings beyond seas was that he might get help and relief to the Christians living under their rule. He cared for the Church of St. Peter the Apostle at Rome above all other holy and sacred places, and heaped high its treasury with a vast wealth of gold, silver, and precious stones. He sent great and countless gifts to the popes; and throughout his whole reign the wish that he had nearest his heart was to reestablish the ancient authority of the city of Rome under his care and by his influence, and to defend and protect the Church of St. Peter, and to beautify and enrich it out of his own store above all other churches. Nevertheless, although he held it in such veneration, only four times did he repair to Rome to pay his vows and make his supplications during the whole forty-seven years that he reigned.

The Missi Dominici (802)

The greatness of a ruler has often been determined not just by how much territory he conquered, but by how well he maintained it. The administration of an empire as vast as Charlemagne's depended on efficient servants of the king. The selections below testify to Charlemagne's organization and efficient rule. The Missi Dominici were members of the church and nobility who traveled throughout the realm administering justice by acting as an appellate court; it was an attempt to inject the presence of the king directly into the law and affairs of the realm.

Concerning the embassy sent out by the lord emperor. Therefore, the most serene and most Christian lord emperor Charles has chosen from his nobles the wisest and most prudent men, both archbishops and some of the other bishops also, and venerable abbots and pious laymen, and has sent them throughout his whole kingdom, and through them by all the

"The Missi Dominici" is from Dana Munro, ed., *Translations and Reprints from the Original Sources of European History*, vol. 6, pt. 5 (Philadelphia: University of Pennsylvania, 1899), p. 16.

following chapters has allowed men to live in accordance with the correct law. Moreover, where anything which is not right and just has been enacted in the law, he has ordered them to inquire into this most diligently and to inform him of it; he desires, God granting, to reform it. And let no one, through his cleverness or astuteness, dare to oppose or thwart the written law, as many would like to do, or the judicial sentence passed upon him, or to do injury to the churches of God or the poor or the widows or the wards or any Christian. But all shall live entirely in accordance with God's precept, justly and under a just rule, and each one shall be admonished to live in harmony with his fellows in his business or profession; the canonical clergy ought to observe in every respect a canonical life without seeking base gain, nuns ought to keep diligent watch over their lives, laymen and the secular clergy ought rightly to observe their laws without malicious fraud, and all ought to live in mutual charity and perfect peace.

The Carolingian Renaissance: Education and the Scriptures
CHARLEMAGNE

Charlemagne's involvement in his empire went beyond its administrative regulation. He believed that learning was an essential aspect of life and established palace schools run by great scholars such as Alcuin of York. In these schools, members of the nobility were taught to read and write. In practical terms, this contributed to greater communication and a more efficient administration of the empire. In spiritual terms, the Bible and other Christian writings were now open to study and revision; accuracy was demanded by the emperor. The following selection is from a letter written by Charlemagne to the clergy of his realm. It is a clear statement of his educational policy.

Charles, by the grace of God, King of the Franks and Lombards and Patrician of the Romans, to Abbot Baugulf and to all the congregation, also to the faithful committed to you, we have directed a loving greeting by our ambassadors in the name of omnipotent God.

We, together with our faithful, have considered it to be useful that the bishoprics and monasteries entrusted by the favor of Christ to our control, . . . ought to be zealous in teaching those who by the gift of God are able to learn, . . . so that those who desire to please God by living rightly should not neglect to please him by speaking correctly. . . . For although correct conduct may be better than knowledge, nevertheless knowledge precedes conduct. Therefore, each one ought to study what he desires to accomplish, so that so much the more fully the mind may know what ought to be done, as the tongue hastens in the praises of omnipotent God without the hindrances of errors. . . . For when in the years just passed letters were often written to us from several monasteries in which it was stated that the brethren who dwelt there offered up in our behalf sacred and pious prayers, we have recognized in most of these letters both correct thoughts and uncouth expressions; because what pious devotion dictated faithfully to the mind, the tongue, uneducated on account of the neglect of study, was not able to express in the letter without error. . . . And we all know well that, although errors of speech are dangerous, far more dangerous are errors of the understanding. Therefore, we exhort you not only not to neglect the study of letters, but also with most humble mind, pleasing to God,

"The Carolingian Renaissance: Education and the Scriptures" is from Dana Munro, ed., *Translations and Reprints from the Original Sources of European History*, vol. 6, pt. 5 (Philadelphia: University of Pennsylvania, 1899), pp. 12–14.

to study earnestly in order that you may be able more easily and more correctly to penetrate the mysteries of the divine Scriptures. . . . And may this be done with a zeal as great as the earnestness with which we command it. For we desire you to be, as it is fitting that soldiers of the church should be, devout in mind, learned in discourse, chaste in conduct and eloquent in speech, so that whosoever shall seek to see you out of reverence for God, or on account of your reputation for holy conduct, just as he is edified by your appearance, may also be instructed by your wisdom, which he has learned from your reading or singing, and may g away joyfully giving thanks to omnipotent God. Do not neglect, therefore, if you wish to have our favor, to send copies of this letter to all your fellow-bishops and to all the monasteries . . . farewell.

The Feudal Relationship

Feudalism in its more refined form was born of the chaos caused by the Viking invasions, internal disputes, and poor leadership that together contributed to the destruction of Charlemagne's empire. As central authority (in the person of the king) collapsed, there evolved rather naturally a system of decentralized rule in which the most important nobles of the realm (lords) *protected their own regional holdings by contracting with lesser nobles* (vassals) *who fought for them. This involved an expression of homage, in which the vassal promised* fealty *(loyalty) to the lord. In return, he was usually granted a* fief *(parcel of land) from which he derived an income and, depending on the size of his land holdings, some measure of prestige. The vassal, in turn, might have other vassals pledged to himself in a hierarchy of support. This process was called* subinfeudation *and became quite complex since vassals could contract with several lords at once. In that case, one's ultimate fealty belonged to the original or most important noble, called the* liege lord.

Feudalism, then, is the political, military, and legal relationship between a lord and a vassal. It had existed rather informally since the later Roman Empire, but became more sophisticated and widespread during the ninth century as the Viking invasions demanded some form of defense. The lords provided the leadership, the vassals composed the army, and the people sought the protection of such regional strongmen. In return for this protection, the free peasant often gave up his land and labored on the fief of a noble for a specified amount of time. The peasant thus became a serf and was responsible for the production and upkeep of the lord's manor. The social, economic, and legal relationship between a serf and a member of the fighting nobility for whom he worked is called manorialism. *The following selections are representative of various aspects of medieval feudalism.*

Legal Rules for Military Service
KING LOUIS IX

The baron and all vassals of the king are bound to appear before him when he shall summon them, and to serve him at their own expense for forty days and forty nights, with as many knights as each one owes; and he is able to extract from them these services when he wishes and when he has need of them. And if the king wishes to keep them more than forty days at their own expense, they are not bound to remain if they do not wish it. And if the king wishes to keep them at his expense for the defence of the realm, they are bound to remain. And if the king wishes to lead them outside of the kingdom, they need not go unless they wish to, for they have already served their forty days and forty nights.

"Legal Rules for Military Service" is from Edward P. Cheyney, ed., *Translations and Reprints from the Original Sources of European History*, vol. 4, pt. 3 (Philadelphia: University of Pennsylvania, 1897), p. 30.

Liege Homage

I, John of Toul, make known that I am the liege man of the lady Beatrice, countess of Troyes, and of her son, Theobald, count of Champagne, against every creature, living or dead, save my allegiance to lord Enjorand of Coucy, lord John of Arcis, and the count of Grandpre. If it should happen that the count of Grandpre should be at war with the countess and count of Champagne on his own quarrel, I will aid the count of Grandpre in my own person, and will send to the count and countess of Champagne the knights whose service I owe to them for the fief which I hold of them. But if the count of Grandpre shall make war on the countess and the count of Champagne on behalf of his friends and not in his own quarrel, I will aid in my own person the countess and count of Champagne, and will send one knight to the count of Grandpre for the service which I owe him for the fief which I hold of him, but I will not go myself into the territory of the count of Grandpre to make war on him.

"Liege Homage" is from Oliver Thatcher and Edgar McNeal, eds., *A Source Book of Medieval History* (New York: Charles Scribner's Sons, 1905), pp. 364–365.

SECTION II: THE HIGH MIDDLE AGES (1000–1300)

THE MEDIEVAL CHURCH IN ASCENDANCY

The Crusades

The first expedition to free the Holy Land from the control of the Infidel Muslim was launched in 1095 at the Council of Clermont. Pope Urban II presided and in a rousing speech excited the crowd with this impassioned plea for action. Although we are not sure about the accuracy of the text (we have five contemporary versions), the following account by Robert the Monk is credible and clearly illustrates Urban's justification for the First Crusade as well as his popular appeal.

Launching the Crusades (1095): "It Is the Will of God!"

ROBERT THE MONK

In 1095 a great council was held in Auvergne, in the city of Clermont. Pope Urban II, accompanied by cardinals and bishops, presided over it. It was made famous by the presence of many bishops and princes from France and Germany. After the council had attended to ecclesiastical matters, the pope went out into a public square, because no house was able to hold the people, and addressed them in a very persuasive

"Launching the Crusades" is from Oliver Thatcher and Edgar McNeal, eds., *A Source Book of Medieval History* (New York: Charles Scribner's Sons, 1905), pp. 518–520.

speech, as follows: "O race of the Franks, O people who live beyond the mountains [the Alps], O people loved and chosen of God, as is clear from your many deeds, distinguished over all other nations by the situation of your land, your catholic faith, and your regard for the holy church, we have a special message and exhortation for you. For we wish you to know what a grave matter has brought us to your country. The sad news has come from Jerusalem and Constantinople that the people of Persia, an accursed and foreign race, enemies of God, a generation that set not their heart aright, and whose spirit was not steadfast with God [Ps. 78:8], have invaded the lands of those Christians and devastated them with the sword, rapine, and fire. Some of the Christians they have carried away as slaves, others they have put to death. The churches they have either destroyed or turned into mosques. They desecrate and overthrow the altars. They circumcise the Christians and pour the blood from the circumcision on the altars or in the baptismal fonts. Some they kill in a horrible way by cutting open the abdomen, taking out a part of the entrails and tying them to a stake; they then beat them and compel them to walk until all their entrails are drawn out and they fall to the ground. Some they use as targets for their arrows. They compel some to stretch out their necks and then they try to see whether they can cut off their heads with one stroke of the sword. It is better to say nothing of their horrible treatment of the women. They have taken from the Greek empire a tract of land so large that it takes more than two months to walk through it. Whose duty is it to avenge this and recover that land, if not yours? For to you more than to other nations the Lord has given the military spirit, courage, agile bodies, and the bravery to strike down those who resist you. Let your minds be stirred to bravery by the deeds of your forefathers, and by the efficiency and greatness of [Charlemagne], and of Ludwig his son, and of the other kings who have destroyed Turkish kingdoms, and established Christianity in their lands. You should be moved especially by the holy grave of our Lord and Saviour which is now held by unclean peoples, and by the holy places which are treated with dishonor and irreverently befouled with their uncleanness.

"O bravest of knights, descendants of unconquered ancestors, do not be weaker than they, but remember their courage. If you are kept back by your love for your children, relatives and wives, remember what the Lord says in the Gospel: 'He that loveth father or mother more than me is not worthy of me' [Matt. 10:37]; 'and everyone that hath forsaken houses, or brothers, or sisters, or father, or mother, or wife, or children, or lands for my name's sake, shall receive a hundredfold and shall inherit everlasting life' [Matt. 19:29]. Let no posses-

sions keep you back, no solicitude for your property. Your land is shut in on all sides by the sea and mountains, and is too thickly populated. There is not much wealth here, and the soil scarcely yields enough to support you. On this account you kill and devour each other, and carry on war and mutually destroy each other. Let your hatred and quarrels cease, your civil wars come to an end, and all your dissensions stop. Set out on the road to the holy sepulchre, take the land from that wicked people, and make it your own. . . . This land our Saviour made illustrious by his birth, beautiful with his life, and sacred with his suffering; he redeemed it with his death and glorified it with his tomb. This royal city is now held captive by her enemies, and made pagan by those who know not God. She asks and longs to be liberated and does not cease to beg you to come to her aid. She asks aid especially from you because, as I have said, God has given more of the military spirit to you than to other nations. Set out on this journey and you will obtain the remission of your sins and be sure of the incorrigible glory of the kingdom of heaven."

When Pope Urban had said this and much more of the same sort, all who were present were moved to cry out with one accord, "It is the will of God, it is the will of God!" When the pope heard this he raised his eyes to heaven and gave thanks to God, and, commanding silence with a gesture of his hand, he said: "My dear brethren, today there is fulfilled in you that which the Lord says in the Gospel, 'Where two or three are gathered in my name, there am I in the midst' [Matt. 18:20]. For unless the Lord God had been in your minds you would not all have said the same thing. For although you spoke with many voices, nevertheless it was one and the same thing that made you speak. So I say unto you, God, who put those words into your hearts, has caused you to utter them. Therefore let these words be your battle cry, because God caused you to speak them. Whenever you meet the enemy in battle, you shall all cry out, 'It is the will of God! It is the will of God!'"

Theme: Imperialism

The Historical Intersection

THE UNITED STATES: 1900

"The Hand of God":
American Imperialism in the Philippines

ALBERT J. BEVERIDGE

Through much of the nineteenth century, the United States was involved with establishing its own borders "from sea to shining sea," but did not try to expand internationally. In 1898, however, because of the Spanish-American War, the United States inaugurated a policy of foreign imperialism. One of the Spanish colonies ceded to the United States was the Philippine Islands. There was a strong independence movement in the islands, however, and actual warfare broke out in 1899 between Filipinos and American forces. Congress was divided about setting up a government for the newly acquired territory. One of the champions of imperialism was Albert J. Beveridge, senator from Indiana. In January 1900, he addressed Congress in support of a resolution that decreed that the United States "establish and maintain such government control throughout the archipelago as the situation may demand."

Compare and Contrast:

- Compare Senator Beveridge's justification for U.S. imperialism in the Philippines with the argument of Pope Urban II in justifying the First Crusade to the Holy Land in 1095. How is God invoked in both excerpts to sanction violence and invasion?

Mr. President, the times call for candor. The Philippines are ours forever, "territory belonging to the United States," as the Constitution calls them. And just beyond the Philippines are China's illimitable markets. We will not retreat from ei-

(contd)

ther. We will not repudiate our duty in the archipelago. We will not abandon our opportunity in the Orient. We will not renounce our part in the mission of our race, trustee under God, of the civilization of the world. And we will move forward to our work, not howling our regrets like slaves whipped to their burdens, but with gratitude for a task worthy of our strength, and thanksgiving to Almighty God that He has marked us as His chosen people, henceforth to lead in the regeneration of the world. . . .

Senators, it would be better to abandon this combined garden and Gibraltar of the Pacific, and count our blood and treasure already spent a profitable loss, than to apply any academic arrangement of self-government to these children. They are not capable of self-government. How could they be? They are not of a self-governing race. They are Orientals, Malays, instructed by Spaniards in the latter's worst estate.

They know nothing of practical government except as they have witnessed the weak, corrupt, cruel, and capricious rule of Spain. What magic will anyone employ to dissolve in their minds and characters those impressions of governors and governed which three centuries of misrule have created? What alchemy will change the Oriental quality of their blood and set the self-governing currents of the American pouring through their Malay veins? How shall they, in the twinkling of an eye, be exalted to the heights of self-governing peoples which required a thousand years for us to reach, Anglo-Saxon though we are? . . .

Mr. President, self-government and internal development have been the dominant notes of our first century; administration and the development of other lands will be the dominant notes of our second century. And administration is as high and holy a function as self-government, just as the care of a trust estate is as sacred an obligation as the management of our own concerns. . . .

The Declaration of Independence does not forbid us to do our part in the regeneration of the world. If it did, the Declaration would be wrong, just as the Articles of Confederation, drafted by the very same men who signed the Declaration, were found to be wrong. The Declaration has no application to the present situation. It was written by self-governing men for self-governing men. . . .

Mr. President, this question is deeper than any question of party politics; deeper than any question of the isolated policy of our country even; deeper even than any question of constitutional power. It is elemental. It is racial. God has not been preparing the English-speaking and Teutonic peoples for a thousand years for nothing but vain and idle self-contemplation and self-admiration. No! He has made us the master organizers of the world to establish system where chaos reigns. He has given the spirit of progress to overwhelm the forces of reaction throughout the earth. He has made us adept in government that we may administer government among savage and senile peoples. Were it not for such a force as this the world would relapse into barbarism and night. And of all our race He has marked the American people as His chosen nation to finally lead in the regeneration of the world. This is the divine mission of America, and

(contd)

it holds for us all the profit, all the glory, all the happiness possible to man. We are trustees of the world's progress, guardians of its righteous peace. The judgment of the Master is upon us: "Ye have been faithful over a few things; I will make you ruler over many things."

What shall history say of us? Shall it say that we renounced that holy trust, left the savage to his base condition, the wilderness to the reign of waste, deserted duty, abandoned glory, forgot our sordid profit even, because we feared our strength and read the charter of our powers with the doubter's eye and the quibbler's mind? Shall it say that, called by events to captain and command the proudest, ablest, purest race of history in history's noblest work, we declined that great commission? Our fathers would not have had it so. No! They founded no paralytic government, incapable of the simplest acts of administration. They planted no sluggard people, passive while the world's work calls them. They established no reactionary nation. They unfurled no retreating flag. . . .

Blind indeed is he who sees not the hand of God in events so vast, so harmonious, so benign. Reactionary indeed is the mind that perceives not that this vital people is the strongest of the saving forces of the world; that our place, therefore, is at the head of the constructing and redeeming nations of the earth; and that to stand aside while events march on is a surrender of our interests, a betrayal of our duty as blind as it is base. Craven indeed is the heart that fears to perform a work so golden and so noble; that dares not win a glory so immortal. . . .

Mr. President and Senators, adopt the resolution offered, that peace may quickly come and that we may begin our saving, regenerating, and uplifting work. . . . Reject it, and the world, history, and the American people will know where to forever fix the awful responsibility for the consequences that will surely follow such failure to do our manifest duty. How dare we delay when our soldiers' blood is flowing?

Consider This:

- Note the appeal in both excerpts to past heritage, to "the deeds of your forefathers." Why is this technique often effective in focusing national will for a cause?

"The Hand of God" is from *Congressional Record*, vol. 33 (1900), pp. 704–705, 708, 710–712.

The Fall of Jerusalem (1099)

The Crusaders who set out at the behest of Pope Urban II in 1096 were quite successful in defeating Muslim armies, capturing territory along the pilgrimage route into Syria, and maintaining it with defensive castles established at Edessa and Antioch. Their ultimate goal, however, was Jerusalem, a

"The Fall of Jerusalem" form Hill, Rosalind–© Rosalind Hill 1962. Reprinted from *Gesta Francorum: The Deeds of the Franks and the other Pilgrims to Jerusalem*, edited by Rosalind Hil l(1962) by permission of Oxford University Press.

city sacred to Christian, Jew, and Muslim alike. Its bloody fall to the Christian forces in 1099 is described in the following account known as the Gesta Francorum.

During this siege, we suffered so badly from thirst that we sewed up the skins of oxen and buffaloes, and we used to carry water in them for the distance of nearly six miles. We drank the water from these vessels, although it stank, and what with foul water and barley bread we suffered great distress and affliction every day, for the Saracens used to lie in wait for our men by every spring and pool, where they killed them and cut them to pieces; moreover, they used to carry off the beasts into their caves and secret places in the rocks.

Our leaders then decided to attack the city with engines, so that we might enter it and worship at our Savior's Sepulchre. They made two wooden siege-towers and various other mechanical devices. Duke Godfrey filled his siege-tower with machines, and so did Count Raymond, but they had to get the timber from far afield. When the Saracens saw our men making these machines, they built up the city wall and its towers by night, so they were exceedingly strong. When, however, our leaders saw which was the weakest spot in the city's defenses, they had a machine and a siege-tower transported round to the eastern side one Saturday night. They set up these engines at dawn, and spent Sunday, Monday, and Tuesday in preparing the siege-tower and fitting it out, while the count of St. Gilles was getting his engine ready on the southern side. All this time we were suffering so badly from the shortage of water that for one penny a man could not buy sufficient to quench his thirst.

On Wednesday and Thursday we launched a fierce attack upon the city, both by day and by night, from all sides, but before we attacked, our bishops and priests preached to us, and told us to go in procession round Jerusalem to the Glory of God, and to pray and give alms and fast, as faithful men should do. On Friday at dawn we attacked the city from all sides but could achieve nothing, so that we were all astounded and very much afraid, yet, when that hour came when our Lord Jesus Christ deigned to suffer for us upon the cross, our Knights were fighting bravely on the siege-tower, led by Duke Godfrey and Count Eustace his brother. At that moment one of our knights, called Lethold, succeeded in getting on to the wall. As soon as he reached it, all the defenders fled along the walls and through the city, and our men went after them, killing them and cutting them down as far as Solomon's Temple, where there was such a massacre that our men were wading up to their ankles in enemy blood.

Count Raymond was bringing up his army and a siege-tower from the south to the neighborhood of the wall, but . . . when he heard that the Franks were in the city he said to his men, Why are you so slow? Look! All the other Franks are in the city already! Then the amir who held David's Tower surrendered to the count, and opened for him the gate where the pilgrims used to pay their taxes, so our men entered the city, chasing the Saracens and killing them up to Solomon's Temple, where they took refuge and fought hard against our men for the whole day, so that all the temple was streaming with their blood. At last, when the pagans were defeated, our men took many prisoners, both men and women, in the temple. They killed whom they chose, and whom they chose they saved alive. On the roof of the Temple of Solomon were crowded great numbers of pagans of both sexes. . . .

After this our men rushed round the whole city, seizing gold and silver, horses and mules, and houses full of all sorts of goods, and they all came rejoicing and weeping from excess of gladness to worship at the Sepulchre of our Saviour Jesus, and there they fulfilled their vows to him. Next morning they went cautiously up on to the Temple roof and attacked the Saracens, both men and women, cutting off their heads with drawn swords. Some of the Saracens threw themselves down headlong from the temple. . . .

Our leaders then took counsel and ordered that every man should give alms and pray that God would choose for himself whomsoever he wished, to rule over the other and to govern the city. They also commanded that all the Saracen corpses should be thrown outside the city because of the fearful stench, for almost the whole city was full of their dead bodies. So the surviving Saracens dragged the dead ones out in front of the gates, and piled them up in mounds as big as houses. No-one has ever seen or heard of such a slaughter of pagans, for they were burned on pyres like pyramids, and no-one save God alone knows how many there were. . . .

The Protection of Allah

USAMAH IBN-MUNQIDH

It has been said that history is often written through the eyes of the conquerors. And although one cannot speak of a "winner" or "loser" in the Crusades because of the complexities of the issues, it is true that there were distinct Christian and Islamic perspectives. Usamah Ibn-Munqidh, an Arab who lived through most of the twelfth century, was a keen observer of the Crusaders. The following accounts give a particularly interesting view of the Christians, their customs, and Muslim confidence in the protection of Allah.

I saw a proof of the goodness of Allah and of his splendid protection when the Franks (the curse of Allah upon them!) encamped against us with knights and foot-soldiers. We were separated from one another by the Orontes River, whose waters were so swollen that the Franks could not reach us and we were prevented from reaching them. They pitched their tents on the mountain, while some took up their position in the gardens in their neighborhood, set their horses free in the meadows and went to sleep. Some young foot-soldiers from Schaizar took off their clothes, took their swords, swam towards these sleepers and killed several of them. Then a number of our enemies rushed at our companions, who took to the water and returned, while the Frankish army rushed down the mountain on horseback like a flood. Near them there was a mosque, the mosque of Abou'l-Madjd ibn Soumayya, in which there was a man named Hasan az-Zahid (the ascetic), who lived on a flat roof and used to retire to the mosque to pray. He was dressed in black woollen clothes. We saw him, but we had no means of reaching him. The Franks came, got down at the gate of the mosque and went towards him, while we said, "Power and might belong to Allah alone! The Franks will kill him." But he, by Allah, neither stopped praying nor moved from his position. The Franks stopped, turned away, remounted their horses and rode off, while he remained motionless in the same place, continuing to pray. We did not doubt that Allah (glory be to him!) had blinded the Franks with regard to him and had hidden him from their sight. Glory to the Almighty, the Merciful!

The Franks: "Superior in Courage, But Nothing Else"

USAMAH IBN-MUNQIDH

Glory be to Allah, the creator and author of all things! Anyone who is acquainted with what

Potter, G.R., trans, *The Autobiography of Ousama (1095–1188)*, 1929, Routledge. Reprinted with permission.

Potter, G.R., trans, *The Autobiography of Ousama (1095–1188)*, 1929, Routledge. Reprinted with permission.

concerns the Franks can only glorify and sanc-
tify Allah the All-Powerful; for he has seen in
them animals who are superior in courage and
in zeal for fighting but in nothing else, just as
beasts are superior in strength and aggressive-
ness.

I will report some Frankish characteristics
and my surprise as to their intelligence. . . .
Among the curiosities of medicine among the
Franks, I will tell how the governor of
Al-Mounaitira wrote to my uncle to ask him to
send him a doctor who would look after some
urgent cases. My uncle chose a Christian doctor
named Thabit. He remained absent only ten
days and then returned to us. There was a general exclamation: "How rapidly you have cured
your patients!" Thabit replied: "They brought
before me a knight with an abscess which had
formed in his leg and a woman who was wasting
away with a consumptive fever. I applied a little
plaster to the knight; his abscess opened and
took a turn for the better; the woman I forbade
certain food and improved her condition." It
was at this point that a Frankish doctor came up
and said: "This man is incapable of curing
them." Then, turning to the knight, he asked,
"Which do you prefer, to live with one leg or
die with two?" "I would rather live with one
leg," the knight answered. "Bring a stalwart
knight," said the Frankish doctor, "and a sharp
hatchet." Knight and hatchet soon appeared. I
was present at the scene. The doctor stretched
the patient's leg on a block of wood and then
said to the knight, "Strike off his leg with the
hatchet; take it off at one blow." Under my eyes
the knight aimed a violent blow at it without
cutting through the leg. He aimed another
blow at the unfortunate man, as a result of
which his marrow came from his leg and the
knight died instantly. As for the woman, the
doctor examined her and said, "She is a woman
in whose head there is a devil who has taken
possession of her. Shave off her hair!" His pre-
scription was carried out, and like her fellows,
she began once again to eat garlic and mustard.
Her consumption became worse. The doctor

then said, "It is because the devil has entered
her head." Taking a razor, the doctor cut open
her head in the shape of a cross and scraped
away the skin in the centre so deeply that her
very bones were showing. He then rubbed the
head with salt. In her turn, the woman died instantly. After having asked them whether my
services were still required and obtained an answer in the negative, I came back, having learnt
to know what I had formerly been ignorant of
about their medicine.

At Neapolis, I was once present at a curious
sight. They brought in two men for trial by battle, the cause being the following. Some Mo-
hammedan brigands had raided some property
in the neighborhood of Neapolis. A farmer was
suspected of having guided the brigands to this
spot. The farmer took flight but soon returned,
the king having had his children imprisoned.
"Treat me with equity," said the accursed, "and
allow me to fight with him who has named me
as the person who brought the brigands into the
village." The king then said to the lord who had
received the village as a fief: "Send for his opponent." The lord returned to his village, picked
out a blacksmith who was working there, and
said to him, "You must go and fight a duel." For
the owner of the fief was primarily anxious to
see that none of his labourers got himself killed,
for fear his crops should suffer.

I saw this blacksmith. He was a strong young
man, but one who, walking or sitting, was always
wanting something to drink. As for the other,
the challenger to single combat, he was an old
man of great courage, who snapped his fingers
as a token of defiance and prepared for the
fight without perturbation. The sheriff [and]
governor of the town appeared, gave each of the
two fighters a cudgel and shield and made the
crowd form a ring round them.

The fight started. The old man forced the
blacksmith backwards, throwing him on to the
edge of the crowd, and then returned to the middle of the ring. The exchange of blows was so violent that the rivals, who remained standing,
seemed to make up one pillar of blood.

The fight continued, while the sheriff urged them to force a conclusion. "Quicker," he shouted to them. The blacksmith profited by his experience at wielding a hammer. When the old man was exhausted, the blacksmith aimed a blow at him which overthrew him, making the cudgel, which he was holding in his hand, fall behind him. The blacksmith crouched over the old man so as to put his fingers into eyes, but he could not reach them because of the streams of blood which were flowing from them; he got up and struck his head so violently with his cudgel that he finished him off.

At once they put a rope round the neck of the corpse, which they took away and hung on a gibbet. The lord who had chosen the blacksmith gave him a considerable piece of property, made him get on a horse with his followers, took him off and went away. See from this example what law and judicial proceedings mean among the Franks (the curse of Allah upon them!).

Medieval Monasticism

Monasticism arose in Egypt and western Asia and was practiced by monks who were true hermits. Their life was one of ascetic denial and personal devotion to God. As the movement spread to the West in the middle of the fourth century and became more popular, the monks began to live together in houses. Although they preserved as much of their personal isolation as possible, it became necessary to formulate rules of conduct. These rules, however, were not severe or even binding in most cases; monks did not even have to take a vow to remain in the monastery. The reforms of Saint Benedict were designed to remedy this problem and other abuses that permeated the monastic life. Benedict moved away from the hermetic emphasis of the East in favor of a common experience among the brothers in the order. His strict rule was popularized by Pope Gregory I (himself a Benedictine) and became the basis for all reforms in monasticism for several centuries. The following excerpts provide a glimpse into this structured life of contemplation and isolation from the world.

The Rule of Saint Benedict (530)

Ch. 1. The kinds of monks: There are four kinds of monks. The first kind is that of the cenobites, those who live in a monastery according to a rule, and under the government of an abbot. The second is that of the anchorites, or hermits, who have learned how to conduct the war against the devil by their long service in the monastery and their association with many brothers, and so, being well trained, have separated themselves from the troop, in order to wage single combat, being able with the aid of God to carry on the fight alone against the sins of the flesh. The third kind (and a most abominable kind it is) is that of the sarabites, who have not been tested and proved by obedience to the rule and by the teaching of experience, as gold is tried in the furnace, and so are soft and pliable like a base metal; who in assuming the tonsure are false to God, because they still serve the world in their lives. They do not congregate in the master's fold, but dwell apart without a shepherd, by twos and threes, or even alone. Their law is their own desires, since they call that holy which they like, and that unlawful which they do not like. The fourth kind is composed of those who are called gyrovagi (wanderers), who spend their whole lives wandering about through different regions and living three or four days at a time in the cells of different monks. They are always wandering about and

"The Rule of Saint Benedict" is from Oliver Thatcher and Edgar McNeal, eds., *A Source Book of Medieval History* (New York: Charles Scribner's Sons, 1905), pp. 434–438, 445–447, 457, 459, 461–462, 467–468, 471–474.

never remain long in one place, and they are governed by their own appetites and desires. They are in every way worse than the sarabites. But it is better to pass over in silence than to mention their manner of life. Let us, therefore, leaving these aside, proceed, with the aid of God, to the consideration of the cenobites, the highest type of monks.

Ch. 6. Silence: . . . It is the business of the master to speak and instruct, and that of the disciples to hearken and be silent. And if the disciple must ask anything of his superior, let him ask it reverently and humbly, lest he seem to speak more than is becoming. Filthy and foolish talking and jesting we condemn utterly, and forbid the disciple ever to open his mouth to utter such words.

Ch. 7. Humility: . . . The sixth step of humility is this, that the monk should be contented with any lowly or hard condition in which he may be placed, and should always look upon himself as an unworthy laborer, not fitted to do what is intrusted to him. . . . The seventh step of humility is this, that he should not only say, but should really believe in his heart that he is the lowest and most worthless of all men. . . . The eighth step of humility is this, that the monk should follow in everything the common rule of the monastery and the examples of his superiors. . . .

The twelfth step of humility is this, that the monk should always be humble and lowly, not only in his heart, but in his bearing as well. Wherever he may be, in divine service, in the oratory, in the garden, on the road, in the fields, whether sitting, walking, or standing, he should always keep his head bowed and his eyes upon the ground. He should always be meditating upon his sins and thinking of the dread day of judgment, saying to himself as did that publican of whom the gospel speaks: "Lord, I am not worthy, I a sinner, so much as to lift mine eyes up to heaven" [Luke 18:13]; and again with the prophet: "I am bowed down and humbled everywhere" [Ps. 119:107]. . . .

Ch. 22. How the monks should sleep: The monks shall sleep separately in individual beds, and the abbot shall assign them their beds according to their conduct. If possible all the monks shall sleep in the same dormitory, but if their number is too large to admit of this, they are to be divided into tens or twenties and placed under the control of some of the older monks. A candle shall be kept burning in the dormitory all night until daybreak. The monks shall go to bed clothed and girt with girdles and cords, but shall not have their knives at their sides, lest in their dreams they injure one of the sleepers. They should be always in readiness, rising immediately upon the signal and hastening to the service, but appearing there gravely and modestly. The beds of the younger brothers should not be placed together, but should be scattered among those of the older monks. When the brothers arise they should gently exhort one another to hasten to the service, so that the sleepy ones may have no excuse for coming late. . . .

Ch. 33. Monks should not have personal property: The sin of owning private property should be entirely eradicated from the monastery. No one shall presume to give or receive anything except by the order of the abbot; no one shall possess anything of his own, books, paper, pens, or anything else; for monks are not to own even their own bodies and wills to be used at their own desire, but are to look to the father [abbot] of the monastery for everything. So they shall have nothing that has not been given or allowed to them by the abbot; all things are to be had in common according to the command of the Scriptures, and no one shall consider anything as his own property. If anyone has been found guilty of this most grievous sin, he shall be admonished for the first and second offence, and then if he does not mend his ways he shall be punished.

Ch. 38. The weekly reader: There should always be reading during the common meal, but it shall not be left to chance, so that anyone may take up the book and read. On Sunday one of the brothers shall be appointed to read during the following week. . . . At the common meal, the strictest silence shall be kept, that no whispering or speaking may be heard except the voice of the reader. The brethren shall mutually wait upon one another by passing the articles of food and drink, so that no one shall have to ask for anything; but if this is necessary, it shall be done by a sign rather than by words, if possible. In order to avoid too much talking no one shall interrupt the reader with a question about the reading or in any other way, unless perchance the prior may wish to say something in the way of explanation. . . .

Ch. 39. The amount of food: Two cooked dishes, served either at the sixth or the ninth hour, should be sufficient for the daily sustenance. We allow two because of differences in taste, so that those who do not eat one may satisfy their hunger with the other, but two shall suffice for all the brothers, unless it is possible to obtain fruit or fresh vegetables, which may be served as a third. . . . In the case of those who engage in heavy labor, the abbot may at his discretion increase the allowance of food, but he should not allow the monks to indulge their appetites by eating or drinking too much. For no vice is more inconsistent with the Christian character. . . .

Ch. 48. The daily labor of the monks: Idleness is the great enemy of the soul, therefore the monks should always be occupied, either in manual labor or in holy reading. . . . When the ninth hour sounds they shall cease from labor and be ready for the service at the second bell. After dinner they shall spend the time in reading the lessons and the psalms. During Lent the time from daybreak to the third hour shall be devoted to reading, and then they shall work at their appointed tasks until the tenth hour. At the beginning of Lent each of the monks shall be given a book from the library of the monastery which he shall read entirely through. One or two of the older monks shall be appointed to go about through the monastery during the hours set apart for reading, to see that none of the monks are idling away the time, instead of reading, and so not only wasting their

own time but perhaps disturbing others as well. . . . Sunday is to be spent by all the brothers in holy reading, except by such as have regular duties assigned to them for that day. And if any brother is negligent or lazy, refusing or being unable profitably to read or meditate at the time assigned for that, let him be made to work, so that he shall at any rate not be idle. . . .

Ch. 58. The way in which new members are to be received: Entrance into the monastery should not be made too easy. . . . So when anyone applies at the monastery, asking to be accepted as a monk, he should first be proved by every test. He shall be made to wait outside four or five days, continually knocking at the door and begging to be admitted; and then he shall be taken in as a guest and allowed to stay in the guest chamber a few days. If he satisfies these preliminary tests, he shall then be made to serve a novitiate of at least one year, during which he shall be placed under the charge of one of the older and wiser brothers, who shall examine him and prove, by every possible means, his sincerity, his zeal, his obedience, and his ability to endure shame. And he shall be told in the plainest manner all the hardships and difficulties of the life which he has chosen. If he promises never to leave the monastery the rule shall be read to him after the first two months of his novitiate, and again at the end of six more months, and finally, four months later, at the end of his year. Each time he shall be told that this is the guide which he must follow as a monk, the reader saying to him at the end of the reading: "This is the law under which you have expressed a desire to live; if you are able to obey it, enter; if not, depart in peace." Thus he shall have been given every chance for mature deliberation and every opportunity to refuse the yoke of service. But if he still persists in asserting his eagerness to enter and his willingness to obey the rule and the commands of his superior, he shall then be received into the congregation, with the understanding that from that day forth he shall never be permitted to draw back from the service or to leave the monastery. . . .

The Canticle of Brother Sun (1225)

SAINT FRANCIS OF ASSISI

One of the most remarkable figures in the world of the medieval church was Saint Francis. Born in 1181 to a wealthy merchant in the little town of Assisi, Saint Francis eventually rejected his prescribed role as heir to the family business, gave his belongings to the poor, and became a barefoot preacher. He quickly gained adherents by advocating a simple rule of poverty and complete service to God. His order received the approval of Pope Innocent III in 1209. He died in 1226 and was canonized in 1228. He was buried in the basilica San Francesco in Assisi, an ironic turn, since Saint Francis had always preached the virtues of poverty and simplicity.

The Franciscans were not a monastic order, but rather considered their business to be within the world. They were called friars, or brothers, and combined the asceticism and simplicity of a regular order of monks with the popular contact that was the preserve of the secular order of priests. With a foot in both worlds of the church and a dedication to poverty and simplicity, the Franciscans were a kind of hybrid, both reviled and admired by competing forces within the church.

Saint Francis' great love of nature and the purity of his devotion to God are distilled in perhaps the most articulate and sensitive of his poems, "The Canticle of Brother Sun." He began it in 1225, during his last illness amid intense physical suffering, and added the final verses about Sister Death shortly before his own death. The "Canticle," for all the depth of feeling it evokes about nature and the creatures he cared so much about, is an earnest prayer and hymn of praise to God.

Most high, all-powerful, all good, Lord!
    All praise is yours, all glory, all honour
    And all blessing.
To you, alone, Most High, do they belong.
    No mortal lips are worthy
    To pronounce your name.
All praise be yours, my Lord, through all
    that you have made,
    And first my lord Brother Sun,
    Who brings the day; and light you give
    to us through him.
How beautiful is he, how radiant in all his
    splendour!
    Of you, Most High, he bears the
    likeness.
All praise be yours, my Lord, through
    Sister Moon and Stars;
    In the heavens you have made them,
    bright
    And precious and fair.
All praise be yours, my Lord, through
    Brothers Wind and Air,

And fair and stormy, all the weather's
    moods,
    By which you cherish all that you have
    made.
All praise be yours, my Lord, through
    Sister Water,
    So useful, lowly, precious and pure.
All praise be yours, my Lord, through
    Brother Fire,
    Through whom you brighten up the
    night.
    How beautiful is he, how gay! Full of
    power and strength.
All praise be yours, my Lord, through
    Sister Earth, our mother,
    Who feeds us in her sovereignty and
    produces
    Various fruits with coloured flowers and
    herbs.
All praise be yours, my Lord, through
    those who grant pardon

Habig, Marion A., ed., *St. Francis of Assisi, Writings and Early Biographies: English Omnibus of Sources for the Life of St. Francis*, 1991, pp. 130–131. Reprinted with permission of the Franciscan Press.

For love of you; through those who
  endure
Sickness and trial.
Happy those who endure in peace,
  By you, Most High, they will be
  crowned.
All praise be yours, my Lord, through
  Sister Death,
  From whom no mortal can escape.
Woe to those who die in mortal sin!
  Happy those She finds doing your will!
  The second death can do no harm to
  them.
Praise and bless my Lord, and give him
  thanks,
  And serve him with great humility.

The cathedral at Reims, where the kings of France were crowned, is a good example of the beauty and majesty of Gothic architecture. Medieval civilization flowed from a spiritual base. (*Art Resource*)

Mind and Society in the Middle Ages

The World of Thought

The Existence of God

SAINT THOMAS AQUINAS

The twelfth century was truly remarkable for its intellectual focus and development of thought. The new commitment to learning was reflected in a system of argument and study called Scholasticism. Scholars edited and commented on ancient writers, methodically arguing for the acceptance or rejection of such philosophers as Aristotle and Plato. No longer was it enough simply to accept the existence of God without a rational argument of proof. Saint Thomas Aquinas (1225–1274) is generally regarded as the most insightful and important philosopher of the Middle Ages. The following excerpts from his Summa Theologica *demonstrate the structure of Scholastic argument and relate his conclusions on the existence of God. Saint Bernard's passage on the love of God reflects the argument of faith.*

Pegis, A.C., trans., *Basic Writings of Saint Thomas Aquinas*, Vol. I. Copyright © 1945 by Hackett PUblishing Company, Inc. Reprinted by permission of Hackett Publishing Company, Inc. All rights reserved.

Third Article: Whether God exists?

Objection 1: It seems that God does not exist; because if one of two contraries be infinite, the other would be altogether destroyed. But the name God means that He is infinite goodness. If, therefore, God existed, there would be no evil discoverable; but there is evil in the world. Therefore God does not exist.

Objection 2: Further, it is superfluous to suppose that what can be accounted for by a few principles has been produced by many. But it seems that everything we see in the world can be accounted for by other principles, supposing God did not exist. For all natural things can be reduced to one principle, which is human reason, or will. Therefore there is no need to suppose God's existence.

I Answer That: The existence of God can be proved in five ways: The first and more manifest way is the argument from motion. It is certain, and evident to our senses, that in the world some things are in motion. . . . [Now], whatever is moved must be moved by another. If that by which it is moved be itself moved, then this also must needs be moved by another, and that by another again. But this cannot go on to infinity, because then there would be no first mover, and, consequently, no other mover, seeing that subsequent movers move only inasmuch as they are moved by the first mover; as the staff moves only because it is moved by the hand. Therefore it is necessary to arrive at a first mover, moved by no other; and this everyone understands to be God.

The second way is from the nature of efficient cause. In the world of sensible things we find there is an order of efficient causes. There is no case known (neither is it, indeed, possible) in which a thing is found to be the efficient cause of itself; for so it would be prior to itself, which is impossible. Now in efficient causes it is not possible to go on to infinity, because in all efficient causes following in order, the first is the cause of the intermediate cause and the intermediate is the cause of the ultimate cause, whether the intermediate cause be several, or

one only. Now to take away the cause is to take away the effect. Therefore, if there be no first cause among efficient causes, there will be no ultimate, nor any intermediate, cause. . . . Therefore it is necessary to admit a first efficient cause, to which everyone gives the name of God.

The third way is taken from possibility and necessity, and runs thus. We find in nature things that are possible to be and not to be, since they are found to be born, and to die, and consequently they are possible to be and not to be. But it is impossible for these always to exist, for that which is possible not to be at some time is not. Therefore, if everything is possible not to be, then at one time there could have been nothing in existence. Now, if this were true, even now there would be nothing in existence, because that which does not exist only begins to exist by something already existing. Therefore, if at one time nothing was in existence, it would have been impossible for anything to have begun to exist; and thus even now nothing would be in existence—which is clearly false. Therefore, not all beings are merely possible, but there must exist something the existence of which is necessary. But every necessary thing either has its necessity caused by another, or not. Now, it is impossible to go on to infinity in necessary things which have their necessity caused by another, as has been already proved in regard to efficient causes. Therefore, we must admit the existence of some being having of itself its own necessity, and not receiving it from another, but rather causing in others their necessity. This all men speak of as God.

The fourth way is taken from the gradation to be found in things. Among beings there are some more and some less good, true, noble, and the like. But "more" and "less" are predicated on different things, according as they resemble in their different ways something which is the maximum, as a thing is said to be hotter according as it more nearly resembles that which is hottest. There is then something which is truest, something best, something noblest, and, consequently, something which is most being; for those things that are greatest in truth are greatest in being. . . . Therefore, there must also be something which is to all beings the cause of their being, goodness, and every other perfection. And this we call God.

The fifth way is taken from the governance of the world. We see that things which lack knowledge, such as natural bodies, act for an end, and this is evident from their acting always, or nearly always, in the same way, so as to obtain the best result. Hence it is plain that they achieve their end, not fortuitously, but designedly. Now whatever lacks knowledge cannot move towards an end, unless it be directed by some being endowed with knowledge and intelligence; as the arrow is directed by the archer. Therefore some intelligent being exists by whom all natural things are directed to their end; and this being we call God.

Reply to Objection One: As Augustine says: "Since God is the highest good, He would not allow any evil to exist in His works, unless His omnipotence and goodness were such as to bring good even out of evil." This is part of the infinite goodness of God; that He should allow evil to exist, and out of it produce good.

Reply to Objection Two: Since nature works for a determinate end under the direction of a higher agent, whatever is done by nature must be traced back to God, as to its first cause. . . . For all things that are changeable and capable of defect must be traced back to an immovable and self-necessary first principle, as was shown in the body of this Article.

The Love of God

SAINT BERNARD OF CLAIRVAUX

You would hear from me, then, why and how God is to be loved? I answer: The cause of loving God is God; the manner is to love without measure. Is this enough? Yes, perhaps, for the wise. But I am debtor to the unwise as well; where enough is said for the wise, we must comply with the others also. Therefore I will not refuse to repeat it, more fully rather than more deeply, for the sake of the slower in apprehension. I may say that God is to be loved for His own sake for a double reason: because nothing can be loved more justly, nothing more fruitfully. . . . Assuredly I find no other worthy cause of loving Him, save Himself. . . .

"The Love of God" is from E. G. Gardner, trans., *On the Love of God* (London: J. M. Dent and Sons, 1916), p. 27. Reprinted by permission of the publisher.

The Dialectical Method: Sic et Non

PETER ABELARD

One of the greatest minds of the Middle Ages belonged to Peter Abelard. He was a renowned scholar and teacher whose method of inquiring into spiritual issues often created formidable enemies (among them, Saint Bernard of Clairvaux). Abelard's method of applying critical thought to the interpretation of sacred texts is best revealed in his famous work Sic et Non *(Yes and No). Abelard would pose a problem and then cite arguments, supported by the most revered church fathers, that the statement was true. He then produced another series of logical and well-supported arguments that proved it false. Abelard did not want to reconcile the conflicting views, but by this dialectical process he hoped to "sharpen the minds" of his students. The pathway to Truth had to be critically examined. The following excerpts demonstrate his method and are good examples of Scholastic argument.*

Bainton, Roland, H., ed., *The Medieval Church.* Copyright © 1962 by Krieger Publishing Company. Reprinted with permission.

Inasmuch as among the multitudinous words of the saints there are some which . . . not only [differ] but actually [contradict one another], we are not to judge lightly of these saints who themselves will judge the world. . . . If there are divine mysteries which we cannot understand in the spirit in which they were written, better to reserve judgment than to define rashly. We are not to rely on apocryphal writings and we must be sure that we have the correct text on the canonical. For example, Matthew and John say that Jesus was crucified at the sixth hour, but Mark at the third. This is an error of transcription in Mark. We are to observe because he carelessly incorporated the work of someone else, as Augustine confessed he had done with reference to Origen. We must bear in mind the diversity of situation in which particular sayings were uttered. In case of controversy between the saints, which cannot be resolved by reason, we should hold to that opinion which has the most ancient and powerful authority. And if sometimes the fathers were in error we should attribute this not to duplicity but ignorance, and if sometimes they were absurd, we are to assume that the text is faulty, the interpreter in error or simply that we do not understand.

Therefore it has seemed to us fitting to collect from the holy fathers apparently contradictory passages that tender readers may be incited to make inquiry after the truth. . . . By doubting we come to inquire, and by inquiry we arrive at the truth. . . . We are including nothing from the Apocrypha and nothing from the writings of Augustine which he later retracted.

Example XXXII. That God may do all things and that He may not.

Chrysostom said that God is called almighty because it is impossible to find anything that is impossible for Him. Nevertheless He cannot lie, or be deceived, He cannot be ignorant. He cannot have a beginning or an end.

He cannot forget the past, be involved in the present or be ignorant of the future. Finally, He cannot deny Himself. Augustine said there are some things God can do as to His power, but not as to His justice. Being himself justice He cannot commit injustice. He is omnipotent in the sense that He can do what He wants. But He cannot die, He cannot change and He cannot be deceived.

Example XI. That the divine persons differ from each other and that they do not.

Athanasius said there is one person of the Father, one of the Son and one of the Holy Spirit. The Father is not made, created or begotten. The son comes solely from the Father. He is not made or created but He is begotten. The spirit proceeds from the Father and the Son. He is not begotten or created but proceeding. But Pope Leo I said, "In the divine Trinity nothing is dissimilar, nothing unequal."

The Medieval Woman

Chivalric Ideals: The Function of Knighthood
JOHN OF SALISBURY

The High Middle Ages saw the transition from a rather crude and barbaric nobility to one controlled by ideals of right action and proper conduct. Knights were expected to comport themselves with dignity and spiritual devotion, especially in the presence of ladies. Knighthood became a rigorous trial, and tales of the "quest" for the Holy Grail or the mystical unicorn became popular. The following account of John of Salisbury presents the ideal of knighthood.

"Chivalric Ideals: The Function of Knighthood" is from Frederick Ogg, ed., *A Source Book of Medieval History* (New York: American Book Company, 1907), p. 401.

But what is the office of the duly ordained soldiery? To defend the Church, to assail infidelity, to venerate the priesthood, to protect the poor from injuries, to pacify the province, to pour out their blood for their brothers (as the formula of their oath instructs them), and, if need be, to lay down their lives. The praises of God are in their throat, and two-edged swords are in their hands to execute punishment on the nations and rebuke upon the peoples, and to bind their kings in chains and their nobles in links of iron. But to what end? To the end that they may serve madness, vanity, avarice, or their own private self-will? By no means. Rather to the end that they may execute the judgment that is committed to them to execute; wherein each follows not his own will but the deliberate decision of God, the angels, and men, in accordance with equity and the public utility. . . . For soldiers that do these things are "saints," and are the more loyal to their prince in proportion as they more zealously keep the faith of God; and they advance the more successfully the honour of their own valour as they seek the more faithfully in all things the glory of their God.

Noblewomen watching a tournament. This painting reflects chivalric ideals of the knight and his lady. In fact, these mock battles served a useful purpose in providing a semi-controlled outlet for the aggression of the nobility. (*Bettmann*)

To His Love Afar

JAUFRE RUDEL

The chivalric ideal of the High Middle Ages enhanced the position of women in medieval society. With the popularity of the Virgin Mary in the twelfth and thirteenth centuries, women were viewed less as temptresses who encouraged sinful thoughts and acts and more as respected individuals, worthy of love and adoration. Knights fought for the honor of their Lady, whom they set on a pedestal and worshiped from afar. The first poem reflects this idealistic detachment. Yet some women were becoming less inhibited about their feelings, and "love from afar" was not necessarily preferred—at least not for the Countess de Dia!

When the days lengthen in the month of
   May,
Well pleased am I to hear the birds
   Sing far away.

And when from that place I am gone,
I hang my head and make dull moan,
Since she my heart is set upon
   Is far away.

So far, that song of birds, flower o'the
   thorn,
Please me no more than winter morn,
   With ice and sleet.
Ah, would I were a pilgrim over sea,
With staff and scrip and cloak to cover me,
That some day I might kneel me on one
   knee
   Before her feet.

Most sad, most joyous shall I go away,
Let me have seen her for a single day,
   My love afar.
I shall not see her, for her land and mine
Are sundered, and the ways are hard to
   find,
So many ways, and I shall lose my way,
   So wills it God.

Yet shall I know no other love but hers,
And if not hers, no other love at all.
   She hath surpassed all.
So fair she is, so noble, I would be
A captive with the hosts of paynimrie
In a far land, if so be upon me
   Her eyes might fall.

God, who hath made all things in earth
   that are,
That made my love, and set her thus afar,
   Grant me this grace,
That I may some day come within a room,

Or in some garden gloom
   Look on her face.

It will not be, for at my birth they said
That one had set this doom upon my
   head,
   —God curse him among men!—
That I should love, and not till I be dead,
   Be loved again.

A Distressed Lover
THE COUNTESS DE DIA

I've lately been in great distress
over a knight who once was mine,
and I want it known for all eternity
how I loved him to excess.
Now I see I've been betrayed
because I wouldn't sleep with him;
night and day my mind won't rest
to think of the mistake I made.

How I wish just once I could caress
that chevalier with my bare arms,
for he would be in ecstasy
if I'd just let him lean his head against my
   breast.
I'm sure I'm happier with him
than Blancaflor with Floris.
My heart and love I offer him,
my mind, my eyes, my life.

Handsome friend, charming and kind
when shall I have you in my power?
If only I could lie beside you for an hour
and embrace you lovingly—
know this, that I'd give almost anything
to have you in my husband's place,
but only under the condition
that you swear to do my bidding.

SECTION III: THE LATE MIDDLE AGES (1300–1450)

The Waning of the Medieval Church

The struggle for supremacy between church and state, which had stirred such dissension in the eleventh and twelfth centuries, seemed settled by the strong leadership of Pope Innocent III in the early thirteenth century. Innocent simply dominated the secular world without a moment of hesitation. But conditions had changed by the late thirteenth century. The forceful kings of England and France were constantly in need of money and began levying taxes against the clergy of their realms. Boniface VIII (1294–1303), in the papal bull (decree) "Clericis Laicos," viewed this as an encroachment upon the liberty of the church.

The second selection, "Unam Sanctam," was another decree wherein Boniface promulgated the famous "Doctrine of the Two Swords," designed to promote the unity of Christianity and the supremacy of the pope. This policy eventually failed, as Boniface was attacked, captured, and humiliated by agents of the French king, Philip IV; Boniface died soon after. The days of papal supremacy were over.

Clericis Laicos (1298)

POPE BONIFACE VIII

It is said that in times past laymen practiced great violence against the clergy, and our experience clearly shows that they are doing so at present, since they are not content to keep within the limits prescribed for them, but strive to do that which is prohibited and illegal. And they pay no attention to the fact that they are forbidden to exercise authority over the clergy and ecclesiastical persons and their possessions. But they are laying heavy burdens on bishops, churches, and clergy, both regular and secular, by taxing them, levying contributions on them, and extorting the half, or the tenth, or the twentieth, or some other part of their income and possessions. They are striving in many ways to reduce the clergy to servitude and to subject them to their own sway. And we grieve to say it, but some bishops and clergy, fearing where they should not, and seeking a temporary peace, and fearing more to offend man than God, submit, improvidently rather than rashly, to these abuses [and pay the sums demanded], with-

out receiving the papal permission. Wishing to prevent these evils . . . by our apostolic authority, we decree that if any bishops or clergy, regular or secular, of any grade, condition, or rank, shall pay, or promise, or consent to pay laymen any contributions, or taxes, or the tenth, or the twentieth, or the hundredth, or any other part of their income or of their possessions, or of their value, real or estimated, under the name of aid, or loan, or subvention, or subsidy, or gift, or under any other name or pretext, without the permission of the pope, they shall, by the very act, incur the sentence of excommunication. And we also decree that emperors, kings, princes, dukes, counts, barons, [etc.] . . . who shall impose, demand, or receive such taxes, or shall seize . . . the property of churches or of the taxes, or shall seize . . . the property of churches or of the clergy . . . shall . . . incur the sentence of excommunication. We also put under the interdict all communities which shall be culpable in such matters. And under the threat of deposition we strictly command all bishops and clergy, in accordance with their oath of obedience, not to submit to such taxes without the express permission of the pope. . . . From this sentence of excommunication and interdict no one can be absolved except in the moment of death, without the authority and special permission of the pope. . . .

"Clericis Laicos" is from Oliver Thatcher and Edgar McNeal, eds., *A Source Book of Medieval History* (New York: Charles Scribner's Sons, 1905), pp. 311–313.

Unam Sanctam (1302)

POPE BONIFACE VIII

The true faith compels us to believe that there is one holy catholic apostolic church, and this we firmly believe and plainly confess. And outside of her there is no salvation or remission of sins. . . . In this church there is "one Lord, one faith, one baptism" [Eph. 4:5]. . . . Therefore there is one body of the one and only church, and one head, not two heads, as if the church were a monster. And this head is Christ and his vicar, Peter and his successor. . . . If therefore Greeks or anyone else say that they are not subject to Peter and his successors, they thereby necessarily confess that they are not of the sheep of Christ. For the Lord says in the Gospel of John, that there is one fold and only one shepherd [John 10:16]. By the words of the gospel we are taught that the two swords, namely, the spiritual authority and the temporal are in the power of the church. . . . Both swords, . . . the spiritual and the temporal, are in the power of the church. The former is to be used by the church, the latter for the church; the one by the hand of the priest, the other by the hand of kings and knights, but at the command and permission of the priest. Moreover, it is necessary for one sword to be under the other, and the temporal authority to be subjected to the spiritual; for the apostle says, "For there is no power but of God: and the powers that are ordained of God" [Rom. 13:1]; but they would not be ordained [i.e., arranged or set in order] unless one were subjected to the other, and, as it were, the lower made the higher by the other. . . . And we must necessarily admit that the spiritual power surpasses any earthly power in dignity and honor, because spiritual things surpass temporal things. We clearly see that this is true from the paying of tithes, from the benediction, from the sanctification, from the receiving of the power, and from the governing of these things. For the truth itself declares that the spiritual power must establish the temporal power and pass judgment on it if it is not good. Thus the prophecy of Jeremiah concerning the church and the ecclesiastical power is fulfilled: "See, I have this day set thee over the nations and over the kingdoms, to root out, and to pull down, and to destroy, and to throw down, to build, and to plant" [Jer. 1:10]. Therefore if the temporal power errs, it will be judged by the spiritual power, and if the lower spiritual power errs, it will be judged by its superior. But if the highest spiritual power errs, it can not be judged by men, but by God alone. For the apostle says: "But he that is spiritual judgeth all things, yet he himself is judged of no man" [1 Cor. 2:15]. Now this authority, although it is given to man and exercised through man, is not human, but divine. For it was given by the word of the Lord to Peter, and the rock was made firm to him and his successors, in Christ himself, whom he had confessed. For the Lord said to Peter: "Whatsoever thou shalt bind on earth shall be bound in heaven: and whatsoever thou shalt loose on earth shall be loosed in heaven" [Matt. 16:19]. Therefore, whosoever resisteth this power thus ordained of God, resisteth the ordinance of God [Rom. 13:2]. . . . We therefore declare, say, and affirm that submission on the part of every man to the bishop of Rome is altogether necessary for his salvation.

"Unam Sanctam" is from Oliver Thatcher and Edgar McNeal, eds., *A Source Book of Medieval History* (New York: Charles Scribner's Sons, 1905), pp. 314–317.

The Babylonian Captivity in Avignon (1309–1377)

PETRARCH

One of the great spiritual crises of the Late Middle Ages was known as the "Babylonian Captivity." From 1309 to 1377, the popes resided not in Rome, but in southern France, in the town of Avignon.

"The Babylonian Captivity in Avignon" is from James H. Robinson, ed., *Readings in European History*, vol. 1 (Boston: Ginn and Company, 1904), pp. 502–504.

They established a papal palace there, and the city became the haunt of pleasure seekers who were indulged by the luxuriant and corrupt papacy. This period of self-imposed exile from the spiritual seat of the papal power in Rome irreparably damaged the church. One of the greatest critics of this situation was the humanist Petrarch, who grew up in Avignon and wrote this letter between 1340 and 1353, just before he moved to Rome.

Now I am living in France, in the Babylon of the West. The sun in its travels sees nothing more hideous than this place on the shores of the wild Rhone, which suggests the hellish streams of Cocytus and Acheron. Here reign the successors of the poor fishermen of Galilee: they have strangely forgotten their origin. I am astounded as I recall their predecessors, to see these men loaded with gold and clad in purple, boasting of the spoils of princes and nations; to see luxurious palaces and heights crowned with fortifications, instead of a boat turned downwards for shelter. We no longer find the simple nets which were once used to gain a frugal sustenance from the lake of Galilee, and with which, having labored all night and caught nothing, they took, at daybreak, a multitude of fishes, in the name of Jesus. One is stupified nowadays to hear the lying tongues, and to see worthless parchments turned by a leaden seal into nets which are used, in Christ's name, but by the arts of [the Devil], to catch hordes of unwary Christians. These fish, too, are dressed and laid on the burning coals of anxiety before they fill the insatiable [mouth] of their captors.

Instead of holy solitude we find a criminal host and crowds of the most infamous satellites; instead of soberness, licentious banquets; instead of pious pilgrimages, preternatural and foul sloth; instead of the bare feet of the apostle, the snowy coursers of brigands fly past us, the horses decked in gold and fed on gold, soon to be shod with gold, if the Lord does not check this slavish luxury. . . .

Here I am, at a more advanced age, back in the haunts of my childhood, dragged again by fate among the disagreeable surroundings of my early days, when I thought I was freed from them. I have been so depressed and overcome that the heaviness of my soul has passed into bodily afflictions, so that I am really ill and can only give voice to sighs and groans. . . . Sweet water cannot come from a bitter source. Nature has ordered that the sighs of an oppressed heart shall be distasteful, and the words of an injured soul harsh.

Disease and History:
The Black Death

Behold, a pale horse; and his name that sat on him was Death.

—Revelation 6:8

There is a Reaper whose name is Death,
And, with his sickle keen,
He reaps the bearded grain at a breath,
And the flowers that grow between.

—Henry Wadsworth Longfellow

We all labour against our own cure, for death is the cure of all diseases.

—Thomas Browne

Ring around the rosie,
Pocket full of posies,
Ashes, Ashes,
We all fall down. . . .

—Children's rhyme

In October 1347, a Genoese fleet docked in Sicily at the port of Messina. The entire crew was either dead or dying, afflicted with a disease that clung, as the chronicler noted, "to their very bones." The ship had arrived from the Black Sea region and was filled with grain for ready distribution. Also aboard were the omnipresent rats, black rats, infested with fleas that, in turn, harbored the Yersinia pestis bacillus. Before the fleet could be quarantined, the rats had run down the ropes and into the city. Over the next four years, the scene would be repeated again and again. The Black Death had arrived.

The mere words "Black Death" have an ominous ring about them. They dredge up images of rotting corpses, broken families, and despair. The people of Europe were devastated by a disease they did not understand nor were prepared to suffer. It was an epidemic of such magnitude that one-third to one-half of the population of Europe was killed. In a recent study by the Rand Corporation, the Black Death ranked as one of the three greatest catastrophes in the history of the world. It did much more than eliminate people; it altered the very foundation of medieval life and jeopardized the unity of Western civilization.

Historians can document some of the changes explicitly; other changes were more ephemeral and are subject to varying opinion. The depopulation of the cities, where the plague hit hardest, caused a crisis in trade and economic exchange. Production of goods was often curtailed with the death of skilled artisans, and those who replaced them offered work of inferior quality. The medieval church grew wealthier from the accumulation of property of those who willed it as a last token of faith before they died. But the church also had difficulty explaining the pestilence and was hard-pressed to defend against the argument that God was taking vengeance for the sins of humanity. The papacy itself was battered by criticism and charges of corruption that were proved daily during its residence in Avignon from 1303 to 1377. What the church gained in wealth, it lost in prestige. The plague also affected the political relationship between church and state that had been under dispute since the eleventh century. The question of whether the secular or spiritual realm had greater authority on earth had already been answered by the mid-fourteenth century, since popes no longer challenged the military might of kings. But this status was confirmed by the results of the Black Death. The traditional containers of monarchical power were the nobility and the clergy. Both groups depended on the strength that numbers and unity gave them in their struggles with the king. The plague reduced their numbers, thus allowing kings to secure their realms more easily.

Perhaps the greatest changes, however, were in the fabric of society. On a personal level, the plague destroyed patterns of life that contributed to social stability. Familial ties were shattered as people refused to care for their relatives out of fear of contracting the disease themselves. Whole families were destroyed; we can truly speak of "lost generations." Survivors were often left in psychological and moral crisis. It was evident to all that Europe was in the throes of change by forces that could not be understood, moving toward a future that could not be guaranteed.

"A Most Terrible Plague"

GIOVANNI BOCCACCIO

Giovanni Boccaccio is best known as a humanist of the Italian Renaissance. The following excerpt is from his most famous work, The Decameron. *Written during the plague years between 1348 and 1353, it is a collection of stories told intimately between friends while they passed the time away from Florence in the solitude and safety of the country. It begins with a detailed description of the pestilence. Over two-thirds of the population of Florence died of the plague.*

In the year then of our Lord 1348, there happened at Florence, the finest city in all Italy, a most terrible plague; which, whether owing to the influence of the planets, or that it was sent from God as a just punishment for our sins, had broken out some years before in the Levant, and after passing from place to place, and making incredible havoc all the way, had now reached the west. There, in spite of all the means that art and human foresight could suggest, such as keeping the city clear from filth, the exclusion of all suspected persons, and the publication of copious instructions for the preservation of health; and notwithstanding manifold supplications offered to God in processions and otherwise, it began to show itself in the spring of the aforesaid year, in a sad and wonderful manner. Unlike what had been seen in the east, where bleeding from the nose is the fatal prognostic, here there appeared certain tumours in the groin or under the armpits, some as big as a small apple, others as an egg; and afterwards purple spots in most parts of the body; in some cases large and but few in number, in others smaller and more numerous—both sorts the usual messengers of death. To the cure of this malady, neither medical knowledge nor the power of drugs was of any effect; whether because the disease was in its own nature mortal, or that the physicians (the number of whom, taking quacks and women pretenders into the account, was grown very great) could form no just idea of the cause, nor consequently devise a true method of cure; whichever was the reason, few escaped; but nearly all died the third day from the first appearance of the symptoms, some sooner, some later, without any fever or accessory symptoms. What gave the more virulence to this plague, was that, by being communicated from the sick to the healthy, it spread daily, like fire when it comes in contact with large masses of combustibles. Nor was it caught only by conversing with, or coming near the sick, but even by touching their clothes, or anything that they had before touched. . . .

These facts, and others of the like sort, occasioned various fears and devices amongst those who survived, all tending to the same uncharitable and cruel end; which was, to avoid the sick, and every thing that had been near them, expecting by that means to save themselves. And some holding it best to live temperately, and to avoid excesses of all kinds, made parties, and shut themselves up from the rest of the world; eating and drinking moderately of the best, and diverting themselves with music, and such other entertainments as they might have within doors; never listening to anything from without, to make them uneasy. Others maintained free living to be a better preservative, and would baulk no passion or appetite they wished to gratify, drinking and revelling incessantly from tavern to tavern, or in private houses (which were frequently found deserted by the owners, and

---

"'A Most Terrible Plague'" is from Giovanni Boccaccio, *The Decameron*, in *Stories of Boccaccio*, trans. John Payne (London: Bibliophilist Library, 1903), pp. 1–6.

The "Danse Macabre" was a common art motif in the fourteenth century. Death seemed to mock the living and the "grim reaper" took his toll indiscriminately. (*Woodcut by Mich. Wohlgemuth, 1493. Bettmann*)

therefore common to every one), yet strenuously avoiding, with all this brutal indulgence, to come near the infected. And such, at that time, was the public distress, that the laws, human and divine, were no more regarded; for the officers, to put them in force, being either dead, sick, or in want of persons to assist them, every one did just as he pleased. A third sort of people chose a method between these two: not confining themselves to rules of diet like the former, and yet avoiding the intemperance of the latter; but eating and drinking what their appetites required, they walked everywhere with [fragrances and nose-coverings], for the whole atmosphere seemed to them tainted with the stench of dead bodies, arising partly from the distemper itself, and partly from the fermenting of the medicines within them. Others with less humanity, but . . . with more security from danger, decided that the only remedy for the pesti-

lence was to avoid it: persuaded, therefore, of this, and taking care for themselves only, men and women in great numbers left the city, their houses, relations, and effects, and fled into the country; as if the wrath of God had been restrained to visit those only within the walls of the city. . . .

I pass over the little regard that citizens and relations showed to each other; for their terror was such, that a brother even fled from his brother, a wife from her husband, and, what is more uncommon, a parent from his own child. Hence numbers that fell sick could have no help but what the charity of friends, who were very few, or the avarice of servants supplied; and even these were scarce and at extravagant wages, and so little used to the business that they were fit only to reach what was called for, and observe when their employer died; and this desire of getting money often cost them their lives. . . .

It fared no better with the adjacent country, for . . . you might see the poor distressed labourers, with their families, without either the aid of physicians, or help of servants, languishing on the highways, in the fields, and in their own houses, and dying rather like cattle than human creatures. The consequence was that, growing dissolute in their manners like the citizens, and careless of everything, as supposing every day to be their last, their thoughts were not so much employed how to improve, as how to use their substance for their present support.

What can I say more, if I return to the city, unless that such was the cruelty of Heaven, and perhaps of men, that between March and July following, according to authentic reckonings, upwards of a hundred thousand souls perished in the city only; whereas, before that calamity, it was not supposed to have contained so many inhabitants. What magnificent dwellings, what noble palaces were then depopulated to the last inhabitant! What families became extinct! What riches and vast possessions were left, and no known heir to inherit them! What numbers of both sexes, in the prime and vigour of youth . . . breakfasted in the morning with their living friends, and supped at night with their departed friends in the other world!

"God's Hand Was Unstrung"

MATTEO VILLANI

Matteo Villani was the brother of Giovanni Villani, the first great chronicler of Florence. Giovanni had described the beginnings of the plague before he himself died of it. Matteo continued his brother's work and devoted two chapters to the effects of the plague. He succumbed to the disease in 1363. The confused reactions to the plague were often either to lead a very temperate life in hopes that God would approve and lift his ban against humanity or conversely to enjoy life to the utmost before Death knocked on the door. Villani describes the scene in Florence.

Those few discreet folk who remained alive expected many things, all of which, by reasons of the corruption of sin, failed among mankind, whose minds followed marvellously in the contrary direction. They believed that those whom God's grace had saved from death, having beheld the destruction of their neighbors, and having heard the same tidings from all the nations of the world, would become better-conditioned, humble, virtuous, and Catholic; that they would guard themselves from iniquity and sins, and would be full of love and charity one towards another. But no sooner had the plague ceased than we saw the contrary; for, since men were few, and since, by hereditary succession, they abounded in earthly goods, they forgot the past as though it had never been, and gave themselves up to a more shameful and disordered life than they had led before. For, mouldering in ease, they dissolutely abandoned themselves to the sin of gluttony, with feasts and taverns and delight of delicate foods; and again to games of hazard and to unbridled lechery, inventing strange and unaccustomed fashions and indecent manners in their garments, and changing all their household stuff into new forms. And the common folk, both men and women, by reason of the abundance and superfluity that they found, would no longer labour at their accustomed trades, but demanded the dearest and most delicate foods for their sustenance; and they married at their will, while children and common women clad themselves in all the fair and costly garments of the ladies dead by that horrible death. Thus, almost the whole city, without any restraint whatsoever, rushed into disorderliness of life; and in other cities or provinces of the world things were the same or worse. Therefore, according to such tidings as we could hear, there was no part of the world wherein men restrained themselves to live in temperance, when once they had escaped from the fury of the Lord; for now they thought that God's hand was unstrung. . . . Again, men dreamed of wealth and abundance in garments and in all other things . . . beyond meat and drink; yet, in fact, things turned out widely different; for most [luxury] commodities were more costly, by twice or more, than before the plague. And the price of labour, and the work of all trades and crafts, rose in disorderly fashion beyond the double. Lawsuits and disputes and quarrels and riots arose everywhere among citizens in every land, by reason of legacies and successions; the law-courts of our own city of Florence were long filled with such [cases], to our great expense and unwanted discomfort. Wars and . . . scandals arose throughout the world, contrary to men's expectation.

CHRONOLOGY: Medieval Civilization in the West: The Sword of Faith

527–565   Reign of Justinian in Constantinople. Reconquest of North Africa and Italy, codification of Roman law, and building of the church, Hagia Sophia.

530   Monastic rule of Saint Benedict established in the West. Emphasis on a common experience among monks, rather than the heremitic emphasis in the eastern Mediterranean.

570–632   Life of Muhammad, who—according to the Qur'an (650)—received revelations from the angel Gabriel, attacked idolatry in Mecca, was driven out in 622 (hegira), and established himself at Medina, where he began the spread of Islam.

732   Charles Martel ("The Hammer") defeats Muslims at Poitiers.

751   Pepin the Short, formerly Mayor of the Palace under the Merovingian Dynasty, becomes King of the Franks. Establishes Carolingian Dynasty and serves as papal protector.

768–814   Reign of Charlemagne, King of the Franks. Defeats Lombards in northern Italy (774) and establishes empire throughout modern-day France, parts of Germany and eastern Europe, Italy, and northern Spain. Charlemagne crowned emperor by Pope Leo III (800). Establishment of Carolingian Renaissance under the direction of Alcuin of York.

814–840   Louis the Pious succeeds Charlemagne as emperor.

843   Treaty of Verdun partitions Carolingian Empire among sons of Louis the Pious. Disagreement and chaos follow.

910   Foundation of the monastery of Cluny with its strict emphasis on the rule of Saint Benedict. Cluny provides basis for general reform of the church.

962	Saxons under Otto II succeed Carolingians in Germany.
987	Capetian dynasty succeeds Carolingians in France.
1066	Norman invasion of Britain by William the Conqueror results in victory over Anglo-Saxon king, Harold Godwinson.
1075–1122	Investiture controversy between Pope Gregory VII and Holy Roman Emperor Henry IV, which carried on to their successors. Resolution in the Concordat of Worms: Church would elect prelates and invest them with spiritual authority, emperor invests prelate with secular lands, goods, and privileges.
1091–1153	Saint Bernard founds monastery at Clairvaux (1115) and leads monastic reform movement throughout Europe.
1095	At the Council of Clermont, Pope Urban II calls for a crusade to free the Holy Land from Muslim control.
1099	Jerusalem falls to the Crusaders. Forty-five years of Western rule begins in the Holy Land.
1154–1189	Reign of King Henry II of England and his wife Eleanor of Aquitaine. Henry's difficult Archbishop of Canterbury, Thomas Becket, murdered (1170) and subsequently canonized.
1182–1226	Life of Saint Francis of Assisi, founder of the Franciscan order of Friars.
1189–1192	Third Crusade, which was attended by King Richard III of England, King Philip Augustus of France, and Holy Roman Emperor, Frederick Barbarossa, fails to recover Holy Land from Muslims.
1198–1216	Papacy of Innocent III, the most powerful and influential medieval pope.
1215	Magna Carta signed by King John of England. Rights of Englishmen established.
1225–1274	Life of Saint Thomas Aquinas, generally regarded as the most insightful and important medieval philosopher.
1337–1453	Hundred Years' War between France and England rages intermittently for 116 years over disputed claims to the French throne.
1346	English victory at Crécy.
1347–1351	Black Death first strikes in Sicily and moves north throughout Europe. Successive but less devastating plagues occur into the next century. Giovanni Boccaccio writes *The Decameron.*
1381	John Ball and Wat Tyler lead the English Peasant Revolt in protest over new taxes, tolls, and reduced wages. Short-lived and brutally crushed by aristocrats, it leaves the country divided for years. Black Death returns.
1415	English victory at Agincourt under the leadership of King Henry V.
1429	Joan of Arc leads French to victory at Orléans. She is executed as a heretic in 1431.

STUDY QUESTIONS

I: The Early Middle Ages (500–1000)

1. Why was the Arian heresy such a threat to the religious unity of Christianity? How did the Nicene Creed solve the controversy? How would you interpret the statement that Jesus was "begotten not made"? What was the emperor Constantine's role in the Council of Nicaea, and how does this reflect the principles of Caesaro-papism?

2. What are the basic tenets of Islam as noted in the selections from the *Qur'an* and from Al-Ghazzali on "The Love of Allah"? Was Muhammad, like Jesus, considered to be divine in nature? How do you interpret the phrase "Fight for the sake of God those that fight against you, but do not attack them first. God does not love the aggressors"? The next statement reads: "Slay them wherever you find them. Drive them out of places from which they drove you." Do you find these ideas to be contradictory? Why or why not? How are women viewed by the Qur'an? Do women have legal rights? Do they assume equal status with men?

3. What does the adventure of Sinbad the Sailor tell us about Arab exploration and trade? Why did Sinbad venture to the East Indies? Why was trade so important in promoting the expansion of Islam?

4. According to the account of Al-Bakri, why did the West African King of Malal decide to convert to Islam? Even if the king's subjects remained polytheists, why was his conversion important to the success of Islamic conversion?

5. What do the selections on mathematics and the scientific description of smallpox tell you about Islamic values? According to Al-Ghazzali, should mathematics and religion be separated? Why or why not?

6. In what ways does Charlemagne's administration of his empire reflect authority and structure? What was the "Carolingian Renaissance," and what do these aspects of Charlemagne's rule say about life in the Dark Ages? According to the sources, why did Charlemagne demand attention to reading and writing? Was the church at risk when more people could read the Bible and other Christian literature? Why?

7. Define feudalism. What conditions contributed to the rise of this system? Be specific in citing appropriate sources. How does homage differ from liege homage? What were some of the obligations of a vassal to his lord? Construct a sequence of contemporary events in the United States that could result in the imposition of feudal government. How realistic a proposal is this? Could it happen?

II: The High Middle Ages (1000–1300)

8. Carefully read the Clermont speech of Urban II. What specific reasons are given for the necessity of a Crusade to the Holy Land? How does he justify a military expedition in which bloodshed could be expected?

9. Who was Usamah Ibn-Monqidh and what was his general impression of the western Crusades? What theme seems to dominate his accounts of his contact with Europeans?

10. What is monasticism and what medieval values does it represent? Why was the monastic movement so popular? Which of the rules of Saint Benedict impress you most and why? Compared to other lifestyles in the Middle Ages, was it hard being a monk?

11. What is Saint Thomas Aquinas' essential argument for the existence of God? Does it sound logical to you? Is it persuasive, or can you find defects in the proof? Is Saint Bernard's argument more satisfying? Peter Abelard summed up his attitude in this way: "By doubting, we

come to inquire, by inquiring, we come to the truth." Saint Anselm said, "I believe in order that I may understand." What is the essential difference between the two statements? Do you believe that Abelard was seeking to undermine faith in God? What is the "truth" he sought?

12. Explain the concept of chivalry. What were the most important functions of knighthood? Why was it important to provide an ideal for knights? Analyze the love poems by Jaufre Rudel and the Countess de Dia. What is their basic theme, and what do they say about the positions of women in the High Middle Ages?

III: The Waning of the Middle Ages (1300–1450)

13. Carefully read the papal decrees "Clericis Laicos" and "Unam Sanctam." What concepts was Boniface VIII trying to promote? Is he persuasive in the logic of his argument? What does the "Doctrine of the Two Swords" entail? What do those who defy the decrees risk? Why would a king be willing to risk such a penalty?

14. What common actions or occurrences do the various accounts of the Black Death identify? Is there a theme that pervades the material? Which account or passage makes the greatest impression on you, and why?

15. In what ways were the interests of both church and state affected by the Black Death? Religion is often considered a stabilizing force in society. How was faith a casualty of this disease? How did the plague disrupt the balance between religious and secular forces that helped resolve the standoff between church and state? What is the role of disease in history? How potent is disease as a force for historical change?

7

Mysteries of the Maya

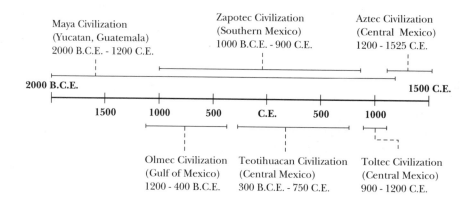

Between about 150 C.E. and 900 C.E., when the Chinese empires of the Qin, Han, and Tang dynasties held sway in the East and the Roman Empire gave way to Germanic and Islamic control in Europe, the civilizations of Mesoamerica entered into a Classic period of strength and cultural prominence. In the valleys of Mexico and Oaxaca, between the Pacific Ocean and the Gulf of Mexico, Native American societies grew to maturity, flourished, and died, absorbed by other rising native powers or destroyed by external invasion. Although historians can often trace and link the mythology, religion, and artistic achievements of these cultures, it is also true that much remains shrouded in mystery.

One of the most interesting and important of these American cultures flourished in the lowlands of Yucatan, Guatemala, and Belize. The Maya civilization consisted of several tribes joined by two related languages and a common cultural tradition. Modern exploration and archeological excavation of the Maya civilization began about 1840 with the efforts of John Lloyd Stephens and Frederick Catherwood. They discovered the ruins of Palenque in eastern Mexico and Chichén Itzá in the Yucatan peninsula. Others followed in the 1850s through 1880s, finding such isolated lost cities as Uxmal and Tikál.

The latter was the largest of Maya cities with a population of perhaps 50,000–70,000 people. Modern archaeologists have found evidence of agricultural technologies, such as terrace farming and irrigation systems, that would have supported dense populations. The most famous cities of Tikál and Chichén Itzá were ruled by powerful families and retainers who were supported by a larger class of common farmers. Warfare between cities was chronic and rulers recounted their glory on stone tablets in hieroglyphs. These rulers were shaman priest-kings who served not only as the font of political authority, but also as the intermediaries between the physical and spirit worlds. Through painstaking research in the mid-twentieth century, archaeologists were able to decipher the Maya scripts and unlock the key to much of what we know about Maya civilization today. As murals and sculptures show, prisoners were often sacrificed to appease the gods and glorify the rulers. This focus on blood ritual is common among other Mesoamerican cultures such as the Toltecs and Aztecs.

The Maya civilization remains a wonder to historians. In the midst of the difficult rainforest climate and vegetation, Mayans built sophisticated cities that adapted to the terrain. These were talented astronomers and mathematicians who invented the concept of zero, developed an absolute calendar (known as the Long Count) to a fixed point in the past, and also created a sophisticated lunar calendar with adjustment provisions to the actual length of the solar year. But between 800 and 900 c.e., this Classic Period civilization collapsed. The exact causes still remain a mystery. Some archaeologists have suggested that overfarming or drought may have led to soil exhaustion that crippled agricultural production. Chichén Itzá declined after 1200. By the beginning of the Spanish conquest of Mesoamerica in 1517, only a few Maya towns remained and many of these were destroyed by the conquerors. But the ruins of this civilization continue to speak to us over the centuries. It remains a fascinating tale.

MAYA ORIGINS: *POPUL VUH*

When Hernando Cortés had completed his conquest of Mexico in 1524, he sent his most fearless captain, Pedro de Alvarado, east to a region in modern Guatemala occupied by the descendants of the once powerful Maya civilization. These Quiché Mayans put up a vigorous defense but finally surrendered in the face of superior Spanish weaponry. Alvarado seized the kings and executed them in the presence of their people. Their city was razed to the ground and the site abandoned.

Two hundred years later in the eighteenth century, the Spanish friar, Father Francisco Ximénez, who had lived with the remnants of the Quiché in the area and had learned their language, was busy converting them to Christianity. In winning their confidence, these Indians offered Ximénez a sacred book that contained the stories and traditions of their ancestors. This book, called the Popul Vuh, *was written shortly after the Spanish conquest by a Quiché Indian who had learned to read and write Spanish. Father Ximénez transcribed the text and returned the book to its owners where it has been lost to history. But Ximénez' transcription still exists and it is an amazing document. It contains the Maya cosmogeny, creation myths, and a chronology of their kings down to the year 1550. The following selections from the* Popul Vuh *reveal much about the Mayan conception of the world and the origins of ritual blood sacrifice.*

The Creation of the World

Keep in Mind. . .

- According to the *Popul Vuh*, who created the world?

- Who were the first men and why were they unacceptable to the gods? How were the first men destroyed?

This is the account of how all was in suspense, all calm, in silence; all motionless, still, and the expanse of the sky was empty.

This is the first account, the first narrative. There was neither man, nor animal, birds, fishes, crabs, trees, stones, caves, ravines, grasses, nor forests; there was only the sky.

The surface of the earth had not appeared. There was only the calm sea and the great expanse of the sky.

There was nothing brought together, nothing which could make a noise, nor anything which might move, or tremble, or could make noise in the sky.

There was nothing standing; only the calm water, the placid sea, alone and tranquil. Nothing existed.

There was only immobility and silence in the darkness, in the night. Only the Creator, the Maker, Tepeu, Gucumatz, the Forefathers, were in the water surrounded with light. They were hidden under green and blue feathers, and were therefore called Gucumatz. By nature they were great sages and great thinkers. In this manner the sky existed and also the Heart of Heaven, which is the name of God and thus He is called.

Then came the word. Tepeu and Gucumatz came together in the darkness, in the night, and Tepeu and Gucumatz talked together. They

Popul Vuh: The Sacred Book of the Ancient Quiché Maya, English version by Delia Goetz and Sylvanus G. Morely from the translation of Adrian Recinos. Copyright © 1950, 1977 by the University of Oklahoma Press. Reprinted by permission.

talked them, discussing and deliberating; they agreed, they united their words and their thoughts.

Then while they meditated, it became clear to them that when dawn would break, man must appear. Then they planned the creation, and the growth of the trees and the thickets and the birth of life and the creation of man. Thus it was arranged in the darkness and in the night by the Heart of Heaven who is called Huracan. . . .

Thus let it be done! Let the emptiness be filled! Let the water recede and make a void, let the earth appear and become solid; let it be done. Thus they spoke. Let there be light, let there be dawn in the sky and on the earth! There shall be neither glory nor grandeur in our creation and formation until the human being is made, man is formed. So they spoke.

Then the earth was created by them. So it was, in truth, that they created the earth. Earth! they said, and instantly it was made.

Like the mist, like a cloud, and like a cloud of dust was the creation, when the mountains appeared from the water; and instantly the mountains grew.

Only by a miracle, only by magic art were the mountains and valleys formed; and instantly the groves of cypresses and pines put forth shoots together on the surface of the earth. . . .

First the earth was formed, the mountains and the valleys; the currents of water were divided, the rivulets were running freely between the hills, and the water was separated when the high mountains appeared. Thus was the earth created, when it was formed by the Heart of Heaven, the Heart of Earth, as they are called who first made it fruitful, when the sky was in suspense, and the earth was submerged in the water.

So it was that they made perfect the work, when they did it after thinking and meditating upon it.

Then they made the small wild animals, the guardians of the woods, the spirits of the mountains, the deer, the birds, pumas, jaguars, serpents, snakes, vipers, guardians of the thickets. . . .

"Let Us Make Him Who Will Nourish and Sustain Us!"

"Let us try again! Already dawn draws near: Let us make him who shall nourish and sustain us! What shall we do to be invoked, in order to be remembered on earth? We have already tried with our first creations, our first creatures; but we could not make them praise and venerate us. So, then, let us try to make obedient, respectful beings who will nourish and sustain us." Thus they spoke.

Then was the creation and the formation. Of earth, of mud, they made [man's] flesh. But they saw that it was not good. It melted away, it was soft, did not move, had no strength, it fell down, it was limp, it could not move its head, its face fell to one side, its sight was blurred, it could not look behind. At first it spoke, but had no mind. Quickly it soaked in the water and could not stand.

And the Creator and the Maker said: "Let us try again because our creatures will not be able to walk nor multiply. Let us consider this," they said.

Then they broke up and destroyed their work and their creation. And they said: "What shall we do to perfect it, in order that our worshipers, our invokers, will be successful?". . .

Beginning the divination, they said: "Get together, grasp each other! Speak, that we may hear." They said, "Say if it is well that the wood be got together and that it be carved by the Creator and the Maker, and if this [man of wood] is he who must nourish and sustain us then there is light when it is day! . . . These were the first men who existed in great numbers on the face of the earth.

Immediately the wooden figures were annihilated, destroyed, broken up, and killed.

Popul Vuh: The Sacred Book of the Ancient Quiché Maya, English version by Delia Goetz and Sylvanus G. Morely from the translation of Adrian Recinos. Copyright © 1950, 1977 by the University of Oklahoma Press. Reprinted by permission.

A flood was brought about by the Heart of Heaven; a great flood was formed which fell on the heads of the wooden creatures. . . . Those that they had made, that they had created, did not think, did not speak with their Creator, their Maker. And for this reason they were killed, they were deluged. . . .

This was to punish them because they had not thought of their mother, nor their father, the Heart of Heaven, called Huracan. And for this reason the face of the earth was darkened and a black rain began to fall, by day and by night. . . .

The desperate ones [the men of wood] ran as quickly as they could; they wanted to climb to the tops of the houses, and the houses fell down and threw them to the ground; they wanted to climb to the treetops, and the trees cast them far away; they wanted to enter the caverns, and the caverns repelled them.

So was the ruin of the men who had been created and formed, the men made to be destroyed and annihilated; the mouths and faces of all of them were mangled.

And it is said that their descendants are the monkeys which now live in the forests; these are all that remain of them because their flesh was made only of wood by the Creator and the Maker.

And therefore the monkey looks like man, and is an example of a generation of men which were created and made but were only wooden figures.

Compare and Contrast:

• Note the phrases: "Then came the word" and "Let there be light." Compare this with the Biblical account of the creation of the world on pp. 32–33, and the African and Hindu creation stories on pp. 34–35 and 47 respectively. In what ways are these stories similar and different from the Maya epic? Why are floods common to creation epics (see the story of Gilgamesh on pp. 9–11)?

- Why did the gods have such difficulty with the formation of human beings? What did the creator gods require of them?

- Why is the concept of creation so important to each culture? How does creation define the religious parameters of society?

The Story of Blood Woman

Keep in Mind. . .

- How does Cuchumaquic [Blood Woman] become impregnated? Why was this necessary?

This is the story of a maiden, the daughter of a lord named Cuchumaquic. A maiden, then, daughter of a lord heard this story. The name of the father was Cuchumaquic [Blood Father] and that of the maiden was Xquic [Blood Woman]. When she heard the story of the fruit of the tree which her father told, she was amazed to hear it.

"Why can I not go to see this tree which they tell about?"

The girl exclaimed. "Surely the fruit of which I hear tell must be very good." Finally she went alone and arrived at the foot of the tree which was planted in Pucbal-Chah.

"Ah!" she exclaimed. "What fruit is this which this tree bears? Is it not wonderful to see how it is covered with fruit? Must I die, shall I be lost, if I pick one of this fruit" said the maiden.

Then the skull which was among the branches of the tree spoke up and said: "What is it you wish? Those round objects which cover the branches of the trees are nothing but skulls." So spoke the head of Hun Hunahpu turning to the maiden. "Do you, perchance, want them?" it added.

"Yes, I want them," the maiden answered.

"Very well," said the skull. "Stretch your right hand up here."

"Very well," said the maiden, and with her right hand reached toward the skull.

In that instant the skull let a few drops of saliva fall directly into the maiden's palm. She looked quickly and intently at the palm of her hand, but the saliva of the skull was not there.

"In my saliva and spittle I have given you my descendants," said the voice in the tree. "Now my head has nothing on it any more, it is nothing but a skull without flesh. So are the heads of the great princes, the flesh is all which gives them a handsome appearance. And when they die, men are frightened by their bones. So, too, is the nature of the sons, which are like saliva and spittle, they may be sons of a lord, of a wise man, or of an orator. They do not lose their substance when they go, but they bequeath it; the image of the lord, of the wise man, or of the orator does not disappear, nor is it lost, but he leaves it to the daughters and to the sons which he begets. I have done the same with you. Go up, then, to the surface of the earth, that you may not die. Believe in my words that it will be so," said the head of Hun-Hunahpu. . . .

And so the girl returned home, and after six months had passed, her father, who was called Cuchumaquic, noticed her condition. At once the maiden's secret was discovered by her father when he observed that she was pregnant.

Then the lords, Hun-Came and Vucub-Came, held council with Cuchumaquic.

"My daughter is pregnant, sirs; she has been disgraced," exclaimed Cuchumaquic when he appeared before the lords.

"Very well," they said. "Command her to tell the truth, and if she refuses to speak, punish her; let her be taken far from here and sacrifice her."

"Very well, Honorable Lords," he answered. Then he questioned his daughter."

"Whose are the children that you carry, my daughter?" And she answered, "I have no child, my father, for I have not yet known a youth."

"Very well," he replied. "You are really a whore. Take her and sacrifice her, Ahpop Achih; bring me her heart in a gourd and return this very day before the lords," he said to the two owls.

The four messengers took the gourd and set out carrying the young girl in their arms and also taking the knife of flint with which to sacrifice her.

And she said to them: "It cannot be that you will kill me, oh, messengers, because what I bear in my belly is no disgrace, but was begotten when I went to marvel at the head of Hun-Hunahpu which was in Pucbal-Chah. So, then, you must not sacrifice me, oh, messengers!" said the young girl, turning to them.

"And what shall we put in place of your heart? Your father told us: 'Bring the heart, return before the lords, do your duty, all working together, bring it in the gourd quickly, and put the heart in the bottom of the gourd.' Perchance, did he not speak to us so? What shall we put in the gourd? We wish too, that you should not die," said the messengers.

"Very well, but my heart does not belong to them. Neither is your home here, nor must you let them force you to kill men. . . . So, then, the blood and only the blood shall be theirs and shall be given to them. Neither shall my heart be burned before them. Gather the product of this tree," said the maiden.

The red sap gushing forth from the tree fell in the gourd and with it they made a ball which glistened and took the shape of a heart. The tree gave forth sap similar to blood, with the appearance of real blood. Then the blood, or that is to say the sap of the red tree, clotted, and formed a very bright coating inside the gourd, like clotted blood; meanwhile the tree glowed at the work of the maiden. It was called the "red tree of cochineal," but [since then] it has taken the name of Blood Tree because its sap is called Blood.

"There on earth you shall be beloved and you shall have all that belongs to you," said the maiden to the owls.

"Very well, girl. We shall go there, we go up to serve you; you, continue on your way, while we go to present the sap, instead of your heart, to the lords," said the messengers.

When they arrived in the presence of the lords, all were waiting. "You have finished?" asked Hun-Came.

"All is finished, my lords. Here in the bottom of the gourd is the heart."

"Very well. Let us see," exclaimed Hun-Came. And grasping it with his fingers he raised it, the shell broke and the blood flowed bright red in color.

"Stir up the fire and put it on the coals," said Hun-Came.

As soon as they threw it on the fire, the men of Xibalba began to sniff and drawing near to it, they found the fragrance of the heart very sweet.

And as they sat deep in thought, the owls, the maiden's servants, left, and flew like a flock of birds from the abyss toward earth and the four became her servants.

In this manner the lords of Xibalba were defeated. All were tricked by the maiden.

Consider This:

- Note the importance of sacrifice in Maya society. Why was Blood Woman to be sacrificed? What does this say about Maya society?

- In the children's story "Snow White" the guard is instructed by the witch to kill the maiden and bring back her heart. But he cannot do this and substitutes an animal heart for her human heart. How is the concept of justice defined in Snow White and in the story of Blood Woman?

THE LOST CITY OF TIKÁL

*Deep in the dense jungles of Guatemala lie the ruins of the largest Maya city, Tikál. The first arche-
ologists who hacked their way into the rainforests of Mesoamerica in the mid-nineteenth century believed that Tikál was simply a religious center, where priests scoured the heavens from temple pyramids and sacrificed captured war prisoners. Later, archeologists discovered housing and water
cisterns that led them to the conclusion that Tikál was in fact a great political and economic center
that included 50,000 to 70,000 inhabitants. Its political control extended almost a thousand
square miles and held sway over perhaps 360,000 people. The city itself is situated near swamps
that could have aided agriculture and had access to river systems that promoted trade between the
Gulf and Carribean coasts.*

*Tikál has been thoroughly excavated and its five massive temple pyramids continue to impress
visitors who marvel at the sophistication of Maya culture. The following selection by the British
archeologist, Alfred Maudslay, describes his first visit to Tikál in 1893.*

"Completely Covered over with Forest"

ALFRED MAUDSLAY

Keep in Mind. . .

- According to archeologist, Alfred Maudslay,
  what was the most difficult problem he encountered while exploring the ruins of Tikál?

The whole site of the ancient town was so completely covered over with forest that it took us
some time to discover the position of the more
important buildings and clear away the trees
which covered them. As neither of my visits was
over a week in length the plan of the ruins here
given is very imperfect; it merely indicates the
shape and size of the principal group of stone
buildings near the house in which I took up my
quarters, and gives approximately the position
of the five great pyramidal temple mounds. . . .

The lofty foundation mounds of the principal
temples are terraced and faced with well-
wrought stone arranged in panels, somewhat in
the same manner as that shown in the photograph of the Castillo at Chichén Itzá. At Tikál,
however, access to the temple is gained by a single stairway only, instead of by four stairways,
one on each side of the mound, as is usual at
Chichén [Itzá]. . . .

There is, however, no other group of temples
in Central America which offers such support to
the theory that the position and form of the
buildings is due to astronomical considerations.
The lofty elevation so as to secure a clear view,
the evident desire to gain length of axis, and the
fact that all the temples may be roughly said to
face the cardinal points favor this theory, and it
may be that we can trace the sequence of the
structures by their position. . . .

Tikál is not rich in carved stone
monuments. . . . The most important inscriptions, and they are among the best examples of
Maya art, were found in the carved wooden
beams which spanned the doorways of the temples. Many of these beams have decayed, but the
best specimens were removed. . . .

The greatest discomfort in exploring the ruins
of Tikál is due to the want of a good supply of
water. Every drop of water we used had to be
brought the distance of a mile and a half from an
overgrown muddy lagoon not more than one
hundred fifty yards wide, and it was so thick and
dirty that I never dared to drink it until it had first
been boiled and then filtered, and my Indian
workmen who refused to take any precautions
suffered considerably from fever. The Indians seldom drink cold water when they are at work, and

"Completely Covered over with Forest" is from Alfred
Percival Maudslay, *A Glimpse at Guatemala* (London: John
Murray, 1899), pp. 232–235.

during a journey they will make frequent halts by the roadside to light fires and prepare warm drinks; but notwithstanding this prevalent habit, when we were encamped in places where the water was indubitably bad, I was never able to persuade my attendants that any advantage would be gained by actually bringing the water to a boil and then allowing it to stand and cool.

A few years before the date of my visit to Tikál, a party of Indians from the borders of the lake had attempted to form a settlement in the neighborhood of the ruins. The solitary survivor of this party accompanied me as a guide, all the others having died of fever.

Consider This:

*   How does the geography of an area limit or enhance the prospects of establishing a successful civilization?

The Great Temple at Tikál

The five temple pyramids at Tikál were built over a period of five hundred years from 300 to 800 c.e. Rising over two hundred feet, this temple served as an astronomical observatory and religious center where the priest kings communed with the gods and sacrificial rituals took place.

Keep in Mind. . .

*   Why did the Mayas construct this temple?

Consider This:

*   What does the Great Temple at Tikál say about the values and interests of Maya civilization?

The Great Temple at Tikál

Theme: Historical Change and Transition

The Historical Intersection

TROY: 1873

The Excavation of Troy

HEINRICH SCHLIEMANN

The exploration of ancient civilizations gained momentum in the mid-nineteenth century as the emerging discipline of archeology competed with the unbridled enthusiasm of amateurs questing for adventure and treasure throughout the world.

One of the most actively debated events was the destruction of the fabled city of Troy as chronicled by the poet Homer in the Iliad. *Was this hard-fought war between the Greeks and Trojans about 1200 B.C.E. just a legend, or was it an actual historical event? Were the stories of Achilles and Hector, Odysseus and Agamemnon simply poetic fantasy, or were these heroes historical figures?*

The wealthy German businessman, linguist, and amateur archeologist, Heinrich Schliemann, set out to find ancient Troy. During excavations in Turkey from 1871 to 1873, Schliemann recklessly uncovered Troy VIIA and found that this settlement had been destroyed in a violent conflagration. He was convinced that Homer was correct and that he had found actual history, not mere legend. Archaeologists and historians have since been persuaded that ancient Troy existed and that it was destroyed about 1200 B.C.E. This account by Heinrich Schliemann attests to the power of myth and the tenacity of one man's personality to bring the past to life.

Compare and Contrast. . .

- Compare accounts of the early descriptions of Tikál and Chichén Itzá respectively by Alfred Maudslay and Désiré Charnáy with this account of the excavation of Troy by Heinrich Schliemann. What was important to these early explorers and archeologists?

(contd)

Troy, June 17th, 1873

In excavating this wall further and directly by the side of the Palace of King Priam, I came upon a large copper article of the most remarkable form, which attracted my attention all the more since I thought I saw gold behind it. . . . In order to withdraw the treasure from the greed of my workmen, and to save it for archaeology, I had to be most expeditious, and although it was not yet time for breakfast, I immediately [called for a break].

While the men were eating and resting, I cut out the treasure with a large knife, which it was impossible to do without the very greatest exertion and the most fearful risk of my life, for the great fortification wall, beneath which I had to dig, threatened every moment to fall down upon me. But the sight of so many objects, every one of which is of inestimable value to archaeology, made me foolhardy, and I never thought of any danger. It would, however, have been impossible for me to have removed the treasure without the help of my dear wife, who stood by me ready to pack the things which I cut out in her shawl and to carry them away. . . .

As I found all the articles together, forming a rectangular mass, or packed into one another, it seems to be certain that they were placed on the city wall in a wooden chest, such as those mentioned by Homer as being in the palace of King Priam. This appears to be the more certain, as close by the side of these articles I found a copper key about 4 inches long, the head of which greatly resembles a large safe-key of a bank. . . .

It is probable that some member of the family of King Priam hurriedly packed the treasure into the chest and carried it off without having time to pull out the key; that when he reached the wall, however, the hand of an enemy or the fire overtook him, and he was obliged to abandon the chest, which was immediately covered to a height of from 5 to 6 feet with the red ashes and the stones of the adjoining royal palace. . . .

That the treasure was packed together at terrible risk of life, and in the greatest anxiety, is proved among other things also by the contents of the silver case, at the bottom of which I found two splendid gold diadems, and four beautiful gold ear-rings of most exquisite workmanship: upon these lay 56 gold ear-rings of exceedingly curious form and 8,750 small gold rings, perforated prisms and dice, gold buttons and similar jewels, . . . six gold bracelets, and on the top of all the two small gold goblets. . . .

The person who endeavored to save the treasure had fortunately the presence of mind to stand the silver vase, containing the valuable articles described above, upright in the chest, so that not so much as a bead could fall out, and everything has been preserved uninjured. . . .

I should in a few weeks have uncovered the most remarkable buildings in Troy, namely, the Palace of King Priam, the Scaean Gate, the Great Surrounding Wall, and the Great Tower of Ilium.

(contd)

Consider This:

- Was Heinrich Schliemann a destroyer of culture or a preserver and protector of the past? Did he perform a service to archeology?
- Is archeology an "Indiana Jones" adventure, or a difficult and methodical scientific discipline?

"The Excavation of Troy" is from Heinrich Schliemann, *Troy and Its Remains*, trans. L. Dora Schmitz; ed. Philip Smith (London: John Murray, 1875), pp. 224–230.

CHICHÉN ITZÁ

Between 800 and 900 C.E., Maya civilization in the southern lowlands of Guatemala collapsed. The ruling dynasties disintegrated into political chaos, monumental architecture ceased, and great cities like Tikál declined and were eventually abandoned. Historians cannot offer definitive reasons for this collapse, but a variety of factors from intensifying warfare to growing population, soil exhaustion, and a drought may have combined to end the Maya dominance.

The center of Maya civilization then shifted to the northern jungles of Yucatan. The primary site of Chichén Itzá, watered by a sacred well, flourished from 800 to about 1200 before it too declined. By 1517, when Cortés and other Spanish conquistadors landed in Mesoamerica, there were only a few Maya cities in existence. Nevertheless, the Spanish prohibited the Maya language and defaced Maya monuments in an effort to eradicate a culture they found perverse and ungodly.

This section begins with a description of the primary temple/fortress at Chichén Itzá, called "El Castillo" by the French explorer and photographer Désiré Charnáy about 1850. His diagrams of El Castillo and Chichén-Chob, the prison at Chichén Itzá, reflect the impressive nature of Maya architecture.

El Castillo: "The Mysterious Past of a Dead City"

DÉSIRÉ CHARNÁY

Keep in Mind. . .

- According to Désiré Charnáy, why was El Castillo (the fortress) an appropriate name for this temple at Chichén Itzá?

El Castillo: "The Mysterious Past of a Dead City" is from Désiré Charnáy, *The Ancient Cities of the New World*, translated by J. Gonino and Helen S. Conant (New York, 1887), pp. 324–325; 333–338.

- Why did the Spanish deface the inscriptions and hieroglyphs on El Castillo and Chichén-Chob, the prison at Chichén Itzá?

This was not my first visit to Chichén, nevertheless my emotion was profound on beholding again the gigantic outline of El Castillo, which we had decided beforehand should be our headquarters, as from its elevated position it offered many strategical advantages, which would secure us against surprise. It was with considerable difficulty that we climbed the steps, which are steep and completely invaded by a vigorous vegetation; as for our great quantity of baggage, none but nimble, sure-footed natives could have

El Castillo at Chichén Itzá

succeeded in hauling it up on to the platform of the monument. . . .

It may seem unworthy to have been put out by such trivial details with the grand spectacle we had before us: a glorious moon had risen, sailing on her course with her brilliant retinue of scintillating stars, illuminating the vast wooded expanse, like a boundless, heaving ocean on a calm day; fragments of walls, mounds, eminences, shrouded in a somber vegetation, were distinctly visible, which I pointed out one by one to my companions who, unlike myself, beheld them for the first time. El Castillo occupies nearly the center of the ruins; below it to the east was the Marketplace, and two small palaces which belonged to it; to the north, a stately but ruinous building, the cenote [well] and the temple attached; to the northwest, the famous Tennis Court; to the west and southwest, the Chichén-Chob [prison], . . . and further south, the hacienda, which has long been abandoned.

We were conversing in subdued tones of the mysterious past of this dead city, which perhaps our studies and explorations would bring to life again; all was hushed, and the death-like silence was only broken at regular intervals by the cry of our sentinels; and these very cries carried us back to the far gone days, when the city was perhaps similarly guarded against a sudden inroad from her jealous neighbors.

The morning effects of light and shade were no less beautiful; the broad level wrapped in a transparent mist, pierced here and there by the pyramids and the wooded eminences, looked like a whitening sea interspersed with green islets; while the horizon was gilded with the brightness of the rising sun, who seemed to create, to raise suddenly into life all the objects touched with his golden wand; presently, like a mighty giant he tore asunder and burned up the white vapor, and lit up the whole sky. . . .

[To return to our excavations], the Castillo, or rather temple, is reared on a pyramid, facing north and south, and is the most interesting monument at Chichén; its four sides are occupied with staircases, facing the cardinal points. Our drawing shows the western facade. The base of the pyramid measures 175 feet. . . . The upper platform is 68 feet above the level of the plain, having a flight on ninety steps, 39 feet wide, leading up to it.

The name of El Castillo (the fortress), given to this building is appropriate enough; since throughout Central America, temples, in times of war, became real strongholds, on whose gigantic terraces the last desperate conflict was waged against an invading and victorious foe. The struggle might last some time, but was always attended with heavy loss, for each terrace had to be carried against men resolved to die. In the assault on the great temple in Mexico, the Spaniards were several times repulsed before they could get possession of the four esplanades of the pyramid; and when these were taken a fierce encounter followed on the upper platform, which only ended with the utter annihilation of the Aztecs, who were either slaughtered on the spot or hurled down the sides of the pyramid. . . .

In [El Castillo] are curious traces of masonry out of character with the general structure, showing the place to have been occupied at two different epochs.

The second construction, or rather restoration, was effected with the materials of the ancient building, as is seen in the fragments of sculptured stones which in the later construction are identical with those of the first, save that they were put up haphazard, so that the systematic ornamentation of the older structure is no longer reproduced, but in places a thick plaster coating was laid over the whole. The

rebuilding may have been the work of the natives, since we know that Chichén was abandoned and reoccupied towards the middle of the fifteenth century; or, more likely still, the clumsy restoration may have been the work of the Spaniards during their sojourn in the city, when [El Castillo] from its elevated position, constituted a valuable fortress. Traces of the Spanish passage are observable . . . where their natural fanaticism, coupled with their ignorance, caused them to see in the portraiture of the national and religious life of the Mayas, representations of the devil. This could not be suffered to remain, and as they were unable to demolish the temples and palaces in which they lived, they whitewashed the ornamentation, in order that their eyes might not be constantly offended by the subjects therein represented.

We try with small success to undo their savage work by means of daggers, brushes, and repeated washes, taking up much time, but in most cases the relief is lost to science, being much too defaced to allow us to take squeezes. The idea that the chiefs who erected these monuments were the authors of their defacement is too absurd for serious consideration.

Compare and Contrast:

- Compare the diagram of El Castillo and with the earlier photograph of the temple at Tikál. Compare these with reference to their appearance and functionality.

Ball Court Action

ANTONIO DE HERRERA Y TORDESILLAS

The world of the Maya was never separated between the physical and spiritual realms. In fact, rulers combined political and religious authority by mediating with the gods and overseeing rituals through which the society was sustained in its divine relationships. These rituals included bloodletting ceremonies, human sacrifice, and even athletic contests.

"Ball Court Action" is from Alfred Percival Maudslay, *A Glimpse at Guatemala* (London: John Murray, 1899), pp. 205–206.

Chichén Itzá housed the largest ball playing court of all Maya cities. The people would wager on the contests and the stakes were often life or death. A losing team might find itself proscribed for sacrifice. This appeasement of the gods found justification in the Maya creation myth as noted earlier in the selection from the Popul Vuh.

The following account is by a Spanish historian who described the action. Note the diagram of the Great Ball Court at Chichén Itzá.

Keep in Mind...

•   How was the Maya game of Tlachtli played? Was it a difficult game? What were the risks and rewards?

The game was called "Tlachtli," which is the same as "Trinquete" in Spanish. The ball was made of the gum from a tree which grows in the hot country. This tree, when tapped, exudes some large white drops, which soon congeal and when mixed and kneaded become as black as pitch; of this material the balls are made, and, although heavy and hard to the hand, they bound and rebound as lightly as footballs, and are indeed better, as there is no need to inflate them. They do not play for "chases" but to make a winning stroke—that is, to strike the ball against or to hit it over the wall which the opposite party defend. The ball may be struck with any part of the body, either such part as is most convenient or such as each player is most skillful in using. Sometimes it is arranged that it should count against any player who touches the ball otherwise than with his hip, for this considered by them to show the greatest skill, and on this account they would wear a piece of stiff raw hide over the hips, so that the ball might better rebound. The ball might be struck as long as it bounded, and it made many bounds one after the other, as though it were alive.

They played in parties, so many on each side, and for such a stake as a parcel of cotton cloths, more or less, according to the wealth of the players. They also played for articles of gold and

The Great Ball Court

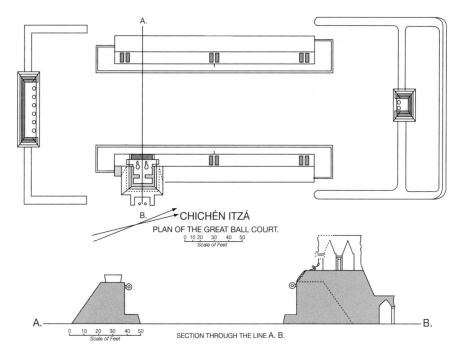

CHICHÉN ITZÁ
PLAN OF THE GREAT BALL COURT.
0 10 20 30 40 50
Scale of Feet

0 10 20 30 40 50
Scale of Feet

SECTION THROUGH THE LINE A. B.

for feathers, and at times staked their own persons. The place where they played was a court on the level of the ground, long, narrow, and high, but wider above than below, and higher at the sides than at the ends. So that it should be better to play in, the court was well cemented, and the walls and floors made quite smooth. In the side walls were fixed two stones like millstones, with a hole pierced through the middle, through which there was just room for the ball to pass, and the player who hit the ball through the hole won the game; and as this was a rare victory, which few gained, by the ancient custom and law of the game, the victor had a right to the mantles of all the spectators. . . .

To those who saw the feat performed for the first time it seemed like a miracle, and they said that a player who had such good luck would become a thief or an adulterer, or would die soon. And the memory of such a victory lasted many days, until it was followed by another, which put it out of mind.

Compare and Contrast:

• Compare the Maya game of Tlachtli and the Great Ball Court at Chichén Itzá with the Roman chariot races or the gladiatorial contests in the Coliseum described on p. 159. How are such contests of skill and risk reflective of the respective values of Maya and Roman society?

• Compare the Maya ball games with the combat of a medieval joust as reflected in the picture on p. 224. Why were such contests important and necessary for those societies? Why are football and ice hockey popular in the United States and Canada?

The Spanish Arrive: "Obliged to Seek Them with the Sword"

JOHN LLOYD STEPHENS

After Cortés had defeated the powerful Aztecs in Central Mexico in 1520, Spanish conquistadors continued their consolidation of the region by traveling east to the once impressive Maya sites that had by this time declined or been abandoned. Still, the Spanish were insistent on looting the area and encountered aggressive resistence by Maya descendants as noted in this account recorded by the earliest excavator of Chichén Itzá, John Lloyd Stephens.

Keep in Mind. . .

• Why did the Spaniards decide to occupy Chichén Itzá about 1520?

Having regard, however, to the circumstances of the occupation and abandonment of Chichén by the Spaniards, their silence is perhaps not extraordinary. I have already mentioned that at this place the [commander of the advance force] made a fatal mistake and, lured by the glitter of gold in another province, divided his forces and sent one of his best captains, with fifty men, in search of it. From this time calamities and dangers pressed upon him; altercations and contests began with the Indians; provisions were withheld, the Spaniards were obliged to seek them with the sword, and all that they ate was procured at the price of blood. At length the Indians determined upon their utter destruction. Immense multitudes surrounded the camp of the Spaniards, hemming them in on all sides. The Spaniards, seeing themselves reduced to the necessity of perishing by hunger, deter-

"The Spanish Arrive" is from John Lloyd Stephens, *Incidents of Travel in Yucatan*, Volume 2 (London: John Murray, 1842), pp. 207–208.

mined to die bravely in the field and went out to give battle. The most sanguinary fight they had ever been engaged in then took place. The Spaniards fought for their lives, and the Indians to remain masters of their own soil. Masses of the latter were killed, but great slaughter was made among the Spaniards, and, to save the lives of those who remained, the commander retreated to the fortifications. One hundred and fifty of the conquerors were dead; nearly all the rest were wounded, and if the Indians had attacked them in their retreat they would have perished to a man.

Unable to hold out any longer, they took advantage of a night when the Indians were off their guard, and making sallies in the evening so as to keep them awake, that weariness might afterward overtake them, as soon as all was still they tied a dog to the clapper of a bell-rope, putting some food before him, but out of his reach, and with great silence marched out from the camp. The dog, when he saw them going, pulled the cord in order to go with them, and afterward to get at the food. The Indians, sup-posing that the Spaniards were sounding the alarm, remained quiet, waiting the result, but a little before daylight, perceiving that the bell did not cease ringing, they drew near the fortification, and found it deserted. In the meantime the Spaniards escaped toward the coast, and in the meager and disconnected accounts of their dangers and escape, it is, perhaps, not surprising that we have none whatever of the buildings, arts, and sciences of the fierce inhabitants of Chichén.

Consider This:

- Why was John Lloyd Stephens not surprised that we have no Spanish accounts "of the buildings, arts, and sciences of the fierce inhabitants of Chichén Itzá"?

- Compare this account of Spanish occupation with the actions of Hernando Cortés against the Aztecs on pp. 362–363. Did this incident at Chichén Itzá contribute to the "Black Legend" of Spain?

8

Imperial China and the Mongol Empire: (589–1368)

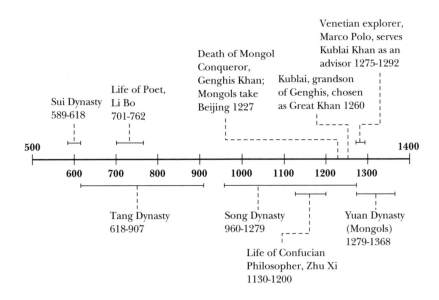

Wealth and rank are what man desires, but if he cannot obtain them in a moral way, he should not enjoy them. Poverty and meanness are what man hates, but if he can only avoid them by departing from the Way, he should not avoid them.

—Mou Zi

For autumn is the minister of punishments, the dark Yin among the four seasons. It is said to be the breath of justice between Heaven and Earth, and its eternal purpose is stern execution. By Heaven's design for all things, spring gives birth, autumn ripens.

—Ouyang Xiu

As the Yin and the Yang govern the way of Heaven and as hardness and softness govern the way of Earth, love and righteousness should govern the way of man. Once realizing that beginning inevitably leads to end and vice versa, one masters the meaning of life and death.

—Zhao Dunyi

I am the scourge of God! If you had not committed great sins, God would not have sent a punishment like me upon you.

—Genghis Khan

CHAPTER THEMES

- *Systems of Government:* For centuries, both the Tang and Song dynasties maintained impressive control of territory often in the face of popular uprisings and external invaders. What is the foundation of stable rule? Does it have more to do with individual leadership or the success of an administrative system?

- *Imperialism:* How did Genghis Khan and his successors establish the largest empire in world history? How was it consolidated? Can an empire built on the personal dynamism of a great leader sustain after the death of its founder? Must there always be a chaotic power vacuum that undermines the foundation of the empire?

- *Beliefs and Spirituality:* During this period, Buddhism was integrated into the social and intellectual fabric of China. What competition from traditional Confucian values did Buddhism encounter and why was it able to permeate Chinese society? How fluid was the intellectual and spiritual environment during this period? How successful was Christianity in gaining adherents in China?

- *Historical Change and Transition:* Genghis Khan called himself the "Scourge of God." What impact did the Mongol hordes have on the political and social history of China and Islamic civilization in Persia and India? Were the Mongols simply a great destructive force? What was their legacy in the Yuan dynasty of China?

- *The Big Picture:* The Tang and Song dynasties have been included by historians among the most progressive and successful civilizations in history. What made them so? Why were they unable to sustain against the Mongols and what legacy did they pass to the Ming dynasty? Should the evaluation of a civilization be tied to its success in overcoming adversity? Given this standard, can the Tang and the Song be considered great Chinese dynasties?

One of the great developmental periods in Chinese history ended in 220 C.E. with the collapse of the Later Han dynasty. The Han emperors had provided strong, centralized rule until the first century when palace intrigues and an increasingly independent aristocracy contributed to political instability and social dislocation. For almost four centuries after the fall of the Han, China was disunited. The great aristocratic families managed their affairs beyond the control of local governments with their own vast estates, fortified manors, and private armies. This feudal structure provided local security amidst periodic invasions by mobile nomadic tribes.

In many ways, these conditions mirrored the problems encountered by Europeans after the breakup of the Roman empire in the third to fifth centuries C.E. Early medieval Western societies struggled to survive the disruptive invasions of Germanic tribes and cope with the degenerating economic conditions and subsequent social dislocation. Just as Western civilization began the long road to recovery through the military efforts and administrative talents of such leaders as Justinian and Charlemagne, and through the spiritual unity provided by the Christian church, so too did China establish new foundations.

A general of mixed Chinese-Turkic ancestry, Sui Wenti (d. 605), reunified China and established the Sui dynasty from 589 to 618. The Great Wall was rebuilt and a Grand Canal that connected the Yellow and Yangtze rivers provided commercial opportunities that linked the interests of northern and southern China. But this dynasty broke down amid corruption and the competing interests of aristocratic families. After a series of rebellions, new leadership established a dynasty called the Tang.

Under the Tang dynasty (618–907) and its successor, the Song dynasty (960–1279), China reached new heights of administrative excellence, economic prosperity, and cultural radiance. It is hard to argue against the brilliance of the Tang dynasty. This was a confident, expressive, cosmopolitan culture. Expansionist and creative, it influenced the formation of cultures in Japan, Korea, and Vietnam. During the Tang, secular scholarship flourished and poetry was unmatched in its expressive power. This was also the golden age of Buddhism in China. The Song dynasty, while weak militarily, saw the most significant developments in philosophy since the Zhou (1050–256 B.C.E.). And it was arguably the greatest age of Chinese painting.

This cultural brilliance could not be sustained by the successors of the Song. The Yuan dynasty (1279–1368) lasted only about a hundred years, and although its impact was not cultural, the world was brought to attention. These were the Mongols, who had been organized into formidable fighting units by the brutal genius of Genghis Khan (1167–1223). During the thirteenth century, Mongol warriors swept through the steppes, destroying everything in their path. Kublai Khan, grandson of Ghengis, moved his capital from Mongolia to Beijing in 1264. In 1271, he adopted the Chinese dynastic name Yuan and went to war with the southern Song. He conquered the last Song stronghold in 1279 and established the new Mongol dynasty. China became the most important political unit in the largest empire in history.

This chapter will focus on some of the most important political, economic, and cultural developments during this significant and exciting period of Chinese history. Tang and Song China would set standards of administrative excellence and cultural brilliance for centuries to come. And the Mongols would also set new standards for psychological and physical destruction that would be burned into the history of the world from Japan to the great Islamic empires and beyond to the gates of Europe.

THE ESTABLISHMENT AND MAINTENANCE OF EMPIRE

The Tang Dynasty (618–907)

After the fall of the Han dynasty in 220 C.E., China began a long period of political chaos and so-cial dislocation. For nearly three centuries, from 311 to 589, China was divided into independent kingdoms of the North and South. This division, which fell along natural geographic lines, not only dissolved centralized government, but also resulted in the growth of regional economies with greater class distinctions. In the North, the rulers were not ethnically Chinese, and this allowed for the incorporation of many different customs and social institutions.

When China was finally unified through the military efforts of Sui Wenti in 589, many hoped for a stable political and economic foundation. But this hope proved illusory as the Sui dynasty ex-pended its human and financial resources in trying to conquer Korea.

Such short-sighted efforts were not lost on the new Tang dynasty that succeeded in 618. The rulers of the Tang emphasized organization and restraint. They were generally successful in limit-ing the private power and status of the aristocracy and taxed the peasantry directly in an efficient and equitable manner. Because of these efforts, the dynasty succeeded in stimulating trade through-out the empire by the eighth and ninth centuries. The capital cities of Qiangan and Luoyang be-came thriving metropolitan centers that fostered a cultural flowering in literature and the arts.

In the following document, Tang Daizong, a founder of the Tang dynasty, set the tone for his new administration to his chosen officials. His emphasis on honesty and open communication con-trasts the single-minded and obsessive rule of the former Sui dynasty.

The Art of Government

TANG DAIZONG

Different people are bound to have different opinions; the important thing is that differ-ences in opinion should not degenerate into personal antagonism. Sometimes to avoid the possibility of creating personal grievances or causing embarrassment to a colleague, an offi-cial might decide to go ahead with the imple-mentation of a policy even though he knows that the policy is wrong. Let us remember that preservation of a colleague's prestige, or the avoidance of embarrassment to him, cannot be compared with the welfare of the nation in im-portance, and to place personal consideration above the well-being of the multitude will lead to defeat for the government as a whole. I want

all of you to understand this point and act ac-cordingly.

During the Sui dynasty, all officials, in the central as well as the local governments, adopted an attitude of conformity to the gen-eral trend in order to be amiable and agreeable with one another. The result was disaster as all of you well know. Most of them did not under-stand the importance of dissent and comforted themselves by saying that as long as they did not disagree, they could forestall harm to them-selves that might otherwise cross their path. When the government, as well as their families, finally collapsed in a massive upheaval, they were severely but justifiably criticized by their con-temporaries for their complacency and inertia, even if they themselves may have been fortunate enough to escape death through a combination of circumstances. This is the reason that I want all of you to place public welfare above private interest and hold steadfastly the principle of righteousness, so that all problems, whatever they are, will be resolved in such a way as to bring about a most beneficial result. Under no circumstances are you allowed to agree with one another for the sake of agreement.

As for Sui Wenti, I would say that he was politically inquisitive, but mentally closed. Being close-minded, he could not see truth even if it were spotlighted for him; being over inquisitive, he was suspicious even when there was no valid reason for his suspicion. He rose to power by trampling on the rights of orphans and widows and was consequently not so sure that he had the unanimous support of his own ministers. Being suspicious of his own ministers, he naturally did not trust them and had to make a decision on every matter himself. He became a hard worker out of necessity and, having overworked, could not make the right decision every time. Knowing the kind of man he was, all his ministers, including the prime minister, did not speak as candidly as they should have and unanimously uttered "Yes, sir" when they should have registered strong dissent.

I want all of you to know that I am different. The empire is large and its population enormous. There are thousands of matters to be taken care of, each of which has to be closely coordinated with the others in order to bring about maximum benefit. Each matter must be thoroughly investigated and thought out before a recommendation is submitted to the prime minister, who, having consulted all the men knowledgeable in this matter, will then present the commendation, modified if necessary, to the emperor for approval and implementation. It is impossible for one person, however intelligent and capable, to be able to make wise decisions by himself. . . .

I want all of you to know that whenever an imperial decree is handed down you should carefully study its content and decide for yourselves whether all or part of it is or is not wise or feasible. If you have any reservations, postpone the enforcement and petition me immediately. You can do no less as my loyal ministers.

Governing a country is like taking care of a patient. The better the patient feels, the more he should be looked after, lest in a moment of complacency and neglect one irrevocably reverse the recovery process and send him to death. Likewise, when a country has only recently recovered from chaos and war, those responsible for running the country should be extremely diligent in their work, for false pride and self-indulgence will inevitably return the country to where it used to be and perhaps make it worse.

I realize that the safety of this nation relies to a great extent on what I can or may do and consequently I have not relaxed for a moment in doing the best I can. But I cannot do it alone. You gentlemen are my eyes and ears, legs and arms, and should do your best to assist me. If anything goes wrong anywhere in the empire, you should let me know immediately. If there is less than total trust between you and me and consequently you and I cannot do the best we can, the nation will suffer enormous damage.

Ballad of the War Chariots

DU FU

Tang rulers succeeded in establishing an impressive political control over China during the period 618 to 755. This golden age produced a calm throughout the land that was founded on full granaries and empty jails. It was an era of great poets like Li Bo (701–762) and Du Fu (712–770), who felt confident enough to criticize the constancy of fighting and express the fatigue and loneliness of those who vigilantly maintained the empire. The following poems testify not only to the cultural brilliance of the period, but also to the depth of personal sacrifice for security and stability.

Du Fu, *Selected Poems*, Alley, Rewi, trans., 1964, pp. 12–13.

The jingle of war chariots,
Horses neighing, men marching,
Bows and arrows slung over hips;
Beside them stumbling, running
The mass of parents, wives and children
Clogging up the road, their rising dust
Obscuring the great bridge at Hsienyang;
Stamping their feet, weeping
In utter desperation with cries
That seem to reach the clouds;

Ask a soldier: Why do you go?
Would simply bring the answer;
Today men are conscripted often;
Fifteen-year-olds sent up the Yellow River
To fight; men of forty marched away
To colonize the western frontier;
Village elders take young boys,
Do up their hair like adults
To get them off; if they return
It will be white with age, but even then
They may be sent off to the frontier again;

Frontiers on which enough blood has
  flowed
To make a sea, yet our Emperor still would
Expand his authority! Have you not heard
How east of Huashan many counties
Are desolate with weeds and thorns?
The strongest women till the fields,
Yet crops come not as well as before;

Lads from around here are well known
For their bravery, but hate to be driven
Like dogs or chickens; only because
You kindly ask me do I dare give vent
To grievances; now for instance
With the men from the western frontier
Still not returned, the government
Demands immediate payment of taxes,
But how can we pay when so little
Has been produced?

Now, we peasants have learned one thing:
To have a son is not so good as having
A daughter who can marry a neighbor
And still be near us, while a son

Will be taken away to die in some
Wild place, his bones joining those
That lie bleached white on the shores
Of Lake Kokonor, where voices of new
  spirits
Join with the old heard sadly through
The murmur of falling rain.

"Fighting and Marching Never Stop"

LI BO

Last year we were fighting at the source of
  the Sang-kan;
This year we are fighting on the Onion
  River road.
We have washed our swords in the surf of
  Parthian seas;
We have pastured our horses among the
  snows of the Tien Shan,
The King's armies have grown grey and old
Fighting ten thousand leagues away from
  home.
The Huns have no trade but battle and
  carnage;
They have no fields or ploughlands,
But only wastes where white bones lie
  among yellow sands.
There the House of Qin built the great
  wall that was to keep away the Tatars.
There, in its turn, the House of Han lit
  beacons of war.
The beacons are always alight, fighting
  and marching never stop.
Men die in the field, slashing sword to
  sword;
The horses of the conquered neigh
  piteously to Heaven.
Crows and hawks peck for human guts,
Carry them in their beaks and hang them
  on the branches of withered trees.
Captains and soldiers are smeared on the
  bushes and grass;
Generals schemed in vain.

Know therefore that the sword is a cursed
   thing
Which the wise man uses only if he must.

"Sorrow, Sorrow Like Rain"

LI BO

By the North Gate, the wind blows full of
   sand,
Lonely from the beginning of time until
   now!
Trees fall, the grass goes yellow with
   autumn.
I climb the towers and towers
   to watch out the barbarous land:
desolate castle, the sky, the wide desert.
There is no wall left to this village.
Bones white with a thousand frosts,
High heaps, covered with trees and grass;
Who brought this to pass?
Who has brought the flaming imperial
   anger?
Who has brought the army with drums
   and with
   kettle-drums?
Barbarous kings.
A gracious spring, turned to blood-
   ravenous autumn,
A turmoil of wars-men, spread over the
   middle kingdom,
Three hundred and sixty thousand,
And sorrow, sorrow like rain.
Sorrow to go, and sorrow, sorrow
   returning.

McNaughton, William, ed., *Chinese Literature.* Copyright
© 1974 Charles E. Tuttle Co., Inc. of Boston, Massachusetts
and Tokyo, Japan. Reprinted with permission.

This portrait by an unknown court painter of Taizu,
the first emperor of the Song dynasty, depicts him as
a benign father figure. Yet he was a skilled general,
who seized power in 960 and used his military and
diplomatic skills to bring local warlords to heel and
reunite the nation. (*National Palace Museum, Taipei,
Taiwan*)

Desolate, desolate fields,
And no children of warfare upon them,
   No longer the men for offence and
   defense.
Ah, how shall you know the dreary sorrow
   at the
   North Gate,
With Rihaku's name forgotten,
And we guardsmen fed to the tigers.

The Song Dynasty (960-1279)

*The Tang dynasty, which had so effectively ruled China for nearly three hundred years, progres-
sively lost control of the country beginning in the mid-ninth century. It fell, as so many other dynasties before it, the victim of ambitious generals who had seized on popular discontent. From 906 to
960, the North of China labored under five successive dynasties that were prime examples of arbitrary rule for short-term gain.*

They reflected the increasing non-Chinese influence of Turkic, Tibetan, and Mongol tribes in the arid regions of northern China. In 960, the new Song dynasty reunified China and established its capital at Gaifeng on the Yellow River. By efficiently organizing its bureaucratic and military resources, the Northern Song, as it became known, was able to rule China for 170 years. Then in 1127, most of northern China was lost to a semi-nomadic confederation of tribes known as the Jurchen. For the next 150 years, the dynasty ruled the South from its capital in Hangzhou as the Southern Song. But drastic change was imminent as the Jurchen fell to the Mongol onslaught in 1234 and the Southern Song collapsed by 1279.

The Song dynasty saw many fundamental changes in Chinese society. It was a period of great commercial success as technological innovations resulted in a commercial revolution that included advances in industry and wet-field rice cultivation. The fast-growing cities brought together different social groups in relationships built more on commercial contracts than on paternalistic traditions.

The Song era saw perhaps most importantly the flourishing of literature and the arts. The invention of printing, and by extension the publication of ancient texts and current commentaries, broke down class barriers and undermined the aristocratic monopoly on education. Popular handbooks filled with moral or economic advice certainly contributed to a more expansive vision of the world.

The Examination System: Two Views

It has been said that the Song dynasty, founded by a scholarly general, was the quintessence of the Confucian ideal state. This was a dynasty that so emphasized the prestige of intellectual accomplishment that it was managed by scholars for the benefit of scholars. The road to success was paved with the accumulated knowledge of centuries as aspiring students were drilled in the Confucian classics: literature, poetry, philosophy, and political theory. Visions of wealth and power hinged on passing the civil service examinations that granted access to the elite governmental bureaucracy.

Although these examinations had existed under the Tang as well, the Song had raised the bar both in difficulty level and in prestige. With so much at stake, the examinations, and in particular, preparation for the examinations, became a controversial subject. The debate swirled around not only the kinds of tests to be given, and the emphasis (prose or poetry), but also around the value of a quota system. Since the southern Chinese were more affluent and consequently more able to secure the advantages of elite education, were they given an unfair advantage? Should there be proportional representation from throughout China in a quota system that was designed to level the field and provide a wise political benefit?

Two outstanding statesmen of the period, Sima Guang (1018–1086), and his friend and colleague, Ouyang Xiu (1007–1072), debated some of these issues in the following selections.

Sima Guang

In each of the metropolitan examinations, the examiners who make up the test are without exception chosen from the scholars in the Hanlin Academy or one of the Three Insinuates. What these scholars like inevitably becomes the academic fashion of the time. This gives the examination candidates in the capital an undisputed advantage over those in more distant areas since they, being knowledgeable of the change of academic trends, adjust their writing style accordingly and will, in due course, be able to write in such a way as to enhance their chance of success in the examinations. How can the candidates in a remote province, denied this advantage, possibly compete with them?. . .

Sometimes an entire province cannot produce a single successful candidate, indicating clearly that something is wrong with the examination system itself. According to the way we are recruiting governmental personnel today, a man cannot obtain a position of importance with the government unless he has passed the metropolitan examination and received the "advanced scholarship" degree. But he cannot pass the metropolitan examination and receive the "advanced scholarship" degree unless he knows how to write prose and poetry in a way that conforms to the academic trend prevalent in the capital at that time. . . .

Ouyang Xiu

The examination system we are practicing today is more impartial and less subject to foul play than in any of the preceding dynasties. For this we should be most grateful to the emperors of the past who did their utmost to perfect this system. The principle that underlies this system is very simple: that an emperor, being the sovereign of all men, should regard all of his subjects as members of one family and treat them equally, without discrimination. Candidates from all the provinces are encouraged to gather in the capital to compete, and the only criterion for their success or failure is the amount of talent they have. To assure objectivity, not only are the names of the candidates covered up, but also the answers to the questions are copied before the copied answers are presented to the examiners in charge to be evaluated. The examiners in charge, consequently, have no idea whose papers they are reading, let alone where these candidates come from or whose sons they are. In short, in no way can personal bias or prejudice play any role in the evaluation process. The examination system we are practicing today may or may not be as good as some ancient system for the same purpose; but, in terms of fairness and objectivity, we cannot do better with any other system. Since the founding of this dynasty, it has been more than adequate to meet our needs.

Life in the City of Hangzhou (1235)

Life in the busy commercial centers of Song China accentuated the changing nature of social relationships during the period. In the city one could find a variety of food, entertainment, and some very shady characters. This description of the city of Hangzhou, written in 1235, reveals the vibrancy of urban society.

Commercial Establishments

In general, the capital attracts the greatest variety of goods and has the best craftsmen. For instance, the flower company at Superior Lane does a truly excellent job of flower arrangement, and its caps, hair-pins, and collars are unsurpassed in craftsmanship. Some of the most famous specialties of the capital are the sweet-bean soup at the Miscellaneous Market, the pickled dates of the Ge family, the thick soup of the Guang family at Superior Lane, the fruit at the Great Commons marketplace, the cooked meats in front of Eternal Mercy Temple, Sister Song's fish broth at Penny Pond Gate, the juicy lungs at Flowing Gold Gate, the "lamb rice" of the Zhi family at Central Square, the boots of the Peng family, the fine clothing of the Xuan family at Southern Commons, the sticky rice pastry of the Zhang family, the flutes made by

Gu the Fourth, and the Chu family's Tatar whistles at the Great Commons.

Teahouses

In large teahouses, there are usually paintings and calligraphies by famous artists on display. In the old capital, only restaurants had them, to enable their patrons to while away the time as the food was being prepared, but now it is customary for teahouses as well to display paintings and the like.

The teahouses also sell salted soybean soup in the winter and plum-flower wine in the summer. During the Shaoxing reign [1131–1162], teahouses used to play the plum-flower wine tune and serve tea with a ladle just as in wine shops.

Often many young men gather in teahouses to practice singing or playing musical instruments. To give such amateur performances is called "getting posted."

A "social teahouse" is more of a community gathering place than a mere place that sells tea. Often tea-drinking is but an excuse, and people are rather generous when it comes to the tips.

There is a special kind of teahouse where pimps and gigolos hang out. Another kind is occupied by people from various trades and crafts who use them as places to hire help, buy apprentices, and conduct business. These teahouses are called "trade heads."

"Water teahouses" are in fact pleasure houses, the tea being a cover. Some youths are quite willing to spend their money there, which is called "dry tea money."

Other jargon calls for explanation: a "teakettle carrier" does more than just bring wine and tea to private households; he also carries messages and functions as a social go-between. "Dirty tea" designates the kind of street vagabonds who, in the name of selling tea, actually beg for cash or gifts.

Hustlers

[These people] have no regular profession, but live off of other people by providing trivial services. Some of these hustlers are students who failed to achieve any literary distinction. Though able to read and write, and play musical instruments and chess, they are not highly

This detail from a scroll painting by Zhang Zeduan entitled *Going Upriver at the Qing Ming Festival* depicts the busy commercial life in the Song capital of Gaifeng in the late eleventh or early twelfth century. (*Wang-go Weng, The Palace Museum, Beijing*)

skilled in any art. They end up being a kind of guide for young men from wealthy families, accompanying them in their pleasure-seeking activities. Some also serve as guides or assistants to officials on business from other parts of the country. The lowliest of these people actually engage themselves in writing and delivering invitation cards and the like for brothels.

There are others who make their living entertaining at private parties. In the past some of these people were quite well versed in activities such as play-acting, jesting, playing musical instruments, juggling, singing, reciting poems, playing wine games, swimming, and boxing. Some who specialize in training birds are called leisure practitioners. They train hawks, eagles, pigeons, doves, quail, and cocks for fighting and gambling.

There are also professional go-betweens, nicknamed "water-treaders," whose principal targets are pleasure houses, where they flatter the wealthy young patrons, run errands for them, and help make business deals. Some gather at brothels or scenic attractions and accost the visitors. They beg for donations for "religious purposes," but in fact use the money to make a living for themselves and their families. If you pay attention to them, they will become greedy; if you ignore them, they will force themselves on you and will not stop until you give in. It requires art to deal with these people appropriately.

The Problems of Women

YUAN ZAI

Since women in China rarely kept diaries or wrote about their lives, it is difficult to assess the struggles they faced or how they reacted to opportunities or setbacks. The following source is from a manual by Yuan Zai, who lived in the twelfth century and offered his practical advice on some of the issues facing women and the proper response of their families.

Women Should Not Take Part in Affairs Outside the Home

Women do not take part in extrafamilial affairs. The reason is that worthy husbands and sons take care of everything for them, while unworthy ones can always find ways to hide their deeds from the women.

Many men today indulge in pleasure and gambling; some end up mortgaging their lands, and even go so far as to mortgage their houses without their wives' knowledge. Therefore, when husbands are bad, even if wives try to handle outside matters, it is of no use. . . .

For women, these are grave misfortunes, but what can they do? If husbands and sons could only remember that their wives and mothers are helpless and suddenly repent, would that not be best?

Women's Sympathies Should Be Indulged

Without going overboard, people should marry their daughters with dowries appropriate to their family's wealth. Rich families should not consider their daughters outsiders but should give them a share of the property. Sometimes people have incapable sons and so have to entrust their affairs to their daughters' families; even after their deaths, their burials and sacrifices are performed by their daughters. So how can people say that daughters are not as good as sons?

Generally speaking, a woman's heart is very sympathetic. If her parents' family is wealthy and her husband's family is poor, she wants to take her parents' wealth to help her husband's family prosper. If her husband's family is wealthy but her parents' family is poor, then she wants to take from her husband's family to enable her parents to prosper. Her parents and husband should be sympathetic toward her feelings and indulge some of her wishes. When her own sons and daughters are grown and married, if either her son's family or her daughter's family is wealthy while the other is poor, she wishes to take from the wealthy one to give to the poor one. Her sons and daughters should understand her feelings and be somewhat indulgent. But taking from the poor to make the rich richer is unacceptable, and no one should ever go along with it.

For Women Old Age Is Particularly Hard to Bear

People say that, though there may be a hundred years allotted to a person's life, only a few reach seventy, for time quickly runs out. But for those destined to be poor, old age is hard to endure. For them, until about the age of fifty, the passage of twenty years seems like only ten; but after that age, ten years can feel as long as twenty. For women who live a long life, old age is especially hard to bear, because most women must rely on others for their existence. Before a woman's marriage, a good father is even more important than a good grandfather; a good brother is even more important than a good father; a good nephew is even more important than a good brother. After her marriage, a good husband is even more important than a good father-in-law;

a good son is even more important than a good husband; and a good grandson is even more important than a good son. For this reason women often enjoy comfort in their youth but find their old age difficult to endure. It would be well for their relatives to keep this in mind.

It Is Difficult for Widows to Entrust Their Financial Affairs to Others

Some wives with stupid husbands are able to manage the family's finances, calculating the outlays and receipts of money and grain, without being cheated by anyone. Of those with degenerate husbands, there are also some who are able to manage the finances with the help of their sons without ending in bankruptcy. Even among those whose husbands have died and whose sons are young, there are occasionally women able to raise and educate their sons, keep the affection of all their relatives, manage the family business, and even prosper. All of these are wise and worthy women. But the most remarkable are the women who manage a household after their husbands have died leaving them with young children. Such women could entrust their finances to their husbands' kinsmen or their own kinsmen, but not all relatives are honorable, and the honorable ones are not necessarily willing to look after other people's business.

When wives themselves can read and do arithmetic, and those they entrust with their affairs have some sense of fairness and duty with regard to food, clothing, and support, then things will usually work out all right. But in most of the rest of the cases, bankruptcy is what happens.

THE THOUGHT OF THE AGE

The Balance of the Mind

For nearly eight hundred years, from the fall of the Han dynasty in 220 C.E. to the rise of the Song in 960, Buddhism was the dominant religious and intellectual movement. The Tang era was in fact the golden age of Buddhism. Patronized by emperors and the aristocracy, Buddhist temples and monasteries became a common sight throughout China and attracted pilgrims from afar. Some of the greatest Chinese minds studied Buddhist texts and even developed new schools of Buddhist philosophy. Progressive styles in art and architecture were most often reflected in monuments to the Buddha.

Buddhism entered China in the first century C.E. and spread rapidly after the fall of the Han dynasty in 220. By the fifth century C.E., Buddhism had spread throughout China, aided by the occasional persecutions of Daoist emperors. But the Buddhism that entered China was not a formalized and unified religion. Upon the final passing of the Buddha about 486 B.C.E., the religion formed into separate sects that emphasized particular teachings or other aspects of Buddha's thought. There were several disparate and conflicting traditions that made it difficult to provide a consonant explanation of Buddhism. These sects became essentially different schools of thought rather than contending religious denominations. The Chinese proved adept at syncretizing many of these schools and adapting them to Chinese culture and intellectual traditions.

Yet in spite of this devotion to Buddhism, Confucian intellectuals still provided an undercurrent to scholarship and imperial administration. During the Tang and especially during the Song dynasty, there was a reappearance of secular scholarship and letters. Those who moved in this tradition were not ideologically anti-Buddhist, but reflected worldly values that enabled them to reform and administer a complex bureaucracy. There existed, then, a kind of intellectual rivalry between Buddhism and Confucian traditions that energized intellectual debate.

The first selection reflects the contentious intellectual battleground of the sixth century C.E. after Buddhism had been established in China and had become a threat to the traditional Confucian education and values. It is an attempt to explain and defend the principles of Buddhism. According to Mou Zi, it was possible to be a good Chinese and a good Buddhist. The second selection by the Confucian scholar and bureaucrat, Ouyang Xiu (1007–1070) of the Song dynasty, argues that centuries of Buddhism had had a corrupting effect and had reduced political efficiency and social stability. He hoped that a solid moral and institutional reform program would lead people to reject Buddhism and to adopt the Confucian ways of their ancestors.

A Defense of Buddhism

MOU ZI

Why Is Buddhism Not Mentioned in the Chinese Classics?

The Questioner said: If the way of the Buddha is the greatest and most venerable of ways, why did Yao, Shun, the Duke of Zhou, and Confucius not practice it? In the seven [Confucian] Classics one sees no mention of it. You, sir, are fond

of the Book of Odes and the Book of History [two of the Confucian Classics], and you take pleasure in rites and music. Why, then, do you love the way of the Buddha and rejoice in outlandish arts? Can they exceed the Classics and commentaries and beautify the accomplishments of the sages? Permit me the liberty, sir, of advising you to reject them.

Mou Zi said: All written works need not necessarily be the words of Confucius, and all medicine does not necessarily consist of the formulae of [the famous physician] Pianchuje. What accords with principle is to be followed, what heals the sick is good. The gentleman-scholar draws widely on all forms of good, and thereby benefits his character. . . How. . .may one reject the

Buddha, whose distinguishing marks are extraordinary and whose superhuman powers know no bounds! How may one reject him and refuse to learn from him? The records and teachings of the Five Classics to not contain everything. Even if the Buddha is not mentioned in them, what occasion is there for suspicion?

Why Do Buddhist Monks Not Marry?

The Questioner said: Now of joy there is none greater than the continuation of one's line, of unfilial conduct there is none worse than childlessness. The monks forsake wife and children, reject property and wealth. Some do not marry all their lives. How opposed this conduct is to felicity and filial piety! . . .

Mou Zi said: Wives, children, and property are the luxuries of the world, but simple living and inaction are the wonders of the Way. Laozi has said "Of reputation and life, which is dearer? Of life and property, which is worth more?". . . The monk practices the way and substitutes that for the pleasures of extending himself in the world. He accumulates goodness and wisdom in exchange for the joys of wife and children.

Death and Rebirth

The Questioner said: The Buddhists say that after a man dies he will be reborn. I do not believe in the truth of these words. . . .

Mou Zi said: The spirit never perishes. Only the body decays. The body is like the roots and leaves of the five grains, the spirit is like the seeds and kernels of the five grains. When the roots and leaves come forth they inevitably die. But do the seeds and kernels perish?. . . Of one who has achieved the Way, only the body perishes. . . .

The Questioner said: If one follows the Way, one dies. If one does not follow the Way, one dies. What difference is there?

Mou Zi said: You are the sort of person who, having not a single day of goodness, yet seeks a lifetime of fame. If one has the Way, even if one dies one's soul goes to an abode of happiness. If one does not have the Way, when one is dead one's soul suffers misfortune.

Why Should a Chinese Allow Himself to be Influenced by Indian Ways?

The Questioner said: I have heard of using what is Chinese to change what is barbarian, but I have never heard of using what is barbarian to change what is Chinese. You, sir, at the age of twenty learned the way of Yao, Shun, Confucius, and the Duke of Zhou. But now you have rejected them, and instead have taken up the arts of the barbarians. Is this not a great error?

Mou Zi said: The land of China is not necessarily situated under the center of heaven. According to the Buddhist scriptures, above, below, and all around, all beings containing blood belong to the Buddha-clan. Therefore, I revere and study these scriptures. Why should I reject the Way of Yao, Shun, Confucius, and the Duke of Zhou? Gold and jade do not harm each other, crystal and amber do not cheapen each other. You say that another is in error when it is you yourself who err.

Why Must a Monk Renounce Worldly Pleasures?

The Questioner said: Of those who live in the world, there is none who does not love wealth and position and hate poverty and baseness, none who does not enjoy pleasure and idleness and shrink from labor and fatigue. . . . But now the monks wear red cloth, they eat one meal a day, they bottle up the six emotions, and thus they live out their lives. What value is there in such an existence?

Mou Zi said: [Confucius once noted:] "Wealth and rank are what man desires, but if he cannot obtain them in a moral way, he should not enjoy them. Poverty and meanness are what man hates, but if he can only avoid them by departing from the Way, he should not avoid them.". . . Can these words possibly be vain? Liuxia Hui would not exchange his way of life for the rank of the three highest princes of the realm. Duangan Mu would not exchange his for the wealth of Prince Wen of Wei. . . . All of them followed their ideals, and cared for nothing more. Is there no value in such an existence?

"Buddha Was a Barbarian!"

OUYANG XIU

The cult of Buddhism has plagued China for over a thousand years. In every age men with the vision to see through its falseness and the power to do something about it have all sought to drive it out. But though they drove it out, it reappeared in greater force; though they attacked and crushed it for a time, it grew only stronger. It has been struck at but not wiped out, and indeed seems rather to grow more prevalent, until in the end it seems as if nothing could be done about it. But is the situation really hopeless, or is it simply that we have not used the proper methods?. . . .

When one seeks to remedy the illnesses of the nation, one must ascertain their origins and heal the areas that are affected.

Buddha was a barbarian who was far removed from China and lived long ago. In the age of Yao, Shun, and the Three Dynasties, kingly rule was practiced, government and the teachings of rites and righteousness flourished in the world. At this time, although Buddhism existed, it was unable to penetrate into China. But some two hundred years after the Three Dynasties had fallen into decay, when kingly rule ceased, and rites and righteousness were neglected, Buddhism came to China. It is clear then that Buddhism took advantage of this time of decay and

neglect to come and plague us. This was how the illness was first contracted. And if we will but remedy this decay, revive what has fallen into disuse, and restore once again to the land kingly rule in its brilliance and rites and righteousness in their fullness, then although Buddhism continues to exist, it will have no hold upon our people. This will also come about as a natural consequence. . . .

Happily there may be one man who is not deceived and who, fired with anger, cries, "What is this Buddhism? I shall seize my spear and drive it out!" or another who says, "I shall repulse it with reason!" But Buddhism has plagued the world for a thousand years. What can one man in one day do? The people are drunk with it, and it has seeped into their bones and marrow so that it cannot be vanquished by mouth and tongue.

What then can be done? I say there is nothing so effective in overcoming it as practicing what is fundamental. . . . These days a tall warrior clad in armor and bearing a spear may surpass in bravery a great army, yet when he sees the Buddha he bows low and when he hears the doctrines of the Buddha he is sincerely awed and persuaded. Why? Because though he is indeed strong and full of vigor, in his heart he is confused and has nothing to cling to. But when a scholar who is small and frail and afraid to advance hears the doctrines of Buddhism his righteousness is revealed at once in his countenance, and not only does he not bow and submit, but he longs to rush upon them and destroy them. Why? It is simply because he is enlightened in learning and burns with a belief in rites and righteousness, and in his heart he possesses something which can conquer these doctrines. This rites and righteousness are the fundamental things whereby Buddhism may be defeated. If a single scholar who understands rites and righteousness can keep from submitting to these doctrines, then we have but to make the whole world understand rites and righteousness and these doctrines will, as a natural consequence, be wiped out.

Yin and Yang: The Revival of Confucianism

ZHOU DUNYI

The concept of Yin and Yang finds expression in some of the earliest philosophy of China. The wishes of Heaven, expressed in the interaction between opposite forces, govern everything on earth. Yang is a positive force that generates life; it is male and is represented by the season of summer when everything grows. Yin is a dark, negative force, passive, feminine, resembling death, winter, punishment. Life can be reduced to the fluctuations between opposites. In the opposition between one extreme and the other is the balance of existence: male and female, life and death, good and bad–all compete for dominance. These forces are in perpetual interplay, struggling toward the balance that permits and enhances life. This theory explained the unity of man and nature, and gave a cosmological basis for ethical and social teachings.

The first source describes this theory in connection with the Absolute or governing life principle. The author, Zhou Dunyi (1012–1073), was instrumental in the revival of Confucianism during the Song, giving it a more abstract and metaphysical foundation. The second selection is by the great philosopher, Zhu Xi (1130–1200), whose neo-Confucian philosophy helped stabilize late imperial China and remained influential into the twentieth century. His concept of the "Great Ultimate" as the principle of the mind that itself has no opposite, helped unify Chinese thought.

The Absolute originates from the Infinite. It generates the *Yang* when it is active. Activity, when maximized, leads to inactivity. When the Absolute is inactive, it generates the *Yin*. When maximized, inactivity in turn leads to activity. Thus, the generation of the *Yang* leads to the generation of the *Yin* and vice versa, just as activity leads to inactivity and vice versa. One is the foundation upon which the other is built. Jointly the *Yin* and the *Yang* are referred to as the Two Forces (*Liang yi*).

The interactions between the *Yin* and the *Yang* create the Five Primary Elements, namely, water, fire, wood, metal, and earth. Their permutations give birth to the physical universe and also enable it to function in an orderly manner, including the orderly appearance and disappearance of the Four Seasons.

In short, the Five Primary Elements are united in, and trace their origin to, the *Yin* and the *Yang*. The *Yin* and the *Yang* are united in, and trace their origin to, the Absolute. The Absolute originates in the Infinite.

As the Infinite is true, each of the Five Primary Elements has its own characteristics. Ingenious and sedulous, they combine with one another to form a multitude of other objects. During the process of formation, the *Yin* and the *Yang* interact with each other. Males are created when [these forces] interact with each other in a positive manner; females are created when they interact with each other in a negative manner. Once an object is created, it changes constantly, in an infinite number of ways.

Of all the substances that come about as a result of the *Yin-Yang* interactions, man is the finest and the most ingenious. He has not only a form but also a spirit. He possesses the Five Temperaments [quietude, nervousness, strength, hardness, and wisdom] and knows the difference between right and wrong. To stabilize him, the sages teach him the virtues of moderation, uprightness, love, and righteousness. The motto for man is inactivity and quietude.

A sage reflects the virtue of Heaven and Earth, the brightness of the sun and the moon, and the orderliness of the Four Seasons. He knows what gods have ordained in terms of fortunes and misfortunes. While a small man works against the wishes of gods and thus incurs misfortunes, a gentleman abides by them and brings about good fortunes.

As the *Yin* and the *Yang* govern the way of Heaven and as hardness and softness govern the way of Earth, love and righteousness should govern the way of man. Once realizing that beginning inevitably leads to end and vice versa, one masters the meaning of life and death. How enormously important change is!

"The Mind Is the Great Ultimate"

ZHU XI

Question: The Great Ultimate is not a thing existing in a chaotic state before the formation of Heaven and earth, but a general name for the principles of Heaven and earth and the myriad things. Is that correct?

Answer: The Great Ultimate is merely the principle of Heaven and earth and the myriad things. With respect to the myriad things, there is the Great Ultimate in them. With respect to the myriad things, there is the Great Ultimate in each and every one of them. Before Heaven and earth existed, there was assuredly this principle. It is the principle that through movement generates the yang. It is also this principle that through tranquillity generates the yin. . . .

The Great Ultimate is spatially conditioned; it has neither corporeal form nor body. There is no spot where it may be placed. When it is considered in the state before activity begins, this state is nothing but tranquillity. Now activity, tranquil-

The Song philosopher, Zhu Xi (1130–1200), was a towering intellectual figure who joined traditional Confucian thought with certain Buddhist elements. This neo-Confucianism won many adherents and became the standard interpretation used in the civil service examinations until the twentieth century. (*National Palace Museum, Taipei, Taiwan*)

lity, yin and yang are all within the realm of corporeality. However, activity is after all the activity of the Great Ultimate and tranquillity is also its tranquillity, although activity and tranquillity themselves are not the Great Ultimate. . . .

The principle of the mind is the Great Ultimate. The activity and tranquillity of the mind are the yin and yang. Mind alone has no opposite.

The Golden Age of Chinese Literature

The Tang and Song dynasties combined to form perhaps the most creative and brilliant age of Chinese literary and artistic accomplishment. The poetry of the Tang, as represented by Li Bo and Du Fu, whom we encountered earlier in the chapter, reflected a sophistication and purpose that set a difficult standard to emulate. The writers of the Song often saw themselves diminished in comparison, but their poetry and prose is among China's finest. Song ceramics, painting (especially landscapes), and calligraphy also sought to grasp the inner dimensions of life without being distracted by surface details.

We can see this focus on the depth of inner expression in the following selections. The first is a powerful prose poem from the multidimensional Song official and scholar, Ouyang Xiu (1007–1072). The second is a love poem by Qin Guang (1040–1100) that reflects the directness and deceptive simplicity that characterizes Song poetry.

The Sound of Autumn

OUYANG XIU

One night when I was reading I heard a sound coming from the southwest. I listened in alarm and said:

"Strange! At first it was a patter of drops, a rustle in the air; all at once it is hooves stamping, breakers on a shore; it is as though huge waves were rising startled in the night, in a sudden downpour of wind and rain. When it collides with something, it clatters and clangs, gold and iron ring together; and then it is as though soldiers were advancing against an enemy, running swiftly with the gag between their teeth, and you hear no voiced command, only the tramping of men and horses."

I said to the boy, "What is this sound? Go out and look."

The boy returned and told me:

"The moon and stars gleam white and pure, the bright river is in the sky, nowhere is there any sound of man; the sound is over among the trees."

"Alas, how sad!" I answered. "This is the sound of autumn, why has it come? If you wish to know the signs which distinguish autumn, its colors are pale and mournful, mists dissolve and the clouds are gathered away; its face is clear and bright, with the sky high overhead and a sun of crystal; its breath is harsh and raw, and the mountains and rivers lie desolate.

Therefore the sound which distinguishes it is keen and chill, and bursts out in shrieks and screams. The rich, close grass teems vivid green, the thriving verdure of splendid trees delights us; then autumn sweeps the grass and its color changes, touches the trees and their leaves drop. The power by which it lays waste and scatters far and wide is the unexpended fury of the breath of heaven and earth. For autumn is the minister of punishments, the dark Yin among the four seasons. It is said to be the breath of justice between Heaven and Earth, and its eternal purpose is stern execution. By Heaven's design for all things, spring gives birth, autumn ripens. . . .

"Alas! The plants and trees feel nothing, whirling and scattering when their time comes; but mankind has consciousness, the noblest of all intelligences. A hundred cares move his heart, a myriad tasks weary his body; the least motion within him is sure to make his spirit waver, and how much more when he thinks of that which is beyond the reach of his endeavor, worries over that which his wisdom is powerless to alter! It is natural that his glossy crimson changes to withered wood, that his ebony black is soon flecked with stars! What use is it for man, who is not of the substance of metal and stone, to wish to vie for glory with the grass and trees? But remembering who it is who commits this violence against us, why should we complain against the sound of autumn?"

The boy did not answer, had dropped his head and fallen asleep. I heard only the sound of the insects chirping from the four walls, as though to make a chorus for my sighs.

Fickle Youth

QIN GUANG

With the mountains touched up with
   traces of clouds,
And the horizons bordered with withered
   grass,
The painted bugles murmured
   intermittently from the watchtower.
I stop my journey here for a while
And drink my parting wine.

Endless memories of old fairyland
Are now recalled

McNaughton, William, ed., *Chinese Literature*. Copyright © 1974 Charles E. Tuttle Co., Inc. of Boston Massachusetts and Tokyo, Japan. Reprinted with permission.

Faint and fleeting like haze;
Beyond the setting sun,
A few specks of cold crows,
A stream flowing around a lone hamlet.

Soul-stirring recollections:
Especially the moment
Her sachet was detached
And her sash loosened!
All I've won is
The long-lasting name of the "fickle one";
Once departed when will I see her again?
My sleeves and lapel are still tinted with
   her tears.
Steeped in sadness,
The tall city, now barely visible,
Already glows with its dim yellow
   lamplights.

THE MONGOL EMPIRE

Piercing the solid rock of the Caucasus, they poured forth like devils from the hell of Tartarus. They swarmed locust-like over the face of the earth and brought terrible devastation to the eastern part of Europe, laying it waste with fire and carnage.

—Matthew Paris

The greatest joy a man can have is victory: to conquer one's enemy's armies, to pursue them, to deprive them of their possessions, to reduce their families to tears, to ride on their horses, and to make love to their wives and daughters.

—Genghis Khan

Images of the Mongols

"I am the scourge of God! If you had not committed great sins, God would not have sent a punishment like me upon you." So spoke the Mongol leader Genghis Khan to refugees huddled together in the mosque of the central Asian city of Bukhara in 1219. There were few of them left, for the Great Khan had just slaughtered 30,000 of the city's defenders and herded the remnants together to be used as a human shield in his next conquest.

For over fifty years, from the first decade of the thirteenth century, the fate of Bukhara was shared by cities from China and Korea in the East, through Persia to Russia, Poland, and Hungary in the West. The great Islamic capitals of Samarkand and Baghdad, the palaces of Beijing, and the riches of India were plundered by the Mongol hordes who laid waste with such savagery that they were known by the Muslims as "the accursed of God."

The Mongols were not so much a race of peoples, but a confederation of tribes, numbering about two million, that was welded together by the will and dynamism of a man who became known as Genghis Khan, the Khan of Khans, or "Universal Ruler" of the Mongol confederation. According to legend, Temujin, as he was first known, entered the world gripping a clot of blood. Although he was born into a clan of authority, he barely survived his younger years after his father's death and learned to adapt amidst abandonment, starvation, tribal feuds, and the competition of family members.

The thirteenth century chronicle, Secret History of the Mongols *(1240), is the only native source of information about the life of Temujin. A compilation of legend and history, it describes Temujin, not only as a destroyer, but also as a military organizer of genius and a wise interpreter of human nature. By the age of forty-five in 1260, he had ended the intertribal rivalry and focused the energy of this diverse people. The presiding shaman declared him to be the representative on earth of the heavenly Eternal Blue Sky, destined to conquer and rule the world. Resistence to the will of God was futile. With the most efficient war machine of his age, Genghis Khan set out to achieve his destiny.*

By the time of his death in 1227, the Great Khan had broken the power of Islam in central Asia and had destroyed Jurchen authority in North China. His empire divided into separate Khanates and were ruled by his sons and grandsons. Under their leadership, and pursuing the same tactics that had served Genghis Khan so well, the Mongol empire grew. Among the most impressive of the descendants of Genghis Khan was his grandson, Kublai. In 1264, after a civil war lasting four years, Kublai won supremacy. Although he never achieved the kind of universal sovereignty that his grandfather had enjoyed, Kublai Khan was successful in his own right. He was cast in a different mold from his rough and unsophisticated ancestors. Kublai was literate, cultured, and politically astute. He rejected the nomadic life on the Asian steppes in favor of a settled existence in China. He had grown up in China, been educated by a Confucian scholar, and embraced Chinese thought and culture. By 1279, seventy years after Genghis's first invasion, Kublai completed the conquest of China, thus ending the Song dynasty and establishing the Yuan.

We know so much about the rule of Kublai Khan because of the accounts of the Christian friar, William of Rubruck, and the Venetian adventurer, Marco Polo. Polo's travels to China in 1266 were detailed in A Description of the World. *Marco Polo spent seventeen years in the court of the Great Khan, even serving as an official envoy to Burma and southern China. He was overwhelmed at the opulence of Kublai's court and was especially amazed at the porcelain, coal, silk, and use of paper money. But few of these wonders can be attributed to the Mongols. They were products of China, a civilization that was, in many ways, far more sophisticated and advanced than was Europe at the time.*

The Great Khan

MARCO POLO

Kublai Khan, it is to be understood, is the lineal and legitimate descendent of Genghis Khan the first emperor, and the rightful sovereign of the Tatars. He is the sixth Great Khan, and began his reign in the year 1256. He obtained the sovereignty by his consummate valor, his virtues, and his prudence, in opposition to the designs of his brothers, who were supported by many of the great officers and members of his own family. But the succession was his in law and right.

It is forty-two years since he began to reign to the present year, 1298, and he is fully eighty-five years of age. Previously to his ascending the throne he had served as a volunteer in the army, and endeavored to take a share in every enterprise. Not only was he brave and daring in action, but in point of judgment and military skill he was considered to be the most able and successful commander that ever led the Tatars [Mongols] in battle.

Politics and Religion

MARCO POLO

The Great Khan, having obtained this signal victory, returned with great pomp and triumph to

"The Great Khan" is from Thomas Wright, ed. *The Travels of Marco Polo* (London: George Bell & Sons, 1899), p. 133.

"Politics and Religion" is from Thomas Wright, ed. *The Travels of Marco Polo* (London: George Bell & Sons, 1899), pp. 139-142.

the capital city of Kanbalu [Beijing]. This took place in the month of November, and he continued to reside there during the months of February and March, in which latter was our festival of Easter. Being aware that this was one of our principal solemnities, he commanded all the Christians to attend him, and to bring with them their Book, which contains the four Gospels of the Evangelists. . . .

Upon being asked his motive for this conduct, he said: "There are four great Prophets who are reverenced and worshiped by the different classes of mankind. The Christians regard Jesus Christ as their divinity; the Saracens, Muhammad; the Jew, Moses; and the idolaters [Persians], Sogomombar-kan, the most eminent among their idols. I do honor and show respect to all the four, and invoke to my aid whichever among them is in truth Supreme in Heaven." But from the manner in which his majesty acted towards them, it is evident that he regarded the faith of the Christians as the truest and the best; nothing, as he observed, being enjoined to its professors that was not filled with virtue and holiness.

By no means, however, would he permit them to bear the cross before them in their processions, because upon it, so exalted a personage as Christ had been scourged and put to death. It may perhaps be asked by some, why, if he showed such a preference to the faith of Christ, he did not conform to it, and become a Christian? . . .

"Should I become a convert to the faith of Christ, and profess myself a Christian, the nobles of my Court and other persons who do not incline to that religion will ask me what sufficient motives have caused me to receive baptism, and to embrace Christianity. 'What extraordinary powers,' they will say,' what miracles have been displayed by its ministers? 'Whereas the idolaters declare that what they exhibit is performed through their own sanctity, and the influence of their idols."

"To this I shall not know what answer to make, and I shall be considered by them as laboring under a grievous error, while the idolaters, who by means of their profound arts can effect such wonders, may without difficulty compass my death. But return you to your pontiff, and request of him, in my name, to send hither a hundred persons well skilled in your law, who being confronted with the idolaters shall have power to restrain them, and showing that they themselves are endowed with similar art, but which they refrain from exercising, because it is derived from the agency of evil spirits, shall compel them to desist from practices of such a nature in their presence. When I am witness of this, I shall place them and their religion under a ban, and shall allow myself to be baptized. Following my example, all my nobility will then in like manner receive baptism, and this will be imitated by my subjects in general. In the end the Christians of these parts will exceed in number those who inhabit you own country."

From this discourse, it must be evident that if the Pope had sent out persons duly qualified to preach the gospel, the Great Khan would have embraced Christianity, for which, it is certainly known, he had a strong predilection.

Consolidation: Messengers of the Khan

MARCO POLO

Under the leadership of Genghis Khan, the Mongol nation was completely geared for war. Warriors and nomadic hunters by nature, they were unencumbered by material possessions and were expertly trained horsemen from youth. When on the move, Mongols lived in the saddle sometimes advancing sixty miles a day. Mongol cavalry moved in huge separate columns and their speed and coordinated maneuverability in battle could make their numbers seem doubled. Every soldier was equipped for

"Consolidation" is from Thomas Wright, ed. *The Travels of Marco Polo* (London: George Bell & Sons, 1899), pp. 177-181.

battle and self-sustained, carrying bows, arrows, shields, lassos, javelins, and daggers, as well as food and clothes. They perfected the technique of shooting from a standing position on horseback, and heavy cavalry were clad in mail, wielding scimitars and maces. The whole column was supported by carts, carrying tents, food, and fodder for the horses. Women cooked the food and mended the clothes, but also participated in mopping up operations, such as slitting the throats of enemy wounded.

The following accounts by Marco Polo and the Christian friar, William of Rubruck, focus on the nature of Mongol communication and the role of women in maintaining the disciplined structure of society.

From the city of Kanbalu [Beijing], there are many roads leading to the different provinces, and upon each of these, that is to say, upon every great high road, at the distance of twenty-five or thirty miles, accordingly as the towns happen to be situated, there are stations, with houses of accommodation for travelers. These are called *yamb* or post-houses. They are large and handsome buildings, having several well-furnished apartments, hung with sills, and pro-

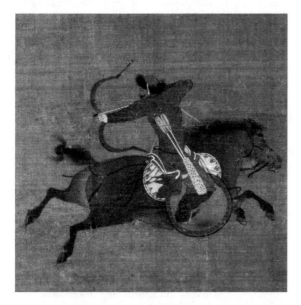

This painting of a Mongol warrior at full gallop demonstrates the mobility and firepower that struck terror into opposing armies on the battlefields of Asia and Europe. (*National Palace Museum, Taipei, Taiwan*)

vided with everything suitable to persons of rank. Even kings may be lodged at these stations in a becoming manner, as every article required may be obtained from the towns and strong places in the vicinity; and for some of them the court makes regular provision.

At each station four hundred good horses are kept in constant readiness, in order that all messengers going and coming upon the business of the Great Khan, and all ambassadors, may have relays, and, leaving their tired horses, be supplied with fresh ones. Even in mountainous districts, remote from the great roads, where there were no villages, and the towns are far distant from each other, His Majesty has equally caused buildings of the same kind to be erected, furnished with everything necessary, and provided with the usual supply of horses.

He sends people to dwell upon the spot, in order to cultivate the land and attend to the service of the post; by which means large villages are formed. In consequence of these regulations, ambassadors to the court, and the royal messengers, go and return through every province and kingdom of the Empire with the greatest convenience and facility. In the management of all this, the Great Khan exhibits a superiority over every other emperor, king, or human being.

In his dominions no fewer than two hundred thousand horses are thus employed in the department of the post, and ten thousand buildings, with suitable furniture, are kept up. It is indeed so wonderful a system, and so effective in its operation, as it is scarcely possible to describe. If it be questioned how the population of the country can supply sufficient numbers of these duties, and by what means they can be supported, we may answer, that all the Idolaters, and likewise the Saracens, keep six, eight, or ten women. According to their circumstances, by whom they have a prodigious number of children. Some of them have as many as thirty sons capable of following their fathers in arms; whereas with us a man has only one wife, and even although she should prove barren, he is obliged to pass his life with her, and is by that means deprived of the chance of raising a family. Hence it is that our population is so much inferior to theirs. . . .

When it is necessary that the messengers should proceed with extraordinary dispatch, as in cases of giving information of disturbance in any part of the country, the rebellion of a chief, or other important matter, they ride two hundred, or sometimes two hundred and fifty miles in the course of a day. . . . And when there are two messengers, they take their departure together from the same place, mounted upon good fleet horses; and they gird their bodies tight, bind a cloth round their heads, and push their horses to the greatest speed. They continue thus till they come to the next post-house, at twenty-five miles distant, where they find two other horses, fresh and in a state for work; they spring upon them without taking any repose, and changing in the same manner at every stage, until the day closes, they perform a journey to two hundred and fifty miles. . . . Messengers qualified to undergo this extraordinary degree of fatigue are held in high estimation.

Women among the Mongols
WILLIAM OF RUBRUCK

It is the duty of the women to drive the carts, to load the tents onto them and to unload them, to milk the cows, to make the butter and [cheese], to dress the skins and to sew them, which they do with thread made out of tendons. They split the tendons into very thin threads and then twist

Dawson, Christopher, ed., *The Mongol Mission*. Copyright © 1955 by Sheed & Ward Ltd. Reprinted with permission of the Continuum International Publishing Company.

these into one long thread. They also sew shoes and socks and other garments. They never wash their clothes, for they say that that makes God angry and that it would thunder if they hung them out to dry; they even beat those who do wash them and take them away from them. They are extraordinarily afraid of thunder. At such a time they turn all strangers out of their dwellings and wrap themselves in black felt in which they hide until it has passed over. They never wash their dishes, but when the meat is cooked, they wash out the bowl in which they are going to put it with some boiling broth from the cauldron which they afterwards pour back. The women also make the felt and cover the tents.

The men make bows and arrows, manufacture stirrups and bits and make saddles; they build the tents and carts, they look after the horses and milk the mares, churn the *cosmos*, that is the mares' milk, and make the skins in which it is kept, and they also look after the camels and load them. Both sexes look after the sheep and goats, and sometimes the men, sometimes the women, milk them. They dress skins with the sour milk of ewes, thickened and salted.

When they want to wash their hands or their head, they fill their mouth with water and pouring this little by little from their mouth into their hands, with it they wet their hair and wash their head.

As for their marriages, you must know that no one there has a wife unless he buys her, which means that sometimes girls are quite grown up before they marry, for their parents always keep them until they sell them. They observe the first and second degrees of consanguinity, but observe no degrees of affinity; they have two sisters at the same time or one after the other. . . .

And so when anyone has made an agreement with another to take his daughter, the father of the girl arranges a feast and she takes flight to relations where she lies hidden. Then the father declares: "Now my daughter is yours; take her wherever you find her." Then he searches for her with his friends until he finds her; then he has to take her by force and bring her, as though by violence, to his house.

The Mongol Assault and Decline

Although the Mongols were great conquerors, they showed little talent or patience for government. Even Kublai Khan, who became more identified with Chinese culture, failed to establish an efficient system of agricultural production and favored non-Chinese commercial interests to such a degree that profits from foreign trade drained out of the country. Kublai Khan's costly military campaigns also proved ruinous. The Chinese regarded their Mongol rulers as barbarians, yet were the ones treated as inferior in the eyes of Mongol custom and law. The Mongol Yuan dynasty survived for almost ninety years from 1279 to 1368, but was never powerful enough to seek new conquests and its decline was hastened by rivalries among the descendants of Kublai Khan. In 1368, a huge peasant army led by a former Buddhist novice, Zhu Yuanzhang, defeated a new generation of Mongol warriors lacking in discipline and with little appetite for war.

The new Ming Dynasty (1368–1644) would reestablish China as a premier cultural civilization. But rather than view the weakened Mongol state at the end of its life, it is perhaps more important to remember the qualities that inspired terror throughout the world. The following accounts from Muslim historians testify to the horror of the Mongol threat. In 1260, at the battle of Ayn Jaut in Palestine, the 10,000-man Mongol force under the leadership of Hulagu Khan was engaged by the army of the Mamluk Sultan of Egypt, Qutuz. This Muslim victory destroyed the Mongols' reputation for invincibility and ended their expansion toward the Mediterranean.

The Fall of Baghdad (1258)

IBN AL-ATHIR

The arrival of Hulagu Khan at Baghdad with all his troops, numbering nearly 200,000 fighting men, occurred on January 19, 1258. . . . He came to Baghdad with his numerous infidel, profligate, tyrannical, brutal armies of men, who believed neither in God nor in the Last Day, and invested Baghdad on the western and eastern sides. The armies of Baghdad were very few and utterly wretched, not reaching 10,000 horsemen. . . . Poets were reciting elegies on them and mourning for Islam and its people. . . .

The Mongols came down upon the city and killed all they could, men, women, and children, the old, the middle-aged, and the young. Many of the people went into wells, latrines, and sewers and hid there for many days without emerging. . . . The Mongols opened the gates by either breaking or burning them. When they entered, the people in them fled upstairs and the Mongols killed them on the roofs until blood poured from the gutters into the street. . . . And Baghdad, which had been the most civilized of all cities, became a ruin with only a few inhabitants, and they were in fear and hunger and wretchedness and insignificance.

The Muslim Defense of Egypt (1260)

AL-MAQRIZI

In 1260, the envoys of Hulagu arrived in Egypt with a letter, the text of which was as follows:

From the King of Kings in the East and the West, the mighty Khan:
In your name, O God, You who laid out the earth and raised up the skies.

Islam: From the Prophet Muhammad to the Capture of Constantinople, Vol. 1 by Bernard Lewis, ed. and trans. Copyright © 1974 by Bernard Lewis, pp. 82–84. Used by permission of HarperCollins Publishers, Inc.

Islam: From the Prophet Muhammad to the Capture of Constantinople, Vol. 1 by Bernard Lewis, ed. and trans. Copyright © 1974 by Bernard Lewis, pp. 84–88. Used by permission of HarperCollins Publishers, Inc.

Let Sultan al-Malik al-Muzaffar Qutuz [the Muslim leader] . . . know, as well as the amirs of his state and the people of his realms, in Egypt and in the adjoining countries, that we are the army of God on His earth. He created us from His wrath and urged us against those who incurred His anger. In all lands there are examples to admonish you and to deter you from challenging our resolve. Be warned by the fate of others and hand over your power to us before the veil is torn and you are sorry and your errors rebound upon you. For we do not pity those who weep, nor are we tender to those who complain. You have heard that we have conquered the lands and cleansed the earth of corruption and killed most of the people. Yours to flee; ours to pursue. And what land will shelter you, what road save our swords, no escape from the terror of our arms. Our horses are swift in pursuit, our arrows piercing, our swords like thunderbolts, our hearts like rocks, our numbers like sand. Fortresses cannot withstand us; armies are of no avail in fighting us. . . .

Those who make war against us are sorry; those who seek our protection are safe. If you submit to our orders and conditions, then your rights and your duties are the same as ours. If you resist, you will be destroyed. Do not, therefore, destroy yourselves with your own hands. He who is warned should be on his guard. You are convinced that we are infidels, and we are convinced that you are evil-doers. God, who determines all, has urged us against you. Before us, your many are few and your mighty ones are lowly, and your kings have no way to us but that of shame. Do not debate long, and hasten to give us an answer before the fires of war flare up and throw their sparks upon you. Then you will find no dignity, no comfort, no protector, no sanctuary. You will suffer at our hands the most fearful calamity, and your land will be empty of you. By writing to you we have dealt equitably with you and have awakened you by warning you. Now we have no other purpose but you. . . . :

Say to Egypt, Hulagu has come,
With swords unsheathed and sharp.
The mightiest of her people will become humble,
He will send their children to join the aged."

In Cairo and the rest of Egypt, proclamations were issued to go out on the Holy War for the cause of God and to defend the religion of the Prophet of God, may God bless and save him. Qutuz sent orders to the governors to rouse the troops for the campaign. Those who hid themselves and were discovered were to be flogged. . . .

Qutuz then summoned the amirs, and he urged them to fight the Mongols. He reminded them of the carnage, the enslavement, and the fire which had befallen other lands and struck fear in them with the thought that the same could happen again. He urged them to save Syria from the Tatars and to defend Islam and the Muslims, and he warned them of God's punishments. They burst into tears and swore together that they would strive to fight the Tatars and drive them out of the land. . . .

When Kitbugha and Baydara, the two deputies of Hulagu, learned of the advance of the [Muslim] army, they gathered together the Tatars who were scattered through Syria and set out to fight the Muslims. The vanguard of the Muslim army met the Tatar vanguard and defeated them. . . .

The army pursued the Tatars as far as the neighborhood of Baysan, where they turned and fought an even fiercer battle than the first. But God defeated the Tatars, and their chiefs and many of them were killed. The Muslims had been violently shaken. The Sultan cried out three times in a loud voice, heard by most of the army, "O Islam! O God, give your servant Qutuz victory over the Mongols." When the Mongols had been defeated for the second time, the Sultan dismounted from his horse, rubbed his face in the dust, kissed it, and recited a prayer with two prostrations, in thanksgiving to God, and then rode on. The troops advanced, their hands full of booty.

CHRONOLOGY: Imperial China and the Mongol Empire (589-1368)

570–632	Life of Muhammad, who—according to the *Qur'an* (650)—received revelations from the angel Gabriel, attacked idolatry in Mecca, was driven out in 622 (*Hegira*), and established himself at Medina, where he began the spread of Islam.
589–618	Sui Dynasty in China.
618–907	Tang Dynasty in China.
710	First Muslim invasion of India.
710–784	Nara Court, the first permanent capital established in Japan.
750–1258	Abbasids seize Caliphate from Umayyads and establish new Islamic dynasty with its capital at Baghdad under the progressive leadership of Harun al-Rashid (750–809). Golden Age of Muslim learning.
ca. 750	Introduction of paper manufacture from China to Islamic world.
768–814	Reign of Charlemagne, King of the Franks. Defeats Lombards in northern Italy (774) and establishes empire throughout modern-day France, parts of Germany, and eastern Europe, Italy, and northern Spain. Charlemagne crowned emperor by Pope Leo III (800). Establishment of Carolingian Renaissance under the direction of Alcuin of York.
794–1185	Heian (Kyoto) Court in Japan.
845	Official repression of Buddhism in China.
856–1086	Fujiwara clan dominates Heian Court in Japan.
960–1279	Song Dynasty in China. Period of Confucian revival begins in the eleventh century.
1000–1500	Development of "Great Zimbabwe," the center of the Bantu kingdom in southwestern Africa.
1054	Christian schism between Latin and Greek churches.
1055–1194	Seljuk rule in Baghdad.
1066	Norman invasion of Britain by William the Conqueror results in victory over Anglo-Saxon king, Harold Godwinson.
1096–1270	Crusades fought between Europeans and Muslims for control of the Holy Land.
1099	Jerusalem falls to the Crusaders. Forty-five years of Western rule begins in the Holy Land.
1130–1200	Life of Zhu Xi, great Song philosopher in China.
1167–1227	Life of Genghis Khan, founder of the Mongol empire.
1174–1193	Rule of Islamic leader, Saladin.

1189–1192	Third Crusade, which was attended by King Richard III of England, King Philip Augustus of France, and Holy Roman Emperor, Frederick Barbarossa, fails to recover Holy Land from Muslims.
1192	Muslim conquerors end Buddhism in India.
1185–1333	Kamakura Shogunate in Japan.
1194–1221	Kanem empire in Africa reaches greatest expansion.
1198–1216	Papacy of Innocent III, the most powerful and influential medieval pope.
1215	Magna Carta signed by King John of England. Rights of Englishmen established.
1220	Mongol invasions of Iran, Iraq, Syria, and India. Japan invaded in 1274 and 1281.
1230–1255	King Sundiata becomes first ruler of African kingdom of Mali. Timbuktu becomes center of trade and culture.
1258	Hulagu Khan, Mongol leader captures Baghdad.
1264	Kublai Khan established as Mongol leader and embraces Chinese thought and culture. Establishes Yuan dynasty of China (1279–1368).
1307–1332	Reign of Mansa Musa, greatest king of Mali in Africa.
1325	Founding of Aztec capital of Tenochtitlán.
1347–1351	Black Death first strikes in Sicily and moves north throughout Europe.
1350–1533	Inca Empire in Peru.

STUDY QUESTIONS

1. The founder of the Tang dynasty, Tang Daizong, in the instructions to his advisors at the outset of his reign was careful to set the tone for his new administration. What mistakes had his predecessor, Sui Wenti, made and what approach to the art of government was initiated by the new emperor? What were the responsibilities of Tang government officials and how were they to take care of their "patient"?

2. Although the Tang dynasty provided security from foreign invasion and stability within the borders of its empire, there was a price to pay. In the poetry of Du Fu and Li Bo, what issues are of most concern to the common people? Who were the enemies of the Tang and what price did they exact from the villages and the families of China? Was the price worth it?

3. Why was the examination system during the Tang and Song dynasties such an important component of bureaucratic efficiency? Why was it so controversial and what were the specific arguments provided by Sima Guang and Ouyang Xiu? Which argument is more persuasive?

4. The city of Hangzhou was typical of the teeming commercial centers of China during the Song. What purpose did the teahouses serve and who were some of the characters frequenting them?

5. According to Yuan Zai, what were some of the issues facing women during the Song? What were their responsibilities and how could families help reduce the stress on women?

6. Mou Zi in the fifth century B.C.E. sought to defend Buddhism through logic in a question-and-answer format. What were his primary arguments in countering the fears of those who sought to expel Buddhism from China? How do you define his concept of the Way? Six hundred years later, Buddhism had become entrenched in China and Ouyang Xiu complained that people were "drunk with Buddhism" and that it was a "cult" centered around the ideas of a barbarian. As a Confucian, why was he so upset and how did he think Buddhism should be driven from China?

7. How would you define the concept of yin and yang? What do they represent and how do they interact? What are the Five Primary Elements? How do yin and yang govern the "way of Heaven"? How does one master the meaning of life and death? What is the essence of life? How does Zhu Xi define the "Great Ultimate"? How does it relate to yin and yang? What does he mean when he says, "mind alone has no opposite"?

8. In his prose poem, "The Sound of Autumn," Ouyang Xiu tries to define the sound of a season. How does he contrast spring with autumn and what meaning does this have for human beings? How do you interpret his last line: "Why should we complain against the sound of autumn?" How does the poem entitled "Fickle Youth" by Qin Guang reflect the same sensitivity expressed by Ouyang Xiu? For Qin Guang, what was important in life?

9. After reading the accounts of Marco Polo, how would you describe Mongol society? Was Kublai Khan a religious man? If, as Marco Polo says, he regarded the Christian faith "as the truest and the best," why did he not convert?

10. How did the Mongols organize their empire and maintain control over such an expanse of territory? What was a post house and how did the message system work? Would you consider this a sophisticated system of communication?

11. What was the role of women in Mongol society and how did they contribute to the stability of the culture? What was considered women's work as opposed to men's work and what rituals were particularly important?

12. According to the Muslim historians, why were the Mongols such an impressive and violent force? How did the Mongols use terror and intimidation to gain advantage before the fighting even began? Note that both the Mongol and Muslim armies claim to be fighting in the name of God. Why? How important is it for an army to have God on its side?

9

"Samurai!": The Development of Classical and Medieval Japan (600–1467)

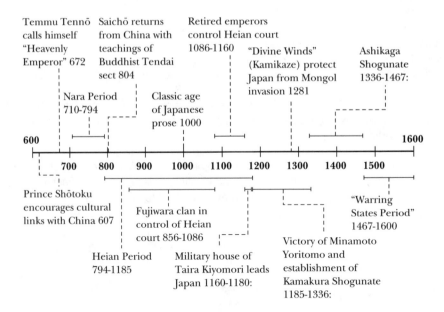

Temmu Tennō calls himself "Heavenly Emperor" 672

Saichō returns from China with teachings of Buddhist Tendai sect 804

Retired emperors control Heian court 1086-1160

"Divine Winds" (Kamikaze) protect Japan from Mongol invasion 1281

Ashikaga Shogunate 1336-1467:

Nara Period 710-794

Classic age of Japanese prose 1000

600

1600

700   800   900   1000   1100   1200   1300   1400   1500

Prince Shōtoku encourages cultural links with China 607

Fujiwara clan in control of Heian court 856-1086

"Warring States Period" 1467-1600

Heian Period 794-1185

Military house of Taira Kiyomori leads Japan 1160-1180:

Victory of Minamoto Yoritomo and establishment of Kamakura Shogunate 1185-1336:

The Way of the Samurai consists in reflecting on his own station in life, in discharging loyal service to his master, in deepening his fidelity to his friends, and in devoting himself to duty above all.

—Yamaga Sokō

Born, reborn, reborn, reborn,
Whence they have come, they do not know.
Dying, dying, ever dying,
They see not where it is they go.

—Kūkai

Looking at the leaves
  on the autumn hillsides,
I picked the yellowed ones
  and admire them,
leaving the green ones
  there with a sigh.
That is my regret.
But the autumn hills are for me.

—Princess Nukada

The sound of the bell echoes the impermanence of all things. The hue of flowers of the teak-tree declares that they who flourish must be brought low. Yea, the proud ones are but for a moment, like an evening dream in springtime. The mighty are destroyed at the last, they are but dust before the wind.

—The Tale of Heike

CHAPTER THEMES

- *Beliefs and Spirituality:*   How did Shintoism and Buddhism provide spiritual foundations for Japanese society? In what ways did these religions affect the arts of Japan? How were samurai warriors influenced by spiritual values?

- *Church/State Relationships:*   What was the role of the emperor in Japanese politics and society? How did his divine status influence his political role in the state? Why did Buddhist "warrior monks" become a disruptive force in the civil wars of medieval Japan?

- *Systems of Government:*   After encountering the political structure and administrative models of Tang China, how did Japan adapt them to their own culture? What role did the Japanese nobility (*daimyo*) play in the administration of the state and how did the *bakufu* or "tent government" originate? What were the responsibilities of the shōgun and how did they differ from those of the emperor?

- *Women in History:*   What various roles did women play in Japanese society and how did these change from the classical and medieval periods to the Tokugawa era? How were women instrumental in establishing the high standards of classical prose during the Heian period?

- ***Historical Change and Transition:*** What were the main transition points when Japanese society changed to incorporate new ideas or political models? In the face of great political upheaval from bloody civil wars during the twelfth and fifteenth centuries, why has there been such continuity of Japanese cultural traditions? How did foreign influence from Dutch and Portuguese traders and missionaries affect Japanese life?

- ***The Big Picture:*** In its geography, political, and spiritual development, how has Japan remained a land of distinct contrasts? How has the Japanese affinity for restricting and adapting foreign political and spiritual influences been instrumental in the development of a unique culture?

Japan—Land of the Rising Sun—is a country of distinct contrasts. Geographically, it is a curve of four main volcanic islands separated from the Asian mainland at its narrowest point by the hundred-mile-wide Strait of Korea. Japan is a land of remarkable beauty, with a temperate climate, consistent rainfall, and fertile valleys. But it is also a violent land, square in the path of hurricanes and vulnerable to the danger of active volcanoes and earthquakes. The geographical isolation of these islands, protected from easy invasion and yet separated from each other, promoted the slow development of Japanese political unity. Possessing a homogeneous population, a common language and religious traditions, Japan developed a deep, layered culture. The beauty of Japanese painting, the delicate brush strokes of calligraphy, the paper art of origami, and the austere beauty of a Zen rock garden, all can be juxtaposed with the belligerence and treachery of its civil wars, not to mention Japan's later role in world war. The intense political competition for the military supremacy of shōgun during the medieval period from about 1200 to 1600 must be balanced with the dignified and aloof position of emperor. Perhaps the greatest contradictions can be found within the warrior elite of Japan—the samurai. Bound to their lords through oaths and a rigid code of honor, these disciplined masters of the sword were among the most respected and lethal of the world's warriors—discipline and destruction. A culture with loving devotion to the strictures of courtesy, the delicacy of flower arrangement, all juxtaposed with a ferocity of spirit rarely matched on the world stage. In this chapter we will focus on some of these contradictions in the development of classical and medieval Japan.

Although Japan was isolated geographically, it nevertheless had established relations with cultures on the Korean peninsula during the period 300 to 600 C.E. This contact was especially important because Korean visitors brought with them to Japan elements of Chinese civilization. Chinese writing was introduced to Japan in the fifth century C.E. and Confucianism entered in 513. This contact with China would prove to be of seminal importance in Japanese history. By the eighth century, Japan had imported Chinese political institutions of the Tang dynasty and by the eleventh century, it had adapted these and other intellectual and religious influences to achieve a truly distinctive Japanese culture.

It is difficult to separate Japanese history into rigid time periods because there is such a continuity of overlapping development, but the period from 710 to about 1200 has been termed the Classical Age of Japan because it saw the introduction of political institutions and the establishment of a cultural seedbed that provided a foundation for later variations. This period is also called Nara and Heian Japan because the political capitals were established first at Nara in 710, and then at Heian-kyō (near Kyoto) in 794.

The organization of the Nara and Heian courts centered around the position of emperor. He ruled with great majesty and respect, a political leader on the Chinese model, but also a religious figure descended from the Sun Goddess. The religion of early Japan was called

Shinto, "the way of the gods." Shinto is an animistic religion that sees the powerful forces of nature embodied in the mountains, trees, winds, and waterfalls. These forces became personified as deities and worshiped by Japanese clans or extended families. The most important clan about 300 C.E., the Yamato, established its patron deity, the Sun Goddess, as the center of a national myth that embodied Japan and justified the authority of Yamato descendants. All Japanese history constitutes the development of a single line of divine emperor, descended from the sun—Japan's "Rising Sun."

During the Nara and Heian periods, the emperor made political appointments and shared power with the various heads of clans, the great lords or *daimyo*. Sometimes the emperor took an active role in running the government, but more often after the mid-ninth century, he reigned but did not rule. Much of the political administration was left to a Council of State, where the *daimyo* exercised their influence and manipulated the emperor. This structure of an emperor, Council of State, and various ministries below was based on the Chinese model of administration under the Tang dynasty (618–907). Likewise, the land distribution and taxation system of Nara and Heian Japan was similar to the "equal field system" of China with some distinct modifications.

By about 856, the Fujiwara clan became the most important political force and from 986 to 1056, dominated the royal court and monopolized key government positions. Resented by the imperial family and the lesser noble houses, Fujiwara rule gave way to the control of a series of retired emperors from 1086 to 1160. The year 1160 marked an important change in Japanese history as rule by the civil aristocracy gave way to centuries of control by a military aristocracy. Japan entered a feudal age of civil war and blood-letting that saw the establishment of the *bakufu* or "Tent Government" shortly after the victory of Minamoto Yoritomo in 1185. With his capital at Kamakura (near Tokyo), he assumed the title of shōgun, supreme military commander, and appointed governors throughout the provinces of Japan.

Minamoto's authority was centered around his relationship with his vassals or retainers who fought for him out of personal loyalty and contractual obligation. These warriors, called samurai ("those who serve") were not a new institution of medieval Japan. In fact they had existed since the Heian period about 792, when the court abolished conscription and adopted a new system of defense that relied on local mounted warriors. Some of these minor aristocracy, who supplied their own armor and wielded their swords with amazing precision, were disruptive forces that were used by local nobility to defy provincial governors. By the tenth century, these local bands had been formed into regional coalitions and had assumed a loyalty toward a lord based on strict codes of honor and rights to income from land. The samurai provided the muscle for Minamoto and others like him to compete for the supreme military position of shōgun.

The term "medieval Japan" is a rather misleading term, for it implies a distinct break with classical Japan when they were both a part of a continuing process of evolution. In fact, the literature and the arts of the classical period, as well as the development of Buddhism throughout Japan, testify to the continuity of tradition. Yet the transition to feudal militarism in Japan, especially after 1200, did produce changes in outlook and focus that were important in later history. The Kamakura shogunate (1185–1336) and the successor Ashikaga shogunate (1336–1467) were often times of turmoil, armed uprising, and even foreign invasion by the Mongols from China. Ultimately, the political control of the Ashikaga shōguns broke apart and Japan entered a "warring states" period from 1467 to 1600, which saw changes in military organization, agriculture, and the establishment of the new Tokugawa shogunate from 1600 to 1868. During this latter period, Japan isolated itself from the outside influences of world civilization. Yet amidst all of this political and social change, the arts of Japan, influenced as they were by the meditative aspects of Buddhism, became some of the greatest cultural monuments in world history. Japanese society remains a fascinating study in contrast.

CLASSICAL JAPANESE CIVILIZATION (600–1185)

The Earliest Records

The oldest extant primary sources for Japanese history are the Records of Ancient Matters *(712 C.E.) and the* Chronicles of Japan *(720). Both begin with mythological origins during an "age of the gods." Little of this information can be taken as actual history, but the early stories of any culture provide insight into fundamental beliefs and values that are reflected in the later development of the civilization.*

One of the most intriguing aspects of early Japanese history is the origin and development of the religion of Shinto, "the way of the gods." Shinto was not an organized and structured religion with a congregation, but rather an aggregate of many animistic cults that developed to serve the religious needs of early Japanese communities. There is no central belief system or doctrine and scholars are hard pressed to provide any coherent definition of Shintoism. Suffice it to say that the objects of worship in all Shinto cults were known as kami *or nature spirits found in objects like trees, plants, seas, mountains, animals, and even humans. These spirits possessed superior powers for good or evil and shrines were made for their worship by families, villages, or regions. In the nineteenth century, Western scholars termed Shinto the "National Faith of Japan," since it was promoted by the Japanese government itself as a "purely Japanese" component of national unity linked around the emperor, who was descended from the Sun Goddess, Amaterasu. But there is no evidence of the "pure" Japanese origins of Shinto because it is also found in Korea and throughout northeast Asia. The attempt to consolidate Shinto into a national religion is hardly in keeping with its personal and decentralized nature. The first selection is from a later Japanese compilation of Shinto folklore called* Nihongi. *The influence of Chinese thought is evident as the paired male and female creator gods of Japan, Izanagi and Izanami, reflect the yin and yang principles of balance so prominent in Chinese cosmology. It is instructive to compare this story of creation with those of Mesopotamian, Hebrew, and Mayan creation myths mentioned in earlier chapters.*

The second selection is from a Chinese dynastic history of the Sui dynasty about 630 C.E. Historians often must rely on such Chinese records in order to piece together early Japanese history. These Chinese records are in the form of footnotes that discuss neighboring peoples; in the case of Japan, the Chinese called this an account of the "Eastern Barbarians."

Early Shinto and the Birth of Japan

Izanagi and Izanami stood on the floating bridge of Heaven, and held counsel together, saying:

"Is there not a country beneath?"

Thereupon they thrust down the jewel-spear of Heaven, and groping about therewith found the ocean. The brine which dripped from the point of the spear coagulated and became an island which received the name of Ono-goro-jima.

The two Deities thereupon descended and dwelt in this island. Accordingly, they wished to become husband and wife together, and to produce countries.

So they made Ono-goro-jima the pillar of the center of the land.

Now the male deity turning by the left, and the female deity by the right, they went round the pillar of the land separately. When they met together on one side, the female deity spoke first and said: "How delightful! I have met with a lovely youth." The male deity was displeased and said: "I am a man, and by right should have spoken first. How is it that on the contrary you, a woman, should have been the first to speak? This was unlucky. Let us go round again." Upon this the two deities went back, and having met anew, this time the male deity spoke first, and said: "How delightful! I have met a lovely maiden."

Then he inquired of the female deity, saying: "In your body is there anything formed?" She answered, and said: "In my body there is a place which is the source of femininity." The male deity said: "In my body again there is a place which is the source of masculinity. I wish to unite the source-place of my body to the source-place of your body." Thereupon the male and female first became united as husband and wife.

Now when the time of birth arrived, first of all the island of Ahaji was reckoned as the placenta, and their minds took no pleasure in it. Therefore it received the name of Ahaji no Shima ["my shame"].

Next there was produced the island of Ō-yamato no Toyo-aki-tsu-shima ["rich harvest"].

Next they produced the island of Iyo no futana [Shikoku], and next the island of Tsukushi [Kyushu]. Next the islands of Oki and Sado were born as twins. This is the prototype of the twin-births which sometimes take place among mankind. Next was born the island of Koshi, then the island of Ō-shima, then the island of Kibi no Ko. Hence first arose the designation of the Great Eight-island Country.

Then the islands of Tsushima and Iki, with the small islands in various parts, were produced by the coagulation of the foam of the salt-water.

Chinese Imperial Perspectives on Japan (630)

The [Chinese] Emperor ordered the appropriate official to make inquiries about the manners and customs [of the Japanese people]. The envoy reported thus: "The King of Wa [Japan] deems heaven to be his elder brother and the sun, his younger. Before break of dawn he attends the court, and, sitting cross-legged, listens to appeals. Just as soon as the sun rises, he ceases these duties, saying that he hands them over to his brother." Our just Emperor said that such things were extremely senseless, and he admonished [the King of Wa] to alter his ways.

[According to the envoy's report], the King's spouse is called Kemi. Several hundred women are kept in the inner chambers of the court. The heir apparent is known as Rikamitahori. There is no special palace. There are twelve grades of court officials. . . .

There are about 100,000 households. It is customary to punish murder, arson, and adultery with death. Thieves are made to make restitution in accordance with the value of the goods stolen. If the thief has no property with which to make payment, he is taken to be a slave. Other offenses are punished according to their nature—sometimes by banishment and sometimes by flogging. In the prosecution of offenses by the court, the knees of those who plead not guilty are pressed together by placing them between pieces of wood, or their heads are sawed with the stretched string of a strong bow. Sometimes pebbles are put in boiling water and both parties to a dispute made to pick them out. The hand of the guilty one is said to become inflamed. Sometimes a snake is kept in a jar, and the accused is ordered to catch it. If he is guilty, his hand will be bitten. The people are gentle and peaceful. Litigation is infrequent and theft seldom occurs.

As for musical instruments, they have five-stringed lyres and flutes. Both men and women paint marks on their arms and spots on their faces and have their bodies tattooed. They catch fish by diving into the water. They have no written characters and understand only the use of notched sticks and knotted ropes. They revere Buddha and obtained Buddhist scriptures from Paekche [Korea]. This was the first time that they came into possession of written characters. They are familiar with divination and have profound faith in shamans, both male and female. . . .

In [607], King Tarishihoko sent an envoy to the [Chinese] court with tribute. The envoy said: "The King has heard that to the west of the ocean a Bodhisattva of the Sovereign reveres and promotes Buddhism. For that reason he has sent an embassy to pay his respects. Accompanying the embassy are several tens of monks who have come to study Buddhism." [The envoy brought] an official message which read: "The Son of Heaven in the land where the sun rises [Japan] addresses a letter to the Son of Heaven in the land where the sun sets [China]. We hope you are in good health." When the Emperor saw this letter, he was displeased and told the official in charge of foreign affairs that this letter from the barbarians was discourteous, and that such a letter should not again be brought to his attention.

The Constitution of Prince Shōtoku (604)

The earliest Japanese sources of their own history describe the mythological foundation of Japan and give a general picture of the social and political arrangements of the early Yamato kings, starting about the fifth century C.E. The picture that emerges is of an aristocratic society based around uji *or clans that were supported by workers* (be). *What little is known about Yamato court politics indicates a constant struggle for power between these clans. In the late sixth century, the Soga clan headed by Soga no Umuko, installed a woman, Empress Suiko (reigned 592–628), as ruler to be guided by the imperial Prince Shōtoku (574–622) as regent. Under Shōtoku's influence, Japan opened itself to the cultural influence of China, promoting political and diplomatic delegations, a quickening flow of technology, writing, art, Buddhism, and the adoption of Tang legal and administrative institutions. The following constitution, promulgated by Prince Shōtoku in 604, reflects the influence of Chinese Confucian and Daoist thought, but also blends this with a Japanese emphasis on nature.*

The Prince Imperial, in person, prepared for the first time laws:

1. Harmony is to be valued, and an avoidance of wanton opposition to be honored. All men are influenced by class-feeling, and there are few who are intelligent. Hence there are some who disobey their lords and fathers, or who maintain feuds with the neighboring villages. But when those above are harmonious and those below are friendly, and there is concord in the discussion of business, right views of things spontaneously gain acceptance. Then what is there which cannot be accomplished!

2. Sincerely reverence the three treasures. The three treasures: the Buddha, the Law, and the Priesthood, are the final refuge . . . and are the supreme objects of faith in all countries. What man in what age can fail to reverence this law? Few men are utterly bad. They may be taught to

"The Constitution of Prince Shōtoku" is from W.G. Aston, trans., *Nihongi: Chronicles of Japan from the Earliest Times to A.D. 697,* volume 2 (London: Kegan, Paul, Trench, Truebner and Co., 1896), pp. 128–132. Translation modernized by editor.

follow it. But if they do not go to the three treasures, how shall their crookedness be made straight?

3. When you receive the Imperial commands, to not fail to obey them. The lord is Heaven, the vassal is Earth. Heaven overspreads, and Earth upbears. When this is so, the four seasons follow their due course, and the powers of Nature obtain their efficacy. If the Earth attempted to overspread, Heaven would simply fall in ruin. Therefore is it that when the lord speaks, the vassal listens; when the superior acts, the inferior yields compliance. Consequently when you receive the Imperial commands, do not fail to carry them out scrupulously. Let there be a want of care in this matter, and ruin is the natural consequence.

4. The Ministers and functionaries should make decorous behavior their leading principle, for the leading principle of the government of the people consists in decorous behavior. If the superiors do not behave with decorum, the inferiors are disorderly: if inferiors are wanting in proper behavior, there must necessarily be offenses. Therefore, it is that when lord and vassal behave with propriety, the distinctions of rank are not confused: when the people behave with propriety, the Government of the Commonwealth proceeds of itself. . . .

6. Punish that which is evil and encourage that which is good. This was the excellent rule of antiquity. Do not conceal, therefore, the good qualities of others, and do not fail to correct that which is wrong when you see it. . . . [Flatters and

deceivers] are all wanting in fidelity to their lord, and in benevolence toward the people. From such an origin great civil disturbances arise.

7. Let every man have his own charge, and let not the spheres of duty be confused. When wise men are entrusted with office, the sound of praise arises. If unprincipled men hold office, disasters and tumults are multiplied. In this world, few are born with knowledge: wisdom is the product of earnest meditation. In all things, whether great or small, find the right man, and they will surely be well managed: on all occasions, be they urgent or the reverse, meet but with a wise man, and they will of themselves be amenable. In this way, the Temples of the Earth and of Grain will be free from danger. Therefore did the wise sovereigns of antiquity seek the man to fill the office, and not the office for the sake of the man. . . .

10. Let us cease from wrath, and refrain from angry looks. Nor let us be resentful when others differ from us. For all men have hearts, and each heart has its own leanings. Their right is our wrong, and our right is their wrong. We are not unquestionably sages, nor are they unquestionably fools. Both of us are simply ordinary men. How can anyone lay down a rule by which to distinguish right from wrong? For we are all, one with another, wise and foolish, like a ring which has no end. Therefore, although others give way to anger, let us on the contrary dread our own faults, and though we alone may be in the right, let us follow the multitude and act like them.

Pilgrimage to China (840)
ENNIN

Ennin (793–864) was a Buddhist monk who traveled in Tang China from 838–847 in search of knowledge about his religion. In this letter to the regional magistrate, Ennin asked for permission to visit several monasteries and shrines. In just this way, the Japanese imported ideas and institutions from China before adapting them to their own culture.

Source: Reischauer, Edwin O., trans., *Ennin's Diary: The Record of a Pilgrimage to China in Search of the Law,* 1955, pp. 179–180.

To the Magistrate, His Honor, Jiexia, with humble respect:

In order to seek the Buddha's teachings, Ennin has come here from afar, moved by your virtue, and has tarried in your region. . . . Humbly he presents this letter, stating his thanks. Respectfully written in brief.

The said Ennin and [his disciples and servant] are solely devoted to the Buddhist teaching and to practicing the Buddha's Way. From afar they heard of Wutai and other places in China. These are the sources of the Buddhist Law, the places where the great saints have manifested themselves. Eminent monks of India have come there from afar, crossing precipitous slopes; famous patriarchs of China have there obtained enlightenment. Ennin and the others of old have admired these places and, crossing the sea, have come to visit them, but they have of yet accomplished their long-cherished wish. . . . Separated by the ocean wastes from the land of their birth and forgetting their beloved land on this ocean shore, they reached the Korean Cloister at Mt. Qia. Fortunately, they were free to travel and were able to come to the Magistrate's enlightened territory.

They now wish to go to various regions to worship at the holy sites and to seek teachers and to study the Law [the tenets of Buddhism], but they fear that everywhere in the prefectures and subprefectures, the barriers and fords, the passes and market places, and the monasteries and temples, their reasons for traveling will not be honored, so they humbly hope that the Magistrate, out of his magnanimity, will especially grant them official credentials to serve as verification, and they humbly ask for a decision regarding this. The said matter is as stated above. Humbly written.

"Dwellers among the Clouds": The Elegance of the Heian Court

The poetry of Japan has its roots in the human heart and flourishes in the countless leaves of words. . . . It is poetry which, without exertion, moves heaven and earth, stirs the feelings of gods and spirits invisible to the eye, softens the relations between men and women, calms the hearts of fierce warriors.

—*Ki no Tsurayuki (868?–945?)*

The political history of Japan from about 600 to 1200 is a tangle of ambition and deceit, of the rivalry between noble families who competed for influence at the Nara and Heian courts. The Fujiwara clan in particular proved dominant and controlled the political agenda through their manipulation, both subtle and overt, of the emperor and his advisors. The Fujiwara married their daughters into the imperial family and served as regents to the emperors, who largely became ceremonial figures. By 858, the Fujiwara family had established itself as a hereditary civil dictatorship.

The Fujiwara and other clans gained tax-free parcels of land through special dispensations of the emperor and acquired provincial estates (called shōen*) that were mostly free of imperial control. By 1150, the landed nobility, supported by their relations at court, managed a patchwork of five thousand* shōen*; imperial land had all but disappeared. In the countryside, these provincial lords sometimes broke into open rebellion, pillaging coastal areas and fighting against one another with their armed retainers called* samurai. *Even in the capital, Heian-kyō, robbery and petty crimes were common.*

Beginning about 1068, there were attempts to curb the power of the Fujiwara clan and reassert imperial control, most notably by the emperor Go-Sanjō Tennō, and his son Shirakawa (1072–1086). Although their establishment of a "cloistered government" of emperors who ruled, then abdicated their formal position to control affairs from "retirement," maintained political stability for over a hundred years, it eventually fell to the ambitions of other provincial clans in the mid-twelfth century.

This resurgence of the power of the clans eventually brought about the demise of the Heian court by 1185; but what a dazzling world it had been! Amidst all of the machinations and undercurrents of Heian politics, there existed a unique atmosphere at court, serene and elegant, where strict rules of decorum governed every move. The Heian court, turbulent and teeming with political intrigue, evinced an image of refined elegance on the surface. Those who lived at court or served the emperor and his noble advisors referred to themselves as "dwellers among the clouds." They were governed by a code of miyabi *or courtly refinement that emphasized grace and precision, elaborate attention to the sleeve length of a gown, to the subtleties of color or scent, to the beauty of calligraphy and the proper form and intimation of a poetic couplet.*

Religious and cultural ceremonies filled the court calendar, and banquets among the nobility were opportunities to flaunt one's erudition in verbal contests of wit and nuance. Poetry was the language of flirtation and seduction, of lament and melancholy. This languid pace of court life belied the active political agenda of the Fujiwara clan, but produced a rich store of refined poetry and prose that set high literary standards in Japan for centuries to come.

Kokinshū: "Scattered Blossoms of a Spring Morning"

The Kokinshū, *or "Collection of Ancient and Modern Poems," was compiled by imperial order and completed in 905. It contains over 1,100 poems. In his preface to the work, Ki no Tsurayuki (d. 946) listed the circumstances under which the poets expressed themselves: "when they looked at the scattered blossoms of a spring morning; when they listened of an autumn evening to the falling of the leaves; when they were startled into thoughts of the brevity of life by seeing the dew on the grass or the foam on the water." Many of the poems in this collection are anonymous and they are characterized by a gentle melancholy truly expressive of the subtleties of the Heian court.*

Like the ice which melts
When spring begins
Not leaving a trace behind,
May your heart melt toward me!
—Anonymous

My love
Knows no destination
And has no goal;
I think only
Of meeting as its limit.
—Ōshikōchi no Mitsune (859-907)

Thinking about him
I sleep, only to have him
Appear before me—
Had I known it was a dream,
I should never have wakened.
—Ono no Komachi

Whipped by a fierce wind
And dashed like the ocean waves
Against the rocks—
I alone am broken to bits
And now am lost in longing.
—Minamoto no Shigeyuki (d. 1000)

To what shall I compare
This world?
To the white wake behind
A ship that has rowed away
At dawn!
—The Priest Mansei (c.720)

I should not have waited.
It would have been better
To have slept and dreamed,
Than to have watched night pass,
And this slow moon sink.
–Lady Akazome Emon

The Pillow Book

SEI SHŌNAGON

The Pillow Book of Sei Shōnagon was written about 1002 when the Heian court was dominated by the civil dictatorship of the Fujiwara clan. We know little of Shōnagon's life, although her father, a scholar and poet, was a member of the Kiyowara clan and worked as a provincial official. Sei Shōnagon served as lady-in-waiting to the Empress Sadako during the last decade of the tenth century and compiled her observations about life at court, her loves and annoyances, her travels and assessments of court officials. The Pillow Book is infused with wit and fun, but also reveals the class intolerance and social expectations of life at the Heian court.

Hateful Things

A lover who is leaving at dawn announces that he has to find his fan and his paper. "I know I put them somewhere last night," he says. Since it is pitch dark, he gropes about he room, bumping into the furniture and muttering, "Strange! Where on earth can they be?" Finally he discovers the objects. He thrusts the paper into the breast of his robe with a great rustling sound; then he snaps open his fan and busily fans away with it. Only now is he ready to take his leave. What charmless behavior! "Hateful" is an understatement. . . .

A good lover will behave as elegantly at dawn as at any other time. He drags himself out of bed with a look of dismay on his face. The lady urges him on: "Come, my friend, it's getting light. You don't want anyone to find you here." He gives a deep sigh, as if to say that the night has not been nearly long enough and that it is

agony to leave. Once up, he does not instantly pull on his trousers. Instead he comes close to the lady and whispers whatever was left unsaid during the night. Even when he is dressed, he still lingers, vaguely pretending to be fastening his sash.

Presently he raises the lattice, and the two lovers stand together by the side door while he tells her how he dreads the coming day, which will keep them apart; then he slips away. The lady watches him go, and this moment of parting will remain among her most charming memories.

Indeed, one's attachment to a man depends largely on the elegance of his leave-taking. When he jumps out of bed, scurries about the room, tightly fastens his trouser sash, rolls up the sleeves of his Court cloak, over-robe, or hunting costume, stuffs his belongings into the breast of his robe and then briskly secures the outer sash—one really begins to hate him.

From *The Pillow Book of Sei Shongaon* by Ivan Morris, trans. & ed., © 1991 Columbia University Press. Reprinted with permission of the publisher.

The Japanese wonder at the power and beauty of nature is reflected in this hanging scroll entitled "Li Tai-Po Looking at a Waterfall" by the painter, poet and garden designer, Sōami (1485?-1525). Ink on paper. (*Asian Art Museum, San Francisco*)

Shameful Things

A man's heart is a shameful thing. When he is with a woman whom he finds tiresome and distasteful, he does not show that he dislikes her, but makes her believe she can count on him. Still worse, a man who has the reputation of being kind and loving treats a woman in such a way that she cannot imagine his feelings are anything but sincere. Yet he is untrue to her not only in his thoughts but in his words; for he speaks badly about her to other women just as he speaks badly about those women to her. The woman, of course, has no idea that she is being maligned; and, hearing his criticisms of the others, she fondly believes he loves her best. The man for his part is well aware that this is what she thinks. How shameful!

When a woman runs into a lover with whom (alas!) she has broken for good, there is no reason for her to be ashamed if he regards her as heartless. But if the lover shows that he has not been even slightly upset by their parting, which to her was so sad and painful and difficult, she is bound to be amazed by the man and to wonder what sort of a heart he can have. Oblivious of his own callous attitude, her abandoned lover carried on a glib conversation in which he criticizes the behavior of other men.

How shameful when a man seduces some helpless Court lady and, having made her pregnant, abandons her without caring in the slightest about her future!

In Spring It Is the Dawn

In spring it is the dawn that is most beautiful. As the light creeps over the hills, their outlines are dyed a faint red and wisps of purplish cloud trail over them.

In summer the nights. Not only when the moon shines, but on dark nights too, as the fireflies flit to and fro, and even when it rains, how beautiful it is!

In autumn the evenings, when the glittering sun sinks close to the edge of the hills and the crows fly back to their nests in threes and fours and twos; more charming still is a file of wild geese, like specks in the distant sky. When the sun has set, one's heart is moved by the sound of the wind and the hum of the insects.

In winter the early mornings. It is beautiful, indeed, when snow has fallen during the night, but splendid too when the ground is white with frost; or even when there is no snow or frost, but it is simply very cold and the attendants hurry from room to room stirring up the fires and bringing

This detail of a painting by Toyoharu (1735–1814) entitled "Wintertime Party," recalls the delicacy of life at the Heian court inspired by the accounts of Sei Shōnagon and Murasaki Shikibu. Ink color and gold on silk. (*Freer Gallery of Art, Washington, DC*)

charcoal; how well this fits the season's mood! But as noon approaches and the cold wears off, no one bothers to keep the braziers alight, and soon nothing remains but piles of white ashes.

Things That Have Lost Their Power

A large boat which is high and dry in a creek at ebb-tide.

A woman who has taken off her false locks to comb the short hair that remains.

A large tree that has been blown down in a gale and lies on its side with its roots in the air.

The retreating figure of a *sumō* wrestler who has been defeated in a match.

A man of no importance reprimanding an attendant.

An old man who removes his hat, uncovering his scanty topknot.

A woman, who is angry with her husband about some trifling matter, leaves home and goes somewhere to hide. She is certain that he will rush about looking for her; but he does nothing of the kind and shows the most infuriating indifference. Since she cannot stay away for ever, she swallows her pride and returns.

Women at the Imperial Court

MURASAKI SHIKIBU

Perhaps the most talented literary artist of the Heian court was Murasaki Shikibu (978–1010?), who served as a lady-in-waiting to the empress Akiko. She was a contemporary of Sei Shōnagon and described her as "a gifted woman," but "self-satisfied" and "frivolous." Certainly no one could accuse Murasaki of frivolity. She was a poet, diarist, and author of The Tale of Genji, *a massive recounting of the adventures and romances of Prince Genji. This was the world's first novel and has attained universal recognition as a masterpiece of psychological insight. The first selection by Murasaki is from her diary as she characterizes various figures at court (including Sei Shōnagon) and then reflects on the expectations of women in Japanese society. It is followed by an excerpt from*

"Women at the Imperial Court" is from Annie Shepley Omori and Kochi Doi, trans., *Diaries of Court Ladies of Old Japan* (Boston: Houghton Mifflin, 1920), pp. 71–73; 89–90; 132–134.

The Tale of Genji *where she discusses the art of the novel. Murasaki Shikibu was truly among the greatest representatives of the literary flowering of the Heian court.*

The ladies waiting upon her honored presence are talking idly. The Queen hears them; she must find them annoying, but she conceals it calmly. Her beauty needs no words of mine to praise it, but I cannot help feeling that to be near so beautiful a queen will be the only relief from my sorrow [due to the death of her husband]. So in spite of my better desires [for a religious life], I am here. Nothing else dispels my grief—it is wonderful! . . .

I can see the garden from my room beside the entrance to the gallery. The air is misty, the dew is still on the leaves. The Lord Prime Minister is walking there; he orders his men to cleanse the brook. He breaks off a stalk of *omenaishi* [flower maiden] which is in full bloom by the south end of the bridge. He peeps in over my screen! His noble appearance embarrasses us, and I am ashamed of my morning face. He says, "Your poem on this! If you delay so much the fun is gone!" and I seize the chance to run away to the writing-box, hiding my face–

Flower-maiden in bloom—
Even more beautiful for the bright dew,
Which is partial, and never favors me.

"So prompt!" said he, smiling, and ordered a writing-box to be brought for himself.
His answer:

The silver dew is never partial.
From her heart
the flower-maiden's beauty.

One wet and calm evening I was talking with Lady Saisho. The [Prime Minister's son] sat with the curtain partly rolled up. He seemed more mature than his age and was very graceful. Even in light conversation such expressions as "Fair soul is rarer than fair face" come gently to his lips, covering us with confusion. It is a mistake to treat him like a young boy. He keeps his dig-

nity among ladies, and I saw in him a much-sought-after romantic hero when once he walked off reciting to himself:

Linger in the field where flower-maidens
    are blooming
And your name will be tarnished with tales
    of gallantry.

Some such trifle as that sometimes lingers in my mind when really interesting things are soon forgotten—why? . . .

Lady Izumi Shikibu corresponds charmingly, but her behavior is improper indeed. She writes with grace and ease and with a flashing wit. There is fragrance even in her smallest words. Her poems are attractive, but they are only improvisations which drop from her mouth spontaneously. Every one of them has some interesting point, and she is acquainted with ancient literature also, but she is not like a true artist who is filled with the genuine spirit of poetry. Yet I think even she cannot presume to pass judgment on the poems of others.

Lady Sei Shōnagon. A very proud person. She values herself highly, and scatters her Chinese writings all about. Yet should we study her closely, we should find that she is still imperfect. She tries to be exceptional, but naturally persons of that sort give offense. She is piling up trouble for her future. One who is too richly gifted, who indulges too much in emotion, even when she ought to be reserved, and cannot turn aside from anything she is interested in, in spite of herself will lose self-control. How can such a vain and reckless person end her days happily? . . .

Having no excellence within myself, I have passed my days without making any special impression on anyone. Especially the fact that I have no man who will look out for my future makes me comfortless. I do not wish to bury myself in dreariness. Is it because of my worldly mind that I feel lonely? On moonlit nights in autumn, when I am hopelessly sad, I often go out on the balcony and gaze dreamily at the moon. It makes me think of days gone by. People say that it is dangerous to look at the moon in solitude, but something impels me, and sitting a little withdrawn, I muse there. In the wind-cooled evening I play on the koto [a stringed instrument], though others may not care to hear it. I fear that my playing betrays the sorrow which becomes more intense, and I become disgusted with myself—so foolish and miserable am I. . . .

The Tale of Genji: Art of the Novel

MURASAKI SHIKIBU

One day Genji, going the round with a number of romances which he had promised to lend, came to Tamakatsura's room and found her, as usual, hardly able to lift her eyes from the book in front of her. "Really, you are incurable," he said, laughing. "I sometimes think that young ladies exist for no other purpose than to provide purveyors of the absurd and improbable with a market for their wares. I am sure that the book you are now so intent upon is full of the wildest nonsense. Yet knowing this all the time, you are completely captivated by its extravagances and follow them with the utmost excitement. . . . Now for a confession. I too have lately been studying these books and have, I must tell you, been amazed by the delight which they have given me. There is, it seems, an art of so fitting each part of the narrative into the next that, though all is mere invention, the reader is persuaded that such things might easily have happened and is as deeply moved as though they were actually going on around him. . . . Or again we may be persuaded by a writer's eloquence into accepting the crudest absurdities,

From *Sources of Japanese Tradition* by William Theodore de Bary, ed., © 1958 Columbia University Press. Reprinted with permission of the publisher.

our judgment being as it were dazzled by sheer splendor of language.

"I have lately sometimes stopped and listened to one of our young people reading out loud to her companions and have been amazed at the advances which this art of fiction is now making. How do you suppose that our new writers come by this talent? It used to be thought that the authors of successful romances were merely particularly untruthful people whose imaginations had been stimulated by constantly inventing plausible lies. But that is clearly unfair. . . ."

Genji continued: "So you see as a matter of fact I think far better of this art than I have led you to suppose. Even its practical value is immense. Without it what should we know of how people lived in the past, from the Age of the Gods down to the present day? For history books such as the *Chronicles of Japan* show us only one small corner of life; whereas these diaries and romances which I see piled around you contain, I am sure, the most minute information about all sorts of people's private affairs . . ." He smiled and went on: "But I have a theory of my own about what this art of the novel is, and how it came into being. To begin with, it does not simply consist in the author's telling a story about the adventures of some other person. On the contrary, it happens because the storyteller's own experience of men and things, whether for good or ill—not only what he has passed through himself, but even events which he has only witnessed or been told of—has moved him to an emotion so passionate that he can no longer keep it shut up in his heart. Again and again something in his own life or in that around him will seem to the writer so important that he cannot bear to let it pass into oblivion. There must never come a time, he feels, when men do not know about it. This my view of how this art arose. . . .

"The outward forms of this art will not of course be everywhere the same. At the court of China and in other foreign lands both the genius of the writers and their actual methods of composition are necessarily very different from ours; and even here in Japan the art of story-telling has in course of time undergone great changes. There will, too, always be a distinction between the lighter and the more serious forms of fiction. . . . Well, I have said enough to show that when at the beginning of our conversation I spoke of romances as though they were mere frivolous fabrications, I was only teasing you."

MEDIEVAL JAPAN (1185–1467)

Shōgun and Samurai

Once the will is resolved, one's spirit is strengthened. Even a peasant's will is hard to deny, but a samurai of resolute will can sway ten thousand men.

—Yoshida Shōin

From the beginning of the year to the end, day and night, morning and evening, in action and in repose, in speech and in silence, the warrior must keep death constantly before him and have ever in mind that the one death which he has to give, should not be suffered in vain.

—Yoshida Shōin

"I spurred my horse on, careless of death in the face of the foe. I braved the dangers of wind and wave, not thinking that my body might sink to the bottom of the sea, and be devoured by the monsters of the deep. My pillow was my harness, arms my trade."

These words from a twelfth century warrior recounted in The Tale of the Heike, *vividly recount the utter contempt for death that was held as a matter of personal honor among samurai. As the Heian period came to an end about 1160, the refined court elegance of the "Dwellers among the Clouds" gave way to a period of vicious blood-letting that matched military rivals like the Minamoto and Taira factions against one another. Japan was entering a feudal age that lasted from about 1185 to 1467, where the control of a civil aristocracy was replaced by the* bakufu *or "tent government" run by military leaders and their retainers.*

These retainers, called samurai ("those who serve"), had existed since the eighth century, but their full mystique and importance in Japanese history was not realized until after the twelfth century. Wealthier samurai, attached to their lord through vows and a personal code of honor, fought on horseback clad in helmet and flexible armor, while others served as foot soldiers and personal bodyguards. In many ways, the mounted samurai outwardly resembled the knights of medieval Europe, but except for their devotion to their overlords, Japanese samurai were motivated by other principles. European knighthood was based on an ideal of chivalry and religious fervor that had no counterpart among the Japanese. When a samurai warrior plunged into battle, he was not invoking the protection of God, but sought to strike terror in his enemies by shouting his own name, asserting his own prowess and the exploits of his illustrious ancestors.

The material symbol of this martial spirit was the warrior's primary weapon, his sword. Forged from many layers of hard and soft steel for strength and flexibility, the samurai honed his technique to fight with devastating efficiency and economy of movement. A skilled swordsman with a disciplined spirit and technique could quickly cut a foe to pieces on the battlefield.

The razor-sharp sword was not, however, only a weapon. It was the central object in an elaborate ritual of honor. For a samurai to be separated from his sword was to lose his honor. The warrior slept with his sword beside his pillow and when he died it was placed on his deathbed. Swords were thought to have miraculous powers and were handed down from father to son, or from warrior to warrior, covered with the glory of an illustrious past. The brutal war sagas of this age, recounted in The Tale of the Heike, *emphasize honor and sacrifice, the fall of the mighty from power, and the basic Buddhist idea that life is short and full of sorrow and suffering.*

But those war tales of samurai in service to their lords were more than just popular entertainment. They had profound influence in shaping the modern Japanese character. By idealizing the virtues of personal loyalty, self-sacrifice, and contempt for death in deference to the larger needs of the shōgun or emperor as the embodiment of the Japanese nation, samurai traditions inspired soldiers and civilians of the twentieth century, who were willing to sacrifice themselves in kamikaze *suicide attacks on U.S. war ships or by cutting themselves open rather than endure the dishonor of surrender.*

The following selections highlight the values of medieval Japan that continue to influence Japanese culture. The first is from The Tale of the Heike, *recounting the wars between Minamoto Yoritomo (1147–1199) and his rivals that established him as Japan's first shōgun or supreme military leader, the founder of the Kamakura shogunate (1192–1336). In this story, Yoshinaka, a leader of Minamoto's forces, together with his friend and retainer, Kanehira, are killed by rivals of the same faction who are jealous of Yoshinaka's success. Note carefully the role played in the battle by the woman, Tomoe. Many of the heroes in these war tales of the twelfth century were women. They had not yet been reduced to the humble submissiveness that would characterize their role in Japanese society during later centuries. The women demonstrated the same values of loyalty and bravery that were expected of the men.*

The Tale of the Heike:

"Cut off My Head and Show It to Yoritomo!"

Yoshinaka had brought with him from Shinano Province two beautiful women, Tomoe and Yamabuki. Of the two, Yamabuki had become ill and had remained in the capital.

Tomoe was indescribably beautiful; the fairness of her face and the richness of her hair were startling to behold. Even so, she was a fearless rider and a woman skilled with the bow. Once her sword was drawn, even the gods and devils feared to fight against her. Indeed, she was a match for a thousand. Thus it was that whenever a war broke out, she armed herself with a strong bow and a great sword, and took a position among the leaders. In many battles she had won matchless fame. This time too she had

From *The Tale of the Heike* translated by Hiroshi Kitagawa and Bruce T. Tsuchiida, © 1975 Columbia University Press. Reprinted with permission of the publisher.

survived, though all her companions had been killed or wounded. . . . Tomoe was [a survivor].

Yoshinaka called her to his side and said: "You are a woman—leave now for wherever you like, quickly! As for me, I shall fight to the death. If I am wounded, I will kill myself. How ashamed I would be if people said that Yoshinaka was accompanied by a woman in his last fight."

Tomoe would not stir. After repeated pleas, however, she was finally convinced to leave.

"I wish I could find a strong opponent!" she said to herself. "Then I would show my master once more how well I can fight." She drew her horse aside to wait for the right opportunity.

Shortly thereafter, Moroshige of Musashi, a warrior renowned for his great strength, appeared at the head of thirty horsemen. Galloping alongside Moroshige, Tomoe grappled with him, pulled him against the pommel of her saddle, and giving him no chance to resist, cut off his head. The fight concluded, she threw off her armor and fled to the eastern provinces.

Among the remaining retainers of Yoshinaka, Tezuka no Tarō was killed, and his uncle took flight, leaving only Kanehira. When Yoshinaka found himself alone with Kanehira, he sighed: "My armor has never weighed upon me before, but today, it is heavy."

"You do not look tired at all, my lord," replied Kanehira, "and your horse is still fresh. What makes it feel so heavy? If it is because you are discouraged at having none of your retainers but me, please remember that I, Kanehira, am a match for a thousand. Since I still have seven or eight arrows left in my quiver, let me hold back the foe while you withdraw to the Awazu pine wood. Now I pray you to put a peaceful end to yourself."

No sooner had he spoken to his master than another band of soldiers confronted them. "Please go to the pine wood, my lord," said Kanehira again. "Let me fight here to keep them away from you."

"I would have died in the capital!" replied Yoshinaka. "I have come this far with no other hope but to share your fate. How can I die apart from you? Let us fight until we die together!"

With these words, Yoshinaka tried to ride neck and neck with Kanehira. Now Kanehira alighted from his horse, seized the bridle of his master's mount, and pleaded in tears: "Whatever fame a warrior may win, a worthless death is a lasting shame for him. You are worn out, my lord. Your horse is also exhausted. If you are surrounded by the enemy and slain at the hand of a low, worthless retainer of some unknown warrior, it will be a great shame for you and me in the days to come. How disgraceful it would be if such a nameless fellow could declare, 'I cut off the head of Yoshinaka, renowned throughout the land of Japan!'"

Yoshinaka finally gave in to Kanehira's entreaty and rode off toward the pine wood of Awazu. Kanehira, riding alone, charged into the band of some fifty horsemen. Rising high in his stirrups, he cried out in a thunderous voice: "You have often heard of me. Now take a good look. I am Imai no Shirō Kanehira, aged thirty-three, a foster brother of Lord Yoshinaka. As I am a valiant warrior among the men of Lord Yoshinaka, your master, Yoritomo, at Kamakura must know my name well. Take my head and show it to him!"

Kanehira had hardly uttered these words when he let fly his remaining eight arrows one after another without pause. Eight men were shot from their horses, either dead or wounded. He then drew his sword and brandished it as he galloped to and fro. None of his opponents could challenge him face to face, though they cried out: "Shoot him down! Shoot him down!"

Sanemori's soldiers let fly a shower of arrows at Kanehira, but his armor was so strong that none of them pierced it. Unless they aimed at the joints of his armor, he could never be wounded.

Yoshinaka was now all alone in the pine wood of Awazu. It was the twenty-first day of the first month. Dusk had begun to fall. Thin ice covered the rice fields and the marsh, so that it was hard to distinguish one from the other. Thus is was that Yoshinaka had not gone far before his horse plunged deep into the muddy slime. Whipping and spurring no longer did any good. The horse could not stir. Despite his predicament, he still thought of Kanehira. As Yoshinaka was turning around to see how he faired, Tamehisa, catching up with him, shot an arrow under his helmet. It was a mortal wound. Yoshinaka pitched forward onto the neck of his horse. Then two of Tamehisa's retainers fell upon Yoshinaka and struck off his head. Raising it high on the point of his sword, Tamehisa shouted: "Kiso no Yoshinaka, renowned throughout the land of Japan as a valiant warrior, has been killed by Miura no Ishida Jirō Tamehisa!"

Kanehira was fighting desperately as these words rang in his ears. At that moment he ceased fighting and cried out: "For whom do I have to fight now? You, warriors of the east, see how the mightiest warrior in Japan puts an end to himself!" Trusting the point of his sword into his mouth, he flung himself headlong from his horse so that the sword pierced his head.

Yoshinaka and Kanehira died valiant deaths at Awazu. Could there have been a more heroic battle?

The Training of a Samurai

KUMAZAWA BANZAN

Kumazawa Banzan (1619-1691) was a low-ranking samurai with the status of rōnin, that is, having no allegiance to a particular lord. In his youth, Kumazawa pursued a rigorous training program in the military arts and broadened his perspective under various masters by studying the Chinese classics. He was concerned that years of peace and indolence during the Tokugawa era in the seventeenth century had had a debilitating effect on the samurai class. A reformer, he sought in this passage from his memoirs to inspire a rededication to the discipline that had made the samurai feared warriors of legend.

When I was about sixteen I had a tendency toward corpulence. I had noticed a lack of agility in other fleshy persons and thought a heavy man would not make a first class samurai. So I tried every means to keep myself agile and lean. I slept with my belt drawn tight and stopped eating rice. I took no wine and abstained from sexual intercourse for the next ten years. While on duty at Edo, there were no hills or fields at hand where I could hunt and climb, so I exercised with spear and sword. When I was on the night watch at my master's residence in Edo, I kept a wooden sword and a pair of straw sandals in my bamboo hamper, and with these I used to put myself through military drill in the darkened court after every one was asleep. I also practiced running about over the roofs of the out-buildings far removed from the sleeping rooms. This I did so as to be able to handle myself nimbly if a fire should break out. There were a few who noticed me at these exercises and they were reported to have said that I was probably possessed by a hobgoblin. This was before I was twenty years old. After that I hardened myself by going into the fields on hot summer days and shooting skylarks with a gun, since I did not own a falcon for hawking. In the winter months I often spent several days in the mountains taking no night clothes or bed quilt with me, and wearing only a lined jacket of cotton over a thin cotton shirt . . . . I stayed overnight in any house I came across in my ramble. In such a way I disciplined myself until I was thirty-seven or -eight years old and avoided becoming fleshy. I was fully aware of my want of talent and believed I could never hope to be of any great service to my country, so I was all the more resolved to do my best as a common samurai.

The Way of the Samurai

YAMAGA SOKŌ

Yamaga Sokō (1622-1685) was a celebrated figure in Japanese history who was, along with Kumazawa Banzan and Yui Shōsetsu, one of the "three great rōnin" of the Tokugawa period. He was also concerned with the inactivity of the warrior class under Tokugawa rule in the seventeenth century and believed that they had a special status and role to perform. To Yamaga, the samurai represented the ideal of balance and commitment so important to enhancing the stature of Japan. A life of austerity, temperance, self-discipline, and readiness to meet death were bound into a creed known as bushidō, the "Way of the Warrior."

The master once said: The generation of all men and of all things in the universe is accomplished by means of the marvelous interaction of the two forces [yin and yang]. Man is the most highly endowed of all creatures, and all things culminate in man. Generation after generation, men have taken their livelihood from tilling the soil, or devised and manufactured tools, or produced profit from mutual trade, so that peoples' needs were satisfied. Thus the occupations of farmer, artisan, and merchant necessarily grew up as complementary to one another. However the samurai eats food without growing it, uses utensils without manufacturing them, and profits without buying or selling. What is the justification for this?... The samurai is one who does not cultivate, does not manufacture, and does not engage in trade, but it cannot be that he has no function at all as a samurai. He who satisfied his needs without performing any function at all would more properly be called an idler. Therefore, one must devote all one's mind to the detailed examination of one's calling .... One must first establish the basic principle of the samurai.

The business of the samurai consists in reflecting on his own station in life, in discharging loyal service to his master if he has one, in deepening his fidelity in associations with friends, and, with due consideration of his own position, in devoting himself to duty above all. However, in one's own life, one becomes unavoidably involved in obligations between father and child, older and younger brothers, and husband and wife. Though these are also the fundamental moral obligations of everyone in the land, the farmers, artisans, and merchants have no leisure from their occupations, and so they cannot constantly act in accordance with them and fully exemplify the Way. The samurai dispenses with the business of the farmer, artisan, and merchant and confines himself to practicing this Way; should there be someone in the three classes of common people who transgresses against these moral principles, the samurai summarily punishes him and thus upholds proper moral principles in the land. It would not do for the samurai to know the martial and civil virtues without manifesting them. Since this is the case, outwardly he stands in physical readiness for any call to service and inwardly he strives to fulfill the Way of the lord and subject, friend and friend, father and son, older and younger brothers, and husband and wife. Within his heart he keeps to the ways of peace, but without he keeps his weapons ready for use. The three classes of the common people make him their teacher and respect him. By following his teachings, they are enabled to understand what is fundamental and what is secondary.

Herein lies the Way of the samurai, the means by which he earns his clothing, food, and shelter; and by which his heart is put at ease, and he is enabled to pay back at length his obligation to his lord and the kindness of his parents. . . .This then is the samurai's calling. The man who takes or seeks the pay of a samurai and is covetous of salary without in the slightest degree comprehending his function must feel shame in his heart. Therefore I say that that which the samurai should take as his fundamental aim is to know his own function.

Zen Buddhism and the Arts of Medieval Japan

Buddhism as a religious movement spread during the sixth century B.C.E. from its origins in northern India throughout Asia. Perhaps the most contemplative of the world's religions, the goal of Buddhism is for all humans to become enlightened and to realize, through meditation and compassion for all living things, spiritual joy and release from the constancy of birth and rebirth.

Japanese civilization encountered Buddhism through its contacts with China in the sixth, seventh, and eighth centuries C.E. Soon after, the Japanese adapted several Chinese sects to their own culture, among them Tendai and Shingon during the ninth and tenth centuries, and later Amida ("Pure Land") in the twelfth and thirteenth centuries. Zen doctrines also originated in China (where they were known as Chan) and made their way into the monasteries of Japan. The two most influential individuals in transplanting Zen doctrines from Song China to Japan were Eisai (1141–1215) and Dōgen (1200–1253).

Zen Buddhism seeks enlightenment from within. It teaches that the historical Buddha was not some austere god, but a man who attained enlightenment through his own disciplined efforts. Each person can become enlightened through a regimen of meditation and physical labor. Self-understanding and self-reliance are the keynotes of Zen.

In many ways, Zen is a paradoxical religion. Zen monks are well educated, yet they emphasize a pureness of mind, almost a return to ignorance, and a reliance on natural intuition as the most essential requirements of knowing. The pursuit of the "original mind," free from cluttered detail that dulls the senses and clouds judgment, is the ideal—simple, natural, and intuitive. Zen monks emphasize compassion, yet at the same time are intolerant of words and sutras that imprison the soul with their mindless repetition. Words mean nothing—it is the spiritual voyage of the centered individual that is crucial to enlightenment.

The absorption and development of Zen Buddhism in Japan remains visible in every branch of its culture, especially in the arts. The freedom of mind gained through meditation is transferred by the Zen artist to the moment. The brush of the calligrapher acts merely as an extension of the soul, unencumbered by the mind, for the intellect is controlled, subdued. The beauty of Zen painting, the "disciplined freedom" of an austere rock garden, and the dramatic opportunities of the Nō play—all reflect the spirit of Zen Buddhism as the following selections testify.

"Great Is Mind"

EISAI

Great is Mind. Heaven's height is immeasurable, but Mind goes beyond heaven; the earth's depth is also unfathomable, but Mind reaches below the earth. The light of the sun and moon cannot be outdistanced, yet Mind passes beyond the light of sun and moon. The macrocosm is limitless, yet Mind travels outside the macrocosm. How great is Space! How great the Primal Energy! Still Mind encompasses Space and generates the Primal Energy. Because of it heaven covers and earth upbears. Because of it the sun and moon move on, the four seasons pass in succession, and all things are generated. Great indeed is Mind! Of necessity we give such a name to it, yet there are many others: the Highest Vehicle, the First Principle, the Truth of Inner Wisdom, the One Reality, the Peerless Bodhi, the way to Enlightenment. . . .

As in India, so in China this teaching has attracted followers and disciples in great numbers.

It propagates the Truth as the ancient Buddha did, with the robe of authentic transmission passing from one man to the next. In the matter of religious discipline, it practices the genuine method of the sages of old. Thus the Truth it teaches, both in substance and appearance, perfects the relationship of master and disciple. In its rules of action and discipline, there is no confusion of right and wrong. . . . Outwardly it favors discipline over doctrine, inwardly it brings the Highest Inner Wisdom. This is what the Zen sect stands for. . . .

There are, however, some persons who malign this teaching, calling it "the Zen of dark enlightenment." There are also those who question it on the ground that it is "utter Nihilism." Still others consider it ill-suited to these degenerate times, or say that it is not what our country needs. Or else they may express contempt for our mendicant ways and our alleged lace of documentary support for our views. Finally there are some who have such a low opinion of their own capabilities that they look upon Zen as far beyond their power to promote. Out of their zeal for upholding the Law, these people are actually suppressing the treasures of the Law.

From *Sources of Japanese Tradition* by William Theodore de Bary, ed., © 1958 Columbia University Press. Reprinted with permission of the publisher.

They denounce us without knowing what we have in mind. Not only are they thus blocking the way to the gate of Zen, but they are also ruining the work of our great forebear at Mt. Hiei [Saichō]. Alas, alas, how sad, how distressing!

The Zen Link: Body and Mind
DŌGEN

Is the Way [of liberation] achieved through the mind or through the body? The doctrinal schools speak of the identity of mind and body, and so when they speak of attaining the Way through the body, they explain it in terms of this identity. Nevertheless this leaves one uncertain as to what "attainment by the body" truly means. From the point of view of our school, attainment of the Way is indeed achieved through the body as well as the mind. So long as one hopes to grasp the Truth only through the mind, one will not attain it even in a thousand existences or in eons of time. Only when one lets go of the mind and ceases to seek an intellectual apprehension of the Truth is liberation attainable. Enlightenment of the mind through the sense of sight and comprehension of the Truth through the sense of hearing are truly bodily attainments. To do away with mental deliberation and cognition, and simply to go on sitting, is the method by which the Way is made an intimate part of our lives. Thus attainment of the Way becomes truly attainment through the body. That is why I put exclusive emphasis upon sitting.

From *Sources of Japanese Tradition* by William Theodore de Bary, ed., © 1958 Columbia University Press. Reprinted with permission of the publisher.

Sage Kūya Invoking the Amidoo Buddha. Painted wood. (*Rokuharamitsu-ji, Kyoto*).

Zen and the Dramatic Arts
SEAMI

As the preceding selections indicate, the relationship between the body and mind is a crucial component of Zen Buddhism. The Zen artist is so skilled that he does not "think" technique, but simply paints. This ideal can be applied to other areas as well. The art of acting consists of proceeding intuitively from

From *Sources of Japanese Tradition* by William Theodore de Bary, ed., © 1958 Columbia University Press. Reprinted with permission of the publisher.

a state of being, of releasing the enlightened mind. Zen became popular in Japan partly because it was not exclusive and could be applied to almost any aspect of life with a refreshing perspective by any individual. Archery, flower arrangement, gardening, martial arts—Zen grants them all a natural dignity.

The first selection is by Seami (1363–1443), who authored several Nō plays. Following this is a piece by Takuan Sōhō (1573–1645), a Zen master who lived later during the "Warring States" period when Japan was once again besieged by domestic chaos and warfare. What do these two selections have in common?

Sometimes spectators of the Nō say, "The moments of 'no action' are the most enjoyable." This is an art which the actor keeps secret. Dancing and singing, movements, and the different types of miming are all acts performed by the body. Moments of "no-action" occur in between. When we examine why such moments without actions are enjoyable, we find that it is due to the underlying spiritual strength of the actor which unremittingly holds the attention. He does not relax the tension when the dancing or singing come to an end or at intervals between the dialogue and the different types of miming, but maintains an unwavering inner strength. This feeling of inner strength will faintly reveal itself and bring enjoyment. However, it is undesirable for the actor to permit this inner strength to become obvious to the audience. If it is obvious, it becomes an act, and is no longer "no-action." The actions before and after an interval of "no-action" must be linked by entering the state of mindlessness in which one conceals even from oneself one's intent. This, then, is the faculty of moving audiences, by linking all the artistic powers with one mind.

> Life and death, past and present—
> Marionettes on a toy stage.
> When the strings are broken,
> Behold the broken pieces.

This is a metaphor describing human life as it transmigrates between life and death. Marionettes on a stage appear to move in various ways, but in fact it is not they who really move—they are manipulated by strings. When these strings are broken, the marionettes fall and are dashed to pieces. In the art of the Nō too, the different sorts of miming are artificial things. What holds the parts together is the mind. This mind must not be disclosed to the audience. If it is seen, it is just as if a marionette's strings were visible. The mind must be made the strings which hold together all the powers of the arts. If this is done, the actor's talent will endure. This resolution must not be confined to the times when the actor is appearing on the stage. Day or night, wherever he may be, whatever he may be doing, he should not forget this resolution, but should make it his constant guide, uniting all his powers. If he unremittingly works at this his talent will steadily grow. This article is the most secret of the secret teachings.

Zen and the Samurai
TAKUAN SŌHŌ

Where should a swordsman fix his mind? If he puts his mind on the physical movement of his opponent, it will be seized by the movement; if he places it on the sword of his opponent, it will be arrested by the sword; if he focuses his mind on the thought of striking his opponent, it will be carried away by the very thought; if the mind stays on his own sword, it will be captured by his sword; if he centers it on the thought of not being killed by his opponent, his mind will be overtaken by this very thought; if he keeps his mind firmly on his own or on his opponent's posture, likewise, it will be blocked by them. Thus the mind should not be fixed anywhere.

CHRONOLOGY: The Development of Classical and Medieval Japan (600–1467)

300 B.C.E.–300 C.E.	Yayoi culture. Regional states with a ruling class of aristocratic warriors. Development of regional tribal confederations by a shaman-queen named Pimiko.
300–680	Tomb culture and the Yamato state with regional rulers and incessant power struggles.
513	Confucianism enters Japan.
538	First image of Buddha arrives in Japan
604	Prince Shotoku writes a seventeen-article constitution. Begins sending regular embassies to China in 607.
672	Temmu Tenno usurps the throne and styles himself "Heavenly Emperor" of Japan. Uses Chinese administrative systems to consolidate power.
710–794	Nara period. Capital established at Nara with architectural influence of China.
712–720	*Records of Ancient Matters* and *Records of Japan* compiled, which talk of mythological origins of the early history of Japan.
785	Saichō founds a temple on Mount Hiei. Returns from China in 804 with Buddhist teachings of the Tendai sect.
794–1185	Heian period begins with establishment of the capital at Heian-kyō (Kyoto). Rule of Fujiwara nobles (856–1086). Go-Sanjō begins to curb the power of the Fujiwara clan at court and his son, Shirakawa, establishes the "cloistered government" of retired emperors (1086–1160). Rule of the Taira military house (1160–1180). Classic age of Japanese prose with the influence of Murasaki Shikibu (*The Tale of Genji*) and Sei Shonagon (*The Pillow Book*). Buddhism imported and modified by Saicho (Tendai sect) and Kukai (Shingon sect).
1185	Victory of Minamoto Yoritomo and the establishment of the military "tent government" system (*bakufu*) at Kamakura, near Tokyo. Minamoto becomes first shōgun (1192).
1191	Eisai returns from China bringing tea. Founds Rinzai branch of Zen Buddhism.
1200—1270	Influence of Buddhist religious sect leaders Hōnen and Shinran (Amida), Nichiren (Sun Lotus), and Eisai and Dōgen (Zen). Nō plays popular during this period.

1274 and 1281	Unsuccessful invasions by Mongols from China as *kamikaze* or "divine winds" sink a portion of the Mongol fleet in 1281.
1336–1467	Ashikaga *bakufu* begun by Ashikaga Takauji. Regional lords (*daimyo*) contend for power.
1467–1600	"Warring States Period." Dispute over succession results in civil war and destruction of Ashikaga shogunate. Inaugurates a long period of civil strife where "the strong eat and the weak become the meat." Replacement of aristocratic mounted warrior with the foot soldier as the backbone of the military.
1600–1868	Tokugawa Era. Japan slowly becomes pacified and unified under the direction of Toyotomi Hideyoshi and his successors. Japan closes itself to the world, reengineers its society, and its political and agrarian systems, allowing for vigorous growth during the seventeenth and eighteenth centuries.

STUDY QUESTIONS

1. How would you define Shintoism? In the selection on the "Birth of Japan," why is the courtship between the male and female deities so formal? What does this selection tell you about the relationship between men and women in early Japan? What role does shame play in the creation? Compare this creation account with those of African civilization on pp. 34–35, Maya civilization on pp. 240–241 and the Hebrews on pp. 32–33. Are there any similarities?

2. The early contact between Japan and China was most important to the development of Japanese culture. How did the Chinese emperor view the delegation of Japanese envoys to the Imperial court in 630? What did the Japanese want to learn and how, according to these Chinese records, was the Japanese king presumptuous? What do we learn about the administration of justice in early Japan? Compare the tenor of this message to the Buddhist monk Ennin's request for credentials to travel in China. How important was respect and decorum to the Chinese?

3. What is the most important message in the constitution of Prince Shōtoku? Why is this message of greatest importance in the organization of society? In what ways does this constitution reflect the influence of Chinese Confucian and Daoist thought?

4. Among the poems in the collections entitled *The Ten Thousand Leaves* and *Kokinshū*, which are your favorites and why? How are the poems structured? What makes them so memorable?

5. How do the observations of Sei Shōnagon and Murasaki Shikibu about life and love reflect the code of *miyabi*, or refinement, that was so prominent at the Heian court? What was important to these ladies? In what ways was this a competitive existence? What does the fact that many of the most prominent writers of the period were women say about Japanese society?

6. How would you define the position of shogun? Who were the samurai and what were the values that defined their existence? According to Yamaga Sokō, what was the Way of the Samurai (*bushidō*)? In what ways was a samurai warrior bound by spiritual more than contractual obligations to his lord?

7. In the excerpt from *The Tale of the Heike*, how did Yoshinaka and Kanehira, demonstrate the ideals of the samurai? Compare the actions of the woman, Tomoe. Why was Yoshinaka so insistent that he not be accompanied by a woman in his last battle? Was she not a worthy warrior? Note how important the concept of shame was to both men and women in Japanese society.

8. According to the Zen masters, Eisai and Dōgen, what is the relationship between the body and the mind? How did Eisai define the concept of "mind"? Is this the same idea that Aristotle referred to as the "unmoved mover" and the Judeo-Christian tradition calls "God"? According to Seami, how important is "no-action" to the actor? How does an actor become truly effective? How does Zen apply to the samurai warrior? How will he survive combat with his opponent?

Part IV

TRANSITIONS TO THE MODERN WORLD (1450-1650)

10

The Age of the Renaissance and Reformation

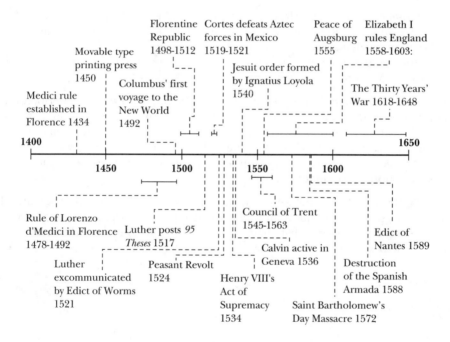

Florentine Republic 1498-1512

Cortes defeats Aztec forces in Mexico 1519-1521

Peace of Augsburg 1555

Elizabeth I rules England 1558-1603:

Movable type printing press 1450

Jesuit order formed by Ignatius Loyola 1540

Medici rule established in Florence 1434

Columbus' first voyage to the New World 1492

The Thirty Years' War 1618-1648

1400

1650

1450   1500   1550   1600

Rule of Lorenzo d'Medici in Florence 1478-1492

Luther posts *95 Theses* 1517

Council of Trent 1545-1563

Edict of Nantes 1589

Luther excommunicated by Edict of Worms 1521

Peasant Revolt 1524

Calvin active in Geneva 1536

Destruction of the Spanish Armada 1588

Henry VIII's Act of Supremacy 1534

Saint Bartholomew's Day Massacre 1572

CHAPTER THEMES

- *Systems of Government:* How did the Medici family control Florence? Was their influence based on their "power" or on their "authority"? How could this be compared to the rule of the Roman emperor Augustus?

- **Church/State Relationships:** Could the Renaissance papacy be described as primarily secular and not spiritual? Had the Christian church during the Renaissance become essentially another secular institution in order to compete with European monarchs? Were the Renaissance popes secular rulers?

- **Beliefs and Spirituality:** What were the fundamental tenets of humanism, and why were they considered radical, especially to the church? Why did the Reformation occur? What led Martin Luther to challenge the belief system of the church? To what extent can faith and personal commitment to a religion change the course of history? Is faith a more powerful force than any army?

- **Revolution:** Was the Protestant Reformation a spiritual revolution, which consequently altered the political and economic institutions of Europe? Or was it a spiritually based reform movement that sought limited change in religious matters? Was Luther a revolutionary who was just as influential as Robespierre, Napoleon, or Lenin?

- **Church/State Relationships:** How did secular rulers benefit from the division of Christianity during the Reformation era? Which monarchs became "defenders of the church" and which aided the Reformers? Why? How did King Henry VIII of England solve the competition between church and state? Were his actions based on a sincere spirituality or on pure political expediency?

- **Historical Change and Transition:** The Renaissance has been seen as a period of transition between the "static" Middle Ages and the "vibrant" modern world. Is this a reasonable interpretation? How was progress measured during the Renaissance, and what drawbacks were evident? What debt does our contemporary world owe to the Renaissance? To what extent was the printing press more essential to the success of this transitional movement than any other factor?

- **The Big Picture:** Why was the Renaissance period so creative? Is artistic and cultural creativity best served by political and religious stability, or is the progress of civilization best served by the energy that chaos promotes? Was the Protestant Reformation ultimately the best thing that could have happened to the Christian church in the West?

SECTION I: THE RENAISSANCE MOVEMENT

Learning is the only thing the mind never exhausts, never fears and never regrets.

—*Leonardo da Vinci*

What a piece of work is man, how noble in reason, how infinite in faculty; in form and moving, how express and admirable, in action how like an angel, in apprehension how like a god: a beauty of the world, the paragon of animals!

—*William Shakespeare, Hamlet*

Apart from man, no being wonders at his own existence.

—Arthur Schopenhauer

Man is the measure of all things.

—Protagoras

Man—a creature made at the end of the week's work when God was tired.

—Mark Twain

The Late Middle Ages, from about 1300 to 1450, was a time of great struggle and calamity in western Europe. The fabric of medieval civilization was gradually torn apart by a plentitude of simultaneous catastrophes that oppressed the spirit and augured the decline of an age of faith. The great political debacle of the period was the Hundred Years' War, which began in 1337 over English claims to the French throne and did not end until 1453. Though battles were fought only intermittently during this period, the war sapped the economic resources of the developing nation-states and directed the energy of Europe onto a path of self-destruction. No longer were Europeans united in some foreign crusade against the enemies of God; they now tore each other apart in rather mindless confusion. But wars are made by people, and at least they have some foreknowledge of the destruction that inevitably ensues. No one, however, could have predicted the devastating effects of the Black Death. From 1347 to 1351, it raged throughout Europe, destroying one-third to one-half of the population. Apart from the physical agony of the disease, the mental terror of an unseen, unknown enemy was enough to divert the energy of life into a dance of death. No one was exempt from the potential of its destruction. God seemed to forsake his flock, and the church was hard-pressed to explain or prevail against the "grim reaper." But the church's credibility as the instrument of God had already been called into question by corruption and disunity. In 1309, the papacy was transferred from its traditional seat in Rome to the city of Avignon, France. This "Baby-lonian Captivity," as it was called, deprived the papacy of authority and contributed to its loss of respect as prelates became known for their licentiousness and corruption. In 1378, the papacy was transferred back to Rome. But political maneuvering resulted in a "schism" that split Western Christianity into two camps, led by two popes, one in Rome and one in Avignon. This spiritual calamity was finally resolved by a series of councils of the church that were empowered to pass judgments on the papacy itself. In effect, they declared their superiority over the pope in spiritual affairs. The reformist zeal of these councils, however, did little but underscore the need for widespread change in the church. The papacy continued to degenerate: Pope Alexander VI fathered several children and Pope Julius II, bedecked in full armor, led papal armies against the French.

These political, social, and spiritual calamities sapped the energy of medieval civilization and destroyed the spiritual foundation that had inspired people to build the cathedrals and to resist the barbarism that came close on the heels of Rome's decline. The focus of Western civilization was shifting from a dutiful devotion to God to an emphasis on the worth and importance of humanity. This transformation was centered, at the outset, in Italy and began during the calamitous fourteenth century. By 1450, the Renaissance was in full bloom.

The term *renaissance* means "rebirth"; it was coined by scholars in the fifteenth and sixteenth centuries who felt a new inspiration. They viewed the medieval world as one of mindless chanting and uncreative introspection. According to Renaissance man, the preceding centuries were "Middle Ages" between the brilliance of the ancient Greeks and Romans and the reflection of that light in the culture of fifteenth-century Italy. The Middle Ages became synonymous with the "Dark Ages." For the scholars of the Renaissance, the hope of Western civilization lay in a cultivation of the classical works of antiquity. The masters of thought and erudition were figures like Cicero, Aristotle, Plato, Virgil, and Thucydides. They became models and authorities for argument, insight, and eloquence. No longer was it enough to be able to read Cicero: One was now expected to imitate his Latin style. A cult of the classics developed as people admired the ancient monuments of Roman civilization and sought copies of the ancient texts. The Renaissance movement was primarily a scholarly pursuit of the ideals and values of classical civilization.

Chief among those values was the emphasis on human worth; this led to the movement known as humanism. The Renaissance emphasized the most positive aspects of humanity. Rational thought and creative instinct were prized. Human beings were composed of two natures: the brutal force of the animal and some of the divine qualities of God. Most important, they had the free will to pursue their own path. The course of life was determined not by God, but by ambition, talent, or deceit. The glory of humanity was portrayed in the poetry and astoundingly rich art of the period. The names of Leonardo, Raphael, and Michelangelo evoke mastery of technique and perfection of style. But perhaps the most transparent assessment of reality was made by Niccolò Machiavelli. For him, power and control were the watchwords of existence. This was humanity, stripped of its embellishment and conscious of the political realities of life. The *Prince* was Machiavelli's manual on practical survival in a chaotic age. Glory could also be attained by strong, competent rule.

Machiavelli made people aware of the realities of power politics, and in doing so he was fulfilling a need in society. For Italy was not a united kingdom, but rather a disjointed chaotic grouping of city-states, led variously by despots, oligarches, and republicans. It is a curious paradox that societal chaos seems to breed creativity. Michelangelo, for example, painted the Sistine Chapel while Rome was in peril of being taken by French armies. The relationship between chaos and creativity is a question worth pursuing, for it precedes discussion of a wider issue: the progress of civilization. Why was the Renaissance such a creative period, artistically, technologically, and politically? Is creativity truly an ingredient of progress, or is the progress of civilization best served by solid administration and continuity, as we found during the height of the Roman Empire? The first section of this chapter will investigate some of the ideas and attitudes that influenced European Renaissance society and beyond.

The Humanist Movement

Oration on the Dignity of Man (1486)

PICO DELLA MIRANDOLA

Perhaps the supreme statement of the Renaissance idolization of man is an extended essay by Pico della Mirandola, a linguist and philosopher who lived from 1463 to 1494. Note Pico's conception of man's relationship to God in this excerpt from the Oration on the Dignity of Man.

At last it seems to me I have come to understand why man is the most fortunate of creatures and consequently worthy of all admiration and what precisely is that rank which is his lot in the universal chain of Being—a rank to be envied not only by brutes but even by the stars and by minds beyond this world. It is a matter past faith and a wondrous one. Why should it not be? For it is on this very account that man is rightly called and judged a great miracle and wonderful creature indeed. . . .God the Father, the supreme Architect, had already built this cosmic home we behold, the most sacred temple of His godhead, by the laws of His mysterious wisdom. The region above the heavens He had adorned with Intelligences, the heavenly spheres He had quickened with eternal souls, and the . . . filthy parts of the lower world He had filled with a multitude of animals of every kind. But, when the work was finished, the Craftsman kept wishing that there were someone to ponder the plan of so great a work, to love its beauty, and to wonder at its vastness. Therefore, when everything was done . . . He finally took thought concerning the creation of man. But there was not among His archetypes that from which He could fashion a new offspring, nor was there in His treasure houses anything which He might bestow on His new son as an inheritance, nor was there in the seats of all the world a place where the latter might sit to contemplate the universe. All was now complete; all things had been assigned to the highest, the middle, and the lowest orders. But in its final creation it was not the part of the Father's power to fail as though exhausted. It was not the part of His wisdom to waver in a needful matter through poverty of counsel. It was not the part of His kindly love that he who was to praise God's divine generosity in regard to others should be compelled to condemn it in regard to himself. At last the best of artisans ordained that the creature to whom He had been able to give nothing proper to himself should have joint possession of what ever had been peculiar to each of the different kinds of being. He therefore took man as a creature of indeterminate nature and, assigning him a place in the middle of the world, addressed him thus: . . . "The nature of all other beings is limited and constrained within the bounds of laws prescribed by Us. Thou, constrained by no limits, in accordance with thine own free will, in whose hand We have placed thee, shalt ordain for thyself the limits of thy nature. We have set thee at the world's center that thou mayest from thence more easily observe whatever is in the world. We have made thee neither of heaven nor of earth, neither mortal nor immortal, so that with freedom of choice and with honor, as though the maker and molder of thyself, thou mayest fashion thyself in whatever shape thou shalt prefer. Thou shalt have the power to degenerate into the lower forms of life, which are brutish. Thou shalt have the power, out of thy soul's judgment, to be reborn into the higher forms, which are divine." O supreme generosity of God the Father, O highest and most marvelous felicity of man! To him it is granted to have whatever he chooses, to be whatever he wills.

The Soul of Man (1474)

MARSILIO FICINO

The ideas of the Greek philosopher Plato were revived during the Renaissance by Neoplatonists who applied his theory on transmigration of the soul to Christian concepts of resurrection. The leading exponent of this philosophy was Marsilio Ficino. Some of his ideas on God and man follow.

Burroughs, Josephine, trans. "Marsilio Ficino's Platonic Theology," *Journal of the History of Ideas* 5 (1944), 234–236. © Journal of the History of Ideas, Inc. Reprinted by permission of the Johns Hopkins University Press.

Man is really the vicar of God, since he inhabits and cultivates all elements and is present on earth without being absent from the ether. He uses not only the elements, but also all the animals which belong to the elements, the animals of the earth, of the water, and of the air, for food, convenience, and pleasure, and the higher celestial beings for knowledge and the miracles of magic. Not only does he make use of the animals, he also rules them. It is true, with the weapons received from nature some animals may at times attack man or escape his control. But with the weapons he has invented himself man avoids the attacks of wild animals, puts them to flight and tames them. Who has ever seen any human beings kept under the control of animals, in such a way as we see everywhere herds of both wild and domesticated animals obeying men throughout their lives? Man not only rules the animals by force, he also governs, keeps and teaches them. Universal providence belongs to God, who is the universal cause. Hence man who provides generally for all things, both living and lifeless, is a kind of god. Certainly he is the god of the animals, for he makes use of them all, and instructs many of them. It is also obvious that he is the god of the elements for he inhabits and cultivates all of them. Finally, he is the god of all materials for he handles, changes and shapes all of them. He who governs the body in so many and so impor-

tant ways, and is the vicar of the immortal God, he is no doubt immortal. . . .

Individual animals are hardly capable of taking care of themselves or their young. Man alone abounds in such a perfection that he first rules himself, something that no animals do, and thereafter rules the family, administers the state, governs nations and rules the whole world. . . .

We have shown that our soul in all its acts is trying with all its power to attain the first gift of God, that is, the possession of all truth and all goodness. Does it also seek His second attribute? Does not the soul try to become everything just as God is everything? It does in a wonderful way; for the soul lives the life of a plant when it serves the body in feeding it; the life of an animal, when it flatters the senses; the life of a man, when it deliberates through reason on human affairs; the life of the heroes, when it investigates natural things; . . . the life of the angels, when it enquires into the divine mysteries; the life of God, when it does everything for God's sake. Every man's soul experiences all these things in itself in some way, although souls do it in different ways, and thus the human species strives to become all things by living the lives of all things. . . . Man is a great miracle, a living creature worthy of reverence and adoration, for he . . . transforms himself into God as if he were God himself.

The Political Life of Florence

The Rule of Cosimo d'Medici

VESPASIANO

Florence was perhaps the city most representative of Renaissance activity and inspiration. This was the home of the statesman Leonardo Bruni, the sculptor Michelangelo, the political scientist Machiavelli, and the greatest literary figure of the age, Dante. But during this era, Florence truly belonged to one family—the Medici. They were led by Cosimo d'Medici, who developed the family's financial interests, and they eventually became the bankers of the papacy. Cosimo and his son Lorenzo (the Magnificent) wrote poetry, discussed philosophy, and heavily patronized the great artists of Florence.

"The Rule of Cosimo d'Medici" is from Vespasiano da Bisticci, *Lives of Illustrious Men of the XV Century*, trans. W. George and E. Waters (London: Routledge and Kegan Paul, Ltd., 1926), pp. 213, 217, 222–224.

They were truly humanists in their own right. Although Florence was ostensibly a republic, it was in fact dominated by the Medici family. In their reign, they applied a valuable lesson of "controlled freedom" from the Roman emperor Augustus. In many ways Florence owed her greatness to their efforts. The portrait of Cosimo below is by the Renaissance biographer Vespasiano.

Cosimo di Giovanni dé Medici was of most honourable descent, a very prominent citizen and one of great weight in the republic. . . .

He had a knowledge of Latin which would scarcely have been looked for in one occupying the station of a leading citizen engrossed with affairs. He was grave in temperament, prone to associate with men of high station who disliked frivolity, and averse from all buffoons and actors and those who spent time unprofitably. He had a great liking for men of letters and sought their society. . . . His natural bent was to discuss matters of importance; and, although at this time the city was full of men of distinction, his worth was recognised on account of his praiseworthy qualities, and he began to find employment in affairs of every kind. By his twenty-fifth year he had gained great reputation in the city. . . . Cosimo and his party took every step to strengthen their own position. . . . Cosimo found that he must be careful to keep their support by temporising and making believe that [they would] enjoy power equal to his own. Meantime he kept concealed the source of his influence in the city as well as he could. . . .

I once heard Cosimo say that the great mistake of his life was that he did not begin to spend his wealth ten years earlier; because, knowing well the disposition of his fellow-citizens, he was sure that, in the lapse of fifty years, no memory would remain of his personality or of his house save the few fabrics he might have built. He went on, "I know that after my death my children will be in worse case than those of any other Florentine who has died for many years past; moreover, I know I shall not wear the crown of laurel more than any other citizen." He spake thus because he knew the difficulty of ruling a state as he had ruled Florence, through the opposition of influential citizens who rated themselves his equals in former times. He acted privately with the greatest discretion in order to safeguard himself, and whenever he sought to attain an object he contrived to let it appear that the matter had been set in motion by some one other than himself and thus he escaped envy and unpopularity. His manner was admirable; he never spoke ill of anyone, and it angered him greatly to hear slander spoken by others. He was kind and patient to all who sought speech with him: he was more a man of deeds than of words: he always performed what he promised, and when this had been done he sent to let the petitioner know that his wishes had been granted. His replies were brief and sometimes obscure, so that they might be made to bear a double sense. . . .

So great was his knowledge of all things, that he could find some matter of discussion with men of all sorts, he would talk literature with a man of letters and theology with a theologian, being well versed therein through his natural liking, and for the reading of the Holy Scripture. With philosophy it was just the same. . . . He took kindly notice of all musicians, and delighted greatly in their art. He had dealings with painters and sculptors and had in his house works of diverse masters. He was especially inclined towards sculpture and showed great favour to all worthy craftsmen, being a good friend to Donatello and all sculptors and painters; and because in his time the sculptors found scanty employment, Cosimo, in order that Donatello's chisel might not be idle, commissioned him to make the pulpits of bronze in St. Lorenzo and the doors of the sacristy. He ordered the bank to pay every week enough money to Donatello for his work and for that of his four assistants. . . . He had a good knowledge of architecture, as may be seen from the buildings he left, none of which were built without consulting him; moreover, all those who were about to build would go to him for advice.

Precepts of Power:
"Everyone Sees What You Appear to Be,
Few Perceive What You Are"

NICCOLÒ MACHIAVELLI

Over the centuries, the name of Machiavelli has become synonymous with evil. The adjective "Machiavellian" still evokes images of deceit and political backstabbing. Machiavelli's ideas were condemned by the church as immoral and inspired by Satan himself. In reality, Niccolò Machiavelli (1469–1527) was a loyal citizen of Florence who had been schooled in the classics and had chosen a career in public service. He disliked the rule of the Medici and was a great advocate of republicanism. After Savonarola's fall from power in 1498, his theocracy was replaced by a true republic, led by elected officials of the people. Machiavelli became ambassador to France, and this duty served as a laboratory for the science of politics where he could observe men and governments in action. The Florentine republic was successful until 1512, when a Spanish mercenary army defeated Machiavelli's personally trained Florentine militia. They reinstalled Medici rule, and Machiavelli was tortured on the rack and thrown into prison for a time. He retired to the country and wrote a little book entitled The Prince. *In it, Machiavelli gives the wisdom of his experience in politics. It is a manual of power: how to obtain it, maintain it, and lose it. In his analysis, Machiavelli is brutally realistic about the nature of human beings and the world of power politics: Learn the rules and you may survive and prosper. In the political chaos of Renaissance Italy, where alliances shifted frequently and distrust prevailed, such a guide proved useful and popular. Some of Machiavelli's most important ideas from* The Prince *are excerpted below.*

On Those Who Have Become Princes by Crime

It is to be noted that in taking a state its conqueror should weigh all the harmful things he must do and do them all at once so as not to have to repeat them every day, and in not repeating them to be able to make men feel secure and to win them over with the benefits he bestows upon them. Anyone who does otherwise, either out of timidity or because of poor advice, is always obliged to keep his knife in his hand; nor can he ever count upon his subjects, who, because of their fresh and continual injuries, cannot feel secure with him. Injuries, therefore, should be inflicted all at the same time, for the less they are tasted, the less they offend; and benefits should be distributed a bit at a time in order that they may be savored fully. And a prince should, above all, live with his sub-

jects in such a way that no unforseen event, either good or bad, may make him alter his course; for when emergencies arise in adverse conditions, you are not in time to resort to cruelty, and what good you do will help you little, since it will be judged a forced measure and you will earn from it no thanks whatsoever.

On Cruelty and Mercy

A prince must be cautious in believing and in acting, nor should he be afraid of his own shadow; and he should proceed in such a manner, tempered by prudence and humanity, so that too much trust may not render him imprudent nor too much distrust render him intolerable.

From this arises an argument: whether it is better to be loved than to be feared, or the contrary. I reply that one should like to be both one and the other; but since it is difficult to join them together, it is much safer to be feared than to be loved when one of the two must be lacking. For one can generally say that about men: that they are ungrateful, fickle, simulators and deceivers, avoiders of danger, greedy for gain; and while you work for their good they are completely yours, offering you their blood, their property, their lives, and their sons, as I said earlier, when danger is far away; but when it comes nearer to you they turn away. And that prince who bases his power entirely on their words, finding himself stripped of other preparations, comes to ruin; for friendships that are acquired by a price and not by greatness and nobility of character are purchased but are not owned, and at the proper moment they cannot be spent. And men are less hesitant about harming someone who makes himself loved than one who makes himself feared because love is held together by a chain of obligation which, since men are a sorry lot, is broken on every occasion in which their own self-interest is concerned; but fear is held together by a dread of punishment which will never abandon you.

A prince must nevertheless make himself feared in such a manner that he will avoid hatred, even if he does not acquire love; since to be feared and not hated can very well be combined; and this will always be so when he keeps his hands off the property and the women of his citizens and his subjects. And if he must take someone's life, he should do so when there is proper justification and manifest cause; but, above all, he should avoid the property of others; for men forget more quickly the death of their father than the loss of their patrimony. Moreover, the reasons for seizing their property are never lacking; and he who begins to live by stealing always finds a reason for taking what belongs to others; on the contrary, reasons for taking a life are rarer and disappear sooner. . . . I conclude, therefore, returning to the problem of being feared and loved, that since men love at their own pleasure and fear at the pleasure of the prince, a wise prince should build his foundation upon that which belongs to him, and not upon that which belongs to others: he must strive only to avoid hatred, as has been said.

How a Prince Should Keep His Word

How praiseworthy it is for a prince to keep his word and to live by integrity and not by deceit everyone knows; nevertheless, one sees from the experience of our times that the princes who have accomplished great deeds are those who have cared little for keeping their promises and who have known how to manipulate the minds

Niccolò Machiavelli: "Let a prince therefore act to seize and to maintain the state; his methods will always be judged honorable and will be praised by all; for ordinary people are always deceived by appearances and by the outcome of a thing; and in the world there is nothing but ordinary people." (Art Resource)

of men by shrewdness; and in the end they have surpassed those who laid their foundations upon honesty.

You must, therefore, know that there are two means of fighting: one according to the laws, the other with force; the first way is proper to man, the second to beasts; but because the first, in many cases, is not sufficient, it becomes necessary to have recourse to the second. Therefore, a prince must know how to use wisely the natures of the beast and the man. . . .

Since, then, a prince must know how to make good use of the nature of the beast, he should choose from among the beasts the fox and the lion; for the lion cannot defend itself from traps and the fox cannot protect itself from wolves. It is therefore necessary to be a fox in order to recognize the traps and a lion in order to frighten the wolves. Those who play only the part of the lion do not understand matters. A wise ruler, therefore, cannot and should not keep his word when such an observance of faith would be to his disadvantage and when the reasons which made him promise are removed. And if men were all good, this rule would not be good; but since men are a sorry lot and will not keep their promises to you, you likewise need not keep yours to them. A prince never lacks legitimate reasons to break his promises. Of this one could cite an endless number of modern examples to show how many pacts, how many promises have

been made null and void because of the infidelity of princes; and he who has known best how to use the fox has come to a better end. But it is necessary to know how to disguise this nature well and to be a great hypocrite and a liar: and men are so simpleminded and so controlled by their present necessities that one who deceives will always find another who will allow himself to be deceived. . . .

A prince, therefore, must be very careful never to let anything slip from his lips which is not full of the five qualities mentioned above: he should appear, upon seeing and hearing him, to be all mercy, all faithfulness, all integrity, all kindness, all religion. And there is nothing more necessary than to seem to possess this last quality. And men in general judge more by their eyes than their hands; for everyone can see but few can feel. Everyone sees what you seem to be, few perceive what you are, and those few do not dare to contradict the opinion of the many who have the majesty of the state to defend them; and in the actions of all men, and especially of princes, where there is no impartial arbiter, one must consider the final result. Let a prince therefore act to seize and to maintain the state; his methods will always be judged honorable and will be praised by all; for ordinary people are always deceived by appearances and by the outcome of a thing; and in the world there is nothing but ordinary people

Renaissance Arts and Manners

The Notebooks of a Universal Man

LEONARDO DA VINCI

The Renaissance produced several outstanding artists, scholars, and statesmen, but no one seemed to imprint this creative age as did Leonardo da Vinci (1452–1519). Leonardo was a painter of great talent. He was especially innovative in his naturalistic backgrounds, his perfection of the techniques of perspective and geometric arrangement of figures, and the subtle treatment of light and shade. But Leonardo never really considered himself to be primarily a painter. His curiosity for the world around him was too great. He wanted to "learn the causes of things." Toward that end he ob-

"The Notebooks of a Universal Man" is from Edward McCurdy, ed., *Leonardo Da Vinci Notebooks* (New York: Empire State Book Co., 1922), pp. 150–153, 188–189, 197–199.

Theme: Historical Change and Transition

The Historical Intersection

FRANCE: 1796

The Realities of Power

NAPOLEON BONAPARTE

In 1796, France was reeling from the violent Reign of Terror that had seen the execution of over 25,000 aristocrats and other "enemies of the French Revolution" from 1793 to 1794. Napoleon Bonaparte, a young artillery officer at the time later fashioned his own political autocracy through his military victories and positions as Consul (1799) and Emperor (1804). The following excerpt is from a conversation Napoleon had with one of his confidants in 1796, while a government called the Directory was in control of France, three years before he himself came into power. It reveals much about Napoleon's ambition.

Compare and Contrast:

- Compare Napoleon's account carefully with Machiavelli's ideas from *The Prince*. Must the goals of power always be "cleverly disguised"? How important is deceit in gaining and maintaining power?

What I have done so far is nothing. I am but at the opening of the career I am to run. Do you suppose that I have gained my victories in Italy in order to advance the lawyers of the Directory? Do you think, either, that my object is to establish a Republic? What a notion! A republic of thirty million people, with our morals and vices! How could that ever be? It is a chimera with which the French are infatuated but which will pass away in time like all others. What they want is glory and the gratification of their vanity; as for liberty, of that they have no conception. Look at the army! The victories which we have just gained have given the French soldier his true character. I am everything to him. Let the Directory attempt to deprive me of my command and they will see who is master. The na-

(contd)

tion must have a head, a head rendered illustrious by glory and not by theories of government, fine phrases, or the talk of idealists, of which the French understand not a whit. Let them have their toys and they will be satisfied. They will amuse themselves and allow themselves to be led, provided the goal is cleverly disguised.

Consider This:

- What does this excerpt reveal about Napoleon's commitment to the democratic ideals of the French Revolution? Was Machiavelli correct? Must any ideal in the political world remain of secondary importance to the necessity of gaining and maintaining power?
- Has the nature of political power changed in our contemporary world or has technology simplified the "creation of belief" and thus made personal freedom even more difficult to maintain?

"The Realities of Power" is from *Memoires of Miot de Melito*, in James H. Robinson, ed., *Translations and Reprints from the Original Sources of European History*, rev. ed., vol. 2, pt. 2 (Philadelphia: University of Pennsylvania Press, 1900), pp. 2–3.

served and made notes in a book for future reference and was constantly inventing machines that he believed would have military value; his sketches of helicopters, tanks, and submarines were far beyond the realities of his times. Leonardo's notebooks give fascinating insight into the workings of his fertile mind. Some of his comments on birds, flight, sketching, and painting are offered below.

The Observation of Birds and Thoughts of Flight

The thrushes and other small birds are able to make headway against the course of the wind, because they fly in spurts; that is they take a long course below the wind, by dropping in a slanting direction towards the ground, with their wings half closed, and they open the wings and catch the wind in them with their reverse movement, and so rise to a height; and then they drop again in the same way.

Remember that your bird should have no other model than the bat, because its membranes serve as an armor or rather as a means of binding together the pieces of its armor, that is the framework of the wings.

And if you take as your pattern the wings of feathered birds, these are more powerful in structure of bone and sinew because they are penetrable, that is to say the feathers are separated from one another and the air passes through them. But the bat is aided by its membrane which binds the whole together and is not penetrated by the air.

Of whether birds when continually descending without beating their wings will proceed a greater distance in one sustained curve, or by frequently making some reflex movement; and whether when they wish to pass in flight from one spot to another they will go more quickly by making impetuous, headlong movements, and then rising up with reflex movement and again making a fresh descent, and so continuing.—To speak of this subject you must . . . in the first book explain the nature of the resistance of the air, in the second the anatomy of the bird and of its wings, in the third the method of working of the wings in their various movements, in the fourth the power of the wings and of the tail, at such time as the wings are not being moved and the wind is favourable, to serve as a guide in different movements.

Dissect the bat, study it carefully, and on this model construct the machine.

There is as much pressure exerted by a substance against the air as by the air against the substance. Observe how the beating of its wings against the air suffices to bear up the weight of the eagle in the highly rarefied air which borders on the fiery element! Observe also how the air moving over the sea, beaten back by the bellying sails, causes the heavily laden ship to glide onwards! So that by adducing and expounding the reasons of these things you may able to realise that man when he has great wings attached to him, by exerting his strength against the resistance of the air and conquering it, is enabled to subdue it and to raise himself upon it.

The Importance of Sketching

When you have thoroughly learnt perspective, and have fixed in your memory all the various parts and forms of things, you should often amuse yourself when you take a walk for recreation, in watching and taking note of the attitudes and actions of men as they talk and dispute, or laugh or come to blows one with another, both their actions and those of the bystanders who either intervene or stand looking on at these things; noting these down with rapid strokes in this way, in a little pocket-book, which you ought always to carry with you. And let this be tinted paper, so that it may not be rubbed out; but you should change the old for a new one, for these are not things to be rubbed out but preserved with the utmost diligence; for there is such an infinite number of forms and actions of things that the memory is incapable of preserving them, and therefore you should keep those [sketches] as your patterns and teachers.

The Way to Paint a Battle

Show first the smoke of the artillery mingled in the air with the dust stirred up by the movement of the horses and of the combatants. . . . The smoke which is mingled with the dust-laden air will as it rises to a certain height have more and more the appearance of a dark cloud, at the summit of which the smoke will be more distinctly visible than the dust. The smoke will assume a bluish tinge, and the dust will keep its natural colour. From the side whence the light comes this mixture of air and smoke and dust will seem far brighter than on the opposite side.

As for the combatants, the more they are in the midst of this turmoil the less they will be visible, and the less will be the contrast between their lights and shadows. You should give a ruddy glow to the faces and the figures and the air around them, and to the gunners and those near to them, and this glow should grow fainter as it is further away from its cause. The figures which are between you and the light, if far away, will appear dark against a light background, and the nearer their limbs are to the ground the less will they be visible, for there the dust is greater and thicker. And if you make horses galloping away from the throng make little clouds of dust as far distant one from another as is the space between the strides made by the horse, and that cloud which is further away from the horse should be the least visible, for it should be high and spread out and thin, while that which is nearer should be more conspicuous and smaller and more compact.

Let the air be full of arrows going in various directions, some mounting upwards, other falling, others flying horizontally, and let the balls shot from the guns have a train of smoke following their course. Show the figures in the foreground covered with dust on their hair and eyebrows and such other level parts as afford the dust a space to lodge.

Make the conquerors running, with their hair and other things streaming in the wind, and with brows bent down; and they should be thrusting forward opposite limbs, that is, if a man advances the right foot the left arm should also come forward. If you represent any one fallen you should show the mark where he has been dragged through the dust, which has become changed to bloodstained mire, and round about in the half-liquid earth you should show the marks of the tramping of men and horses who have passed over it. Make a horse dragging the dead body of his master, and leaving behind him in the dust and mud the track of where the body was dragged along.

Make the beaten and conquered pallid, with brows raised and knit together, and let the skin above the brows be all full of lines of pain; at the sides of the nose show the furrows going in an arch from the nostrils and ending where the eye begins, and show the dilation of the nostrils which is the cause of these lines; and let the lips be arched displaying the upper row of teeth, and let the teeth be parted after the manner of such as cry in lamentation. Show some one using his hand as a shield for his terrified eyes, turning the palm of it towards the enemy, and having the other resting on the ground to support the weight of his body; let others be crying out with their mouths wide open, and fleeing away. Put all sorts of arms lying between the feet of the combatants, such as broken shields, lances, broken swords, and other things like these. Make the dead, some half buried in dust, others with the dust all mingled with the oozing blood and changing into crimson mud; and let the line of the blood be discerned by its colour, flowing in a sinuous stream from the corpse of the dust. Show others in the death agony grinding their teeth and rolling their eyes, with clenched fists grinding against their bodies, and with legs distorted . . . but see that there is no level spot of ground that is not trampled over with blood.

Book of the Courtier (1518)

BALDASSARE CASTIGLIONE

With the growing emphasis on diplomacy and contact with ambassadors of other states during the Renaissance, rules of etiquette were established. The new age demanded that knights become gentlemen and that the relationship between the sexes be redefined. Baldassare Castiglione provided the instruction in his Book of the Courtier.

I wish, then, that this Courtier of ours should be nobly born and of gentle race; because it is far less unseemly for one of ignoble birth to fail in worthy deeds, than for one of noble birth, who, if he strays from the path of his predecessors, stains his family name, and not only fails to achieve but loses what has been achieved already; for noble birth is like a bright lamp that manifests and makes visible good and evil deeds, and kindles and stimulates to virtue both by fear of shame and by hope of praise. . . .

But to come to some details, I am of the opinion that the principal and true profession of the Courtier ought to be that of arms; which I would have him follow actively above all else, and be known among others as bold and strong, and loyal to whomsoever he serves. And he will win a reputation for these good qualities by exercising them at all times and in all places, since one may never fail in this without severest censure. And just as among women, their fair fame once sullied never recovers its first lustre, so the repu-

"Book of the Courtier" is from Baldassare Castiglione, *Book of the Courtier,* trans. Leonard Opdycke (New York: Horace Liveright, 1903), pp. 22, 25–26, 28–31.

tation of a gentleman who bears arms, if once it be in the least tarnished with cowardice or other disgrace, remains forever infamous before the world and full of ignominy. Therefore the more our Courtier excels in this art, the more he will be worthy of praise; and yet I do not deem essential in him that perfect knowledge of things and those other qualities that befit a commander; since this would be too wide a sea, let us be content, as we have said, with perfect loyalty and unconquered courage, and that he be always seen to possess them. . . .

Therefore let the man we are seeking, be very bold, stern, and always among the first, where the enemy are to be seen; and in every other place, gentle, modest, reserved, above all things avoiding ostentation and that impudent self-praise by which men ever excite hatred and disgust in all who bear them. . . .

Then coming to the bodily frame, I say it is enough if this be neither extremely short nor tall, for both of these conditions excite a certain contemptuous surprise, and men of either sort are gazed upon in much the same way that we gaze on monsters. Yet if we must offend in one of the two extremes, it is preferable to fall a little short of the just measure of height than to exceed it, for besides often being dull of intellect, men thus huge of body are also unfit for every exercise of agility, which thing I should much wish in the Courtier. And so I would have him well built and shapely of limb, and would have him show strength and lightness and suppleness, and know all bodily exercises that befit a man of war: I think the first should be to handle every sort of weapon well on foot and on horse, to understand the advantages of each, and especially to be familiar with those weapons that are ordinarily used among gentlemen; for besides the use of them in war, where such subtlety in contrivance is perhaps not needful, there frequently arise differences between one gentleman and another, which afterwards result in duels often fought with such weapons as happen at the moment to be within reach: thus knowledge of this kind is a very safe thing. . . .

It is fitting also to know how to swim, to leap, to run, to throw stones, for besides the use that may be made of this in war, a man often has occasion to show what he can do in such matters; whence good esteem is to be won, especially with the multitude, who must be taken into account withal. Another admirable exercise, and one very befitting a man at court, is the game of tennis, in which are well shown the disposition of the body, the quickness and suppleness of every member, and all those qualities that are seen in nearly every other exercise. Nor less highly do I esteem vaulting on horse, which although it be fatiguing and difficult, makes a man very light and dexterous more than any other thing; and besides its utility, if this lightness is accompanied by grace, it is to my thinking a finer show than any of the others.

On the Nature and Purpose of Women and Men

BALDASSARE CASTIGLIONE

"Now you said that Nature's intention is always to produce the most perfect things, and therefore she would if possible always produce men, and that women are the result of some mistake or defect rather than of intention. But I can only say that I deny this completely. You cannot possible argue that Nature does not intend to produce the women without whom the human race cannot be preserved, which is something that Nature desires above everything else. For by means of the union of male and female, she produces children, who then return the benefits received in childhood by supporting their parents when they are old; then they renew them when they themselves have children. . . . In this way Nature, as if moving in a circle, fills out eternity and confers immortality on mortals. And since woman is as necessary to this process as man, I do not see how it can be that one is more the fruit of mere chance than the other. It is certainly true that Nature always intends to produce the most perfect things, and therefore always intends to produce the species man, though not male rather than female; and indeed, if Nature always produced males this would be imperfection: for just as there results from body and soul a composite nobler than its parts, namely man himself, so from the union of male and female there results a composite that preserves the human species, and without which its parts would perish. Thus male and female always go naturally together, and one cannot exist without the other. . . ."

Then signor Gaspare said: "I do not wish us to go into such subtleties because these ladies would not understand them; and though I were to refute you with excellent arguments, they would still think that I was wrong, or pretend to at least; and they would at once give a verdict in their own favor. However, since we have made a beginning, I shall say only that, as you know, it is the opinion of very learned men that man is as the form and woman as the matter, and therefore just as form is more perfect than matter,

and indeed it gives it its being, so man is far more perfect than woman. . . ."

The Magnifico Guiliano at once replied: "The poor creatures do not wish to become men in order to make themselves more perfect but to gain their freedom and shake off the tyranny that men have imposed on them by their one-sided authority. Besides, the analogy you give of matter and form is not always applicable; for woman is not perfected by man in the way that matter is perfected by form. . . . Woman does not receive her being from man but rather perfects him just as she is perfected by him, and thus both join together for the purpose of procreation which neither can ensure alone. Moreover, I shall attribute woman's enduring love for the man with whom she has first been, and man's detestation for the first woman he possesses, . . . but to the resolution and constancy of women and the inconstancy of men. And for this, there are natural reasons: for because of its hot nature, the male sex possesses the qualities of lightness, movement and inconstancy, whereas from its coldness, the female sex derives its steadfast gravity and calm and is therefore more susceptible."

SECTION II: THE REFORMATION ERA

I am more afraid of my own heart than of the pope and all his cardinals. I have within me the great pope—Self.

—*Martin Luther*

Whatever your heart clings to and confides in, that is really your God.

—*Martin Luther*

All religions must be tolerated for every man must get to heaven his own way.

—*Frederick the Great*

During the Middle Ages, the church was the focal point of society. One's life was inextricably bound to the dictates of religion from the baptism that followed birth to the last rites that accompanied death. But by the sixteenth century, the omnipotence of the church, both in a spiritual sense and in the political realm, had been called into question. The church had lost much of the authority that had allowed it, in the eleventh through the thirteenth centuries, to claim superiority in the ongoing struggle between church and state. By the middle of the fifteenth century, the papacy was occupied with finding new sources of income that would help it fend off political challenges to its territory and increase its influence in the secular realm. The Renaissance papacy became infamous in its corruption and succumbed to the sensual delights of the world, as well as to the more traditional abuses of simony (the selling of church offices) and pluralism (allowing an individual to hold more than one position).

These actions resulted in a plentitude of criticism from within the church and especially from Christian humanists such as Desiderius Erasmus. Perhaps the most controversial practice of the church was the sale of indulgences. An indulgence was a piece of paper, signed by the pope, that remitted punishment in Purgatory due to sin. It was based on the theory that all humans are by nature sinful and after death will have to undergo a purgation of sin before being allowed to enter the Kingdom of Heaven. The pope, however, controlled an infinite "treasury of grace" that could be dispensed to mortals, thus removing the taint of sin and freeing the soul from Purgatory. By the late fifteenth century, the remission of sin was extended to both the living and the dead, and one could therefore liberate the soul of a relative "trapped" in Purgatory by purchasing an indulgence. The sale of indulgences became a routine affair of peddling forgiveness of purgatorial punishment, and the papacy came to rely on it as a necessary source of income. In 1507, Pope Julius II issued a plenary indulgence in order to obtain funds for the construction of Saint Peter's Basilica in Rome. Leo X renewed the indulgence in 1513, and subcommissioners actively began the sale to the faithful. It was in response to this sale that a young monk named Martin Luther protested and nailed his *Ninety-five Theses* to the door of the Wittenberg church.

It is important to note that although Luther called into question the sale of indulgences, the main issue was salvation. Salvation, he reasoned, was cheap indeed if it could be purchased. Luther was tortured by the demands of God for perfection and worried that his own righteousness was insufficient for salvation in the sight of God. The church taught that in addition to winning grace through faith, one could also merit God's grace through good works or the remission of sin by indulgence. In fact, the purchase of an indulgence was considered a good work. But to Luther's mind, salvation required more, much more, and had nothing to do with deeds. While studying Saint Paul's Epistle to the Romans (1:17), Luther achieved a breakthrough that freed him from his torment: By the grace of God alone could one be saved, and this salvation was obtained only through faith in Christ. Neither good works nor indulgences could have anything to do with salvation. This stand called into question the very foundation of established Christian belief. Was the pope the true Vicar of Christ who spoke the words of God? If so, why did he advocate indulgences as a means of salvation? Was he in fact infallible on such matters of faith? The corruption of the papacy was also troubling, yet Luther's objective was not to overthrow the church, but to reform it from within.

The church replied to such a challenge with what it considered swift and appropriate action. Luther was excommunicated and his writings were condemned as heretical. It became evident to Luther that his desire to reform the church could be achieved only by defying the authority of the pope and starting a new church. Supported by the Holy Roman Emperor Charles V, the church sought to eliminate the root of the controversy. However, Luther was hidden, protected by the secular princes in Germany who, because of their location and traditional independence, were willing to defy their emperor and promote a religion that to them served a secular purpose. Yet Luther's movement was spiritual in nature, and he decried such political connections even as he sought the aid of the princes and nobility.

This section of the chapter seeks to explore the spiritual and political foundations of the Reformation and the Protestant movement, from its inception by Martin Luther through its development under John Calvin to its royal imposition in England under Henry VIII and Elizabeth I. The Reformation era must also be viewed in its proper context, noting that during this period the Catholic Church made significant strides toward reform in its own right. The themes presented in this section include the role of the individual in changing history and the impact of religion on the political framework and social fabric of the times. The Reformation era was one of transition and instability that eventually led to war and bloodshed as nations fought during the sixteenth and seventeenth centuries in support of the "true religion." This bloody future was far from Martin Luther's mind when he nailed his Ninety-five Theses on the Wittenberg church door in 1517 and thus started a movement that shook the spiritual foundations of Christendom and altered the political face of Europe for centuries to come.

The Lutheran Reformation

The Indulgence Controversy

The controversy over the sale of indulgences was the spark that set the Reformation in motion. In 1515, Pope Leo X made an agreement with Archbishop Albert to sell indulgences in Mainz and other areas of northern Germany, with half the proceeds going to support Leo's construction of Saint Peter's Basilica in Rome and half going to pay for the debts that Albert had incurred in securing his church offices. In the first selection, Archbishop Albert gives instructions to those subcommissioners who actually sold the indulgences in 1517. One of the most successful subcommissioners was Johann Tetzel, prior of the Dominican monastery at Leipzig. His oratorical ability is evident in the second passage.

Instructions for the Sale of Indulgences (1517)

ARCHBISHOP ALBERT

Here follow the four principal graces and privileges, which are granted by the apostolic bull, of which each may be obtained without the other. In the matter of these four privileges preachers shall take pains to commend each to believers with the greatest care, and, in-so-far as in their power lies, to explain the same.

The first grace is the complete remission of all sins; and nothing greater than this can be named, since no man who lives in sin and forfeits the favor of God, obtains complete remis-

sion by these means and once more enjoys God's favor: moreover, through this remission of sins the punishment which one is obliged to undergo in Purgatory on account of the affront to the divine Majesty, is all remitted, and the pains of Purgatory completely blotted out. And although nothing is precious enough to be given in exchange for such a grace—since it is a free gift of God and grace is beyond price—yet in order that Christian believers may be the more easily induced to procure the same, we [offer them the following guidance]. . . . Because the conditions of men, and their occupations, are so various and manifold, and we cannot consider and assess them individually, we have therefore decided that the rates can be determined thus, according to recognized classifications: [Then follows a graded schedule of rates: kings and their families, bishops, etc., 25 Rhenish gold guilders; abbots, counts, barons,

"Instructions for the Sale of Indulgences" is from James H. Robinson, ed., *Translations and Reprints from the Original Sources of European History*, vol. 2, no. 6 (Philadelphia: University of Pennsylvania, 1902), pp. 4–9.

etc., 10; lesser nobles and ecclesiastics and others with incomes of 500, 6 guilders; citizens with their own income, 1 guilder; those with less, ½. Those with nothing shall supply their contribution with prayer and fasting, "for the kingdom of heaven should be open to the poor as much as the rich."]

The second grace is a confessional letter containing the most extraordinarily comforting and hitherto unheard of privileges, and which also retains its virtue even after our bull expires at the end of eight years, since the bull says: "they shall be participators now and for ever...."

The third most important grace is the participation in all the possessions of the church universal, which consists herein, that contributors toward the said building, together with their deceased relations, who have departed this world in a state of grace, shall from now and for eternity be partakers in all petitions, intercessions, alms, fasting, prayers, in each and every pilgrimage, even those to the Holy Land; furthermore, in the stations at Rome, in the masses, canonical hours, flagellations, and all other spiritual goods which have brought forth or which shall be brought forth by the universal most holy church militant or by any of its members. Believers will become participants in all these things who purchase confessional letters.

The fourth distinctive grace is for those souls which are in purgatory, and is the complete remission of all sins, which remission the pope brings to pass through his intercession to the advantage of said souls, in this wise; that the same contribution shall be placed in the chest by a living person as one would make for himself.... Moreover, preachers shall exert themselves to give this grace the widest publicity, since through the same, help will surely come to departed souls, and the construction of the Church of St. Peter will be abundantly promoted at the same time.

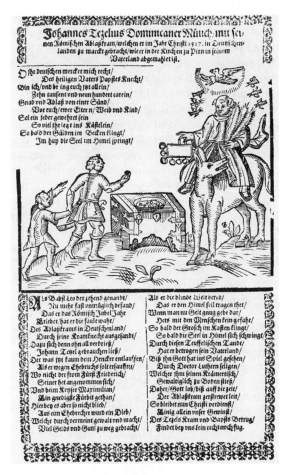

Caricature of Johann Tetzel, the indulgence preacher who spurred Luther to publish his *Ninety-five Theses.* The last line of the caption reads: "As soon as gold in the basin rings, right then the soul to heaven springs." (Staatliche Lutherhalle, Wittenberg)

"How Many Sins Are Committed in a Single Day?" (1517)

JOHANN TETZEL

Venerable Sir, I pray you that in your utterances you may be pleased to make use of such words as shall serve to open the eyes of the mind and cause your hearers to consider how great a grace and gift they have had and now have at

"'How Many Sins Are Committed in a Single Day?'" is from James H. Robinson, ed., *Translations and Reprints from the Original Sources of European History,* vol. 2, no. 6 (Philadelphia: University of Pennsylvania, 1902), pp. 9–10.

their very doors. Blessed eyes indeed, which see what they see, because already they possess letters of safe conduct by which they are able to lead their souls through that valley of tears, through that sea of the mad world, where storms and tempests and dangers lie in wait, to the blessed land of Paradise. Know that the life of man upon earth is a constant struggle. We have to fight against the flesh, the world and the devil, who are always seeking to destroy the soul. In sin we are conceived,—alas! what bonds of sin encompass us, and how difficult and almost impossible it is to attain to the gate of salvation without divine aid; since He causes us to be saved, not by virtue of the good works which we accomplish, but through His divine mercy, it is necessary then to put on the armor of God.

You may obtain letters of safe conduct from the vicar of our Lord Jesus Christ, by means of which you are able to liberate your soul from the hands of the enemy, and convey it by means of contrition and confession, safe and secure from all pains of Purgatory, into the happy kingdom. For know that in these letters are stamped and engraven all the merits of Christ's passion there laid bare. Consider, that for each and every mortal sin it is necessary to undergo seven years of penitence after confession and contrition, either in this life or in Purgatory.

How many mortal sins are committed in a day, how many in a week, how many in a month, how many in a year, how many in the whole course of life! They are well-nigh numberless, and those that commit them must needs suffer endless punishment in the burning pains of Purgatory.

But with these confessional letters you will be able at any time in life to obtain full indulgence for all penalties imposed upon you, in all cases except the four reserved to the Apostolic See. Therefore throughout your whole life, whenever you wish to make confession, you may receive the same remission, except in cases reserved to the Pope, and afterwards, at the hour of death, a full indulgence as to all penalties and sins, and your share of all spiritual blessings that exist in the church militant and all its members.

Do you not know that when it is necessary for anyone to go to Rome, or undertake any other dangerous journey, he takes his money to a broker and gives a certain percent—five or six or ten—in order that at Rome or elsewhere he may receive again his funds intact, by means of the letter of this same broker? Are you not willing, then, for the fourth part of a florin, to obtain these letters, by virtue of which you may bring, not your money but your divine and immortal soul safe and sound into the land of Paradise?

Salvation Through Faith Alone

MARTIN LUTHER

Martin Luther's transformation from monk to reformer was not a preconceived act; it developed gradually not only as a result of corruption around him, but especially because of a spiritual awakening. Luther struggled with the need to imitate the perfection of Christ, which was important in the eyes of the church for salvation. Luther realized that because of his nature as a human, he was too sinful, and that no amount of prayer or good works could help him achieve the Kingdom of Heaven. After much study and pain, he came to the conclusion that salvation was a free gift of God and that a person was saved by faith in Christ alone. In the first selection, Luther explains his enlightenment. The second document is his answer to the indulgences being sold by Johann Tetzel. When Luther posted the Ninety-five Theses *on the church in Wittenberg, the Reformation began in earnest.*

Reprinted from Luther's Works, Vol. 54 edited by Theodore G. Tappert, © 1967 Fortress Press. Used by permission of Augsburg Fortress.

I, Martin Luther, entered the monastery against the will of my father and lost favor with him, for he saw through the knavery of the monks very well. On the day on which I sang my first mass he said to me, "Son, don't you know that you ought to honor your father?" . . . Later when I stood there during the mass and began the canon, I was so frightened that I would have fled if I hadn't been admonished by the prior. . . .

When I was a monk I was unwilling to omit any of the prayers, but when I was busy with public lecturing and writing I often accumulated my appointed prayers for a whole week, or even two or three weeks. Then I would take a Saturday off, or shut myself in for as long as three days without food and drink, until I had said the prescribed prayers. This made my head split, and as a consequence I couldn't close my eyes for five nights, lay sick unto death, and went out of my senses. Even after I had quickly recovered and I tried again to read, my head went 'round and 'round. Thus our Lord God drew me, as if by force, from that torment of prayers. . . .

The words "righteous" and "righteousness of God" struck my conscience like lightning. When I heard them I was exceedingly terrified. If God is righteous [I thought], he must punish. But when by God's grace I pondered, in the tower and heated room of this building, over the words, "He who through faith is righteous shall live" [Rom. 1:17] and "the righteousness of God" [Rom. 3:21], I soon came to the conclusion that if we, as righteous men, ought to live from faith and if the righteousness of God should contribute to the salvation of all who believe, then salvation won't be our merit but God's mercy. My spirit was thereby cheered. For it's by the righteousness of God that we're justified and saved through Christ. These words [which had before terrified me] now became more pleasing to me. The Holy Spirit unveiled the Scriptures for me in this tower.

God led us away from all this in a wonderful way; without my quite being aware of it he took me away from that game more than twenty years ago. How difficult it was at first when we journeyed toward Kemberg after All Saints' Day in the year 1517, when I first made up my mind to write against the crass errors of indulgences! Jerome Schurff advised against this: "You wish to write against the pope? What are you trying to do? It won't be tolerated!" I replied, "And if they have to tolerate it?" Presently Sylvester, master of the sacred palace, entered the arena, fulminating against me with this syllogism: "Whoever questions what the Roman church says and does is heretical. Luther questions what the Roman church says and does, and therefore [he is a heretic]." So it all began.

The Ninety-five Theses (1517)

MARTIN LUTHER

In the desire and with the purpose of elucidating the truth, a disputation will be held on the underwritten propositions at Wittenberg, under the presidency of the Reverend Father Martin Luther, Monk of the Order of St. Augustine, Master of Arts and of Sacred Theology, and ordinary Reader of the same in that place. He therefore asks those who cannot be present and discuss the subject with us orally, to do so by letter in their absence. In the name of our Lord Jesus Christ, Amen. . . .

5. The Pope has neither the will nor the power to remit any penalties except those which he has imposed by his own authority, or by that of the canons.

6. The Pope has no power to remit any guilt, except by declaring and warranting it to have been remitted by God; or at most by remitting cases reserved for himself; in which cases, if his power were [disregarded], guilt would certainly remain. . . .

20. Therefore the Pope, when he speaks of the plenary remission of all penalties, does not really mean of all, but only of those imposed by himself.

"The Ninety-five Theses" is from H. Wace and C. A. Buchheim, eds., *First Principles of the Reformation* (London: John Murray, 1883), pp. 6–13.

21.   Thus those preachers of indulgences are in error who say that by the indulgences of the Pope a man is freed and saved from all punishment.

22.   For in fact he remits to souls in Purgatory no penalty which they would have had to pay in this life according to the canons.

23.   If any entire remission of all penalties can be granted to any one it is certain that it is granted to none but the most perfect, that is to very few.

24.   Hence, the greater part of the people must needs be deceived by his indiscriminate and high-sounding promise of release from penalties.

25.   Such power over Purgatory as the Pope has in general, such has every bishop in his own diocese, and every parish priest in his own parish. . . .

27.   They are wrong who say that the soul flies out of Purgatory as soon as the money thrown into the chest rattles.

28.   It is certain that, when money rattles in the chest, avarice and gain may be increased, but the effect of the intercession of the Church depends on the will of God alone. . . .

32.   Those who believe that, through letters of pardon, they are made sure of their own salvation will be eternally damned along with their teachers.

33.   We must especially beware of those who say that these pardons from the Pope are that inestimable gift of God by which man is reconciled to God. . . .

35.   They preach no Christian doctrine who teach that contrition is not necessary for those who buy souls (out of Purgatory) or buy confessional licenses.

37.   Every true Christian, whether living or dead, has a share in all the benefits of Christ and of the Church, given by God, even without letters of pardon. . . .

42.   Christians should be taught that it is not the wish of the Pope that buying of pardons should be in any way compared to works of mercy.

43.   Christians should be taught that he who gives to a poor man, or lends to a needy man, does better than if he bought pardons. . . .

45.   Christians should be taught that he who sees any one in need, and, passing him by, gives money for pardons, is not purchasing for himself the indulgences of the Pope but the anger of God. . . .

50.   Christians should be taught that, if the Pope were acquainted with the exactions of the Preachers of pardons, he would prefer that the Basilica of St. Peter should be burnt to ashes rather than that it should be built up with the skin, flesh, and bones of his sheep. . . .

62.   The true treasure of the Church is the Holy Gospel of the glory and grace of God. . . .

66.   The treasures of indulgences are nets, wherewith they now fish for the riches of men. . . .

86.   Again; why does not the Pope, whose riches are at this day more ample than those of the wealthiest of the wealthy, build the Basilica of St. Peter with his own money rather than with that of poor believers. . . .

94.   Christians should be exhorted to strive to follow Christ their head through pains, deaths, and hells.

95.   And thus not trust to enter heaven through many tribulations, rather than in the security of peace.

Address at the Diet of Worms (1521)

MARTIN LUTHER

Within a period of six months in 1520, Luther finished three important treatises that sealed his break with the Roman church. In the Address to the Christian Nobility of the German Nation *Luther advocated that the secular authorities in Germany undertake the reform that the church would not. The treatise* On Christian Liberty *described the liberating effect that pure faith in Christ has on an individual. Luther had written an accompanying letter to Pope Leo X stating that his writings were directed at the false doctrine and corruption surrounding the church and not meant as a personal slight against Leo; nevertheless, the break with Rome was complete, as events in the next year proved.*

After his excommunication by Leo X in June 1520, Luther was summoned to appear before a diet (assembly) of prelates and officials of the Holy Roman Empire in the city of Worms to answer questions about his heretical writings. His safe conduct to the meeting was guaranteed by the Holy Roman Emperor Charles V, who presided over the Diet. Accompanied by his secular protector, Frederick the Wise, Elector of Saxony, Luther appeared on April 17, 1521. When asked whether he wished to defend all his writings or retract some, Luther delivered this famous speech. On April 23, Luther secretly left Worms and was hidden by friends at Wartburg castle. Charles V's edict against Luther is the second selection.

"Most serene emperor, most illustrious princes, most clement lords, obedient to the time set for me yesterday evening, I appear before you, beseeching you, by the mercy of God, that your most serene majesty and your most illustrious lordships may deign to listen graciously to this my cause—which is, as I hope, a cause of justice and truth. If through my inexperience I have either not given the proper titles to some, or have offended in some manner against court customs and etiquette, I beseech you to kindly pardon me, as a man accustomed not to courts but to the cells of monks. I can bear no other witness about myself but that I have taught and written up to this time with simplicity of heart, as I had in view only the glory of God and the sound instruction of Christ's faithful. . . .

"[A] group of my books attacks the papacy and the affairs of the papists as those who both by their doctrines and very wicked examples have laid waste the Christian world with evil that affects the spirit and the body. For no one can deny or conceal this fact, when the experience of all and the complaints of everyone witness that through the decrees of the pope and the doctrines of men the consciences of the faithful have been most miserably entangled, tortured, and torn to pieces. Also, property and possessions, especially in this illustrious nation of Germany, have been devoured by an unbelievable tyranny and are being devoured to this time without letup and by unworthy means. [Yet the papists] by their own decrees . . . warn that the papal laws and doctrines which are contrary to the gospel or the opinions of the fathers are to be regarded as erroneous and reprehensible. If, therefore, I should have retracted these writings, I should have done nothing other than to give strength to this [papal] tyranny and I should have opened not only windows but doors to such great godlessness. It would rage further and more freely than ever it has dared up to this time. Yes, from the proof of such a revocation on my part, their wholly lawless and unrestrained kingdom of wickedness would become still more intolerable for the already wretched people; and their rule would be further strengthened and established, especially if it should be reported that this evil deed had been done by me by virtue of the authority of your

Luther's Work, Vol. 2 © 1960, 1988 Concordia Publishing House. Used with permission.

Martin Luther by Lucas Cranach the Elder (1521). This picture of Luther was painted in the same year that he defied the pope and the Holy Roman Emperor at the Diet of Worms. His complete break with Rome ushered in an age of religious reform. (Galleria Uffizi)

most serene majesty and the whole Roman Empire. Good God! What a cover for wickedness and tyranny I should have then become.

"I have written a third sort of book against some private and (as they say) distinguished individuals—those, namely, who strive to preserve the Roman tyranny and to destroy the godliness taught by me. Against these I confess I have been more violent than my religion or profession demands. But then, I do not set myself up as a saint; neither am I disputing about my life, but about the teachings of Christ. It is not proper for me to retract these works, because by this retraction it would again happen that tyranny and godlessness would, with my patronage, rule and rage among the people of God more violently than ever before.

"However, because I am a man and not God, I am not able to shield my books with any other protection than that which my Lord Jesus Christ himself offered for his teaching. When questioned before Annas about his teaching and struck by a servant, he said: 'If I have spoken wrongly, bear witness to the wrong' [John 18:19–23]. If the Lord himself, who knew that he could not err, did not refuse to hear testimony against his teaching, even from the lowliest servant, how much more ought I, who am the lowest scum and able to do nothing except err, desire and expect that somebody should want to offer testimony against my teaching! Therefore, I ask by the mercy of God, may your most serene majesty, most illustrious lordships, or anyone at all who is able, either high or low, bear witness, expose my errors, overthrowing them by the writings of the prophets and the evangelists. Once I have been taught I shall be quite ready to renounce every error, and I shall be the first to cast my books into the fire.

"From these remarks I think it is clear that I have sufficiently considered and weighed the hazards and dangers, as well as the excitement and dissensions aroused in the world as a result of my teachings, things about which I was gravely and forcefully warned yesterday. To see excitement and dissension arise because of the Word of God is to me clearly the most joyful aspect of all in these matters. For this is the way, the opportunity, and the result of the Word of God, just as He [Christ] said, 'I have not come to bring peace, but a sword. For I have come to set a man against his father, etc.' [Matthew 10:34–35]. . . . Therefore we must fear God. I do not say these things because there is a need of either my teachings or my warnings for such leaders as you, but because I must not withhold the allegiance which I owe my Germany. With these words I commend myself to your most serene majesty and to your lordships, humbly asking that I not be allowed through the agitation of my enemies, without cause, to be made hateful to you. I have finished."

When I had finished, the speaker for the emperor said, as if in reproach that I had not answered the question, that I ought not call into question those things which had been condemned and defined in councils; therefore what was sought from me was not a horned response, but a simple one, whether or not I wished to retract.

Here I answered:

"Since then your serene majesty and your lordships seek a simple answer, I will give it in this manner, neither horned nor toothed: Unless I am convinced by the testimony of the Scriptures or by clear reason (for I do not trust either in the pope or in councils alone, since it is well known that they have often errored and contradicted themselves), I am bound by the Scriptures I have quoted and my conscience is captive to the Word of God. I cannot and I will not retract anything, since it is neither safe nor right to go against conscience.

"I cannot do otherwise, here I stand, may God help me, Amen."

The Edict of Worms (1521)

EMPEROR CHARLES V

In view of . . . the fact that Martin Luther still persists obstinately and perversely in maintaining his heretical opinions, and consequently all pious and God-fearing persons abominate and abhor him as one mad or possessed by a demon . . . we have declared and made known that the said Martin Luther shall hereafter be held and esteemed by each and all of us as a limb cut off

"The Edict of Worms" is from James H. Robinson, ed., *Readings in European History,* vol. 2 (Boston: Ginn and Company, 1906), pp. 87–88.

from the Church of God, an obstinate schismatic and manifest heretic. . . .

And we publicly attest by these letters that we order and command each and all of you, as you owe fidelity to us and the Holy Empire, and would escape the penalties of the crime of treason, and the ban and over-ban of the Empire, and the forfeiture of all regalia, fiefs, privileges, and immunities, which up to this time you have in any way obtained from our predecessors, ourself, and the Holy Roman Empire—commanding, we say, in the name of the Roman and imperial majesty, we strictly order that immediately after the expiration of the appointed twenty days, terminating on the fourteenth day of May, you shall refuse to give the aforesaid Martin Luther hospitality, lodging, food, or drink; neither shall any one, by word or deed, secretly or openly, succor or assist him by counsel or help; but in whatever place you meet him, you shall proceed against him; if you have sufficient force, you shall take him prisoner and keep him in close custody; you shall deliver him, or cause him to be delivered, to us or at least let us know where he may be captured. In the meanwhile you shall keep him closely imprisoned until you receive notice from us what further to do, according to the direction of the laws. And for such holy and pious work we will indemnify you for your trouble and expense. . . .

And in order that all this may be done and credit given to this document we have sealed it with our imperial seal, which has been affixed in our imperial city of Worms, on the eighth day of May, after the birth of Christ 1521, in the second year of our reign over the Roman Empire, and over our other lands the sixth.

By our lord the emperor's own command.

Social and Political Aspects of the Lutheran Reformation

The Lutheran Reformation was not simply spiritual or corrective in nature, for it had many political and social repercussions as well. In response to the celibacy demanded of priests by the church, Luther advocated that clergy be allowed to marry. He himself married a former nun. Such defiance in one sphere was confusing for certain elements of society that saw Luther as their champion as well. In 1524, a major peasant revolt broke out in Germany as social and economic conflicts came to a head. The peasants demanded freedom from the long-standing feudal obligations of serfdom. Luther understood that the survival of his movement depended on the political influence and protection of the nobility. Although Luther sympathized with the peasants, he clearly sided with the nobility, and they savagely crushed the revolt.

On Celibacy and Marriage

MARTIN LUTHER

First, not every priest can do without a woman, not only on account of the weakness of the flesh but much more because of the needs of the household. If, then, he is to keep a woman, and the pope grants him permission to do so, but he may not have her in marriage, what is this but leaving a man and a woman alone and forbidding them to fall? It is like putting fire and straw together and commanding that there shall be neither smoke nor fire. Secondly, the pope has as little power to give this command as he has to forbid eating, drinking, the natural process of bodily elimination or becoming fat. No one, therefore, is in duty bound to keep this commandment and the pope is responsible for all the sins that are committed against this ordinance, for all the souls lost thereby, and for all consciences thereby confused and tortured. Consequently, he undoubtedly has deserved long ago that someone should drive him out of the world, so many souls has he strangled with this devilish snare; although I hope that God has been more gracious to many of them at their end than the pope had been during their life. Nothing good has ever come out of the papacy and its laws, nor ever will.

Listen! In all my days I have not heard the confession of a nun, but in the light of Scripture I shall hit upon how matters fare with her and know I shall not be lying. If a girl is not sustained by great and exceptional grace, she can live without a man as little as she can without eating, drinking, sleeping, and other natural necessities. Nor, on the other hand, can a man dispense with a wife. The reason for this is that

procreating children is an urge planted as deeply in human nature as eating and drinking. That is why God has given and put into the body the organs, arteries, fluxes, and everything that serves it. Therefore what is he doing who would check this process and keep nature from running its desired and intended course? He is attempting to keep nature from being nature, fire from burning, water from wetting, and a man from eating, drinking, and sleeping.

Whoever intends to enter married life should do so in faith and in God's name. He should pray that it may prosper according to His will and that marriage may not be treated as a matter of fun and folly. It is a hazardous matter and as serious as anything on earth can be. Therefore we should not rush into it as the world does, in keeping with its frivolousness and wantonness and in pursuit of its pleasure; but before taking this step we should consult God, so that we may lead our married life to His glory. Those who do not go about it in this way may certainly thank God if it turns out well. If it turns out badly, they should not be surprised; for they did not begin it in the name of God and did not ask for His blessing.

Condemnation of the Peasant Revolt (1524)

MARTIN LUTHER

In my preceding pamphlet [on the "Twelve Articles"] I had no occasion to condemn the peasants, because they promised to yield to law and better instruction, as Christ also demands (Matt. 7.1). But before I can turn around, they go out and appeal to force, in spite of their promises and rob and pillage and act like mad

What Luther Says, Vol. 2 © 1959, 1987 Concordia Publishing House. Used with permission.

"Condemnation of the Peasant Revolt" is from James H. Robinson, ed., *Readings in European History*, vol. 1 (Boston: Ginn and Company, 1904), pp. 106–108.

dogs. From this it is quite apparent what they had in their false minds, and that what they put forth under the name of the gospel in the "Twelve Articles" was all vain pretense. In short, they practice mere devil's work, and it is the arch-devil himself who reigns at Muhlhausen, indulging in nothing but robbery, murder, and bloodshed; as Christ says of the devil in John 8.44, "he was a murderer from the beginning." Since, therefore, those peasants and miserable wretches allow themselves to be led astray and act differently from what they declared, I likewise must write differently concerning them; and first bring their sins before their eyes, as God commands (Isa. 58.1; Ezek. 2.7), whether perchance some of them may come to their senses; and, further, I would instruct those in authority how to conduct themselves in this matter.

With threefold horrible sins against God and men have these peasants loaded themselves, for which they have deserved a manifold death of body and soul.

First, they have sworn to their true and gracious rulers to be submissive and obedient, in accord with God's command (Matt. 22.21), "Render therefore unto Caesar the things which are Caesar's," and (Rom. 13.1), "Let every soul be subject unto the higher powers." But since they have deliberately and sacrilegiously abandoned their obedience, and in addition have dared to oppose their lords, they have thereby forfeited body and soul, as perfidious, perjured, lying, disobedient wretches and scoundrels are wont to do. Wherefore St. Paul judges them saying (Rom. 13.2), "And they that resist shall receive to themselves damnation." The peasants will incur this sentence, sooner or later; for God wills that fidelity and allegiance shall be sacredly kept.

Second, they cause uproar and sacrilegiously rob and pillage monasteries and castles that do not belong to them, for which, like public highwaymen and murderers, they deserve the twofold death of body and soul. It is right and lawful to slay at the first opportunity a rebellious person, who is known as such, for he is already under God's and the emperor's ban. Every man is at once judge and executioner of a public rebel; just as, when a fire starts, he who can extinguish it first is the best fellow. Rebellion is not simply vile murder, but is like a great fire that kindles and devastates a country; it fills the land with murder and bloodshed, makes widows and orphans, and destroys everything, like the greatest calamity. Therefore, whosoever can, should smite, strangle, and stab, secretly or publicly, and should remember that there is nothing more poisonous, pernicious, and devilish than a rebellious man. Just as one must slay a mad dog, so, if you do not fight the rebels, they will fight you, and the whole country with you.

Third, they cloak their frightful and revolting sins with the gospel, call themselves Christian brethren, swear allegiance, and compel people to join them in such abominations. Thereby they become the greatest blasphemers and violators of God's holy name, and serve and honor the devil under the semblance of the gospel, so that they have ten times deserved death of body and soul, for never have I heard of uglier sins. And I believe also that the devil foresees the judgment day, that he undertakes such an unheard-of measure; as if he said, "It is the last and therefore it shall be the worst; I'll stir up the dregs and knock the very bottom out." May the Lord restrain him! Lo, how mighty a prince is the devil, how he holds the world in his hands and can put it to confusion; who else could so soon capture so many thousands of peasants, lead them astray, blind and deceive them, stir them to revolt, and make them the willing executioners of his malice. . . .

And should the peasants prevail (which God forbid!),—for all things are possible to God, and we know not but that he is preparing for the judgment day, which cannot be far distant, and may purpose to destroy, by means of the devil, all order and authority and throw the world into wild chaos,—yet surely they who are found, sword in hand, shall perish in the wreck with clear consciences, leaving to the devil the kingdom of this world and receiving instead the eternal kingdom. For we are come upon such strange times that a prince may more easily win heaven by the shedding of blood than others by prayers.

In the Wake of Luther

John Calvin and the Genevan Reformation

Although Lutheranism formed the basis of the Reformation, by the mid-sixteenth century it had lost much of its energy and was confined to Germany and Scandinavia. The movement was spread throughout Europe by other reformers, the most influential of whom was John Calvin (1509–1564).

A trained lawyer and classical scholar, Calvin had been a convert to Luther's ideas and was forced to leave France, eventually settling in Geneva in the 1530s. There in the 1540s he established a very structured society that can best be described as a theocracy. Calvin's strict adherence to biblical authority and his singular strength of personality can be seen in his treatise, On the Necessity of Reforming the Church. *In it he defines the church as "a society of all the saints, a society spread over the whole world, and existing in all ages, yet bound together by the one doctrine and the one Spirit of Christ." In the words of Saint Cyprian, which Calvin often quoted, "We cannot have God for our Father without having the Church for our mother." The importance of this idea cannot be overestimated in Calvin's understanding of doctrine and of the reform of the church. In the following excerpt from his famous treatise, which was addressed to the Holy Roman Emperor Charles V in 1544, Calvin expressed disgust that the church had become divorced from the society of saints it was supposed to serve. The continuity of the church as a universal embodiment of all believers had to be reestablished through clerical reform and a reconceptualization of Spirit.*

On the Necessity of Reforming the Church (1544)

JOHN CALVIN

In the present condition of the empire, your Imperial Majesty, and you, Most Illustrious Princes, necessarily involved in various cares, and distracted by a multiplicity of business, are agitated, and in a manner tempest-tossed. . . . I feel what nerve, what earnestness, what urgency, what ardor, the treatment of this subject requires. . . . First, call to mind the fearful calamities of the Church, which might move to pity even minds of iron. Nay, set before your eyes her squalid and unsightly form, and the sad devastation which is everywhere beheld. How long, pray, will you allow the spouse of Christ, the mother of you all, to lie thus protracted and afflicted—thus, too, when she is imploring your protection, and when the means of relief are at hand? Next, consider how much worse calamities impend. Final destruction

"On the Necessity of Reforming the Church" is from John Calvin, *Tracts and Treatises on the Reformation of the Church*, trans. by Henry Beveridge, vol. 1 (Edinburgh: Calvin Translation Society, 1844), pp. 231-234.

cannot be far off, unless you interpose with the utmost speed. Christ will, indeed, in the way which to him seems good, preserve his Church miraculously, and beyond human expectation; but this I say, that the consequence of a little longer delay on your part will be, that in Germany we shall not have even the form of a Church. Look round, and see how many indications threaten that ruin which it is your duty to prevent, and announce that it is actually at hand. These things speak loud enough, though I were silent. . . .

Divine worship being corrupted by so many false opinions, and perverted by so many impious and foul superstitions, the sacred Majesty of God is insulted with atrocious contempt, his holy name profaned, his glory only not trampled under foot. Nay, while the whole Christian world is openly polluted with idolatry, men adore, instead of Him, their own fictions. A thousand superstitions reign, superstitions which are just so many open insults to Him. The power of Christ is almost obliterated from the minds of men, the hope of salvation is transferred from him to empty, frivolous, and insignificant ceremonies, while there is a pollution of the Sacraments not less to be execrated.

Baptism is deformed by numerous additions, the Holy Supper [communion] is prostituted to all kinds of ignominy, religion throughout has degenerated into an entirely different form. . . .

In the future, therefore, as often as you shall hear the croaking note—"The business of reforming the Church must be delayed for the present"—"there will be time enough to accomplish it after other matters are transacted"—remember, Most Invincible Emperor, that the matter on which you are to deliberate is, whether you are to leave to your posterity some empire or none. Yet, why do I speak of posterity? Even now, while your own eyes behold, it is half bent, and totters to its final ruin. . . .

But be the issue what it may, we will never repent of having begun, and of having proceeded thus far. The Holy Spirit is a faithful and unerring witness to our doctrine. We know, I say, that it is the eternal truth of God that we preach. We are, indeed, desirous, as we ought to be, that our ministry may prove salutary to the world; but to give it this effect belongs to God, not to us. If, to punish, partly the ingratitude, and partly the stubbornness of those to whom we desire to do good, success must prove desperate, and all things go to worse, I will say what it befits a Christian man to say, and what all who are true to this holy profession will subscribe: We will die, but in death even be conquerors, not only because through it we shall have a sure passage to a better life, but because we know that our blood will be as seed to propagate the Divine truth which men now despise.

Predestination: Institutes of the Christian Religion (1536)

JOHN CALVIN

Calvin's doctrines were primarily Lutheran in nature, but Calvin went a step beyond and stressed the doctrine of predestination: One's salvation had already been determined by God, and those elect who had been "chosen" gave evidence of their calling by living exemplary lives. Calvinism became popular in the Netherlands and Scotland and it formed the core of the Puritan belief that was to be so influential in the colonization of America. The following excerpts reveal Calvin's justification for reform, his concept of predestination, and his strict regulation of lives and beliefs in Geneva.

The covenant of life is not preached equally to all, and among those to whom it is preached, does not always meet with the same reception. This diversity displays the unsearchable depth of the divine judgment, and is without doubt subordinate to God's purpose of eternal election. But it is plainly owing to the mere pleasure of God that salvation is spontaneously offered to some, while others have no access to it, great and difficult questions immediately arise, questions which are inexplicable, when just views are not entertained concerning election and predestination. . . . By predestination we mean the eternal decree of God, by which he determined with himself whatever he wished to happen with regard to every man. All are not created on equal terms, but some are preordained to eternal life, others to eternal damnation; and, accordingly, as each has been created for one or other of these ends, we say that he has been predestined to life or to death. . . .

We say, then, that Scripture clearly proves this much, that God by his eternal and immutable counsel determined once for all those whom it was his pleasure one day to admit to salvation, and those whom, on the other hand, it was his pleasure to doom to destruction. We maintain that this counsel, as regards the elect, is founded on his free mercy, without any respect to human worth, while those whom he dooms to destruction are excluded from access to life by a just

"Predestination" is from John Calvin, *Institutes of the Christian Religion*, vol. 2, trans. Henry Beveridge (Edinburgh: Calvin Translation Society, 1845), pp. 529, 534, 540.

and blameless, but at the same time incomprehensible judgment. In regard to the elect, we regard calling as the evidence of election, and justification as another symbol of its manifestation, until it is fully accomplished by the attainment of glory. But as the Lord seals his elect by calling and justification, so by excluding the reprobate either from the knowledge of his name or the sanctification of his Spirit, he by these marks in a manner discloses the judgment which awaits them. I will here omit many of the fictions which foolish men have devised to overthrow predestination. There is no need of refuting objections which the moment they are produced abundantly betray their hollowness. I will dwell only on those points which either form the subject of dispute among the learned, or may occasion any difficulty to the simple. . . .

The Genevan Catechism: Concerning the Lord's Supper (1541)

JOHN CALVIN

The minister: Have we in the supper simply a signification of the things above mentioned, or are they given to us in reality?

"The Genevan Catechism" is from James H. Robinson, ed., *Translations and Reprints from the Original Sources of European History*, vol. 3 (Philadelphia: University of Pennsylvania, 1902), pp. 8–9.

The child: Since Jesus Christ is truth itself there can be no doubt that the promises he has made regarding the supper are accomplished, and that what is figured there is verified there also. Wherefore according as he promises and represents I have no doubt that he makes us partakers of his own substance, in order that he may unite us with him in one life.

The minister: But how may this be, when the Body of Jesus Christ is in heaven, and we are on this earthly pilgrimage?

The child: It comes about through the incomprehensible power of his spirit, which may indeed unite things widely separated in space.

The minister: You do not understand then that the body is enclosed in the bread, or the blood in the cup?

The child: No. On the contrary, in order that the reality of the sacrament be achieved our hearts must be raised to heaven, where Jesus Christ dwells in the glory of the Father, whence we await him for our redemption; and we are not to seek him in these corruptible elements.

The minister: You understand then that there are two things in this sacrament: the natural bread and wine, which we see with the eye, touch with the hand and perceive with the taste; and Jesus Christ, through whom our souls are inwardly nourished?

The child: I do. In such a way moreover that we have there the very witness and so say a pledge of the resurrection of our bodies; since they are made partakers in the symbol of life.

The English Reformation

The Protestant Reformation has often been viewed as essentially a spiritual movement that had fundamental political and social impact throughout Europe. But the motives of some reformers were not purely spiritual, and they sought a more expedient premise. As the Reformation spread to Switzerland, northern Germany, and Scandinavia, it met with little organized opposition. But England, it seemed, was prepared to resist any incursion. Its monarch, Henry VIII, was a gregarious and dynamic king who had grown up amidst political intrigue and international power plays in the court of his father, Henry Tudor (VII). Henry VIII knew how to handle himself politically and sought to maintain domestic tranquility by promoting secure alliances abroad.

Henry VIII had himself been a pawn in his father's political accommodations. In order to preserve an alliance with Spain, Henry had been allowed to marry his brother's widow, Catherine of Aragon, through a special papal dispensation. For a time, this arrangement seemed to work all around.

Theme: Church/State Relationships

The Historical Intersection

FRANCE: 1806

The Imperial Catechism

NAPOLEON BONAPARTE

Five years after Napoleon became head of the French government as first consul, he moved to expand his power, and on May 18, 1804, the Senate decreed that he should be made emperor of the French. The people of France overwhelmingly approved of this measure through a plebiscite. Napoleon now had complete control of France's government and fate. In fact, Napoleon crowned himself emperor since he did not recognize the pope's authority as superior to his own. Appropriately, Napoleon found divine sanction for his power. The following recounts a catechism written during the reign of Louis XIV and modified to meet Napoleon's particular needs. Its questions and answers address the duties of French citizens toward their emperor.

Compare and Contrast:

- Compare the structure of John Calvin's Genevan Catechism with that of Napoleon's Imperial Catechism. What do they demand respectively of the citizens of Geneva and the populace of France?

Question: What are the duties of Christians toward those who govern them, and what in particular are our duties towards Napoleon I, our emperor?

Answer: Christians owe to the princes who govern them, and we in particular owe to Napoleon I, our emperor, love, respect, obedience, fidelity, military service, and the taxes levied for the preservation and defense of the empire and of his throne. We also owe him fervent prayers for his safety and for the spiritual and temporal prosperity of the state.

(contd)

Question: Why are we subject to all these duties toward our emperor?

Answer: First, because God, who has created empires and distributes them according to his will, has, by loading our emperor with gifts both in peace and in war, established him as our sovereign and made him the agent of his power and his image on earth. To honor and serve our emperor is therefore to honor and serve God himself. Secondly, because our Lord Jesus Christ himself, both by his teaching and his example, has taught us what we owe to our sovereign. Even at his very birth he obeyed the edict of Caesar Augustus; he paid the established tax; and while he commanded us to render to God those things which belong to God, he also commanded us to render unto Caesar those things which are Caesar's.

Question: Are there not special motives which should attach us more closely to Napoleon I, our emperor?

Answer: Yes, for it is he whom God has raised up in trying times to reestablish the public worship of the holy religion of our fathers and to be its protector; he has reestablished and preserved public order by his profound and active wisdom; he defends the state by his mighty arm; he has become the anointed of the Lord by the consecration which he has received from the sovereign pontiff, head of the Church universal.

Question: What must we think of those who are neglecting their duties toward our emperor?

Answer: According to the apostle Paul, they are resisting the order established by God himself, and render themselves worthy of eternal damnation.

Consider This:

- Should we characterize Calvin as a spiritual leader and Napoleon as a political leader? How do these documents blur the boundaries of such designations? In order to obtain effective control over people, must spiritual leaders grant themselves political power and must political leaders claim spiritual authority?

"The Imperial Catechism" is from James H. Robinson and Charles A. Beard, eds., *Readings in Modern European History*, vol. 1 (Boston: Ginn and Company, 1908), pp. 351–352.

Henry VIII had proved a dutiful son of the church by writing a religious tract supporting the pope, which earned him the title "Defender of the Faith." But Henry became concerned when Catherine suffered a series of miscarriages and was unable to provide a male heir to the Tudor throne. Although she bore Henry a daughter named Mary, this did not conciliate the English king. To secure the succession, he needed a male heir, so he turned to a young favorite at court named Anne Boleyn. When Henry wanted an annulment of his marriage to Catherine on the grounds that his union with his brother's widow was incestuous and accursed by God, the pope could not renege on his earlier dispensation. The pathway to a workable solution seemed closed. Henry became increasingly consumed with the need to stabilize the future of England with a male heir. He finally decided to break with Rome and found the Church of England with himself as head. He granted himself a divorce from Catherine and married Anne in 1533. He was excommunicated by the pope "with the sword of eternal damnation" that same year. Henry did not buckle. The Protestant Reformation had come to England, although through political expediency rather than through spiritual commitment.

The following sources are essential in understanding the English Reformation. The first is the Act of Supremacy (1534), which recognized Henry VIII as the supreme head of the Church of England. He had already extorted from the English bishops, abbots, and priests written declaration that the pope had no more authority in England than any other foreign bishop. The next source is an excerpt from "The Act of Succession" (1534), which declared his marriage with Catherine void and provided for the royal succession: Anne's daughter, the princess Elizabeth, would succeed unless Anne should have sons by the king. Note the harsh provisions should anyone not accept the arrangement. Anne, indeed, failed to produce a son and paid for it with her life as Henry accused her of adultery and moved on to more fertile pastures. Elizabeth was then bumped down the succession ladder.

The Supremacy Act (1534): "The Only Supreme Head of the Church of England"

Albeit the king's majesty firstly and rightfully is and ought to be the supreme head of the Church of England, and so is recognized by the clergy of this realm in their Convocations . . . ; be it enacted by authority of this present Parliament, that the king our sovereign lord, his heirs and successors, kings of this realm, shall be taken, accepted, and reputed the only supreme head in earth of the Church of England . . . and shall have and enjoy, annexed and united to the imperial crown of this realm, as well the title and style thereof, as all honors, dignities, pre-eminences, jurisdictions, privileges, authorities, immunities, profits, and commodities to the said dignity of supreme head of the same Church . . . ; and that our said sovereign lord, his heirs and successors, kings of this realm, shall have full power and authority from time to time to visit, repress, redress, reform, order, correct, restrain, and amend all such errors, heresies, abuses, offenses, contempts, and enormities, whatsoever

they be. . . to the pleasure of Almighty God, the increase of virtue in Christ's religion, and for the conservation of the peace, unity, and tranquility of this realm. . . .

The Act of Succession (1534)

If any person or persons, of what estate, dignity, or condition whosoever they be, maliciously, by writing, print, deed, or act, procure or do any thing or things to the prejudice, slander, or derogation of the said lawful matrimony solemnized between your Majesty and the said Queen Anne, or to the peril or slander of any of the heirs of your Highness, being limited by this act to inherit the crown of this realm, every such person and persons, and their aiders and abettors, shall be adjudged high traitors, and every such offense shall be adjudged high treason, and the offenders . . . shall suffer pain of death, as in cases of high treason.

All are to be sworn truly, firmly, and constantly, without fraud or guile, to observe, fulfill, maintain, and keep, . . . to the utmost of their powers, the whole effects and contents of this present act.

"The Supremacy Act" is from *Statutes of the Realm*, vol. 3, no. 492, in Henry Gee and W. J. Hardy, eds., *Documents Illustrative of English Church History* (London: Macmillan and Co., Ltd., 1896), pp. 243–244.

"The Act of Succession" is from *Statutes of the Realm*, vol. 3, no. 471, in Henry Gee and W. J. Hardy, eds., *Documents Illustrative of English Church History* (London: Macmillan and Co., Ltd., 1896), p. 240.

The Enforcement of the Elizabethan Settlement (1593):
"Divine Service According to Her Majesty's Laws"

Henry VIII was certainly no Protestant, although he utilized the political and economic advantages of declaring himself a Protestant. He enforced Catholic doctrine in his Church of England while rejecting the control of the pope. But after his death, his son Edward VI (1547–1553), embraced Protestantism and issued an official Book of Common Prayer and several statutes establishing the primacy of Protestant doctrine. Upon Edward's death in 1553, Henry VIII's daughter by Catherine, Mary Tudor, became queen. She had been raised a Catholic and was married to Philip II, King of Spain. Her brutal attempts to reinstate Catholicism in England by burning heretics earned her the epithet "Bloody Mary."

After Mary's unsettling reign, Henry VIII's daughter by Anne Boleyn came to the throne as Elizabeth I (1558–1603). A talented and diligent queen, she became one of the greatest of all English monarchs, and her reign established England as the most formidable political power of its age. Her religious solution to the struggle between Catholicism and Protestantism was a compromise: The Church of England would be Protestant in doctrine and Catholic in ritual. This "Anglican Settlement" would endure, though Catholic dissent and Protestant attempts at "purifying" or purging Catholic elements from the Church of England would not be settled for nearly two centuries. The following selection demonstrates Elizabeth's commitment to enforcing her religious compromise by demanding Catholic allegiance to the authority of the English crown. Other statutes demanding Puritan obeisance were likewise initiated.

For the better discovering and avoiding of all such traitorous and most dangerous conspiracies and attempts as are daily devised and practiced against our most gracious sovereign lady the queen's majesty and the happy estate of this commonweal, by sundry wicked and seditious persons, who, terming themselves Catholics, and being indeed spies and intelligencers, not only for her majesty's foreign enemies, but also for rebellious and traitorous subjects born within her highness's realms and dominions, and hiding their most detestable and devilish purposes under a false pretext of religion and conscience, do secretly wander and shift from place to place within this realm, to corrupt and seduce her majesty's subjects, and to stir them to sedition and rebellion: Be it ordained and enacted by our sovereign lady the queen's majesty, and the Lords spiritual and temporal, and the Commons, in this present Parliament assembled, and by the authority of the same, that every person above the age of sixteen years, born within any of the queen's majesty's realms and dominions. . . shall come to some parish church on some Sunday or other festival day, and then and there hear divine service, and . . . make public and open submission and declaration of his and their conformity to her majesty's laws and statutes. . . .

The Catholic Reformation

The Society of Jesus

During the Protestant movement, the Catholic church was active in its own efforts to reform from within. The Society of Jesus (Jesuits) was a religious order founded by Ignatius Loyola in 1540.

"The Enforcement of the Elizabethan Settlement" is from *Statutes of the Realm*, vol. 4, pt. 2, p. 843, in Henry Gee and W. J. Hardy, eds., *Documents Illustrative of English Church History* (London: Macmillan and Co., Ltd., 1896), pp. 499, 506.

Loyola (1491–1556) was a soldier who had turned to religion while recovering from wounds. Under Loyola's firm leadership, the Jesuits became a disciplined organization that was dedicated to serving the pope with unquestioned loyalty. The next two selections from the constitution of the society and the famous spiritual exercises of Loyola demonstrate the purity and determination of these Catholic reformers.

Constitution (1540)

He who desires to fight for God under the banner of the cross in our society,—which we wish to distinguish by the name of Jesus,—and to serve God alone and the Roman pontiff, his vicar on earth, after a solemn vow of perpetual chastity, shall set this thought before his mind, that he is a part of a society founded for the especial purpose of providing for the advancement of souls in Christian life and doctrine and for the propagation of faith through public preaching and the ministry of the word of God, spiritual exercises and deeds of charity, and in particular through the training of the young and ignorant in Christianity and through the spiritual consolation of the faithful of Christ in hearing confessions; and he shall take care to keep first God and next the purpose of this organization always before his eyes. . . .

All the members shall realize, and shall recall daily, as long as they live, that this society as a whole and in every part is fighting for God under faithful obedience to one most holy lord, the pope, and to other Roman pontiffs who succeed him. And although we are taught in the gospel and through the orthodox faith to recognize and steadfastly profess that all the faithful of Christ are subject to the Roman pontiff as their head and as the vicar of Jesus Christ, yet we have adjudged that, for the special promotion of greater humility in our society and the perfect mortification of every individual and the sacrifice of our own wills, we should each be bound by a peculiar vow, in addition to the general obligation, that whatever the present Roman pontiff, or any future one, may from

time to time decree regarding the welfare of souls and the propagation of the faith, we are pledged to obey without evasion or excuse, instantly, so far as in us lies, whether he send us to the Turks or any other infidels, even to those who inhabit the regions men call the Indies; whether to heretics or schismatics, or, on the other hand, to certain of the faithful.

Spiritual Exercises (1548)
IGNATIUS LOYOLA

1. Always to be ready to obey with mind and heart, setting aside all judgement of one's own, the true spouse of Jesus Christ, our holy mother our infallible and orthodox mistress, the Catholic Church, whose authority is exercised over us by the hierarchy.

2. To commend the confession of sins to a priest as it is practised in the Church; the reception of the Holy Eucharist once a year, or better still every week, or at least every month, with the necessary preparation.

4. To have a great esteem for the religious orders, and to give the preference to celibacy or virginity over the married state.

5. To approve of the religious vows of chastity, poverty, perpetual obedience, as well as the other works of perfection and supererogation. Let us remark in passing, that we must never engage by vow to take a state (such e.g. as marriage) that would be an impediment to one more perfect. . . .

6. To praise relics, the veneration and invocation of Saints: also the stations, and pious pilgrimages, indulgences, jubilees, the custom of

"Constitution" is from James H. Robinson, ed., *Readings in European History*, vol. 1 (Boston: Ginn and Company, 1904), pp. 162–163.

Bettenson, Henry, ed., *Documents of the Christian Church*, Second Edition. Copyright © 1963. Reprinted by permission of Oxford University Press.

lighting candles in the churches, and other such aids to piety and devotion. . . .

9. To uphold especially all the precepts of the Church, and not censure them in any manner; but, on the contrary, to defend them promptly, with reasons drawn from all sources, against those who criticize them.

10.   To be eager to commend the decrees, mandates, traditions, rites and conduct; although there may not always be the uprightness of conduct that there ought to be, yet to attack or revile them in private or in public tends to scandal and disorder. Such attacks set the people against their princes and pastors; we must avoid such reproaches and never attack superiors before inferiors. The best course is to make private approach to those who have power to remedy the evil.

The Council of Trent (1545–1563)

The Council of Trent was an involved effort by the Catholic church to clarify its doctrine and bring about internal reform. The Church sought to make its own stand in the face of the Protestant threat, and thus its traditional doctrinal views are set forth with firmness and confidence, as the first excerpt indicates. One of the most significant actions of Trent was its reorganization and codification of laws concerning censorship and the prohibition of books. The second selection, published after the Council closed, sets out some of the restrictions. These general rules were in force until they were replaced with new decrees in 1897.

The Profession of Faith

I profess . . . that true God is offered in the Mass, a proper and propitiatory sacrifice for the living and the dead, and that in the most Holy Eucharist there are truly, really and substantially the body and blood together with the soul and divinity of Our Lord Jesus Christ, and that a conversion is made of the whole substance of bread into his body and of the whole substance of wine into his blood, which conversion the Catholic Church calls transubstantiation. I also confess that the whole and entire Christ and the true sacrament is taken under the one species alone.

I hold unswervingly that there is a purgatory and that the souls there detained are helped by the intercessions of the faithful; likewise also that the Saints who reign with Christ are to be venerated and invoked; that they offer prayers to God for us and that their relics are to be venerated. I firmly assert that the images of Christ and of the ever-Virgin Mother of God, as also those of the older Saints, are to be kept and retained, and that due honour and veneration is to be accorded them; and I affirm that the power of indulgences has been left by Christ in the Church, and that their use is very salutary for Christian people.

I recognize the Holy Catholic and Apostolic Roman Church as the Mother and mistress of all churches; and I vow and swear true obedience to the Roman Pontiff, the successor of blessed Peter, the chief of the Apostles and the representative [*vicarius*] of Jesus Christ.

I accept and profess, without doubting the traditions, definitions and declarations of the sacred Canons and Oecumenical Councils and especially those of the holy Council of Trent. . . .

The Tridentine Index of Books (1564)

The holy council in the second session, celebrated under our most holy Lord, Pius IV, commissioned some fathers to consider what ought

Bettenson, Henry, ed., *Documents of the Christian Church,* Second Edition. Copyright © 1963. Reprinted by permission of Oxford University Press.

"The Tridentine Index of Books" is from J. Barry Colman, ed., *Readings in Church History,* rev. ed., vol. 2 (Westminster, MD: Christian Classics, Inc., 1985), pp. 705–706, 708.

to be done concerning various censures and books either suspected or pernicious and to report to this holy council. . . .

1. All books which have been condemned either by the supreme pontiffs or by ecumenical councils before the year 1515 and are not contained in this list, shall be considered condemned in the same manner as they were formerly condemned.

2. The books of those heresiarchs, who after the aforesaid year originated or revived heresies, as well as those who are or have been the heads or leaders of heretics, as Luther, Zwingli, Calvin, Balthasar Friedberg, Schwenkfeld, and others like these, whatever may be their name, title or nature or their heresy, are absolutely forbidden. The books of other heretics, moreover, which deal professedly with religion are absolutely condemned. Those on the other hand, which do not deal with religion and have by order of the bishops and inquisitors been examined by Catholic theologians and approved by them, are permitted. Likewise, Catholic books written by those who afterward fell into heresy, as well as by those who after their fall returned to the bosom of the Church, may be permitted if they have been approved by the theological faculty of a Catholic university or by the general inquisition.

3. The translations of writers, also ecclesiastical, which have till now been edited by condemned authors, are permitted provided they contain nothing contrary to sound doctrine. Translations of the books of the Old Testament may in the judgment of the bishop be permitted to learned and pious men only. . . . Translations of the New Testament made by authors of the first class of this list shall be permitted to no one, since great danger and little usefullness usually results to readers from their perusal. . . .

4. Since it is clear from experience that if the Sacred Books are permitted everywhere and without discrimination in the vernacular, there will by reason of the boldness of men arise therefrom more harm than good, the matter is in this respect left to the judgment of the bishop

or inquisitor, who may with the advice of the pastor or confessor permit the reading of the Sacred Books translated into the vernacular by Catholic authors to those who they know will derive from such reading no harm but rather an increase of faith and piety, which permission they must have in writing. Those, however, who presume to read or possess them without such permission may not receive absolution from their sins until they have handed them over to the authorities. . . .

5. Those books which sometimes produce the works of heretical authors, in which these add little or nothing of their own but rather collect therein the sayings of others, as lexicons, concordances, apothegms, parables, tables of contents and such like, are permitted if whatever needs to be eliminated in the additions is removed and corrected in accordance with the suggestions of the bishop, the inquisitor and Catholic theologians. . . .

7. Books which professedly deal with, narrate or teach things lascivious or obscene are absolutely prohibited, since not only the matter of faith but also that of morals, which are usually easily corrupted through the reading of such books, must be taken into consideration, and those who possess them are to be severely punished by the bishops. Ancient books written by heathens may by reason of their elegance and quality of style be permitted, but may by no means be read to children.

8. Books whose chief contents are good but in which things have incidentally been inserted which have reference to heresy, ungodliness, divination or superstition, may be permitted if by the authority of the general inquisition they have been purged by Catholic theologians. . . . Finally, all the faithful are commanded not to presume to read or possess any books contrary to the prescriptions of these rules or the prohibition of this list. And if anyone should read or possess books by heretics or writings by any author condemned and prohibited by reason of heresy or suspicion of false teaching, he incurs immediately the sentence of excommunication. . . .

CHRONOLOGY: The Age of the Renaissance and Reformation

1265–1321   Life of poet Dante Alighieri (*Divine Comedy*).

1294–1303   Pope Boniface VIII boldly reasserts church's claim to temporal power in Clericis Laicos (1298) and Unam Sanctam (1302). Boniface attacked, captured, and beaten by agents of the French king, Philip IV (1303).

1309–1377   "Babylonian Captivity": Residency of popes transferred to Avignon, France.

1304–1374   Life of poet and papal critic, Petrarch, who is considered to be the "Father of Humanism."

1337–1453   Hundred Years' War rages intermittently between England and France over English claims to the French throne.

1374–1444   Life of Leonardo Bruni, scholar and Chancellor of Florence, who gave definition to the humanist movement.

1378–1417   Great Schism, or division, between supporters of the popes in Rome and those who again reside in Avignon. Dispute has political ramifications as countries develop military alliances based on support of Rome or Avignon. Issue finally resolved by councils of the church.

1415   Execution of Czech reformer John Huss for heresy. After a decade of belligerent protests, the Hussites win significant religious reforms in Bohemia.

1434   Medici rule of Florence established by Cosimo d'Medici, banker to the popes, and patron of the arts.

1435–1455   Technology invented for movable type printing press by Johannes Gutenberg.

1452–1519   Life of Leonardo da Vinci, artist, scientist, and inventor.

1463–1494   Life of Pico della Mirandola, whose *Oration on the Dignity of Man* (1486) is the quintessential expression of humanism.

1478–1492   Florence ruled by Lorenzo d'Medici, called "The Magnificent." Florence at height of political and artistic influence.

1492   Columbus' first voyage to the eastern Bahamas in search of a route to India.

1492–1503   Corrupt papacy of Alexander VI.

1494–1498   Florence controlled by Dominican friar Girolamo Savonarola. He is excommunicated after a series of sermons condemning the pope. Savonarola welcomes French invasion of Charles VIII, but loses confidence of Florentines and is executed.

1498–1512   Florence survives as a true republic. Niccolò Machiavelli organizes the Florentine militia, which is defeated by Spanish mercenary forces (1512). Machiavelli looks toward a strong, practical rule and writes *The Prince* (1513).

1501–1504   Michelangelo's statue of David completed.

1503–1513 Papacy of Julius II, "Warrior Pope" and patron of the arts (commissions Michelangelo's painting of the Sistine Chapel, among other works).

1509 Desiderius Erasmus, a northern humanist, writes *The Praise of Folly*, a satire that criticizes abuses within the Church.

1510–1511 Raphael's "School of Athens" completed.

1517 Martin Luther posts his *Ninety-five Theses*, a list of grievances against indulgences, on the door of Wittenberg church in hopes of engaging clerical authorities in debate.

1519 Luther challenges authority of the pope and the inerrency of Church councils at the Leipzig Debate.

1519–1521 Hernando Cortés lands on the coast of Mexico and brutally defeats Aztec forces.

1520 Luther publishes two works: *Address to the Christian Nobility of the German Nation* and *On Christian Liberty*.

1521 Luther is excommunicated by order of the pope. Diet of Worms called to question him about his heretical writings. Luther is condemned and secretly leaves Worms.

1521–1522 Edict of Worms issued imposing the "ban of Empire" on Luther. Luther is hidden by friends at Wartburg Castle, where he translates the New Testament into German.

1523 Ulrich Zwingli active as Protestant reformer in Switzerland. Issues *Sixty-seven Articles*.

1524–1525 Peasant Revolt breaks out in Germany as peasants demand freedom from the long-standing feudal obligations of serfdom. Luther sides with aristocracy and condemns violence of peasants.

1529 Marburg Colloquy called by Philip of Hesse, who sought to unite Luther and Zwingli. Luther leaves thinking Zwingli a dangerous fanatic.

1534 Act of Supremacy declares Henry VIII of England "the only supreme head of the Church of England." Henry's political need for an heir forces his religious break with the Catholic church.

1534–1535 Anabaptists assume political power in the city of Münster. Theocracy imposed and polygamy practiced. Shocked Protestant and Catholic armies unite to crush the radicals.

1536 John Calvin arrives in Geneva. Publishes *Institutes of the Christian Religion*, which contains the doctrine of predestination.

1540 Jesuit order formed by Ignatius Loyola is recognized by the pope. The Jesuits became a disciplined organization that was dedicated to serving the pope with unquestioned loyalty.

1545–1563 Council of Trent is called to clarify Catholic doctrine and bring about internal reform.

1546	Death of Martin Luther.
1553–1558	Mary I restores Catholic doctrine to England.
1555	Peace of Augsburg recognizes the rights of Lutherans to worship as they please. Principle of *cuius regio, eius religio* is established: "The ruler of a land would determine the religion of the land."
1558–1603	Elizabeth I of England fashions an Anglican religious compromise settlement.
1572	Saint Bartholomew's Day Massacre in which 3,000 Huguenots in Paris and 20,000 throughout France are killed.
1588	Destruction of the Spanish Armada by English navy.
1589	Edict of Nantes legally recognizes the legitimacy of Calvinism.
1618-1648	The Thirty Years' War fought between Catholic and Protestant forces primarily in northern Europe.

STUDY QUESTIONS

Section I: The Renaissance Movement

1. How would you define "humanism"? Give examples of its most important tenets from the many sources offered in the section entitled "The Humanist Movement." According to Pico della Mirandola, what is man's relationship to God? The humanists were criticized by the church for their secular interest at the expense of devotion to God. Do you agree with this criticism? Were the humanists disrespectful of God and irreligious? Note especially Marsilio Ficino on this point. In his opinion, what is man's position with respect to God?

2. Niccolò Machiavelli has been called "the disciple of the Devil." After reading the excerpts from *The Prince*, why do you think this view has prevailed? Is it better for a prince to be loved or feared? Why kill all enemies or potential enemies when you come into power through crime? Interpret the phrase "the ends justify the means." How does Machiavelli's view of human nature compare with that of other Renaissance humanists? Do you see Machiavelli as moral, immoral, or amoral? Why did he write *The Prince*?

3. Why has Leonardo da Vinci been called a "universal man"? After reading the selections from his sketchbook, what impressions do you have of him? In answering this, make specific reference to passages in the sources. Leonardo was an illegitimate child and was very pleased with that fact. Why was illegitimacy beneficial for the aspiring Renaissance man?

4. Politically, the Renaissance in Italy was an insecure, chaotic period, with shifting alliances and numerous invasions. Amid all this disunity, an intense cultural creativity was reflected in the art and music of the period. Do you think that chaos is a prerequisite for creativity or at least a contributor to creative energy? Or are great art, literature, and music best fostered in an atmosphere of relative calm and security? Relate this question specifically to the Renaissance, but also give contemporary examples when possible.

5. What was a courtier, and what did Castiglione require of him? Why do you think Castiglione's book was so popular? What values of Renaissance society does it promote? According to Castiglione, what should be the relationship between women and men?

6. In 1929, the British author Virginia Woolf commented in her book *A Room of One's Own* that "women have served all these centuries as looking-glasses possessing the magic and delicious power of reflecting the figure of man at twice its natural size." How would you compare this idea to Castiglione's view that "woman does not receive her being from man, but rather perfects him just as she is perfected by him." Do you agree that the relationship between men and women is symbiotic or have women been held in lesser esteem throughout the centuries because they have been expected to enhance the image of men? How modern is Castiglione in his thinking?

Section II: The Reformation Era

7. Why were indulgences so detested by critics of the church? Can you construct a logical argument in support of indulgences with which the church could have satisfactorily defended itself against criticism? Is the principle of indulgences at issue here, or just the manner in which they were sold?

8. What would you identify as the underlying causes for the Reformation, and what is the "spark" that set things in motion? To what extent was Martin Luther's action directed against abuses within the church?

9. What were Luther's arguments against the peasants in 1524? Are they persuasive? What does Luther's condemnation of the Peasants' Revolt tell you about his reform movement? Do you regard Luther as a hypocrite or not?

10. In the treatise *On the Necessity of Reforming the Church*, what is John Calvin's primary message to the Holy Roman Emperor Charles V? Do you think Calvin was exaggerating when he reminded the Emperor that "the matter on which you are to deliberate is, whether you are to leave to your posterity some empire or none"?

11. How would you define the concept of predestination and why is it so efficient as a device for controlling a congregation? What was the basis for the success of the Calvinist movement?

12. Did the English Reformation involve personal conscience or political expediency? How was the religious authority of the monarch achieved?

13. Read carefully the sections on the Society of Jesus and the Council of Trent. What specifically do Loyola and the Council of Trent demand from the Catholic faithful? Was the Catholic Reformation progressive in its intent? Why then does the Tridentine Index of Books seem so repressive? Can faith be enforced in this manner? Some historians have called the Catholic reform movement the "Counter Reformation." Do you think a reformation of the church would have occurred without Martin Luther? How important was Luther in changing history?

14. A critical issue of the Reformation era centered on the diverse means of attaining salvation. How is this issue reflected in the sources? According to Luther, Calvin, Loyola, and the Catholic church, how is one saved? Be specific in your documentation.

15. One of the most important questions of this period that separated the reformers from the church centered on religious authority. In spiritual matters, did religious authority rest in the church (as dictated by the pope), in church councils (such as Trent), in scripture, or in individual conscience? How is this problem reflected in the sources?

16. Edward Bulwer-Lytton once said, "A reform is a correction of abuses; a revolution is a transfer of power." Under this definition, would you consider the Protestant Reformation to be a revolution?

11

East and West: The Interaction of New Worlds

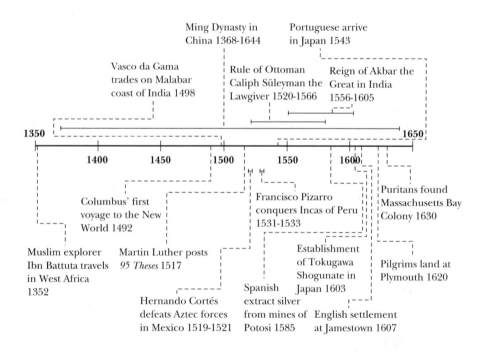

They are poor discoverers who think that there is no land when they see nothing but sea.

—*Sir Francis Bacon*

The destiny of nations depends on how they nourish themselves.

—*Jean Anthelme Brillat-Savarin*

It should be noted that when he seizes a state, the new ruler ought to determine the injuries that he will need to inflict. He should then inflict them all at once, and not have to renew them everyday.

—*Niccolò Machiavelli*

The use of force is but temporary. It may subdue for a moment; but it does not remove the necessity of subduing again—and a nation is not governed, which is perpetually to be conquered.

—*Edmund Burke*

I teach kings the history of their ancestors so that the lives of the ancients might serve them as an example, for the world is old, but the future springs from the past.

—*The Griot, Mamoudou Kouyaté*

CHAPTER THEMES

- *Systems of Government:* How did political and economic rivalry among world powers provide motives for exploration and conquest? How did the centralization of monarchies during the sixteenth and seventeenth centuries contribute to the acquisition and maintenance of empire?

- *Imperialism:* Why did Europeans explore, conquer, and settle lands in the new worlds of America, Africa, and Asia? Why were they particularly successful in suppressing natives? How important is technology as a factor in progress and destruction? What were the motives behind Chinese or Muslim exploration? Is imperialism a process that inherently carries the seeds of genocide? What are those components?

- *Propaganda:* How did Europeans justify their exploitation of the Americas? In order to justify conquest or genocide, must the conquered be methodically dehumanized? How has this process been repeated throughout history and in other world societies?

- *Church/State Relationships:* What role did the Catholic Church and Protestant religious exiles play in world exploration and in the settlement of the Americas? Are missionary motives simply another justification for conquest? Or did religious representatives work for accommodation and coexistence? How did the Chinese and Japanese react to Western missionaries? Were they a positive force in the settlement of the Americas? Was religion the primary motive in the creation of the great Islamic empires of the sixteenth and seventeenth centuries?

- *Historical Change and Transition:* What impact did the European exploration and conquest of the Americas have on the cultures of both regions? What are some of the "seeds of change" that ultimately linked these continents? Is the interaction between cultures both a beneficial and dangerous process? How and why did the Japanese isolate themselves from outside influences? In our modern world, can a culture be truly homogeneous? What are the challenges of cultural integration and diversity?

- ***The Big Picture:*** Must exploration always result in exploitation? How have world civilizations been changed through "first contact" over the last seven hundred years?

"Discovery! To know that you are walking where no others have walked; that you are beholding what the human eye has not seen before; to give birth to an idea, to discover a great thought. To be the first—that is the idea!" The wit and insight of Mark Twain have often been invoked to reflect on the motivations of the human heart and the condition of human societies. Twain, in his experience as an adventurer and observer of people, did not shield us from the glory and foibles of human endeavor. Perhaps central to our human nature is the need to know, our curiosity that motivates discovery and interaction, that equates the encounter with new and different peoples, customs, and traditions, with the fulfillment of the progressive spirit of adventure. But perhaps this is only the first phase of a process that also opens the door to the darker dimensions of the human soul and unleashes the destructive passions of greed, lust for conquest, and cultural domination.

The history of human beings records a great conflict of opposites as societies struggle for political, social, and economic balance. Stability affords security and strength that often results in risk—exploration, trade, and then exploitation, destruction, and a new resolution. Balance to imbalance to balance. The Chinese vision of yin and yang, of the necessity and interaction of opposites, defines the catalyst called curiosity.

In this chapter we will explore the interactions of Western and Eastern societies. The cultures of Europe, America, Asia, and Africa all existed by about the thirteenth century in "old worlds" with more or less established societies, religions, and political organizations. Of course, there had been military, economic, and cultural contact between these regions for centuries as evidenced by the Phoenician circumnavigation of Africa, Chinese trade with the Roman Empire, the Mongol conquests, and the images of Eastern Buddhist statuary that bear a striking resemblance to Alexander the Great. But a more concerted effort to explore the horizons of the world began in the eleventh century with the voyages of the Vikings to North America and especially with the travels of the Venetian trader Marco Polo to the court of the Mongol chieftain Kublai Khan about 1275. Polo's *A Description of the World* was translated into most European languages and opened a new vision of wealth and culture to the West that excited an interest in geography. Christopher Columbus set sail in 1492 to find the wealth of Chipangu, Polo's name for an outer island of Japan.

One of the most famous world travelers was Ibn Battuta, a Muslim native of Tangier in northern Africa. His long years of exploration down the coasts of Africa and into India and China in the early fourteenth century provide one of the great compendiums of cultural observation and interaction.

These voyages of discovery were certainly not limited to westerners. In fact, some of the most significant indicators of the strength of the Ming dynasty in China were the maritime expeditions commanded by the eunuch, Zheng He, between 1405 and 1433. Navigating by compass along sea routes established by Arab traders, Zheng He led hundreds of ships to Southeast Asia, India, the Arabian Gulf, and East Africa. He set out to demonstrate the glory of the Ming dynasty and to enroll other kingdoms in a tribute system. These voyages were successful in presenting the Chinese court with exotic animals, hostile kings, and some tributary states, but they were short-lived since they were expensive and came at a time when the dynasty needed to focus its resources toward building programs and defensive arrangements. It is interesting to note that although the Chinese possessed the technical knowledge for such expeditions, they lacked the decisive combination of greed, faith, and curiosity that gave rise to the Portuguese trading empire fifty years later.

Exploration was only a means to an end for the Portuguese and Spanish who were motivated by the lure of wealth, the spice trade in India, the gold and silver in the Americas, the slaves of Africa. After Hernando Cortés and Francisco Pizarro conquered respectively the Aztecs in 1519 and the Incas in 1531, the door lay open for the European domination of a continent. Spanish conquistadores, French trappers, Dutch traders, and English religious refugees all sought to establish themselves on territory that was already occupied by indigenous peoples. Europeans ravaged their land, mocked their gods, banished their languages, decimated their populations through disease, and subjugated their children to a subservient and dependent status that is still in evidence today.

This dominance was certainly disproportionate to the geographic size or population of Europe. Although European apologists would concoct theories that explained and justified the domination of "inferior races," their conquest was not the result of racial superiority, but of technological supremacy. Gunpowder and naval power proved to be the decisive forces in the eradication of Native American cultures.

This interactive relationship between the European and American worlds can be attested by the exchange of crops and animals, but perhaps might best be noted in the specter of disease. Although there is continuing controversy about what diseases were introduced by outsiders into the Americas, it is generally held that smallpox, cholera, measles, diphtheria, typhoid fever, some strains of influenza, and the bubonic plague originated in Asia, Europe, or Africa. The affect of these diseases on American populations without previous exposure or immunity was devastating. Native populations may have declined by 75 percent.

The influx of spices into Europe from the Malabar coasts of India and the precious metals delivered by the Spanish treasure fleets from the Americas proved to be a mixed blessing for the economy of Europe and highlights the importance of interdisciplinary study. The increase in gold and silver bullion certainly paid for innovations in printing, shipping, mining, textile manufacturing, and weapons development. The influx of bullion alone allowed Spain to launch the Spanish Armada against England in 1588, France to develop its silk industry, and all of Europe to gorge on the bloody seventeenth century wars of religion. But it also contributed to serious inflation that saw prices doubling in Spain by 1600, and the cost of food and clothing increasing by 100 percent in Germany by 1540.

Such complex societal change may help explain the fateful decision made by the Japanese to retreat from this exchange of "new worlds." Having just survived a long period of civil strife, the Tokugawa Shogunate isolated Japan by restricting the influence of Western religion and trade. From about 1635 to 1865, Japan maintained political unity and a homogeneous domestic culture in isolation. This flight from curiosity was to be decisive in the history of the world.

This chapter offers us an opportunity to analyze some of the benefits and attendant atrocities of cultural interaction. History is a reflection of the complexity of human environments and as such is necessarily interactive. This is a story of greed, destruction, and ultimately of cultural awareness that affords perspective and presents new possibilities for the progress of world civilization.

EXPLORATION AND ENCOUNTER

The adventures and achievements of Christopher Columbus have stirred controversy among historians for over a century. The 1992 quincentenary recognition of his four voyages to the New World reignited debate between those who regard him as a great explorer and true embodiment of the Renaissance spirit of discovery and others who regard him as an exploiter, leader of the first invasion of European barbarians, which resulted in the sixteenth-century conquests of the Aztecs under Hernando Cortés and the Incas at the hands of Francisco Pizarro. Columbus remains an enigmatic figure. His reputation as a skilled navigator has been challenged, and his handling of his men was inept at best. Still, he provides an important example of an individual who, through a supreme confidence in his abilities and in the rightness of his vision, altered the course of history. But just what was his vision, and how positive were his contributions to history?

Columbus expected that since the world was round, he could sail west and arrive at Chipangu, the Japan mentioned by Marco Polo. There the wealth of the East would justify his risk and hardship. Columbus' principal illusion, that he had successfully made the voyage to Asia, was fostered by his need to provide evidence of a wealth that would in turn justify the backing for future exploration. But the islands in the Caribbean that he "discovered" were not rich. The gold he claimed to be just about ready to discover was always on the next island. Ultimately, he was arrested in Santo Domingo for misgovernment and sent home in chains. Yet even this turned to his advantage as Columbus was viewed, even by his enemies, as a man of destiny who had vastly extended the domain of Christianity.

The first selection from Columbus' initial voyage in 1492 is a digest of his lost logbook made by Bartolomé de Las Casas, a friend of the Columbus family. The second source is a letter written by Columbus to various supporters in Spain on his return journey from the New World. These documents justify his actions but also provide insight into this controversial historical figure.

Christopher Columbus: "Admiral of the Ocean Sea" (1492)

BARTOLOMÉ DE LAS CASAS

On 2 January in the year 1492, when your Highnesses had concluded their war with the Moors [Muslims in Spain] who reigned in Europe, I saw your Highnesses' banners victoriously raised on the towers of the Alhambra, the citadel of that city, and the Moorish king come out of the city gates and kiss the hands of your Highnesses and the prince, My Lord. And later in that same month, on the grounds of information I had given your royal Highnesses concerning the

The Four Voyages of Christopher Columbus translated by J.M. Cohen (Penguin Classics, 1958) copyright © J.M. Cohen 1958, pp. 37–38, 43, 51–53. Reproduced with permission of Penguin Books Ltd.

lands of India and a prince who is called the Great Khan—which means in Spanish "King of Kings"—and of his and his ancestors' frequent and vain application to Rome for men learned in the holy faith who should instruct them in it, your Highnesses decided to send me, Christopher Columbus, to see these parts of India and the princes and peoples of those lands and consider the best means for their conversion. For, by the neglect of the Popes to send instructors, many nations had fallen to idolatry and adopted doctrines of perdition, and your Highnesses as Catholic princes and devoted propagators of the holy Christian faith have always been enemies of the sect of Mahomet [Muhammad] and of all idolatries and heresies.

Your Highnesses ordained that I should not go eastward by land in the usual manner but by the western way which no one about whom we have positive information has ever followed. Therefore having expelled all the Jews from your dominions in that same month of January, your Highnesses commanded me to go with an adequate fleet to those parts of India. In return you granted me great favors bestowing on me the titles of Don and High Admiral of the Ocean Sea and Viceroy and perpetual governor of such islands and mainland as I should discover and win or should in future be discovered and won in the Ocean Sea, and that these rights should be inherited by my eldest son and so on from generation to generation.

I departed from the city of Granada on Saturday, 12 May, and went to the seaport of Palos, where I prepared three ships very suitable for such a voyage and set out from that port well supplied both with provisions and seamen. Half an hour before sunrise on Friday, 3 August, I departed on a course for the Canary Islands, from which possession of your Highnesses I intended to set out and sail until I reached the Indies, there to deliver your Highnesses' letters to their princes and to fulfil your other commands. . . .

TUESDAY, 18 SEPTEMBER

During that day and night they made more than fifty-five leagues but he reckoned only forty-eight. On these days the sea was as smooth as the river at Seville. That day Martin Alonso called ahead in the Pinta, which was a fast ship; because, as he called to the Admiral from his ship, he had seen a great flock of birds flying westward and hoped to sight land that night; this was his reason for not holding back. To the north there appeared a great bank of clouds, which is a sign that land is near. . . .

WEDNESDAY, 10 OCTOBER

He sailed west-south-west, making ten miles an hour but sometimes dropping to seven and sometimes rising to twelve, and in the day and night together they went fifty-nine leagues, which he counted as no more than forty-four for the men. Here the men could bear no more;

they complained of the length of the voyage. But the Admiral encouraged them as best he could, holding out high hopes of the gains they could make. He added that it was no use their complaining, because he had reached the Indies and must sail on until with the help of Our Lord he discovered land.

THURSDAY, 11 OCTOBER

He sailed west-south-west. They ran into rougher seas than any they had met with on the voyage. They saw petrels and a green reed near the ship. The men of the Pinta saw a cane and a stick and picked up another small stick, apparently shaped with an iron tool; also a piece of cane and some land-grasses and a small board. Those on the caravel Nina saw other indications of land and a stick covered with barnacles. At these signs, all breathed again and were rejoiced. That day they went twenty-seven leagues before sunset and after sunset he resumed his original western course. They made twelve miles an hour and up to two hours before midnight had gone ninety miles, which are twenty-two leagues and a half. The caravel Pinta, being swifter and sailing ahead of the Admiral, now sighted land and gave the signals which the Admiral had commanded.

The first man to sight land was a sailor call Rodrigo from Triana, who afterwards vainly claimed the reward, which was pocketed by Columbus. The Admiral, however, when on the sterncastle at ten o'clock in the night, had seen a light, though it was so indistinct he would not affirm that it was land. He called Pero Gutierrez, butler of the King's table, and told him that there seemed to be a light and asked him to look. He did so and saw it. He said the same to Rodrigo Sanchez of Segovia, whom the King and Queen had sent in the fleet as accountant, and he saw nothing because he was not in a position from which anything could be seen. After the Admiral spoke, this light was seen once or twice and it was like a wax candle that went up and down. Very few thought that this was a sign of land, but the Admiral was quite certain that they were near land. Accordingly, after the recitation of the Salve in the usual manner by the assembled sailors, the Admiral most seriously urged them to keep a good lookout from the forecastle and to watch carefully for land. He promised to give a silk doublet to the first sailor who should report it. And he would be entitled also to the reward promised by the sovereigns, which was an annual payment of ten thousand maravedis [a small copper coin].

Two hours after midnight land appeared, some two leagues away. They took in all sail, leaving only the mainsail, which is the great sail without bonnets, and lay close-hauled waiting for day. This was Friday, on which they reached a small island of the Lucayos, called in the Indian language Guanahani [Watling Island in the Bahamas]. Immediately some naked people appeared and the Admiral went ashore in the armed boat, as did Martin Alonso Pinzon and Vincente Yanez his brother, captain of the Nina. The Admiral raised the royal standard and the captains carried two banners with the green cross which were flown by the Admiral on all his ships. On each side of the cross was a crown surmounting the letters F and Y (for Ferdinand and Isabella [Ysabela]). On landing they saw very green trees and much water and fruit of various kinds.

The "New World"

CHRISTOPHER COLUMBUS

All these islands are very beautiful, and distinguished by a diversity of scenery; they are filled with a great variety of trees of immense height, and which I believe to retain their foliage in all seasons. . . . The inhabitants of both sexes in this island, and in all the others which I have seen, or of which I have received information, go always naked as they were born, with the excep-

---

"The 'New World'" is from R. H. Major, ed., *Select Letters of Christopher Columbus* (London: The Hakluyt Society, 1847), pp. 5–9.

tion of some of the women, who use the covering of a leaf or small bough, or an apron of cotton which they prepare for that purpose. None of them . . . are possessed of any iron, neither have they weapons, . . . [for] they are timid and full of fear. They carry however in lieu of arms canes dried in the sun, on the ends of which they fix heads of dried wood sharpened to a point, and even these they dare not use habitually. . . . As soon as they see that they are safe, and have laid aside all fear, they are very simple and honest and exceedingly liberal with all they have. . . . They exhibit great love towards all others in preference to themselves; they also give objects of great value for trifles, and content themselves with very little or nothing in return. I however forbade that these trifles and articles of no value (such as pieces of dishes, plates, and glass, keys, and leather straps) should be given to them, although if they could obtain them, they imagined themselves to be possessed of the most beautiful trinkets in the world. . . . Thus they bartered, like idiots, cotton and gold for fragments of bows, glasses, bottles, and jars; which I forbade as being unjust, and myself gave them many beautiful and acceptable articles which I had brought with me, taking nothing in return. I did this in order that I might the more easily conciliate them, that they might be led to become Christians, and be inclined to entertain a regard for the King and Queen, our Princes and all Spaniards, and that I might induce them to take an interest in seeking out, and collecting, and delivering to us such things as they possessed in abundance, but which we greatly needed. They practice no kind of idolatry, but have a firm belief that all strength and power, and indeed all good things would come to them after they had thrown aside their fears. Nor are they slow or stupid, but of very clear understanding; and those men who have crossed to the neighboring islands give an admirable description of everything they observed; but they never saw any people clothed, nor any ships like ours. On my arrival at that sea, I had taken some Indians by force from the first island that I came to, in order that they might learn our language, and communicate to us what they knew respecting the country; this plan succeeded excellently, and was a great advantage to us, for in a short time, either by gestures and signs, or by words, we were enabled to understand each other. These men are still travelling with me, and although they have been with us now a long time, they continue to entertain the idea that I have descended from heaven; and on our arrival at any new place they published this, crying out immediately with a loud voice to the other Indians, "Come, come and look upon beings of a celestial race": upon which both women and men, children and adults, young men and old, when they got rid of the fear they at first entertained, would come out in throngs, crowding the roads to see us.

"CITIES OF GOLD": THE EUROPEAN DOMINATION OF AMERICA

Hernando Cortés and the Conquest of Mexico

A primary area of historical controversy and dissension in the twenty-first century concerns the Spanish conquest of Mexico and Peru and the subsequent administration of Spanish domains in the Western Hemisphere collectively called "New Spain." The role of the Spanish explorers and conquistadors as agents of destruction or purveyors of progress has been hotly disputed in recent years. Subsidized by Spanish royalty, explorers such as Hernando Cortés and Francisco Pizarro landed in Mexico (1519) and Peru (1531), respectively, with lofty dreams and visions of enormous wealth to be extracted from the inhabitants of this mythic land. The Spanish monarchy itself sought the wealth and geopolitical advantage that such a presence in the New World could bring, while the church saw an opportunity to spread the Christian faith to new lands without the stifling competition and dissension that the Protestant Reformation had engendered in Europe.

But it is dangerous to narrow the perspective, and the Spanish presence in New Spain surely combined national interest, religious zealotry, and personal greed. This was an encounter of unparalleled importance, and in the process of consolidating their claims, the Spanish destruction of native peoples and their cultures reflected a European arrogance and confirmation of the Machiavellian principle that the "ends justify the means." Indeed, the Catholic Church had difficulty tolerating the exploitation of native populations it was trying to convert. A "Black Legend" of Spanish abuse and butchery soon developed and, through the propaganda of Anglo-Dutch rivals, colored the Spanish national profile for centuries. This encounter between forces of the Old World and the New inaugurated centuries of exploitation and rigid consolidation that set precedents for slaughter and fueled competition among European powers.

The first source describes the initial encounter of the Aztecs with the Spanish explorers in 1519. The Franciscan friar Bernardino de Sahagún was instrumental in preserving information about Aztec culture and the history of this period. His intention was to understand native culture and religious beliefs in order to more effectively convert the Indians to Christianity. His General History of the Things of New Spain *was based on information gained from Aztec eyewitnesses and surviving participants to the conquest of Mexico from 1519 to 1521.*

The succeeding sources are excerpted from letters by Mexico's Spanish conqueror, Hernando Cortés. They lend a valuable perspective to the motives and methods of Spanish conquest in the New World.

The Aztec Encounter: "This Was Quetzalcoatl Who Had Come to Land"

BERNARDINO DE SAHAGÚN

When the first Spanish ships were seen in this land, Montezuma's stewards and captains who lived along the coast of Veracruz immediately assembled and took counsel among themselves, deciding whether they should give this news to their lord Montezuma, who was in the city of Mexico. The chief among them said, "In order for us to take an accurate report of this matter, it seems to me proper that we should see with our own eyes what this is; this we can do if we go to them on the pretext of selling them some things that they have need of." This seemed like a good idea to the others, and at once they took articles of food and clothing, and loaded into canoes what they were going to sell them and went to them by water. When they arrived at the flagship (to which they directed their canoes because of the banner they saw on it), immediately upon arriving they paid homage and gave signs that they came in peace to sell them food and clothing. [It was thought that this was Quetzalcoatl who had come to land.] The Spaniards asked them where they were from and what they came for. They said, "We are Mexicans." The Spaniards said, "If you are Mexicans, tell us who the lord of Mexico is."

The Indians said, "Gentlemen, the lord of Mexico is called Montezuma." Then the Spaniards answered, "Well, come and sell us some things that we need; climb up here and we shall look at them. Have no fear that we shall do you harm." . . . Then [the Indians] climbed into the ship and took with them certain bundles of rich [capes] that they had brought.

They spread them out in front of the Spaniards, who liked them and agreed to buy them, for which they gave the Indians strings of fake precious stones, some red, others green, some blue, others yellow. As they seemed to the Indians to be precious stones, they accepted

Reprinted courtesy of the University of Utah Press and the School of American Research.

them, and gave them the capes. . . . Finally the Spaniards said to them, "God go with you and take those stones to your master and tell him that we are unable to see him now . . . ; we will come again and go to see him in Mexico."

With this they departed in their canoes, and upon reaching land they got ready and departed for Mexico to give the news to Montezuma. . . .

Montezuma: "We Shall Obey You and Hold You As Our God"

HERNANDO CORTÉS

After we had crossed this bridge, Montezuma came to greet us and with him some two hundred lords, all barefoot and dressed in a different costume, but also very rich in their way and more so than the others. They came in two columns, pressed very close to the walls of the street, which is very wide and beautiful and so straight that you can see from one end to the other. . . . Montezuma came down the middle of this street with two chiefs, one on his right hand and the other on his left. . . . When we met I dismounted and stepped forward to embrace him, but the two lords who were with him stopped me with their hands so that I should not touch him; and they likewise all performed the ceremony of kissing the earth. . . .

When at last I came to speak to Montezuma himself I took off a necklace of pearls and cut glass that I was wearing and placed it round his neck; after we had walked a little way up the street a servant of his came with two necklaces, wrapped in a cloth, made from red snails' shells, which they hold in great esteem; and from each necklace hung eight shrimps of refined gold almost a span in length. . . . [Montezuma] took me by the hand and led me to a great room facing the courtyard through which we entered. And he bade me sit on a very rich throne . . . and addressed me in the following way:

Hernando Cortes, *Letters from Mexico*, Pagden, A. R., trans. & ed. Copyright © 1986 by Yale University Press. Reprinted with permission.

"For a long time we have known from the writings of our ancestors that neither I, nor any of those who dwell in this land, are natives of it, but foreigners who came from very distant parts; and likewise we know that a chieftain, of whom they were all vassals, brought our people to this region. And he returned to his native land and after many years came again, by which time all those who had remained were married to native women and had built villages and raised children. And when he wished to lead them away again they would not go nor even admit him as their chief; and so he departed. And we have always held that those who descended from him would come and conquer this land and take us as their vassals. So because of the place from which you claim to come, namely from where the sun rises, and the things you tell us of the great lord or king who sent you here, we believe and are certain that he is our natural lord, especially as you say that he has known of us for some time. So be assured that we shall obey you and hold you as our lord in place of that great sovereign of whom you speak; and in this there shall be no offense or betrayal whatsoever. And in all the land that lies in my domain, you may command as you will, for you shall be obeyed; and all that we own is for you to dispose of as you choose. Thus, as you are in your own country and your own house, rest now from the hardships of your journey and the battles which you have fought. . . . "

Human Sacrifice: "A Most Horrid and Abominable Custom"

HERNANDO CORTÉS

JULY 10, 1519

Most High, Mighty and Excellent Princes, Most Catholic and Powerful Kings and Sovereigns: [The Aztecs] have a most horrid and abominable

custom which truly ought to be punished and which until now we have seen in no other part, and this is that, whenever they wish to ask something of the idols, in order that their plea may find more acceptance, they take many girls and boys and even adults, and in the presence of the idols they open their chests while they are still alive and take out their hearts and entrails and burn them before the idols, offering the smoke as sacrifice. Some of us have seen this, and they say it is the most terrible and frightful thing they have ever witnessed.

This these Indians do so frequently that . . . not one year passes in which they do not kill and sacrifice some fifty persons in each temple. . . . Your Majesties may be most certain that, as this land seems to us to be very large, and to have many temples in it, not one year has passed, as far as we have been able to discover, in which three or four thousand souls have not been sacrificed in this manner.

Let Your Royal Highnesses consider, therefore, whether they should not put an end to such evil practices, for certainly Our Lord God would be well pleased if by the hand of Your Royal Highnesses the people were initiated and instructed in our Holy Catholic Faith, and the devotion, trust and hope which they have in these their idols were transferred to the divine power of God. . . . And we believe that it is not without cause that Our Lord God has been pleased that these parts be discovered in the name of Your Royal Highnesses so that Your Majesties may gain much merit and reward in the sight of God by commanding that these barbarous people be instructed and by Your hands be brought to the True Faith. For, as far as we have been able to learn, we believe that had we interpreters and other people to explain to them the error of their ways and the nature of the True Faith, many of them, and perhaps even all, would soon renounce their false beliefs and come to the true knowledge of God; for they live in a more civilized and reasonable manner than any other people we have seen in these parts up to the present.

The Destruction of Tenochtitlán:
"And Their Mothers Raised a Cry of Weeping"

BERNARDINO DE SAHAGÚN

The following accounts of the brutal destruction of the Aztec capital of Tenochtitlán, first from the native perspective and then from that of Cortés, demonstrate the advantages that the Spanish enjoyed with their armor, weaponry, horses, and sophisticated manipulation of the rivalries and animosities of Aztec enemies. Cortés had difficulty controlling the anger and brutality of his native allies who were released to fight against their Aztec rulers.

The greatest evil that one can do to another is to take his life when [the victim] is in mortal sin. This is what the Spaniards did to the Mexican Indians because they provoked them by being faithless in honoring their idols. [The Spaniards], catching [the Indians] enclosed [in the courtyard] for the feast [of Huitzilopochtli], killed them, the greater part of whom were unarmed, without their knowing why.

When the great courtyard of the idol, Huitzilopochtli, god of the Mexicans, was full of nobles, priests, and soldiers, and throngs of other people, intent upon the idolatrous songs to that idol, whom they were honoring, the Spaniards suddenly poured forth ready for combat and blocked the exits of the courtyard so that no one could escape. Then they entered with their weapons and ranged themselves all along the inner walls of the courtyard. The Indians thought that they were just admiring the style of their dancing and playing and singing, and so continued the style of their dancing and playing and singing, and so continued with their celebration and songs.

At this moment, the first Spaniards to start fighting suddenly attacked those who were playing the music for the singers and dancers. They chopped off their hands and their heads so that they fell down dead. Then all the other Spaniards began to cut off heads, arms, and legs and to disembowel the Indians. Some had their heads cut off, others were cut in half, and others had their bellies slit open, immediately to fall dead. Others dragged their entrails along until they collapsed. Those who reached the exits were slain by the Spaniards guarding them; and others jumped over the walls of the courtyard; while yet others climbed up the temple; and still others, seeing no escape, threw themselves down among the slaughtered and escaped by feigning death.

So great was the bloodshed that rivers of blood ran through the courtyard like water in a heavy rain. So great was the slime of blood and entrails in the courtyard and so great was the stench that it was both terrifying and heartrending. Now that nearly all were fallen and dead, the Spaniards went searching for those who had climbed up the temple and those who had hidden among the dead, killing all those they found alive. . . .

Seeing themselves hotly pursued by the Mexicans, the Spaniards entered the royal houses and fortified and barricaded themselves as best they could to keep the Indians out. From inside they began to defend themselves, firing off crossbows, [rifles], and cannon, and even aiming stones from the rooftop to drive off the Indians struggling to break down the wall and force their way in.

Having a convenient opportunity, the Spaniards conferred with each other, and also with

Reprinted courtesy of the University of Utah Press and the School of American Research.

Montezuma and his courtiers, and decided to put them in irons. Meanwhile, the Mexicans were busy performing burial ceremonies for those who had been killed in the ambush and so delayed a few days before returning to do battle with the Spaniards. Great was the Indians' mourning over their dead. . . . [And their mothers, their fathers raised a cry of weeping. There was weeping for them. There was weeping.]

"We Could No Longer Endure the Stench of Dead Bodies"

HERNANDO CORTÉS

AUGUST 12, 1521

On leaving my camp, I had commanded Gonzalo de Sandoval to sail the brigantines [ships] in between the houses in the other quarter in which the Indians were resisting, so that we should have them surrounded, but not to attack until he saw that we were engaged. In this way they would be surrounded and so hard pressed that they would have no place to move save over the bodies of their dead or along the roof tops. They no longer had nor could find any arrows,

Hernando Cortes, *Letters from Mexico*, Pagden, A. R., trans. & ed. Copyright © 1986 by Yale University Press. Reprinted with permission.

javelins or stones with which to attack us; and our allies fighting with us were armed with swords and bucklers, and slaughtered so many of them on land and in the water that more than forty thousand were killed or taken that day. So loud was the wailing of the women and children that there was not one man among us whose heart did not bleed at the sound; and indeed we had more trouble in preventing our allies from killing with such cruelty than we had in fighting the enemy. For no race, however savage, has ever practiced such fierce and unnatural cruelty as the natives of these parts. Our allies also took many spoils that day, which we were unable to prevent, as they numbered more than 150,000 and we Spaniards were only some nine hundred. Neither our precautions nor our warnings could stop their looting, though we did all we could. One of the reasons why I had avoided entering the city in force during the past days was the fear that if we attempted to storm them they would throw all they possessed into the water, and, even if they did not, our allies would take all they could find. For this reason I was much afraid that Your Majesty would receive only a small part of the great wealth this city once had, in comparison with all that I once held for Your Highness. Because it was now late, and we could no longer endure the stench of the dead bodies that had lain in those streets for many days, which was the most loathsome thing in all the world, we returned to our camps.

The Devastation of Smallpox

BERNARDINO DE SAHAGÚN

It would be narrow and simplistic to view the Spanish conquest of Mexico and Peru from a military or even cultural perspective alone. For there were even more encompassing societal changes that affected both Europe and the Americas as a result of the encounter. Recent research has noted the importance of the Spanish introduction of horses to the Americas and especially the impact of these horses on the Native American cultures of the Southwest and Plains. In addition, the crops that poured into Europe from the Americas after 1492 included maize, potatoes, sweet potatoes, tomatoes, peanuts, and various kinds of peppers, beans, and squashes. When one considers that the four chief staples of the human diet in our contemporary world are wheat, rice, maize, and potatoes, the impact of the New World on the Old becomes apparent.

But perhaps the most immediate factor in the exchange of European and American cultures was disease. It has been proposed by scholars that syphilis, a disease unknown in Europe before the end of the fifteenth century, was brought to Europe by the Spaniards from America. The Indians suffered from it in a mild form, but it attacked the Spanish more severely. Next to tobacco, it may have been the most harmful gift of the New World to the Old. By the same token, the Spanish brought with them diseases against which the Indians had no resistance. The smallpox as described in the following selection by Sahagún certainly devastated the Aztecs and may have been the pivotal factor in Cortés' success.

After the previously mentioned hardships that befell the Spaniards in the year 1519, at the beginning of the year 1520 the epidemic of smallpox, measles, and pustules broke out so virulently that a vast number of people died throughout this New Spain. This pestilence began in the province of Chalco and lasted for sixty days. Among the Mexicans who fell victim to this pestilence was the lord Cuitlahuactzin, whom they had elected a little earlier. Many leaders, many veteran soldiers, and valiant men who were their defense in time of war, also died.

During this epidemic, the Spaniards, rested and recovered, were already in Tlaxcala. Having taken courage and energy because of the ravages of the [Mexican] people that the pestilence was causing, firmly believing that God was on their side, being again allied with the Tlaxcalans, and attending to all the necessary preparations to return against the Mexicans, they began to construct the brigantines [ships] that they would need in order to wage war by water.

The Spanish Empire in America

With the exploration of America by Christopher Columbus in 1492, the subsequent Spanish conquest of the Aztecs by Hernando Cortés in 1519, and the Incas by Juan Pizarro in 1531, perspectives suddenly changed. This "New World" fired the imagination with the abstraction of discovery—the encounter with strange peoples of different color, perspective, customs, and religions. But it also presented unique tangible opportunities to realize immense national and personal power through regional conquest and consolidation and of untold, mythic wealth through the exploitation and extraction of natural resources.

Thus began one of the most brutal episodes in modern Western history. The Spanish conquistadores *("conquerors") methodically organized the region in order to extract the gold and silver that would allow Spain to surpass its rivals for European power. This was an economy of exploitation that was primarily focused on mining, agriculture, and shipping. There was little accommodation to the native population on the part of the Spanish as European language, values, and religion became the dominant culture of what would be called Latin America.*

Although the Spanish were particularly attracted to gold, silver became the primary metal of Mexico and Bolivia. Since the Spanish crown received one-fifth (the quinto*) of all mining revenues, it imposed a monopoly over the production and sale of mercury, which was essential in the process of mining silver. The extraction of silver was such a labor-intensive process that the Spanish developed various systems to compel and organize native workers.*

One of the most important was the encomienda. *Influential businessmen (*encomenderos*) received formal grants to the labor of a specified number of Indians for a limited time. In the silver* *mines of Potosí, Bolivia, the* mita *or "labor tax" placed on Indians required that they contribute a certain number of days of labor annually to the Spanish authorities. Many of these Indians did not survive their* mita *as conditions in the mines were dangerous and the overseers harsh in their demands.*

The Extraction of Mercury

ANTONIO VASQUEZ DE ESPINOSA

Antonio Vasquez de Espinosa (d. 1630) was a Spanish friar and missionary in the Americas who sought to convert the Indians to Christianity. He returned to Spain in 1622 and wrote several accounts of his experiences. In the following excerpt, he describes the mita *system of forced Indian labor used in the dangerous process of extracting mercury from the mines. He then describes Potosí, the richest silver mine in the world. Such wealth allowed the Spanish government to wage wars in Europe against Protestant forces and contributed to the stability of the Spanish crown.*

And so at the rumor of the rich deposits of mercury . . . in the years 1570 and 1571, they started the construction of the town of Huancavelica de Oropesa in a pleasant valley at the foot of the range. It contains 400 Spanish residents, as well as many temporary shops of dealers in merchandise and groceries, heads of trading houses, and transients, for the town has a lively commerce. . . .

Every two months His Majesty sends by the regular courier from Lima 60,000 pesos to pay for the mita of the Indians, for the crews are changed every two months, so that merely for the Indian mita payment (in my understanding of it) 360,000 pesos are sent from Lima every year, not to speak of much besides, which all crosses at his risk that cold and desolate mountain country which is the puna [high plateau] and has nothing on it but llama ranches.

Up on the range there are 3,000 or 4,000 Indians working in the mine; it is colder up there than in the town, since it is higher. The mine where the mercury is located is a large layer which they keep following downward. When I was in that town (which was in the year 1616) I went up on the range and down into the mine, which at that time was considerably more than 130 stades deep [about 104 miles]. The ore was

very rich black flint, and the excavation so extensive that it held more than 3,000 Indians working away hard with picks and hammers, breaking up that flint ore; and when they have filled their little sacks, the poor fellows, loaded down with ore, climb up those ladders or rigging, some like masts and others like cable, and so trying and distressing that a man empty-handed can hardly get up them. That is the way they work in this mine, with many lights and the loud noise of the pounding and great confusion. Nor is that the greatest evil and difficulty; that is due to thievish and undisciplined superintendents. As that great vein of ore keeps going down deeper and they follow its rich trail, in order to make sure that no section of that ore shall drop on top of them, they keep leaving supports or pillars of the ore itself, even if of the richest quality, and they necessarily help to sustain and insure each section with less risk. This being so, there are men so heartless that for the sake of stealing a little rich ore, they go down out of hours and deprive the innocent Indians of this protection by hollowing into these pillars to steal the rich ore in them, and then a great section is apt to fall in and kill all the Indians, and sometimes the unscrupulous and grasping

"The Extraction of Mercury" from de Espinosa, Antonio Vasquez, *Compendium and Description of the West Indies* 1942, pp. 621-625.

superintendents themselves, as happened when I was in that locality; and much of this is kept quiet so that it shall not come to the notice of the manager and cause the punishment of the accomplices. . . .

This is how they extract the mercury. On the other side of the town there are structures where they grind up the mercury ore an then put it in jars with molds like sugar loaves on top of them, with many little holes, and others on top of them, flaring and plastered with mud, and a channel for it to drip into and pass into the jar or place where it is to fall. Then they roast the ore with a straw fire. . . . Under the onset of this fire it melts and the mercury goes up in vapor . . . until it cools and coagulates and starts falling downward again. Those who carry out the reduction of this ore have to be very careful and test cautiously; they must wait till the jars are cold before uncovering them for otherwise they may easily get mercury poisoning and if they do, they are of no further use; their teeth fall out, and some die. After melting and extracting the mercury by fire, they put it in dressed sheepskins to keep it in His Majesty's storehouses, and from there they usually transport it on llamaback to the port of Chincha . . . where there is a vault and an agent appointed by the royal Council, and he has charge of it there; then they freight it on shipboard to the port of San Marcos de Arica, from which it is carried by herds of llamas and mules to Potosi.

"The Extraction of Mercury" from de Espinosa, Antonio Vasquez, *Compendium and Description of the West Indies* 1942, pp. 621-625.

The Silver Mines of Potosi

ANTONIO VASQUEZ DE ESPINOSA

The famous Potosi range, so celebrated all over the world for the great wealth which God has created unique in its bowels and veins, lies in the Province of the Charcas, 18 leagues form the city of Chuquisaca, which was later called La Plata, on account of the great richness of this range. . . .

According to His Majesty's warrant, the mine owners on this massive range have a right to the mita of 13,300 Indians in the working and exploitation of the mines, both those which have been discovered, those now discovered, and those which shall be discovered. It is the duty of the Corregidor of Potosi [a district military officer] to have them rounded up and to see that they come in from all the provinces between Cuzco over the whole of El Collao and as far as the frontiers of Tarija and Tomina; this Potosi Corregidor [official] has power and authority over all the Corregidors in those provinces mentioned; for if they do not fill the Indian mita allotment assigned each of them in accordance with the capacity of their provinces as indicated to them, he can send them, and does, salaried inspectors to report upon it, and when the remissness is great or remarkable, he can suspend them, notifying the Viceroy of the fact.

These Indians are sent out every year under a captain whom they choose in each village or tribe, for him to take them and oversee them for the year each has to serve; every year they have a new election, for as some go out, others come in. This works out very badly, with great losses and gaps in the quotas of Indians, the villages being depopulated; and this gives rise to great extortions and abuses on the part of the inspectors toward the poor Indians, ruining them and thus depriving the chief Indians of their property and carrying them off in chains because they do not fill out the mita assignment, which they cannot do, for the reason given and for others which I do not bring forward.

These 13,300 are divided up every four months into three mitas, each consisting of 4,443 Indians, to work in the mines on the range and in the 120 smelters in the Potosi and Tarapaya areas; it is a good league [three miles] between the two. These mita Indians earn each day, or there is paid each one for his labor, four reals [Spanish silver coins]. . . .

After each [Indian] has eaten his ration, they climb up the hill, each to his mine, and go in, staying there from that hour until Saturday evening without coming out of the mine; their wives bring them food, but they stay constantly underground, excavating and carrying out the ore from which they get the silver. They all have tallow candles, lighted day and night; that is the light they work with, for as they are underground, they have need of it all the time. . . .

So huge is the wealth which has been taken out of this range since the year 1545, when it was discovered, up to the present year of 1628, which makes 83 years that they have been working and reducing its ores, that merely form the registered mines, as appears from an examination of most of the accounts in the royal records, 326,000,000 pesos have been taken out.

Over and above that, such great treasure and riches have come from the Indies in gold and silver from all the other mines in New Spain and Peru, Honduras, the New Kingdom of Granada, chile, New Galicia, New Vzcaya [north central and northwestern Mexico], and other quarters since the discovery of the Indies, that they exceed 1,800 millions.

The Barbarians of the New World: "They Are Slaves by Nature"

JUAN GINES DE SEPULVEDA

Juan Gines de Sepulveda (1490–1573) was a scholar and apologist for the Spanish treatment of Indians in the Americas. His argument, in essence, is one that would be echoed by conquerors of later ages, from the nineteenth century British imperialists and American Social Darwinists, to the Nazis of the twentieth century: Superior peoples had the right to enslave inferior peoples. For Sepulveda, the Aztecs were stupid, cruel, immoral, and deserved destruction; they were "natural slaves." Note how his argument is repeated four hundred years later by Sir Frederick Lugard in East Africa and countered by Bartolomé de Las Casas in the succeeding source.

Turning then to our topic, whether it is proper and just that those who are superior and who excel in nature, customs, and laws rule over their inferiors, you can easily understand . . . if you are familiar with the character and moral code of the two peoples, that it is with perfect right that the Spaniards exercise their dominion over those barbarians of the New World and its adjacent islands. For in prudence, talent, and every kind of virtue and human sentiment they are as inferior to the Spaniards as children are to adults, or women to men, or the cruel and inhumane to the very gentle, or the excessively intemperate to the continent and moderate. . . .

And what shall I say of [Spanish] moderation in rejecting gluttony and lasciviousness, inasmuch as no nation or very few nations of Europe can compare with the frugality and sobriety of the Spaniards? I admit that I have observed in these most recent times that through contact with foreigners luxury has invaded the tables of our nobles. Still, since this is reproved by good men among the people, it is to be hoped that in a short while they may return to the traditional and innate sobriety of our native custom. . . .

As for the Christian religion, I have witnessed many clear proofs of the firm roots it has in the hearts of Spaniards, even those dedicated to the military. . . . What shall I say of the Spanish soldiers' gentleness and humanitarian sentiments? Their only and great solicitude and care in the battles, after the winning of the victory is to save the greatest possible number of vanquished and free them from the cruelty of their allies. Now compare these qualities of prudence, skill, magnanimity, moderation, humanity, and religion with those of those little men [of America] in whom one can scarcely find any remnants of humanity. They not only lack culture but do not even use or know about writing or preserve records of their history—save for some obscure memory of certain deeds contained painting. They lack written laws and their institutions and customs are barbaric. And as for their virtues, if you wish to be informed of their moderation and mildness, what can be expected of men committed to all kinds of passion and nefarious lewdness and of whom not a few are given to the eating of human flesh. Do not believe that their life before the coming of the Spaniards was one of . . . . peace, of the kind that poets sang about. On the contrary, they made war with each other almost continuously, and with such fury that they considered a victory to be empty if they could not satisfy their prodigious hunger with the flesh of their enemies. . . . But in other respects they are so cowardly and timid that they can scarcely offer any resistance to the hostile presence of our side, and many times thousands and thousands of them have been dispersed and have fled like women, on being defeated by a small Spanish force scarcely amounting to one hundred. . . .

Could there be a better or clearer testimony of the superiority that some men have over others in talent, skill, strength of spirit, and virtue? Is it not proof that they are slaves by nature? For the fact that some of them appear to have a talent for certain manual tasks is no argument for their greater human prudence. We see that certain insects, such as the bees and the spiders, produce works that no human skill can imitate. . . .

I have made reference to the customs and character of the barbarians. What shall I say now of the impious religion and wicked sacrifices of such people, who, in venerating the devil as if he were God, believed that the best sacrifice that they could placate him with was to offer him human hearts? . . . Opening up the human breasts they pulled out the hearts and offered them on their heinous altars. And believing that they had made a ritual sacrifice with which to placate their gods, they themselves ate the flesh of the victims. These are crimes that are considered by the philosophers to be among the most ferocious and abominable perversions, exceeding all human iniquity. . . .

How can we doubt that these people—so uncivilized, so barbaric, contaminated with so many impieties and obscenities—have been justly conquered by . . . a nation excellent in every kind of virtue, with the best law and best benefit for the barbarians? Prior to the arrival of the Christians they had the nature, customs, religion, and practice of evil sacrifice as we have explained. Now, on receiving with our rule our writing, laws, and morality, imbued with the Christian religion, having shown themselves to be docile to the missionaries that we have sent them, as many have done, they are as different from their primitive condition as civilized people are from barbarians, or as those with sight from the blind, as the inhuman from the meek, as the pious from the impious, or to put it in a single phrase, in effect, as men from beasts.

Theme: Imperialism

The Historical Intersection

EAST AFRICA: 1893

"A Natural Inclination to Submit to a Higher Authority"

SIR FREDERICK DEALTRY LUGARD

Probably the most obvious motive for imperialism is in the economic profit to be made from the colonization of territory and the subjugation of people. Sir Frederick Lugard, soldier and administrator of some of Britain's colonial possessions in the late nineteenth century, analyzed the European "scramble for Africa" in the nineteenth century.

Compare and Contrast:

- Compare Lugard's assessment of Africans with Juan Gines de Sepulveda's opinion of Native Americans in the preceding account. What are the arguments for European supremacy? Why must African natives and American Indians be deprived of their independence and subdued?

The "Scramble for Africa" by the nations of Europe—an incident without parallel in the history of the world—was due to the growing commercial rivalry, which brought home to civilised nations the vital necessity of securing the only remaining fields for industrial enterprise and expansion. It is well, then, to realise that it is for our advantage—and not alone at the dictates of duty—that we have undertaken responsibilities in East Africa. It is in order to foster the growth of the trade of this country, and to find an outlet for our manufactures and our surplus energy, that our far-seeing statesmen and our commercial men advocate colonial expansion. . . .

There are some who say we have no right in Africa at all, that "it belongs to the natives." I hold that our right is the necessity that is upon us to provide for our ever-growing population—either by opening new fields for emigration, or

(contd)

by providing work and employment which the development of over-sea extension entails—and to stimulate trade by finding new markets, since we know what misery trade depression brings at home.

While thus serving our own interests as a nation, we may, by selecting men of the right stamp for the control of new territories, bring at the same time many advantages to Africa. Nor do we deprive the natives of their birthright of freedom, to place them under a foreign yoke. It has ever been the key-note of British colonial method to rule through and by the natives, and it is this method, in contrast to the arbitrary and uncompromising rule of Germany, France, Portugal, and Spain, which has been the secret of our success as a colonising nation, and has made us welcomed by tribes and peoples in Africa, who ever rose in revolt against the other nations named. In Africa, moreover, there is among the people a natural inclination to submit to a higher authority. That intense detestation of control which animates our Teutonic races does not exist among the tribes of Africa, and if there is any authority that we replace, it is the authority of the Slavers and Arabs, or the intolerable tyranny of the "dominant tribe."

Consider This:

- The "dehumanization" of an enemy has been standard procedure for nations engaged in war or imperialistic activities. How did Lugard and Sepulveda dehumanize natives? To what extent must war be accompanied by the justification of propaganda?

And How About . . .

- The dehumanization of American Indians by the United States government in the late nineteenth century?
- The Japanese dehumanization of the Chinese and "Rape of Nanjing" during the invasion of Manchuria in 1936?
- The Serbian dehumanization of ethnic Albanians in Kosovo in 1998?

"'A Natural Inclination to Submit to a Higher Authority'" is from Sir Frederick Dealtry Lugard, *The Rise of Our East African Empire*, vol. 1 (London: William Blackwood and Sons, 1893), pp. 380–382.

The "Black Legend" of Spain

BARTOLOMÉ DE LAS CASAS

More than any other single individual, the Dominican friar Bartolomé de Las Casas was responsible for the birth of the "Black Legend," the vicious Spanish reputation that developed during the sixteenth and seventeenth centuries. Although the Black Legend became primarily an instrument of Anglo-Dutch propaganda against the Spanish, which Las Casas probably would never have ac-

A Short Account of the Destruction of the Indies by Bartholome dé Las Casas, translated by Nigel Griffin (Penguin Classics, 1992) copyright © Nigel Griffin, 1992, pp. 14–15. Reproduced with permission of Penguin Books Ltd.

cepted, his influence in its creation is undeniable. After witnessing the ravages and atrocities of Spanish colonists, Las Casas dedicated himself to the protection and defense of the Indians. He wrote the Short Account of the Destruction of the Indies *in 1542 and dedicated it to the Spanish king Philip II in an effort to inform the crown of atrocities in the New World that, if not curtailed, would result in God's destruction of Spain. This book, a fierce and deeply atmospheric anatomy of genocide, established the image of the Spanish conquest of America for the next three centuries. It is testimony to the persuasive and enduring influence of the Black Legend that the Spanish government hoped to amend this pejorative image by hosting the 1992 Olympics in Barcelona.*

As we have said, the island of Hispaniola was the first to witness the arrival of Europeans and the first to suffer the wholesale slaughter of its people and the devastation and depopulation of the land. It all began with the Europeans taking native women and children both as servants and to satisfy their own base appetites; then not content with what the local people offered them of their own free will (and all offered as much as they could spare), they started taking for themselves the food that natives contrived to produce by the sweat of their brows, (which was in all honesty little enough). . . . Some of them started to conceal what food they had, others decided to send their women and children into hiding, and yet others took to the hills to get away from the brutal and ruthless cruelty that was being inflicted on them. The Christians punched them, boxed their ears and flogged them in order to track down the local leaders, and the whole shameful process came to a head when one of the European commanders raped the wife of the paramount chief of the entire island. It was then that the locals began to think up ways of driving the Europeans out of their lands and to take up arms against them. Their weapons, however, were flimsy and

Bartolomé de Las Casas: "[The Spaniards] spared no one, erecting especially wide gibbets on which they could string their victims up with their feet just off the ground and then burn them alive." (*Engraving by Flemish engraver Theodor de Bry taken from a sixteenth-century Dutch edition of the* Short Account of the Destruction of the Indies *by Bartolomé de Las Casas. The British Library*)

ineffective both in attack and in defense (and, indeed, war in the Americas is no more deadly than our jousting, or than many European children's games) and, with their horses and swords and lances, the Spaniards easily fended them off, killing them and committing all kind of atrocities against them.

They forced their way into native settlements, slaughtering everyone they found there, including small children, old men, pregnant women, and even women who had just given birth. They hacked them to pieces, slicing open their bellies with their swords as though they were so many sheep herded into a pen. They even laid wagers on whether they could manage to slice a man in two at a stroke, or cut an individual's head from his body, or disembowel him with a single blow of their axes. They grabbed suckling infants by the feet and, ripping them from their mothers' breasts, dashed them headlong against the rocks. . . . They slaughtered anyone and everyone in their path, on occasion running through a mother and her baby with a single thrust of their swords. They spared no one, erecting especially wide gibbets on which they could string their victims up with their feet just off the ground and then burn them alive thirteen at a time, in honor of our Savior and the twelve Apostles, or tie dry straw to their bodies and set fire to it. Some they chose to keep alive and simply cut their wrists, leaving their hands dangling, saying to them: "Take this letter"—meaning that their sorry condition would act as a warning to those hiding in the hills. The way they normally dealt with the native leaders and nobles was to tie them to a kind of griddle consisting of sticks resting on pitchforks driven into the ground and then grill them over a slow fire, with the result that they howled in agony and despair as they died a lingering death.

LINKS TO AFRICA AND INDIA

Mali: "The Land of Gold"

The kingdom of Mali near the Niger River region of West Africa was founded in the mid-thirteenth century by the Keita ruling clan, which had converted to Islam about 1100. Agriculture provided the foundation of Mali's economy, but it was a monopoly of the lucrative north-south gold trade that allowed the Keita kings to prosper. Ultimately, Mali controlled all trade on the upper Niger river and linked it to western markets served by the Gambia and Senegal rivers.

Mali's imperial power was founded primarily by the Keita King Sundiata (r. 1230–1255), who established a vast network of influence, including provinces and tribute-paying kingdoms whose chieftains recognized the sovereignty of the sacred mansa *or supreme emperor of all the Malian realms. Perhaps the greatest of Sundiata's successors was the famous Mansa Musa (r. 1312–1337). A devout Muslim, Mansa Musa consolidated his realm and with the blessings of peace, imported Muslim scholars and architects, poets and scientists. The fabled trading city of Timbuktu, with its splendid libraries and Islamic schools, became the intellectual center of sub-Saharan Islam. By the fifteenth century, however, factional fighting for succession to the* mansa's *throne had sent Mali into sharp decline.*

The following source is an excellent example of what has been termed "historical oratory." Although western scholars have concentrated primarily on written sources of history, the stories of African tribes were handed down through oral traditions by griots *or singers, who might be likened to poets or troubadours in the West. The African* griot *was, in fact, a most respected and valued member of society. He was often the advisor and tutor of kings and was appointed to preserve the traditions of the tribe. The following selection is perhaps the greatest epic of old Mali to have been preserved by this oral tradition. It is the story of the Lion King, Sundiata. It begins with the words of the* griot, *Mamoudou Kouyaté, who then launches into the tale of Sundiata's struggle for power against Soumaoro Kanté, the sorcerer king of Sasso.*

The Victory of Sundiata

MAMOUDOU KOUYATÉ

I am a griot. It is I, Djeli Mamoudou Koyaté, son of Bintou Kouyaté and Kedian Kouyaté, master in the art of eloquence. Since time immemorial the Kouyatés have been in the service of the Keita princes of Mali; we are vessels of speech, we are the repositories which harbor secrets many centuries old. The art of eloquence has no secrets for us; without us the names of kings would vanish into oblivion, we are the memory of mankind; by the spoken word we bring to life the deeds and exploits of kings for younger generations. . . .

Listen to my word, you who want to know; by my mouth you will learn the history of Mali. Listen now to the story of Sundiata, the Na'Kamma, the man who had a mission to accomplish.

At the time when Sundiata was preparing to assert his claim over the kingdom of his fathers, Soumaoro was the King of Kings, the most powerful king in all the lands of the setting sun. The fortified town of Sosso was the bulwark of fetishism against the word of Allah. For a long time Soumaoro defied the whole world. Since his accession to the throne of Sosso he had defeated nine kings whose heads served him as fetishes in his macabre chamber. Their skins served as seats and he cut his footwear from human skin. Soumaoro was not like other men, for his power was beyond measure. So his countless warriors were very brave since they believed their king to be invincible. But Soumaoro was an evil demon and his reign had produced nothing but bloodshed. Nothing was taboo for him. His greatest pleasure was publicly to flog venerable old men. He had defiled every family and everywhere in his vast empire there were villages populated by girls whom he had forcibly abducted from their

families without marrying them. Oh! How power can pervert a man. . . .

Soumaoro proclaimed himself king of Mali by right of conquest, but he was not recognized by the populace and resistance was organized in the bush. Soothsayers were consulted as to the fate of the country. The soothsayers were unanimous in saying that it would be the rightful heir to the throne who would save Mali. This heir was "The Man with Two Names." The man with two names was no other than Maghan Sundiata. . . .

Soumaoro sent a detachment under his son, Sosso Balla, to block Sundiata's route Tabon. Sosso Balla was about the same age as Sundiata. He promptly deployed his troops at the entrance to the mountains to oppose Sundiata's advance to Tabon.

In the evening, after a long day's march, Sundiata arrived at the head of the great valley which led to Tabon. The valley was quite black with men, for Sosso Balla had deployed his men everywhere in the valley, and some were positioned on the heights which dominated the way through. When Sundiata saw the layout of Sosso Balla's men, he turned to his generals laughing.

"Why are you laughing, brother," said one of his generals, "you can see that the road is blocked."

"Yes, but no mere infantrymen can halt my course towards Mali," replied Sundiata.

The troops stopped. All the war chiefs were of the opinion that they should wait until the next day to give battle because, they said, the men were tired.

"The battle will not last long," said Sundiata, "and the men will have time to rest. We must not allow Soumaoro the time to attack Tabon."

Sundiata was immovable, so the orders were given and the war drums began to beat. On his proud horse, Sundiata turned to right and left in front of his troops. . . . Having drawn his sword, Sundiata led the charge, shouting his war cry.

The Sossos were surprised by this sudden attack for they all thought that the battle would be joined the next day. The lightning that flashes across the sky is slower, the thunderbolts less frightening and flood waters less surprising than Sundiata swooping down on Sosso Balla and his warriors. In a second, Sundiata was in the middle of the Sossos like a lion in the sheepfold. The Sossos, trampled under the hooves of his fiery charger, cried out. When he turned to the right the warriors of Soumaoro fell in their tens, and when he turned to the left his sword made heads fall as when someone shakes a tree of ripe fruit. The horsemen of Mema [Sundiata's army] wrought a frightful slaughter and their long lances pierced flesh like a knife.... Charging ever forward, Sundiata looked for Sosso Balla; he caught sight of him and like a lion bounded towards the son of Soumaoro, his sword held aloft. His arm came sweeping down, but at that moment a Sosso warrior came between him and Sosso Balla and was sliced like a calabash. Sosso Balla did not wait and disappeared from amidst his warriors. Seeing their chief in flight, the Sossos gave way and fell into a terrible rout. . . . The Sossos were pursued until nightfall and several of them were taken prisoner.

The victory had fallen to Sundiata, the son of Sogolon, [and] there was an all-night celebration in the very valley where the Sossos had been defeated. . . . At break of day, the victors entered impregnable Tabon to the cheering of women standing on the ramparts.

The news of the battle of Tabon spread like wildfire throughout the plains of Mali. It was known that Soumaoro was not present at the battle, but the mere fact that his troops had retreated before Sundiata sufficed to give hope to all the peoples of Mali. Soumaoro realized that from now on he would have to reckon with this young man, Sundiata. When Sosso Balla returned with the remnant [of his army] he had managed to save at Tabon, he said to Soumaoro: "Father, he is worse than a lion; nothing can withstand him."

The Kingdom of Mali

IBN BATTUTA

For Muslim traders from North Africa, the kingdom of Mali loomed large in the imagination. Trading salt across the Sahara desert for the gold of Mali was a difficult but rewarding opportunity that inspired a linkage between different cultural worlds.

The following sources are from the pen of Abu Abdallah Muhammad ibn Battuta (1304-1369), who lived a life of great adventure. In 1325, he left home in Morocco on a pilgrimage to Mecca. Inspired by what he saw along the way, he continued to travel, moving mostly within the cultural boundaries of Islam from Spain to Russia and India, to southeast Asia, all the way to China. In 1352, before he settled down to write about all that he had seen, he left by caravan for Mali, the fabled "land of gold." His observations of the customs of Africans often shocked him, but give real indication of the variety of life within the Islamic world.

We set out thereafter from Karsakhu and came to the river of Sansara, which is about ten miles from Mali. . . . I saw a crocodile in this part of the Nile, close to the bank; it looked just like a small boat. One day I went down to the river to satisfy a need, and lo, one of the blacks came and stood between me and the river. I was amazed at such lack of manners and decency on his part, and spoke of it to someone or other. He answered, "His purpose in doing that was

"The Kingdom of Mali" is from H.A.R. Gibb, trans., *Travels of Ibn Battuta in Asia and Africa* (London: Routledge Kegan & Paul, 1927), p. 52.

solely to protect you from the crocodile, by placing himself between you and it.". . .

The Negroes [of Mali] possess some admirable qualities. They are seldom unjust, and have a greater abhorrence of injustice than any other people. The sultan of Mali [called *mansa*] shows no mercy to anyone who is guilty of the least act of it. There is complete security in their country. Neither traveler nor inhabitant in it has anything to fear from robbers or men of violence. They do not confiscate the property of any white man who dies in their country, even if it be accounted wealth. On the contrary, they give it into the charge of some trustworthy person among the whites, until the rightful heir takes possession of it. They are careful to observe the hours of prayer, and assiduous in attending them in congregations, and in bring up their children to them. On Fridays, if a man does not go early to the mosque, he cannot find a corner to pray in, on account of the crowd. It is a custom of theirs to send each man his boy (to the mosque) with his prayer-mat; the boy spreads it out for his master in a place befitting him and remains on it (until his master comes to the mosque). The prayer-mats are made of the leaves of a tree resembling a date-palm, but without fruit.

Another of their good qualities is their habit of wearing clean white garments on Fridays. Even if a man has nothing but an old worn shirt, he washes it and cleans it, and wears it at the Friday service. Yet another is their zeal for learning the Qur'an by heart. They put their children in chains if they show any backwardness in memorizing it, and they are not set free until they have it by heart. I visited his house on the day of the festival. His children were chained up, so I said to him, "Will you not let them loose?" He replied, "I shall not do so until they learn the Qur'an by

heart." Among their bad qualities are the following. The women servants, slave-girls, and young girls go about in front of everyone naked, without a stitch of clothing on them. Women go into the sultan's presence naked and without coverings, and his daughters also go about naked. Then there is the custom of their putting dust and ashes on their heads as a mark of respect, and the grotesque ceremonies we have described when the poets recite their verses. Another reprehensible practice among many of them is the eating of carrion, dogs, and asses.

The Women of Mali

IBN BATTUTA

The women have their "friends" and "companions" among the men outside their own families, and the men in the same way have "companions" among the women of other families. A man may go into his house and find his wife entertaining her "companion" but he takes no objection to it. One day at Walata, I went into the *qadi's* [Muslim judge] house; after asking his permission to enter, and found with him a young woman of remarkable beauty. When I saw her I was shocked and turned to go out, but she laughed at me, instead of being overcome by shame, and the *qadi* said to me, "Why are you going out? She is my companion." I was amazed at their conduct, for he was a theologian and a pilgrim to boot. I was told that he had asked the sultan's permission to make the pilgrimage that year with his "companion" (whether this one or not I cannot say), but the sultan would not grant it.

"The Women of Mali" is from H.A.R. Gibb, trans., *Travels of Ibn Battuta in Asia and Africa* (London: Routledge Kegan & Paul, 1927), pp. 56-58.

The Portuguese in Africa and India

Portugal was to play a primary role in the exploration of new worlds. The Portuguese had traditionally made their living on the sea both as fishermen and as traders, but the leadership of Prince Henry the Navigator (reigned 1394–1468) organized and intensified Portuguese exploration. Henry, inspired both by mercenary motives and missionary ideals sponsored a series of explorations of the African coast in an effort to compete with Muslims, who controlled the land routes of the gold trade. In addition to the lure of gold, the Portuguese saw opportunity in the spice trade of the East and sought to establish outposts that would provide access to new markets and the possibility of commercial dominance.

Explorers such as Bartholomew Dias in 1487 and Vasco da Gama in 1498 rounded the Cape of Good Hope at the tip of Africa and sailed east to India. The first ventures were especially lucrative; da Gama returned with a cargo worth sixty times the cost of the voyage. The Portuguese soon established themselves on the Malabar coast of western India with colonies in Goa and Calcutta. So effective were they in organizing and exploiting commercial links that by the sixteenth century, the Portuguese had successfully challenged the Arabs and Venetians for control of the European spice trade. By the next century, Portuguese contact extended to Japan and other lands in the Far East.

But the establishment of these commercial colonies came at a distinct price for the inhabitants of those regions. In the following selection, Duarte Barbosa (ca. 1480–1521), an agent of the Portuguese government who helped establish commercial contacts along the east African coast, gives a description of the people and products of the area and of Portuguese methods for controlling trade.

The East Coast of Africa

DUARTE BARBOSA

Sofala

Going forward in the direction of India there is a river of no great size upon which up the stream is a town of the Moors [African Muslims] which they call Sofala, close to which the King our Lord [Portuguese King Manuel I] possesses a fort. These Moors have dwelt there a long time by reason of the great traffic which they carried on with the heathen of the mainland. The Moors of this place speak Arabic and have a king over them who is subject to the King our Lord.

And the manner of their traffic was this: they came in small vessels named zambucos from the kingdoms of Kilwa, Mombasa, and Malindi, bringing many cotton cloths, some spotted and others white and blue; also some of silk, and many small beads, grey, red, and yellow, which things come to the said kingdoms from the great kingdom of Cambay [on the coast of northwest India] in other greater ships. And these wares the said Moors who came from Malindi and

Mombasa paid for in gold at such a price that those merchants departed well pleased. . . .

Kilwa

Going along the coast from the town of Mozambique, there is an island hard by the mainland which is called Kilwa, in which is a Moorish town with many fair houses of stone and mortar, with many windows after our fashion, very well arranged in streets, with many flat roofs. The doors are of wood, well carved, with excellent joinery. Around it are streams and orchards and fruit-gardens with many channels of sweet water. It has a Moorish king over it. . . . Before the King our Lord sent out his expedition to discover India, the Moors of Sofala, Cuama, Angoya and Mozambique were all subject to the King of Kilwa, who was the most mighty king among them. And in this town was great plenty of gold, as no ships passed toward Sofala without first coming to this island. . . .

This town was taken by force from its king by the Portuguese, as, moved by arrogance, he refused to obey the King our Lord. There took many prisoners and the king fled from the island, and His Highness ordered that a fort should be built there, and kept it under his rule and governance. . . .

"The East Coast of Africa" is from *The Book of Duarte Barbosa: An Account of the Countries Bordering the Indian Ocean*, 2 vols. (London: Hakluyt Society, 1918, 1921).

Mombasa

Further on, an advance along the coast toward India, there is an isle hard by the mainland, on which is a town called Mombasa. . . . This Mombasa is a land very full of food. Here are found many very fine sheep with round tails, cows and other cattle in great plenty, and many fowls, all of which are exceedingly fat. There is much millet and rice, sweet and bitter oranges, lemons, pomegranates, Indian figs, vegetables of diverse kinds, and much sweet water. The men are often times at war . . . but at peace with those of the mainland, and they carry on trade with them, obtaining great amounts of honey, wax, and ivory.

The king of this city refused to obey the commands of the King our Lord, and through this arrogance he lost it, and our Portuguese took it from him by force. He fled away, and they slew many of his people and also took captive many, both men and women, in such sort that it was left ruined and plundered and burned. Of gold and silver great booty was taken here, bangles, bracelets, earrings and gold beads, also great store of copper with other rich wares in great quantity, and the town was left in ruins.

The City of Brava

Yet further along the coast, beyond these places, is a great town of Moors, of very fine stone and mortar houses, called Brava. It has no king, but is ruled by elders, and ancients of the land, who are the persons held in the highest esteem, and who have the chief dealings in merchandise of diverse kinds. And this place was destroyed by the Portuguese, who slew many of its people and carried many into captivity, and took great spoil of gold and silver and goods. Thenceforth many of them fled away toward the inland country, forsaking the town; yet after had been destroyed the Portuguese again settled and peopled it, so that now it is as prosperous as it was before.

"Our Kingdom Is Being Lost"

NZINGA MBEMBA (AFONSO I)

The next selection is a letter from the African King of Kongo, Nzinga Mbemba, who had converted to Christianity and adopted the name Afonso I (reigned ca. 1506–1543). Afonso had hoped to develop a prosperous state by cooperating with the Europeans. But by the time of his death, his kingdom had almost disintegrated. His concerns are expressed in a letter to the Portuguese king, Joao III, in 1526. It was evident that Portuguese exploitation and aggressive pursuit of slaves resulted in dissension and instability throughout the region.

Sir, Your Highness should know how our Kingdom is being lost in so many ways that it is convenient to provide for the necessary remedy, since this is caused by the excessive freedom given by your agents and officials to the men and merchants who are allowed to come to this Kingdom to set up shops with goods and many things which have been prohibited by us, and which they spread throughout our Kingdoms and Domains in such an abundance that many of our vassals, whom we had in obedience, do not comply because they have the things in greater abundance than we ourselves; and it was with these things that we had them content and subjected under our vassalage and jurisdiction, so it is doing a great harm not only to the service of God, but the security and peace of our Kingdoms and State as well.

And we cannot reckon how great the damage is, since the mentioned merchants are taking every day our natives, sons of the land and the sons of our noblemen and vassals and our relatives, because the thieves and men of bad conscience grab them wishing to have the things and wares of this Kingdom which they are ambitious of; they grab them and get them to be sold; and so great, Sir, is the corruption and licentiousness that our country is being completely depopulated, and Your Highness should not agree with this nor accept it as in your service. And to avoid it we need from your Kingdoms no more than some priests and a few people to teach in schools, and no other goods except wine and flour for the holy sacrament. That is why we beg of Your Highness to help and assist us in this matter, commanding your factors [agents] that they should not send here either merchants or wares, because it *our will that in these Kingdoms there should not be any trade of slaves nor outlet for them.* Concerning what is referred [to] above, again we beg of Your Highness to agree with it, since otherwise we cannot remedy such an obvious damage. Pray Our Lord in his mercy to have Your Highness under His guard and let you do forever the things of His service. . . .

Moreover, Sir, in our Kingdoms there is another great inconvenience which is of little service to God, and this is that many of our people, keenly desirous as they are of the wares and things of your Kingdoms, which are brought here by your people, and in order to satisfy their voracious appetite, seize many of our people, freed and exempt men, and very often it happens that they kidnap even noblemen and the sons of noblemen, and our relatives, and take them to be sold to the white men who are in our Kingdoms; and for this purpose they have concealed them; and others are brought during the night so that they might not be recognized.

And as soon as they are taken by the white men they are immediately ironed and branded with fire, and when they are carried to be embarked, if they are caught by our guards' men the whites allege that they have bought them but they cannot say from whom, so that it is our duty to do justice and to restore to the freemen their freedom, but it cannot be done if your subjects feel offended, as they claim to be.

And to avoid such a great evil we passed a law so that any white man living in our Kingdoms and wanting to purchase goods in any way should first inform three of our noblemen and officials of our court whom we rely upon in this matter, and these are Dom Pedro Manipanza and Dom Manuel Manissaba, our chief usher, and Gocalo Pires our chief freighter, who should investigate if the mentioned goods are captives or free men, and if cleared by them there will be no further doubt nor embargo for them to be taken and embarked. But if the white men do not comply with it they will lose the aforementioned goods. And if we do them this favor and concession it is for the part Your Highness has in it, since we know that it is in your service too that these goods are taken from our Kingdom, otherwise we should not consent to this. . . .

"Cut Off Their Ears, Hands and Noses!"

GASPAR CORREA

The following selection is an excerpt from the journals of Gaspar Correa, who sailed with Vasco da Gama in 1502. This incident occurred after a group of Portuguese had been killed in the trading station of Calcutta. Vasco da Gama sought to control the situation by exacting a bloody vengeance.

"Cut Off Their Ears, Hands and Noses!" is from H.E.J. Stanley, ed., *The Three Voyages of Vasco da Gama* (London: The Hakluyt Society, 1869), pp. 328-332.

The captain-major [Vasco da Gama], on arriving at Calecut, was in the passion because he found the port cleared, and in it there was nothing to which he could do harm, because the Moors, knowing of his coming, had all fled, and hid their vessels and sambuks in the rivers.... The King of Calecut thought that he might gain time, so that the captain-major should not do him harm; and when his fleet arrived he sent him a Brahman [religious official] of his in a boat with a white cloth fastened to a pole, as a sign of peace. This Brahman came dressed in the habit of a friar, one of those who had been killed in the country; and on reaching the ship, he asked for a safe conduct to enter. When it was known that he was not a friar—for the captain-major and everyone had been joyful, thinking that he was one of our friars—seeing that he was not, the captain-major gave him a safe conduct, and bade him enter the ship.... He then ordered all the fleet to draw in close to the shore, and all day, till night, he bombarded the city, by which he made a great destruction....

While they were doing this business, there came in from the offing two large ships and twenty-two sambuks and Malabar vessels, which came from Coromandel laden with rice, which the Moors of Calecut had ordered to be laden there;... but our fleet having sighted them, the [Portuguese] caravels went to them, and the Moors could not fly, as they were laden, and the caravels brought them to the captain-major, and all struck their sails....

Then, the captain-major commanded them to cut off the hands and ears and noses of all the crews, and put all that into one of the small vessels, into which he ordered them to put the friar, also without ears, or nose, or hands, which he ordered to be strung round his neck, with a palm-leaf for the King, on which he told him to have a curry made to eat of what his friar brought him. When all the Indians had been thus executed, he ordered their feet to be tied together, as they had no hands with which to untie them: and in order that they should not untie them with their teeth he ordered them to strike upon their teeth with staves, and they knocked them down their throats; and they were thus put on board, heaped up upon the top of each other, mixed up with the blood which streamed from them; and he ordered mats and dry leaves to be spread over them, and the sails to be set for the shore, and the vessel set on fire; and there were more than eight hundred Moors; and the small vessel with the friar, with all the hands and ears, was also sent on shore under sail, without being fired. These vessels went at once on shore, where many people flocked together to put out the fire, and draw out those whom they found alive, upon which they made great lamentations.

The Prospects of Christian Conversion

SAINT FRANCIS XAVIER

My own and only Father in the Heart of Christ, I think that the many letters from this place which have lately been sent to Rome will inform you how prosperously the affairs of religion go on in these parts, through your prayers and the good bounty of God. But there seem to be certain things which I ought myself to speak about to you; so I will just touch on a few points relating to these parts of the world which are so distant from Rome. In the first place, the whole race of the Indians, as far as I have been able to see, is very barbarous; and it does not like to listen to anything that is not agreeable to its own manners and customs, which, as I say, are barbarous. It troubles itself very little to learn anything about divine things and things which concern salvation. Most of the Indians are of vicious disposition, and are adverse to virtue. Their instability, levity, and inconstancy of mind are incredible; they have hardly any honesty, so inveterate are their habits of sin and cheating. We have hard work here, both in keeping the Christians up the mark and in this account you

"The Prospects of Christian Conversion" is from Henry James Coleridge, ed., *The Life and Letters of St. Francis Xavier,* 2nd edition (London: Burns and Oates, 1890), p. 86.

should take great care of us and help us continually by your prayers to God. You know very well what a hard business it is to teach people who neither have any knowledge of God nor follow reason, but think it a strange and intolerable thing to be told to give up their habits of sin, which have now gained all the force of nature by long possession. . . .

The experience which I have of these countries makes me think that I can affirm with truth, that there is no prospect of perpetuating our Society out here by means of the natives themselves, and that the Christian religion will hardly survive us who are now in the country; so that it is quite necessary that continual supplies of ours should be sent out from Europe. . . .

The Portuguese in these countries are masters only of the sea and of the coast. On the mainland they have only the towns in which they live. The natives themselves are so enormously addicted to vice as to be little adapted to receive the Christian religion. They so dislike it that it is most difficult to get them to hear us if we begin to preach about it, and they think it like death to be asked to become Christians. So for the present, we devote ourselves to keeping the Christians whom we have. Certainly, if the Portuguese were more remarkable for their kindness to the new converts, a great number would become Christians; as it is, the heathen see that the converts, are despised and looked down upon by the Portuguese, and so, as is natural, they are unwilling to become converts themselves. For all these reasons there is no need for me to labor in these countries, and as I have learned from good authorities that there is a country near China called Japan, the inhabitants of which are all heathen, quite untouched by Muslims or Jews, and very eager to learn what they do not know both in things divine and things natural, I have determined to go thither as soon as I can. . . .

THE LIGHT IN THE EAST

The Ming Dynasty of China (1368-1644)

By about 1365, Mongol control of China under the Yuan dynasty had collapsed amidst the furious rioting of peasants, who had for decades endured the dislocation of floods, famines, brigands, and political instability. In 1368, power finally passed to Zhu Yuanzhang, one of the leaders of the Red Turban secret society, who had struggled for years against Yuan warlords of southern China. "Proclaim yourself emperor slowly," one of his counselors suggested and Zhu consolidated his gains carefully from his capital at Nanjing. This new dynasty would be known by the epithet of Ming, or "brilliant."

The Ming dynasty (1368–1644) truly lived up to the dimensions of this epithet. In the year 1600, the Chinese empire was the largest and most sophisticated of all unified realms in the world. Its population of over 120 million was greater than the population of all European countries combined. The era of the Ming and its successor dynasty, the Qing (1644–1911), represent the longest period of good government in Chinese history. While rulers in Europe, India, Japan, and the Ottoman Empire were struggling to develop stable models of imperial rule, China retained its traditions of systematic bureaucracy, law, and provincial administration that had existed for over a millennium. Historians have described this as the "perfected" late imperial system of government, since it represented an improved continuation of the structure that had been so successful during the Han, Tang, and Song dynasties. Ming emperors generally maintained a Confucian approach to progressive government. The civil service examinations became ever more intense and competitive, since the rewards of public service were so great. These administrators were generally produced from a strong gentry class of urban, well-educated individuals.

At the center of power was the emperor, whose position became even more despotic and was maintained by a sophisticated secret police and brutal prison system. The third Ming emperor moved his capital from Nanjing to Beijing and constructed an elaborate Forbidden Palace. The entire complex redefined the majesty of the emperor as absolute ruler. The palace had over 6,000 cooks who served 10,000 persons daily and included an enormous harem with a staff of about 70,000 eunuchs. This isolation and reverence of the emperor promoted the political unity of China, but later contributed to the decline of the regime during the Qing as emperors were increasingly isolated from political and social realities.

Like other Chinese dynasties, the Ming and Qing passed through what historians refer to as a "dynastic cycle." At the outset, the dynasties consolidated political authority and began expansive periods characterized by energetic reforms and ambitious projects. As the dynasties aged, political and social stability fell prey to corruption, popular discontent, eventual decline, and failure. In foreign affairs, the beginning of the cycle saw an expansive energy only to decline into an isolationist stance. For all of the impressive Chinese political stability and wonderful artistic contributions, the dynamic momentum of civilization resided in Europe during these centuries. The western Renaissance, Reformation, scientific revolution, Enlightenment, democratic and industrial revolutions all happened concurrent to Ming and Qing rule. The West had accelerated while China was withdrawing from the world stage, becoming increasingly conservative and isolationist.

The Voyages of Zheng He

ZHANG TINGYU

Perhaps the most ambitious decision of the early Ming dynasty was the promotion of Zheng He's Seven Voyages to the Western Ocean. In some of the largest and best constructed ships in the world at the time, the eunuch, Zheng He (ca. 1373–1435), sailed to such remote locations as the Persian Gulf, the Red Sea, and the eastern coast of Africa. He returned with dozens of foreign kings, who in turn, paid tribute to the Chinese emperor. When Zheng He set out on his last voyage in 1430, the fortunes of the Ming had already started to decline, and such ambitious and expensive voyages could no longer be financed. Still, they demonstrate that world exploration was certainly not an exclusive European or Islamic preserve. Such ventures also flowed from the East to the West. The historian Zhang Tingyu provides the following account of these impressive voyages.

After his accession to the throne, Emperor Yunglo, suspected that his defeated predecessor Xuiti might have escaped from Nanking and be residing somewhere in the South Seas and wanted very much to know his whereabouts. Besides, he wished to glorify Chinese arms in the remote regions and show off the wealth and power of the Central Kingdom. It was this combination of motives that prompted him to launch Zheng He's voyages.

In the sixth month of 1405, Zheng He and his deputy Wang Jinghong, as ordered by the emperor, proceeded with their journey to the Western Ocean [areas of South and Southeast Asia]. Well furnished with treasure and accompanied by more than 27,800 officers and men, they sailed in sixty-two giant ships, each of which measured [517 feet] in length and [212 feet] in width. The ships left the Liuchia River [near modern Shanghai] for the sea and then sailed southward to . . . Champa [Vietnam]. From Champa, the Chinese envoys visited one country after another. They read the imperial decree that demanded the submission of the kingdoms they visited and rewarded generously those rulers who agreed to submit. As for those who chose not obey, force was used to assure their compliance.

In the ninth month of [1407], Zheng He returned to the capital and presented to the emperor tribute-bearing envoys from the kingdoms he had visited. The emperor was greatly pleased and granted titles and financial rewards to all of those who had been presented to him. Zheng He also brought back many prisoners of war, including the captured king of Palembang [Indonesia].

[Palembang's ruler], a Chinese named Chen Zuyi, had been active as a pirate in the South Seas before he was captured by Zheng He. When Zheng He demanded his surrender, he said he would, but in secret he was planning to launch an attack upon Zheng He's ships. Once the perfidy was recognized, Zheng He attacked and won a decisive victory. Chen Zuyi was captured alive and later bought to Beijing. He was executed shortly afterward. . . .

In the eleventh month of [1412], the emperor again ordered Zheng He to proceed to Sumatra. Zheng He arrived at a time when Sekeander, son of a former ruler of that kingdom,

was plotting the overthrow of the reigning prince so as to establish himself as the king. Resenting Zheng He for having failed to give him any gold or silk, he ordered his men to attack Chinese troops. Zheng He responded vigorously, defeated his army, and pursued him until, he, together with his family, was captured at Lambri. The Chinese envoy returned to Beijing in the seventh month of [1415], to be welcomed by a pleased emperor who rewarded all the officers and men for their efforts. . . .

Zheng He served three emperors with distinction and conducted seven voyages altogether, [visiting thirty kingdoms]. . . . The amount of treasure he brought to China from these kingdoms was of course enormous, but the expense to China herself was even more staggering. [From 1426–1435], these kingdoms, occasionally, still sent tribute missions to China, but they could not be compared with the tribute missions [from 1403 to 1424] that were not only more sumptuous but also more frequent. By then Zheng He had become too old to undertake any strenuous task. Long after his death, however, his achievement was still so highly regarded that Chinese generals and admirals, whenever serving abroad, kept mentioning it as a way to impress foreigners. Even laymen spoke of the Seven Voyages . . . as a most outstanding event of the Ming dynasty.

Gentleman Wang: The Noble Merchant

DAOKUN

The following portrait of a revered Chinese merchant reveals much about business practices during the Ming. Note especially the qualities of character that were esteemed in China.

In 1556, Mr. Wang, who was ninety years old at the time, was given the highest prefectural title by imperial decree and from that time on has been treated with the courtesies due an elder. As the histories testify, in ancient times emperors often honored venerable old men so as to receive the

benefit of their constant advice. Even at his great age, Mr. Wang is a man of the highest integrity; therefore I now extol his deeds in order to show my respect for virtuous old men. . . .

Mr. Wang lives in Shanghai. Being open and confident he has attracted the respect of many capable and prosperous people who compete to attach themselves to him. At first, Mr. Wang's capital was no greater than the average person's. Later, as he grew more prosperous every day, the number of his associates also steadily increased. To accommodate his apprentices, Mr. Wang built buildings with doors on four sides. Whenever customers came, they could be taken care of from all four directions; thus, no one ever had to wait very long.

Mr. Wang set up the following guidelines for his associates: do not let anyone who lives in another county control the banking; when lending money, never harass law-abiding people unnecessarily or give them less than they need; charge low interest on loans; do not aim at high profit and do not ask for daily interest. These principles led customers to throng to him, even ones from neighboring towns and provinces. Within a short time, Mr. Wang accumulated great wealth; in fact, of all the rich people in that area he became the richest.

Mr. Wang liked to help people and to give assistance to the poor. If anyone among his kinsmen could not afford a funeral for his parents, Mr. Wang would always buy some land and build a tomb for him. As soon as he heard someone could not make ends meet, he would buy land to rent to him. Whenever he was out traveling and met some unburied spirit, he would bid his servants bury it and present some offerings. . . .

When Mr. Wang is at home he is always in high spirits. He likes to make friends with the chivalrous youths. In his later years he has become particularly fond of chess, often staying up all night until he either wins or loses a game. The youths say that Mr. Wang is no ordinary person, that he must have received instruction from Heaven.

Now Mr. Wang is almost one hundred years old. He has at least thirty sons and grandsons living at home with him. It is said, "One who seeks perfection will attain it." This describes Mr. Wang perfectly.

The Coming of the West and the "Portuguese Problem"

Portuguese explorers were often the first Europeans to encounter the peoples and develop the markets of India and Africa. When Portuguese traders arrived at Canton, China in the early 1500s, the Chinese believed that they had come to pay tribute and "partake of a superior civilization." The Chinese soon discovered that the Portuguese sought to exploit the region with actions that bordered on piracy. Still, the Portuguese brought with them goods and spices that were greatly desired. And although the Chinese government imposed severe restrictions on foreigners, other coastal Chinese were willing to trade with the "red-haired barbarians." The following accounts from two officials testify to the ambivalence of Chinese policy. The "Portuguese Problem" remained a source of irritation for the Chinese that was exacerbated in the early seventeenth century by the arrival of the Dutch, who were themselves aggressive traders.

Zhang Tingyu: Censor Ho Ao also presented a memo [to the emperor] in connection with the Fu-lang-chi [Portuguese] problem. "The people of Portugal are as brutal as they are treacherous, and their military equipment is far superior to that of other foreigners," said the memorialist. "Sometimes, borne on large ships, they suddenly burst into the capital of Canton: the sound of their cannons could be heard far and wide. The Portuguese who remained at Huaiyuan I violated the law by communicating with the Chinese, and those who went to the capital [Beijing] were arrogant enough to show off their so-called talents. If we allow them to travel freely and trade, strife

"The Coming of the West" is from Dun J. Li, ed. and trans., *China in Transition: 1517-1911* (New York: Van Nostrand Reinhold Company, 1969), pp. 5-7. Copyright © 1969 by Litton Educational Publishing, Inc. Reprinted by permission.

is bound to break out, and the mischief they can start among the people in the south will never come to an end. The ancestors of our dynasty specified the years when tribute missions were allowed and provided us with guides to keep our national defense strong. As a result, the visits of tribute missions from foreign countries have been infrequent. Lately, . . . we have allowed these Portugese people to come and trade in any year they choose. The result is that foreign ships keep sailing into our rivers and seas, and foreigners themselves live side by side with the Chinese in our towns and cities. As we continue to relax our defense measures, foreigners have become more and more familiar with our waterways. This is the reason why the Portuguese were able to make intrusions into our territory without our advance knowledge. I accordingly suggest that all foreign ships currently anchored in our bays and harbors should be expelled at once and that all foreigners who live in China without permission should be deported immediately. Clandestine communication with foreigners should be prohibited, and our defense should be further strengthened. Only in this way can our coastal areas again enjoy peace and security." . . . The emperor replied: "Let this be done."

Huo Ruxia: What then should we do? There are three measures we can take, each exclusive of the others. The best measure would be to govern them in the same manner as we govern our own people: to convert the territory they have occupied into a subprefecture and to place them under the jurisdictional control of duly appointed government officials. The next best measure would be to expel them and make sure that they never come back again. The worst measure would be to cut off their food supply, which would force them to revolt, and then use armed forces to exterminate them. . . .

Some people may say that once these barbarians are expelled from China, there will be no further disturbances on our frontier and our people will be much better off. How, they may ask, can expulsion be regarded as the second best course? I reply that to have confidence in the barbarians' natural goodness for our own defense is reflective of the greatness of the Son of Heaven, that to welcome all barbarians to partake of our civilization is indicative of the benign nature of the Celestial King, and that to provide food for our enemy so as to pacify the frontier betokens the farsightedness of a powerful nation. . . . In short, to construct cities for them and to govern them with Chinese officials in accordance with the Chinese law will be the best policy to follow. It is best because it is a policy of kindness by which peace can be secured without great effort.

The Jesuits

ZHANG TINGYU

Not all Europeans who ventured to China were out simply for financial gain. In addition to traders, the Catholic church, smarting from European setbacks during the Protestant Reformation, sought new converts in the East. The Jesuit order, founded about 1540 by Ignatius Loyola, provided most of these missionaries. One of the most respected Jesuits, Matteo Ricci, arrived in China in 1583 and stayed there until his death in 1610. Ricci became fluent in Chinese and so impressed the emperor with his knowledge that he was made a court mathematician and astronomer. His journals were published in 1615 and offer us a detailed glimpse into the life of Ming China. The first selection by the court historian Zhang Tingyu describes the influence of Matteo Ricci from a Chinese

"The Jesuits" is from Dun J. Li, ed. and trans., *China in Transition: 1517–1911* (New York: Van Nostrand Reinhold Company, 1969), pp. 14-15; 17. Copyright © 1969 by Litton Educational Publishing, Inc. Reprinted by permission.

perspective. This is followed by an excerpt from Ricci's own journals about the extraordinary gifts of China.

Italy is located in the Great Western Ocean and had no relationship with China in ancient time. During the Wanli period [1573-1619], an Italian named Li Mazou [Matteo Ricci] came to the capital [Beijing] and presented an atlas of the world. "There are five continents in the world," he said. "The first continent is Asia, consisting of more than one hundred countries, including China. The second continent is Europe, consisting of more than seventy countries, including Italy. The third continent, Africa, also has more than one hundred countries. The fourth continent, America, is even larger and has two constituent parts, North and South America. The last or fifth continent is Australia. These five continents are all the land in this world." His words were so vague and incoherent that they could not be verified in any of the books then in existence. But the fact that people from these remote lands did roam about in China seemed to indicate that there was some truth in his remarks.

All these people came from European counties and believed in a religion called Roman Catholicism. Jesus, the man whom they worshiped, was born . . . in a country called Judea. Fifteen hundred eighty-one years later, in [1581], Li Mazou sailed across the ocean and arrived a Macao off Canton. With his arrival in China came his religion. . . .

The tribute this man has presented consists of the images of a Heavenly Lord and His Mother [Mary, Mother of Jesus], a tribute that is highly irregular. He has also brought with him "bones of the immortals [relics]." The term "bones of the immortal" is self-contradictory since a true immortal can fly by himself without any bones. . . .

Later, the emperor, pleased that this man had come such a long way to visit China, granted him living quarters and a food allowance, plus numerous gifts. All the ministers at court thought highly of the man and associated with him. Li Mazou was so happy with his new home that he decided to stay until the end of his life. He died in [1610] and was buried in the western suburb of Beijing. . . .

The people who came from the Great Western Ocean [Jesuit missionaries] were mostly intelligent and highly knowledgeable. They were only interested in spreading their religion and did not care for fame or wealth. The books they wrote dealt with topics which the Chinese rarely mentioned, and those who loved different and strange things were anxious to learn from them. . . . As a result, this religion, called Roman Catholicism, suddenly flourished in China.

The Life of China
MATTEO RICCI

This country is so thoroughly covered by an intersecting network of rivers and canals that it is possible to travel almost anywhere by water. Hence, an almost incredible number of boats of every variety pass hither and thither. Indeed, there are so many of them that one of the writers of our day does not hesitate to affirm that there are as many people living on the water as there are dwellers on land. This may sound like an exaggeration and yet it all but expresses the truth, as it would seem, if one were to travel here only by water. In my opinion, it might be said with greater truth and without fear of exaggeration, that there are as many boats in this kingdom as can be counted up in all the rest of the world. . . .

"The Life of China" is from Louis J. Gallagher, trans., *The China That Was* (Milwaukee: The Bruce Publishing Company, 1942), pp. 18-19; 22; 25-26; 32-33. Copyright © 1942 by The Bruce Publishing Company. Reprinted by permission.

The ordinary tableware of the Chinese is clay pottery. It is not quite clear to me why it is called porcelain in the West. There is nothing like it in European pottery either from the standpoint of the material itself or its thin and fragile construction. The finest specimens of porcelain are made from clay found in the province of Kiam, and these are shipped not only to every part of China, but even to the remotest corners of Europe where they are highly prized by those who appreciate elegance at their banquets rather than pompous display. This porcelain, too, will bear the heat of hot foods without cracking and, what is more to be wondered at, if it is broken and sewed with a brass wire, it will hold liquids without any leakage. . . .

Two or three things are entirely unknown to Europeans of which I must give a brief account. First, there is a certain bush from the leaves of which is decocted that celebrated drink, known to the Chinese, the Japanese, and to their neighbors as tea. Its use cannot be of long duration among the Chinese, as no ideography in their old books designates this particular drink and their writing characters are all ancient. Indeed, it might be that this same plant can be found in our own fields. Here they gather its leaves in the springtime and place them in a shady place to dry, and from the dried leaves they brew a drink which they use at meals and which is served to friends when they come to visit. On such occasions, it is served continually as long as they remain together engaged in conversation. This beverage is sipped rather than drunk and it is always taken hot. It is no unpleasant to the taste, being somewhat bitter, and it is usually considered to be wholesome even if taken frequently. . . .

Finally we should say something about the saltpeter, which is quite plentiful but which is not used extensively in the preparation of gunpowder, because the Chinese are not expert in the use of guns and artillery and make but little use of these in warfare. Saltpeter, however, is used in lavish quantities in making fireworks for display at public games and on festival days. The Chinese take great pleasure in such exhibitions and make them the chief attraction of all their festivities. Their skill in the manufacture of fireworks is really extraordinary, and there is scarcely anything which they cannot cleverly imitate with them. They are especially adept in reproducing battles and in making rotating spheres of fire, fiery trees, fruit, and the like, and they seem to have no regard for expense where fireworks are concerned. When I was in Nanjing, I witnessed a pyrotechnic display for the celebration of the first month of the year, which is their great festival, and on this occasion, I calculated that thy consumed enough powder to carry on a sizable war for a number of years. . . .

The art of printing was practiced in China at a date somewhat earlier than that assigned to the beginning of printing in Europe, which was about 1405. It is quite certain that the Chinese knew the art of printing at least five centuries ago, and some of them assert that printing was known to their people before the beginning of the Christian era, about 50 B.C. . . .

Their method of making printed books is quite ingenious. The text is written in ink, with a brush made of very fine hair, on a sheet of paper which is inverted and pasted on a wooden tablet. When the paper has become thoroughly dry, its surface is scraped off quickly and with great skill, until nothing but a fine tissue bearing the characters remains on the wooden tablet. Then, with a steel graver, the workman cuts away the surface following the outlines of the characters until these alone stand out in low relief. From such a block a skilled printer can make copies with incredible speed, turning out as many as fifteen hundred copies in a single day. Chinese printers are so skilled in engraving these blocks, that no more time is consumed in making one of them than would be required by one of our printers in setting up a form of type and making the necessary corrections. . . .

The simplicity of Chinese printing is what accounts for the exceedingly large number of books in circulation here and the ridiculously low prices at which they are sold. Such facts as these would scarcely be believed by one who had not witnessed them. . . .

The Grand Eunuch Wei and Ming Decline

ZHANG TINGYU

The Ming dynasty saw the expansion of the autocratic power of the Chinese emperor. As Sons of Heaven, they were entitled to the best amenities in life, from extraordinary personal power to the pleasures of food and sex. Their harems numbered in the thousands and were composed of women chosen for their beauty and charm. How best to oversee the purity of such valuable amenities? The Chinese solution was to castrate low-born males during childhood and train them to manage the "interior bureaucracy" of the palace, which, of course, included the harem. Powerful and competent emperors controlled the influence of their most devoted eunuchs, but weak emperors, as in the Roman Empire, fell prey to the machinations of ambitious servants. One of the most legendary of these eunuchs was Wei Zhongxian. His power was unrivaled and contributed to political instability and the decline of the Ming.

Selected as a palace eunuch [under the Emperor Wanli (1573–1619)], Wei Zhongxian moved quickly to ingratiate himself with those who could help his cause. An excellent cook, he was particularly patronized by Princess Wang, mother of the crown prince designate, later known as Emperor Ming Xizun. Subsequently he became a lover to the prince's wet nurse name Ke, who had abandoned an earlier lover on his behalf. As later events proved, this alliance between a eunuch and a wet nurse, based upon a relationship of illicit love, formed the basis of Wei Zhongxian's emergence to power.

Within a month after Ming Xizun's accession to the throne, wet nurse Ke was titled Madame Fengsheng and eunuch Wei received three simultaneous appointments, including the appointment as administrator of rites. Normally only a man of great learning could be privileged to occupy that post; eunuch Wei acquired that post only because of Ke's insistence. Meanwhile the close relatives of both, including an elder brother of the eunuch, were promoted to lucrative positions and titled accordingly. The increasing influence of Ke alarmed many members of the censorate who, noting the forthcoming royal marriage, maintained that the emperor had no more need of his wet nurse and that she, indeed, should be ousted from the palace. The emperor, in reply, stated that he could no more dispense with the service of his wet nurse than he could with that of his own mother. In view of the love and protection that the wet nurse had provided for him when he was a child, he, the emperor, could not but be eternally grateful.

As long as Ke's influence over the emperor continued, Wei Zhongxian could do whatever he pleased with his rivals or enemies inside the palace. All of them, one after another were ousted from positions of power and influence, including Ke's former lover previously mentioned. Having thus secured his own position inside the palace, Wei Zhongxian received permission from the emperor to train the eunuchs under his control in the use of military weapons and other martial arts. To keep the emperor busy, he led the young man to a variety of dissipations, such as sex, music, hunting, and gambling. . . .

So far the power of eunuch Wei was confined to the palace. To explain its extension to the imperial government and eventually the country as a whole, we have to review the development of events toward the end of the Wanli period. Later in his life Emperor Wanli increasingly lost interest in the management of state affairs and seldom bothered to read the memorials that had been presented to him. As he gradually moved away from political activities, factions began to develop among his ministers, each of whom resorted to the expression of radical ideas to gain attention and influence. . . .

Those who opposed the Grand Eunuch were dismissed from their posts, while those who supported him were either appointed to new positions or promoted to greater responsibility. To impress others with his own importance, the Grand Eunuch increased his personal retainers to ten thousand and was always escorted by armed guards, whether inside or outside the palace. Meanwhile his palace ally Ke was doing her utmost to make sure that the royal weakling could not produce a legitimate heir. Concubine Chang was executed in secret when it was learned that she had become pregnant; when the empress was also found to have become pregnant, Ke made sure that a miscarriage would occur. Thus the boy emperor, despite the size of his harem, was never able to produce an heir. . . .

The Grand Eunuch [decided] to purge or physically eliminate all of his opponents. . . . By 1626, not only the officials in the imperial government, but also those on the local level had become devoted followers of the Grand Eunuch. In the sixth month of that year Ban Ruzhen, Governor of Zhekiang [province], petitioned for the erection of a living shrine in honor of the Grand Eunuch. . . . Before long, living shrines in honor of the Grand Eunuch

mushroomed all over the empire. From every corner of the empire came eulogies, the writers of which competed with one another in extolling the Grand Eunuch's virtues. Those who disagree openly were arrested on trumped-up charges and punished accordingly. A political machine was thus established, which functioned effectively, though ruthlessly, throughout the empire. Its top echelon consisted of a military as well as a civilian group. . . .

Great though it was, the power of the Grand Eunuch Wei fell as precipitously as it had risen. In 1627, emperor Ming Xizun died and was succeeded by Prince Xing who, after accession, was known as Emperor Ming Zhongxian [1627–1644]. When serving as a crown prince, Zhongxian detested Grand Eunuch Wei for his evil ways but was careful enough not to offend him until he, upon becoming an emperor, could do something about his misgivings. Indictments against the Grand Eunuch soon appeared on [the Emperors's] desk. . . . The Emperor summoned the Grand Eunuch to his presence and asked one of the officials to read the indictment aloud. Realizing that the walls had finally closed in on him, the Grand Eunuch offered heavy bribes to . . . the Emperor's own eunuch and confidant and the Grand Eunuch's one-time gambling partner, hoping to ease the pressure. The Emperor learned about the bribe and reprimanded [his eunuch] for accepting it. In 1627, the Grand Eunuch was exiled to Fengyang.

A Plan for the Prince

ZHANG TINGYU

The historian Zhang Tingyu (1610–1675), who contributed many of the selections in this section, was the son of a high Ming official. His father died in prison at the hands of powerful eunuchs. At age eighteen, after the fall of the Grand Eunuch Wei, he avenged his father's death by bringing to justice those who were responsible. Upon the collapse of the Ming dynasty in 1644, he led unsuccessful guerilla operations against the new Manchu dynasty and then settled down at age fifty-two to write the history of the Ming. Perhaps his most impressive work, A Plan for the Prince, analyzes political and economic weaknesses of seventeenth century China.

From *Sources of Chinese Tradition* by William Theodore de Bary, ed. © 1960 Columbia University Press. Reprinted with permission of the publisher.

In many ways, Zhang's life parallels another impressive political observer, the Florentine Niccolò Machiavelli (1469–1527). After serving the republic of Florence, Machiavelli was imprisoned by the restored Medici family in 1512, tortured, and forced from power. He returned and wrote a short political manual entitled The Prince *(1519), offering advice on gaining and maintaining power. In the following selection, note carefully Zhang Tingyu's Confucian emphasis on the importance of character in good government, both in the position of the Prince and in his ministers. Machiavelli would reject such notions, arguing that politics was an amoral game of survival.*

In ancient times, the people were considered hosts and the prince was the guest. All of his life the prince spent working for the sake of the people. Now the prince is host and the people are guests. Because of the prince, people can find peace and happiness nowhere. In order to achieve his ends, people must be harmed and killed and their families broken up—all for the aggrandizement of one man's fortune. Without feeling the least pity for mankind, the prince says: "I want only to establish this estate for the sake of my descendants." Yet when he has established it, the prince still wrings every drop of blood and marrow from the people and takes away their sons and daughters to serve his excessive pleasures. It seems entirely proper to him. It is, he says, the interest on his estate. Thus the greatest enemy of mankind is the prince and nothing but the prince.

If there had been no rulers, each man would have lived for himself and secured what was to his own benefit. Could it be that the institution of rulership was meant to work out like this? In ancient times men loved their prince, thought of him as a father, likened him to God; and truly this was no more than just. Now men hate their prince, think of him as a mortal foe, call him an "outcast." . . .

It is not easy to make plain the function of the prince, but any fool can see that a brief moment of excessive pleasure is not worth an eternity of sorrows.

The reason for ministership lies in the fact that the world is too big for one man to govern and that it is necessary to share the work with others. Therefore, when I come forth to serve, it is for the whole world and not for the prince; it is for all men and not for one family. . . .

But those who act as ministers today do not understand this concept. They say that a minister is created for the prince, that he rules only because the prince shares part of the world with him and delegates to him some leadership over the people. They look upon the world and its people as personal property in the prince's pouch. . . .

Whether there is peace or disorder in the world does not depend on the rise and fall of dynasties, but upon the happiness or distress of the people. . . .

If a minister ignores the plight of the people, then even if he succeeds in assisting his prince's rise to power or follows him to final ruin, it still can never be said that he has followed the [True] Way of the Minister. . . . Alas, the insolent princes of later times indulge themselves [in the same way] and do not tend to the business of the world an its people. From among the men of the country they seek out only such as will be servile errand-boys. And if from the country those alone respond who are of the servile errand-boy type, then when they are protected from cold and hunger for a while, they feel eternally grateful for his majesty's kindness. Such men will not care whether they are treated by the prince with due respect, and will think it no more than proper to be relegated to a servant's status. . . .

The terms "prince" and "minister" derive their significance from service to mankind. If I have no sense of duty to mankind I am an alien to the prince. If I come to serve him without any consideration for the welfare of mankind, then I am merely the prince's menial servant. If, on the other hand, I have the people's interest at heart, then I am the prince's mentor and colleague. Only then may I really be called a minister.

The Establishment of Tokugawa Japan

The medieval period in Japan, from the twelfth to the sixteenth centuries, was a complex time of in-cessant change. Although the emperor reigned over Japan, the administrative and military affairs of the state were controlled by the shōgun, chosen for his preeminent authority and influence among the great lords (daimyō) of the realm. The Ashikaga Shogunate that had ruled Japan since the four-teenth century from its capital in Kyoto had never really been able to control the political indepen-dence of regional daimyō. By the first half of the sixteenth century, the worst period of disorder, there was virtually no unified leadership in Japan and the country degenerated into over sixty indepen-dent domains, each ruled by local lords with aspirations of greatness. There began a contest of elimi-nation to determine the political future of the state, a contest remarkable for its bloody ferocity. Out of this chaos emerged three generals whose vigor, ambition, and ruthlessness led to the reorganiza-tion of Japan and the establishment of a unified nation.

One of the great figures in the process of political unification was Oda Nobunaga (1534–1582). Born into a rather obscure family, his ambition was "to bring the entire country under one sword," a motto inscribed on his personal seal. Nobunaga, determined and tenacious in the pursuit of his goals, showed amazing flexibility in his methods. His audacity on the battlefield won him the sup-port of many local lords, and he eliminated rivals with ruthless treachery.

Perhaps the most illustrative example of his vindictiveness was the destruction of the famous Buddhist stronghold on Mount Hiei. Contending Buddhist sects had played a crucial role in the struggle for power over the Ashikaga Shogunate. Although many of these Buddhist religious commu-nities were peaceful and set themselves apart from the political fray, others supplied "warrior-monks," who fought as mercenaries. Nobunaga harbored a deep resentment for Buddhism and con-sidered it a threat to political stability. The fate of the monastery on Mount Hiei demonstrates the ruthlessness that made Nobunaga both feared and successful.

The Slaughter on Mount Hiei (1571)

On September 11, [1571], Nobunaga en-camped . . . in Seta and ordered his principal re-tainers to set fire to and to destroy all temples, halls, and quarters on Mount Hiei and to anni-hilate all monks and inmates. Devoid of compas-sion, he relentlessly commanded his men to has-ten with the destruction. Although vassals close to him, armed and confounded, admonished him not to go ahead with the order, Nobunaga's indignation increased and he could not be re-strained. Thus, all helplessly acceded to his order. Then [Sakuma] Nobumori and [Sekian] of Higo came forward . . . to rebuke Nobunaga. They told him that this mountain center, since its founding . . . had been the guardian of the

From *Sources of Japanese Tradition* by William Theodore de Bary, ed., © 1958 Columbia University Press. Reprinted with permission of the publisher.

imperial palace for eight hundred years, and that its complaints to the Throne—even the most audacious—had not gone unheeded. "Although it is said that ours is a degenerate age," they con-tinued, "such an act as the destruction of the center is an unprecedented, unheard-of act." In the face of this strong rebuke, Nobunaga ex-plained that he was not entirely insensitive to the warning, but he requested that they listen calmly to what he had to say. He said, "I am not the destroyer of this monastery. The destroyer of the monastery is the monastery itself. As you know, I am one who has not known a moment of peace. I have risked my life. I have devoted myself to hard work and to a life of denial of my personal desires. I have given myself to the hard-ships of warrior life in order that I might re-strain the turbulence within the land, check the decline of imperial prestige and restore it, im-prove the prevailing manners and customs, and perpetuate the benefits of government and religion. But last year, when Noda and Fukushima of Settsu Province [enemies] were about to be subdued and their strongholds about to fall, Asakura and Asai seized the opportunity of my absence to invade Shiga in this province at the head of several tens of thousands of mounted troops. Thus, I was compelled to return here and to expel them from Sakamoto. The following day I drove the rebels to the hilltop of Tsubogusa. The deep snows retarded their flight and they were about to be slain by our men when the monastic inmates of Mt. Hiei came to their assistance. You were sent to dissuade and to reason with the monks, but they would not listen. Whereupon, I sent another envoy—Inaba—to inform them that if they persisted in their decision, all buildings without exception, including the central cathedral and the Shrine of the Mountain King [a Shinto deity], would be burned and destroyed, and all inmates—clergy and otherwise—would be decapitated. Still they would not yield. I do not speak falsehoods. It is they who obstruct the maintenance of law and order in the country. Those who would help

rebels are themselves traitors to the country. If, moreover, they are not destroyed now, they will again become a peril to the nation. Therefore not a single life should be spared." So convincing was his reasoning that even Sekian, succumbed to his arguments without a word of protest. . . .

Everything, everywhere, from the central cathedral to the twenty-one shrines of the Mountain King, the bell tower and the library, were burned to the ground. Moreover, the holy scriptures . . . and the records of the imperial capital under generations of emperors were destroyed at once. Great scholars, men of rare talents, aged priests and young boys—still with their innocent, delicate features—were either beheaded or taken captive. . . .

The roar of the huge burning monastery, magnified by the cries of countless numbers of the old and the young, sounded and resounded to the ends of heaven and earth. The noise was at once deafening and pathetic. . . . Thus, it may be said that the destruction of the mountain center was its own doing and not that of Nobunaga.

The Introduction of Firearms

NAMPO BUNSHI

Nobunaga's hostility to tradition and convention left him receptive to new ideas and helped him adapt successfully to changing circumstances. His hostility toward Buddhism was contrasted with his cordiality toward Christian missionaries. He was particularly generous with Portuguese Jesuits and was receptive to European technology.

Firearms were introduced to Japan in 1542 by Portuguese adventurers and immediately stirred controversy. Many soldiers despised the new matchlock guns called arquebuses *as weapons for cowards. In Japan, the sword of the samurai had over the centuries become a quasi-religious symbol of fear and class dominance. But Nobunaga and commanders like him quickly saw the advantage of pressing peasants into military service and training them in new tactics. The gun invested the common soldier with power and purpose that Nobunaga used to advantage. In 1575, at the Battle of Nagashino, a small force of Nobunaga's musketeers mowed down four waves of samurai horsemen with their disciplined volleys. Cavalry quickly became only a ceremonial fixture. In the following selection dated about 1600, a chronicler describes the introduction of firearms into Japan and the adaptations made by a regional lord named Tokitada.*

There are two leaders among the traders, the one called Murashusa, and the other Christian Mota. In their hands they carried something two or three feet long, straight on the outside with a passage inside, and made of a heavy substance. The inner passage runs through it although it is closed at the end. At its side there is an aperture which is the passageway for fire. Its shape defies comparison with anything I know. To use it, fill with powder and small lead pellets. Set up a small white target on a bank. Grip the object in you hand, compose your body, and closing one eye, apply fire to the aperture. Then the pellet hits the target squarely. The explosion is like lightning and the report like thunder. Bystanders must cover their ears. . . . This thing with one blow can smash a mountain of silver and a wall of iron. . . .

Lord Tokitada saw it and though it was the wonder of wonders. He did not know its name at first nor the details of its use. Then someone called it "iron-arms". . . . Thus, one day Tokitada spoke to the two alien leaders through an interpreter: "Incapable though I am, I should like to learn about it.". . .

Disregarding the high price of the arms, Tokitada purchased from the aliens two pieces of the firearms for his family treasure. As for the art of grinding, sifting, and mixing of the powder, Tokitada let his retainer, Shinokawa Shoshiro, learn it. Tokitada occupied himself, morning and night, and without rest in handling the arms. As a result, he was able to convert the misses of his early experiment into hits—a hundred hits in a hundred attempts. . . .

It is more than sixty years since the introduction of this weapon into our country. There are some gray-haired men who still remember the event clearly. The fact is that Tokitada procured two pieces of the weapon and studied them, and with one volley of the weapon, startled sixty provinces of our country.

The Sword Collection Edict (1588)

TOYOTOMI HIDEYOSHI

Perhaps the greatest success story in Japanese history belongs to Toyotomi Hideyoshi (1536–1598), who rose from a menial position under Nobunaga to undisputed master of Japan by 1590, eight years after Nobunaga's death. Born into obscurity, homeless and without even a family name, Hideyoshi had the consuming ambition of Nobunaga, but achieved a reputation for magnanimity by using his diplomatic abilities to persuade and compromise. He achieved a settlement with the Buddhist religious communities and strengthened the internal administration of the country. Through a series of ordinances on land reform, he sought to establish a stable tax basis, confirm local autonomy, and reward his loyal retainers. In many ways, Hideyoshi's rule reinforced feudal society, and his financial support of the shogunate in Kyoto maintained social and political stability during a dangerous period. On his death in 1598, he was granted the posthumous Shinto title, Hōkoku, or "Wealth of the Nation."

Hideyoshi's domestic agenda supported an ambitious world vision of controlling all of East Asia. To quell civil disturbances at home, he issued the following sword collection order in 1588. The ensuing "Sword Hunt" deprived the peasants of their weaponry and made fighting once again the exclusive prerogative of an hereditary class. Note how he even supplied a popular and pious motive in justifying the collection of swords; they were to be recast as a great Buddha image.

From *Sources of Japanese Tradition* by William Theodore de Bary, ed., © 1958 Columbia University Press. Reprinted with permission of the publisher.

1. The people of the various provinces are strictly forbidden to have in their possession any swords, short swords, bows, spears, firearms, or other types of arms. The possession of unnecessary implements [of war] makes difficult the collection of taxes and dues and tends to foment uprisings. Needless to say, the perpetrators of improper acts against official agents shall be summarily punished, but in that event the paddy fields and farms of the violators will remain unattended and there will be no yield of crops. Therefore, the heads of provinces, official agents, and deputies are ordered to collect all the weapons mentioned above and turn them over to the government.

2. Swords and short swords thus collected will not be wasted. They shall be used as nails and bolts in the construction of the Great Image of Buddha. This will benefit the people not only in this life, but also in the life hereafter.

3. If the people are in possession of agricultural implements only and devote themselves exclusively to agriculture, they and their descendants will prosper. Sincere concern for the well-being of the people is the motive for the issuance of this order, which is fundamental for the peace and security of the country and the happiness of the people. . . .

All implements mentioned above shall be collected and submitted forthwith.

Hideyoshi

Seventh Month, 8th day

Laws Governing Military Households (1598)

HIDETADA

After the death of Hideyoshi in 1598, Tokugawa Ieyasu (1542–1616), a protege of Nobunaga and commander of ability, defeated a powerful coalition of rivals and was appointed shōgun in 1603. Less impetuous than Nobunaga and less colorful than Hideyoshi, Ieyasu proved himself to be an astute politician with the vision and abilities to mold a lasting peace. From 1616 to 1868, Japan remained prosperous and at peace largely through the stable influence of Ieyasu and his successors.

The first selection is an edict promulgated in 1615, a year before Ieyasu's death by his immediate successor as shōgun, Hidetada. The object of this law was to ensure peace and order among feudal domains. It also served as a moral guide for the feudal nobility with an emphasis on loyalty, martial valor, and personal honor. The last selection by Ieyasu's son and eventual successor, Iemitsu, reflects the continued desire to maintain domestic stability by limiting and controlling the foreign influence of priests and commercial interests. Japan became isolated from the world, comfortable in its traditions and domestic stability, protected from the threat of foreign contamination. When Japan awoke in 1853 upon the arrival of the American commander, Matthew Perry, its introduction to the modern world was both traumatic and decisive.

1. The arts of peace and war, including archery and horsemanship, should be pursued single-mindedly. From of old the rule has been to practice "the arts of peace on the left hand, and the arts of war on the right"; both must be mastered. Archery and horsemanship are indispensable to military men. Though arms are called instruments of evil, there are times when they

must be resorted to. In peacetime, we should not be oblivious to the danger of war. Should we not, then, prepare ourselves for it?

2. Drinking parties and wanton revelry should be avoided. In the codes that have come down to us this kind of dissipation has been severely proscribed. Sexual indulgence and habitual gambling lead to the downfall of a state.

3. Offenders against the law should not be harbored or hidden in any domain. Law is the basis of social order. Reason may be violated in the name of the law, but law may not be violated in the name of reason. Those who break the law deserve heavy punishment.

4 Great lords (*daimyō*), the lesser lords, and officials should immediately expel from their domains any among their retainers or henchmen who have been charged with treason or murder. Wild and wicked men may become weapons for overturning the state and destroying the people. How can they be allowed to go free?

7. Immediate report should be made of innovations which are being planned or of factional conspiracies being formed in neighboring domains. "Men all incline toward partisanship; few are wise and impartial. There are some who refuse to obey their masters, and others who feud with their neighbors." Why, instead of abiding by the established order, do they wantonly embark upon new schemes?

8. Do not enter into marriage privately [i.e., without notifying the Shogunate authorities]. Marriage follows the principle of harmony between yin and yang, and must not be entered into lightly. In the *Book of Changes* it says, "Marriage should not be contracted out of enmity [against another]. Marriages intended to effect an alliance with enemies [of the state] will turn out badly." The "Peach Blossom" ode in *The Book of Poetry* also says that "When men and women are proper in their relationships and marriage is arranged at the correct time; then throughout the land there will be no loose women." To form an alliance by marriage is the root of treason.

9. Visits of the daimyō to the capital are to be in accordance with regulations. The *Chronicles of Japan* contains a regulation that "Clansmen should not gather together whenever they please, but only when they have to conduct some public business; and also that the number of horsemen serving as an escort in the capital should be limited to twenty. . . . " Daimyō should not be accompanied by a large number of soldiers. Twenty horsemen shall be the maximum escort for daimyō?. . . . On official missions, however, they may be accompanied by an escort proportionate to their rank.

10. Restrictions on the type and quality of dress to be worn should not be transgressed. Lord and vassal, superior and inferior, should observe what is proper to their station in life.

12. The samurai of the various domains shall lead a frugal and simple life. When the rich make a display of their wealth, the poor are humiliated and envious. Nothing engenders corruption so much as this, and therefore it must be strictly curbed.

Closed Country Edit (1635)

TOKUGAWA IEMITSU

1. Japanese ships are strictly forbidden to leave for foreign countries.

2. No Japanese is permitted to go abroad. If there is anyone who attempts to do so secretly, he must be executed. The ship so involved must be impounded and its owner arrested, and the matter must be reported to the higher authority.

3. If any Japanese returns from overseas after residing there, he must be put to death.

4. If there is any place where the teachings of the [Catholic] priests is practiced, the two of you must order a thorough investigation.

5. Any informer revealing the whereabouts of the followers of the priests must be rewarded accordingly. If anyone reveals the whereabouts of a high ranking priest, he must be given one hundred pieces of silver. For those of lower

Lu, David John, *Sources in Japanese History,* Vol. I. Copyright © 1974 by The McGraw-Hill Companies, Inc. Reprinted with permission.

ranks, depending on the deed, the reward must be set accordingly. . . .

7. If there are any Southern Barbarians [Westerners] who propagate the teaching of the priests, or otherwise commit crimes, they may be incarcerated in the prison. . . .

8. All incoming ships must be carefully searched for the followers of the priests. . . .

10. Samurai [military nobility] are not permitted to purchase any goods originating from foreign ships directly from Chinese merchants in Nagasaki. . . .

14. The date of departure homeward of foreign ships shall not be later than the twentieth day of the ninth month. Any ships arriving in Japan later than usual shall depart within fifty days of their arrival. As to the departure of Chinese ships, you may use your discretion to order their departure after the departure of the Portuguese [galleons]. . . .

17. Ships arriving in Hirado [an island near Nagasaki] must sell their raw silk at the price set in Nagasaki, and are not permitted to engage in business transactions until after the price is established in Nagasaki.

You are hereby required to act in accordance with the provisions set above. It is so ordered.

CHRONOLOGY: "An Embarrassment of Riches": The Interaction of New Worlds

1230–1255	Reign of Sundiata, who established Mali's imperial power.
1312–1337	Reign of Mansa Musa, the great Keita King of Mali, who established Timbuktu as the leading Muslim intellectual center in sub-Saharan Africa.
1352	Muslim adventurer, Ibn Battuta, explorers West Africa and records his travel throughout the Islamic world from Africa and Persia, to India and southeast Asia.
1368–1644	Ming Dynasty of China.
1394–1468	Reign of Portuguese Prince Henry the Navigator, who organized and sanctioned Portuguese exploration on the coasts of Africa and India.
1478–1492	Florence ruled by Lorenzo d'Medici, called "The Magnificent." Florence at height of political and artistic influence.
1487	Bartholomew Dias opens spice routes to the East.
1492	Columbus' first voyage to the eastern Bahamas in search of a route to India.
1498	Vasco da Gama trades on Malabar coast of India.
1500–1772	Safavid Shi'ite rule in Iran.
1517	Protestant reformer Martin Luther posts *Ninety-five Theses* on Wittenberg church door in hopes of engaging clerical authorities in debate.
1519–1521	Hernando Cortés lands on the coast of Mexico and brutally defeats Aztec forces.
1520–1566	Reign of Ottoman Caliph Süleyman the Lawgiver.
1526	Afonso I, King of Kongo, writes to Portuguese King Joao III requesting him to condemn slavery.

1531–1533   Francisco Pizarro conquers Incas in Peru.

1543   Portuguese arrive in Japan.

1556–1605   Reign of Akbar the Great of the Mughal dynasty in India.

1558–1603   Reign of Queen Elizabeth of England, last Tudor monarch.

1585   Silver mines of Potosi, Bolivia bring extraordinary wealth to Spain.

1600–1868   Warring States Era in Japan ends (1603) with the establishment of the Tokugawa Shogunate in Edo.

1607   English settlement of Jamestown.

1620   Pilgrims land at Plymouth.

1624   Dutch colony New Netherland founded.

1628–1630   Puritans establish Massachusetts Bay Colony near Boston.

1642–1649   English Civil War and establishment of the Commonwealth.

1643–1715   Reign of French King Louis XIV.

1644–1911   Qing (Manchu) dynasty in China.

1660–1856   Omani state centered in Zanzibar dominates East Africa and takes Mozambique from Portuguese control in 1698.

1699   British East India Company arrives in China.

STUDY QUESTIONS

1. In the logbook of Columbus' first voyage to the New World, what are the primary reasons he gives for wanting to sail to "the lands of India"? Do you think he was revealing the truth? What other motives might have influenced his decision to sail? Can you find evidence of them in this source? How did Columbus treat the inhabitants of the islands? Was Columbus a great explorer who reflected the adventurous spirit of the Renaissance or an exploiter of peoples?

2. Analyze the sources in the section on the conquest of Mexico. What were Cortés' motives in sailing to Mexico? Why did he decide to destroy the Aztecs after having been accepted as conqueror by Montezuma? Compare the two accounts of Cortés and Sahagún regarding the destruction of Tenochtitlán by the Spanish. How do you explain Cortés' statements that "there was not one man among us whose heart did not bleed at the sound" of the slaughter? Who bears the primary responsibility for the Aztec destruction? Cortés? His Indian allies? Or Montezuma himself? Is Cortés' attitude toward the Amerindians consistent with that of Columbus'? Were they explorers or exploiters?

3. How was Cortés able to defeat thousands of Aztec warriors with only a few hundred soldiers? What role did smallpox play in the destruction of the Aztec civilization in Mexico? Do you agree with William McNeill that "the main destructive role was certainly played by epidemic disease"? How important is disease as an agent of change in history?

4. What was the *encomienda* system and how were it and the *mita* used to exploit Indian labor? How was the mercury extracted from the mines and why was this a dangerous process? Why were the silver mines of Potosi so important to the Spanish and what made them such a lucrative operation?

5. What was the "Black Legend" of Spain? What types of atrocities were committed by the Spanish conquistadores? Study the pictures accompanying the accounts of Bartolomé de Las Casas. Was this an attempt at genocide, or have these atrocities been blown out of proportion by Las Casas and inflated as anti-Spanish propaganda? Do the arguments of Juan Gines de Sepulveda effectively counter those of Las Casas? How does Sepulveda justify Spanish treatment of the Indians?

6. In the griot account of the struggle between the sorcerer king, Soumaoro, and Sundiata for the control of Mali, what qualities of heroism did Sundiata display? Compare Sundiata's achievements with those of the Greek heroes, Achilles and Odysseus, on pages 90–95 Why are heroes important to each civilization? The African griot, Mamoudou Koyaté, was aware of his value as the "memory of mankind." Do you regard oral history as legitimate history? Must history be based on written sources?

7. In the description of the east coast of Africa by Duarte Barbosa, what does he find most important and impressive? What is the Portuguese method of doing business? How does Barbosa justify the destruction of African cities?

8. In his correspondence with the Portuguese king, what matters were of the gravest concern to the King of Kongo, Afonso I? Why was his kingdom "out of balance" and what reforms did he suggest? Does Afonso's predicament reveal a Portuguese policy of political and commercial exploitation consistent with the description given by Duarte Barbosa in the previous selection? What does the account of mutilation in the following selection by Gaspar Correa say about Portuguese methods of control? Is a trading relationship based on fear a good commercial policy?

9. Why did the Chinese emperor decide to sponsor the voyages of Zheng He? Where did Zheng travel and which of his actions were particularly impressive? What do his voyages say about the strength and vision of the early Ming dynasty?

10. What were some of the reasons that the merchant Wang prospered in his business practices? Would you say that such principles are still important in contemporary society? How does this account demonstrate the Confucian virtue of *jen* (humanity) and how does it reflect the Chinese respect for the elderly?

11. What was the "Portuguese Problem" and what options did the Chinese government explore in order to control their actions? Compare Portuguese actions in China with those in India and Africa. What was the Portuguese mode of operation?

12. Who was Matteo Ricci and why was he respected by the Chinese? What does the account by Zhang Tingyu reveal about the Chinese view of the world about 1600? In Matteo Ricci's journal, what specifically does he advise about the Chinese and their way of life?

13. According to the account of Zhang Tingyu, how did the Grand Eunuch Wei achieve such overwhelming influence over the emperor? How did he exploit his power and how did this contribute to the instability of the dynasty? What was Wei's ultimate fate?

14. According to Zhang Tingyu, what is the function of the Chinese emperor or "Prince" as he calls him? Why do people hate their Prince? What are the responsibilities of the ministers of the Prince? The Italian political philosopher, Niccol" Machiavelli, argued that a Prince must always be wary of advisors who seek only his approval and "yes men" who offer nothing but flattery. Would Zhang Tingyu have agreed?

15. Why did Nobunaga destroy the Buddhist monastery on Mount Hiei in 1571? What do you learn about the character of Nobunaga through this act? Do you agree that the destruction of this mountain center "was its own doing and not that of Nobunaga"? In his rise to power, Nobunaga profited from his use of firearms. Why was the introduction of firearms to Japan such an important event? How did Japanese society change as a result?

16. Analyze the "Sword Collection Edit" of Hideyoshi and Hidetada's laws to govern military households. Why were these domestic plans enforced? Were they necessary? What does this say about Tokugawa rule? Compare Iemitsu's "Closed Country Edict" in 1635. Why was it so important to isolate Japan from the world? How did this isolation affect the nation? What were the benefits and drawbacks from such enforced isolation?

12

The Great Islamic Empires

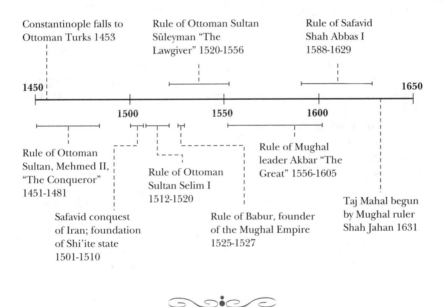

Constantinople falls to Ottoman Turks 1453

Rule of Ottoman Sultan Süleyman "The Lawgiver" 1520-1556

Rule of Safavid Shah Abbas I 1588-1629

1450   1500   1550   1600   1650

Rule of Ottoman Sultan, Mehmed II, "The Conqueror" 1451-1481

Rule of Ottoman Sultan Selim I 1512-1520

Rule of Mughal leader Akbar "The Great" 1556-1605

Safavid conquest of Iran; foundation of Shi'ite state 1501-1510

Rule of Babur, founder of the Mughal Empire 1525-1527

Taj Mahal begun by Mughal ruler Shah Jahan 1631

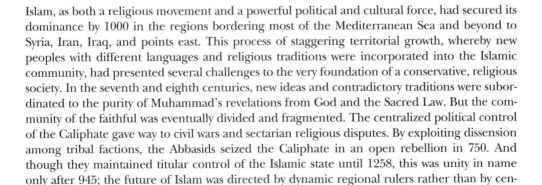

Islam, as both a religious movement and a powerful political and cultural force, had secured its dominance by 1000 in the regions bordering most of the Mediterranean Sea and beyond to Syria, Iran, Iraq, and points east. This process of staggering territorial growth, whereby new peoples with different languages and religious traditions were incorporated into the Islamic community, had presented several challenges to the very foundation of a conservative, religious society. In the seventh and eighth centuries, new ideas and contradictory traditions were subordinated to the purity of Muhammad's revelations from God and the Sacred Law. But the community of the faithful was eventually divided and fragmented. The centralized political control of the Caliphate gave way to civil wars and sectarian religious disputes. By exploiting dissension among tribal factions, the Abbasids seized the Caliphate in an open rebellion in 750. And though they maintained titular control of the Islamic state until 1258, this was unity in name only after 945; the future of Islam was directed by dynamic regional rulers rather than by centralized political authority. Indeed, by 1200, there were many threats on the horizon for Islam, the most serious of which was the unrelenting pressure and devastation of the Mongols.

The rise of the vast Mongol empire under the leadership of Ghengis Khan (ca. 1162–1227) threatened the eastern borders of Islamic control in Transoxiana and the Indus as the Great Khan plundered the area mercilessly from 1219–1222. Then Hulagu Khan (r. 1256–1265), a grandson of Ghengis, led Mongol armies west across the Oxus River, destroying every Islamic army he encountered. In 1258, the Abbasid caliph refused to surrender the capital city of Baghdad and met with the full fury of Hulagu's armies, which plundered the city and killed over 80,000 men, women, and children.

Although such destruction, and more to come under the brutal forces of Tamerlane (1336–1405), shook the foundations of Islamic control in eastern lands, nevertheless, the period from 1000–1500 saw the growth of a truly international Islamic community. Conquests and conversions followed Islamic armies from the Caspian and Black Seas north to Moscow and into Greece and the Balkans. India, Indonesia, Malaysia, and the coasts of East Africa fell to the commercial and political interests of Islam. Muslim traders were perhaps the major agents of Islamization during this time.

From 1400 to 1600, the Islamic heartlands were consolidated into three great empires. The Ottoman Turks, led by Sultan Mehmed II "The Conqueror" (r. 1451–1481), captured Constantinople, the last remnant of the Byzantine Empire, and renamed it Istanbul. To the east of Ottoman lands, the Persian emperor Shah Isma'il I created the Safavid empire in the early sixteenth century, which was fervently devoted to the Shi'ite Islamic sect. The third great Islamic empire was founded in India through the conquests of Babur from 1525–1527. He established the Mughal dynasty, which would include Akbar "the Great" (r. 1556–1605), the most influential Indian ruler since Asoka (ca. 264–223 B.C.E.).

The Ottomans, Safavids, and Mughals, the last great Islamic empires, were built by leaders of unquestionable energy and ability. They fashioned the greatest cities of their time, patronized the arts, and even stimulated new traditions in Islamic literature. But they were essentially conservative societies that had difficulty competing with the new pressures of European expansionism. These were culminating Islamic empires that fell to the relentless energy of Western industrial, military, and commercial forces that would come to dominate the regions from the nineteenth to the mid-twentieth centuries. It is perhaps this Islamic cultural culmination, this legacy statement, that makes studying the last Muslim empires so rewarding.

THE OTTOMAN EMPIRE OF TURKEY

The Ottomans were a Turkish dynasty founded by Osman about 1280. He led a core of rugged frontier warriors from Asia Minor and fought Christians in the region about 1291. Within a hundred years, Ottoman control extended from the Danube river east to the Upper Euphrates. Despite a significant defeat at the hands of the Mongol warrior Tamerlane in 1402, which truly shattered the confidence of the Ottoman state, it was restored by the will and efficiency of Mehmed II, who came to power in 1451 and captured the great city of Constantinople in 1453. Under Selim I (r. 1512–1520) and Süleyman "The Lawgiver" (r. 1520–1566), the Ottoman state was established as a major Asian and European power as it annexed North Africa, Egypt, and Syria, as well as Iraq, Kurdistan, and Georgia in the Caucasus. The Ottomans nearly took Vienna by siege in 1526–1529 and controlled virtually all of Hungary by 1540. At this time, no other world power with the possible exception of China could match Ottoman strength. The Ottoman state was organized as one great military institution with a discipline and administrative infrastructure that was most impressive and maintained its influence for centuries before a long decline commenced in the late seventeenth century. The Ottoman empire simply could not sustain an income through its external trade and domestic agrarian economy that offset its expensive wars. It fell prey to the rising European industrial powers and collapsed in 1918 at the conclusion of World War I.

Sunni versus Shi'ite: "We Exhort You to Embrace the True Faith!"

SULTAN SELIM I

One of the most important factors in the successful establishment and perpetuation of the Islamic empires of the fifteenth through eighteenth centuries was leadership. These states were organized first around the religious tenets of Islam as interpreted by the ulama *or religious leadership, and then around the secular interests of the political leadership. There was plenty of room for disagreement and competition as Islam labored under sectarian religious disputes that had dramatic political implications. Perhaps the most serious of these religious disputes divided Islam between two factions: Sunnis and Shi'ites.*

According to the Shi'ites, shortly before the death of Muhammad in 632, he revealed secret instructions and teachings to his son-in-law Ali, who was the just successor (or "caliph") to the Prophet. Ali was subsequently murdered, but still managed to pass on these revelations to religious leaders called imams *who were in fact the true guardians of Islam. Shi'ites believe that although the last of these* imams *had died in the ninth century, he was expected to reappear in the future as the* mahdi *or savior of humanity.*

The Sunnis, on the other hand, reject the notion that Muhammad had entrusted any secret prophecy to Ali and that all of Muhammad's revelations can be found in the Qur'an, *Islamic traditions, and the Sacred Law codes* (Shari'a). *The vast majority of Muslims today are of the Sunni sect, but an ample minority of Shi'ites exist primarily in modern day Iran, the successor state to the heart of the Safavid Shi'ite empire.*

The first selection is a letter from the Ottoman ruler, Selim I to his Persian rival, Isma'il I, leader of the Shi'ite Safavid state. Ismail had entered Ottoman territory and had demanded that Ottoman subjects accept Shi'ism. This response by Selim I, a committed Sunni, reveals the divisive competition among Islamic religious sects and political leaders. Selim I won the battle of Chaldiran in 1514 and protected his territory from Shi'ite encroachment.

Keep in Mind . . .

- What is the purpose of this warning to Amir Isma'il from Sultan Selim I?

- How does Selim use the *Qur'an* to justify his actions?

The Supreme Being who is at once the sovereign arbiter of the destinies of men and the source of all light and knowledge, declares in the *Qur'an* that the true faith is that of the Muslims, and that whoever professes another religion, far from being hearkened to and saved, will on the contrary be cast out among the re-

---

"Sunni versus Shi'ite" is from C. T. Foster and F. H. Blackburne Daniell, *The Life and Letters of Ogier Ghiselin de Busbecq*, vol. 1 (London: Hakluyt Society, 1881), pp. 152-156; 219-221.

jected on the great day of the Last Judgment; He says further, this God of truth, that His designs and decrees are unalterable, that all human acts are perforce reported to Him, and that he who abandons the good way will be condemned to hell-fire and eternal torments. Place yourself, O Prince, among the true believers, those who walk in the path of salvation, and who turn aside with care from vice and infidelity. May the purest and holiest blessings be upon Muhammad, the master of the two worlds, the prince of prophets, as well as upon his descendants and all who follow his Law!

I, sovereign chief of the Ottomans, master of the heroes of the age . . . I, the exterminator of idolaters, destroyer of the enemies of the true faith, the terror of the tyrants and pharaohs of the age; I, before whom proud and unjust kings have humbled themselves . . . and whose hand breaks the strongest scepters; . . . I address myself graciously to you, Amir Isma'il, chief of the troops of Persia . . . and predestined to perish . . . in order to make known to you that the works emanating from the Almighty are not the fragile products of caprice or folly, but make up an infinity of mysteries impenetrable to the human mind. The Lord Himself says in His holy book: "We have not created the heavens and the earth in order to play a game" [*Qur'an*, 21:16]. Man, who is the noblest of the creatures and the summary of the marvels of God, is in consequence on earth the living image of the Creator. It is He who has set up Caliphs on earth, because, joining faculties of soul with perfection of body, man is the only being who can comprehend the attributes of the divinity and adore its sublime beauties; but because he possesses this rare intelligence, he attains this divine knowledge only in our religion, and by observing the precepts of the prince of prophets, the Caliph of Caliphs, the right are of the God of Mercy; it is then only by practicing the true religion that man will prosper in this world and merit eternal life in the other. As to you, Amir Isma'il, such a recompense will not be your lot; because you have denied the sanctity of the divine laws; because you have deserted the path of salvation

and the sacred commandments; because you have impaired the purity of the dogmas of Islam; because you have dishonored, soiled, and destroyed the altars of the Lord, usurped the scepter of the East by unlawful and tyrannical means; because coming forth from the dust, you have raised yourself by odious devices to a place shining with splendor and magnificence; because you have opened to Muslims the gates of tyranny and oppression; because you have joined iniquity, perjury, and blasphemy to your sectarian impiety; because under the cloak of the hypocrite, you have sowed everywhere trouble and sedition; because you have raised the standard of irreligion and heresy; because yielding to the impulse of your evil passions, and giving yourself up without rein to the most infamous disorders, you have dared to throw off the control of Muslim laws and to permit lust and rape, the massacre of the most virtuous and respectable men, the destruction of pulpits and temples . . . the repudiation of the *Qur'an*, the cursing of the legitimate Caliphs. Now as the first duty of a Muslim and above all of a pious prince is to obey the commandment, "O, you faithful who believe, be the executors of the decrees of God!" the *ulama* [religious leadership] and our doctors have pronounced sentence of death against you, perjurer and blasphemer, and have imposed on every Muslim the sacred obligation to arm in defense of religion and destroy heresy and impiety in your person and that of all your partisans.

Animated by this [religious decree], conforming to the *Qur'an*, the code of divine laws, and wishing on one side to strengthen Islam, on the other to liberate the lands and peoples who writhe under your yoke, we have resolved to lay aside our imperial robes in order to put on the shelf and coat of mail, to raise our ever victorious banner, to assemble our invincible armies, to take up the gauntlet of the avenger, to march with our soldiers, whose sword strikes mortal blows. . . . In pursuit of this noble resolution, we have entered upon the campaign, and guided by the hand of the Almighty, we hope soon to strike down your tyrannous arm, blow away the clouds of glory and grandeur which trouble your head and cause your fatal blindness, release from your despotism your trembling subjects, smother you in the end in the very mass of flames which your infernal [spirit] raises everywhere along your passage, accomplishing in this way on you the maxim which says: "He who sows discord can only reap evils and afflictions." However, anxious to conform to the spirit of the law of the Prophet, we come, before commencing war, to set out before you the words of the *Qur'an*, in place of the sword, and to exhort you to embrace the true faith; this is why we address this letter to you. . . .

But if, to your misfortune, you persist in your past conduct; if, puffed up with the idea of your power and your foolish bravado, you wish to pursue the course of your iniquities, you will see in a few days your plains covered with our tents and inundated with our battalions. Then prodigies of valor will be done, and we shall see the decrees of the Almighty, Who is the God of Armies, and sovereign judge of the actions of men, accomplished. For the rest, victory to him who follows the path of salvation!

Consider This:

- Aren't Sunnis and Shi'ites both Muslims? What was the reason for this confrontation?

- Why was Selim I so sure that he embodied the "true religion" and that this justified his military threat?

Süleyman "The Lawgiver" and the Advantages of Islam
OGIER DE BUSBECQ

The energy of the Ottoman Empire perhaps reached its zenith under the direction of Sultan Süleyman "The Lawgiver" (r. 1520–1566). One of the most important assessments of Süleyman's influence came from Ogier Ghiselin de Busbecq, the ambassador from Austria to Süleyman's court at Istanbul from 1554–1562. Busbecq had been dispatched in the recent wake of the unsuccessful Ottoman siege of Vienna in 1529. His mission was to use his diplomatic skills to prevent another possible attack on the city. Busbecq's letters reveal much about Süleyman, his court, capital, Islamic traditions, and treatment of women.

Keep in Mind . . .

- What are the most important qualities for success and advancement in the Ottoman empire?

The Sultan [Süleyman "The Lawgiver"] was seated on a very low ottoman, not more than a foot from the ground, which was covered with a quantity of costly rugs and cushions of exquisite workmanship; near him lay his bow and arrows. . . . The Sultan then listened to what I had to say; but the language I used was not at all to his taste, for the demands of his Majesty breathed a spirit of independence and dignity, which was by no means acceptable to one who deemed that his wish was law; and so he made no answer beyond saying in an impatient way, "Giusel, giusel," that is, well, well. After this we were dismissed to our quarters.

The Sultan's hall was crowded with people, among whom were several officers of high rank. Besides these, there were all the troopers of the Imperial guard, and a large force of Janissaries

"Süleyman "the Lawgiver" is from C. T. Foster and F. H. Blackburne Daniell, *The Life and Letters of Ogier Ghiselin de Busbecq*, vol. 1 (London: Hakluyt Society, 1881), pp. 152-156.

[the elite infantry corps], but there was not in all that great assembly a single man who owed his position to anything save his valor and his merit. No distinction is attached to birth among the Turks; the respect to be paid to a man is measured by the position he holds in the public service. There is no fighting for precedence; a man's place is marked out by the duties he discharges. . . . It is by merit that men rise in the service, a system which ensures that posts should only be assigned to the competent. Each man in Turkey carries in his own hand his ancestry and his position in life, which he may make or mar as he will. Those who receive the highest offices from the Sultan are for the most part the sons of shepherds or herdsmen, and so far from being ashamed of their parentage, they actually glory in it, and consider it a matter of boasting that they owe nothing to the accident of birth; for they do not believe that high qualities are either natural or hereditary, nor do they think that they can be handed down from father to son, but that they are partly the gift of God, and partly the result of good training, great industry, and unwearied zeal; arguing that high qualities do not descend from a father to his son or heir, any more than a talent for music, mathematics, or the like. . . . Among the Turks, therefore, honors, high posts, and judgeships are the rewards of great ability and good service. If a man is dishonest, or lazy, or careless, he remains at the bottom of the ladder, an object of contempt; for such qualities there are no honors in Turkey!

This is the reason that they are successful in their undertakings, that they lord it over others, and are daily extending the bounds of their empire. These are not our ideas, with us there is no opening left for merit; birth is the standard for everything; the prestige of birth is the sole key to advancement in the public service.

The Turkish monarch going to war takes with him over 40,000 camels and nearly as many baggage mules, of which a great part, when he is invading Persia, are loaded with rice and other kinds of grain. These mules and camels also serve to carry tents and armor, and likewise

Süleyman "The Lawgiver." This miniature shows the great Ottoman leader offering advice to his son, the Crown Prince Mehmed Khan. (Folio 79a of the Talkizade Shenamesi, *Library of the Topkapi Palace Museum, A3592/Photograph courtesy of Talat Halman*)

tools and munitions for the campaign. . . . The invading army carefully abstains from encroaching on its supplies at the outset, as they are well aware that, when the season for campaigning draws to a close, they will have to retreat over districts wasted by the enemy, or scraped as bare by countless hordes of men and droves of baggage animals, as if they had been devastated by locusts; accordingly they reserve their stores as much as possible for this emergency. . . .

From this you will see that it is the patience, self denial, and thrift of the Turkish soldier that enable him to face the most trying circumstances, and come safely out of the dangers that surround him. What a contrast to our men! . . .

For each man is his own worst enemy, and has no foe more deadly than his own intemperance, which is sure to kill him, if the enemy be not quick. It makes me shudder to think of what the result of a struggle between such different systems must be; one of us must prevail and the other be destroyed, at any rate we cannot both exist in safety. On their side is the vast wealth of their empire, unimpaired resources, experience and practice in arms, a veteran soldiery, an uninterrupted series of victories, readiness to endure hardships, union, order, discipline, thrift, and watchfulness. On ours are found an empty exchequer, luxurious habits, exhausted resources, broken spirits, a raw and insubordinate soldiery, and greedy generals; there is no regard for discipline, license runs riot, the men indulge in drunkenness and debauchery, and, worst of all, the enemy are accustomed to victory, we, to defeat. Can we doubt what the result must be?

Consider This:

- Busbecq maintained that between Christians and Muslims, "one of us must prevail and the other be destroyed." Why did he think Christian nations were at a disadvantage? By painting such a picture, was Busbecq hoping to frighten European nations into reform?

Women in Ottoman Society
OGIER DE BUSBECQ

Keep in Mind . . .

- What is the role of woman in Ottoman society?

"Women in Ottoman Society" is from C. T. Foster and F. H. Blackburne Daniell, *The Life and Letters of Ogier Ghiselin de Busbecq*, vol. 1 (London: Hakluyt Society, 1881), pp. 219-221.

The Turks are the most careful people in the world of the modesty of their wives, and therefore keep them shut up at home and hide them away, so that they scarce see the light of day. But if they have to go into the streets, they are sent out so covered and wrapped up in veils that they seem to those who meet them mere gliding ghosts. They have the means of seeing men through their linen or silken veils, while no part of their own body is exposed to men's view. For it is a received opinion among them, that no woman who is distinguished in the very smallest degree by her figure or youth, can be seen by a man without his desiring her, and therefore without her receiving some contamination; and so it is the universal practice to confine the women to the harem. Their brothers are allowed to see them, but not their brothers-in-law. Men of the richer classes, or of higher rank, make it a condition when they marry, that their wives shall never set foot outside the threshold, and that no man or woman shall be admitted to see them for any reason whatever, not even their nearest relations, except their fathers and mothers, who are allowed to pay a visit to their daughters at the [festival of Bairam].

On the other hand, if the wife has a rather high rank, or has brought a larger dowry than usual, the husband promises on his part that he will take no concubine, but will keep to her alone. Otherwise, the Turks are not forbidden by any law to have as many concubines as they please in addition to their lawful wives. Between the children of wives and those of concubines there is no distinction, and they are considered to have equal rights. As for concubines, they either buy them for themselves or win them in war; when they are tired of them there is nothing to prevent their bringing them to market and selling them; but they are entitled to their freedom if they have borne children to their master. . . . The only distinction between the lawful wife and the concubine, is that the former has a dowry, while the slaves have none. A wife who has a portion settled on her [a dowry] is mistress of her husband's house, and all the other women have to obey her orders. The husband, however, may choose which of them shall spend the night with him. He makes known his wishes to the wife, and she sends to him the slave he has selected. . . . Only Friday night . . . is supposed to belong to the wife; and she grumbles if her husband deprives her of it. On all the other nights he may do so as he pleases.

Divorces are granted among them for many reasons which it is easy for the husbands to invent. The divorced wife receives back her dowry, unless the divorce has been caused by some fault on her part. There is more difficulty in a woman's getting a divorce from her husband.

Consider This:

- Why are women completely covered in Ottoman society? What were the expectations for women at this time and what distinctions were made between wives and concubines?

THE SAFAVID SHI'ITE EMPIRE OF PERSIA

The Safavid state in Persia had been built upon a fervent commitment to the Shi'ite sect of Islam. The greatest Safavid ruler, Shah Abbas I (r. 1588–1629) had inherited his throne at a difficult time. His father had been forced to abdicate and much of his empire was on the brink of disintegration. Ottoman invaders from the west and Uzbecs from the east had placed tremendous pressure on the new monarch. But within fifteen years, Abbas I had defeated both groups and the Mughals in India as well by 1621, securing more territory and trading posts in the Persian Gulf. He then focused on international trade and manufacturing and on protecting his territories through diplomatic contacts.

In executing this strategy, Shah Abbas I cultivated relations with several European countries whose skills in war and technology were of the highest importance. Abbas was more interested in European gunsmiths than in the vagaries of Muslim doctrine. As a result, he allowed European missionaries to visit his realm and openly seek converts among his Muslim population. The following accounts are from Fathers Simon and Vincent, Carmelite friars dispatched to Abbas's capital at Isfahan in 1605. They spent six months gathering information and then made their report to Pope Paul V.

Shah Abbas I

FATHER SIMON

Keep in Mind . . .

- What qualities made Shah Abbas I an effective leader?

The king, Shah Abbas . . . is [43] years old . . . of medium height, rather thin than fat, his face round and small, tanned by the sun, with hardly

"Shah Abbas I" is from Robert Simon, *A Chronicle of the Carmelites in Persia and the Papal Mission of the Seventeenth and Eighteenth Centuries* (London: Eyre and Spottiswoode, 1939), pp. 158-161.

any beard; very vivacious and alert, so that he is always doing something or other. He is sturdy and healthy, accustomed to much exercise and toil: many times he goes about on foot, and recently he had been forty days on pilgrimage, which he made on foot the whole time. He has extraordinary strength, and with his scimitar can cut a man in two and a sheep with its wool on at a single blow—and the Persian sheep are of large size. He has done many other feats and has found no one to come up to him in them. In his food he is frugal, as also in his dress, and this to set an example to his subjects; and so in public he eats little else than rice, and that cooked in water only. His usual dress is of linen, and very plain: similarly the nobles and others in his realm follow suit, whereas formerly they used to go out dressed in brocade with jewels and other fopperies: and if he sees anyone who is overdressed, he takes him to task, especially if it be a soldier. But in private, he eats what he likes.

He is sagacious in mind, likes fame and to be esteemed: he is courteous in dealing with everyone and at the same time very serious. For he will go through the public streets, eat from what they are selling there and other things, speak at ease freely with the lower classes, cause his subjects to remain sitting while he himself is standing, or will sit down beside this man and that. He says that is how to be a king, and that the king of Spain and other Christians do not get any pleasure out of ruling, because they are obliged to comport themselves with so much pomp and majesty.

He causes foreigners to sit down beside him and to eat at his table. With that and accompanying all such informality he requires that people shall not [lack] respect toward him and, should anyone fail in this regard, he will punish the individual severely. So the more he demonstrates kindliness to his subjects and the more familiarly he talks with them, they tremble before him, even the greatest among them, for, while joking, he will have their heads cut off. He is very strict in executing justice and pays no regard to his own favorites in this respect; but rather is the stricter with them in order to serve an example to others. So he has no private friends, nor anyone who has influence with him. . . . While we were at Court, he caused the bellies of two of his favorites to be ripped open, because they behaved improperly to an ordinary woman. From this it comes about that there are so very few murderers and robbers. In all the time I was at Isfahan, there was never a case of homicide.

He is very speedy in dispatching business: when he gives audience, which he does at the gate of his palace, . . . he finishes off all the cases that are brought to him. The parties stand present before him, the officers of justice, and his own council, with whom he consults when it

pleases him. The sentence which he gives is final and is immediately executed. If the guilty party deserves death, they kill him at once. . . .

Because of the great obedience [the nobles] pay the Shah, when he wills to have one of the nobles killed, he dispatches one of his men to fetch the noble's head: the man goes off to the grandee, and says to him: "The Shah wants your head." The noble replies: "Very well," and lets himself be decapitated—otherwise he would lose it and with it, all his family would become extinct. But, when [the nobles] allow themselves to be decapitated, [the Shah] aggrandizes the children. . . .

Regarding the religion of the king, I think that no one knows what he believes: he does not observe the Muslim law in many things, nor is he a Christian. Six or seven years ago he displayed many signs of not being averse to our Faith: God knows whether they were feigned, or came from his heart. In his [harem] he has many Christian Armenian, Georgian, and Circassian women. I think that he lets them live as they wish, because when I enquired what the Shah did with so many [holy] pictures that were presented to him as gifts and some relics of the Saints, for which he asked, the answer was made to me that he used to give them to the women in his harem. Besides that he is well informed regarding the mysteries of our holy Faith and discourses on the mystery of the most holy Trinity: he knows many examples and allusions which the Saints give in order to prove it, and discourses about the other mysteries—which we know from a man who had the opportunity of hearing him—if he does not talk about the women in his harem or about some demon or other. On account of the many disappointments which he asserts the Christians have caused him all this fervor has cooled. With all that he does not detest them. For he converses and eats with them, he suffers us to say frankly what we believe about our Faith and his own: sometimes he asks us about this. To us he has given a house: he knows that we say Mass publicly, he allows whoever may wish among the Persians to come to it, and we can teach them freely regarding our holy Faith, whenever they make inquiries about it. . . . I believe that the king realizes the objective with which our friars go out there. Till now none of them has been converted: I think they are waiting for one of the nobles or of their [religious leaders] to break the ice. . . .

Compare and Contrast:

- According to Father Simon, why was Shah Abbas I both loved and feared? Compare the qualities of his leadership with those noted by Niccolò Machiavelli on pp. 318–320 Would Machiavelli have admired Shah Abbas I?

- Father Simon noted that "no one knows what [Shah Abbas I] believes." Was the Shah a devout Muslim? Why did he provide Christian churchmen with such flexibility in trying to convert Muslims in his realm? What does this say about Shah Abbas I as a political and religious leader?

The Worship of Idols

FATHER VINCENT

Keep in Mind . . .

- What was Father Vincent's argument in rejecting the charge that Catholics were idolaters?

Two days previously the English had been with the king and discoursed at great length on the matter of religion and spoken ill of the Catholics saying that they were idolaters, who adored pictures and images, and made the sign of the cross, etc. The Shah had said that he would bring the Fathers together with them, so that they might hold a disputation on these matters.

"The Worship of Idols" is from Robert Simon, *A Chronicle of the Carmelites in Persia and the Papal Mission of the Seventeenth and Eighteenth Centuries* (London: Eyre and Spottiswoode, 1939), pp. 248-255.

This was the motive why the king of Persia asked the Fathers about the difference there is between Catholics and English. The Father Visitor answered that the English are heretics and false Christians and that Roman Catholics are the true Christians. . . .

In order to convince him, the Fathers put the question to the king: "Because your Highness and your people prostrate yourselves and worship seals and beads made of earth, would it be right for us to call your Highness and your people idolaters? Certainly not, because we know that, when you perform that act of adoration, you do not mean by it that the seal and stone are God, but do it out of piety and reverence for that soil, as it comes from the places of sepulture of your ancestors and that great men whom you consider saints." The Shah answered: "That is not the chief reason and intention we have for worshiping on earthen seals and beads, but rather in that act of veneration we make an act of recognizing that we are clay, and that from earth God created us, and we adore the Creator of this: and the reason why in the mosques and in our houses while we say our prayers on matting and carpets, our prayers would not be lawful and acceptable, unless we said them [touching] the earth. With this in view, for more convenience and cleanliness we use the earthen medallions [to touch with our foreheads during prayer] and beads: and that they are of this or that soil is an accidental matter: it suffices that it be earth. And so, when we have any other sort of stone, even if it be a piece of rock, we have no need of a seal. It is also true that we venerate it (the seal) as a memorial and a pious object, as you say, but no mainly for that reason."

To this the Fathers replied: "Very good! And thus our Christian religion does not adore nor serve images, as if they were gods, nor does it expect from them the future judgment (God preserve us from such a thing!), but it venerates images for the things they represent. They serve us also as memorials to remind us of the virtues of those saints they represent, in order that we may imitate them and beg them to intercede by their prayers with our Lord God, that He will grant us what we ask and that we may be good and his servants, as they have been, so that we may attain the glory which they now enjoy. So that, just as your Highness and your people do not say that the earthen medallion is God, no more do we say that the statues of the saints are gods, nor do we adore them as such." With these reasonings the Shah and his courtiers remained content.

Consider This:

- Father Vincent stated that "the English are heretics and False Christians and that Roman Catholics are the true Christians." Compare this with Sultan Selim I's argument in rejecting the Shi'ite sect that Sunni Muslims were the "true religion." What does this tell you about sectarian disputes within a religion? Which is the "true religion"?

THE MUGHAL EMPIRE OF INDIA

The Mughal rulers of India claimed their authority and descent from the great Mongol warriors, Ghengis Khan and Tamerlane. The founder of the dynasty was Babur (r. 1525–1527), who carved his empire out of northwest India. The family power was consolidated by his grandson Akbar the Great (r. 1556–1605), who established a stable administrative structure and efficient army that supported a progressive social and cultural tradition. Akbar was an engaged ruler, perhaps the most powerful in the world at the time, whose discriminating artistic sense and vision of tolerance were widely admired. Born a Muslim, Akbar ruled a region where the vast majority of the population was Hindu. The following selections by a variety of authors give testimony to his authority and wisdom. The first excerpt is from a Jesuit missionary, Father Monserrate, who visited Akbar's court in the 1580s.

Akbar the Great and His Dominions

FATHER MONSERRATE

Keep in Mind . . .

- What qualities made Akbar an effective ruler?

He is a great patron of learning, and always keeps around him erudite men, who are directed to discuss before him philosophy, theology, and religion, and to recount to him the history of great kings and glorious deeds of the past. He has an excellent judgment and a good memory, and has

"Akbar the Great" is from Father Monserrate, *Commentary on His Journey to the Court of Akbar from 1580 to 1583*, edited by S.N. Banjerjee, trans. by J.S. Hoyland (London: Oxford University Press, 1922), pp. 213-214; 219.

attained to a considerable knowledge of many subjects by means of constant and patient listening to such discussions. Thus he not only makes up for his ignorance of letters (for he is entirely unable either to read or write), but he has also become able clearly and lucidly to expound difficult matters. He can give his opinion on any question so shrewdly and keenly, that no one who did not know that he is illiterate would suppose him to be anything but very learned and erudite. And so indeed he is, for in addition to his keen intellect, of which I have already spoken, he excels many of his most learned subjects in eloquence, as well as in that authority and dignity which befits a King. The wise men are wont every day to hold disputations on literary subjects before him. He listens with delight, not to actors, but to mimics and jesters, thinking their style of speaking to have a literary flavor. . . .

The King exacts enormous sums in tribute from the provinces of his empire, which is wonderfully rich and fertile both for cultivation and pasture, and has a great trade both in exports and imports. He also derives much revenue from the hoarded fortunes of the great nobles, which by law and custom all come to the King on their owners' death. In addition, there are the spoils of conquered kings and chieftains, whose treasure is seized, and the great levies exacted, and gifts received, from the inhabitants of newly subdued districts in every part of his dominions. These gifts and levies are apt to be so large as to ruin outright many of his new subjects. He also engages in trading on his own account, and thus increases his wealth to no small degree; for he eagerly exploits every possible source of profit.

Moreover, he allows no bankers or money-changers in his empire except the superintendents and tellers of the royal treasuries. This enormous banking-business brings the King great profit; for at these royal treasuries alone may gold coin be changed for silver or copper, and vice versa. The government officers are paid in gold, silver or copper according to their rank. Thus it comes about that those who are paid in one type of coin need to change some of it into another type. . . .

To say something about Indian towns: they appear very pleasant from afar; for they are adorned with many towers and high buildings, in a very beautiful manner. But when one enters them, one finds that the narrowness, aimless crookedness, and ill-planning of the streets deprive these cities of all beauty. Moreover the houses are purposely built without windows on account of the filth of the streets. . . . Such houses will show nothing in their facades or entrances by which the eye of the passer-by might be attracted, and nothing by which it might be known that inside is anything out of the ordinary.

Consider This:

- What were the specific measures that increased Akbar's wealth and administrative control over his empire?

Reforms of Akbar:
The Abolition of Slavery
ABÛ'L FAZL

Abû'l Fazl ibn Mubârak (1550–1602) wrote an extensive history of Akbar and his court. Although patronized by Akbar, the flattering portrayal by Abû'l Fazl of Akbar's reforms and legacy upon his death has much to commend it since Akbar was genuinely successful in reconciling negative forces that sought to divide Mughal society in India. Certainly the last selection, a memoir by Akbar's son, Jahangir (r. 1605–1627), gives testimony to his father's influence in promoting tolerance between Muslims and Hindus.

Keep in Mind . . .

- Why was slavery abolished by Akbar?

One of the glorious benefits of His Majesty the Shâhinshâh, which shone forth in this auspicious year, was the abolition of enslavement. The victorious troops which came into the wide territories of India used in their tyranny to make prisoners of the wives and children and other relatives of the people of India, and used to enjoy them or sell them. His Majesty the Shâhinshâh, out of his

"Reforms of Akbar" is from Abû'l Fazl ibn Mubârak, trans. by H. Beveridge, *The Akbarnâmâ* (Calcutta: The Asiatic Society, 1905), Vol. 2, pp. 92-93.

thorough recognition of and worship of God, and from his abundant foresight and right thinking gave orders that no soldier of the victorious armies should in any part of his dominions act in this manner. Although a number of savage natures who were ignorant of the world should make their fastnesses a subject of pride and come forth to do battle, and then be defeated by virtue of the emperor's daily increasing empire, still their families must be protected from the onset of the world-conquering armies. No soldier, high or low, was to enslave them, but was to permit them to go freely to their homes and relations. It was for excellent reasons that His Majesty gave his attention to this subject, for although the binding, killing or striking the haughty and the chastising the stiff-necked are part of the struggle for empire—and this is a point about which both sound jurists and innovators are agreed—yet it is outside of the canons of justice to regard the chastisement of women and innocent children of the rebellious.

If the husbands have taken the path of insolence, how is it the fault of the wives, and if the fathers have chosen the road of opposition what fault have the children committed? Moreover the wives and innocent children of such factions are not munitions of war! In addition to these sound reasons there was the fact that may covetous and blind-hearted persons from vain imagining or unjust thoughts, or merely out of cupidity attacked villages and estates and plundered them, and when questioned about it said a thousand things and behaved with neglect and indifference. But when final orders were passed for the abolition of this practice, no tribe was afterwards oppressed by wicked persons on suspicion of sedition. As the purposes of the Shâhinshâh were entirely right and just, the blissful result ensued that the wild and rebellious inhabitants of portions of India placed the ring of devotion in the ear of obedience, and became the materials of world-empire. Both was religion set in order, for its essence is the distribution of justice, and things temporal were regulated, for their perfection lies in the obedience of mankind.

Consider This:

- Because of his abolition of slavery, could Akbar be considered a just and progressive ruler?

- Was Akbar's abolition of slavery a measure to promote more effective administration of India? By abolishing slavery, how did Akbar place "the ring of devotion in the ear of obedience"?

"Good God! What a Personality He Was!"

ABÛ'L FAZL

On the eve of Wednesday, 15th October, 1605, His Majesty withdrew the shade of his heavenly self from the heads of mortals, and spread out the shadow of his beneficence over the heads of the celestials. The men of this world sat down in the dark days of failure, while the inhabitants of the other world attained their long-cherished wishes. The report of this disaster caused lamentation in heaven and earth. There was a daily bazaar of consternation and terror, and sorrow and affliction became active. Darkness took possession of the earth, and the evening of sorrow fell upon mortals in the midday of contentment. The lightning of labor and sorrow struck mankind's harvest of joy. The stone of violence and oppression smote on the vases of the hearts of the sincere. Good God! What a personality he was! He was pure from every stain and endowed with all perfections. What a jewel free from every blemish and pure of every stain! Lofty prestige, a happy horoscope, and awakened fortune, complete auspiciousness, a daily-increasing dominion, mounting victoriousness, pleasant friendship, a love of pleasantry, friend- cherishing, foe-destroying, a kingdom-bestowing liberality, a might that overthrew enemies, a world-

"Good God!" is from Abû'l-Fazl ibn Mubârak, trans. by H. Beveridge, *The Akbarnâmâ* (Calcutta: The Asiatic Society, 1905), Vol. 3, pp. 1260-1261.

embracing majesty, a world-conquering resolution, a firmness and gravity together with the working of conspicuous miracles, lofty conversation, an illuminated mind, a God-given understanding, an enlightened soul, a taste for knowledge, and expounder of mysteries, and an opener of mysteries, conquest over difficulties—all these were gathered together in that sublime personality and created astonishment among the lords of insight.

The Toleration of Hindus

JAHANGIR

Keep in Mind . . .

* What was Akbar's advice to his son Jahangir regarding tolerance?

I am here led to relate that at the city of Banaras, a temple had been erected [where there existed a] . . . principal idol and four other images of solid gold, each crowned with a tiara . . . with precious stones. It was the belief of these non-believers that a dead Hindu, provided when alive he had been a worshiper, when laid before this idol would be restored to life. As I could not possibly give credit to such a pretense, I employed a confidential person to ascertain the truth; and, as I justly supposed, the whole was detected to be an impudent fraud. . . .

On this subject I must, however, acknowledge that having on one occasion asked my father the reason why he had forbidden anyone to prevent or interfere with the building of these haunts of idolatry, his reply was in the following terms: "My dear child," said he, "I find myself a power-

ful monarch, the shadow of God upon earth, I have seen that he bestows the blessing of his gracious providence upon all his creatures without distinction. . . . With all of the human race, with all of God's creatures, I am at peace: why then should I permit myself, under any consideration, to be the cause of molestation or aggression to any one? Besides, are not five parts in six . . . either Hindus or aliens to the faith; and were I to be governed by motives of the kind suggested in your inquiry, what alternative can I have but to put them all to death! I have thought it therefore my wisest plan to let these men alone. Neither is it to be forgotten, that the class of whom we are speaking . . . are usefully engaged, either in the pursuits of science or the arts, or of improvements for the benefit of mankind, and have in numerous instances arrived at the highest distinctions in the state, there being, indeed, to be found in this city men of every description, and of every religion on the face of the earth." . . .

In the practice of being burnt on the funereal pyre of their husband as sometimes exhibited among the widows of the Hindus, I had previously directed that no woman who was the mother of children should be thus made a sacrifice, however willing to die; and I now further ordained, that in no case was the practice to be permitted, when compulsion was in the slightest degree employed, whatever might be the opinions of the people. In other respects they were in no way to be molested in the duties of their religion, nor exposed to oppression or violence in any manner whatever. . . .

Consider This:

* In what ways was the tolerance of Hinduism an important principle of effective Muslim political control?

Price, David, trans., *Memoirs of the Emperor Jahangueir Written by Himself*, 1829, pp. 33–36, 51–53.